SOVIET ECONOMIC
DEVELOPMENT
SINCE 1917

SOVIET ECONOMIC DEVELOPMENT SINCE 1917

by MAURICE DOBB, M.A.

LECTURER AND FELLOW OF TRINITY COLLEGE, CAMBRIDGE

INTERNATIONAL PUBLISHERS

New York

CONTENTS

PART ONE

PART TWO

v

PREFACE

The present work treads the ground of my study of *Russian Economic Development since the Revolution*, written twenty years ago, and goes beyond it. Some of the material from this earlier work (which owes much to the assistance which the author then had from Mr. H. C. Stevens) is embodied in Chapters Four to Nine ; as are also a few passages from a war-time booklet, *Soviet Planning and Labour in Peace and War*, in Chapter Sixteen. But the historical story of the first decade after the Revolution has been completely re-worked and re-written as well as being extended over a further twenty years, and the design of the book changed.

The various sections of this book may prove of unequal interest to different types of reader. Chapters One, Thirteen and Fourteen will probably be of interest mainly to economists, and Chapter Fifteen to the economic geographer. If an economic historian should be persuaded to open the book, such matters as may hold his attention will probably lie somewhere between Chapters Two and Twelve ; while Chapters Eight to Ten, and possibly the four which precede them, may have some interest for the student of comparative economic policies. About the relevance of a study of Soviet economic development to problems which concern the world to-day I have ventured to say something in the introductory · chapter. I can only hope that readers with special angles of interest will not be deterred by the amount of detail which had necessarily to be included if this study was to be complete.

It remains for me to express my indebtedness to Dr. Alexander Baykov, of the University of Birmingham, for invaluable criticism and advice at various stages in the preparation of this work ; to both Mr. Andrew Rothstein, of the University of London School of Slavonic Studies, and Mr. Jacob Miller, of the Russian Department of Glasgow University, for information most generously supplied, for loan of books and periodicals and for the painstaking reading of large sections of my manuscript ; and also to the librarians of the School of Slavonic Studies and of Chatham House. For the two maps which form the end-papers of the book I am indebted to my wife.

M. H. D.

Cambridge, July 1947

In the new (fourth) edition of this work, no rewriting of the old (save for a few minor corrections and additions) has been attempted. But a new chapter has been added (Chapter Thirteen) summarising the main events of the past decade.

M. H. D.

December 1956

In this latest edition the historical chapters have been left substantially unaltered and (apart from a very few and minor changes, *e.g.* to allow for revised agricultural figures for the pre-war period) no attempt has been made to rewrite them. This applies even to the first, and introductory, chapter, where some generalisations relevant to the pre-war period of intensive industrialisation and construction require qualification in the light of post-war experience, especially of the past ten years. Later chapters, however, in particular Chapters Thirteen and Fourteen, have either been rewritten or been extended to deal with changes over the past decade and to bring information up to date (*i.e.* to 1965).

M. H. D.

September 1965

PART ONE

CHAPTER ONE

INTRODUCTION

The Significance of a Study of Soviet Economic Development for the Problems of Our Time

I

When we contemplate the economic and social changes which have taken place during the past thirty years over the area which used to be called the Russian Empire, novelty and magnitude compete for our attention. It is doubtful whether in any previous age so profound a change, affecting so large an area of the world's surface, has ever occurred within such a narrow span of time. Until recent years—virtually until the war years of 1941 to 1945—the extent of this transformation in the social and economic face of the former Russian Empire was little appreciated in western countries. Scepticism about official accounts of plans and achievements was almost universal ; and even those with access to information, claiming the title of expert, greatly underestimated the extent and durability of the changes that had occurred. For some this disbelief rested on genuine ignorance. In the case of many it was probably the fruit of wishful thinking. But there were also those among the sceptics who lacked the excuse either of ignorance or of deficient training in the objective approach to facts. In view of so much of what had been privately said and both privately and publicly written during the 1930's about the economic condition of the U.S.S.R., it is hardly surprising that authoritative military forecasts in Washington and London in 1941 as to Soviet powers of resistance to Germany should have been so grotesquely pessimistic as they can now be seen to have been.

The story of the economic development of what at first was Soviet Russia and since 1923 has been the U.S.S.R. holds a special interest for our times for two main reasons. Firstly, it provides the first case in history of a working-class form of State (under the slogan of " the dictatorship of the proletariat ") carrying out the expropriation of the former propertied class and establishing a socialist form of economy. This alone would suffice to give it a unique interest : an interest for economists and economic historians of our century at least as great as that of post-1789 France for political theorists and historians in the last century. But secondly, it affords a unique example of the transformation of a formerly backward country to a country of extensive industrialisation and modern technique at an unprecedented *tempo* : a transformation unaided by any considerable import of capital from abroad, but effected under the guidance and control of a national economic plan, instead of in the conditions of *laissez-faire* and atomistic capitalist enterprise which characterised the classic industrial revolutions of the past. As such it seems likely in turn to become the classic type for the future industrialisation of the countries of Asia. Already it has profoundly influenced the discussion of projects for the economic development of India and those for south-eastern Europe. It may well have the effect to-morrow of shifting the focus of economic inquiry ; furnishing it with an entirely new set of questions and new perspectives on economic development.

Since the *tempo* of industrial growth in the U.S.S.R. in the dozen years before the war was so exceptional, its main interest for the economist will be the light it can throw on the factors governing economic development. Until quite recently economists in this country have been concerned with considerations of equilibrium rather than with those of change. Even when the equilibrium which occupied their attention was a " moving equilibrium ", this was conceived simply in terms of a series of adjustments to certain " arbitrary " shifts in some given factor (e.g. demand, population, technique, capital) ; the relations of adjustment being such that vectors of movement were generally smooth and continuous. The situation where the rate of movement was greater than the rate of adjustment was seldom considered ; although in the last few years there has been a certain amount of attention paid to fluctuating series and the influence of time-lags in adjustment (along the lines of the so-called " cobweb theorem "). It seems not untrue to say that, as a result of this preoccupation with a certain analytical method, some of the most essential features of economic development, especially those which dominate crucial periods of transition, like the transition from an agricultural to an industrial economy or from a backward to an advanced level of technique, were never examined. Economists for the most part were preoccupied with the notion that the heart of the economic problem lay in securing an *optimum* allocation of resources between alternative uses, with both resources and uses treated as given. The economists who in the period between wars discussed the comparative merits of different economic systems (including at one time the present writer) generally assumed that the success of any system was mainly to be judged by its success in so doing (usually with the implication that this could only be adequately performed by the operation of a pricing system, not only for consumers' goods, but for intermediate products and factors of production).[1] The notion that successful development from one economic situation, with its given combination of resources and configuration of demand, to another might be a more crucial test of the contribution made by an economic system to human welfare than the attainment of perfect equilibrium in any given situation seldom commanded attention.[2] It was as though one were to concentrate on the perfection of instruments whereby the summit of any mountain could be precisely located rather than ascertaining which was the highest mountain in the neighbourhood and which was the quickest way to the top.

But the issue is not simply between sacrificing equilibrium-conditions in favour of progress and making the most of what one has at any given time. When we shift the focus of attention to problems of economic development, a more fundamental issue than this appears. One is very soon struck with the fact that the picture of the economic world presented by these problems does not seem at all to resemble the picture which economists have usually presented. In actuality these problems seldom or never seem to have the form of choosing that one among an indefinitely large number of economic patterns or routes which is the best according to some ideal standard. They seem rather to be con-

[1] For example, in his *Russian Economic Development since the Revolution* in 1928 the present writer wrote as follows: "The chief aspects of any economic planning must be the regulation of the relative *proportions* in which things are produced, and arising therefrom, the proportions in which economic resources are distributed between the various branches of production. . . . There are certain objective quantities which should be represented in prices to provide the basis for an adequate social accounting." It was added, however (unwisely as it now seems) that the inclusion in costs of a capital charge was probably undesirable, because this would "limit the intensive use of capital"; and that the desirable principle was to require "each enterprise to extend its production and the use of its capital equipment up to the point where the marginal prime costs rose to the level of selling-prices and so made further extension undesirable"; deciding whether to increase or decrease capital equipment according to the size of the resulting surplus over average cost when output had been fixed in this way (pp. 168, 176, 179, 180).

[2] A notable exception to this statement is Schumpeter, who has used the notion of development as the justification of the capitalist *entrepreneur*—the pioneer of *new* economic patterns and *new* combinations of resources—and also for monopoly, on the ground that monopoly gives the *entrepreneur* control of a wider range of resources and so enables him to carry out such developments and also to face the risks and uncertainties attending economic change.

cerned with discovering how the situation confronting one *limits* what it is possible to choose. Instead of an indefinitely large number of ends and limited means to be distributed between them, with an indefinitely large number of possible patterns to choose between, essential problems seem to turn upon the fact that the ends which it is practicable to choose are themselves fairly straitly limited by the means available and that the number of possible combinations which can be chosen is small rather than large. If this is the case, the emphasis of economic inquiry is inevitably shifted to a study of how these limits upon economic action are actually defined : a study of the characteristics of particular types of situation which determine the sort of development that is possible.

This is not the place to venture upon a discussion of the basic premises of economic method. It must suffice to indicate what this issue amounts to in terms of different assumptions about the texture of economic events, and to stress some of the implications of this difference. The traditional approach, with its treatment of economic quantities as subject to continuity of variation, requires that the nature of production (and also of consumers' wants) should be such that the distribution of productive resources between different sorts of production must be susceptible of variation that is very large (relatively to the scale of wants). Productive resources must be tractable in a high degree ; and the possible patterns into which the distribution of them can be woven must be very numerous. On the side of consumers' wants there must be an analogous flexibility in the degree to which the variety of things which cater for those different wants can be combined without damage to consumers. This picture of the economic situation seems to rest, *inter alia*, on an implicit assumption that on the side of production " indivisibilities ", occasioned by the size of the basic technical units, or interdependencies between different lines of production (e.g. joint supply relationships) are small relatively to the scale on which things are being viewed ; while on the side of demand the particular needs of consumers for particular commodities are for the most part independent of one another, in the sense that each is rival to the rest and the number of possible combinations of these commodities which would be equally satisfying to consumers is very large.

If, on the other hand, so-called " indivisibilities " in production are large relatively to the scale on which problems are being viewed, the situation has a quite different aspect ; as it also will have if the items which compose consumers' aggregate demand to any large extent form a closely interrelated set, bound together, e.g. by social convention or by links of complementarity between particular wants into " modes of life " or patterns of behaviour which assume the character of organic wholes.[1] In this kind of situation, it will not be possible with limited resources to produce *some* of *each* of *n* commodities which consumers may desire if they can get them. To produce any (or most) of them at all will require that production of them be undertaken on a minimum scale that is sufficiently large to reduce drastically the number of different things that it is practicable to put simultaneously into production. To produce some of *a* may not merely reduce the quantity of *b* that can be produced : it may preclude the possibility of producing any of *b* at all. The possible patterns of allocation of productive resources will then be relatively small. The production can be undertaken only of a fraction of *n* commodities, and those which are produced must be turned out in certain minimum quantities, so that for practical purposes the relative proportions in which different products can be placed on the market are not capable of any very large degree of variation, but are determined within fairly narrow limits by technical conditions of production.[2] If, on the side of consumers, wants for different commodities tend to be grouped into sets which are wanted in combination,[3] the items in each set not being readily combined with items from another set, then the possible combinations of different commodities which confront the framers of a production plan will be further reduced in number. With any given quantity of productive resources, it may be a question of allocating them to the production of Set A of commodities, or of Set B or Set C, the series of alternative sets consisting of relatively few—of opting between a certain number of mutually exclusive menus (as it were) for a *table d'hôte* meal rather than the more complicated task of catering for a lengthy *à la carte* list in proportions adapted to consumers' requirements.

[1] The largeness of the *unit* (measured in its value) in which wants are supplied relatively to consumers' total expenditure (e.g. a motor-car, a house, a refrigerator) will have a similar significance in the context to which we are referring.

[2] For example, if motor-cars (of a certain type) are to be produced at all, it is desirable to produce them at least in quantities equal to the output-capacity of one (large) specialised motor plant. If more are required than this, then the alternative is one of doubling the initial output by constructing a second plant, and then again trebling it ; but intermediate levels of output are for practicable purposes excluded from consideration.

[3] For example, the combined set of wants for houses, furniture, gardening equipment, radio, facilities for cooking and eating at home, which constitutes one " mode of life ", and another set consisting of flats or lodgings, motor-car, restaurant feeding, public places of entertainment, etc.

In the degree that the economic situation approximates to this, problems of economic planning seem to acquire a resemblance to the problems of military strategy, where in practice the choice lies between a relatively small number of plans, which have in the main to be treated and chosen between as organic wholes, and which for a variety of reasons do not easily permit of intermediate combinations.[1] The situation will demand a concentration of forces round a few main objectives, and not a dispersion of resources over a very wide range.

We cannot stay to consider how far in fact productive resources are tractable or intractable, or the pattern of consumers' wants is characterised by flexibility or inflexibility, in relation to fairly long periods of time. But there is a particular consideration which gives the issue that we have just raised a greater relevance to problems of economic planning than at first sight it might seem to have. This is the high degree of intractability attaching to productive resources over a short period of time, by reason of the durability of the patterns into which productive resources have at any given time been woven and the high cost attaching to the transformation of them into other forms within less than a quite fairly considerable interval of time : an interval which will commonly be a matter of a decade and in some cases may amount to as much as several decades. When we combine this with the fact that any economic plan is bounded by a fairly restricted time-horizon (if only because the number of imponderables in the problem increases very rapidly when that horizon is extended beyond a certain point), our tentative analogy between choosing between economic plans and choosing between rival military strategies seems to acquire a reasonable claim upon the attention of economists. At least, it has sufficient plausibility to serve as a warning against introducing a distortion into one's study of the problems of a planned economy by viewing these through the traditional economist's lens.

It is obvious that the amount of new construction which can

---

[1] This is not to say that in certain aspects of military problems analogies cannot be found with the balancing and transfer of small quantities at a margin ; e.g. calculating the comparative advantages of putting an additional gun or battalion or ship in location A or in location B. It is to say that the *essential* part of the problem has no analogy with this ; mainly because each strategic plan requires the use of a certain minimum of forces, which is large relatively to the total available, and a certain combination of different arms (capable of variation outside fairly narrow limits only with damage to the military potential of the force). Hence it is not a question of allocating military resources between various positions from Iceland to Suez so as to equalise their marginal effectiveness at each point, but of choosing between alternative concentrations, e.g. on the " soft under-belly of Europe " or in north-west Europe, each of which is rival to the other.

be put in hand over the next few years will be strictly conditioned (short of import-possibilities) by the existing output capacity of heavy industry ; although there will be some margin for variation if one is willing and able to forgo repair and replacement work in any sector of the economy at the expense of future productivity in that sector. Similarly the amount of consumption that is practicable over the near future will be conditioned by the existing output capacity of the consumption goods trades ; and a diminution either of consumption or of construction will have little immediate effect in facilitating an expansion of the other. If, however, the problem which a planning body is considering relates to a period of several decades, the range of alternatives between which it is able to choose will be widened : the number of economic patterns that it will be possible to weave will be multiplied. In those future decades there can be more consumption if in the interim construction has been devoted to the expansion of the equipment of the consumption goods industries : a possible rate of expansion which will be conditioned, however, by the previously existing capacity of plants making equipment for these industries and the rate of their expansion in the interim. As an alternative these future decades could be rendered capable of maintaining a higher rate of investment and construction, if in the meantime resources have been devoted to the expansion of heavy industry, augmenting the number of steel furnaces and of plants capable of manufacturing machine-tools. To each time-horizon of given radius there corresponds its given range of possibilities ; the existing pattern of productive resources and its degree of tractability being the determinants of this range. As the radius of the time-horizon extends, the range of possibilities increases—the number of alternative routes rises by which, when the day arrives, that horizon can be crossed.

In an unplanned economy of atomistic individualism this situation is never one that is consciously envisaged by any single executive person or body of persons ; since output and investment decisions are diffused among numerous autonomous business-units and taken atomistically, and never constitute a co-ordinated and unified decision in the hands of any one body. The range of alternatives and its relation to a given time-horizon is not envisaged as an element in policy-making. If such things are thought of at all, this is not *ex ante* in relation to what can or cannot be written upon the future, but *ex post* by some theorist analysing causal sequences in retrospect. Even in the explanation of a causal-

genetic process in retrospect this method of framing the problem
is unlikely to be very fruitful, since the entrepreneur does not regard
the problem in any such way, still less base his actions upon an
estimate of such possibilities ; but steers his own business according to expectations or guesses about the movement of forces in his
immediate neighbourhood—expectations which will be largely
affected by the probable actions of his neighbours, since these
actions will be so large a factor in determining the movement of
prices.   To discover what are the theoretically possible routes
which the economy as a whole could take will be of little assistance
in forecasting the actual path which a capitalist system will follow
(steered as it is by entrepreneurs who are, as it were, " in blinkers ") ;
even though it be true that to discover this set of theoretically
possible routes would tell an economist the *limits* within which
such an economy could wander.   But in a planned economy such
as developed in the U.S.S.R. after 1928, or indeed in any country
where the government designs to steer economic development in a
particular direction (as is envisaged, for example, in recent plans
for the industrialisation of India), this question as to how the possible routes are limited, and the relation of these limits to the
chronology of one's plan, necessarily becomes the central preoccupation of economic policy.   Economic inquiry is given a quite
new perspective and a quite novel set of questions to answer.
Attention will be focused on such questions as the relation in which
particular alternatives stand to one another, and the extent to which
the choice between alternatives that may become available at a
future date will be conditioned by some crucial decision between a
narrower range of alternatives which has to be made at some earlier
date.   It may even be found that in terms of the answer to questions such as these the variety of economic situations can be
exhaustively classified.

Notions of equilibrium will not, of course, be foreign to the
perspective of economic development which, instead of just happen-
ing as the outcome of " blind " force, is consciously steered.   They
will in one sense come into the picture in the form of certain internal
relationships between its constituent elements to which any scheme
of development must conform.   These relationships will define the
intrinsic " stuff " out of which the schemes of development must
be made.   While the form and pattern of development may be
varied, these cannot be of *any* kind, by reason of the essential texture
of the stuff.   Development must conform to certain internal require-

ments, just as it is subject to the kind of determination of which we have spoken by reason of the mastery of past events over the present. Of the discussions of this matter which at one time filled Soviet planning literature we shall have something more to say later, in Chapter Fourteen. But clearly a notion of equilibrium of this kind, applied to a description of the nature of the material which the economic planner handles, •is very different from notions of equilibrium applied as a deterministic picture of an atomistic system : a system which, because of its essential nature (epitomised by Adam Smith in his famous simile of " the unseen hand "), has been treated in its movement and motivation in terms of mechanical analogies.

In fact, it will be precisely the conscious use of knowledge of these relationships that can enable a planned economy to pursue quite other paths of development than those which an individualist system could normally take. The conscious use of such knowledge amounts to the attempt to substitute *ex ante* co-ordination of the constituent elements in a scheme of development for the tardy *post facto* co-ordinating tendencies that are operated by the mechanism of price movements on a market in a capitalist world—tendencies, moreover, which in the presence of substantial time-lags may merely achieve extensive fluctuations. In this the essential difference between a planned economy and an unplanned evidently consists. The successful employment of such *ex ante* co-ordination may not only enable a given objective to be attained more smoothly and more speedily, but because the degree of uncertainty confronting economic decisions is of a much smaller order of magnitude— uncertainty regarding the character of parallel decisions in other sectors of the economy and regarding future decisions that will be made—it will open the door to certain types of development which would not be possible at all (or at least be extremely unlikely) for an unplanned capitalist economy. In the latter the uncertainty attaching to any substantial departure from the *status quo* will tend to make entrepreneurs prefer the familiar to the novel and incalculable ; while the presence of monopoly may place a premium on retrenchment and restriction instead of pioneering innovation. But apart from this, there are changes beneficial for the whole of an industry or the whole of an economy to make in unison which will not be profitable for an individual to initiate on his own, when he is not certain that others will follow suit and take parallel action which co-ordinates with, and justifies, his own. This fact is attributable to the existence of relations of interdependence[1] between various productive units and sectors of the economic system, which cause cost or productivity at one point to be dependent, not only on the scale of production at that point, but on the scale of production in other production units and in other industries as well.

Such interdependence has long been familiar to economists, and its practical consequences long ago secured recognition in the so-called " infant industry " case, where it was admitted that an industry could remain at an infant level, or even never be brought to birth, although its growth would ultimately yield economic gain to itself and to the community. The reason for this is that no individual acting on his own can reap sufficient of this gain to justify the expansion. In other words, in an individualist economy the unit of decision is *too small* to embrace the full consequences of expansion. It is clear, however, that such relations of interdependence extend beyond the boundaries of a particular industry and moreover can extend over time as well as through space. Such wider types of interdependence between different industries and sectors of an economic system have seldom been given their proper weight in relation to the development of the economic system as a whole. Speaking of the problems of industrialisation in south-eastern Europe, Dr. Rosenstein-Rodan recently put the matter in this way : " If the industrialisation of international depressed areas[2] were to rely entirely on the normal incentive of private entrepreneurs, the process would not only be very much slower, the rate of investment smaller, and (consequently) the national income lower, but the whole economic structure of the region would be different. Investment would be distributed in different proportions between different industries, the final equilibrium would be below the optimum."[3] It accordingly follows that, although (as we have emphasised) the number of plans that a planned economy could choose is in all probability strictly limited, there are economic strategies open to such a system which would be beyond the capacity of any other (apart from some specially favourable constellation

---

[1] This interdependence may be through production (connections of the joint supply kind, which is the sense in which we have spoken of interdependence above) or through market demand, which can affect the cost and prices of the products of other processes or industries by influencing the degree to which certain " indivisible " units involved in their production are utilised fully.

[2] By this the writer refers to areas with large surplus agricultural populations.

[3] " Problems of Industrialisation of Eastern and South-Eastern Europe " in *Economic Journal*, June–Sept. 1943, 206–7. Cf. also K. Mandelbaum on " the difficulties of making a beginning in countries which have once been left behind " in *The Industrialisation of Backward Areas*, 3–11.

of circumstances such as may have been responsible for our own industrial revolution in this country). In having that wider choice and in choosing that path of development which is the *optimum* according to some given canon of social policy from among the possible paths confronting it, a planned economy can claim its essential superiority as an economic mechanism.

II

The detailed form that such problems of development have assumed in the case of the U.S.S.R. will be described in what follows. But in this case special considerations have influenced the objectives of policy and in the two decades between wars have given economic development certain unique features. With respect to its initial situation, Russia prior to 1917 was not unlike a country such as India on the one hand or large areas of south-eastern Europe on the other, which to-day stand upon the threshold of ambitious schemes of development. As we shall see in the next chapter, she was a country with a small national income per head and a low standard of life, by reason of the low level of productivity of labour which prevailed. This in turn depended on the fact that industry was relatively little developed and the overwhelming majority of the population were engaged on the land, for the most part in types of agriculture which had a very low yield in relation both to man-power and to acreage. Together with the low yield of a primitive agriculture went rural over-population : an excess of population relative to the cultivated area available and to the means of production in the hands of the cultivators. Heavy industry in particular was weakly developed, and its past development had been closely geared to the needs of railway construction. Fuel and power development with reference to industry was largely confined to the coal of the Donbas on the south-eastern border of the Ukraine. The eastern regions of the Russian Empire beyond the Urals were scarcely developed industrially at all. Even mining, of which there had been quite early beginnings in Siberia, was relatively backward, and paid more attention to rare and precious metals for export than to raw materials of modern industry. Agriculture was largely dominated by the export market ; and while certain light industries, especially textiles, had reached a fairly advanced level of development, the country remained overwhelmingly dependent on import for the supply of an extensive range of both capital goods and consumers' goods.

Short of large-scale import of machinery and constructional equipment, the possible rate of industrial development was accordingly a slender one. Before any process of industrial development had progressed very far, its further advance was likely to be halted by the relative backwardness of her transport system (where for bulky commodities like grain and timber water transport had always played the leading rôle) and also of her fuel and power base for industry. This backwardness could only in its turn be overcome by diverting the products of heavy industry to railway building and renovation, the improvement of waterways and the construction of roads, and to the opening of new mines and the building of electric power stations. Such diversion of a slender flow of metals, mechanical equipment and constructional materials would inevitably have involved a damping down of the rate of construction in industry itself, perhaps over a period of several quinquennia. The low standard of living meant that any increase of income that the population might enjoy (whether from increased employment or increased remuneration for human effort) was likely to be spent almost wholly on foodstuffs or consumers' goods, thereby requiring either a smaller export of the former or an increased import (or else home manufacture) of the latter at the expense of the rate at which the basic bottlenecks of heavy industry, transport or power, could be widened.

The process of industrialisation of the U.S.S.R. when it came was to be dominated by certain quite distinctive features. In the first place the possibilities of easing the bottleneck of heavy industry by importing capital goods from abroad was severely restricted by reason of the reluctance to grant loans to the U.S.S.R. which prevailed in the surrounding capitalist world. This not only hindered the expansion of normal trade relations (*vide* the campaigns against Soviet timber and oil exports at various periods between the wars), but virtually excluded the possibility of financing an import surplus by foreign borrowing, such as most countries which in the past had followed Britain's industrial revolution had relied upon so largely. The means for industrial construction had therefore to be found almost exclusively from internal resources.

Secondly, the Soviet Government was under the obligation, by reason of its social philosophy and its programme, to give high priority to the extension of collective forms of economy. To a large extent this was, of course, an economic asset, since it facilitated the centralised planning of construction without which the impressive development of the years from 1928 to 1941 would scarcely have been conceivable. But at the same time it had the consequence that an agricultural surplus could not be obtained by permitting or encouraging the growth of large-scale individual farming, as was done in other countries, since this would have opened the door to a revival of Capitalism in the countryside : a Capitalism deeply entrenched in the village and dominating the supply of primary products to industry and the towns. For this reason it proved necessary for Soviet economy simultaneously to carry through a policy of high-speed industrialisation and a socio-economic revolution in the basis of peasant agriculture.

Thirdly, the *tempo* of industrialisation had partly to be dictated by the prospects of war and the needs of defence. While it is very far from being true, as some have asserted, that military considerations were a major motive of industrialisation, such considerations exerted an increasing influence over policy as the decade of the 1930's advanced towards its close. Not only did they dictate a forcing of the pace of development, but they occasioned a diversion of a growing proportion of the fruits of previous construction to the needs of armament and eventually of war.

In at least two respects Soviet experience touches the issue of which we have spoken concerning the nature of the economic problems which confront the framers of an economic plan. In the first place, it seems to indicate the *prima facie* feasibility of planning the allocation of investment without the device of a price for capital as an explicit category of cost. In Soviet economy there is a retail market in which consumer goods are priced, and there is a wage-structure related both to the nature of different types of work and to the relative scarcities of different sorts of labour-power, which form the basis for the calculation of prime costs. But while interest-charges are made on certain types of bank-advances, and interest is paid on savings bank deposits and State loans, the bulk of capital investment has taken the form of interest-free grants from the Budget, and capital charges other than capital-depreciation have not entered into the calculation of costs. (We shall see later, however, that in the light both of experience and of the needs of a period of greater decentralisation this traditional practice is changing.)

Economists in the past have generally maintained that the allocation of capital between industries, involving decisions about the number, type and size of plant in each case, could only be " rationally " arranged (i.e. so as to maximise the effectiveness of those invested resources in terms of total production) if a mechanism existed whereby anticipated productivity in each use could be directly compared with the cost of the resources, when " cost " was so calculated as to reflect the highest potential productivity of those resources in some alternative use. To make this possible, it has been maintained, these capital resources (e.g. machinery or building materials) require to be valued, not only in terms of the amount of labour-power (priced at the current wage) used directly and indirectly in their production, but in terms of a special " capital cost " calculated as some kind of interest-rate expressing the " scarcity " of the total of capital resources available for investment relative to the sum of their potential uses (valued in terms of potential productivity in these uses).

This, however, does not seem necessarily to follow, even if the economic situation, and the problem it holds, is of the character which economists have usually assumed it to have. Provided that data are available about the comparative productivities of different investment-projects and about their construction costs (expressed in terms of the prime costs of building and of building materials and equipment), a basis will exist for calculating the *net productivity*[1] of each project, and for constructing on this basis a priority-list of projects in terms of their comparative yields. Given such a priority-list (which may not, of course, be influenced *solely* by considerations of calculated productivities), the problem of allocation can be decided by working down the list until the resources for investment in that given period are exhausted.[2] If this is done, no project giving prospect of lower yield will have

[1] This being defined as the output (valued at current prices) from the plant over a given period *less* the prime cost of producing that output, expressed as a ratio to the construction cost of the plant, again calculated in terms of current cost in wages and materials involved in construction.

[2] The writer's present opinion (1965) would be that this method might well involve a significant degree of error in many cases, unless the prices of capital goods entering into construction costs as well as prices generally, were constructed on the principle of what Marx termed "prices of production" (thus including in price some general profit-rate on capital). Probably allowance should also be made in prices for certain other types of scarcity, not only natural scarcities but also certain types of fairly enduring scarcity (e.g. newer sources of fuel and power). In other words, unless prices used in calculation include some allowance of this kind, a productivity-ratio as suggested in the text may not suffice as a criterion for allocation even to a "sufficient" degree of approximation (or as affording a so-called "second best" or "third best" solution). This must be taken as a qualification of what is said in the preceding paragraph above. A further qualification is that Soviet experience in the post-war period indicates that, if the enterprise is to have autonomy as an operational unit, the cost of the capital employed by it must be made to impinge in some way on the enterprise financially, in order to encourage the best use of plant and equipment (and *a fortiori* if the enterprise controls, or can influence, any appreciable part of investment decisions). We shall see below that among the changes introduced in September 1965 was a capital charge of this kind, payable by enterprises in proportion to the capital funds at their disposal. See below Chapter Fourteen, pages 376–7, 379–81, also c.f. page 335n.

been preferred to one giving a prospect of higher ; and the condition for the most effective use of the resources available will have been observed. From an administrative standpoint this method has the virtues of simplicity, compared with the other mechanisms that have been proposed ; and it seems capable at least of yielding a result with a sufficient degree of approximation to the ideal one to justify its use. It would be utopian to hope that any system could regularly attain an optimum allocation (however that may be defined) in face of the imperfection of calculating instruments and the number of imponderables which in practice will exist. What is needed is that any considerable departure from an efficient allocation of resources should be quickly registered and corrected ; and this such a priority-list mechanism, resting on a direct comparison of productivities, seems to be quite capable of doing. About the actual financial arrangements in Soviet economy by which costs and prices are calculated and compared something will be said in a later chapter (Chapter Fifteen). These arrangements, as we shall see, are consistent with the use of a priority-list method of the type of which we have spoken; and there is reason to think that some method of this sort has formed the basis on which investment decisions at top levels have been made.[1]

In the second place, there is a good deal to support the analogy which we suggested in the first part of this chapter between the general shape of economic problems and the problems of military strategy. We have seen that if the economic situation has this shape, it cannot be pictured in terms of continuous variation of economic quantities, even as an approximation. The problem of pricing factors of production as economists have posed it will accordingly lack any simple solution, owing to the presence of substantial discontinuities, which render a marginal technique of equilibrating costs and returns inapplicable to certain major sectors

---

[1] As an accounting technique the notion of a "rate of return" on an investment has been customarily used in the preparation of Soviet investment plans as a criterion for choosing between various technical types of constructional projects. This has taken the form of requiring a certain minimum "term of repayment" (apart from amortisation) of the initial investment. Strumilin speaks of an annual rate of return of 6 per cent. as being at first required and later 8 or 10 per cent. (S. G. Strumilin, "The Time Factor in Planning Capital Investment" in *Izvestia Academii Nauk S.S.S.R.*, Economics and Law Series, 1946, No. 3, 196.) Strumilin proceeds to criticise this device of a "term of repayment" (for one reason because the results it yields in choosing between different technical projects are dependent on the level of selling-price, relatively to cost, which in Soviet economy is an "arbitrary", planned price). He suggests that the criterion as to what degree of economy in prime production costs ought at any time to be demanded as a minimum condition for investment projects should be the expected rate at which labour productivity is likely to rise in the economy at large as a result of technical progress. On this cf. the present writer's *Essay on Economic Growth and Planning*, pp. 26–7.

of the terrain. We have also seen that a principal reason for such discontinuities may be the existence of large-scale technical units, which, because of technical indivisibilities of equipment, are not capable of being operated below a certain minimum size ; this minimum size being fairly large relatively to the total output of the product in question. In a socialist economy one could reasonably expect the degree of specialisation of particular plants to be much greater than it is under Capitalism, where the uneconomic multiplication of variety by a firm is favoured, both as a form of " monopolistic competition " and as a means of spreading the risks of market fluctuations. One would expect a particular industrial plant to specialise on one type or line or variety of product, unless the existence of significant elements of joint supply and joint cost in the production process rendered the manufacture of several types of product in one plant specially advantageous. If for technical reasons the minimum practicable size of a plant were large, investment decisions would be primarily concerned with the question whether to put that product into production and to manufacture it in quantities corresponding to the output capacity of this minimum-sized plant or to refrain from putting it into production at all. Decisions about the distribution of a given total of investible resources, in other words, would be primarily concerned with the question as to how many product-types or product-varieties (each in most cases the work of a specialised plant) to put into production, rather than with the proportions in which different commodities were to be produced. True, there would usually be the alternative of constructing a plant of more primitive technical type with a much smaller output capacity, if the need and the available resources did not seem to warrant the larger. But in most cases the number of practicable alternatives seems likely to be fairly small, and the choice between them unlikely to be very long in doubt once the larger dimensions of the economic situation are known, even if only approximately.

The amount of standardisation of products arose as an issue of policy at a quite early stage of Soviet planning ; and a decision was taken in favour of combining a high degree of standardisation with the adoption wherever possible of the latest American technique in the construction of industrial plants. At the beginning of the First Five-Year Plan a Soviet writer presented the issue in this way : " At the present time, at the beginning of the carrying out of an extensive plan of reconstruction, it is necessary to decide the problem : on what levels of quality or on what standards to maintain development ? Here two roads are possible : the road of English industry of producing dear things of specially high quality and the road of American industry, developed on the simplified production of products of mass consumption. . . . Taking account of the general problems involved in the industrialisation of the country, the insufficiency of capital and the necessity for maximum economy of means, and also the swift *tempo* of technical progress in which the period of ' psychological depreciation ' of things is extremely short, one is bound to conclude that with regard to the question before us we must choose the American road."[1] The industrial development during the period of the Five-Year Plans accordingly took the form mostly (apart from local industries and lines of production little fitted for highly mechanised methods) of constructing large specialised plants. For example, during the First Five-Year Plan three main tractor plants were put under construction, each of them specialised to a particular type of tractor, and two main motor plants, each specialised if not to one type at least to a very narrow range of types of motor vehicles. In the Second Five-Year Plan it was designed that " only 4 types of tractors " should be produced, as compared with 80 types produced in U.S.A. in 1929 ; and that motor plants should " produce in the main 3 standard types of trucks and buses : model GAZ (' Ford AA ') manufactured by the Gorky Automobile Plant, 1·5 ton ; model ZIS-3-5 manufactured by the Stalin Automobile Plant in Moscow, 3 ton ; and model YG-5 manufactured by the Yaroslavl Truck Plant, 5 ton". In addition to this, " two standard types of passenger cars of model GAZ " were to be put into production and some " 3-axle truck sub-types, traction automobiles, trailers, etc."[2] Of steam railway locomotives 4 types were in production, two of them for freight and two for passengers. Similarly in the cotton industry it was designed that by 1937 the " average number of yarn numbers per spinning mill " should be reduced to 4 and the average number of grades of cloth per weaving mill to scarcely more than 2.[3] It is of interest to notice that at the end of the decade of the '30's M. Molotov was demanding that the question

[1] M. Aronovitch, " Problems of Standardisation in the Reconstruction of Industry " in *Planovoe Khoziaistvo* [Planned Economy], 1929, No. 5, 122–3. This writer cites some examples of recent standardisation : the reduction of the types of cotton cloth from 2,600 in 1924 to 187 in 1927 ; in one factory at Tver from 500 to 42 ; in a spinning factory a concentration on only two counts of yarn ; in rolling mills a reduction of standards in one case to 4 per cent. and in another to 6 per cent. of the previous number, and of the flow of production in some rolling mills proceeding, in consequence, for ten days or more without an interruption (111–12).
[2] *The Second Five-Year Plan for the Development of the National Economy of the U.S.S.R.* (Gosplan, 1936), 358, also 139, 143. [3] *Ibid.*, 615.

of building parallel or duplicate plants should be placed on the agenda in the case of certain key products;[1] but presumably for reasons of military security rather than for economic reasons, and at any rate with the intention that each of the parallel plants should serve a distinct regional market.

The significance of such a high degree of specialisation as this for investment-policy is twofold. Firstly, it means that when a particular plant has been built and is working to full capacity, the question of increasing the output of that commodity by less than twice its existing output cannot for most practical purposes appear on the planning agenda. It is commonly held by economists to-day that the notion of " full capacity output " is much more capable of being given a precise meaning[2] than used to be thought ; and the present writer has elsewhere[3] suggested that in many types of modern production there is little choice for practiçal purposes between a zero output and production at, or close to, the limit of full capacity. Hence, changes in the output of that commodity have virtually to occur in fairly large and discontinuous jumps. In practice the question seems likely to present itself always as whether to use this second (or third or fourth, as the case may be) plant to augment the supply of the identical product which the first plant turned out, or to take advantage of the possibility of building a new plant to extend the range of variety and to adapt the new plant to the production of some new distinctive species of product within the same larger genus.

Secondly, if it be true that the most important issue in all questions of capital-allocation upon the planning agenda is the amount of variety in production which the community at any one time can afford, then this major issue is one which in practice can never be satisfactorily decided by any verdict of the market.[4] It is not a problem in the adaptation of supply to an already established

---

[1] Report to 18th Party Congress in March 1939 on the Third Five-Year Plan.

[2] This is usually described by stating that the " short period cost curve " (defining the prime cost of various scales of output from a given plant) has the shape of an inverted L. By contrast this curve used to be conceived as having the shape of a very shallow U.

[3] *Studies in the Development of Capitalism*, 359–65.

[4] For the reason that (i) " new wants " are something of which the consumer cannot be regarded as having previously been conscious, and which cannot be said to exist until the new commodity has been introduced upon the market (I am not aware that any exponent of a subjective theory of value has seriously maintained that the want for, say, a television set was somehow " latent " in the minds of consumers before television was invented, and hence that this " want " was an element in the consumers' " indifference map " prior to, and independently of, the impact of the first appearance on the market of television sets) ; (ii) if a new variety is introduced on the market, individual consumers will transfer to it so long

pattern of demand as the *datum* of the problem : it is concerned with a developing process in which the pattern of demand is itself changing in reciprocal interaction with the development of production, as new varieties of a commodity and new wants appear by a complex process of " education " in the consciousness of consumers. As economic development proceeds, and the stock of capital equipment in a community grows, the improvement in its standard of life seems likely to take the form as much (if not more) of multiplying the variety of its products as of multiplying the quantity of each particular sort. The investment programme of that community will be occupied with progressing from little variety to more variety at a rate which, though it may be guided by consumers' wishes expressed in various forms and influenced by the results of trial and error, cannot in any simple or precise sense be decided by any form of " consumers' voting " and must to a large extent be left to the initiative of producers.

Thus the alternatives that can appear on the economic agenda at any one time will themselves be conditioned by the means available ; their range extending as economic means grow more plentiful. When a country is still very poor, it will be a matter of producing one type (or at most very few types) of a narrow range of articles of prime necessity ; and the type in each case to be chosen for priority (e.g. the uni-type utility bicycle or the uni-type utility mackintosh) will not call for any very complex decision. Nor in deciding the kind or size of plant to be constructed to produce each type are the practicable alternatives likely to be very numerous. As the country becomes richer in capital equipment, it will each year multiply the variety of its products, both in the sense of adding luxuries to prime necessities and in affording a more luxurious assortment of styles and types of consumers' goods to cater for each main category of wants. The smaller the variety in production, the more obvious and the less controversial is likely to be the decision about what are the essential priorities. To provide an abundance of one-style prefabricated houses but no footwear or to give everyone a bicycle while some still lack a warm suit of clothes, would by universal admission be a miscalculation most damaging to human welfare. But these are hardly miscalculations that any sensible group of planners would make. As primary wants are satisfied and variety

as their preference for it exceeds the difference in price between the new variety and the existing one, irrespective of the fact that the transference of demand will cause the cost of producing existing varieties (if their production is subject to decreasing cost) to *rise* ; whereas this latter effect of multiplying variety must be taken into account in any assessment of what is in the *social* interest.

is multiplied, the alternatives become more numerous and choice between them more controversial and less calculable. At the same time the difference to be made to human welfare by the difference between two alternative solutions of the puzzle will have become a quantity of a relatively small order ;[1] and the country, being relatively rich in capital equipment, will stand to lose much less from misdirection or waste of new equipment than a poor country would have done.[2] Thus as economic development proceeds, the economic problem passes from one of maximum concentration of available resources on a few main objectives towards successively greater dispersion.

Reinforcing these considerations about the shape of economic problems is a particular characteristic of market demand that seems likely to prevail in societies where large inequalities of income are absent. It is a familiar fact that in a society with large inequalities of income the demand for most commodities beyond the essentials of life is determined at least as much by the shape of the income-distribution curve as by the position that these commodities occupy in any scale of preferences of consumers. The demand for most luxuries will be restricted within the bounds of a comparatively limited supply by the fact that their price is beyond the reach of all but a small minority of the population. The nearer that a society approaches to an equality of income-distribution, the more likely is it that market-demand for a very wide range of articles will be characterised by this sort of discontinuity : above a certain price the article (let us suppose it is some new commodity like bicycles, wrist-watches, radio sets or refrigerators) will have scarcely any purchasers at all, because few or none can afford it ; while immediately below this price the demand for it may become almost

---

[1] One may express this by saying that as one passes from primary wants to wants lower in the scale of urgency, and as variety increases, the demand for any one thing becomes progressively more elastic. This means that a consumer comes nearer to the point of indifference between the alternatives placed before him. This will still not be so in the case of primary wants. But the supply to satisfy them is likely to become a matter of routine calculation (in so far as the demand for them, e.g. for bread, has become inelastic with regard both to price and to income ; and the supply has come to be based on a calculation of so much per head of the population). Nor may a consumer remain near to the point of indifference even in the case of luxuries if the departure from a preferred assortment is very large. But at the same time the chance of such a large miscalculation of demand in fact remaining uncorrected for any length of time will be a relatively small one.

[2] Again, this may be expressed in the technical language of economists by saying that, as capital equipment (relatively to labour and natural resources and existing technical possibilities) becomes very plentiful, and the most productive uses for capital are " saturated ", considerations of capital cost (i.e. cost apart from amortisation) tends to become negligibly small by comparison with other costs.

infinitely elastic because everyone will now wish to acquire it, until the supply has become adequate for all, when the demand may once more become quite inelastic. In such circumstances a planning authority would need to be very careful not to put a new article into production until resources were adequate to produce it on a large enough scale to supply the majority of consumers. Until productive resources were adequate to do this, this commodity could not appear on the planning agenda at all. Once it had appeared on the agenda, there would be no alternative than to produce it on a very large scale sufficient for everyone. One seems to have this paradox, which some may find hard to appreciate : the more that the income-distribution of a community approaches equality, the larger is likely to be the number of things that are either not available at all or are in short supply. Yet the existence of these conditions is not necessarily any indication that economic resources are being inefficiently used. Rather is it an indication to the contrary.

Soviet planning in the period with which this book deals was primarily occupied, as we have seen, with such questions as the rate of investment, the location of industry and the development of new sources of power and of raw materials, transforming the very constants of economic geography. These were basic strategic questions, affecting the relative rates of development of different regions and of industry relatively to agriculture, upon which the economic history of decades was to turn. Regarding the production of consumers' goods, the country was still at a stage of economic development where the problem of poverty had still to be tackled and the task of supplying a sufficiency of the main essentials of life took precedence over the extension of variety and over questions about the proper order of that extension. When variety in diet of foodstuffs was still meagre for the mass of the population, the multiplication of styles and types of textile goods and furniture and household ornaments was a luxury which those harassed years could ill afford. This is not to say that problems about quality and range of consumers' goods had no place. We shall see that an increasing attention was being devoted to them in the latter half of the 1930's : an attention which would have been greater had it not been for gathering war clouds and the claims of rearmament. But at a stage of development when output *per capita* of the population still fell a long way below that of Western countries such matters could still occupy only a subordinate place. It has sometimes been assumed that the economic problem was to this extent simplified. In one sense it was, so far as the objectives of planning were relatively simple and unambiguous. At the same time the very backwardness of the country, which the Soviet régime inherited from the past, and its poverty in capital equipment compared with the West, meant that the stakes in the game were high. The economy could the less afford mistakes in planning ; and the difference between a correct estimate or miscalculation, or the incalculable influence of weather upon harvests, could mean the difference between a whole loaf and starvation. In the 1920's at least there was less room to manœuvre, and questions of will had more ruthlessly to be subordinated to the dictates of necessity. A more developed country can afford to brave uncertainty and to learn by trial and error where a poorer country can bet only on a certainty.

III

There is a particular respect in which Soviet experience bears upon an issue that has had some prominence in all the discussions of recent years concerning the industrialisation of formerly backward areas of the world. A notion which at one time was widely held among economists, and which still wields an influence over such discussions, is that economic development, conditioned as it so largely is by growth in the stock of social capital, is essentially limited by what may be termed the " savings fund " of the community, in the sense of the gap between its existing income and its consumption. From this the corollary is drawn that a poor country is generally incapable of maintaining as high a rate of development as a rich one, unless it is willing to adopt coercive measures to reduce absolutely the standard of life of the mass of the population. With reference to the problems of south-eastern Europe, this view has been expressed succinctly in the comment of one recent writer that owing to the low income per head in these predominantly agricultural countries " the rate of capital accumulation is checked ; there is not a sufficient volume of savings—or at least it cannot be mobilised on a large enough scale—to stimulate industrialisation ".[1]

In recent years there has been a growing inclination among economists to regard such a pre-existing " savings fund " as a myth ; and in general terms the argument that a country's potentiality for investment is not limited by any such factor is now sufficiently familiar. This general argument amounts to the contention

[1] Doreen Warriner, *Economics of Peasant Farming*, 50.

that the margin between income and consumption may be enlarged by augmenting income as well as by lowering consumption, and that the carrying out of plans of capital construction will augment income from the moment of their inception. While the margin between income and consumption will thereby be widened, this can occur without any absolute fall in the consumption either of the community as a whole or of any individuals in it. This latter conclusion depends on the assumption that the economic system contains elements of reserve productive capacity (unutilised or under-utilised labour and resources) which can be mobilised for constructional work without competing with the production of consumption goods. Subsequently, as the capital equipment under construction comes into operation, it will have the positive effect of facilitating consumption : new sources of power or new technical equipment will raise the productivity of labour already engaged in the production of consumers' goods.

The experience of economic construction in the U.S.S.R. affords an illustration, firstly of the fact that the period of time in which a programme of capital construction, boldly planned and executed, can become an aid to the output of consumption goods, instead of a competitor with it, is a relatively short one ; and secondly of the fact that the launching of such a programme does not necessarily entail any prior or concurrent fall of consumption, provided that the appropriate measures of economic organisation are taken. The experience of the U.S.S.R. seems to indicate that this is likely to be true, at least to a very large extent, of backward agricultural countries in general when they embark upon the first stages of industrialisation ; and that the previous backwardness of industrial development in such regions has not been due in the final analysis to any financial deficiency (inadequate savings or the absence of financial means for their mobilisation) but to a deficiency of *economic organisation*. It is characteristic of such countries that they tend to have a large " rural over-population " consisting of persons who are either landless, and gain such livelihood as they may by intermittent employment, mainly seasonal, or are cultivators of small plots of land by primitive methods and with inadequate equipment. In either case the productivity of their labour is exceedingly low and their transfer to the work of industrial construction would involve a negligible fall in the output of food. Of south-eastern Europe it has recently been said that " of a total active farm population of rather less than thirty millions between six and eight million active workers are superfluous and could be taken off the land with-

out loss to agriculture ".[1] Given a measure of reorganisation in the
social and property relations of the village—an extension of agricultural co-operation and some consolidation of parcellated and
scattered holdings, permitting a more rational utilisation of labour
—the transfer of labour from village to town can march in company
with an actual increase in the output of agriculture.

In a certain sense the inelastic marketable surplus of agriculture
in the U.S.S.R. in the 1920's (of which we shall have a good deal to
say below) could be regarded as forming " a fund of real working
capital " which acted as the crucial limiting factor upon plans for
industrialisation. As such many of the participants in the intense
controversies of those years treated it ; and the notion that an
enlargement of this surplus must precede any increase of investment (unless grave symptoms of economic crisis and inflation were
to appear) was implicit in the arguments of those who advocated a
low rather than a high *tempo* of industrialisation. But, for the
reasons we have stated, this fund was not necessarily a limiting
factor in the sense that its *prior* enlargement was an essential
condition for more investment, at least so far as food supplies were
concerned. If peasants moved from village to town, they became
consumers of bread in the town instead of in the village. A different
distribution of grain between village and town consumers was
accordingly needed ; but neither the volume of total consumption
nor the consumption per head of the population remaining in the
village were necessarily reduced. Moreover, if changes were simultaneously introduced into the economic and social life of the village,
which simultaneously released both labour and mouths from the
village and raised the productivity of the labour remaining there, a
growth of industrial investment could be accompanied by an actual
growth in total consumption. It is true that none of these results
might follow automatically. They would not necessarily result
alone from a financial policy designed to promote investment, but
would require appropriate measures of economic organisation to
carry them into effect. Without the latter, it might merely happen
that, with new prospects of employment and earnings for some
members of the family in industry, peasant households would take
advantage of the situation to consume more grain themselves
(thereby preventing an enlargement of the marketed food supply

[1] K. Mandelbaum, *op. cit.*, 2 ; also cf. Hugh Seton-Watson, *Eastern Europe
Between the Wars, 1918–1941*, 97–9, who speaks of " rather more than a third "
of the agricultural man-power in Poland, Roumania, Yugoslavia and Bulgaria as
being " superfluous ", and of " the great majority of all small holders in Eastern
Europe " as " permanently under-employed ". Also D. Warriner, *op. cit., passim.*

available to the towns) or alternatively to produce less than they formerly did. Even so, the situation, and the problem it yielded, would be a different one from that which most exponents of a " savings fund theory " seem to have had in mind. Needless to say, those who framed the industrialisation programme of the U.S.S.R. did not wait for any automatic adaptation of marketed food supplies to the financial consequences of a high rate of invest-ment-expenditure. The cornerstone of the First Five-Year Plan was precisely its combination of bold plans for industrial construc-tion with a yet bolder transformation of the property relations of the village and of the traditional forms of rural economy. Measures for raising the productivity of labour in agriculture and at the same time for bringing the marketable surplus of agriculture more directly under planned control (by means of the so-called "forward delivery contracts " which were to become obligatory supply-quotas) had the effect of simultaneously releasing labour to swell the ranks of industrial wage-earners, of reducing the number of mouths in the village and of raising the per man hour productivity of labour on the land.

So far as raw materials are concerned, or equipment for the new industry that has to be imported, the position is a different one. Here there is a more substantial sense in which the marketable surplus of agriculture constitutes a " real fund of investible re-sources ". Once new factories have been constructed, their opera-tion will require additional supplies of raw material as well as of labour ; and if constructional materials and machinery need to be imported, commodities will have to be exported in return.[1] In a backward country such export must generally consist of primary products, which have either to be made available in greater supply or diverted from home consumption. Again, to the extent that transport is a bottleneck, and the haulage of building materials and industrial equipment crowds out the movement of foodstuffs and causes regional shortages (as often tended to happen during the urgent years of the First Five-Year Plan), a heightened rate of investment will be a competitor to consumption.

In contrast to what we have said, the Soviet Five-Year Plans are often cited as an example of a forced *tempo* of industrialisation promoted at the expense of the standard of life of the people. On this whole matter there has been a good deal of loose and ill-

---

[1] Or alternatively other imports cut down, which means a curtailment of consumption of imported consumer goods (or raw materials to be used in making consumer goods).

informed chatter in the West. Actually, as we shall see below, the
First Five-Year Plan as originally drafted (even in its maximum
or " optimal " variant in which it was adopted by the Government
as the definitive programme) provided for a steady increase, and
not a decrease, in consumption from year to year over the quinquennium. Certainly the Plan did not envisage any lowering of
consumption as the *conditio sine qua non* of the high rate of investment for which it budgeted. Although the share of consumption
in the national income was designed to fall from 81 per cent. to
66 per cent. over the quinquennium, the absolute amount of consumption was planned so as to grow by about 6 per cent. even in
each of the first two years, and to grow by a total of 40 per cent. in
values and 75 per cent. in real terms over the quinquennium as
a whole.[1] In so far as a fall in the standard of life occurred in the
"tight" years of the First Five-Year Plan, this was largely due
to what one may call extraneous and "accidental" factors (the
nature of which we shall consider in more detail below) which were
not contemplated in the original Plan. Such factors could not be
regarded as necessary concomitants of industrialisation and are at
any rate without much relevance to an estimate of the consequences
of industrialisation elsewhere.

There remains another and quite distinct sense in which it is
sometimes said that a process of rapid industrialisation necessitates
an increase in the rate of saving. In this sense, increased saving
must accompany a process of increased investment, but it need not
precede it in time (or precede it in the sense of a causal-genetic
chain of events) and it does not represent any absolute reduction
of consumption. The saving which in this sense is stated to be
necessary refers to the extra income which the increased investment
activity *ipso facto* represents. As such, the statement has a purely
formal significance, and merely states that, if the active labour
force is increased by a given percentage as a result of employing
additional labour on constructional work, then the real income of
the community *including* the constructional work will have risen
without the output of consumption goods having risen as well. But
behind it there stands a more substantial point. When labour
moves from the village into industry, and takes employment at a
level of wages appropriate to urban employment, the money income
of the community will almost inevitably be raised. Unless this rise
in money income can be tapped in the form of taxation or voluntary

[1] S. G. Strumilin, *Sotsialnie Problemi Piatiletki, 1928/9–1932/3*, 52 ; cit. below,
page 235.

savings, the increased money-demand for commodities cannot be
immediately satisfied (unless the productivity of labour in agriculture or in consumption goods industries has risen *pari passu*),
and a goods shortage and an upward pressure on prices must result.[1]
Here again there has been some misconceived talk about events in
the U.S.S.R. It has been said that inflation accompanied the
putting into operation of the Five-Year Plans ; sometimes with the
corollary that thereby new sources of finance were mobilised, without which those high rates of investment could not have been
maintained ; sometimes with the corollary that thereby the investment at which the Plan was aiming was shown to be in excess of
real economic possibilities. On this matter, again, we shall have
more to say below. It must suffice at the present stage to say only
this : an expansion of money income (and of the money in circulation) seems likely to be an inevitable consequence of any increased
industrial investment in a backward agricultural economy. This
increase of money income will be a function of the increase of
employment (short of a reduction of wage-rates) and hence of the
wage-bill, not of financial policy ; and there is no fundamental
sense in which the price-rise which may be the consequence of this
larger money income either can augment the real potentialities of
industrial expansion or be a witness that the limits of these potentialities have been passed.[2] We shall also at a later stage adduce
reasons for supposing that in an economy of the type of Soviet
economy any substantial increase in the rate of investment is likely
to raise the ratio of retail prices to costs ; thereby creating a price-

[1] This upward pressure on prices is likely to be the greater if the income-
elasticity of demand is large for those things of which the supply is most restricted;
which may well be the case with people on a low standard of life who are likely to
spend most of any increased income on a few primary foodstuffs.

[2] The war-time Bombay Plan for the Industrialisation of India, for example,
did not explicitly state, but certainly implied, that "inflation" can somehow
provide an additional source to finance investment. In the purely financial sense
that, if "voluntary savings" are likely to be deficient, a price-rise is an alternative
way of equating enhanced money income with the supply of consumption goods,
this can of course be maintained. But the authors of the Bombay Plan based their
conclusion on the statement that the margin between consumption and income
per head would be too narrow to permit of "savings" of an adequate amount. In
then stating that "inflation" could provide an additional source for financing investment, they seemed to ignore the fact that, if the available margin between income
and consumption has been fully estimated, inflation is incapable of widening it,
and if it cannot it is incapable of providing a new source of savings. Alternatively,
it is possible that in estimating the margin between consumption and income they
omitted to take account of the effect of investment in increasing income. Elsewhere the authors spoke of the "hardship to the masses" caused by Soviet
industrialisation due to "over-enthusiasm" and a too high rate of investment: a
result which they prided themselves on avoiding by choosing a lower rate of
investment (1st Penguin Ed., 1944, *A Plan of Economic Development for India*, 44–5,
48).

margin which, in a purely balance-sheet sense, will automatically provide the means whereby that investment is " financed ".

In any such process of economic development there will be two main and conjoint dynamic factors : technical improvement and capital accumulation. The first of these will determine the concrete forms in which the second is embodied, and the progress of the second will determine the extent to which advantage can be taken of the former at any particular point in time. Soviet economists have eschewed Western notions of capital as a factor of production (with a specific cost attaching to its creation or its use, and a specific " yield ") and have treated it as the embodiment of labour (past labour : Marx's " stored-up " or " dead " labour) in the particular form of material aids to current labour in production, and as " costing " the present no more than the labour necessarily devoted to its maintenance or renewal. In a socialist society these durable instruments of production lose the specific historical character which they had when they were in private ownership and they become the property as well as the creation of society as a collective whole. The result of this emphasis has been to focus attention upon increasing the productivity of labour by augmenting and improving the stock of capital equipment with which labour works as the prime objective of economic policy. The existing stock of instruments is regarded as part of the social heritage which any given generation acquires from history, and not as a factor of production which has to " yield " a certain return (i.e. a return *additional* to the cost of its amortisation or depreciation) in order to justify the " cost " that its creation originally involved. Accordingly, since planning attempts to take a long view and has small reason to discount the future,[1] there is little to qualify the priority that is assigned to the task of equipping future decades with productive instruments more richly than the present is equipped. Differences in the incomes of nations or of generations are regarded as deriving primarily from the richness or poverty of this technical heritage ; and to add to this heritage is regarded as the reasoned duty of each decade towards its successors.

There is another consequence of this emphasis which is, perhaps, worthy of remark. Since capital is no longer conceived as a sum of values, separable from concrete instruments of production— alienable " capital claims ", yielding income-rights to their posses-

---

[1] That is to discount the addition to productivity in the future, which will result from an addition to the stock of capital equipment, for any reason *other* than the higher income per head (and hence the smaller urgency of wants) which the future is likely to have as compared with the present.

sors and capable of being trafficked in independently of the properties to which they refer—the pressure to export capital, which has
been so large a factor in shaping the policies of capitalist states,
is absent from Soviet economy. This is not to say that there are
no reasons which may induce the U.S.S.R. to export goods on loan
to other countries. It is to say only that this process will be seen
for what it is : a transfer of products of home industry from home
uses to foreign uses, against no corresponding present import of
products in return. If investment is thought of in real terms, as an
addition to the community's stock of productive instruments, a
diversion of such investment to a foreign sphere will be regarded
as something which impoverishes productive power at home in the
immediate future (even if it brings benefits in the more distant
future from the heightened productivity of a neighbour's industry,
with its cheapened supplies). It will not be thirsted for as a means
of maintaining or enlarging the paper value of capital claims. What
has been a major " expansionist " force in capitalist countries, and
a cause of international rivalries, will accordingly be absent from
Soviet economy.

A question that has been central to most discussions about
economic planning has been the possibility of combining co-ordination of economic decisions at the centre with the exercise of discretion and initiative at the periphery. We have remarked that the
essence of economic planning lies in the fact that decisions which in
a capitalist society are diffused among numerous units are embodied
in a single complex decision which constitutes the plan. Decisions
about price and output and about investment in the renewal or
extension of capital equipment are taken, no longer atomistically
according to a profit-motivation—the motive of maximising profit
in a given market situation—but integrally in accordance with the
dictates of social policy. In practice, however, it will be impossible
for a plan to embody decisions about everything. Its preoccupation will necessarily be with the main contours of the economic
process. The filling out of these main contours with detail, the
adaptation of general directives to the special qualities of a particular
situation, which the most long-sighted planner located at the centre
cannot possibly bring within his focus, must inevitably be decentralised. A plan has to be constructed on the basis of information
that can be expressed in generalised form ; and the decisions it
embraces have to be capable of expression in precise terms. Yet
there will necessarily be much in the economic situation that defies
any such precise description, or which has not yet reached the stage

of digestion in experience where it can be easily described in verbal terms at all. The actual " feel " of the situation by men standing close to events is here essential to any realistic decision. In the adaptation of a plan to a rapidly changing situation, this can be seen to be of special importance. If not in major degree, at least in very large degree the success of any system of economic planning will depend on the character of the personnel near the periphery of economic decision, and on the capacity of the system to provide an adequate motivation for those peripheral decisions to be efficiently taken and implemented. It is from lack of capable lieutenants and sergeants rather than from poor generalship that economic planning runs the danger of failing.

The crucial obstacle to any attempt to impose a set of centralised decisions upon a capitalist economy is the tendency of entrepreneurs, who still hold (or until recently held) rights of economic sovereignty, to obstruct any provisions of an economic plan which run counter to the aim of maximising the profit to be earned upon their property. Quite apart from anything of a sufficiently political and conscious character to justify the name of " economic sabotage ", a concerted passive resistance would probably develop from the play of conditioned entrepreneur-behaviour alone. In such circumstances an economic plan imposed upon the economy from above is likely to have a purely negative character, excluding certain courses of action from the agenda or setting limits within which the autonomous decisions of entrepreneur units can operate. If anything more positive than this is contemplated, enforcing courses of action such as would not normally be taken, it will be necessary for State policy to be backed by extensive coercive powers and by a special apparatus of coercion which duplicates the normal apparatus of economic administration. It is a situation of this type that apparently lies in the background of the mind of those critics who allege that abnormal coercive powers of the State and an inflated bureaucratic apparatus are inevitable accompaniments of any planned economy.

In a socialist economy, by contrast, the managers of industry are no longer persons who either hold rights of ownership over the means of production or are responsible to private owners ; and the motivation of the economic activities which they control is no longer that of maximising profit-earnings on such property. Moreover, an economic system which has passed through the fire of social revolution will enjoy at least this advantage over any other : that the traditions of economic administration, and the traditional forms in which these are embodied and preserved, will

to a very large extent have been broken and the personnel which
rules economic activity at the periphery will have been extensively purged and refreshed by the infusion of fresh blood.   One
can, indeed, say that this cathartic action constitutes a major part
of the historical rôle of social revolutions.   Even so, although the
motive and habit of obstruction may have been exorcised, it does
not follow that the personnel responsible for the management of
economic enterprises will be spontaneously inclined or fitted to
co-operate wholeheartedly with the spirit as well as with the letter
of a central economic plan.   Sectional interests and departmentalism
may give rise to centrifugal tendencies which conflict with co-
ordination, such as we shall see were an important factor in the
early years of Soviet planning.   To achieve the requisite degree of
co-operation, a combination of education and inducement will be
necessary, so that a fairly close-knit identity of aims and of interests
in essential matters between the collectivity which frames the plan
and the individuals and groups which operate the plan may be
created.

In certain respects economic plans in Soviet economy embrace a
greater amount of detail than one might have deemed practicable ;
for example, regarding the costing and pricing and the output of
particular commodities and varieties of commodities, as well as
about new construction projects and the reconstruction of existing
plants.   At the same time, in a number of directions much greater
latitude is given to peripheral initiative, both in the moulding of
plans and in implementing them in detail, than is often supposed.
This applies particularly to the production of things which are
susceptible of greater variety and to industries which both rest
upon local sources of supply and cater for a local market.   Moreover, in all except certain key lines of production, where supplies,
orders and administration are alike centralised in high degree,
this decentralisation of decision applies to a considerable range
of questions including the detailed employment of personnel (within
certain "wage limits"), the detailed choice of supplies of raw
materials, components and fuels and of details of delivery of the
finished product, also choice of methods of production within
the limits set by the investment and construction plan.   Upon
an efficient and untroubled decision of such questions a very
great deal depends.   Stress has been laid in Soviet economic
literature since the early '20's upon the need to combine centralised
control over the main direction-lines of economic policy—" the
orientating directives "—with decentralisation of the managerial

operation of economic activity. In fact, the very word that is usually rendered into English as " control " has in Soviet usage a meaning that goes at least half-way towards what in England would be referred to as " supervision ", and might at any rate be not inappropriately rendered as " steering ". With a passing of the more acute shortages of the construction period, which imposed a necessity for stringent centralised allocation of scarce supplies, the tendency has been to extend this decentralisation of particular detailed decisions involved in current economic activity (we shall speak later of new forms of decentralisation since the middle 'fifties).

The precise measures by which a financial incentive is given to the economic units at the periphery to exercise this discretion along lines which harmonise with the general provisions of a centralised economic plan assume, therefore, a more universal interest and importance than at first glance they might appear to have. These measures were not the *a priori* creation of economic or social doctrine ; they were forged in the light of actual experience of economic administration, and they have emerged in their present shape from a process of continual adaptation and change. Their detailed character will be the subject of a later chapter (Chapter Fifteen); and this more complete account will be anticipated here only by this preliminary observation. The measures to which we have referred have mainly the form of financial induce- ments—inducements both of a group and an individual character ; and the main coercive instrument whereby the centralised direc- tives of the plan are enforced has come to consist of the financial apparatus. To this extent the controlling hand exerts a mediate rather than an immediate influence upon those who manage pro- duction. The essence of this method by which central control is combined with peripheral discretion is the translation of the nominal (limited) autonomy of each economic enterprise into reality by granting it a minimum quantity of its " own " resources, over which it has limited powers of disposal, while at the same time leaving it dependent for a margin of resources upon credit ad- vances from the banking system, over the disposal of which the latter is in a position to exercise a considerable measure of control. The provisions of the production plan are then clothed in financial form, in terms of costs and prices ; and any deviation of the actual from the planned result is accordingly left to express itself in an addition to, or subtraction from, the resources at the disposal of the enterprise. In summary one might, perhaps, hazard this generalisa- tion : the need to combine peripheral discretion with centralised direction is one of two crucial reasons for the prominent, if secondary, place that financial problems and a financial apparatus continue to occupy in Soviet planning. Administrative problems have been extensively transmuted into financial problems.

More important for many than these narrower economic issues will be another claim which Soviet development between the wars is increasingly making upon the attention of the world. Soviet planning in these years was not concerned only with economic problems, in the restricted sense of this term : it was concerned equally, if not more, with wider issues concerning those social relationships which compose the basic texture of society. Soviet economic policy was not something conducted as a calm experiment in a settled society of which the social basis had come to be taken for granted as the constant element in any economic problem. This policy, as we remarked at the opening of this chapter, was part of a process of revolutionary transformation from an old social order to a new one. Society was in transition from a social order which still bore marks of recent Feudalism and of levels of economic development which countries of Western Europe had passed a century or a century and a half ago. Economic policy was necessarily entwined and often dominated by consideration of the effect which an action might have on the relation between classes, on the dying out or the resuscitation of an old class or the bringing to maturity of a new. Whether this entwining of economic with social issues will lower or heighten the interest of an economist in the events which this book describes will no doubt depend upon his point of view. Certainly these events involve considerations which reach beyond what he usually regards as his special field. They relate, moreover, to changes which have aroused more apprehension and hatred in some and more enthusiasm and devoted allegiance in others than any set of events in modern history, not excluding the French Revolution. To describe them in an atmosphere uncharged with controversy is impossible. But one can hope at least to approach an objective study of these historic years by endeavouring to see facts as they were and to present issues of policy as they appeared to the eyes of the participators.

CHAPTER TWO

RUSSIAN ECONOMIC DEVELOPMENT PRIOR TO THE FIRST WORLD WAR

I

In its economic development, as in its geographical position, European Russia in the first decade and a half of the present century was intermediate between the undeveloped lands of Asia and the industrially developed regions of Western and Central Europe. It is true that capitalist industry had in certain regions shown a quite remarkable development, particularly since the 1880's : in the coal and iron region of the Donetz and the Dnieper in the south, in the Moscow region and the neighbourhood of Petersburg, and in Poland. Much of this industry was fairly modern in type, and was marked by a surprisingly high level of concentration both of production and of ownership and control. For example, the proportion of all workers in factories who were employed in enterprises with more than 500 workers reached the surprisingly high figure of 53 per cent. ; as compared with an American figure of 31 per cent. as the proportion of wage earners in manufacture in 1914 who were in establishments employing more than 500.[1] In the iron industry in the south the size of blast furnaces, measured by their output, was greater than in German industry, and about half as large again as those in British industry, and even three fifths of the much larger average size of furnaces in American industry. In 1913 nine iron and steel plants accounted for more than half the production of pig-iron. Nine tenths of the production of rails came from seven firms, and in the oil industry six large enterprises accounted for two thirds of the whole output of the Baku region. Taking Russian factory industry as a whole (exclusive of mining), the horse-power per worker was about three fifths of the equivalent figure in England and only a third of that in American industry, but was on a higher level than French and German industry at the time.[2]

---

[1] Liashchenko, *Narodnoe Khoziaistvo S.S.S.R.*, 559 ; *American Statistical Abstract, 1916,* 177. Liashchenko quotes a figure of 33 per cent. which is apparently a mistake. [2] Liashchenko, *op. cit.,* 560–2.

In the closing decades of the nineteenth century there had been a good deal of railway construction, which in mileage figures reached an impressive total. By 1903 there were some 40,000 miles of railroad in existence (about two thirds State-operated) in the area of the Russian Empire :[1] a figure which by 1914 had been increased by a further 8,000-odd miles. Between 1891 and 1904 the considerable feat of linking Moscow with the Pacific coast by means of the 4,000-mile Trans-Siberian railway[2] was carried through ; and by 1905 Tashkent had been linked with the Volga and further west by the Orenburg–Tashkent line, as well as with the Caspian Sea at Merv by the Turkestan railway across the trans-Caspian desert which had been started in 1884. But despite these achievements, Russia's railway development, whether measured in relation to area or to population, remained the lowest of any European country. On many lines the construction of the permanent way, as regards ballasting and gradients, the weight of rails and the closeness of sleepers, was inferior to the standards in vogue in Central and Western Europe, with slower train-speeds and diminished tractive-power of locomotives as the result ; and in view of the very limited exploitation of coal resources outside Poland and the Donbas in eastern Ukraine, railways in many parts, especially in Siberia, had to operate on wood-fuel. At the time of the Russo-Japanese war there was a railway bridge across the river Volga at only one point (ten years later increased to three). Lines such as the Trans-Siberian, the Tashkent and the Archangel lines were no more than single tracks. Road development was strikingly primitive. There were less than 20,000 miles of regular road, and of these scarcely more than 3,000 were surfaced in the west-European manner. As regards roads Russia was for the most part still in the position that England was in the mid-eighteenth century.

In general it can be said that industrialisation had as yet touched little more than the hem of Russia's economic system ; even if, where matured forms of industrial Capitalism had taken root, this Capitalism was of a fairly advanced type. The patches of factory

---

[1] Of this roughly six sevenths were within the territory of the U.S.S.R. as it existed prior to 1939.

[2] The total distance from Moscow to Vladivostok is about 5,500 miles. Engineering difficulties were very great owing to the rigours of the climate, the existence at some points of soil perpetually frozen a few feet below the surface, and a continual danger of thaws and flooding ; and in the Lake Baikal sector thirty-three tunnels had to be excavated through rock. There was much corruption and inefficiency in the administration, and the total expenditure (amounting to some £40 million) greatly exceeded the estimates.

industry in the Leningrad and Moscow districts and in the south were no more than industrial " islands " in a vast agricultural sea, bordered to the north by deep forests and to the south by mountain or desert. Less than 15 per cent. of the population lived in towns, and less than 10 per cent. derived their livelihood from industry. The total numbers employed in factory industry lay between two and three million (to which are to be added a further million railwaymen and three-quarters of a million miners). The mechanical horsepower in production, when measured per hundred of the population, worked out at only 1·6 in Russia against 13 in Germany, 24 in England and 25 in U.S.A.[1] Even many of the wage-earners in factories were only semi-proletarians, in the sense that they still had economic links with the village and often returned there in the summer to help their families with the harvest. According to an investigation in 1910, as many as two thirds of the factory workers of Petersburg, the capital, retained nominal ownership of some village land, and nearly a fifth of them returned to the village every summer. In the mining industry of the south the migration to the village in the harvest season was even more marked than it was in the factory industry of the Petersburg and Moscow districts. Moreover, twice as many persons were employed (though not always full time) in non-factory handicraft industries as were employed in factories with mechanical power or with more than sixteen employees ; and Capitalism in Russia still very largely took the relatively primitive form of the " putting-out system ", under which work was given out to domestic workers or to small sub-contracting masters, owning handicraft workshops, by capitalists who were as much merchants as manufacturers. The *kustarny* industry was the form which the first considerable development of Capitalism, based on hired labour, had taken in the 30's and 40's of the nineteenth century, captained by merchants or well-to-do peasants ; and its survival was encouraged throughout the century, despite the growth of a landless class in the countryside, by the continued attachment of the rural population to the village, due to restrictions on peasants' movement and on the sale of land by a peasant family, which continued despite the Emancipation of the Serfs in 1861. The factories that existed were frequently foreign importations : foreign-owned, foreign-financed and staffed by foreign managerial and technical personnel.

Not only in this respect, but with regard to her trade relations, Russia represented an economic system that was pendent on the

[1] Liashchenko, *op. cit.*, 562.

West. As an exporter of raw and agricultural products and an importer of finished manufactures, her agriculture had been developed in the course of the nineteenth century under the strong influence of the export market, and her manufactures had mainly grown up in relation to the few main urban markets of western Russia. She led the world as a grain exporter, and supplied nearly a third of the wheat imports and nearly a half of the imports of other grains of Western European countries. Cereals and other foodstuffs accounted for over a half of Russia's total exports in 1914; and goods classified as " raw materials and semi-manufactured goods " for a further 36 per cent. Of imports manufactured goods made up a third and were on the increase ; and raw materials, such as cotton, wool, jute and silk and some non-ferrous metals, together with semi-manufactured goods accounted for nearly a half. So great was the reliance of Russian economy on the German market and on German supplies (which composed half of her peacetime imports) that in the First World War of 1914–18 Russia continued to import certain commodities from Germany (chiefly chemicals, metals and machinery), explicitly exempting these from the general prohibition on trade with enemy countries.[1] The import tariff prior to 1914 was so graded as to lay an almost prohibitive rate of duty on most foodstuffs ; and although in 1896 the tariff had been reformed under the influence of Witte as Minister of Finance to give protection to industry, the average level of duty on industrial raw materials and on manufactured articles was by contrast relatively low. It was common knowledge that the large grain export thrived on the extreme poverty of the mass of the peasants, which combined with the tax system to oblige the poorer peasants to flood local markets with grain at low prices immediately after the harvest in order to acquire cash with which to meet their taxes and to meet debts incurred in the previous sowing period. At the same time, railway rates were adjusted favourably to transport of grain over long distances, thereby extending the area over which grain could be profitably sold for export ;[2] and both railway companies and the State Bank granted credits against consignments

[1] Cf. Baron Boris Nolde, *Russia in the Economic War* (1928), 54–5.
[2] Actually on short hauls the mileage rate worked out higher for export grain than for grain consigned to domestic markets (as a result of railway-rate policies introduced in the '90's) ; the intention of this being to reserve the supplying of the grain-importing regions of Central European Russia and the North and North-west to the agricultural regions on the northern edge of the black-earth belt. But as the distance increased, the difference disappeared, and the mileage rate for grain consigned to the ports fell considerably ; thereby favouring particularly districts a good distance from the Black Sea ports, such as those east of the Volga. (Cf. V. P. Timoshenko, *Agricultural Russia and the Wheat Problem*, 331–2.)

of grain for export. An indication of the tendency for agriculture to
be increasingly geared to the export market rather than to the needs
of mass consumption at home is that in the territories of European
Russia in the two decades prior to 1914 the production of wheat
(the main export crop) rose by about 75 per cent., while that of rye
(the crop consumed by the peasantry and the town workers) increased only a little if at all.[1]

Russia had also been an importer of capital from abroad, to an
average amount of some 200 million roubles annually in the two
decades before the war of 1914. Annual indebtedness on foreign
loans exceeded the annual import of new capital, and hence accounted for part of Russia's surplus of merchandise exports over
imports in her annual trade balance.[2] It has been estimated that
nearly a half of the capital invested in the Donetz coal basin prior
to 1914 was foreign, and over 80 per cent. of the capital in iron
mining, metallurgy and the oil industry. The total foreign capital
invested in Russian industry has been estimated at over 2 milliard
gold roubles, of which 32 per cent. was French and 22 per cent.
British; and a further 5 milliard odd in State and municipal and
State-guaranteed loans.[3] Of the basic capital of 18 leading joint-
stock banks some 42 per cent. was in foreign ownership, firstly
French and secondly German.[4]

But while Tsarist Russia in such respects occupied a semi-
colonial position relatively to the West, she also had her own
imperialist ambitions in the south and south-east and east, and
here even exported a little capital and sought markets for manufactured goods. In the second half of the nineteenth century she

---

[1] Timoshenko, op. cit., 368 ; Pavlovsky, Agricultural Russia on the Eve of the
Revolution, 258–63 ; M. Miller, Economic Development of Russia, 1905–1914,
57–78, 111. Of wheat production between a quarter and a third was exported in
the two decades prior to 1914 and of rye no more than about 5 per cent. Actually
a major part of the extra wheat went to meet urban consumption among the lower
middle and middle class ; but at the same time wheat export increased by approximately a third. Less than 10 per cent. of the rye was marketed at any considerable
distance from the village (i.e. sent to market by rail or water). About half of the
marketed surplus of the four principal grain crops went for export and more than
a half of the grain traffic on the railways. (Timoshenko, op. cit., 372, 578 ; Pavlovsky,
op. cit., 251–3 ; Liashchenko, op. cit., 614–15.) Of flax and hemp sent by rail three
quarters was for export.

[2] Between 1898 and 1913 Russian exports as recorded equalled 17·4 million
roubles and imports 13·3 million. The import of capital (into industry, municipal
and State loans, etc.) was approximately 4 million, and dividend and interest payments sent abroad about 5 million. (Cit. from an article on " Pre-war Russia's
Balance of Payments " in Vestnik Finansov, 1928, No. 5, by Liashchenko, op. cit.,
600–1.) The other large item of " invisible import " seems to have been " expenses
of Russians abroad " which is put at the surprisingly high figure of 2 million roubles.

[3] L. Pasvolsky and H. G. Moulton, Russian Debts and Russian Reconstruction,
175–84.   [4] Liashchenko, op. cit., 591.

followed up her successful penetration of the Amur basin in the Far East and nearer home of Transcaucasia with the subjugation of Central Asia ; and at the turn of the century she was showing signs of extending her economic and political influence into Persia, Mongolia and Manchuria. Lenin had spoken of Russia in 1905 with its " handful of feudal landowners headed by Nicholas II ruling in close alliance with the magnates of finance capital " as playing the rôle of agent to the imperialism of Western Europe ; to which fact he attributed the " military-feudal " character of the Tsarist State and its policies ; adding that Russia represented an economy " in which the latest capitalist imperialism is entwined, so to speak, with a particularly dense network of pre-capitalist relations " and " a very backward agriculture and a very primitive village " co-existed with " a very advanced industrial and financial capitalism ".[1]

The basic reason for the lowness of the average standard of life[2] in Tsarist Russia was the low productivity of her agriculture, which constituted the livelihood of four fifths of her population. For an agricultural country, moreover a grain-exporting country, her population density was relatively great : that of European Russia exclusive of Poland at the end of the nineteenth century being 53·5 per square mile against 31 in U.S.A. Moreover, the proportion of the total land that was cultivated was also relatively small, being no more than 25 per cent. even in European Russia, compared with something like 40 per cent. in France and Germany. The result was that the average area of cultivated land per head of the agricultural population worked out at a figure of only about 3 acres, compared with about 13 acres in U.S.A., 8 acres in Denmark and 4 acres in France and Germany.[3] At the same time the average yield per acre of arable land in European Russia was no more than about 8 to 10 bushels ; below that prevailing in those regions which represent the American extreme of extensive cultivation and scarcely more than a quarter of the yield per acre in the United Kingdom, a third of that of eastern Germany and half that of France. Her wheat yield was below that of Italy and Serbia, little more than a half that of Austria-Hungary and about

---

[1] *Collected Works* (Russian edition), vol. XIX, 136 ; vol. XX, 570.

[2] National income per head, according to the estimate of Prokopovitch, was about 102 roubles a year, or scarcely more than a third that of Germany, less than a quarter that of England and about a seventh that of U.S.A. at that date.

[3] Academician D. Prianishnikov and Prof. A. Lebediantsev in *Planovoe Khoziaistvo*, 1935, No. 3, 69. In the northern part of the Ukraine the area of cultivated land per head of the agricultural population was not much more than 1½ acres, or nearly as low as the equivalent figure for India.

on a level with India.[1]   Her agriculture accordingly " combined
the negative features of European agriculture (relative smallness of
arable area) and of American agriculture (lowness of yield)," with
a resulting level of grain production per head " appropriate to a
country importing grain, instead of exporting it ".[2]

This is surprising in view of the fact that Russia contains in her
black-earth region some of the potentially richest soil for grain
cultivation in Europe.   This belt stretches from Bessarabia across
southern European Russia where it has a maximum breadth of some
400 miles round Kharkov (between Orel and Tula to the north and
just above the coast of the Sea of Azov to the south), across the
Volga between Kazan and Saratov and into western Siberia where
it narrows to a breadth of little more than 100 miles.   But except
in the western Ukraine, west of the Dnieper, fertility of the soil
is offset by the aridity of the climate ; the rainfall in the Volga
region of the black-earth belt being only about a half or even a
third of that in the west and sometimes falling below twelve and
even below ten inches annually.   Even the melting of the snows in
the eastern areas is of little assistance to agriculture, since the thaw
is too rapid and the moisture, instead of penetrating, runs off and
often washes away the soil, forming ravines.   As one moves west
from the Volga across the Dnieper into the western Ukraine, the
yield tends to increase by two or three bushels an acre, or by
approximately 20 or 30 per cent.

But the yield was also maintained at a low level by the primitive
character of farming technique.   The three-field system predominated in most parts of the country, which necessitated one third
of the arable area lying fallow every year.   In some parts of the
southern Ukrainian steppes and the north Caucasus a rotation
system inferior even to the three-field was common : the *perelog*
under which exhaustion of the soil tended to occur after a period
of years, since only a fifth or a quarter of the arable area was left
fallow at one time.   Many village communes continued to practise
periodic redistribution of the land among their members ; and
even in those communes where this did not occur (and its absence
was a characteristic of the west and south-west) a farmer's land was
held in scattered strips, often at long distances (frequently several
miles, and not infrequently five or six miles) from one another
and from the village.   These strips were sometimes very numerous :

---

[1] The lowness of the wheat yield is partly, but far from wholly, due to the
fact that Russia generally produced hard red wheats, the yield of which is always
lower than soft wheats. (Timoshenko, *op. cit.*, 274.)

[2] Prianishnikov and Lebediantsev, *loc. cit.*, 69.

as many as twenty or thirty being not uncommon in some of the
northern provinces, while a hundred strips per household was not
unknown.[1] Of no less importance as a reason for low yield was the
lack of balance in the holding : in particular, the insufficiency of
available pasture for the proper arable–hayland–pasture balance.[2]
In the southern steppe region, in particular, the shortage of pasture,
and hence of livestock, resulted in an extreme shortage of manure ;
and it has been estimated that the amount of manuring of land
was only about one tenth of the traditional amount in east Germany. The adverse factors affecting productivity were therefore
most serious precisely in those regions where the rural population had come to be settled most thickly—the regions of new settlement in the " free frontier " regions of past centuries—and where,
because land was more valuable and more of it had been retained
in the hands of large landowners, peasant holdings on the average
were smallest.[3] On the other hand, in the north and north-west
where available pasture was more plentiful, and meadow lands
were more valuable than arable, it was precisely the former that
the landlord had striven to keep in his own hands at the Emancipation settlement ; so that *peasant* lands remained deficient in suitable
pasture even in these regions where the average of peasant holdings
was generally larger. While livestock could be pastured in the
forests in summer, the number of cattle that a peasant household
could maintain through the long winter was narrowly limited. In
a bad year it was not uncommon for the straw from roofs to be fed
to cattle and for more than a third of the cattle of the village to be
slaughtered or sold, for lack of means to maintain them. The
average number of working horses per peasant household came
out at less than one ; which meant that, if some households had
several horses, a large number were without a horse with which
to plough and bring in the harvest or to take the produce to market.
Moreover, in the last two decades of the nineteenth century the

---

[1] Pavlovsky, *op. cit.*, 82 ; Liashchenko, *op. cit.*, 370.

[2] Cf. : " In a large number of places, sometimes throughout whole districts,
it was not the sizes of the holdings, but the relative shortage in them of this essential
element that was the root of the problem. Here, indeed, one could see the application of 'the law of the minimum ', as enunciated by Liebig with regard to the constitution and fertility of the soil, to the economic aspect of farming. On the average,
under the three-course system, the area of meadows and pastures must be approximately equal to that of arable. . . . By the close of the last century the ratio, in a
great majority of cases, did not exceed one third or one half of the arable. . . . At
its worst in the Province of Kursk that fraction did not exceed one thirtieth.
(Pavlovsky, *op. cit.*, 84–5, who quotes from A. I. Chuprov.)

[3] To some extent the lack of balance in the rotation was a *result* of the pressure
of peasant population on available peasant land, since this had forced the extension
of arable at the expense of grass land.

position in this respect had been deteriorating. The amount of cattle per peasant household is estimated to have declined between 1870 and 1900 by 30 per cent. and the number of working horses per working male in similar proportion and per 1,000 dessiatines by 23 per cent.[1]

To these factors in low productivity was added the chronic deficiency of capital among all peasants except a thin upper stratum. This showed itself not only in the prevalence of extremely primitive implements, but also in the absence of reserves to tide the family over the year and to meet taxes and the provision of seed-corn if the harvest in any year was poor. Half of the peasants still used a primitive type of wooden plough (called the *sokha*). Most sowing was by hand, and only in the south-eastern steppes had seed-drills become at all common even as late as the second half of the 1920's. The major part of the harvesting and even of the threshing was done by hand, laboriously with a sickle and the centuries-old hand-flail. Agricultural surveys indicated that there was on the average about one reaper to every 25 peasant farms, one threshing machine to every 29 and one mower to every 100. In this respect the larger estates and the well-to-do *kulak* farms were better situated, and the yield per acre on them was generally somewhat higher than the average.[2] It was they who were responsible for most of the marketed produce ; while the middling and poorer peasantry were primarily subsistence farmers, selling only so much of their produce as was necessary to procure money for purposes of taxation and the few bare essentials that had to be purchased from outside the village, such as kerosene for lamps. Thus, while some two thirds of all agricultural produce came from peasant lands, and only a third from the large estates, as regards the marketed surplus something approaching the reverse proportions held ; and even of the 30–40 per cent. of the marketed surplus which came from peasant land, by far the greater part of this came from the upper layer of well-to-do *kulak* farms. The tendency of the large estates was to develop the cultivation of specialised crops with an urban or an export market, such as sugar beet, which was

---

[1] Pavlovsky, *op. cit.*, 82–6 ; Mavor, *Economic History of Russia*, vol. II, 99–103, 285, 291.
[2] Taking the average yield per acre for 1901–13 in the black soil belt, this differed in the case of spring wheat from 9·7 bushels on peasant land to 11·5 on the estates, in the case of winter wheat from 13·4 to 14·5 respectively, and of winter rye from 12·4 to 15·2 respectively. (Timoshenko, *op. cit.*, 276.) As an average of the whole country, the difference, according to the official figures, worked out at between 15 and 20 per cent. ; but this may be an under-estimate of the difference owing to the way the statistics were compiled. (Cf. Pavlovsky, *op. cit.*, 218.)

being considerably developed in the west and south-west in the decade and a half prior to 1914 ; also flax and in the north-west dairy farming.[1] Apart from the big estates on the southern steppes, producing wheat for export, grain and especially rye remained essentially a peasant crop, grown to the extent of nearly three fourths[2] of it not for market but for home peasant consumption. Yet even in the case of grain, while the estates accounted for barely one eighth of total production, they supplied nearly one half of the marketed surplus.

All averages about peasant conditions and peasant cultivation are, however, apt to be misleading since they conceal the extensive social differentiation among the peasantry themselves, with the important tendencies in village economy which were the result of this. An official inquiry of the Central Statistical Committee relating to 1905, and covering 50 provinces, showed that a richer 10 per cent. of peasant households, each possessing more than 20 dessiatines (about 55 acres) of cultivated land, owned some 35 per cent. of all land ; while half of all peasant households had holdings of less than 8 dessiatines (about 22 acres), and occupied just over a fifth of the total area. The smallest holders of all, those possessing less than 10 acres, made up one sixth of the peasantry, but covered less than 4 per cent. of the land. In the villages that still undertook periodic redistribution of village land it was customary for larger holdings to be allotted to families having more mouths to feed and more hands to work the land ; so that to some extent the size of holding was apt to vary with the size of the family. However, not all villages practised redistribution ; and even where they did it frequently happened that land allotments went to the families which had horses and implements to work them, and the rich peasant could frequently use his influence over the village commune or *mir* and its officials to secure preferential treatment. Inequalities in the possession of livestock and farming equipment were apt to be greater than inequalities of landholding, and even to some extent to form the basis for the latter. At the end of the nineteenth century nearly a third of all peasant households lacked horses. The rich *kulak*, with horses and carts and ploughs to spare, could loan these to his poorer neighbour who had none, sometimes on a kind of *métayage* system under which the latter yielded a proportion of his produce to the former, or under a labour-rent

---

[1] Even in these specialised crops yield was below that of western countries : e.g. the yield of beet per acre was less than two thirds that of France and little more than a half Germany's.

[2] That is, as a proportion of the gross harvest.

system under which the poorer peasant paid for the plough team or the extra land he hired by himself working a given area of land for his richer neighbour. To work two dessiatines of land for the loan of one dessiatine was a common rate of exchange under these labour-renting bargains ; and it was not unknown for a poorer peasant to have to work three dessiatines for every one used for himself. To this type of contract between rich and poor peasant was frequently added a more usurious one, by which the former advanced to the latter seed-corn in the spring against future repayment in money or in a share of the crop after the harvest. Most of the poor peasants, being in urgent need of cash after the harvest, were apt to glut the market with their grain in these post-harvest months ; with the result that the peasant with capital to spare could buy up the grain at low prices and hold it until the spring when prices were higher, and when the very peasants who had parted with it the previous autumn were often forced into the market again as buyers to tide them over the period of sowing and harvesting ; taking back produce at a higher price (in money or in their own labour or on some kind of loan contract secured on their future labour time) than the price at which they had sold grain six months before. This fluctuation of prices on local markets between autumn and spring was frequently as much as 30–50 per cent. ; and in some provinces, even in those provinces that produced a regular surplus for export, more than a half of the peasant households, and in bad years more than three quarters, had themselves become buyers of grain by the spring.[1]   It was this type of sharp practice, by which profit was made from the necessities of his neighbours, that earned the richer peasant his opprobrious title of *kulak*, or "fist" : a creature characterised, in Stepniak's[2] words, by " the hard unflinching cruelty of a thoroughly uneducated man who . . . has come to consider money-making, by whatever means, as the only pursuit to which a rational being should devote himself ", and affording " fair samples of that rapacious and plundering stage of economic development which occupies a place analogous to that of the Middle Ages in political history ".

An important result was an increasing tendency for the poorer peasantry to seek additional earnings, either by working for wages or by undertaking domestic handicraft industry. For the majority even of the so-called " middle peasants "—the families with a horse or two horses and a twenty-five to forty acre holding—the

[1] Cf. Mavor, *op. cit.*, vol. II, 291 ; G. T. Robinson, *Rural Russia under the Old Regime*, 103.   [2] *Russian Peasantry*, 55.

product of their land was insufficient to maintain a family above the subsistence level. From an official investigation in 1895 it emerged that in 46 provinces of European Russia more than a half of the peasantry lacked the 19 poods of breadstuffs necessary for the needs of a peasant household, and less than a fifth had an excess above the 26–27 poods considered "truly adequate".[1] It has been estimated that the average annual net income of a peasant household from the land amounted to no more than some 150–180 roubles (the equivalent roughly of about £15–£18).[2] In the black-earth belt it was estimated at the end of the nineteenth century that a quarter of the males of working age took employment as agricultural labourers for some period of the year;[3] and the big estates of the southern steppes met their "peak" labour needs at harvest time by the employment of several millions of migratory labourers from villages often hundreds of miles north and north-east. Others moved to factory districts and the mines. But this casual wage labour was not only supplied to the large estates and to industry. About half of it was employed by the local *kulak* in cultivating the additional land he could rent or buy to enlarge his allotment or in the local *kustarny* industry that he had established. Thus, in addition to the industrial proletariat proper, there existed a large rural semi-proletariat drawn from families who were unable to support themselves from their holdings of land, since they lacked the animal-power and equipment with which to work it, and were burdened or dispossessed by taxation and usury. For rising industry and a *kulak* class to feed upon, this rural semi-proletariat represented a rich potential reserve.

II

The condition of the peasantry and peasant discontents at the opening of the present century had their roots in the terms of the Peasant Emancipation of 1861, and in the outcome of the arrangements by which the peasant ceased to be a serf and became in legal title, at least, an independent holder of his allotment-land[4] (subject to the powers vested in the village commune (*mir*) to regulate the

---

[1] Mavor, *op. cit.*, vol. II, 290.   [2] Pavlovsky, *op. cit.*, 94.

[3] *Ibid.*, 199. Lenin in his "Agrarian Question in Russia" quoted figures to show that "seven tenths of the horseless peasants and almost half the one-horse peasants hire themselves out as labourers", these "lower groups of peasantry" occupying the position of "labourers and day labourers with allotments". (*Selected Works,*, vol. I, 190–1.)

[4] It was, however, the family as a unit and not the head of the family (until 1906) in whom the holding was vested.

land allotment among peasant families and to distribute certain collective liabilities laid upon the village as a unit). But the effects
of the Emancipation settlement were far from uniform ; and
some attention is necessary to the peculiarities of the main regions
into which agricultural Russia falls, if the agrarian history of the
second half of the nineteenth century and the peasant movement
which constituted so important an element in the revolutions of
1917 are to be understood.

We have said something of the characteristics of the black-
earth zone and of the difference of climate between the western
districts and the more easterly steppe districts, which made the
latter with their lower rainfall and greater extremes of summer
and winter temperatures a land of low crop-yields and of extensive arable cultivation. This was the region which in earlier
centuries had been an area of recent settlement : the land beyond
the official frontiers to which fugitive serfs had fled from the
exactions of their lords and masters in Central Muscovy and where
squatters' rights prevailed. The regions of the Don and the Yaik
(or Ural) rivers and the Kuban had witnessed the famous Cossack
settlements : largely self-governing communities of colonists who
owed certain military service obligations to the Crown. Much of
the land of this region was cultivated in a form more primitive than
the three-field rotation ; land being ploughed and sown for as
many years as it would yield a crop, and then when its fertility was
exhausted being allowed to revert to grazing land for a period, while
the cultivator and his plough moved on to fresh land. Grazing of
sheep in earlier times also occupied a prominent position in these
regions. As these lands became more thickly settled, however,
regular fallowing of land on some kind of primitive crop rotation
came to be adopted (although the previous system of exhaustive
cropping remained general in the Kuban and Don and eastern
Ukraine); and especially under the attraction of export markets
the arable area was extended at the expense of pasture.[1] Sheep
grazing shrank until it occupied a minor place (except in the Kuban
and Don and Stavropol) ; and on the eve of the Revolution nearly
three quarters of the area was arable and nine tenths of the arable
area was sown with wheat, rye, oats or barley. This was the region
essentially of extensive wheat cultivation and of production for
export through the ports of the Black Sea and the Sea of Azov. It

[1] In the three decades following the Emancipation the arable area in the black-
earth belt grew by as much as a half ; while in the non-black-earth regions it
actually declined—by nearly 10 per cent. (Liashchenko, *op. cit.*, 375.)

was also a region of fairly extensive large-scale capitalist arable farming.

By contrast with this, the western Ukraine, to the west of the Dnieper and particularly west of Kiev, was a region of denser population, of higher yield and of more intensive methods of farming. Not only did grain-yields tend to be higher by something like 20 or 30 per cent., but more attention was paid to the intensive cultivation of non-grain crops like sugar beet and potatoes ; and root crops as well as grass fairly widely had a place in the rotation. Moreover, periodic repartition of land by the village community did not exist in this region.

Quite different from the southern black-earth belt and steppe land, both in historical traditions and agricultural conditions, was the forest region in the northern half of European Russia. Here the proportion of arable is very much smaller than anywhere in the black-earth belt, and the chief grain crop is rye and not wheat. In the north-west, round Petersburg, Novgorod and Pskov, only a relatively small proportion of the land was suitable for the plough. Forests and marshes occupied nearly two thirds of the whole region, and of the remainder meadows and pastures occupied as prominent a place as land under crops. By contrast with the crippling aridity of the eastern steppe regions, the cost of drainage here set a limit to arable farming ; while the abundance of meadow land favoured stock breeding and also dairy farming. On the whole, the methods of cultivation were superior in these regions to those prevalent in the south, the three-course rotation being in many places improved upon by the introduction of multiple grass crops and roots. Flax and potatoes were largely grown, and market gardening was developed in the vicinity of the capital. One has the curious paradox, indeed, that in this region of poor soil for growing crops the actual yield was generally greater than in the steppe region (not only greater than in provinces like Kherson and Taurida but in the case of the Petersburg region greater even than the Kuban) ; thereby illustrating that economic factors, such as nearness to towns, are more important than geographical in determining variations in the yield of land. Moreover, in the centre and north the custom of periodic repartition of land by the village community was more common than in the steppe zone, and in many areas was almost universal.

The geographical division into forest regions and steppe corresponded to the economic distinction between what have been traditionally called the consuming or grain-importing regions and the surplus-producing or grain-exporting regions. In general, the former grew insufficient grain for their needs, even for village needs, and appeared as buyers of grain on the internal market ; while the latter provided a grain surplus for export either abroad or to the grain-importing regions to the north. Generally speaking, the provinces on the northern edge of the black-earth belt (officially known as the Central Agricultural Region) sent their grain surplus northward to the deficiency regions ; and the peculiar construction of railway tariffs, of which we have spoken,[1] encouraged them so to do. The surplus of the central black-earth zone and of the provinces in the extreme south, on the other hand, with their greater concentration on wheat production, gravitated towards southern ports for shipment through the Black Sea.

Intermediate between this northern region and the south was the belt of partly cleared forest land stretching from Minsk through Moscow to Perm. To the west the comparatively poor region of White Russia resembled the north-west in the limited extent of cereal cultivation and its greater attention to crops such as potatoes, to a less extent flax, to pig breeding and also some stock farming. The Moscow region, with a moderately high density of population, had a proportion of arable land that was markedly higher than the north-west or the west, but much smaller than that of the steppe region of the south. Only to the south round Riazan and Tula, on the edge of the black-earth zone, did the region produce a surplus of grain. Land prices, however, were relatively high in this region ; and cattle breeding and dairy farming, and market gardening in the neighbourhood of towns, occupied a fairly important place. Further east the region usually known as the Middle Volga between Nizhni-Novgorod and Samara belonged rather more to the surplus-producing than to the consuming or deficiency zone, although the northern portion of it usually needed to import some grain. About half the total area was arable, and of this four fifths was devoted to cereal crops, principally rye. But as there were possibilities of forest-grazing such as did not exist further south, there was also a moderate amount of livestock breeding. To the east of the Volga towards Perm and Ufa lay more thinly settled country. Round Perm and Viatka population was thinly spread, arable cultivation covered a relatively small area compared to forest land and pasture combined, although it sufficed at least for rural consumption, and dairy farming and cattle occupied a place of some importance. To the south was the country of the Bashkirs : that country of

---

[1] Above, page 37.

virgin land for new settlement in the early nineteenth century of
which we read in Aksakov's genial *Country Gentleman*. The
methods of cultivation here were as extensive as in the south-eastern
steppe, and in some areas wheat was grown for export, being
carried a railway haul of as much as 800 or 900 miles to the Black
Sea ports.

Finally there was Siberia, the region of predatory exploitation
of its mineral and animal wealth in the seventeenth and eighteenth
centuries, when the native population was bled white by tribute
(paid chiefly in furs) and forced trading, and in the late nineteenth
century a region of increasing colonisation for peasants emigrating
from the west. In Western and Central Siberia the forest extends
down until it almost touches the northern fringe of the desert-
steppe ; and the area suitable for agricultural settlement is virtually
confined to the 100-mile-wide belt of black earth which stretches
from the Urals to the river Yenisei. Here, again, richness of the
soil is partly neutralised by insufficient moisture ; and while the
winters are severe (the mean January temperature is a degree or
two below zero Fahrenheit), the depth of snow is too small to give
much protection to crops. But in certain parts, particularly round
the foothills of the Altai mountains, the valleys provide rich meadow
lands for cattle. Land in Siberia had always (with a few trifling
exceptions) been Crown land, not alienable to individuals ; and
the rare settlers in the days of serfdom counted as State peasants,
owing obligation to the State and not to an individual master.
When at the end of the nineteenth century colonisation took place
on an extensive scale, land grants to peasants (made by the Crown
as a virtual grant of right of usage in perpetuity in return for a rent)
were relatively generous, and certain privileges were extended to
the new settlers. But, in addition to the legal settler, a great deal
of illegal settlement took place, and over large areas virtual
squatters' rights prevailed. In the '90's the rate of emigration was
under 100,000 annually. But in 1908 the peak of emigration was
reached with about three quarters of a million emigrants. Between 1897 and 1914 the total population of Siberia increased
by some four million, or by about 75 per cent. ; while in the first
fifteen years of the century the area under crops more than doubled.
Arable cultivation was mainly by the exhaustive cropping system,
although there were certain areas in the west where the three-field
rotation was being introduced ; and wheat cultivation marched
with dairy farming and cattle rearing.

The Emancipation left the relative shares of peasant land (*nadiel*) and landlords' estates and the size of individual peasant holdings very different in different regions. The basic principle of the Emancipation was that the serfs on private estates were to be left in possession of approximately the same amount of land as they had occupied previously. Thus far the peasants were better treated than those in the Baltic States (where at the beginning of the century they had been emancipated without land) or in Prussia. But in return, the peasantry (after an interval during which arrangements for redemption of peasant land were to be made jointly between peasants and landlords) were to compensate their masters for the dues and services which the latter could no longer command by a series of annual money payments extending over forty-nine years.[1] These payments actually represented, not simply a redemption price for the land allotted to them, but a redemption price of their own previous feudal obligations : the peasants in fact had to ransom themselves. The form this redemption took was that the State immediately compensated the landlords with interest-bearing bonds and collected the capital sum plus interest in annual redemption payments for forty-nine years. However, in the detailed application of these principles latitude was allowed for settlement by negotiation between landowners and peasants within certain maximum and minimum limits:[2] limits which were assessed differently for different regions. Between these limits the landlord could in effect choose between granting a larger allotment of land with a larger redemption payment attaching to it and a smaller allotment with a smaller redemption payment attaching to it. But, since the payment the peasant had to make to buy his freedom was intended to represent the price of his own personal obligations of which his master was deprived, the redemption payment did not fall proportionally with the size of the land-allotment ; and the payment represented a proportionally heavier burden on an allotment that was close to the minimum limit than on a larger allotment. There was, in fact, a provision that landlords were able to annex to themselves part of what had previously been peasant land, and the peasantry on their side could escape redemption payments altogether if the latter were willing to accept only a quarter of the

---

[1] At the outset such redemption was intended to be voluntary; an interim arrangement providing for annual dues to be paid as a kind of rent. In view of delays in entering into these voluntary agreements, the law later proceeded to make them obligatory.

[2] Except in certain parts of the south and south-east where a single standard size for allotments was laid down, and in the west where the size of the allotments was based on recently compiled " inventories " of peasant holdings and peasant obligations.

standard allotment of land—the "poverty lots" as they came to be called : a form of settlement, as we shall see, that landlords were inclined to force upon their peasants in regions where land was valuable and hired labour to cultivate their estates was plentiful and cheap.

For the country as a whole the amount of land allotted to the peasantry was only slightly smaller (by some 4 per cent. in 43 provinces of European Russia) than the land they had previously occupied. In the northern regions, where the soil was poor, and in the west the tendency was for the area of land allotted to increase, and individual holdings to be relatively large. But at the same time redemption payments collected from the peasants and paid to the landlords were here equivalently heavier, and on the average were nearly double the market value of the peasants' land. In these regions the peasantry showed strong reluctance to accept the Emancipation settlement ; and we have seen that the tendency was for the lords to retain in their own hands the more valuable meadow-lands and pasture, thereby leaving peasant land with an uneconomic lack of balance. In the black-soil regions, by contrast, the land held by the peasants was reduced by about a quarter; individual holdings on the average were much smaller ; and the " poverty lots " of which we have spoken were very common ; while the total redemption payments exceeded the market value of the land by only about 20 per cent.[1] " Thus in the black-soil belt, where the land was well worth keeping, the landlords cut the peasants off with reduced allotments to be redeemed at a moderate premium ; in the north the allotments were more ample, but the price upon them was nearly double for redemption purposes. North and south the scales were weighted against the peasant."[2]

Peasants on imperial estates or on State land were on the whole little affected by the change. Previously their obligation had almost entirely taken the form of a money payment, and they continued to pay a money rent for their land. In Siberia, in particular, the peasantry were not greatly affected, and continued to occupy much the same area of land as they had previously done and to pay dues to the State Treasury as before. The Cossacks (by a law of

[1] The average excess of redemption payments over land value was approximately 33 per cent for the whole country including the Polish provinces. In the latter the settlement was most favourable to the peasantry (largely as a political measure directed against the Polish nobility for their part in the insurrection of 1863) ; and here the redemption payments were if anything slightly smaller than the value of land allotted to the peasants.

[2] G. T. Robinson, op. cit., 88, also 83 ; also cf. Kluchevsky, History of Russia, vol. V, 271 seq. ; G. Pavlovsky, op. cit., 66 seq.

1869) were allotted about two thirds of all Cossack lands,[1] which were granted in communal tenure to the Cossack *stanitsas* for periodic repartition among the households. In return, they were required to perform twenty years of military duty in service or on the reserve and to provide their own horses and arms. To quote Mr. Tanquery Robinson's comment : " By a combination of generosity and compulsion the government had disciplined the whirlwind : these fighters on horseback who were once the terror of the landlords had now become the scourge of a discontented peasantry."[2]

Two other special classes of serfs received much inferior treatment to the majority of their brethren. The so-called industrial serfs who had been assigned to mines or factories were given smaller allotments than was customary in other places, and in some cases given none at all ; and the household serfs (*dvornie lyudi*) who worked about the houses of their masters were given no land at all and became a landless class : potential wage-workers on the estates or in industry.

Prior to the Emancipation, the peasantry in the northern zone and the centre had for the most part been paying their obligations in the form of money dues (*obrok*) ; and owing to the poor quality of the land many of them even at this early date had engaged in subsidiary occupations such as handicrafts or taken work at wages, paying a proportion of these earnings as additional *obrok* to their masters. In the south, however, where arable farming on the estates was much more extensively developed, serfs were generally required to fulfil their obligations in the form of direct labour services (*barshchina*) in cultivating the lords' estates ; and over a large area of the Ukraine this was almost universal. The effect of the change was that in the north, where the redemption payments were heavy relatively to the productivity of the land, and where in many cases (as we have seen) the balance of arable and meadow on peasant lands was unfavourably affected, the peasantry were forced into renting more land and into seeking new sources of supplementary earnings, either in local *kustarny* industry or in the towns. In many areas of the black-earth district the fact that the redemption payments were lighter relatively to the productivity of the soil was counterbalanced by the smallness of the size of peasant holdings ;[3]

---

[1] The other third chiefly went to the use of the Cossack army or was assigned to Cossack officers and administrators.   [2] *Op. cit.*, 92.

[3] Both because holdings had previously been small, especially in the northern half of the black-earth belt, and because, land being valuable, landlords exerted pressure to reduce the standards of allotments.

and the frequency of the " poverty lots " (which in some provinces applied to more than a third of the peasants[1]) had the result that at least the poorer half of the peasantry was driven into seeking wage employment on the large estates and into renting additional land wherever they could get it. Thus was laid the foundation for that hunger-renting of which we hear so much in the last quarter of the nineteenth century : renting of additional land, usually for short terms, from the landlords at inflated rents—rents which often exceeded the net income of the land, in the sense that after paying the rent there did not remain to the peasant even an equivalent of the customary wage for the labour that he had expended upon it.[2] Towards the end of the century there was also a good deal of selling of land by landlords ; some of this to the urban bourgeoisie and land speculators, but more than half of it to peasants. These sales were assisted by the Peasants' Land Bank which was instituted in 1883 to facilitate land purchase and so maintain the value of land. Some of this was bought by village communes collectively. But of these land sales the richer peasants were the chief beneficiaries ; and it is clear that this transfer of ownership was a factor in accelerating the development of a *kulak* class. For example, of additional peasant land purchased in this way through the Peasants' Land Bank 56 per cent. was transferred in the form of purchases of 100 dessiatines (about 270 acres) or more, and went into the hands of less than 5 per cent. of all peasant families.[3]

As a result of these transfers, the area owned by the nobility, which had been about 274 million acres at the time of the Emancipation, had fallen to 200 million by 1916 ; and land in the ownership of the peasantry had risen by about one fifth to round 447 million. Of the 200 million acres still in the hands of the landed gentry

[1] E.g., Taurida, Saratov, Viatka, Perm, Ufa, Samara, Orenburg. As a percentage of all serfs they applied to 6 per cent. (Pavlovsky, *op. cit.*, 71-3.)

[2] Robinson, *op. cit.*, 100. Mr. Robinson points out that the amount of additional land rented in various districts tended to be inversely correlated with the amount of land owned by the peasants in the district. At the same time he suggests that, as between individual households, the amount of leasing was probably not correlated with the number of *eaters* in the household but with the number of working members in it and with the size of the family's stock of farm equipment and animals. Thus the poorest families probably did not rent additional land since they lacked the means to work it, but instead hired themselves out as wage-workers and even leased some of their own allotment to neighbours. Hence this type of renting was probably most developed among the middle peasantry. The *kulak* rented land in excess of subsistence needs in order to produce a surplus for the market. (Cf. also Lenin, *Selected Works*, vol. I, 168.)

[3] Robinson, *op. cit.*, 114-15. Lenin stated that " poor households representing 50 per cent. of the total possessed from 0·4 per cent. to 15·4 per cent. of the total amount of land purchased by peasants " and that of this purchased land " two thirds to three fourths is in the hands of an insignificant minority of wealthy households ". (" Agrarian Question " in *Selected Works*, vol. I, 174.)

probably slightly over a third was leased to the peasantry and cultivated by them as adjuncts to their own small holdings. But while the land in the ownership of the peasants as a whole had increased, it had failed to increase as fast as the natural increase of population,[1] and emigration into Siberia (which chiefly came from the most overcrowded areas) was insufficient to relieve the pressure on the soil in the parts of European Russia from which the emigrants came. As a result, there was a tendency throughout the last three decades of the nineteenth century for the amount of peasant land per male soul to decrease (probably by about a fifth as a rough average) ; while at the same time the development of inequality among the peasantry themselves had increased the number of families that could not extract a bare subsistence from the land. Such was the background of the revolutionary movement of 1905 so far as the countryside was concerned.

Under the influence of the growing agricultural market, the structure of the old feudal village, much of which had survived the Emancipation, was in process of rapid disintegration by the turn of the century. Large estate farming, though still important in the south and west, was tending to decline, and land of the nobility was being transferred by sale into the hands of a rising urban and village bourgeoisie. In addition to this, something like a third of the land of the nobility was in mortgage to the Nobles' Land Bank. In the village the *otrabotchny* system of hiring land in return for labour rent (which Lenin described as a virtual survival of *barshchina*) was giving way to money renting, on the one hand, and to service at wages for the *kulak*, the landlord or the factory-employer on the part of the impoverished peasant (the *bedniak*), on the other hand. The influence of the village *mir* as an equalising influence had greatly weakened ; and over an increasing area virtual hereditary tenures in the village open fields had replaced the old temporary tenures subject to repartition.[2] The Stolypin policy, which was the answer of the Tsarist regime to the events of 1905, was designed to accelerate these tendencies, and to develop in the village a thriving class of capitalist farmers, producing for the market with the aid of hired labour.[3] Politically these would afford

---

[1] Between 1860 and 1897 the peasant population of European Russia increased by more than a half.

[2] There was still a restriction on the sale of such hereditary tenures. By a law of 1893 hereditary holdings of peasant allotment land could only be sold to peasant buyers.

[3] By a law of June 14, 1910, however, an upper limit was placed on the amount of peasant allotment lands (as distinct from landlord's land) that any one peasant could acquire by purchase—a maximum varying with the district between 50 and 160 acres.

new allies in the countryside for the existing regime and would serve to sap the strength of the revolutionary movement among the peasantry. Economically, by developing commercial farming with more progressive methods the new developments would provide a growing surplus for export and for supplying the needs of an expanding industry. This represented a sharp turn of policy on the part of the Tsarist State. Previously the maintenance of the authority of the village commune had been relied upon as a bulwark of conservatism in rural Russia, as well as a means of maintaining a reserve labour supply for estate-owners in the country districts by attaching the rural population to the land. The essence of the Stolypin legislation of 1906 was that any peasant could now (without waiting upon the consent of the *mir*) demand as a right his share of the village land, not only in hereditary tenure in villages that still practised periodic repartition, but as a single enclosed holding (" so far as possible ") outside the village open fields. In consequence of this policy, by the eve of the 1917 revolution probably rather more than a half of all peasant households having allotment land had come to hold their land in hereditary tenure (not subject to repartition). But the separation of the title of land did not necessarily imply the physical separation of the whole of it from the village open fields and its consolidation. The latter applied only to a smaller number of peasant households— probably to no more than 10 per cent. Here again the regional pattern of these changes is of importance for subsequent events. The development of enclosed farmsteads, often with their separate houses and farm buildings outside the village (the *khutor*) on the English model, was especially advanced in the west, and the enclosure movement also made considerable headway in the southern steppe regions ; while it was least developed on the other hand in Central Russia and in the north-east.[1]

III

The development of industry in eighteenth-century Russia had occupied a prominent place in the " westernising policy " of

[1] The Petersburg region, where production for the market was well developed, showed a high proportion of holdings enclosed, while the south-west, where hereditary tenures had prevailed hitherto and repartition had been absent, showed a relatively low proportion. Apart from *kulaks*, it was apparently peasants with the smaller holdings, most discontented with the *status quo*, who tended to take advantage of the Stolypin law, at least as far as acquiring their land on hereditary tenure was concerned ; the middle peasantry taking relatively little advantage of it. (Cf. Pavlovsky, *op. cit.*, 134–9.)

Peter the Great ; and it was during his reign that the Urals first assumed importance as a centre of iron mining and of a primitive iron industry. In the middle of the century Russia's iron production was several times greater than that of England, and she was competing with Sweden as an exporter of iron. This nascent industry was based on serf labour, which was compulsorily assigned to work in the factories or the mines. In some cases factories were established as State works, conducted by the Treasury, like the Treasury iron works at Tula founded in 1712. In other cases concessions were granted to private entrepreneurs, sometimes foreigners, together with the assignment of a given number of villages of State peasants to supply the labour. By the last decade of the century the number of such assigned serfs reached 300,000, rather more than two thirds of them attached to Treasury works and rather less than one third to private works. But a tendency was developing to dispose of Treasury works to private entrepreneurs. Labour for hire was not unobtainable at this time, and some private entrepreneurs used it side by side with serf labour and regarded it as being more efficient. But it remained very scarce, especially in the remote Urals. The result was that an entrepreneur who was not himself a serf-owner or was not in receipt of a special grant of State serfs from the Tsar was severely handicapped. This handicap was increased by the decrees of 1752 and 1762 which placed a limit upon the number of bonded serfs that any bourgeois factory-owner might possess and prohibited the acquisition of peasants for factories by purchase (except in the case of foreigners). The effect of this legislation was virtually to place a ban on the growth of large-scale industry financed by members of the merchant class, and to give a virtual monopoly in the iron industry to members of the nobility, who being serf-owners were in possession of the requisite labour supply. To this old Urals iron industry, resting on serf labour in remote districts, the Emancipation dealt a blow from which it never properly recovered.[1]

In the central districts round Moscow, however, hired labour was more easily obtainable : the labour of serfs who went by permission of their lords to seek supplementary employment and paid *obrok* on their wage-earnings, or the remnants of old freeholders (*odnodvortsi*), or fugitive or freed serfs. Hence it was here that

[1] The Urals iron industry was also affected by the exhaustion of forest timber in the neighbourhood of the old ironworks. The introduction of coke-smelting favoured other regions where coking coal was available. Even in the 1920's Urals ironworks were mainly of primitive type based on charcoal-smelting.

bourgeois industry, financed by merchants or enriched peasants and staffed by hired wage labour, was able to strike roots ; and it was here that the textile industry, especially cotton, showed considerable development in the early nineteenth century. Even this textile industry, however, at the time was handicapped in its growth by lack of labour ; and although factories were started, merchant capitalists had more frequently to encourage home industry on the putting-out system, sending the work to the village instead of bringing the labour into a single place of production in the town. But with the introduction of the steam-power loom in the '40's, the superiority of factory production became decisive, and its growth at the expense of the village *kustarny* industry was greatly aided as a result of the Emancipation, just as the growing penetration of a money-economy into the village, which followed the Emancipation, enlarged the market for the products of factory industry. By 1866 there were forty-two cotton factories using the new steam-power. Many of the mills started in the nineteenth century were the product of foreign capital and initiative : for example, the mill established by Ludwig Knoop at Narva, one of the largest in the world (and other enterprises financed by him)[1] and the Thornton woollen mills on the Neva. Between the '60's and the end of the century the number of cotton factories showed an expansion of about a half and of workers employed by about three times, thereby indicating a significant degree of concentration.[2] Between the year of Emancipation and the first year of the new century the consumption of raw cotton by Russian mills had grown from 31 thousand tons to 212 thousand : a figure which was to show a further increase to 360 thousand by 1910.

The rebirth of the iron industry was due very largely again to the stimulus of government action : this time less directly than under Peter's westernising policy, as a result of the demand created by the railway building of the '60's and '70's, which was very largely government-financed or else raised under government guarantee of a minimum revenue. But this new iron industry, instead of being in the Urals where coal was deficient and charcoal furnaces had been used, was located in the south between the Donetz and the Dnieper, where there were plentiful sources of good coking coal in the basin of the Donetz and rich iron deposits at Krivoi

[1] Mavor says that " nearly all the cotton mills in Central Russia were founded by Knoop " and that his firm " for a time practically controlled the cotton-factory industry of Russia " ; citing the popular doggerel : " No church without a Pop, no mill without a Knop." (*Op. cit.*, vol. II, 378–9.)   [2] *Ibid.*, 387.

Rog some 200-odd miles to the west. The completion in 1884 of a railway linking Krivoi Rog with the coal region of the Donbas was decisive in encouraging a rapid development of this region. Previously there had been only the ironworks of the Englishman Hughes (who gave his name to Yuzovka, now Stalino) and of Pastukhov. By the end of the '80's there were twenty-nine blast furnaces in operation and another twelve under construction. The new ironworks were built on a giant scale, each of the main works employing 10,000 workers. " In two years the south of Russia has changed its physiognomy," said the *Vestnik Finansov* at the time. Between 1885 and 1898 the output of pig iron increased more than four times. By the latter date it exceeded two million tons : a figure which was to be more than doubled in the next fifteen years, until it stood at 4·7 million, against 5·2 million in France and 10 million in the United Kingdom. As a result of the boom of the 1890's, stimulated by a fresh wave of railway building, the output of Russian factory industry as a whole showed nearly a fourfold increase. Between the turn of the century and the outbreak of the First World War this output probably again almost doubled.[1] Moreover, this development of industry in the first decade and a half of the century was accompanied by a considerable growth in monopolistic organisation, chiefly in the form of cartels.[2]

For all but an upper layer of skilled and responsible workers the wages and living conditions of the growing army of factory workers that the new industry had created were wretched enough. In the textile industry and mining many of these workers retained some attachment to the village, as we have seen, and constituted little more than a semi-industrialised proletariat. But there was also a growing core of permanent town-dwellers, especially among the skilled workers of the metal industry. Many of the temporary town-dwellers or the casually employed lived in barrack-like lodgings of the kind described in Gorky's *Lower Depths*. In the '80's it was estimated that in Moscow and Petersburg there lived some 50,000 persons in each place in underground basement lodgings : most of them fetid, sometimes flooded, cellars below the level of the pavement ; and an investigation of 1908 showed that 60 per

---

[1] Cf. S. N. Prokopovicz, *Russlands Wolkwirtschaft unter den Sowjets*, 173.
[2] Cf. Prof. A. V. Benediktov in *Tiazholaia Industria S.S.S.R.*, 10–32 ; Liaschenko, *op. cit.*, 564–76. For example, the syndicate called *Prodamet*, formed in 1902, controlled four-fifths of the iron and steel output. As regards the influence of banks over industry, " seven Petersburg banks disposed of more than a half of all capital resources directed to the financing of the whole of Russian industry " (*ibid.*, 589).

cent. of textile workers live more than one family to a room (inhabit-
ing curtained-off " corners "), and that on an average a whole
family occupied the incredibly small space of ten square feet.
Another report spoke of barracks for casual workers in Urals mines
as being "in most cases low, close and dirty . . . men lie in them
like herrings in a barrel " ; and an engineer in the '90's said of
workmen's dwellings at Briansk : " they can only be compared,
without exaggeration, to places where cattle are kept ".[1] A few
enlightened firms built blocks of flats for their workmen of a rather
grim Peabody-building type.   But on the whole the living condition of the Russian urban proletariat prior to 1914 belonged to the
period of our own industrial revolution of a century previously and
not to the condition associated in the West with the twentieth
century.

Curiously enough, in urban districts wages seem to have stood
highest in the years following the Emancipation, owing to the
tendency of bonded labour to return to the village.   Later, however,
a renewed influx from village to town, under pressure of the
redemption payments and the growth of economic inequalities in
the village, lowered them again ; and towards the end of the nineteenth century, while money wages rose, the price of bread and
meat rose considerably more, so that real wages fell.   Wage-data
in Tsarist Russia were not too plentiful ; but the average wage in
mines and factories in 1913 is usually estimated to have been
between 20 and 25 roubles per month, or the equivalent of between
40 shillings and 50 shillings in English money at its purchasing
power at the time (i.e. about 10 to 13 shillings a week).   This
represented a figure rather less than a half the level in Britain at
that date.   Even so, considering the condition of the country, it
represented a relatively high figure ; especially when we bear in
mind that the national income per head in 1913 was only about a
quarter that of this country and a seventh that of the U.S.A. Wages
showed considerable variation from 35 roubles a month in the metal
industry to 16 or 17 roubles in textiles (where wages were closer to
the village level, because of the more migratory character of the
labour to and from the village and consequently a more elastic
supply).   In rural districts wages also showed considerable variation ; but rural wages and peasant incomes generally were on
a much lower level.   In rural districts, fairly remote from large
urban centres, the daily wage for labourers even at harvest time
seldom exceeded 80 kopecks (or about 20 roubles a month), and

[1] Mavor, *op. cit.*, 401–27.

in winter was probably only half this figure. Thus in most rural areas wages cannot have been much more than a half and no more than two thirds of the average wage in the large industries. Although there were the beginnings of a Trade Union movement and an incipient strike-movement in the 1870's, any concerted attempts to better these conditions by organisation met with severe police repression ; and save for the officially fostered " Police-Unions " organised by Zubatov in 1904 and 1905, any form of trade unionism remained illegal. Yet this numerically small, but highly concentrated, working class, especially those in the metal factories of Petersburg, Moscow and the Ukraine, was to form the core of the revolutionary movement that brought those fateful changes which are associated in history with the year 1917.

CHAPTER THREE

THE PRELUDE TO NOVEMBER 1917

I

The idea that Russia's historical destiny was essentially different from that of Central and Western Europe had a considerable ancestry. It was the central theme in the famous debate between Slavophils and Westerners in the early nineteenth century ; and it ran through the discussion as to whether feudalism in the Western sense had ever existed in Russia, or whether the system of land-holding and of social obligations in earlier centuries represented something unique so far as European development was concerned. To the school of thought known as *Narodniki*[1] it was the village commune (*mir*) and the important place this held in the agrarian history and the social life of the peasantry that gave Russia the possibility of avoiding the road to industrial capitalism, which had been followed in the West. Once domination of the people by a feudal aristocracy had been terminated, Russia could set a course directly towards a kind of agrarian communism, built upon tradi-tional village institutions. The *mir* had developed in the peasantry a deeply egalitarian and communal instinct, foreign to the indi-vidualism of the German and French peasantry. It had kept alive the notion that the right of holding and using land derives exclusively from working that land : a conception described by Stepniak as " exclusively Russian . . . deeply rooted throughout the Slavonic world, save among the few tribes who have been long subjected to Western influences ".[2] The periodic redistribution

---

[1] The name derived from the movement in student and intellectual circles in the early '70's called *v Narod* : a romantic movement of young intellectuals to go among the peasantry, to gain inspiration from them and in turn to awake in them a sense of their revolutionary mission to overthrow the old order. The movement had little effect among the peasantry, who regarded these urban visitors as strangers to themselves, and it was quickly suppressed by the Tsarist police who undertook wholesale arrests. In 1876 a society called *Zemlya i Volya* (Land and Liberty) was formed to agitate among the peasantry in favour of a redistribution of land. Three years later this split into two wings : the *Chorni Peredel*, favouring peaceful propaganda, and the *Narodnaya Volya* (People's Liberty) which favoured terror-istic action against the leading figure of the aristocracy. For some vivid pictures of this movement cf. D. Footman's study of Zhelyabov, entitled *Red Prelude*.
[2] *Op. cit.*, 10. Stepniak, *alias* Kravchinsky, was a Narodnik who in 1878 assassi-nated the head of the secret police in St. Petersburg and escaped to Italy and then to London, where he died in 1897.

of the land by the *mir* was the instrument for resisting the concentration of land ownership and the formation of a landless proletariat to be a labour reserve for capitalist industry. At the same time this village community formed the foundation upon which co-operative " people's production " could be directly built.

It was to a criticism of this whole conception of historical development that Lenin directed a large part of his energies in the years following his arrival in Petersburg and his adherence to the Marxist movement known as the Emancipation of Labour in the early '90's.[1] The story is told by his sister that when, as a schoolboy, he heard the news of the execution of his elder brother for connection with the *Narodnaya Volya* group, responsible for the assassination of Alexander II, he muttered between set teeth, " we must not go along that road, we need not go along that road ". From his brother's books he imbibed the ideas of Marxism ; but it was to a refutation of the views of the movement to which his brother had adhered that he devoted himself as soon as his university studies were completed.[2] The first few years in the capital were largely occupied with the work of practical organisation and agitation, especially among some of the factory workers of the city. But he had time to take part in a debate with a leading Narodnik writer, Vorontsov (during a visit to Moscow), and to write his *Who are the Friends of the People*, devoted to a sharp attack on what he described as the degeneration of the Narodniki into a reactionary tendency, glorifying the past, encouraging adaptation to the existing order, and acting as a barrier against progress. But when, in 1897, he was sentenced to three years' exile in Siberia (together with his wife, Krupskaya, who followed him in the following year), he was able to complete a study on *The Development of Capitalism in Russia*, in which his views on the controversy with the Narodniki were more fully stated.

In these writings Lenin in the first place maintained that Capitalism, on the contrary to being a forced and " artificial " product of foreign influence and reliant on a foreign market (as Narodnik writers claimed), had already developed in Russia on a

---

[1] This organisation had been originally formed for the study and propagation of Marxism by Plekhanov, formerly a Narodnik of the Chorni Peredel group. The first volume of Marx's *Capital* had appeared in a Russian translation in 1872, and in the ensuing decade began to have an important influence in intellectual circles, especially among the disciples of Lavrov, who was at the time engaged in a controversy with Bakunin.

[2] Expelled from the University of Kazan, he had been obliged to take a degree externally, which he did at the University of St. Petersburg in 1892, after which he moved to the capital, nominally to pursue the calling of a barrister.

considerable scale, and had considerable roots in rural economy itself. Moreover, this growth of Capitalism represented a progressive force, and Capitalism had a definite historical " mission " to perform in the economic development of the country. This progressive rôle he summed up in two brief postulates : " increase in the productive forces of social labour, and the socialisation of labour " (by which he meant the transformation of the productive process from separate and scattered small units into concentrated production in large units, in which labour, instead of being autonomous and individual in character, became the collective labour of a production-team). In particular, Capitalism " squeezes out the forms of personal dependence that were an inseparable part of preceding systems of economy "—" forms of dependence which augment the oppression and degradation of the producer, weaken the powers of independent organisation " and are " a source of . . . innumerable forms of oriental despotism in Russian life ". By creating among the population an industrial proletariat, it transforms the " spiritual make-up of the population " and " gives a tremendous impetus to organisation " among the exploited classes. In the economy of the village itself the process of social differentiation, with its formation of a rural bourgeoisie on the one hand, and of a rural proletariat on the other, represented a disintegration of the old economic forms and the penetration of market relations and of capitalist methods into the village. The old labour-rent system was rapidly giving way before money-renting, at the same time as the middle peasantry and its self-sufficient system of " subsistence farming " went into decline : already " about one fifth of the peasantry [were] already in the position in which their chief occupation [was] that of wage labourers, working for rich peasants and landlords ", and migration of labour in search of employment was assuming large dimensions (and was to be encouraged rather than hindered). Agriculture was increasingly assuming " an entrepreneur character ", land was becoming a commodity to be bought and sold, " the age-long stagnation in agriculture " with its " local isolation and insularity " was being terminated, and large-scale agriculture based on machinery had arrived on the scene. Against such tendencies—even if their progress was " exceedingly slow for a modern capitalist country "—the *mir* as an institution was powerless. So far from preventing the growth of social differentiation in the village, it frequently became dominated by the *kulaks* to further their own interests, and " it serve[d] as a mediaeval obstacle which disunite[d] the peasants who [were] as if

chained to small associations and to categories which [had] lost all
raison d'être ". To attempt to preserve the old institutions would
merely be to " perpetuate the good old system of semi-serf, semi-
free labour—a system which contains all the horrors of exploitation
and oppression, but which holds no possibility of escape from
them ".[1]

From this social diagnosis of economic conditions at the end of
the nineteenth century Lenin drew the conclusion that it was the
proletariat and not the peasantry which was destined to be the
historical motive force of the future. To hope to by-pass Capitalism
and to prevent proletarianisation of the peasantry was Utopian and
reactionary : instead, the political task must be to organise the
proletariat as it grew, and to develop its own independent struggle,
and through struggle class consciousness, so that it might become
capable of fulfilling its historical mission of overthrowing and supplanting Capitalism.   While stressing the progressive rôle of
Capitalism as against Narodnik conceptions, he stressed the importance, even at that stage, of simultaneously developing proletarian organisation and struggle against their exploitation by
capital, and of avoiding any tendency to harness the aims and
activities of the working class o the interests of the bourgeoisie, as
he charged the so-called " legal Marxists ", represented by Peter
Struve, with doing.[2] He did not conclude from this, however, that
the working-class movement had no interest in the popular struggle
for democracy, and no interest in the remedying of peasant
grievances, in particular their desire to take over the land of the
large estates.   On the contrary, it was " the imperative duty of the
working class to fight side by side with radical democracy against
absolutism and the reactionary estates and institutions ".[3]   A firm

---

[1] *Selected Works*, vol. I, 221–385 ; also 146, 396, 400–5, 431.
[2] In 1897, in *Tasks of Russian Social Democrats*, he said : " Our work is
primarily and mainly concentrated on the factory urban workers. The Russian
Social Democrats must not dissipate their forces . . . But while recognising that it
is important to concentrate our forces on the factory workers and decry the dissipa-
tion of forces, we do not for a moment suggest that Russian Social Democrats
should ignore other strata of the Russian proletariat and the working class. Nothing
of the kind."   And in 1899 he wrote : " The proletariat must not regard the
other classes and parties as a ' homogeneous reactionary mass ' [a phrase used in
the Gotha Program of the German Social Democratic Party in 1875 and criticised
by Marx] : on the contrary, it must take part in the whole of political and social
life, support the progressive classes and parties, support every revolutionary
movement against the present system, must champion the interests of every
oppressed nation or race, of every persecuted religion, disfranchised sex, etc."
(*Ibid.*, 498, 522–3.)
[3] " The achievement of democratic demands is necessary for the working
class ", he wrote, " as a means of clearing the road to victory over the chief enemy
of the toilers, viz. capital " ; adding that while capital was " purely democratic

smytchka, or alliance, of the proletariat with the peasantry was to remain a leading and distinctive feature of Lenin's doctrine both after and before 1917 : a principle which sharply differentiated him from the " legal Marxists " and later the Mensheviks, who leaned towards alliance with the liberal bourgeoisie, and also from those among the Marxists who advocated exclusive concentration on proletarian interests and struggles.[1]

In a later study of *The Agrarian Situation in Russia* (written in 1908, but not actually published until ten years later) Lenin gave a striking characterisation of the alternative paths of development facing Russia in the first decade of the new century. These two paths he designated the American and the Prussian ; and the task of the bourgeois-democratic revolution, which it was the function of the proletariat and peasantry in partnership to carry through, was to ensure that the former was chosen in preference to the latter. The Prussian path was " characterised by the fact that medieval relationships in land-ownership are not liquidated at one stroke ; they gradually adapt themselves to Capitalism, and for this reason Capitalism for a long time retains semi-feudal features. Prussian landlordism was not crushed by the bourgeois revolution ; it sur-vived and became the basis of *Junker* economy, which is capitalist at bottom, but which still keeps the rural population in a certain degree of dependence. As a consequence the social and political domination of the *Junker* was strengthened for many decades after 1848, and the development of the productive forces of German agriculture proceeded much more slowly than in America. On the contrary, in America it was not the slave economy of the big land-lords that served as the basis of capitalist agriculture, but the free economy of the free farmer working on free land, land free from all mediaeval features." Hence, " the whole question of the future development of the country can be reduced to this : which of the two paths of development will ultimately prevail, and correspond-ingly which class will carry through the necessary and inevitable

in its nature ", it was " in Russia strongly inclined to sacrifice its democracy and enter into alliance with reaction in order to suppress the workers and to retard the labour movement still further " (*ibid.*, 444–5). Until the " pillars of reaction " were thrown down, " the Russian rural proletarian, whose support is absolutely essential if the working class is to attain victory, will never cease to be a wretched and cowed creature, capable only of acts of sullen desperation, and not of sensible and sturdy protest and struggle " (*ibid.*, 445).

[1] In 1905 he wrote (against Parvus and Trotsky) : " At the present time the Russian proletariat represents a minority of the population. It can become a great overwhelming majority only if it combines with the mass of semi-proletarians and small farm owners, i.e. with the mass of the petty bourgeoisie, urban and rural poor " (in *Vperiod*, March 30, 1905, reprinted in *Selections from Lenin*, vol. II, 69).

change—the old landlord or the free peasant farmer ? " The task which " the nineteenth century is bequeathing to the twentieth century " is one of " completing the process of ' cleaning out ' the mediaeval forms of land ownership " ; and only the victory of the proletarian-peasant alliance in the democratic revolution would decide " whether this ' cleaning ' will be carried out in the form of the peasant nationalisation of the land or in the form of the accelerated plunder of the village commune by the *kulaks* and the transformation of landlord economy into *Junker* economy ".[1] One may say that Stolypin policy followed the latter alternative and the Land Reform of 1917–18 the former.

Consistently with this notion of development, Lenin advocated both in 1905 and 1917 that the proletarian movement must take the leadership of the revolutionary movement, even though purely bourgeois-democratic and not socialist aims were on the immediate agenda. This is what in 1905 had differentiated Bolsheviks from Mensheviks, who argued that at the present stage of the revolution the leadership must necessarily lie with the liberal bourgeoisie, and that the labour movement and socialist parties could act as no more than " pressure groups " in the background. The 1905 revolution Lenin later described as " a peasant revolution led by the proletariat ". When he returned to Russia after the overthrow of Tsardom in the March days of 1917, he surprised and joined issue with many even within the ranks of his own party by formulating the policy, in his famous April Theses, of transferring power at the earliest opportunity from the existing Provisional Government (which he regarded as a government of the bourgeoisie) to a Soviet Government as representative of the proletarian-peasant alliance. " The peculiarity of the present situation in Russia," he wrote, " is that it represents a *transition* from the first stage of the revolution, which, because of the inadequate organisation and insufficient class consciousness of the proletariat, led to the assumption of power by the bourgeoisie, into its second stage which is to place power in the hands of the proletariat and the poorest strata of the peasantry."[2] By contrast, the Menshevik view was expressed by statements such as that of Potresov that the bourgeoisie " is destined to be the lord and master in the immediate future, for the time necessary for the consolidation of the régime of a developed capitalist system in the country ", and of Sukhanov that " the power

---

[1] *Selected Works*, vol. I, 181, 210–11.
[2] *Collected Works*, vol. XX, bk. I, 107. For the effect of Lenin's April speech even on other Bolsheviks, cf. P. N. Miliukov, *Istoria Vtoroi Russkoi Revoliiutsi* (Sofia, 1921), vol. I, Pt. I, 88–9.

which will replace Tsarism must be a bourgeois power. . . . Such is the settlement we must strive for, otherwise the *coup* will fail and the revolution will perish." [1]

During the March days, as previously in 1905, there had come into existence Soviets of workers' delegates, elected from factories and professional organisations, as organising centres of the popular movement. In April an all-Russian Soviet Congress was convened at which representatives from the villages and from soldiers' committees in the army took their places alongside the delegates of the urban workers ; and while the governing authority was vested *de jure* in the Provisional Government, composed of the heads of the former opposition parties in the Duma,[2] an increasing amount of *de facto* influence rested with the Soviets. For example, the famous Order No. 1 of March 14, instructing units of the army to establish soldiers' committees, which was regarded by the military command as the fount of indiscipline and of decay of morale, was issued by the Petrograd Soviet ; and in the course of the summer and autumn it was to the local Soviets that peasants or workers came to look, in taking direct action against landlords' estates or factory managements, for any sanction of authority that they required. This situation constituted that Dual Power of which Lenin spoke as characteristic of this period. " What has made our revolution so strikingly unique ", he wrote in *Pravda* on April 22, " is that it has established Dual Power. What constitutes Dual Power ? The fact that by the side of the Provisional Government, the government of the bourgeoisie, there has developed another, as yet weak, embryonic, but undoubtedly real and growing government—the Soviets of Workers' and Soldiers' Deputies." This was evidently a highly unstable situation, which, as the events of the autumn were to prove, was bound quickly to yield place either to a dictatorship of the Right (as the abortive *coup* of General Kornilov at the end of August attempted) suppressing or at least drawing the teeth of the Soviets, or else a transfer of *de jure*, as well as *de facto*, authority to the Soviets. " It is impossible to stand still in history generally, in war-time particularly : one must go either backward or forward."[3]

---

[1] Cit. in *History of Civil War*, vol. I, 122.
[2] At first under the Premiership of Prince Lvov this excluded the Socialist parties (except for Kerensky who represented the *Trudovik* or Labour group). But in May a coalition government was formed to include representatives of the parties in the Soviet (Miliukov resigning). On July 2 the Cadets, the leading bourgeois party, resigned from the Government, and on July 8 Kerensky became Prime Minister of a Government predominantly composed of Mensheviks and Right S.R.'s.　　　　[3] *Collected Works*, vol. XXI, bk. I, 211.

It was commonly imagined at the time that Lenin's advocacy of the hegemony of the proletariat so fast on the heels of the downfall of the autocracy in March rested on a utopian belief that Socialism could be introduced immediately, despite the immature development of industry in Russia, and that, like Narodnik doctrine, it was designed to by-pass Capitalism and " skip over " historical stages on the road to Communism. Commentators in the West wrote of Bolshevism in this sense.[1] Bolshevism was treated as the creed of socialists of impatient temperament who were too much in a hurry, whose ardour needed the leaven of more sober realists, schooled in the surer methods of Anglo-Saxon " gradualism". Even critics among the " old Bolsheviks " (e.g. Kamenev[2]) accused him of wishing to make the transition to Socialism before the stage of bourgeois-democratic revolution was completed. But this simple view does not do justice to the facts ; and failure to appreciate this has opened the door to a whole family of misunderstandings concerning the events and policies of the ensuing decade. It is, of course, true that Lenin held that the establishment of Soviet power would drastically alter the time-scale of future economic and social development, and he saw in the hegemony of the proletariat a historical guarantee that the transition from the bourgeois to the socialist revolution would be begun. But the placing of Socialism on the immediate agenda was explicitly disclaimed. Clause 8 of the April Theses clearly affirmed : " Not the ' introduction of Socialism ' as an immediate task, but to bring immediately social production and distribution of goods under the *control* of the Soviet of Workers' Deputies."[1] The " amalgamation of all banks into a single national bank, control over which shall be exercised by the Soviet " and national control of syndicates or cartels were called for, but only as " measures which do not in any way imply the ' introduction ' of socialism " and " which have been frequently undertaken during the war by a number of bourgeois States ", which are " entirely feasible economically " and which " are absolutely essential in order to combat complete economic disorganisation and famine which are pending ".[4] Nationalisation of the land was also

---

[1] E.g., R. W. Postgate's *Bolshevik Theory*, where Bolshevism is defined as a doctrine of " Socialism at once " ; and later Norman Angell's *Must Britain Travel the Moscow Road ?*, where it is described as " the policy of establishing Socialism at one stroke, as opposed to its gradual introduction" (115).

[2] L. Kamenev in *Pravda*, April 21, 1917, wrote that Lenin's thesis " proceeds from the assumption that the bourgeois-democratic revolution *has been completed*, and it builds on the immediate transformation of the revolution into a socialist revolution ".   [3] *Ibid.*, vol. XX, bk. I, 108 ; also *Selected Works*, vol. VI, 24.

[4] *Ibid.*, 62 ; and *Collected Works*, vol. XX, bk. I, 144 ; also vol. XX, bk. II, 79, 135.

advocated, but as a measure for " completing the democratic revolution " by extirpating the roots of a landed aristocracy and satisfying the elemental peasant hunger for the distribution of the landed estates among themselves.   Later, writing on the eve of the November revolution on " The Threatening Catastrophe and How to Avert It ", he spoke of the nationalisation of the oil industry and of the coal industry as necessary " to increase the production of fuel " and to combat " the stopping of production by the industrialists " ;   the compulsory syndication of industry under State control—a measure which " has already been put into practice in Germany " and " does not directly, in itself, infringe upon the relations of private property to any degree " ; and the introduction into industry of workers' control " from below ".[1] About the same time he again stated that " the vital matter is, not the confiscation of capitalist property, but universal, all-embracing workers' control over the capitalists. . . . Compulsory syndication under the control of the State, this is what Capitalism has prepared the way for and what the *Junker* State has put into effect in Germany ; this is what will be completely realised in Russia by the Soviets."[2]

II

The Great War placed a grave strain on the slender resources of the Russian Empire, and by the winter of 1916 economic disorganisation had reached an advanced stage.   The weakness of her economic potential was shown in the fact that throughout the first three years of the war her output of rifles was only between a third and a half of her estimated needs.   In the summer of 1915, when the Germans launched their offensive, it was common knowledge that Russian artillery could only fire a hundred shells to several thousand of the Germans, and at the beginning of 1917 no more than 12 per cent. of the programme of machine-gun needs was available.   The gap in supplies was partly filled by imported munitions from the allied countries through Archangel and Vladivostok ; but the rate of flow of these supplies was straitly restricted by the inadequate transport facilities.   Imports through Vladivostok had to travel several thousands of miles along the single-track Trans-Siberian Railway ; and the only contact with Archangel in the first two years of the war was a narrow-gauge railway, with the

[1] *Ibid.*, vol. XXI, bk. I, 190–2, 197, 207.
[2] In *Will the Bolsheviks Maintain State Power ?* (English Ed., 1922), 52–3 ; also in *Selected Works*, vol. VI, 267–8.

result that merchandise arriving from England or America piled up at the port for lack of possibility of moving it to the interior.[1] The early loss of Poland to the Germans meant the loss of a substantial fraction of the country's industrial potential ; and after the disaster of the 1915 campaign the Russian War Minister declared that his sole reliance lay in " immeasurable distances, impassable roads and the mercy of St. Nicholas, patron saint of Holy Russia ". The loss of industry in captured territory was partly balanced by increased employment in industries engaged on war production : for example, in the capital the number of workers employed in large enterprises nearly doubled between 1914 and 1917. But despite the increased war demand, iron and steel production in 1916 was below that of 1914 by as much as a sixth, and coal production by a tenth. Difficulties of transport had been acute from the first. As the war proceeded they were increased by the disrepair of locomotives and of rolling stock, which developed faster than repair shops could handle them. Nearly one fifth of the railway locomotives were out of action by the end of 1916 : a figure which rose to more than one third in the course of the next twelve months. At the same time skilled workers were mobilised for military service and a number of railway shops were transferred to the manufacture of munitions.[2] The Chief of Staff, General Alexeyev, in the summer of 1916 stated in a report to the Tsar that " there is hardly a branch of State and public life at present which is not suffering severe dislocation owing to the fact that the demand for transport facilities is not being properly satisfied ; . . . on an average only 50 or 60 per cent. of the transport requirements of the factories producing military supplies are being satisfied ".[3] Attempts to ration transport space were largely ineffective through inefficiency or corruption. Stories were current about car-loads of fresh roses arriving from the Black Sea coast for the aristocracy in the capital, while in nearby provinces there were no means of shifting grain ; and of desperate attempts to transport wheat from Siberia to the west by the dispatch of officials in special trains across the Urals, armed with large sums of money to ease with bribes the passage of essential supply trains.[4]

---

[1] Cf. *History of Civil War*, vol. I, 27–45. The Archangel railway was only changed over to a broad gauge in 1916. The Murmansk railway was not completed till the end of 1917. A report of Rodzianko, President of the Duma, spoke of supplies at the port " piled mountain high " and " cases lying on the ground, literally pressed deep into the soil from the weight of the goods above ". On the eve of the war the port of Archangel was in a very bad condition.

[2] Shatunovsky in *Yezhegodnik Cominterna*, 1923, 360 seq.

[3] Cit. in *History of Civil War*, vol. I, 35.

[4] Baerlein, *The March of the Seventy Thousand* 45–6.

Lack of armaments, instead of setting a limit to the numbers called to the colours, seems to have encouraged a greater reliance on mere quantity of man-power. Mobilisation reached the large figure of 15 million and involved the withdrawal of more than a third of the male labour force from industry and agriculture. This contributed very largely to the shrinkage of the area under crops in the regions of the south-east where the drain of male labour from the Cossack districts was particularly heavy. By 1916 the contraction in the total area sown to crops had passed 10 per cent., in the case of potatoes it was more than 15 per cent., and of sugar-beet 20 per cent. Only in the single case of flax did the area of cultivation increase ; and this because of the British Government scheme of large-scale direct purchase of the crop. Moreover, after 1916 not only the sown area but also the yield per acre showed a marked decline : in some areas of the steppe zone by as much as a third between 1916 and 1917. More important even than decline in the sown area and in yield was the fall in the proportion of the crop which peasants were willing to market, even where transport was available to move it. By the end of 1916 this seems to have declined in the case of grain by at least a third, and the amount of grain transported on the railways by as much as 60 per cent. True, the export of grain had dwindled to insignificance. On the other hand, with the transfer of millions from the village into the army and into war industry, the demand for grain to supply the towns and the front was much greater than the urban demand had been before.

A major factor in this decline of the marketed surplus was the growing scarcity of manufactured goods available for exchange against the products of agriculture. Until the autumn and winter of 1916 there are signs that the influence of this factor was unimportant ; and until then it is possible that the decline in the supplies becoming available from the villages was primarily due to the greater decline in sown area (as a combined result of loss of man-power and the stopping of export outlets) precisely in those areas which had previously been the main surplus-producing areas. Until the end of 1916 the peasantry were apparently willing to hoard the paper money they received for their crops, and were not deterred from so doing by its diminished purchasing-power in terms of industrial goods. One estimate suggests that such hoarding may have amounted to one half, or even more, of the total currency circulation ;[1] and it is this no doubt which explains the fact

[1] E. Epstein, *Les Banques de Commerce Russes*, 56–8.

that the proportional rise in the general price level was much smaller than the increase in currency-issues. After the winter of 1916 this relationship between price-rise and currency-issues was reversed ; the former rising between March and November 1917 more rapidly than the latter.[1] In the crucial year 1917 the peasantry no longer hoarded, but apparently dishoarded, paper money.[2] The peasant had become aware that money was a wasting asset and the market price of the things that he purchased was rising more steeply than the price he received for the products he sold ; and his reluctance to market his produce accordingly increased. The September programme of State grain purchase was fulfilled to only a third, and the October programme to only a fifth ; little more than a half as much grain having been purchased as in the same month of the previous year.[3]

Growing food shortage increased distress among the working-class populations of the towns in the winter of 1916–17 to the point of desperation. The French Ambassador recorded in his diary at the beginning of March 1917 : " At the present moment 57,000 railway wagons cannot be moved. . . . Extreme cold has put more than 1200 engines out of action owing to boiler tubes bursting and there is a shortage of spare tubes as a result of strikes. . . . Petrograd is short of bread and wood. . . . At the bakery on the Liteiny this morning I was struck by the sinister expression on the faces of the poor folk who were lined up in a queue, most of whom had spent the whole night there."[4] A few days later the patience of these poor folk had become exhausted and bakeries were being looted in the Viborg quarter. At the same time the Tsarina was analysing the increasingly revolutionary situation in a letter to her husband in these classic terms : " This is a hooligan movement ; young people run and shout that there is no bread, simply to create excitement ; along with workers who prevent others from working. If the weather were very cold, they would all probably stay at home. But all this will pass and become calm, if only the Duma will behave itself." In these early days of March the food shortage was aggravated by unemployment caused by the closing of factories

---

[1] Cf. L. N. Yurovsky, *Currency Problems and Policy of the Soviet Union* (1925), 16–19. Between the beginning of 1915 and March 1, 1917, the quantity of paper money in circulation showed a sevenfold increase, and the price-index a threefold increase. Between March 1 and November 1, 1917, the quantity of money increased by 90 per cent. and the price-level by over 200 per cent.

[2] Dr. Baykov has pointed out to the author that this applied to the so-called Kerensky rouble, but not to the rouble of older denomination.

[3] *History of Civil War*, vol. I, 395.

[4] M. Paléologue, *An Ambassador's Memoirs*, vol. III, 213.

owing to scarcity of fuel. At the same time strikes spread until they covered some 100,000 workers in the capital and at one time one third of the workers in Moscow factories. On March 11 (N.S.) the President of the State Duma telegraphed to the Tsar from Petrograd : " Transport and fuel absolutely disorganised. Anarchy in the capital. Government is paralysed. General dissatisfaction is growing. Riots and firing in the streets."[1]

During the Provisional Government (which came into existence after the abdication of the Tsar on March 12, 1917) very little was successfully done to stem the progress of economic decline, and by the end of the year conditions had in many respects deteriorated. The Tsarist Government had already in 1916 adopted measures for controlling the grain trade, even going so far as to impose compulsory purchase of a proportion of farm produce at official prices. On March 25, 1917, the new government took the further step of declaring the grain trade to be a State monopoly and of prohibiting all private trade in grain outside the village. Thenceforth grain surpluses were to be delivered to the State food organisations in each district and to them alone, and were to be paid for at the official control-prices. The measure was, however, weakly enforced under the Provisional Government, and private trade continued. By the end of the summer of 1917 bread prices had increased three times over pre-war, prices of dairy produce about five times and meat about seven ; while manufactured goods and fuel had risen in price by much more. Although money wages had probably increased on the average in greater proportion than bread-prices, this increase was less than that of the price of meat and very much less than prices of industrial products. The very control of grain prices accentuated the discontent among the peasantry and encouraged the beginnings of a " peasant strike " against the government purchasers of grain. By August the general bread ration in Petrograd had been reduced to a half of what it had been in March.

The Provisional Government had also established a Chief Economic Committee charged with the task of introducing " a purposive regulation of economic life ". But this committee met with obstruction from the industrialists, possessed neither a policy nor the will to deal with such obstruction, and exerted little, if any, practical influence. By the autumn the transport situation had grown worse, the average daily wagon-loadings in October being less than two thirds of what they had been two years before. " This was the

[1] J. Mavor, *Russian Revolution*, 51–9 ; *History of Civil War*, vol. I, 87–112; *Illustrated History of the Russian Revolution* (1928), vol. II, 261–92.

beginning of the complete breakdown of the railway system," says a foreign writer of three years later, " which the Bolsheviks in spite of extreme efforts could not check or even retard."[1]   Transport disorganisation and fuel famine reinforced one another in their effects.   Coal production in the Donbas had declined in 1917 compared with the previous year.   Blast-furnaces began to be drawn, and in the Moscow district pig-iron output in 1917 fell even below 20 per cent. of the previous year.   Cotton mills, affected by non-delivery of raw cotton supplies from Turkestan, began in some districts to cease work entirely, and in October even flour mills started to close.[2]   At the beginning of October one half of the factories in the Urals region had closed, and in Petrograd and Moscow manufacturers were taking steps to organise a lock-out as an answer to the claims of their workers.[3]   At the end of September a railway strike was only just avoided by timely concessions. General Denikin states that the production of munitions fell by some 60 per cent. and of aircraft by as much as 80 per cent., while " only 16 per cent. of the actual needs of the army was satisfied ". Industry, he says, was " steadily falling into ruin ".[4]   Professor Prokopovitch estimates that industrial production on the average for 1916–17 was only 71 per cent. of pre-war ;[5] and by the autumn of 1917 it was undoubtedly a good way below the 1916–17 average. Even in May M. Paléologue was writing in his diary : " Anarchy is spreading all over Russia " ; adding that the army was incapable of " any intense and continuous action . . . owing to the anarchy in its rear ".   On May 17 he wrote : " How on earth is he [Kerensky] to cope with the administrative disorganisation, the agrarian movement, the financial crisis, the economic débâcle, the universal spread of strikes and the progress of separatism ? . . . I tell you even a Peter the Great would not suffice."[6]   Miliukov subsequently declared that at the time of the Soviet revolution in November, " the situation was so bad that, in everybody's opinion, it could not be made worse by any new change ".[7]

III

Most powerful of the currents that were carrying events towards the Soviet revolution of November was the elemental

[1] K. Leites, *Recent Economic Developments in Russia*, 52 ; cf. also Shatunovski, *loc. cit.*, 360–1 ; Liashchenko, *op. cit.*, vol. I, 628–55.
    [2] Leites, *op. cit.*, 39–40.   [3] *History of Civil War*, vol. I, 367.
    [4] *The Russian Turmoil*, 117–19. [5] *The Economic Condition of Soviet Russia*, 20.
    [6] *Op. cit.*, 334–5.   [7] *Russia To-day and To-morrow*, 43.

movement among the peasants, who were effecting the seizure of the landed estates by direct action on a growing scale. The Provisional Government had promised that action should be taken in connection with agrarian reform and had in May established both a central and local land committees " to prepare the way for land reform and to draft provisional measures to be adopted ".[1] But little more than preparatory work had in fact been done by these committees, and a final settlement had been explicitly postponed until the meeting of a Constituent Assembly. The peasantry soon showed themselves to be in no mood to wait upon the leisurely progress of legal enactment and sceptical that its outcome would be such as to appease their temper ; and as the fateful year moved from spring into autumn, a spontaneous movement of illegal land reform " from below " gathered cumulative volume and impetus. In this movement, not only local Soviets joined but also the local land committees established by the government, acting independently of central authority and assisting in the organisation of land-confiscation and land-division. Already in April there had been numerous cases of what was called in the terminology of police reports " agrarian lawlessness ". Most of these were of a fairly peaceful character involving the unauthorised seizure of timber from forest land, or the organisation of strikes of labourers on the neighbouring estates ; although in about a quarter of the cases the police reports had referred to some destruction as having occurred. While such disturbances were reported from as many as 174 districts, these were mainly concentrated in the Central Agricultural Region and the Middle Volga. Within a fortnight of the decree of May 3 which had established land committees, a peasant congress at Kazan had resolved to confiscate all estate-land without waiting for the Constituent Assembly, and in June a local landowner reported that this resolution was being put into force and that " local administrative authorities are unable to restrain the local land committees from irregular measures ".

By June the number of districts covered by the reports had increased to over 300, and cases of violence and destruction, which included the burning of manor houses and the actual appropriation of land, had become much more common. Among the reasons for the resignation of Prince Lvov as head of the Provisional Government in early July was his opposition to the tendency of the

[1] The Central Committee had no executive powers ; but the local land committees were entrusted with limited powers of issuing local regulations and of arbitrating in disputes over ownership rights.

Minister of Agriculture in particular " to justify the disastrous seizures of property that are taking place throughout Russia and are confronting the Constituent Assembly with a *fait accompli* ", instead of " combating aggressive tendencies and bringing order into agrarian relations ".   After July there was a slight decline to the June level, possibly occasioned by a proclamation of Kerensky's government of July 8, promising " to abandon entirely the old land policy which ruined and demoralised the peasantry " and to base the future land reform on " the principle that the land is to pass into the hands of those that work it ".   Even so, alarming reports continued to be received in the capital from the provinces. In August a peasant congress at Voronezh had passed a resolution empowering village committees to take over estate-land and divide it on leases at fixed rents ; in the Saratov province the Tsaritsin district was reported to be " a centre of anarchy supported by local committees ".   In September a report came from the League of Landowners in Tambov announcing that twenty-four estates had been burned in three days and the local authority was powerless to prevent the movement.   In October the movement attained a new crescendo, and a proposal was being discussed at the Ministry of the Interior for withdrawing cavalry from the front to the interior.   Of all the cases of destruction and violence reported in these eight months three quarters fell within September and October.   What was of crucial significance was that by this time the peasant move-ment had spread even to the prosperous south-western Ukraine, the stronghold of individual enclosed farming on the Stolypin model.   In October cases of illegal seizure were here between twenty and thirty times as numerous as they had been in April, and in this month this region furnished a quarter of all the reported cases of " destructive activity ".   In the days of serfdom there had been a peasant saying :   " We are the landlord's, but the land we work is ours."   Now the peasants were adapting it to the temper of the times and were declaring : " The landlord is our landlord : we worked for him and his property is ours."[1]

In industry a parallel form of direct action was taking place in

[1] Launcelot Owen, *The Russian Peasant Movement, 1906–17*, 132–52, 196–238 ; *History of Civil War*, vol. I, 424–7 ; *Illustrated History of the Russian Revolution*, vol. II, 275–84.   Dr. Owen points out two further features of this peasant move-ment : (*a*) that after passing from comparatively peaceful measures such as illegal cutting of timber in the forests and strikes to acts of violence and destruction, the tendency in its most advanced stage was to pass from purposeless acts of destruc-tion to organised seizures of land ; (*b*) that while there were burnings of manor houses, there was little actual personal violence against landowners and only a few cases of squires being killed : " during the period February–October there was no *pugachovshchina*, no *jacquerie* ".   (147.)

the summer and autumn, and was gradually undermining the authority of the Provisional Government. An early foretaste of this had occurred in the spring when Moscow industrialists refused to adopt an agreement which Petrograd industrialists had made with the Petrograd Soviet for an 8-hour day, the establishment of factory committees and the submission of wage disputes to arbitration; and the Moscow Soviet decided to enforce the 8-hour day on industry within the district without waiting for the authority of the government. In the summer reports began to multiply of arrests of engineers by workers, acting in the name of local Soviets, and of the forcible expulsion from factories of unpopular foremen. On June 1 a national resolution of the executive committee of the Soviets advised all industrial workers to " create councils at the enterprises, the control embracing not only the course of work at the enterprise itself but the entire financial side of the enterprise ". In the same month the factory and dock committees at Kronstadt were claiming and exercising " the right to inspect the accounts and the books of the management " and to see " that no materials left the premises without good reason " ; while in the cable works the owner had actually been deposed by the local Soviet on the charge of trying to close down his plant and sell it to a foreign bank, and the concern was being administered by its factory committee. In July at Kharkov a conference of factory committees was threatening to remove directors and factory owners who " refuse within the next five days to satisfy the workers' demands " and to replace them by elected engineers, and a Conference of Industrialists sent an angry complaint to the Minister of Labour that " criminal elements are going entirely unpunished ", that the management of one of the largest factories in the city had been kept under arrest by the workers for twenty-four hours, and similarly the directors of the Kharkov locomotive works. When in the autumn certain factories in Petrograd proposed to close down, and others proposed to transfer elsewhere by agreement with the Government, this met with strong opposition and obstruction from the factory committees ; and in the south in a similar case of a large naval shipbuilding yard at Nikolaev, the workers' committee arranged to send delegates to the places from which the yard obtained its raw materials to investigate the raw material position, and in the meantime tried to enforce a ban on any further dismissals. A delegate meeting of leather workers on strike in Moscow instructed factory committees to " proceed immediately to adopt practical measures in preparation for sequestration, such as taking an inventory of goods, machinery, etc." In October, in the Donbas coalfield a wave of strikes was followed by miners taking control of the mines into their own hands, and Ataman Kaledin (later to be a leading figure in the civil war) wired the Minister of War : " At the moment the entire power has been seized by various self-appointed organisations which recognise no other authority than their own."[1]

Besides the Social Democratic Labour Party (which in 1903 had divided into two tendencies, Bolshevik and Menshevik, and later had split into two parties), the Social Revolutionary Party had a large following in pre-1917 days. While the former, having a Marxist tradition, had drawn its supporters mainly from the industrial workers and the urban intelligentsia, the latter had always made its principal appeal to the peasantry. Founded in 1901, it very largely carried on the traditions of the *Narodnaya Volya*, including its policy of individual terrorism ; and among its initial central committee, in addition to Chernov, Gotz and Gershuni, was the notorious Azef, who for a number of years played the dual rôle of organiser-in-chief of its secret terrorist section, plotting assassinations against leading Tsarist officials, and of police agent who betrayed his revolutionary colleagues to the authorities. Among its aims, as stated in a manifesto in the year following its formation, was the socialisation of land, combined with measures of economic co-operation to liberate the peasantry from the power of money capital. " The patience of the peasant masses ", it declared, " is almost exhausted. . . . We shall ourselves set fire to this combustible material with the torch of the struggle for liberty. . . . We call the peasant by Land to Freedom and through Freedom to Land."[2] Since the 1905 revolution the leading bourgeois party had been the Constitutional Democrats, or Cadets, to which had gravitated the so-called " legal Marxists " of the '90's, and the supporters of P. Struve's journal *Ozvobozhdenie*, around which had been formed the Union of Liberation (*Soius Ozvobozhdenie*) in 1904 to work for a democratic constitution. Standing in opposition to Tsarist autocracy in favour of a democratic constitution and an economic policy favourable to the development of industrial Capitalism along western lines, the Cadet party had grown alarmed at the mass movement as this had developed during the events of

---

[1] *History of Civil War*, vol. I, 413–21 ; M. Philips Price, *My Reminiscences of the Russian Revolution*, 39–40, 132–3 ; Piatakov in *Yezhegodnik Cominterna*, 1923, 327.   [2] Cit. J. Mavor, *Economic History of Russia*, vol. II, 177–9.

1905, and had adopted an increasingly conservative position over the course of the next decade. Between March and October 1917, it stood definitely on the Right, as an opponent of the Soviets and of the developing peasant movement; the Cadet ministers had resigned from the Provisional Government at the beginning of May, largely in protest against " the growing strength of those elements which destroy all order and wish to undermine discipline in the army "; and many of its members sympathised with and aided the abortive military *coup* of General Kornilov in September.

But the events of 1917 progressively widened the rift in the party of the peasantry, the Social Revolutionary Party, itself. As so often happens with peasant parties in agricultural countries,[1] the Right-wing tended to adapt its policies to the interests of the more prosperous peasants, and to become a party of the rural bourgeoisie. But as the actual currents among the peasantry which we have described gathered momentum in the summer and autumn of the year, it was the Left-wing section of the party, favouring a revolutionary solution of the agrarian problem, which won adherents in the countryside and became the political spokesman of the mass of peasantry in the rural Soviets and on other local bodies. As far as the immediate objectives of the revolution were concerned, they accordingly found themselves with much more in common with the Bolsheviks than with the Right-wing section of their own party. At the Peasants' Congress which met in the Duma Building in Petrograd on November 18th, a few days after the Bolsheviks in the name of the Soviets had assumed power,[2] the Left Social Revolutionaries had a clear majority, and the Bolsheviks had about one fifth of the delegates. Marie Spiridinova, a leader of the Left-wing, was elected to the chair; Chernov, an old S.R. leader since the inception of the party, was shouted down; and in the course of the Congress the minority section of the S.R.'s, led by the old committee, seceded to form a separate convention of their own. Meanwhile negotiations were in progress at the Soviet headquarters at Smolny between the Bolsheviks and the Left S.R. leaders, the outcome of which was a provisional agreement between them. The Central Committee of the Soviets at Smolny, which had hitherto represented only the soldiers' and workers' councils, was to be broadened to include an equal number of delegates elected from the

---

[1] Cf. H. Seton Watson, *Eastern Europe Between the Wars*, 259.
[2] In the course of the preceding month the Bolsheviks had secured a majority in the Soviets of Petersburg and Moscow and of one or two other cities.

Peasant Congress ; while a certain number of posts in the Government were to be allotted to the Left Social Revolutionaries.[1]

By this compromise, which accorded with Lenin's theory of the *smytchka*, or proletarian-peasant *bloc*, the leading influences in the villages and smaller townships, as well as in the larger industrial centres, had become supporters of the new Soviet régime. At the same time it meant that the implementing, and in part the formulation, of the current policy of the new Government was in the hands of those who were political inheritors of Narodnik doctrines. Among the first acts of the Soviet Government was the Land Decree, signed by Lenin on the day following the revolution.[2] This stated that " the landowners' right to possession of the land is herewith abolished without compensation ",[3] and that " estates of the landowners, together with all Crown lands, monastic lands and Church lands, including all livestock and agricultural equipment and farm buildings, are transferred to the disposition of district Land Committees and the local Soviets of Peasant Deputies ". Any citizen wishing to cultivate the soil was to have the right to apply for the allotment to him of land for so long as he was able and willing to work it. In the meantime " any damage done to confiscated property, which from now on belongs to the whole people, will be treated as a serious crime " ; and district Soviets were charged with taking " all necessary measures for the preservation of the strictest order during the confiscation of estates ". It was the intention of the Bolsheviks, however, that a considerable portion of the estate-lands should not be subject to distribution but be retained as model State farms ; and the annexe to the decree referred explicitly to " territories where cultivation is of a high order : gardens, plantations, nurseries for plants and trees, orchards, etc.", as " not subject to division " but as reserved for " the exclusive use of the State or district as model institutions " ; and similarly " studs, State and private cattle-breeding establishments, poultry farms ". As it turned out, however, under the pressure of peasant influence in the localities, much less was reserved from distribution than was apparently at first intended. For

[1] Cf. Philips Price, *op. cit.*, 169–71 ; *Illustrated History*, vol. II, 431–44, 464–5. The invitation to participate in the Government on the basis of the full recognition of the November revolution and of Soviet power had been extended to all the socialist parties ; but the Mensheviks and the Right S.R.'s had refused to accept this condition and had seceded from the 2nd Soviet Congress which had met on November 7.

[2] Published in *Izvestia* two days later, on November 10 (N.S.).

[3] However, " those who suffer by their dispossession are to have the right of being publicly supported until they adapt themselves to the new conditions ".

example, only between two and three million acres of estates which had been run as beet-sugar farms were retained as State farms, instead of the ten to twelve million acres that had been originally intended.   As an average for the whole country, the land in the use of the peasantry rose from 70 per cent. of the whole cultivated area to 96 per cent.   In the Ukraine the increase was from 56 per cent. to 96 per cent., and in some regions the latter figure reached almost 100 per cent.   Over the economic history of Russia in the following decade this land reform, which in cementing the prole-tarian-peasant alliance in the November Revolution placed agricultural production under the almost complete control of small producers, was to exercise an overshadowing influence.

PART TWO

CHAPTER FOUR

THE FIRST EIGHT MONTHS

I

The *leitmotiv* running through the speeches and writings of Lenin in 1917 was the overshadowing importance of the political issue of the class which held the actual reins of power. For him this issue was paramount, since on it depended the direction in which historical forces would move in the coming historical epoch. Yesterday this power had resided in the landed nobility, with certain of the richer elements of the *parvenu* capitalist class as its junior partner. The March revolution had placed power in the hands of the capitalist class in town and country (though in Lenin's view, because the masses had handed the power to them, rather than because the bourgeoisie had themselves taken it) ; and now the Soviet Revolution of November had transferred power to representatives of the proletariat and the peasantry, representing " the overwhelming majority of the population ". A crucial feature of Lenin's political conception, which many have failed to appreciate, was that this issue was for him independent of the immediate tasks of economic and social policy which were on the historical agenda. The transfer of power to the Soviets, as organs which directly expressed the mood of those who toiled in town and village and which had been in large measure their own spontaneous creation, was required in order to prevent the March revolution from stopping half-way before the economic basis of the old nobility had been destroyed (as so many bourgeois revolutions had previously done), as well as to lay the basis for an eventual transition from Capitalism to Socialism. Not only was the existence of the Provisional Government no guarantee that the bourgeois-democratic revolution would not stop half-way ; but the Kornilov *coup* was witness to the danger of a Russian Thermidor, in the course of which agrarian reform might be submerged and fetters laid upon the working class once more.

At any rate, an immediate transition to a socialist economy was not on the agenda in the early months of the new Soviet régime. Immediate preoccupation was with the seizure of certain economic key positions to consolidate the political power that had already been won, and with measures of control over industry—control " both from above and from below "—designed to keep industry working and to protect the new régime both against the spreading epidemic of economic disintegration and against a possible " strike of capital " aimed to bring the government to its knees. But no sweeping measures of confiscation or nationalisation were immediately proposed. Rather was it a controlled or directed Capitalism, steered by such measures of economic control as had come to be the common stock-in-trade of belligerent governments, that was contemplated. There was little of the rash utopianism sometimes charged against him in the description which Lenin subsequently gave of this period as one in which " the State power made an attempt to pass to the new social relationships, while adapting itself to the conditions then prevailing as much as possible, as gradually as possible and breaking with as little of the old as possible ".[1] An early decree of the new Soviet Government, which called in general terms for " strictest control over production " and appealed to workers and peasants to " guard as the apple of your eye the land, the grain, the factories, the tools, the products, the means of transport ", referred to the transition to Socialism as proceeding " gradually with the consent and confirmation of the majority of the peasants following the teachings of their practical experience and of the workers ".[2] The Decree on Workers' Control of November 14th gave the workers' committees in each enterprise " the right to supervise the management " and " to determine a minimum of production ", and the right to have access to all correspondence and accounts. But at the same time the General Instructions appended to the Decree expressly reserved to the proprietor the executive right of giving orders as to the conduct of the enterprise and forbade the factory committee to interfere in this or to countermand such orders ; while Article 9 forbade committees " to take possession of the enterprise or direct it ", except with the sanction of the higher authorities. The nationalisation of the joint stock banks and their merging in the State Bank, announced on December 17th, was primarily undertaken to counter a strike of

---

[1] *Selected Works*, vol. IX, 284. At the same time he pointed out that " the tactics adopted by the capitalist class were to force us into a desperate and ruthless struggle which compelled us to smash up the old relationships to a far larger extent than we at first intended ". In a pamphlet written in 1918 against the so-called " Left Communists " he spoke of " a whole period of transition from Capitalism to Socialism ", this transitional form of economy containing " elements, particles, pieces of both Capitalism and Socialism ". (*Ibid.*, 165, 170.)

[2] *Izvestia*, November 21, 1917.

civil servants and employees of the State Bank, which was being organised by the League for the Regeneration of Russia, financed by the private banks. As regards the grain trade, Soviet policy reaffirmed what the Provisional Government had already inaugurated, in the shape of State monopoly of trading in grain, and did not introduce any new principle ; although it strengthened this policy by nationalising all grain elevators and warehouses in February 1918. A certain number of individual enterprises that were considered to be of key importance, especially those engaged on war work, were taken into State ownership ; a decree of December 18th, 1917, listing the reasons for which enterprises might be " confiscated ", which included the special importance of the enterprise to the State, refusal of the owner to observe the terms of the Decree on Workers' Control and the closing down or abandonment of the works by its owner. But until May, 1918, there was no case of a whole industry being nationalised ; in that month the sugar industry being placed under the administration of a government body called the Supreme Sugar Committee, to be followed by the oil industry a month later and by the declaration of State monopolies of trade in certain commodities which included matches, coffee, spices and yarn, and also foreign trade.

In one half of the cases where nationalisation of individual enterprises took place in these early months, the reason stated was the " sabotage " of the owner, and not infrequently the fact that he had closed his business and emigrated until counter-revolution should restore for him a more congenial environment. Thus we find the Société Internationale des Wagon-Lits and the Sergiev-Ufalenski mines nationalised because of " the refusal of the management to continue work in the workshops " and because of " the refusal of the management to submit to the Decree on Workers' Control ",[1] and the business of M. Helferich-Sade nationalised in January because the management " had closed down its factory and abandoned its principal office at Kharkov ".[2] Similarly, the aeroplane works of Andreiev Lanski and Company were taken over because of the declared intention of the company to dismiss its workers ; the Sestronetsk Metallurgical Works for refusing to continue production ; the Roentgen tube factory because its owner had abandoned the enterprise ; and the Rostkino dye works for " the categorical refusal of its owner to continue production in spite of the

---

[1] Decree of Dec. 29, 1917, cit. Labry, *Une Législation Communiste*, 96–7.
[2] Decree of Dec. 13, 1918, signed by Lenin and Shliapnikov.

reserves of material and fuel in stock ".[1] On the other hand, the large electrical concern in Moscow, Electro-Peredacha, was taken over " in view of its general importance to the State " ;[2] the Putilov armament works at Petrograd had been taken over in December for a similar reason ; the Chaudoir Company was nationalised by decree of February 27th for " governmental considerations of great importance " ; and the Novorossisk mining and metallurgical works at Yuzovka on March 3rd for the double reason of " the importance of the works to the State " and " the impossibility of the company continuing its operations ".

For certain enterprises, particularly where foreign capital was involved, proposals were canvassed for the creation of " mixed companies " in which the State and private capitalists should participate jointly. In the circumstances of the time very little was to become of these projects, although they were later to be revived on a limited scale after the civil war in the early period of the New Economic Policy. But some abortive negotiations took place in March between the Soviet Government and a group of capitalists, headed by the wealthy Moscow merchant Meshchersky for the formation of a mixed company in which foreign capital should participate, to control a certain group of enterprises in the metal industry (enterprises which were later amalgamated to form the State trust *Gomza*) ; and a similar proposal came from a company known as the Stakhaev Company. In government circles there was apparently some difference of view as to whether to accept or reject these proposals, and Lenin, who was in charge of the negotiations on the government side, opposed their acceptance at a meeting of the Supreme Economic Council on April 27th on the ground that in heavy industry the government wanted engineers, not shareholders. At any rate no agreement was reached ; although Meshchersky had modified his original proposal to give the government only a third of the shares to a proposal that his own group should be allotted only non-voting bonds. In the early summer a commission instituted to frame conditions on which concessions might be given to foreign capital was considering certain proposals made by a Norwegian firm and a Russo-Dutch syndicate for railway extensions in Siberia and the Donetz region.[3] In industries where private concerns continued to exist alongside State enterprises joint

---

[1] Decrees of Jan 16, Feb. 19 and Jan. 13, 1918, signed by Lenin and Shliapnikov.
[2] Decree of Feb. 17, 1918, signed Lomov and Antipov, cit. Labry, *op. cit.*, 105–6.
[3] Labry, *op. cit.*, 168 seq. ; Leites, *op. cit.*, 84 seq. ; S. Zagorsky, *La République des Soviets*, 37 seq. ; Benediktov in *Tyazholaia Industria S.S.S.R.* 81–3.

controlling bodies were set up to exercise general functions and regulations, consisting of representatives of the trade unions, of the private owners and of the government : for example, *Centro-Textil*, established on April 1st, 1918, following a Congress of the Textile Industry in February, which had provisionally instituted a Central Council for the industry consisting of 30 representatives of the trade unions, 15 of the owners and 20 representatives of various governmental bodies.[1]

Something similar to this form of representative controlling board was at first contemplated for the majority of light industries ; and these *Centres* were given fairly considerable powers of regulating their respective industries. They represented, in fact, a decentralised form of industrial control, by contrast with heavy industry where the control from an early date was more centralised, being vested in *Glavki*, or sub-departments of the Supreme Economic Council (*Vesenkha*), which had been instituted in December 1917, consisting of representatives of government departments and trade unions, together with technical experts in an advisory capacity, with the function of co-ordinating the activities of the organs of workers' control and systematising the process of nationalisation. Thus for the metal industry, a special Metal Department of Vesenkha was organised, absorbing the personnel of the pre-existing Fuel and Metal Council, and this became *Glavmetal*, which proceeded to concentrate all orders in its own hands and allocate them among the various enterprises. Similarly in the summer of 1918 *Glavugol* was instituted as the controlling body of the coal industry, with " exclusive rights for the investigation of new coal resources, for control over the private coal industry and its compulsory trustification, for the closing down of technically imperfect enterprises (on confirmation by Vesenkha), for the organisation of new enterprises, the working out of a programme of nationalisation, and the distribution of coal and the regulation of the coal trade ".[2]

But while the constitutions of the Centres and Glavki were generally different, their functions were similar and gradually approximated to one another. In light industry the Centres had power to give instructions to owners of private businesses, to distribute stocks of materials, to fix prices, to effect the amalgamation of enterprises, and finally (with the confirmation of Vesenkha) to

[1] Y. L. Piatakov in *Yezhegodnik Cominterna*, 1923, 329.
[2] Benediktov, *op. cit.*, 74-5.

nationalise any firm which they thought fit. When a firm or industry was nationalised, they organised the financing of enterprises and appointed the factory managers or managing " collegiates ", whose authority was in theory supreme in technical questions, but which were subject in practice on most matters to another body called a " factory collegiate ", composed of representatives of the workers in the factory (including the office staff), of the technical staff, of the local Soviet, of the trade union branch and of the local department of Vesenkha. In some cases Centres had the right of concentrating in their hands the supply of raw materials and fuel to the industry, of marketing the product and of exercising a monopoly of import and export. In the course of the summer of 1918, as industry became more widely nationalised, the Centres responsible for controlling light industry came increasingly to resemble, both in constitution and in functions, the sub-departments of Vesenkha which administered branches of heavy industry. Many of them came to exercise statutory powers, not only over firms within their branch of industry, but over the actions of other bodies ; and as their economic functions were enlarged, they tended to set up subordinate sections or Glavki to undertake more specialised tasks in the administration of production (as Glav-Textil was formed from Centro-Textil). Where Centres did not become virtually industrial sub-departments of Vesenkha, they tended to disappear, leaving only the more specialised Glavki in direct subordination to Vesenkha. Centroresin was given power " to increase, to restrain or to close enterprises " ; Centrokaska " to procure materials, to elaborate a plan of purchase, to control quality, and to arrange a plan for the distribution of products " ; and Centrochai could make " regulations touching tea (and associated goods) obligatory for both private enterprises and persons and also for social and governmental organisations ". Glavki have been described as " plenary organs of government ", having powers within their special spheres similar to those exercised in a wider sphere by Vesenkha.[1] For example, a Vesenkha decree of June 23rd gave authority to Glavsakhar (administering the nationalised sugar industry) to " publish obligatory decrees and instructions for all enterprises concerned with sugar, to regulate the increase, the reduction or the closing down of works, to create new establishments and organise new plantations ", to establish plans of output, transport and delivery, to supervise the finances of businesses, fix the scale of wages in the

[1] L. Kritsman, *Geroicheskoe Period Velikoi Russkoi Revolutsii*, 199.

sugar industry, to concentrate in its hands necessary reserve stocks, and to organise the distribution of labour and materials among the various establishments.[1]

II

This transitional State Capitalism, characterised by control over private trade and industry rather than by extensive socialisation, was to prove an unstable situation. In existing political conditions it could scarcely be more than an uneasy compromise, and it did not survive the summer of 1918. The reason for this breakdown, and for the accelerated transition to general nationalisation in the second half of the year, was twofold. In the first place, many factory committees went beyond the legal powers awarded to them in the Decree on Workers' Control, and eventually took the administration of factories into their own hands. This was a continuation of the spontaneous movement of direct action on the part of peasants and factory workers which had gathered momentum under the Provisional Government. The period was one of which subsequent writers have spoken as the " elemental period " of the revolution, when most things were done by uncoordinated local initiative, and the Soviet authorities at the centre still had no more than a light hand upon the reins. Such elemental tendencies were of course part of the strength of the new régime: the vigour of those spontaneous historical forces without which the revolution would neither have been started nor been completed. In real life social transformations seldom go according to plan ; and when they seem to go smoothly they often have something wrong inside them. But the immediate effect of these elemental tendencies was turbulent. In some cases the new régime of diarchy in industry continued satisfactorily for a period : for example, the case of an engineering firm at Odessa whose English manager submitted to the demand that workers' representatives should be present at Board meetings, and found it " not entirely disagreeable ".[2] It was not unknown for employers to win over the factory committee by personal influence or bribery ; and in " several cases the rôle of the factory committee was purely passive and the former directors or proprietors continued for a long time to enjoy the powers they

---

[1] Labry, *op. cit.*, 83 seq. ; also Zagorsky, *op. cit.*, 22 seq. Actually it is difficult to discover any consistent line of demarcation between the power of the Centres and of the Glavki. Evidently the demarcation differed according to the circumstances of each special case, and changed with the development of the situation.
[2] Article by " A British Manager " in *The Times*, September 4, 1918.

possessed under the old régime.[1] But few employers thought that
the new régime would survive for more than a few weeks ; and
while some owners grudgingly submitted to the orders of the factory
committee to keep their works running instead of closing them,
probably a larger number either defied the factory committees or
took the earliest opportunity of closing down and of moving themselves to another district until more favourable conditions should
return. In fact, manufacturers' associations had from the first
attempted to organise resistance to the Decree on Workers' Control : as, for example, resolutions of the Petrograd Manufacturers'
Association and the All-Russian Commercial and Industrial
Organisation in the previous December, which had advised employers to close their works if attempts were made to enforce the
decree. The retort of the factory committees to obstruction or
attempts to close down production was to invade the office, and
often after ejecting the owner or manager to run the factory on their
own. In the spring of 1918 a syndicalist tendency had become
widespread among factory committees : the notion that factories
should be run directly by the workers in them, and for the benefit
of those workers. The result was a further decline of workshop
discipline and of production, and in many cases the rise of a sectional, proprietorial sentiment on the part of workers towards their
factory, which spurned the interest of the larger community and
jealously resisted attempts at co-ordination and direction from
above. " Another proprietor came," wrote one of the leaders of
the Metal Workers' Union, " who was equally an individualist and
anti-social as the former one, and the name of the new proprietor
was the control committee. In the Donetz area, the metal works
and mines refused to supply each other with coal and iron on
credit, selling the iron to the peasants without regard for the
needs of the State."[2] A subsequent report of Vesenkha[3] summed
up its position at this period in very frank terms. " Vesenkha
clearly realised the necessity for a co-ordinated plan of nationalisation on definite lines. But in the first period it did not have the
statistical apparatus or the administrative apparatus, it did not have
links with the localities, and accordingly, lacking sufficient local
organs and ' cadres ' of workers, it was compelled to bring within
its purview and to try to handle an unnecessarily large number of
ailing economic enterprises : a fact which made the organisation

---

[1] I.L.O., *Labour Conditions in Soviet Russia*, 241 ; cf. also Zagorsky, *op. cit.*, 19.
[2] Cf. Piatakov, *loc. cit.*, 340.
[3] Report to the Eighth Congress of Soviets in December 1920.

of production extremely difficult. This first tempestuous period of industrial administration shattered any systematic organisation of industry and of economic accounting."

Against this illegal nationalisation on the initiative of factory committees or local Soviets the central authorities did what they could to exercise a restraining hand. A leading object in the institution of Vesenkha had been to co-ordinate the process of nationalisation and to give some shape and cohesion to the elemental forces which were riding the economic situation. On February 14th, 1918, an official announcement was issued that enterprises could not be taken over from their previous owners except by joint degree of Vesenkha and the Council of People's Commissars (*Sovnarcom*). Again, on April 27th, local bodies were reminded that no confiscation of industrial plants was permissible without the authority of Vesenkha ; the reminder being issued " in view of the fact that local Soviets continue confiscation of enterprises without notifying Vesenkha ".[1] But the instructions continued to be disobeyed ; and efforts made by Vesenkha in the direction of centralisation met with considerable resistance. The case of a group of factories in the Urals which the central authorities had decided to leave in private hands was not untypical. The local factory committee, declaring that the attitude of the owners was provocative, announced their intention of taking over the factory. The Central Council of Trade Unions sent a delegation from Moscow to dissuade them, but without avail ; and followed this by telegraphing instructions forbidding any action to be taken by the factory committee. To this telegram the only reply was a laconic report announcing the date on which the factory had been taken over on the authority of the local Soviet. Of individual firms that had been nationalised prior to July 1918 only about 100 were nationalised by decree of the centre, while over 400 had been nationalised on the initiative of local organisations.[2] When the starch and molasses factory, *Zhivilov*, was nationalised by the government, the factory committee refused to hand over to the administrator whom Vesenkha had sent to take charge ;[3] and when the District Economic Council of the Northern Region instituted a system of government inspectors to bring the metal works of Petrograd under its control, serious conflicts ensued between the inspectors and the factory committees.[4]

---

[1] *Izvestia*, April 27, 1918.
[2] I.L.O., *op. cit.*, 196 ; Benediktov, *loc. cit.*, 81. Half of the acts of nationalisation fell within the six weeks May 15–June 28.
[3] I.L.O., *op. cit.*, 240.   [4] *British Labour Delegation Report, 1920*, 96.

In the railway shops there actually appeared an organisation grandiloquently terming itself the " Alliance of Workers' Representatives ", which agitated against centralised control in the interests of " the autonomy of the workers' committees ".[1]

Although in February a joint meeting of factory committees and trade unions had agreed upon a subordination of the former to the latter, at the Third Congress of Trade Unions which opened on April 20th some strong opposition was expressed to proposals by the Government to introduce the principle of individual management into industry and to apply methods of payment by results and scientific management. The latter were particularly denounced as " relics of capitalist exploitation " by Riazanov (a Bolshevik who had recently resigned from his Party owing to disagreement on this point) ; and both the Alliance of Workers' Representatives and Maxim Gorky's *Novaya Zhizn* group allied themselves with the opposition. The mention of the need for "Americanising" the railway administration by a Bolshevik delegate at a meeting of the railway committee became a particular target of attack. The counter-proposal was made that the factory committees and trade unions should be entrusted with " collective responsibility " for a certain minimum programme of production, to be fixed in joint consultation between Vesenkha and the union representatives. The government spokesmen on the other hand argued that there was a wide gulf fixed between piece-rates and scientific management as used in the old days and under the new régime. There was now no question of using such methods to extort larger profits for shareholders and no fear of their being used to the detriment of the workers' class interests, seeing that a Workers' State was in being and the trade unions were strongly represented on the Supreme Economic Council. On the contrary, such methods were an essential instrument for increasing production, which would serve to raise the workers' standard of life and strengthen socialist industry. The majority policy of the Bolshevik Central Committee eventually carried the day, although not without some concessions to the objectors. Individual management of factories by managers responsible to the higher economic bodies which appointed them was accepted in principle, and was applied forthwith in cases where the requirements of production made it urgently necessary ; but the principle was not generally applied in industry until 1920, following the discussions at the 9th Party Congress. Payment by results and some features of Taylor-

[1] M. P. Price, *op. cit.*, 279–80.

methods of scientific management were also introduced in some factories and were gradually extended. In the case of the railways, administration was placed in the hands of a permanent railway department, whose decisions on purely administrative matters were to be binding on local trade unions and shop committees. The first round, at least, of the battle of Bolshevism against syndicalist tendencies had been won. Further, in the realm of finance the power of the local Soviets to impose indiscriminate levies on the bourgeoisie and to arrest people as a means of distraining their property, which had been a not uncommon practice in many provinces, was terminated ; and authority to levy taxes was centralised in responsible regional finance departments, charged with conducting their work in conformity with general regulations laid down by the organs of the central government.[1]

But apart from spontaneous tendencies among the workers to force the pace, born of the sharpened temper of class relations, there was a good deal of conscious opposition at the time to the policy which Lenin was advocating : opposition not only from among those outside the ranks of the Bolsheviks who were influenced by the ideas of the Left S.R.'s, but from inside the Party itself among the so-called " Left Communists ". The latter at one time constituted a separate fractional organisation within the Party, ran its own newspaper, *The Communist*, and co-operated with the Left S.R.'s. Its opposition became specially vocal at the time of the Brest-Litovsk Treaty, which they denounced as " a surrender to German Imperialism ", and culminated in the armed revolt of the Left S.R.'s on July 6th, with its plan to overthrow the Government and to arrest Lenin.[2] But they had earlier attacked the slowness of nationalisation, had denounced the negotiations with Meshchersky concerning a mixed company, and although they were not explicitly hostile to the employment of bourgeois technicians and experts in industry (on this point Bukharin apparently once declared he was " more to the Right than Lenin "), many of them seem to have looked askance at Lenin's insistence on generous treatment of " specialists ",[3] unless this was offset by greater

---

[1] M. P. Price, *op. cit.*, 280-5 ; L. Pasvolsky, *Economics of Communism*, 32-5 ; I.L.O., *op. cit.*, 244 seq., 254-7.

[2] Cf. L. Trotsky, *Cours Nouveau*, 37 ; M. P. Price, *op. cit.*, 271 ; evidence of Yakovleva, Ossinsky, Kamkov, Karelin, Bukharin, etc., in *Verbatim Report of the Case of the Anti-Soviet Bloc of Rights and Trotskyites*, 439-509. The leading members of the Left Communists were Bukharin, Radek, Piatakov, Ossinsky, Yakovleva, Lomov. The Hungarian Bela Kun also seems to have belonged to this group (which was apparently formed towards the end of 1917 or early 1918), although he took an active part in suppressing the revolt of the Left S.R.'s.

[3] E.g., in his pamphlet, *The Soviets at Work*.

powers of direct control over production by the factory committees. Karelin, the Left S.R., however, at the Fourth Session of the Soviet Central Executive Committee openly spoke of Lenin's employment of bourgeois engineers and economists as " coalition with the bourgeoisie ", and in May the Left S.R.'s opposed a Bolshevik motion for more centralised control of food supply, and in particular for empowering the Commissariat of Supply to remove local supply commissars and to countermand the orders of local Soviets.

It was against these tendencies that Lenin published his pamphlet[1] in which he spoke of " State Capitalism " as a " gigantic step forward ", and emphasised that the " period of transition between Capitalism and Socialism " would be one in which inevitably " elements of both Capitalism and Socialism " would be mixed. In such circumstances it was urgently necessary both to study and to copy the State Capitalism of the war-time countries of Central and Western Europe, and it was even permissible in certain circumstances to " buy off the bourgeoisie ", especially those " cultured capitalists who agree with State Capitalism, who are capable of putting it into practice, and who are useful to the proletariat as clever and experienced organisers of the largest types of enterprises ". Against those who repeated traditional formulas about the dangers and oppressiveness of State Capitalism he emphasised that such fears were groundless in the novel situation where the working class held State power and occupied the " key positions " from which it could steer the course of development. In such circumstances it was with an " encircled Capitalism " that compromises were being made. Romanticists and " slaves of phrases " he answered with the demand for realism. " When workers' delegations came to me with complaints against the factory owners," Lenin once said, " I always said to them : ' You want your factory nationalised. Well and good. We have the decree ready and can sign it in a moment. But tell me, can you take the organisation into your own hands ? Do you know how and what you produce ? And do you know the relations between your product and the Russian and international market ? ' And inevitably it transpired that they knew nothing. There was nothing written about such matters in the Bolshevik textbooks, or even in those of the Mensheviks."[2]

The second and decisive factor which brought the policies of

[1] " The Principal Tasks of our Day : Left-wing Childishness and Petit-Bourgeois Mentality ", part of which is republished in *Selected Works*, vol. IX, 156–76.
[2] Cit. Farbman, *After Lenin*, 43.

this eight months' breathing space to a close was the outbreak in the summer of 1918 of acute civil war, supported by the armed intervention of foreign powers. On May 29th came news of the revolt of the Czechoslovak troops in the Urals (who had been moving eastward across Siberia prior to their evacuation and re-patriation *via* Vladivostok) ; and on May 30th martial law was declared in Moscow and other leading cities. In the first week of June General Krasnov and his Cossacks in the south attacked Tsaritsin. After the signing of the Brest-Litovsk Treaty in March the Germans had occupied the Ukraine, and in the course of July British troops landed at Archangel[1] in the north, and the Allied forces already in Murmansk since April (when they had first gone there with the agreement of the Soviet authorities to prevent its capture by the Germans in Finland) began to advance south. In August General Denikin's Volunteer Army in the North Caucasus captured Ekaterinodar in the Kuban ; and on September 5th the attempted assassination of Lenin took place. In these circum-stances, not only did the attitude of the bourgeoisie to the new régime harden, and any willingness to co-operate that they had pre-viously shown evaporate overnight, but for the Soviet Government military necessities immediately took precedence over all other considerations. Such captains of industry and big merchants as had not previously done so packed their bags and passed through the White Armies' lines ; while for the Soviet authorities a direct control over production quickly became of urgent necessity, both to combat attempts at ca' canny and sabotage and to ensure priority for military supplies.[2] Where there was sabotage from owners or managerial staff or chaos resulting from the sectional activities of the factory committees, there was now no alternative for the

[1] This landing took place following intrigues with the Whites " helped by the British Secret Service at Petrograd ", which had assisted members of White organisations to move north to Archangel and Murmansk. (Cf. G. Stewart, *The White Armies of Russia*, 91.) Tchaikovsky, the first head of the Archangel White Government, was kidnapped by White officers ; Chaplin, a Russian naval officer on General Poole's staff, being mainly responsible, if not with the connivance of General Poole at least with his subsequent support. Although Tchaikovsky was restored for a time, he was soon forced to resign and a virtual military dictatorship followed. General Poole was succeeded by General Ironside—Lord Ironside of Archangel. (*Ibid.*, 92–3 ; Mavor, *The Russian Revolution*, 352–7.) Cf. also the remarks of Professor P. Sorokin on preparations for a rising against the Bolsheviks in the north during the spring, which under cover of " a purely fictitious neutra-lity " towards the Soviet régime he conducted in Ustyug and Kotlas. (*Leaves from a Russian Diary*, 136 seq., 147.)

[2] Lenin subsequently said that " in March or April 1918, as against methods of gradual transition, we began to discuss . . . methods of struggle to be directed mainly towards the expropriation of the expropriators [i.e. the capitalists]. . . . But we were to see that our work in organising, accounting and control lagged considerably behind." (*Selected Works*, vol. IX, 280.)

central government than to declare the enterprise nationalised and to send down a representative from the centre, armed with powers to restore a degree of order and to harness production to some central programme.

Already in May the pace of nationalisation, even of " galel " nationalisation, had quickened. But at the end of June a governmental measure was precipitately adopted which closed one chapter of policy and opened another. This was the Decree of General Nationalisation of June 28th, which applied nationalisation by a stroke of the pen to practically all large-scale enterprises without distinction. It applied to all companies with more than a million roubles of capital (the equivalent roughly of something in the neighbourhood of £50,000 and £100,000), in mining, metals, textiles, glass, leather, cement, and the timber and electrical trades, and to " all metal-producing enterprises which are the only ones of their kind in Russia ". It might have seemed as if the government had suddenly capitulated to the Left. The immediate reason for the decree, however, was a rather special one, which gave it an emergency character. There were considerable fears in Moscow at this time that the Germans, having already occupied the important industrial regions of the Ukraine, might proceed, here and in other regions as well, to protect important industrial concerns from future nationalisation by transferring them (in actuality, or nominally as a cloak for their original owners) to German firms ; and in the course of June Berlin had witnessed a mild speculative boom in Russian industrial shares. Larin, who was at the time in Berlin on a commercial mission, telegraphed on June 25th to Lenin that there was a likelihood of the German Ambassador in Moscow lodging with the Soviet Government a list of Russian enterprises that were now in the ownership of German citizens, and accordingly exempt from any future nationalisation decree. To counter this move, an all-night sitting of Vesenkha prepared the list of enterprises over which it was desirable that the net of legal nationalisation should be cast, and the Council of People's Commissaries adopted the new decree within forty-eight hours. The decree appeared in *Izvestia* on the very morning on which Count Mirbach may very well have been preparing to deliver his diplomatic note about the safeguarding of German property in Russia from confiscation.[1] Although the terms of the decree were permissive only, and existing proprietors were directed to continue in control, subject to acceptance of financial responsibility by the Government

[1] Zagorsky, *op. cit.*, 40–1 ; M. P. Price, *op. cit.*, 285–6.

until arrangements for nationalisation were completed, once published it was fairly quickly implemented ; and in the next six or nine months a series of particular decrees followed, nationalising whole groups of enterprises or sections of an industry.[1] By the end of the year the number of nationalised concerns reached the figure of 1000, and by the autumn of 1919 some 3000 or 4000. The drift towards nationalised control of industry, centralised allocation of supplies and centralised collection and distribution of products was to be rapid. What came to be known as the period of " War Communism " had been launched : a product of the forcing house of a mortal struggle of the new régime against extinction, when military necessity ruled all and problems of industry were virtually identified with the problem of military supplies.

---

[1] Cf. *Sbornik Dekretov i Postanovlenii po Narodnomu Khoziaistvu, 1918–19* (1920), 83 seq., 112 seq.

CHAPTER FIVE

THE PERIOD OF "WAR COMMUNISM"

I

With the advance of the White Armies, backed by the armed forces of foreign Powers, the process of economic disorganisation moved at headlong speed. To the inevitable disruption caused in the early months by those centrifugal and syndicalist tendencies of which we have spoken were now added the effects of a civil war raging over the most important industrial and agricultural regions of the country. The base of the White Armies in the south was the rich Kuban and the North Caucasus region ; and since the Treaty of Brest-Litovsk the Germans had been in possession of the Ukraine. Following the capture of Ekaterinodar by the Volunteer Army of General Denikin in August 1918, General Krasnov's Cossacks established themselves on the lower Volga ; and in October the White Armies of the south were united under General Denikin, who established over the whole region between the Sea of Azov and the Volga what an American historian of the White Armies has termed " a simple dictatorship of the sword " in which " pillage became the order of the day ".[1] In August of the same year the Czech forces that were operating in conjunction with the White Armies from Siberia occupied Kazan ; and the Urals and Siberia were soon subordinated to the régime of Admiral Kolchak, supported by a mixed expeditionary force of Americans, Canadians, French, and Japanese. Although the British advance in the extreme north made little progress, the forces of General Yudenich in the Baltic States advanced in the following autumn up to the gates of Petrograd itself, while supporting units of the British Navy operated

---

[1] G. Stewart, *The White Armies of Russia*, 66, 69. Of allies and subordinates of Admiral Kolchak (commanding the White forces in Siberia) such as Atamans Semyonov and Kalmykov, General Rosanov and Annenkov, this writer speaks as responsible for deeds which " would have done credit to Genghis Khan " and " guilty of murders and plundering which would have disgraced any mediaeval footpad " (823, also 258–9, 287, 305–6, 315). Cf. also Baerlein, *The March of the Seventy Thousand*, 178–80, 207, on the deeds of Semyonov and others ; and General W. S. Graves, *America's Siberian Adventures, 1918–20*, 127 seq., 203–4, 253–5, 261 seq., 312–14, who speaks of Kalmykov particularly as " the notorious murderer, robber and cut-throat " and " the worst scoundrel I ever saw or heard of " (90).

a blockade of Kronstadt at the entrance to the Neva. At one stage the Soviet Government had lost possession of all but 100 per cent. of the former coal supplies of the country, and retained less than a quarter of its iron foundries, less than a half of its grain area and less than one tenth of its sources of sugar beet.

Shortage of materials threatened to paralyse industry. Famine walked in the streets of Moscow and Petrograd. With the absence of goods for which reliance had always been placed on import from abroad (for example, electric lamps, tubing for boilers, belting, etc., for the lack of which many factories had to close[1]) was combined an acute fuel crisis, following the loss of the Donbas and the stoppage of oil supplies from Baku and Grozny, which necessitated an almost complete transfer to wood fuel on the railways. By 1919 the amount of fuel available for consumption (other than domestic) had shrunk to little more than one half of the amount available in 1917 and to 40 per cent. of 1916.[2] The Donetz basin in 1913 had accounted for 75 per cent. of the iron ore and 60 per cent. of the pig-iron output of the Russian Empire. The Urals, which was a fighting front in 1918–19, accounted for another 19 per cent. of the pig-iron ; while of the remaining 21 per cent. Poland had been responsible for nearly a half.[3] The Powers operated what was virtually a complete blockade of Soviet territory. Cotton no longer came from Turkestan or Transcaucasia to the cotton mills of Vladimir or Ivanovo-Vosnesensk. After Denikin's advance no coal came from the Donetz. In the central area, which remained in the Soviet sphere, the number of blast-furnaces in operation fell from 13 in 1918 to 9 in 1919 and to no more than 5 at the beginning of 1920 ; the number of rolling-mills from 14 in 1918 to 7 in 1920 ; and the production of cast-iron from 3·7 million poods in 1918 to 1·3 million in 1919 and 0·3 million in 1920.[4] The result was starvation for the engineering and munitions industry in metal supplies. Fuel shortage and difficulties in repairs grievously enhanced the disorganisation of transport, as did the added strain on the railway system from the urgent military needs of several fronts. There was also the direct disorganisation and physical destruction resulting from the frequent ebb and flow of the fighting line. Even before

---

[1] A. Heller, *The Industrial Revival in Russia*, 138.
[2] Larin and Kritsman, *Ocherk Khoziaistvennoi Zhizni i Organisatzia Narodnovo Khoziaistva Sov. Russ.*, 28–9. Pre-war consumption of fuels had been in these proportions : coal 65 per cent., oil 20 per cent., wood 13½ per cent., peat 1½ per cent.
[3] M. Miller, *Econ. Development of Russia, 1905–1914*, 288 seq.
[4] Leites, *op. cit.*, 142.

the effects of the civil war had been felt, the Government's chief railway expert, Professor Lomonossov, had reported that an early complete collapse of the railway system was inevitable. To a large extent the civil war was " a railway war ", since it took place along the main lines, and the railway was the only available means for moving troops, munitions and supplies any distance. In 1919 50 per cent. of the locomotives in action were being used for military purposes.[1] The proportion of disabled locomotives awaiting repair, which had stood at about 30 per cent. at the time of the October Revolution, steadily mounted to 47 per cent. in December 1918, to 55 per cent. in December 1919, and to 69 per cent. in 1920. Correspondingly the number of locomotives in the hands of the Government and in running order, which had stood at about 14,500 at the end of 1917, quickly declined to under 5000 by the end of the following year and to under 4000 in January 1920. The proportion of wagons awaiting repair had by 1920 reached more than 20 per cent.[2] The full extent of the disorganisation can be gauged from the fact that in 1918–19 about 60 per cent. of the railroad mileage of Russia was in the territory occupied by the White Armies ; and in 1920 as much as 80 per cent. of the railroad system was within the sphere of military operations. The direct destruction suffered by the transport system was estimated by the Soviet Government to have amounted to 3600 railway bridges, 1200 miles of permanent way, 380 engine depots and railway shops, in addition to the destruction of 3600 ordinary bridges and over 50,000 miles of telegraph and telephone lines.[3]

Shortage of fuel, of materials and of food combined to bring about a disastrous fall in industrial productivity. The transport and industrial difficulties, which were enough to baffle the boldest and wisest efforts, caused congestion and dislocation in the administrative apparatus, which reacted upon and worsened the economic situation. Starvation or semi-starvation grievously lowered the intensity of work and the efficiency of the individual worker, swelled absenteeism and encouraged petty theft and peculation as means of supplementing starvation rations. Professor Prokopovitch estimated that by 1920 the number of workers employed in industry was less than one half the pre-war figure, that the average productivity per worker had fallen to 30–35 per cent., and the total output

---

[1] Larin and Kritsman, *op. cit.*, 35.
[2] Pasvolsky, *op. cit.*, 362 ; Shatunovski, *op. cit.*, 366.
[3] *Ibid.*, 362 ; League of Nations, *Report on Econ. Conditions in Russia*, 14–5; Rudzutak in *Manchester Guardian Commercial*, Russian Supplement June 26, 1924, 919.

of industry to the figure of 14·5 per cent.[1] Absenteeism in industry was sometimes as high as 60 per cent. and quite commonly exceeded 30 per cent. ;[2] while the Moscow worker's monthly wage in 1920 was only sufficient to keep him alive for eleven to thirteen days, so that he was under the necessity of supplementing it, legally or illegally, from other sources.[3] At the worst period the meagre daily bread ration of one eighth of a pound for workers was issued only on alternate days. It is hardly surprising that the towns should have lost between a quarter and a third of their population, largely by migration to the village, and Moscow as much as a half of its population.

With the additional strain that the war situation imposed on Budget expenditure, there was little chance of the Government terminating inflation and arresting the depreciation of the currency. On the contrary, despite the tapping of new (though limited) sources of revenue by special levies on the bourgeoisie, there was increased resort to raising funds by the expedient of printing paper money. During the first eight months of the revolution, up to the outbreak of civil war and armed intervention in June 1918, the rate of increase of paper money was slower than it had been during the Provisional Government. The currency circulation, which had stood at 22·4 milliard roubles on November 1st, 1917, did not pass the 30 milliard figure until March 1918. On June 1st it stood at 40·3 and on January 1st, 1919, at 60·8 milliard ; the increase during 1918 amounting to 119 per cent. compared with 180 per cent. in 1917. But after 1918 inflation proceeded at a disastrously accelerated pace, multiplying three times in the course of 1919 and more than four times in 1920.[4] In October 1920 the purchasing power of the rouble was no more than 1 per cent. of what it had been in October 1917.[5]

Inflation enables a government to procure command over resources by using new paper issues in purchase of what it requires. To the extent that this occurs in conditions of scarcity of commodi-

---

[1] *Economic Conditions in Soviet Russia*, 24. Popov in *Econ. Zhizn*, March 31, 1923, gave 15 per cent. as the average figure, ranging from 6 per cent. in the metal industry (in pig-iron only 2–3 per cent.) and in cotton to 32 per cent. in hemp and 35 per cent. in linen and wool. Chernomordik quotes similar figures ; but speaks of the productivity of labour as being only 20 per cent. of the 1913 level, and real wages as being no more than 35–40 per cent. of pre-war. (*Economicheskaia Politika S.S.S.R.*, 85.) Strumilin writing in 1921 gave higher proportions both for real wages and for the productivity of labour in 1919–20. (Cf. *Na Khoziaistvennom Fronte*, 23.)
[2] Leites, *op. cit.*, 152, 199.   [3] Khalatov in *Yezhegodnik Cominterna*, 1923, 460.
[4] Prof. S. Katzenellenbaum, *Russian Currency and Banking, 1914–1924*, 56–9; Prof. L. N. Yurovsky, *Currency Problems in the Soviet Union*, 25–6.
[5] G. A. Neyman, *Vnutrennia Torgovlia S.S.S.R.* (1935), 84.

ties and of productive-power,[1] less resources will be left available to meet the needs of ordinary consumers. Inflation, therefore, acts as a forced levy or tax upon the community, forcing other people to go without, in order that the government as consumer may command a larger share of the available resources. This reduction of consumption is enforced by the rise of prices which the impact of increased demand from the government upon scarce supplies tends to produce. Those who suffer thereby, and upon whom the incidence of the levy rests, are those whose incomes are fixed in terms of money and those who hold reserves in money form. Such persons find their income or their reserves shrinking in purchasing power as inflation proceeds. In the past it has usually been wage- and salary-earners who have been the principal sufferers, since their rates of pay have tended to lag behind price movements. But in Russia under a Soviet régime every attempt was made to prevent the industrial worker from suffering in this way ; and it was largely in his interests that the practice came to be adopted of giving an increasingly large part of the workers' wages in kind. So severe was the shortage that the worker could not be prevented from losing to a considerable extent. But at least in his case the effect of inflation was cushioned by the practice of wages in kind.[2] The two principal sections, accordingly, on whom the burden of inflation fell were the remnants of the former moneyed class, who were extensively expropriated by the fall in the value of money, and the peasantry. The former lost in so far as they held wealth in money form. The peasantry were damaged in two ways : in so far as, after selling their produce for money, they hoarded their money or at least held it for any substantial interval of time before they subsequently spent it in purchase of other goods, and in so far as the prices of manufactured goods which they bought rose more steeply than the prices of agricultural goods which they sold. We have seen that since before the November Revolution the grain monopoly had been used to curb the rise of grain prices ; and in so far as it was successful in so doing, the effects of inflation were thrown mainly upon the prices of manufactured goods, and the rate of interchange between the products of the town and of the village was turned to the disadvantage of the latter.

[1] The position is, of course, different where excess productive capacity and unemployed man-power exists. Here the effect will be merely to bring this excess capacity into use by expanding market demand.

[2] An I.L.O. estimate of the time stated that in 1918 half of the Russian workers' wages were in kind, in 1919 more than three quarters, and in 1920 round nine tenths. (*Industrial Life in Soviet Russia*, 169.)

One part of the levy imposed by inflation could be evaded if the peasant reduced the balance which he held in money form by dishoarding existing money-reserves and contracting the interval of time between his receipt of money and his spending of it. We have noticed that such evasion of inflationary levies was already beginning in the winter of 1916–17. In the years which followed the process continued. The result of such action was to enhance the shortage of manufactured goods by increased peasant-purchases of them, to accelerate the rise in their market-price and to make it progressively more difficult for the Government to acquire real resources by means of fresh issues of paper money. As prices rise, the Government, in order to acquire the same *quantity* of real things, has to increase progressively the amount of new currency issues. In order to acquire an increasing quantity of real resources, it has to increase its currency issues, not merely by a greater *amount* than before, but in greater proportion to the total currency circulation. The result of this is a shrinkage of the real value, or purchasing power, of the aggregate currency circulation (in terms of the goods available to ordinary consumers) ; and, if private dishoarding is simultaneously occurring, there is likely to be a decrease in the real values yielded to the Exchequer by inflationary issues. The limit to such a process is where no goods are brought on the market for sale against money (but goods are bartered or hoarded instead) and where the purchasing power of money and the ability of the Government to acquire real resources by inflation is reduced to zero. But long before this point has been reached the Government will be faced with the impossibility of obtaining sufficient real resources by inflation to meet its requirements. As a matter of fact, the real values which the Soviet Government was able to raise by means of paper issues fell drastically in the course of 1919 and 1920 ; and in the latter year amounted to little more than a third of the real value of new issues in 1918, and covered less than 8 per cent. of government expenditure.[1]

The economic crux of the system known as "War Communism" accordingly consisted in the relationship with peasant agriculture. In the situation we have just described it had become impossible for the Soviet Government to obtain the resources it needed through the normal processes of the market, even with extensive aid from the money-printing press. It could obtain these resources only by measures of coercion, and by centralised control and distribution

[1] Cf. Y. S. Rozenfeld, *Promishlennaia Politika S.S.S.R.* (1926), 384.

of supplies. The surplus produce of each peasant farm, over and above essential needs of subsistence and seed-corn, was subjected to compulsory requisitioning ; the collection of this produce, and the allocation of it between the army and industry and the main distribution-points for workers' rations, being organised by the Commissariat of Supplies (*Narcomprod*). This centralised collection and distribution of supplies was the keystone of the system. Without it there is small doubt that starvation in the towns in the winter of 1919–20 would have been very much more extensive, and the army might well have collapsed. Towards the latter half of 1920 the collecting apparatus was strengthened and the supplies improved, so that a slight increase in workers' food rations became possible.[1] But it could be no more than a temporary expedient ; since its inevitable effect was to rupture that alliance between the industrial working class and the peasantry upon which the Soviet Revolution had been based. It was this which constituted the Achilles' heel of War Communism. The estrangement of the peasantry was not merely political : an effect which was serious enough for the Soviet régime. Compulsory requisitioning, which often had to be enforced by the dispatch of armed detachments of workers from the towns to the villages, very soon produced a direct economic consequence of the gravest import, which was much harder to combat than the withholding of grain from the market : a shrinkage of the sown area. Not all of the shrinkage of the sown area which occurred could be attributed to a " peasants' strike " against the demands of Narcomprod : some of it was due to the direct destruction of manpower and means of cultivation by the war. But the fact remains that, whereas in 1918 the main problem consisted in the holding back of grain in store by the peasantry, in preference to selling it against paper money, by 1920 it consisted of a halving of the sown area in Siberia and a reduction of it to as little as a quarter in parts of the Volga region and the Caucasus (which had been brought again within the sphere of the Soviet Government). The sugar-beet area was reduced to 30 per cent. of 1913 and the crop to under 10 per cent. ; and already in 1919 the flax crop was less than one fifth of the pre-war level.[2] Since

[1] Khalatov in *Yezhegodnik Cominterna*, 1923, 389 ; Larin and Kritsman, *op. cit.*, 18.
[2] *Soviet Union Yearbook, 1926,* 76 seq. ; I.L.O., *Co-operative Movement in Sov. Russia,* 90–1. Mainly as a result of the breaking of communications between the cotton-manufacturing districts near Moscow and the cotton-growing areas of Turkestan and Transcaucasia, the cotton crop had fallen by 1919 to 6 per cent. of 1913. Almost the only crop to suffer little reduction in cultivated area was hemp. Its yield showed a greater fall than did its area, but not as great as other

the total crop yield had also shrunk by a third or rather more, the total harvest in 1920 was little more than two fifths of the average harvest of the pre-war quinquennium.[1] At the end of the period of War Communism an extension of coercion from the peasant's surplus produce to his sown area was under discussion. This was proposed by Ossinsky of Narcomprod in the form of a compulsory minimum of cultivated area to be assigned to each farm (similarly to measures adopted under the British War Agricultural Committees during the Second World War); and although the proposal was regarded coldly by the Commissariat of Agriculture, it was actually adopted in a modified form by the 8th Soviet Congress.

We have said that the policy of compulsory requisitioning was not a creation of the Soviet Government. Nor was the problem of food shortage a creation of the civil war. What was new was the strictness with which the requisitioning policy came to be enforced ; and what the civil war did was to accentuate the food shortage to a point where it became the dominant obsession of economic policy. On May 14th, 1918, a decree of TSIK (the central executive committee of the Soviets) declared that "in any district the labouring peasants, not employing other citizens' labour, must see that all peasants who have surplus grain stores and refuse to deliver them up at the fixed prices be declared enemies of the people, and be deprived of their rights as citizens of the Republic and be brought before a revolutionary tribunal". This was followed by the decree of June 11th which instituted the Committees of the Village Poor. The intention of their formation was to secure allies inside the village who would be instrumental in enforcing the requisitioning policy upon the well-to-do peasantry in whose hands the surplus stocks chiefly were. In this way the supply-policy would not be something imposed upon the village from without but carried through by the poorer strata of peasants themselves who felt their interests most closely linked with the town workers and with the defence of the revolution. But the formation of these committees was to have serious consequences, not all of which conformed to the original intention. It was this action which precipitated the final breach between the Bolsheviks and the Left Social Revolutionaries, who, following their defeat at the 5th Soviet Congress in July, attempted an armed revolt the in streets of Moscow and the

crops. This was apparently because hemp was cultivated less for the market than for the peasants' own use, and because its chief centres were in central provinces least affected by the fighting, namely Vladimir, Kostroma and Yaroslav.
[1] Cf. League of Nations, *Report on Economic Conditions in Russia*, 20–1.

institution of a new revolutionary government. More serious, it was often responsible for antagonising, not merely the *kulaks*, who though influential were no more than a minority of the village population, but the mass of the middle peasantry who constituted the majority in the countryside and who since the agrarian revolution formed the backbone of agricultural economy. In certain provinces the middle peasantry became the basis for such support as the White Armies when they advanced were able to win in the countryside. More extensively they were a source of recruitment to the various anti-Soviet insurgent movements, often semi-bandit in character and invoking a plague upon Commissars and White officers impartially : for example, the picturesque Anarchist bandit leader Makhno in the southern Ukraine and Antonov in the province of Tambov.[1] In many areas, particularly in the provinces of Tula and Riazan, there were armed clashes between workers' detachments engaged in the collection of supplies and the local peasantry; and officials of Narcomprod seldom went far into the countryside unarmed.

Lenin was quick to see the danger to the *smytchka* latent in this fanning of the class struggle in the village. At the end of the year, accordingly, the Committees of the Village Poor was dissolved ; and at the 8th Party Congress in March 1919 he urged the need to heal the breach with the middle peasantry and to win them as allies in the fight against counter-revolution. " Learn to come to an agreement with the middle peasant," he insisted, " while not for a moment renouncing the struggle against the *kulak* ; and at the same time placing firm reliance solely on the poor peasant." The resolution of the Congress called for " a more correct execution of the Party's policy with regard to the middle peasantry, in the sense of a more attentive attitude to their needs, the elimination of arbitrary conduct on the part of the local authority ". " To confuse the middle peasantry with the *kulaks* . . . represents the crudest violation of the entire policy of the Soviet Government. . . . Soviet policy must reckon with a long period of co-operation with the middle peasantry." There can be little doubt that this shift of

---

[1] Makhno at first held a command in the Red Army in the Ukraine and was dismissed for indiscipline. He and his followers then harried the rear of Denikin's White Armies, with the support of the local peasantry. After the advance of the Red Army, he turned his attention in 1920 to harrying Soviet food collectors and officials, raiding towns and communications in the rear of the Red Army. After a brief period of co-operation with the Red Army against Wrangel in Oct. 1920, fighting between them broke out again before the end of the year. In Aug. 1921 he escaped into Rumania. Antonov was active throughout the winter of 1920–1, and continued into the autumn of 1921. He himself was not captured until June 1922. (Cf. W. H. Chamberlin, *The Russian Revolution, 1917–1921*, vol. II, 233–9, 437–9.)

emphasis, which was subsequently described by Stalin as a shift from a policy of " neutralising " the middle peasant to one of forming a " stable alliance " with him, was a major factor in the success of the Soviet Government in the civil war.   But although the majority of the peasantry were prepared to support the Red Army despite their dislike of requisitioning, especially if they had experienced occupation by the White armies and had been touched by the danger of landlordism restored, the local agents of Narcomprod continued to be unpopular figures who were frequently the victims of attack.   The danger to the *smytchka* remained.

II

With the substitution of requisitioning and centralised allocation of supplies for the ordinary mechanism of the market went both a hypertrophy of centralised administration of economic life and a progressive replacement of money as a means of exchange by direct allocation of supplies and the payment of wages in kind.   The requisitioning policy with regard to agriculture and centrally organised allocation of supplies, alike for industry, the ordinary consumer and the army, can be said to have formed the quintessence of War Communism.   At the same time the nationalisation of industry continued until it embraced, not only large-scale and medium-sized industry, but even quite small factories.   In November, 1920, a decree announced the nationalisation of all enterprises employing more than five workers where mechanical power was used and more than ten workers in purely handicraft workshops ;   and by the end of this year as many as 37,000 enterprises were listed as belonging to the State.   This figure embraced many thousands of quite small workshops : 18,000 of the 37,000 did not use mechanical power, and more than 5000 of them were actually businesses with only one employee.[1]   " Parallel with the nationalisation of productive enterprises, the free exchange of commodities was eliminated, and together with this the apparatus of a free market.   Government measures assisted this tendency by establishing State monopolies in the exchange of various types of commodity ;   and with the establishment of these State monopolies the commodities in question were withdrawn from the sphere of private-enterprise exchange and their distribution among consumers was concentrated in the hands of special organs of State.

[1] L. Kritsman, *Geroicheski Period Velikoi Russkoi Revolutsii*, 62, 127–9 ; also D. I. Chernomordik, *op. cit.*, 80.

In the course of 1918 and 1919 State monopolies were extended to almost all objects of productive and individual consumption—to provisions, to industrial goods, to raw materials, etc. The establishment on a very extensive scale of these State monopolies completely destroyed the supply apparatus peculiar to the structure of commodity-capitalist relations of trade."[1] Already in August, 1918, a decree of Vesenkha had stipulated that " settlements for products delivered or received are to be effected by means of book entries without the use of money ", thereby eliminating money as a medium for transactions between State undertakings. By decree of November 21st of the same year all private internal trade was prohibited, and Narcomprod was made the sole authority for supplying consumption goods to the population. In March, 1919, the co-operatives lost their independent status and were virtually merged in the supply apparatus of Narcomprod. Even the small " bagman " trade—that precursor of the Europe-wide " black market " of the Second World War—which grew to huge proportions in 1920 was illegal. In industry itself, not only did the rations attaching to a job become a more important consideration than the scale of money wages and wage-payment in kind come to be increasingly substituted for payment in depreciating paper roubles, but working conditions approximated to those in the army. Penalties were established for " labour deserters ", and " stern labour discipline was introduced, bearing a semi-military character ".[2]

At first agricultural commodities were divided into three classes ; the degree of State control over their purchase being different in each case. The first consisted of products subject to compulsory requisitioning ; the second of those the purchase of which was monopolised by the State but which were not requisitioned ; and the third of non-monopolised goods free to be sold to or bartered with State supply-organs or co-operatives or private persons. The inevitable tendency was for the peasants to reduce their production of the first two groups and wherever possible to transfer to the production of things in the third group. To counter this tendency, the number of goods included in the category of State monopolies was continually extended, until by the end of the civil war scarcely anything of importance remained in the third category. The collection of goods of the first category was shared between Narcomzem (the Commissariat of Agriculture) and Narcomprod ;

[1] S. I. Asknazii, *Nar. Khoz. Sovetskikh Respublik za 1917–1924 g.* (1925), 7.
[2] Chernomordik, *op. cit.*, 81.

and in order to supplement these collections with additional purchases, Narcomprod organised a fund of industrial goods which
could be sold to the peasantry as an encouragement to them to
place additional produce on the market.   Here it made use of the
co-operatives : the agricultural and handicraft co-operatives for the
purchase of non-requisitioned products and the consumers'
co-operatives for the distribution of industrial goods.   In August,
1918, it was decreed that the latter should only be supplied in
return for receipts for grain deliveries ; and increasingly this
exchange assumed the form of barter, payment being made increasingly in kind and decreasingly in money.   Industry arranged for the
disposal of its output to Narcomprod, which then planned its
distribution to the town and village population.   Industrial organisations, being credited with the value of their output at ruling prices,
came to be increasingly paid in kind in the shape of foodstuffs and
raw materials, collected by Narcomprod, which were then appor-
tioned by the industrial organisations among the factories subordinated to them.   Sometimes workers in a factory were paid in
tickets of purchase at their local co-operative store, and such purchases were debited to the account of the factory in question.

In monopolised goods the co-operatives could only trade by
special licence from Narcomprod ; and therefore in this sphere they
could do little more than carry out the plan of the State organs and
act as agents for the latter.   The non-monopolised articles, in
which they were free to conduct their own transactions, with their
own funds and at their own risk, were being continually narrowed.
Consequently the character of the co-operatives as independent
trading organs became increasingly subordinated to their character
as commission agents for the State.   Transactions which they conducted on order from Narcomprod were generally financed by the
latter ; this financing often taking the form of the supply to them
of a manufactured-goods fund which they could exchange directly
in the villages against peasant produce, their administrative expenses being covered by a percentage commission.   This type of
operation tended to increase at the expense of transactions in
which the co-operatives acted on their own initiative with their
own funds.

Administratively a tendency also developed for the co-operatives
to be subordinated to the central organs of State.   Since they
played such an important rôle in the distributive machinery of the
war-time economy, it was evidently of concern to the Government
in such a critical period that they should be directed by persons

who would work in harmony with the economic plans of the State. It happened that the directors of the co-operatives in 1918 consisted of persons who, while anxious to preserve the prosperity of their organisation by adapting it to the new conditions, were politically hostile to the Soviet Government and reluctant to allow their organisation to be used to assist the new Government in its difficulties, and still more reluctant to surrender any of their independence. While they agreed to co-operate with the State as an independent body, this co-operation in practice was of a half-hearted kind. At the end of 1918, accordingly, attempts were made by the Communists to secure increased control over *Centrosoyus*, the co-operative wholesale society. In December, 1918, at the Congress of Industrial Co-operatives the Communists for the first time secured a small majority ; and the Industrial Co-operatives, as a body affiliated to Centrosoyus, proceeded to place certain demands before the latter for including sufficient representatives of the Industrial Co-operatives on the Board of Centrosoyus to place the supporters of the Government in a majority. Centrosoyus refused to accede to this request *in toto*, but went so far as to concede a minority of seats on the Board to representatives of the affiliated body. This compromise the Industrial Co-operatives refused to accept, and they retaliated by withdrawing their affiliation and setting up a rival trading society, *Centrosection*. The resulting situation was clearly untenable. The new body could not build a new organisation overnight to equal its rival in efficiency, even if it had had the experience and the personnel. The Government was unable to dispense with the assistance of Centrosoyus, and State departments continued to give contracts to it. Between March and May, 1919, the Government took the step of appointing to the Board of Centrosoyus a certain number of Government nominees, so that these appointed members, together with the representatives of the Industrial Co-operatives, which now renewed their affiliation to the larger body, held a majority on the Board. At the same time the Government made membership of the co-operatives compulsory on the whole working population (such membership to be without entrance fee), ordered a regrouping of retail stores so that they could serve the whole population in their various districts, and constituted the co-operative organisation as the sole distributive agent of the State, charged with carrying out the purchase and distributive plans of Narcomprod.[1]

Similar centralisation occurred in the administration of industry,

[1] I.L.O., *Co-operative Movement in Soviet Russia*, 26 seq.

under the so-called Glavki (*Glavnie Upravlenya*), which were sub-departments of Vesenkha specialised to a particular sphere of industry. We have seen that in a number of cases these departments had been instituted prior to the outbreak of civil war : for example, Glavmetal, to distribute orders among enterprises in the metal industry, and Glavugol with extensive powers over the distribution of coal, the closing down of inefficient colleries and the opening of new ones. In other industries such as textiles somewhat broader and more representative bodies, with powers of general supervision over their respective industries, were set up, called Centres (*Tsentralnie Upravlenya*). As the nationalisation of industry extended, the number of such bodies, especially the Glavki, increased ; and from general co-ordination of their respective industries they passed to closer administrative control of individual enterprises. The latter were subordinated more closely to their respective Glavki, and the Glavki and Centres, which had sometimes had a more or less autonomous position before, were more closely subordinated to Vesenkha. At the heart of this centralising tendency was the fact that all orders and all supplies were concentrated in the Glavki, which by the end of 1920 numbered about 50. At first many Glavki made their own supply and delivery arrangements with the co-operatives and other bodies. But with the growing shortage of supplies the actions of the Glavki themselves became subordinated to a supreme Utilisation Commission, attached to Vesenkha : a body set up in November, 1918, to act as a supreme interdepartmental authority concerned with all supply-priorities and allocations. This body has been termed " the crown of the Glavki system ".[1] Moreover, dealings in agricultural products, as we have already seen, came to be virtually concentrated in Narcomprod, from which the Glavki received their allocations, and to which they delivered the output of their several industries for distribution to the town and village population. " Enterprises were deprived of economic independence in operative work and depended on the State budget."[2]

At the same time there was some simplification of the personnel of the central controlling bodies, and at the factory level a substitution of one-man management, or at least of small directorates of about three, for the earlier committee-management, against which Lenin in particular had inveighed so forcibly.[3] The representative

---

[1] Rozenfeld, *op. cit.*, 125.   [2] Chernomordik, *op. cit.*, 80.
[3] By 1920 some 85 per cent. of industrial enterprises were under individual management and no longer under committees. (Cf. Kritsman, *op. cit.*, 201; Y. Piatakov in *Yezhegodnik Cominterna*, 1923, 342.)

boards or councils of which the Centres had consisted were abolished in favour of a smaller Presidium, which now tended to lose its representative character and to be appointed wholly by Vesenkha, even though the latter generally acted in consultation with the trade unions in making these appointments and usually included a certain number of trade union nominees. These Centres, therefore, where they did not disappear altogether, virtually became industrial sub-departments of Vesenkha as a gigantic State department of industry, and thus were either assimilated to Glavki or were replaced by them. These sub-departments usually consisted of a directorate of five to seven persons, of which the president was the chief of the department. At the same time the controlling board of Vesenkha itself was narrowed down from the previous unwieldy representative council, composed of up to fifty persons, to a Presidium of ten to twelve persons. The latter retained, however, something of a representative character, being nominally elected at annual congresses composed of the heads of large enterprises and of representatives of Glavki, of trade unions and of provincial economic councils (called *Gubsovnarhozy*).

These latter bodies were local organs of Vesenkha, consisting of a small Presidium appointed by the local Soviet authority. For purposes of administration industrial enterprises were divided into three categories. Firstly, there were large-scale enterprises of national scale and significance. These were placed immediately under the appropriate Glavki. Secondly, there were those which served a national market but were of medium-size and constituted a highly localised group. Their administration was decentralised to the extent of being placed under special industrial sections of the Gubsovnarhoz (parallel in their organisation to the Glavki at the centre); but at the same time they were nominally subject to general supervision—were " under watchful tutelage "[1]—by the Glavki at the national level. In practice these local industrial sections generally did little more than execute the orders of the central Glavki under whose supervision they came, showed little initiative in acting on their own discretion and served merely as channels through which matters were referred to the central authority for decision. Thus *de facto* the distinction between the first and second categories of enterprises virtually disappeared. The third category consisted of small-scale enterprises that were purely local in character, drawing their material and finding their market in the district. These were entirely within the competence of the

[1] Rozenfeld, *op. cit.*, 123.

Gubsovnarhoz ; and in their case alone was there complete decentralisation.[1]

As the pace of nationalisation quickened, the number of enterprises in the last two categories rapidly increased. With so many and scattered small local factories and workshops to administer, the Gubsovnarhozy had their hands too fully occupied to pay much attention to enterprises in the second group ; and consequently the central Glavki became congested with the work of handling a growing number of medium-sized concerns with which they had slender contacts and about which their information was meagre and sometimes virtually non-existent. When the directives they issued to the local Gubsovnarhozy did not correspond with the local situation (which was more apt to be the case than not), the Gubsovnarhoz became the stage for a prolonged struggle between local bodies and the centre ; and as War Communism advanced, economic administration was increasingly disorganised by a conflict between centre and localities—by the contradiction between regional administration resented by the Gubsovnarhozy and industrial administration represented by the Glavki. " The information possessed at the centre about all the numerous enterprises united under one Glavka was very meagre and in most cases bore a purely formal character ; the technical and productive characteristics of the enterprise were usually lacking ; detailed inventories of property were not even thought of, since there had been no time to compose them since nationalisation and factory records had been disorganised in the years of the world war. To keep an eye on the course of production were also extremely difficult, especially if enterprises were dispersed in distant regions."[2] A committee of investigation set up in June, 1920, reported that many Glavki not only " do not know what goods and in what amounts are kept in the warehouses under their control, but are actually ignorant even of the number of such warehouses ". The storing, receiving and delivery of goods were quite unsystematised ; inventories of current stocks were the exception rather than the rule ; and pilfering and looting of warehouses and secret sale of their contents on the private market were

---

[1] Rozenfeld, op. cit., 122–3 ; Larin and Kritsman, op. cit., 117 seq. The composition of the Boards of Glavki was as follows : 36 per cent. of their personnel were former workers, 34 per cent. engineers, 22 per cent. office workers, and half of 1 per cent. were former directors of businesses. (Pasvolsky, op. cit., 43.) Study of a sample of 160 factory managers in 1920–1 showed that 48 were former workers, 30 former clerks and office workers, 37 former managers and 16 former owners of businesses, and 16 were engineers. 13 per cent. of them only had had higher education and another 24 per cent secondary education. (Econ. Zhizn., 26 Nov., 1922.)

[2] Rozenfeld, op. cit., 123–4.

not uncommon. In textiles, even when stocks of raw material were available, they were not utilised because they lay in the warehouses undistributed. The Petrograd metal section, though it had started to take an inventory of stocks at the factories and in warehouses, did not possess any complete inventory in 1920. In that year the programme of Narcomprod was so little based on actualities that the department utilised only half of the cargo space assigned to it by the railways, with the result that in June there were 35,000 wagons and 300 precious locomotives lying idle ; and in the first five months of the year Narcomprod was unable to fulfil more than 97 per cent. of its programme of supplies to the army, 70 per cent. to transport and 40 per cent. to factories and workshops. Vesenkha itself completely failed to fill the proud rôle originally intended for it—an economic general staff surveying and co-ordinating all economic activities of the State—and became so obsessed with special problems as to constitute in practice merely a Commissariat of Industry. Accordingly, in the relations between it and Narcomprod, which was independent of it, and with transport and the war industries, which came under separate commissariats, there was no co-ordinating body, until towards the end of this period the Council of Defence was broadened into the Council of Labour and Defence (STO) in order to fill this supreme co-ordinating rôle. Meanwhile the number of officials concerned with central administration was swollen. In July, 1920, one out of every four adults in Petrograd was said to be an official ; and in industry the ratio of administrative employees to the total workers employed had doubled.[1] The localities were in no less confusion than the centre. Since the latter was not *au fait* with the local situation, the orders sent out by it " did not correspond with the actual situation in the districts, or arrived late and caused only confusion ".[2] Sometimes the instructions which came from the various Glavki to the corresponding departments of the Gubsovnarhoz did not agree. Krzhizhanovsky points out that the merely *formal* execution of the letter of orders from the centre was often adopted as the line of least resistance ; while heroic individual attempts to clear up the mess by improvisation on individual initiative often ended in worse confusion. He refers

---

[1] Kritsman, *op. cit.*, 194, 208 ; Larin and Kritsman, *op. cit.*, 208 ; Pasvolsky, *op. cit.*, 109, 209, 215 ; *British Labour Delegation Report, 1920*, 102-3. In an attempt to mediate between themselves and thousands of local enterprises some Glavki began to group enterprises into territorial *kusts* or groups, and to devolve certain functions upon them. This represented the first ebbing of the tide of centralisation ; and these *kusts* were to become the nuclei of the later *trusts* of the NEP period. (Cf. Rozenfeld, *op. cit.*, 132.)

[2] Prof. A. N. Dolgov in *Sotsialisticheskoe Khoziaistvo*, March 1923, 22.

to the " heaps of useless report sheets ", " the maintenance of numerous agents " and " documentary circumlocution " as characteristic of the period.[1]

The administrative chaos and delays which resulted from the passing of so many decisions about matters of detail through a few central bottlenecks had their reaction in what came to be known as the " shock " system. These " shock " methods, indeed, were what such unified planning as existed at the period amounted to. To by-pass the administrative congestion when its economic results became alarming, certain enterprises of special importance, usually from the immediate military point of view, were singled out as " shock " enterprises. These were given top priority in the supply of fuel and materials and food rations for their workers, and the best organisers available were assigned to their administration. When applied only to a limited range of industry, it was, of course, a reasonable method of applying priorities and its effect was beneficial (for example, in improving the situation of transport). In the situation of civil war it is difficult to see what other method could have been quickly applied. But in the course of time, as soon as it had come to be applied at all widely, it tended in many cases to increase rather than to lessen the economic confusion. Its weakness was, not that it attempted to enforce a scale of priorities, but that as a priority method it was too crude. The concentration of resources on the " shock " industries inevitably starved all " non-shock " industries and enterprises of essential supplies and often brought them to a standstill. This provoked an agitation for a further widening of the category of " shock " industries ; and each such widening not only worsened the plight of those enterprises which remained outside, but weakened its effect as a priority system inside the " shock " category. The widening went so far as to embrace the manufacture of minor office equipment such as pens and pencils. The Commissariat of Health at one time appealed for the inclusion of mineral waters, and at another time the inclusion of the manufacture of carbolic was considered.[2] Sometimes the concentration of resources on one " shock " industry resulted in the starving of some " non-shock" industry which was an essential subsidiary to the former : as Kritsman quaintly puts it, the problem was " solved " by applying the " shock " to its head, only to find that in doing so one had " tied up its tail ".[3] When the war was at an

---

[1] G. Krzhizhanovsky, *Khoziaistvennie Problemi R.F.S.F.R.*, 67.
[2] Dolgov, *loc. cit.*, 21.
[3] Kritsman, *op. cit.*, 122 ; cf. also Rozenfeld, *op. cit.*, 137–8.

end, the impossibility of continuing it as a normal system became only too clear.

The general result was a negation of the essential principles of economic planning. In the words of Krzhizhanovsky, the State " endeavoured to achieve the greatest quantity of goods without consideration of their costs of production, or whether the limited resources were being used economically or not ", and resources were dissipated in " putting into activity an immeasurably large number of enterprises of an extremely low economy of labour ".[1] Although the distribution of supplies to ordinary consumers according to a rationing system greatly simplified the problem of allocation and of production of consumer goods, the data for estimating demand were frequently not available to the controlling authorities. In a certain local supply department in Tambov *gubernia* the distribution of different commodities was in the hands of different officials. Each of these officials made his own estimate of the population of the *gubernia*, and these estimates varied as widely as 20 per cent.[2] In the distribution of materials and components to factories confusion frequently prevailed, with paralysing results where the productive needs for different things had a joint character (as they so largely did). An enterprise needing lamps might receive from one department 100 per cent. of its need for lamp glass, from another 60 per cent. of its need for containers and perhaps 20 per cent. of its demand for burners from a third.[3] One factory might have sufficient raw material but insufficient fuel ; or sufficient of both, but not enough food supplies to provide its workers with adequate rations, so that it lost most of its labour force by migration to the village.

Aggravating all this was the extreme scarcity of efficient administrative personnel, and lack of political sympathy, amounting in many cases to ill-concealed hostility, among large numbers of those who staffed both the central and local organs. All but a small percentage of the economic experts would probably have misused discretion if this had been granted to them. The old-style *chinovnik*, or civil servant, had a tradition which generally made him worse than useless for purposes of economic administration, requiring initiative and quick decisions without interminable reference. Newly promoted proletarian elements were often rich in " drive " and had genuine organising capacity, but were lacking in experience

[1] G. Krzhizhanovsky, *op. cit.*, 64.
[2] Kritsman, *op. cit.*, 119. One official, in charge of household utensils, confessed to having no knowledge at all on which to base an estimate.
[3] *Ibid.*, 117–19.

and in training and frequently both distrusted and antagonised the older specialists. Kritsman records some interesting results of a confidential enquiry made as late as 1922 among 270 engineers and technicians in responsible positions in Moscow, which probably gives a fairly representative sample of their species. These engineers were divided into two groups : those who had held responsible posts in capitalist industry before the war and those who had been in an employed capacity as technical assistants. The main items in the enquiry were three in number : were they sympathetic to the Soviet Government ; did they consider their work to be of social value ; and did they consider the taking of bribes to be inadmissible ? Those among the first group who answered the three questions affirmatively were 9, 30 and 25 per cent. respectively, and among the second group 13, 75 and 30 per cent.[1] Thus, if these figures are representative, nearly 90 per cent. of such officials were unsympathetic to the Government ; a quarter of one group and over two thirds of the other had no faith in their work ; while two thirds were unwilling to discountenance completely the taking of bribes. In 1918–19 the proportion of such persons hostile to the Soviet régime must have been greater than in 1922. With an administrative personnel in which it could place so little faith, it is hardly surprising that one should find a tendency to refuse discretion to subordinate bodies, and either to bind the latter with detailed regulations or else to concentrate all important decisions at the centre.

III

In the degree that the market was abolished as the link between industry and agriculture and the requisitioning policy was extended, peasant resistance grew and the *smytchka* became increasingly endangered. At first the obligation had been imposed upon the farmer to hand over the whole of the surplus produce above a minimum necessary for his family (calculated according to the number of mouths which the family had to feed). But this proved to be subject to widespread evasion, and came to be replaced by purely arbitrary levies on the initiative of the local collection department. The system saved the towns and the armies from starvation in the blackest months of civil war ; but it could serve as no more than an emergency method of supply. Evasion of the levies became an art, which evoked all the *mouzhik*'s native cunning and resource. The local authorities retaliated by more forcible

[1] Kritsman, *op. cit.*, 144–5.

and inquisitorial methods of collection, and this in turn sharpened peasant hostility and resistance. Evasion seems to have assumed surprising proportions. According to the figures of the Central Statistical Bureau, concealment of actual sowings from the authorities amounted in 1920 to more than 20 million acres, or about 14 per cent. of the sown area ; while Strumilin gives a higher estimate of 20 per cent. Of the gross harvest the amount concealed from the authorities is said to have reached the surprising proportion of 33 per cent.[1]

Nominally the produce handed over to the State was balanced by an equivalent distribution of manufactured goods through the co-operatives in the villages, the receipt for grain deliveries serving as a voucher for purchases at the co-operative store. Larin, writing in 1920, actually maintained that the peasant secured between 1917 and 1920 for each pood of grain supplied to the State twice as much manufactured goods as he received pre-war.[2] But this is a statement about the *values* of manufactured goods received by the peasant at current prices ; and we have seen that the price of manufactured goods had risen much more (by two or three times) than the price of agricultural products. From other estimates it appears that while the towns received from State collections about one third of their pre-war agricultural supplies, the villages received little more than 12 or 15 per cent. of their pre-war supplies of manufactured goods, and certainly no more than 20 per cent.[3] Moreover, the terms of exchange between industry and agriculture seem to have worsened sharply between 1919 and 1920. According to some figures given by Kritsman, the ratio of exchange between a pood of grain and one *arshin* of textiles had been 1 : 3 in 1919, but was 1 : 0·85 in 1920.[4] It has further to be remembered, as Kritsman proceeds to point out, that the most generous portion of manufactured goods assigned to the village went to the village poor, who were given priority of purchase but supplied little or no agricultural produce in return ; while the more well-to-do peasant, who supplied most of the grain, received no more, and sometimes even less, than his poorer neighbour. Again,

---

[1] Kritsman, *op. cit.*, 131–3.

[2] Larin, *op. cit.*, 20–1. Speaking of 1918–19, he says that industrial goods to the value of 4 milliard roubles went to the peasants of the producing districts. " This sum was sufficient according to the fixed prices of the time for the collection of 216 million poods of grain. Meanwhile the State only managed to collect a half of this, or 107 million."

[3] Rozenfeld, *op. cit.*, 165–6 ; also cf. Prokopovitch, *op. cit.*, 110–11. Strumilin indicates that the price of manufactures relatively to the price of rye in 1920 stood at a 2 : 1 ratio compared with pre-war (= 1 : 1). [4] *Op. cit.*, 173–4.

there was a tendency for manufactured goods to go to the " consuming regions " rather than to the " producing regions ", partly because the former were nearer to the centres of manufacture ; so that the regions which had the largest surplus of grain were worse supplied with industrial products. Hence, as Kritsman puts it, the exchange was not so much an exchange between industry and agriculture as an exchange of industrial goods with the services of the poor peasants in extracting produce from the richer farms ;[1] and middle peasants and rich peasants particularly in the producing areas of the south and in Siberia were receiving a rate of interchange even less favourable, compared with pre-war, than was the countryside as a whole. Sharp complaint was already being voiced by peasant delegates at the 8th Soviet Congress ; as for example an outspoken complaint against officials and committees that " there are in a *volost* almost as many as there are households. If the committees were put one on top of the other, they would almost reach the sky. They are standing on the calloused neck of the toiling peasant and his legs are tottering and will soon break down."[2] And while these words were being spoken an epidemic of peasant risings was spreading over the Volga region and west Siberia, and in Tambov *gubernia* and Saratov officials responsible for the food collections were being attacked and tortured and killed.

/ It was not only the peasantry who were coming to be estranged from the régime. The masses of the town workers were beginning to feel a separation between themselves and the State apparatus and between themselves and the Communist Party. One aspect of this was the antagonism between the " centre " and the " provinces " that was characteristic of the time—grumbling in the provinces even among Communists at smartly booted, cake-eating Commissars from the centre such as Yury Libedinsky in *The Week* put into the mouths of his characters Simkhova and Martinov. It showed itself in the factory workers' growing distrust of the higher economic authorities, deluging them with orders and regulations and leaving them idle for want of materials or fuel, forbidding them to buy food on the free market while failing to supply them with even their meagre ration. It was reflected in a growing suspicion of the trade unions as an apparatus designed to secure acquiescence by the workers in the Government's designs, rather than an organ of the rank and file upholding the interests of the masses in State counsels : the trade unions had come to be looked upon as little different from any ordinary State department.

[1] Rozenfeld, *op. cit.*, 174.   [2] Cit. M. Farbman, *Bolshevism in Retreat*, 251–2.

The position of trade unions under war conditions—their co-operation with industry to maintain labour discipline and to recruit labour armies and the fairly general practice of substituting appointment for election to offices—powerfully contributed to this attitude. The régime introduced on the railways by Trotsky was an extreme example of this tendency and was to provoke a considerable volume of protest from the trade union world. Flushed with his success in organising the Red Army, Trotsky at the beginning of 1920 had inaugurated a project of labour conscription and the formation of a labour army to tackle the problems of reconstruction. Special " shock battalions " were formed to supply the driving force for " shock " enterprises ; while units of the Red Army, released from the front, were turned on to the economic front instead of being demobilised, to deal with the fuel and transport crisis which at this time was at its height. In this scheme the trade unions were to provide the organising personnel who would be appointed from above and made subject to military discipline. A certain measure of success was achieved : the gathering of wood fuel was accelerated and urgent repair work in the railway shops and on the permanent way was carried through. But against flagging incentive and physical exhaustion military organisation and compulsion could not avail very much, and very soon brought an unfavourable reaction. In the second half of 1920 strikes became a fairly frequent occurrence. Absenteeism continued to increase. Factory meetings passed opposition resolutions ; protest street demonstrations occurred ; and government speakers were shouted down. When the temporary improvement in the fuel situation, due to the return of the Caucasian oil-fields to Soviet control, showed signs of passing, fresh discontent blazed forth. This time it reached even to Kronstadt, the naval station outside Petrograd, which since the early March days of 1917 had been the pride and glory of the revolution. This was specially significant as a reflection of peasant discontent within the very citadel of Bolshevism ; since the ranks of the Kronstadt sailors, which had supplied contingents to every fighting front during the civil war, had been recently filled by a new recruitment from the villages. A mass meeting of the garrison adopted a resolution for the abolition of the grain monopoly, and for the formation of a new government based on new Soviet elections ; and when these demands were rejected the Kronstadt sailors, under the lead of a handful of Tsarist officers, broke into armed revolt. " Soviets without Communists and Commissars " became their slogan. In the *Journal* of the Kronstadt committee attacks were made upon " the new Communist slavery ", " the bureaucratic trade unions " and the oppression of the peasants.   " An uprising has here begun," it declared, " to throw off the yoke and arbitrary power of the Communists, in comparison with which even the yoke of the monarchy fades into nothing."[1]   Never did it seem, even when the Czechoslovaks had captured Kazan or when Yudenich was at the gates of Petrograd, that the star of the Bolsheviks had fallen so low.   In circles abroad there was fevered talk of the imminence of a Russian *Vendée*.   But the Soviet Government had its ear close to the ground and was alert to the murmurings of the crowd.   Before the last Kronstadt gun had been silenced Lenin was urging upon the 10th Congress of the Communist Party the need to scrap the requisitioning policy which was the keystone of War Communism and was outlining the initial principles of the New Economic Policy.

The general interpretation of War Communism which at the time was current in the West was that the system was product of an attempt to realise an ideal Communism, which, coming into inevitable conflict with realities, had to be scrapped in favour of a retreat in the direction of Capitalism, as represented by the New Economic Policy.   It is true that some justification for this view, at least to a superficial inspection, can be found in certain of the actions of these years and in the expressed opinions of some among the Bolsheviks.   There were, doubtless, those who held at the time that the main features of the war-time system represented the bones and flesh of the ideal communist society at which they were aiming, and which they had been enabled to realise at an unexpected speed owing to the consuming fire of civil war.   This particularly applied to the adoption of State-organised barter and payments in kind, in substitution for monetary transactions.   Towards the end of 1920 steps were deliberately taken to abolish charges for the use of a number of services : not only for postal and telegraph and telephone facilities, water and electricity supply, but even for housing accommodation in municipal dwellings, for railway travel and for the supply of basic food rations.   In the first half of 1920 the State Bank had been merged in the Commissariat of Finance to become what was termed simply " the book-keeping department " of the latter ; and in the early months of 1921 arrangements were actually in preparation for discontinuing all taxation payments on the ground that the State now acquired the supplies it needed by levies

[1] Cit. *Illustrated History of the Russian Revolution*, vol. II, 557.

in kind, distributing them by direct allocations, and accordingly no longer needed to raise money in order to pay for them. It may be held, of course, that this was no more than a recognition of a *fait accompli*—of the *de facto* process of demonetisation as the extreme result of the inflation process—and was not necessarily an *a priori* product of theory. Nevertheless, there were those who welcomed these events as part of a " normal " development towards the ideal society and an anticipation of full Communism. There were " dreamers " (as Lenin afterwards termed them) who deemed it " possible in three years to transform the whole economic foundation ", and who saw the events of the civil war period as the tortured embodiment of their dreams. There still survived strong elements of that " leftism " which during the first eight months had sought to force the pace of events. To some extent these had taken the bit between their teeth during the civil war period and felt that events had justified their previous standpoint.

This " leftism " was characterised by an under-estimation of the importance of the peasantry, an imperfect appreciation of the real nature of the economic factors which they sought to handle, and by the possession of a purely formal conception of what the nature of socialist society would be. It was natural for persons of this tendency to regard War Communism, not as a deviation from the normal line of development, not as a set of emergency measures under stress of war, but as a partial embodiment of their ideal. The abolition of money—was not that a feature of true Communism ? State barter between town and country—was not that merely the higher form of economy which was to replace the anarchy of the market ? The " kindling of the class war " in the villages—was not this an essential stage in eliminating bourgeois influence from the countryside as it had been eliminated in the towns : the inevitable next stage in that process of " permanent revolution " of which Trotsky had written ? Even those who did not argue thus from first principles, since they had become accustomed to the system for two and a half years, tended to identify its main features with the very stuff of the revolution, and so could hardly conceive, let alone countenance, any alternative. " Any retreat from the system which for long seemed to be the primary essence of socialist construction was regarded as an abandonment of conquered positions."[1] For example, the economist Preobrazhensky (whom we shall meet again as a theoretical exponent of Trotskyism in the middle 1920's) preached the inevitable " dying out of money " in Soviet economy and welcomed

[1] Rozenfeld, *op. cit.*, 144.

the inflationary printing press as "that machine-gun which attacked the bourgeois régime in its rear, namely through its monetary system". "Honour to our printing presses," he wrote in a study of paper money in the Soviet epoch. "It is true that only a short life remains to them; but then they have already done three quarters of their job." Larin, another and somewhat erratic economist of the period, wrote in 1920 that "the progressive 'dying out' of money grows in proportion to the growth in organisation of Soviet economy. Money no longer exists as the sole measure of value. Money as a medium of exchange can already be abolished to a considerable extent. Money as a means of payment will cease to exist when the Soviet State can free the workers from the necessity of flocking to the Sukharevsky market [i.e. the 'black market']. Both will be realised in practice in the next few years. Money will then lose its significance as a store of value and will remain merely as what it actually is: coloured paper." Bukharin also expressed similar views about money, if more cautiously. More authoritatively a decree of TSIK, announcing the merging of the Bank in Narcomfin (the Commissariat of Finance), spoke of this as an attempt "to establish moneyless settlements with a view to the total abolition of the money system". A resolution of the 8th Congress of the Party in March 1919 had spoken of "widening the sphere of moneyless settlements" in order to "pave the way for the abolition of money"; and in the early months of 1921 an official committee was considering a scheme for introducing a labour unit of account. Such opinions contributed much to the reluctance in some quarters to accept the change to the New Economic Policy, and caused those who were influenced by such notions to stress only the negative side of the change as a "retreat".[1]

But to a considered view these notions can be seen to have been no more than flights of leftist fancy. If we regard the system of War Communism in its proper setting, both against the economic current of those years and as standing between the events and policies of the first eight months of Soviet economy, on the one hand, and of the New Economic Policy, on the other, it emerges clearly as an empirical creation, not as the *a priori* product of theory: as an improvisation in face of economic scarcity and military urgency in conditions of exhausting civil war. This is, perhaps, something that western opinion is now more ready to understand after the

---

[1] Cf. Chernomordik, *op. cit.*, 82; *Ekonomika Sovetskoi Torgovli* (1934), 36–41, 389–94; G. A. Neyman, *Vnutrennia Torgovlia S.S.S.R.* (1935), 43; also A. Z. Arnold, *Banks, Credit and Money in Soviet Russia*, 103–10.

economic experience of European countries during the Second World War. At any rate, this was evidently the way in which Lenin regarded it (who, in contrast to Preobrazhensky, had said that " the aid of the printing press can only be regarded as a temporary measure ").[1] This is clear, not only from his subsequent judgments on the period, but from all that he had previously said about the transition to Socialism, with which the view of War Communism as a temporary deviation from the normal course under pressure of circumstances is alone consistent. In an article on the Food Tax on April 21st, 1921, Lenin said quite explicitly that " War Communism was thrust upon us by war and ruin. It was not, nor could it be, a policy that corresponded to the economic tasks of the proletariat. It was a temporary measure". In introducing the new policy at the 10th Congress he said : " Some of the things we were compelled to do by necessity. . . . We did much that was simply wrong. . . . We went further than was necessary theoretically and politically."[2] Some months later he referred to it as a " mistake " and a " jump ", " in complete contradiction to all we wrote concerning the transition from capitalism to socialism ".[3]

The adoption in its place of the New Economic Policy was 'accordingly, a reversion to the road which was being travelled during the early months, before the onset of civil war, if at a different point on the road from that at which the excursion had left it and (in view of what had happened in the interim) in an altered stretch of country. Needless to say, this is the view that most Soviet economic writers have subsequently taken. Of these we need quote only two. The author of a textbook of the middle '20's wrote that " the transition to War Communism was a matter of compulsion, imposed on us, first by German Imperialism, and after that by internecine counter-revolution. War Communism was not a normal economic policy. But it was historically and economically inevitable in the conditions of that time."[4] Ten years later another popular textbook contained this judgment: " War Communism fully justified itself in conditions of civil war. But it would have been a mistake to insist on a continuance of the policy of War Communism after those circumstances had disappeared which had necessitated it." As for the New Economic Policy which succeeded it, this " did not flow only from the peculiar national features of Russia. NEP is the normal economic policy of the proletariat after

[1] Cf. G. A. Neyman, op. cit., 43.   [2] Selected Works, vol. IX, 113, 178.
[3] Speech on NEP reported in Izvestia, Oct. 19, 1921.
[4] Smushkov, Economicheskaia Politika S.S.S.R., 16.

revolution. The necessity of NEP flows from the variety of economic strata which exists, not only in backward, but also in very advanced countries (U.S.A., Germany, etc.)."[1]

[1] Chernomordik, *op. cit.*, 84, 95. Cf. also *Economika Sovetskoi Torgovli*, 17–23, for " the necessity of commodity-forms " in Soviet economy. " In the present stage . . . labour in State enterprises will have a particular commodity-money expression."

CHAPTER SIX

THE TRANSITION TO THE NEW ECONOMIC POLICY

I

It was not until an armistice had been signed with Poland in October, 1920, not until the remnant of Baron Wrangel's army at the end of November had abandoned its crusade to win back Russia for civilisation, and the Donbas and the Baku oil-fields and the Turkestan cotton belt and the trans-Ural wheat area had returned to the sphere of the Soviet Government, that attention could seriously be turned to the inadequacies of War Communism as an economic system. Even when attention had been given to such an enquiry, an answer was not easily forthcoming in the circumstances of the time. People were too close to the particular problems of the past two and a half years, which had crowded upon them without giving breathing space for reflection, to be capable at once of evaluating the situation correctly. War Communism, created from the necessities of those years, had served an important function during a crucial period. In the confusion it was not easy to tell how far its disadvantages had been merely incidental or an inseparable product of it, or to judge the degree to which the altered circumstances of peace-time modified the necessities in which it had been cradled.

The first revolt against the crippling centralisation of the Glavki system came at the 8th Soviet Congress in December, 1920. Complaint was specially made of the difficulties of enterprises of that second category[1] which came under the joint control of the Glavki and of the provincial economic councils (*Gubsovnarhozy*), and in practice acted on orders from the former transmitted more or less automatically through the corresponding industrial department of the latter. Here the separation of the enterprise from the competent authority was greatest, as were also confusion and conflict between central and local administrations. Already earlier in the year the 9th Party Congress had criticised the Glavki system in no muted tones. " In view of the hugeness of the country," the

---

[1] See above, page 111.

statement ran, " and the inexactitude of the methods and results of accounting, these centralised methods, which inevitably produced an isolation of enterprises in the localities, led to the monstrous forms of procrastination which are causing so much incurable harm to our economy." The criticisms voiced in December were even more strongly worded. The outcome of the discussion was the transfer of a considerable number of enterprises, about 2000 in all, to the administration of the local Gubsovnarhozy. These included most of the enterprises in the so-called second category and even some of those that had previously been included in the first. Nearly the whole of the textile industry was in this way transferred from central to local administration ; and only electrical engineering and the metal industry remained substantially unaffected by the change. At the same time the Gubsovnarhozy were subordinated to the provincial Soviet authority entirely, and their industrial subdepartments were no longer made subordinate to respective Glavki at the centre as heretofore. Vesenkha itself underwent reorganisation, so as to reduce the number of Glavki from the previous figure of 52 to only 16 in the following year ; each of these covering a branch of industry and exercising general supervision over the activities of the provincial bodies and administering those enterprises that were still subordinated to the centre through regional combines or associations, which grouped together a number of enterprises in the area. In making these changes the Congress emphasised the need to differentiate between the *general direction* of economic activity, which was to remain centralised, and the operative administration, or management, of industry, which should be decentralised to the maximum possible extent, so as to bring those concerned with the latter into the closest possible contact with the productive activities of which they had charge. But as yet this was no more than the enunciation of a principle : a declaration of intention. Its translation into practice required a more fundamental change in economic relationships. As long as supplies and orders remained pendent on the centre, the administrative flesh was bound to conform to the economic bone structure. Until NEP, by reintroducing the market, made it possible to form new economically autonomous units, free to conduct transactions of purchase and sale on their own initiative, the desired decentralisation of operative administration did not become, and scarcely could have become, a reality.[1]

[1] Krzhizhanovsky, *op. cit.*, 11 ; Rozenfeld, *op. cit.*, 147–50 ; Dolgov, *loc. cit.*, 22 ; Piatakov, *loc. cit.*, 342–3.

The crux of centralised supply, as we have seen, was the policy of compulsory requisitioning of the peasant surplus ; and the crux of the restoration of commercial transactions in the economy at large, when this came, was to be the market-relationship between agriculture and industry. Curiously enough, the discussion from which the NEP emerged started, not with the relationship with the peasantry, but with the relationship between State industry and the industrial workers. This took the form of a vigorous discussion of the trade union question—of the precise rôle of trade unions in socialist industry. Preoccupation with this question was evidently connected with those discussions of centralisation and bureaucracy in the administration of industry which accompanied the preparation for the 8th Soviet Congress. The debate had been prompted by the régime introduced on the railways by Trotsky as Commissar of Ways and Communications, and had its first phase in a sharp disagreement on the matter between Trotsky and the trade union leader Tomsky at the 5th Trade Union Conference at the beginning of November, 1920. Trotsky would have made the trade unions into brigades in a labour army, with its officers subject to appointment and removable by the State from above.[1] This precipitated something of a crisis in the Party, which was grave enough to evoke from Lenin the declaration : " We must have the courage to look the bitter truth straight in the face. The Party is sick. The Party is shaking with fever." He even went so far as to speak of " an inevitable split in the Party if it does not prove to be sufficiently sound to heal itself of the sickness quickly and thoroughly".[2] In the course of December the disagreement was discussed at several meetings of the Central Committee of the Party, at which the policy submitted by Trotsky was rejected by 10 votes to 4 in a statement condemning the " degeneration of centralism and militarised forms of work into bureaucracy, petty tyranny and red tape ". At the end of the month Trotsky published his policy-statement as a pamphlet entitled *The Rôle and Tasks of the Trade Unions*, in which he charged the existing trade unions with " craft conservatism " and with " cultivating in their midst the spirit of corporative exclusiveness ", and called for a radical " shaking-up " of the existing trade unions and the harnessing of them more closely to the management of industry. Meanwhile, there had been instituted a special trade union commission of the Party on which

[1] Cf. L. Trotsky in *Econ. Zhizn.*, Feb. 13, 1921 and Feb. 17, 1921, and in *Pravda*, Jan. 29, 1921 ; also Stalin in *Pravda*, Jan. 19, 1921, and Rudzutak, *ibid.*, Jan 30, 1921

[2] *Selected Works*, vol. IX, 28. These statements were made on Jan. 19, 1921

Trotsky had refused to serve ; and this in the course of January, 1921, produced a report, commonly known as " the platform of the ten " and signed among others by Lenin, Zinoviev, Stalin, Tomsky, Kamenev and Rudzutak, which was to become in essentials the official policy of the Party.

Trotsky's policy amounted to what was known as the " State-isation " of the trade unions : their closer identification with and subordination to the State, in the interests of industrial efficiency. But the issue was not a simple two-sided one around this proposal. There were several other standards as well around which the battle raged. Not only was there a "buffer" group, including Bukharin and Zinoviev, which sought a compromise with the Trotsky policy, but there was an important syndicalist group, which virtually advocated the handing over of industrial administration to the trade unions and was opposed to the principle of one-man management in industry. Of this we shall have something more to say in a later chapter. Lenin sharply attacked all three of these tendencies. Meanwhile Rudzutak had outlined a policy which was closely similar to that of Lenin ; advocating that the trade unions, while retaining their independent position, should undertake greater responsibility in organising labour to solve the problems of production, in combating absenteeism and slackness. Labour discipline, he wrote, "cannot be achieved by bureaucratic methods and orders from above " and is " conceivable only if the whole mass of participants in production take a *conscious part* in the fulfilment of these tasks ". There were also two other opposition " platforms " (the " democratic centralism " group of Ossinsky and Sapronov and the " Ignatovists ") which criticised both the centralisation of policy-decisions in the hands of the Political Bureau of the Party and the " bureaucratic deadness of the unions and their lack of contact with local needs and with the broad masses ". As the discussion proceeded, the vacillating " buffer group " divided and went different ways ; Zinoviev joining Lenin, and Bukharin, while presenting to the Congress a separate resolution, inclining towards support of Trotsky. The official "platform of the ten " opposed both the " State-isation " of the trade unions and the syndicalist proposals, advocated the restoration of internal democracy within the unions, and rejected any reconstruction of the unions from above. The rôle of the unions was to form a link with the non-Party masses, drawing them into collective activity while defending their interests against bureaucratic tendencies of the State. At the same time the leaders of the unions should participate in the organs of economic administration, and put forward candidates from among the workers for State economic posts.[1]

By the time of the meeting of the crucial 10th Party Congress on March 8th, 1921, a danger was beginning to be sensed that discussion of the trade union question might obscure wider economic issues ; and on the eve of the Congress *Economicheskaia Zhizn* reminded its readers that " the question of economic policy of the coming year, and not the trade unions, is the key question".[2] Up to this time very little attention had been paid to the question of the peasantry. The protagonists in the discussion had apparently either failed to appreciate the crucial importance of this question or else had concentrated on the problem of industry in the belief that if industrial output could be increased the difficulties of the village would *ipso facto* be solved. In fact, industrial production at the moment was paralysed by the crisis of supplies, and supplies of materials and of food depended in the main upon the peasantry. Moreover, discontent in the countryside rapidly spread its infection to the town workers and members of the army, who were often separated by only a few years from the village and sometimes by less.

With his quite extraordinary capacity for grasping the essentials of a situation, Lenin quickly saw that the restoration of the *smytchka* with the peasantry was the crux of existing difficulties ; and having seen this he was in no two minds as to the course it was necessary to steer. To restore the mass of the peasantry to the position of allies and to revive the exchange of products between town and village, it was necessary to abolish the system of requisitioning and to replace this initially by an agricultural tax in kind. Such was the proposal he submitted to the Party Congress. The proposed tax was to be assessed as a proportion of the net produce above minimum subsistence needs of the family. It would be certain instead of arbitrary, and since it took only a fixed share of the peasant's surplus, the farmer would have an incentive to make this surplus as large as possible so as to enlarge the share which he had at his own disposal.[3] In the explanatory notes accompanying the decree which later announced the change the position was explained as follows : " From now on, by decision of the All-Russian Soviet

---

[1] Cf. Lenin in *Pravda*, Jan. 21, 1921 ; also *Pravda*, Jan. 18, 1921. Cf. also Chernomordik, *op. cit.*, 89.   [2] *Econ. Zhizn*, March 8, 1921.
[3] The tax took into account the number of dependants in the family and was graduated against the rich peasant. At first the tax was of a multiform and complicated character, taking a proportion of each different kind of produce. Later it was simplified into a single tax assessed in money, and after 1923 it was paid entirely in money and not in kind.

Executive Committee and the Council of People's Commissars, requisitioning is abolished and a tax in kind on agricultural products is introduced instead. . . . After the tax has been paid, what remains with the peasant is left at his full disposal. . . . Every peasant must now realise and remember that the more land he plants, the greater will be the surplus of grain which will remain in his complete possession." The tax was assessed so as to yield about a half that of the previous requisitioning quotas, and was based on the minimum food needs of the army and of workers in essential national enterprises. In his speech to the Congress Lenin stated : " The question of substituting a tax in kind for requisitioning is primarily a political one. Its essence lies in the relations between the workers and the peasants. The interests of these classes do not coincide : the small farmer does not desire what the worker is striving for. Nevertheless, only by coming to an agreement with the peasants can we save the socialist revolution. We must either satisfy the middle peasant economically and restore the free market, or else we shall be unable to maintain the power of the working class. . . . If certain Communists were inclined to think it possible in three years to transform the whole economic foundation, to change the very roots of agriculture, they were certainly dreamers; and we must confess to having a few such dreamers among us." A month later he wrote that " the food tax is one of the forms of transition from the peculiar ' War Communism ', which was thrust upon us by extreme want, ruin and war, to the proper socialist interchange of products ". " We are still in such a state of ruin," he went on, " so crushed by the burden of war . . . that we cannot give the peasant manufactured goods for *all* the grain we require. Knowing this, we are introducing the food tax, i.e. we shall take the minimum of grain we require (for the army and the workers) in the form of a tax and will obtain the rest in exchange for manufactured goods."[1]

At first sight this might seem to have represented a comparatively trifling change : the substitution of a predetermined levy which took a share of the peasant's surplus produce for a levy aimed at the whole of that surplus and often arbitrary in its assessment. Lenin himself admitted that it was as yet only a half-hearted change: that it "contains a particle of the previous quota [i.e. the requisitioning system] and a particle of the system which is the only correct system, namely the exchange of manufactures . . . for the products of peasant farming".[2] But it was a step which once taken logically

[1] *Op. cit.*, 178.   [2] *Ibid.*, 152.

implied a whole series of others. In the first place it necessarily implied the restoration for the peasantry of the right to trade in that part of their surplus produce which remained at their disposal (otherwise the leaving of this surplus at their disposal would have been no more than a nominal concession, possessing very little influence as an incentive to increase peasant production). This in turn implied the revival of a market in agricultural produce, the re-creation of market-relations as the essential link between agriculture and industry and a restored sphere of circulation for money. At first the right of free trade in peasant produce was limited to the local market ; but very soon this limitation was removed. The restoration of the peasant's right to trade in his produce as he pleased in turn implied the abolition of the war-time monopoly possessed by Narcomprod in collection or purchase and of the consequent funnelling of all agricultural supplies through that central bottle-neck of Narcomprod allocations. Lenin was quick to stress at the 10th Congress that an immediate corollary of the introduction of the food tax was a separation once again of the co-operatives from Narcomprod and the restoration to them of commercial autonomy—of the right to deal in the market at their own discretion. A further step in the logical train of consequences was the termination of the system of centralised supply of materials and foodstuffs to industrial enterprises through the Glavki network, and its replacement by a decentralised system whereby industrial enterprises made their own contracts for the acquisition of raw materials and the disposal of their products. This occurred by stages in the course of 1921. State organisations were given the right to buy and sell in the open market in the degree to which they ceased to be supplied with rationed allocations from the centre ; and as a first stage, in August, 1921, most branches of industry were allowed to dispose of one half of their output commercially, the other half continuing to be handed over to the central organs in return for that portion of their raw material and fuel needs which continued to be met from centralised supply-allocations. Two months later these enterprises were freed altogether from dependence on centralised supplies of materials and fuel, and the right of disposing of their output on the market was extended to the whole, instead of only a part, of their output. For a few months industrial units tended to make direct barter-deals with other organisations or with the peasantry in order to obtain their needed supplies : a system which was manifestly cumbrous and inefficient. But fairly soon the two sets of transactions, the purchase of supplies and the sale of output, were separated, and normal money-transactions among State institutions, and between industry and agriculture, were restored. As a completion of the process, industry was grouped into financially autonomous units, which (with certain exceptions, including the major part of heavy industry) were " removed from the State budget " and " transferred to a commercial basis ". This implied that they no longer received even money-subventions, but had to balance their own commercial receipts against their outlays, and to reduce the latter to a minimum by exerting every possible economy in production so that the balance should show a margin on the credit side.

II

The new decentralised system of industry for which the introduction of NEP laid the foundations rested upon commercially autonomous units called *trusts*. In the course of the second half of 1921 and the following year these trusts were rapidly formed and chartered in those industries that were freed from dependence on State supplies and from the collateral obligation of handing over their products to the State. By a decree of October 27th, 1921, enterprises were divided into two classes : those still dependent on centralised State supplies and those endowed with complete financial and commercial independence. Fuel and metal were the principal industries which remained in the former category. By a further decree of February 6th, 1922, this category was narrowed and confined to enterprises " the products of which can only be used by the State and cannot be placed on the open market, or else undertakings delivering the greater part of their production to the State". In other words, it was confined to such things as war industries and army supply establishments, certain municipal enterprises, locomotive works, and certain metal works engaged on meeting orders for centralised construction projects such as those included in the electrification plan. These were to be administered by centralised State organs, similar to the former Glavki. At the same time a resolution of the 9th Soviet Congress affirmed the principle that " all State undertakings, whether supplied by the State or not, must be managed on a commercial basis ".

It was to enterprises of the second category, which now embraced the main part of industry, and in particular industry catering for the ordinary consumer, that the new form of organisation applied. Supervision over their activities was in the hands of the sixteen new central industrial departments of Vesenkha which had replaced the fifty-odd Glavki ; their function being to plan and supervise the carrying out of industrial reorganisation along the new lines, and thereafter to exercise a general regulation of the policies and activities of industrial trusts falling within their several spheres. But in many cases the initiative in the reorganisation of industry did not come from above, but from below. The directors of enterprises and the local economic departments seized upon their new-found freedom eagerly, and began to federate enterprises locally into trusts. Some enterprises, in reaction against the former centralism, gaily plunged into the market as independent units, and like guerilla bands operated for several months on their own without being rounded up under any form of disciplined control. But this only applied to concerns which happened to be fairly well placed in the matter of stocks. Others which lacked the means with which to procure supplies on the market for continued production were of necessity forced to join their fortunes in a group and to apply to higher authority, as errant son to a father, for a modicum of working capital to start them on their career. Even so, it was found that, in the haste to take advantage of their independence, enterprises had federated into trusts in a very haphazard way. The principles on which they had been combined were often faulty and inconsistent. Not infrequently they conflicted and overlapped ; and there was a plethora of local trusts—" trustlets " as Rozenfeld calls them[1]—without any *raison d'être* other than the desire for independence. Accordingly, in December, 1922, a central Commission for the Revision of Trusts was set up, which proceeded to reorganise some of those that had been already formed and to eliminate inconsistencies.

The basis on which enterprises were federated into trusts was subject to considerable variation ; and there was a good deal of flexibility according to varying technical and market conditions in different branches of production. In many cases the trusts followed the lines of the earlier *kusts* under the Glavki system,[2] although in their actual functions they were very different. In the case of a homogeneous process of production conducted on a national scale for a national market, a whole branch of an industry might be combined in a single national trust, as with rubber and sugar. Where an industry was localised in certain districts, each of which had special local peculiarities, the industry might be divided among

[1] *Op. cit.*, 216.   [2] See above, page 113, footnote.

several local trusts, each of which combined horizontally similar enterprises in that district. For instance, in the coal-mining industry a large number of the Donetz mines were combined in Donugol and those of the Moscow region in Moscugol ; while Grozneft, Azneft and Embaneft controlled oil boring and refining in the three oil districts of Grozny, Baku and Emba. Sometimes such district trusts were vertical in character where successive processes were localised in one district and subsidiary industries had grown up in close association with the industry in question ; as, for instance, Yugostal, which embraced three of the largest engineering works of the south along with coal mines, coke ovens and auxiliary plants, and Chemugol, which was based on an association of chemical works in the Ukraine with glass and coal and timber. Finally, there were a few trusts of national scope which were organised on a vertical principle, even though their constituent enterprises were separated geographically, when the concerns in practice constituted successive stages in a single process of production which needed to be united under one control for a proper balance between them to be maintained. The flexible variety of principle on which this grouping was based is seen particularly in mining and in textiles. Some mining enterprises, as we have seen, were linked vertically with manufacturing industries to which they were essential subsidiaries, while the remainder were federated horizontally in district trusts. The textile trusts were numerous and were all local and vertical in character ; Russian textile firms (unlike the majority of the English industry) having customarily embraced both spinning and weaving and even finishing as well. In wool the trusts were organised according to the various branches of the industry : for instance, the production of fine cloth in the Moscow, Petrograd and Klintzovsky districts was grouped in a separate trust ; and similarly coarse cloth in Tambov, Penza and Simbirsk ; the long-staple industry of the Moscow district ; and felt production in Yaroslav, Nizhni-Novgorod and Kazan. By the end of 1921 there were 8 wool trusts, covering 78 per cent. of the yarn, 64 per cent. of the coarse cloth and 93 per cent. of the finished goods production. In cotton the chief were the Moscovsky trust covering 7 Moscow factories with 340,000 spindles, 6700 looms and 17 printing machines ; the Orekhovo-Zuyevka, combining 8 factories with 535,000 spindles and 11,000 looms ; and the Bogorodsk of 10 mills with 690,000 spindles and 7700 looms. In a few cases local trusts embraced mills of different branches of textiles, as the largest of the cotton trusts, that of Ivanovo-Voznesensk, which comprised 6 linen mills in the district as well as 29 cotton mills with 788,000 spindles and 19,000 looms.[1]

The first of these trusts to be formed was in July, 1921, the Northern Timber Trust, or Severoles, and a federation of linen factories in Kostroma and Muromsk, close to their sources of raw material and covering 40 per cent. of linen production from the purchase of flax up to finished piece-goods. The most intensive period of trust-building was between December and the following March ; and by the summer of 1923 there were 478 trusts chartered by Vesenkha, embracing 3561 enterprises with about a million workers, or some 75 per cent. of all the workers employed in nationalised industry. Some of these which were national in scale came directly under the control of Vesenkha, while others which were purely local in character were handed over by " mandate " from Vesenkha to the control of the provincial economic councils, the Gubsovnarhozy. Later, after the formation of the federal Union of Soviet Republics, a triple classification was introduced of trusts of Union, of republic and of local significance ; the trusts in each category being subordinated respectively to the all-Union Vesenkha, to the corresponding economic council of the republic and to the local Gubsovnarhoz. The size of these trusts varied widely, both between different industries and according as they were national or local in scale. Of the total production of trusts some 60 per cent. came from all-Union trusts, and some 15 and 25 per cent. respectively from those which were under republican and provincial control. The average number of workers covered by enterprises in national or regional trusts in 1922 was about 440, while in enterprises in purely local federations the figure was only 85. On the average each trust employed just over 2000 workers. But whereas more than a half were quite small trusts, employing 360 workers each on the average but covering only 10 per cent. of trustified industry (measured in terms of its labour-strength), 62 per cent. of the workers involved were in 41 trusts, each of which had 12,500 workers on the average, with an average of 900 workers to each constituent enterprise. These large trusts were chiefly to be found in textiles, metal and engineering, sugar, rubber and wood. At the other end of the scale were 41 very small trusts, federating not more than 5 or 6 enterprises, each with only 10 to 20 workers.[2]

The precise legal status of the new trusts was eventually defined

[1] Rozenfeld, op cit., 214 seq. ; The Russian Economist, vol. II, No. 6, 2020–1.
[2] Rozenfeld, op. cit., 216–20 ; Russkaia Promishlennost, 1922, X.

by a Sovnarcom decree of April 10th, 1923. This gave trusts legal personality as bodies capable of entering into independent contracts, not as owners of property, but as trustees of the State, endowed with terminable powers by the State in the form of a charter. This charter, through which the trust acquired its legal personality, had to be confirmed by Vesenkha, and had to reserve to Vesenkha the right of determining the allocation of profit, of liquidating the trust for certain named reasons, and of terminating the appointment of members of the trust board at the end of any year. The charter was required to contain a valuation of the foundation capital, which was divided into two parts : basic or fixed capital, covering the plant, buildings and immovable property generally, and the turnover or working capital, covering stocks of goods, currency or securities held. The former part of the capital could not, while the latter could, be pledged as security for loans and attached for debt. A trust could issue bonds, but without the power of committing the State thereby to any liability ; and the State was not liable for debts incurred by the trust and was under no obligation to make good any deficit in the year's working. As a check on the financial operations of the trust, Vesenkha was to nominate an Audit Committee of three, one of them selected to represent the trade union of the industry ; this committee being given power to inspect all accounts, books and documents. The Audit Committee was forbidden to interfere in the practical work of the trust, and had no power to override decisions of the trust directors. But it filled the very important rôle of keeping the superior organ informed by periodic reports and consultations concerning the work of the "trustees", and without narrowing the competence of the latter made effective the supervision of general industrial policy by the former.[1]

The trust consisted of a Board appointed by Vesenkha (in consultation with the trade union concerned), the administrative rôle of which resembled that of the Board of Directors of a private company, with the substantial difference that each member to the Board of a trust generally had charge of a department of its work. The appointment of the managers of individual factories was vested in the Board ; these managers being responsible for the internal management of the works, but having no competence in commercial matters of buying and selling, save in special cases. Contracts for sale and purchase on the market were freely made by the trust with other organisations. Wages and

[1] Cf. Rozenfeld, *op. cit.*, 247 seq.

working conditions were regulated by a collective agreement with the trade union. Production plans for the factories under the control of the trust were drawn up by the Board and submitted to Vesenkha for sanction ; and, subject to price-control regulations by State authorities, the operation of these production plans was carried out according to familiar economic principles of maximising the difference between receipts and outlay and of choosing the method of production which involved the least cost.

The trust differed, accordingly, from the old Centres and Glavki in possessing no statutory powers to bind third persons : they " were not organs of State government, but organs of State economy ",[1] possessing only such powers over other parties as they could secure by contract. It differed from the *kust* or group of enterprises under the old Glavki system in its financial and commercial independence. It differed from the private joint stock company, operating a " concession ", or a " mixed company " in having no private capital : in the event of its desiring such private participation, it had to be rechartered as a " mixed company ". Its commercial independence was safeguarded by Clauses 2 and 3 of the decree of April 10th, 1923, which denied the right of any State institution to acquire any property or products of a trust except by contractual agreement (with the exception of special emergencies, and then only by permission of STO or Vesenkha). At the same time a State preference clause (Clause 50 of the decree) provided that " in all buying and selling transactions the trust must give preference, whenever terms and conditions are equal, to State departments and co-operative associations ". Clause 29 stated that " Vesenkha does not interfere in the current administration and managerial work of the Board of the trust ". Clause 44 made obligatory the establishment of an amortisation fund at a given percentage of the basic capital : a charge which in practice entered into the costing calculation of a trust and was a charge on the gross receipts prior to the declaration of net profit.[2] It was provided that 20 per cent. of any profit must be put to reserve until the reserve fund reached one half of the chartered capital, when with the consent of Vesenkha it might be capitalised. The remainder of the profit was to accrue to the State treasury, after the deduction of sums for bonuses to the staff of the enterprise and for workers' welfare ; the proportions in which this distribution of profit should take place to be determined by Vesenkha each year in consultation with Narcomfin. Clause 47 made the trusts " liable to

---

[1] Rozenfeld, *op. cit.*, 251   [2] *Ibid.*, 250.

all forms of taxation, including income and property tax, on the same basis as private undertakings, except where otherwise established by law".

Similarly, the revival of the market under NEP was immediately followed by the restoration of financial and commercial independence to the co-operatives ;[1] and by a general agreement, dated May 25th, 1921, between Narcomprod and Centrosoyus the latter was granted temporarily the sole right among State organs of trading in foodstuffs and raw materials. Narcomprod agreed to hand over to Centrosoyus all stocks of manufactured goods in its possession, which were to be used for purposes of direct barter against agricultural produce. These foodstuffs and raw materials, in return (less a commission), were to be supplied to Narcomprod for distribution to that part of industry which was still dependent on State supplies. But although " by this agreement the co-operative system became no longer a distributive agent of the State, but an independent contractor, as it were, negotiating on a footing of equality ",[2] the transactions of Centrosoyus were still bound by certain conditions. One of these was that the barter-exchange which it conducted through its local organs should be conducted at a " fixed equivalent ". This condition circumscribed very considerably the independence of local buyers in manœuvring on the market at their discretion, and imposed a wooden rigidity on the system which did not correspond to market conditions on the average, let alone to the widely varying conditions in different districts. Largely for this reason the system proved to be a failure ; and after seven months of the agreement (which included the crucial harvest months) the co-operatives had fulfilled only 35 per cent. of their programme of purchases. It was a year of crop failure and famine in certain regions ; and towards the second half of 1921 the prices of agricultural goods on the market rose sharply, and the " fixed equivalent " established by Narcomprod undervalued grain and overvalued manufactures. Consequently, the co-operatives, bound to this " fixed equivalent ", could find few customers ; and the peasants sold their grain instead to the private trader from whom they could obtain a better price. " Traders would barter a scythe for one pood of wheat, whereas the co-operatives asked two poods in accordance with their instructions."[3] An important contributory cause of failure was the inability of

[1] By decree published in *Econ. Zhizn.*, April 9, 1921.
[2] I.L.O., *Co-operative Movement in S.R.*, 136.
[3] *Pravda*, No. 193, 1921, cit. I.L.O., *op. cit.*, 142.

Narcomprod to supply the co-operatives with the agreed quantities of industrial goods, and a consequent deficiency in the barter fund at the disposal of the co-operatives for use in procuring grain and raw materials. The fact that scarcely 25 per cent. of the required fund could be mustered is an eloquent example of that general shortage of working capital which characterised the first few years of the reconstruction period, and about which we shall have more to say below. This shortage in fact may well have been a factor behind the rapid cutting adrift of industry from State supplies in the course of the autumn and winter of 1921 : a development which does not seem to have been contemplated earlier in the year. At the same time as industry was being cut adrift from centralised supplies a similar concession was made to the co-operatives. A new decree of October 26th, 1921 (one day before the decree applying to industry) terminated the May agreement and placed the co-operatives on a basis of complete commercial independence. Centrosoyus was no longer to be financed by the State, and its position of sole State purchaser from the village was abolished. Gone also were the binding conditions such as the " fixed equivalent ". There remained only a preference clause giving to the co-operatives the preference in wholesale contracts of Government departments and State trusts. Such stocks of goods as the co-operatives already possessed, plus a small additional contribution from the State, were assigned to them as working capital ; and with these funds they were now free to trade at their own discretion on the peasant market, on the one hand, and with State institutions, on the other. At the same time the right of formation of agricultural co-operatives on a voluntary basis was recognised, and also of co-operative organisations for peasant home industries ; while legal sanction was granted for the hiring of labour for auxiliary work by industrial co-operatives up to one fifth of their membership.[1] Agricultural co-operatives proceeded to form their own federating body called Selskosoyus ; and in January, 1922, agricultural credit and loan associations were legalised, which came in turn to be assisted by larger Societies for Agricultural Credit, raising capital by the issue of shares to other co-operative institutions and to the State Bank.

This same shortage of resources available for use as working capital showed itself also in the inadequacy of the funds which the newly formed trusts had at their disposal. When a trust was chartered, it was usual for the State to assign to it a certain fund as

[1] I.L.O., *op. cit.*, 132–46 ; A. Orlov in *Russian Economist*, vol. II, 1935.

" turnover capital ". In practice this usually amounted to little more than the stocks of material and fuel and finished goods which the enterprises already had in their possession. The State, as we have seen, had very limited supplies itself, and what it had it wanted to concentrate on the fuel industry and transport and on metal works which were handling urgent railway repairs. In theory the trusts were supposed to supplement their turnover resources by bank credits ; and the State Bank was reopened on November 16th, 1921, as a necessary complement to the restoration of the market, with the express aim of " aiding the development of industry, agriculture and trade by means of credit and other banking operations ".[1] But for several months it was not in a position to make more than trifling advances to industry. At its foundation the only capital assigned to the Bank by the Treasury was a fund of paper roubles amounting to about 50 million pre-war gold roubles, which "by the time the Bank began business and the money was brought to its coffers was only worth about 14 million ".[2] As a result of this shortage of resources, and in order to guard itself against losses on credit operations through rouble depreciation, the Bank proceeded to charge rates of interest as high as 12 to 18 per cent. per month, and later, while keeping its rates fairly high, proceeded to conduct its loan operations in terms of gold, so that repayment had to be made by a sum of paper roubles equivalent to the gold value of the loan at the time of its issue.[3] As a result, the rouble credits advanced to industry were only saved from rapid depreciation if they could be instantaneously converted into goods ; and part, at least, of the losses from rouble depreciation were shifted on to industry. Accordingly, even when the Bank's branch system had been developed—which was not for some months—the aid which the State Bank was able to give to industry was so small and on such onerous terms as to be insignificant in helping the trusts to overcome their difficulties.

Even prior to the reopening of the State Bank, there had been a repeal of all war-time measures limiting the amounts of money

---

[1] The decree on the reopening of the bank was dated Oct. 12, and issued by TSIK. This ratified an earlier Sovnarcom decree of Oct. 4. The State Bank was to be subordinated to Narcomfin, by which its directors were appointed ; it was authorised to open branches and to establish clearing houses ; and one of its first acts was to set up a special Loan and Discount Committee. (Cf. Arnold, op. cit., 118.)   [2] Katzenellenbaum, op. cit., 156.
[3] Ibid., 157–8. If this had not been done, the real resources of the Bank would, of course, have dwindled to insignificance within a few weeks. Later, deposits were also credited to depositors in terms of gold.

deposited in a bank by private individuals and safeguarding such
deposits from any extraordinary taxes and levies.   Charges were
reintroduced for railway services (including charges to State
institutions themselves), for posts and telegraphs, water, electricity,
gas and the renting of sites and buildings to industrial and trading
concerns as well as to individuals.   In June, 1921, a beginning was
made with the reintroduction of a tax system of the traditional kind
by the reimposition of a tax on industrial and trading enterprises
and of certain excise duties on such things as wines and spirits,
tobacco, matches, tea and coffee.   Preliminary steps even began to
be taken in the direction of a balanced budget, in order to obviate
the need for reliance on currency emission as a source of budget
revenue.   Until the end of 1923, however, these steps were to be
very halting ones.   The currency continued to be increased more
rapidly even than before, and the price-level continued to rise at
headlong speed.   But the position soon had this difference from
the situation during the civil war : that, with a considerable
increase in the transactions-demand for money as a result of the
widened area of transactions for which money was now used, the
relation between currency issues and the rise in the price-level was
reversed for the first time since 1916.   The rise in the price-level
began to proceed at a slower rate than the increase in the amount of
currency in circulation, instead of the converse, and the real value
of the total currency in circulation substantially increased.   In the
course of 1921 and 1922 two devaluations of the depreciated
paper rouble were undertaken ; as a combined result of which one
rouble of new notes became equal to one million roubles of the
issues of earlier years, which were withdrawn.[1]   On the eve of the
second of these devaluations, which made one new rouble equal to
a hundred of the previous year's issue, the price-level was about
200,000 times the price-level of 1913.   In 1923 a beginning was
made with the issue of a new stabilised currency-unit through the
State Bank, the *chervonetz* rouble ;[2]   and after a few months'
experience of two parallel monetary units (the old paper roubles
continuing to circulate alongside the new notes, which at first were
issued only in larger denominations, and continuing to depreciate
both in terms of goods and of the new monetary unit) the monetary
reform of 1924 was completed, by which the depreciated rouble

[1] Yurovsky, *op. cit.*, 47-8.
[2] In the last quarter of 1923 less than 10 per cent of budget revenue came
from currency emission, as compared with nearly nine tenths at the beginning of
1922.

was withdrawn entirely and the new stabilised bank-note issue took its place.[1]

Finally, among the changes which accompanied the inauguration of the NEP there was a certain amount of denationalisation, mainly of those small enterprises, mostly workshops rather than factories, that had been swept into the net of nationalisation by the decree of November 29th, 1920. The extent of this denationalisation should not be exaggerated ; and its economic significance was nothing like as great as foreign commentators at the time were inclined to suppose. Many of the leases of small enterprises were to industrial co-operatives, and not to individual owners ; and the policy of granting concessions on a larger scale to foreign companies had little success, apart from one or two special cases, while the concessions which were granted were more often in the sphere of foreign trade than of production. By a decree of May 17th, 1921, all enterprises covered by the earlier decree which had not yet in fact been taken over by the State were forthwith declared restored to their previous owners ; and on December 10th it was laid down that all enterprises with less than 20 workers, whether previously taken over by the State or not, were to be restored to their previous owners or leased to new ones. By the autumn of 1922 some 4000 enterprises had been leased (or more than were organised in State trusts at the time). But they were mostly quite small enterprises, mostly no more than handicraft workshops, and the share of total industrial production which they represented was insignificant. In the spring of 1923 the Central Statistical Department conducted an industrial census, covering all enterprises in towns or suburbs of towns that possessed any kind of productive equipment, with or without mechanical power, or employed hired labour. According to this census, private enterprises covered only 12½ per cent. of all workers employed in enterprises covered by the census, employed on the average only 2 persons each and covered only 5 per cent. of gross production.[2]

It was in trade, and especially in retail trade, that the Nepman, as the private capitalist of the time came to be called, struck his roots and for a few years flourished. In the village he bought the peasants' grain and took it to the nearest town or railhead and sold

---

[1] The new *chervonetz* rouble had partial gold cover ; but it was not convertible into gold. For details of the monetary reform, cf. Yurovsky, *op. cit.*, 85 seq. ; Arnold, *op. cit.* ; and the present writer's *Russian Economic Development* (1928), 252–4, 270.

[2] Cf. Rozenfeld, *op. cit.*, 208–12 ; Kritsman, *op. cit.*, 127–9. The figures for the share of private industry in production referred to Dec. 1922. The average number employed in State enterprises was 155 and in industrial co-operatives 15.

it, and bought the villagers' chickens or vegetables or eggs and sold them at a booth in a nearby market town or in the village or suburban shop which he proceeded to establish.   In the village this was sometimes done by enterprising outsiders, but more often by the well-to-do peasant, who possessed a horse and a cart and a small reserve of capital.   In the towns as well private shops appeared and private merchants invaded wholesale trade, buying from the new trusts that part of their products which they could not as yet dispose of for themselves or supplying them with raw materials. Some trusts set up shops of their own in towns like Moscow and made bulk contracts for sale and purchase with the co-operatives. But in general in the early years of NEP the State and co-operative trading organisation was incapable, either separately or in combination, of providing anything like a complete commercial network for the new decentralised industry.   Hence considerable reliance had to be placed on the private trader, who in these years both assisted State industry to restore its shattered productive apparatus and was in turn kept alive by the economic patronage of State industry.   It has been estimated that in the first year or two of NEP the private trader furnished about a half of the immediate market for the products of industrial trusts ; the wholesale organisation of the co-operatives providing no more than one fifth of this market.[1] Even the consumers' co-operatives in 1922–3 purchased nearly one third of the supplies for their urban shops through private traders. It has been estimated that about nine tenths of all retail trading outlets (including kiosks and stalls as well as shops) about this time were private and that three quarters of the retail turnover was in private hands.   In wholesale trade the Nepman was less strongly entrenched than in retail trade, and by 1923 a fifth and no more of the total turnover in wholesale trade fell to the private trader.   After 1923 the network of State and co-operative trading organisations was considerably expanded.   Not only did industry set up its own wholesale organisations, but various State bodies founded commercial trading companies to engage in both wholesale and retail trade.   For example, both Vesenkha at the national level and various republican and provincial governments founded companies (e.g. Gostorg, Mostorg and Ukraintorg) to operate in the wholesale sphere and to serve the needs of local and rural industry.   In turn these bodies often established retail stores in urban centres.   Within a year their number reached nearly 80, and they handled some 16 per cent. of the commercial turnover, and played an especially

[1] Cf. Bronsky in *Sots. Khoz.*, 1926, No. 5, 18–19.

important rôle in the handling of textiles and foodstuffs. Accordingly by the later '20's the Nepman's sun had already begun to set. Of the wholesale trade turnover on the eve of the First Five Year Plan private enterprise only accounted for 5 per cent. But even as late as 1928 in retail trade the private trader was still responsible for a fifth or a quarter of the total turnover.

III

In foreign bourgeois circles at the time the introduction of NEP was hailed as a retreat, a recognition of failure and an abandonment of positions previously won, which must eventually result in a restoration of Capitalism unless the collapse of production was to be aggravated instead of being overcome. Even with the economy set on its new course, *émigré* writers remained sceptical of any improvement. Miliukov, writing at the beginning of 1922, spoke of NEP as " the beginning of the end " ; and Prokopovitch declared that " there is little hope for the re-establishment of the Russian national and State economy ".[1] Even inside the country there was apprehension and pessimism in certain circles : a tendency to emphasise the new line as a retreat, as a concession to hostile forces, and to mutter that the scrapping of War Communism might be the first chapter in a Russian Thermidor.

How, then, is the complex economic system which was established by the NEP to be described ? Clearly it falls neatly into none of the pigeon-holes which textbooks about economic systems are apt to employ. Nearly all large and medium-scale industry was nationalised ; and to this extent the socialist element in the system was more prominent than it had been in the first eight months of the Soviet régime. On the other hand, agriculture remained stubbornly individualist. Save for a very small area covered by State and collective farms, it consisted of small-scale production by individual working-owners, much of it subsistence farming rather than farming for the market, but some of it *kulak* farming for sale with the aid of hired labour. The essential links between agriculture and industry were once again market links; and we have seen that in the sphere of trade between village and town and between production and the consumer private capital occupied a place of some importance. Clearly it could not be described as a socialist economy, in view of the wide extent of

[1] P. Miliukov, *Russia To-day and To-morrow*, 230, also 295 ; Prokopovitch, *op. cit.*, 229.

individual enterprise.   At the same time, apart from the *kulak* farm
which relied considerably on hired labour, peasant farming, while
it was individualist production, could not be described as capitalist ;
and the elements of actual Capitalism in the system at large were
comparatively insignificant.   Petty production, whether in agriculture or in handicraft production, formed a soil, however, from
which a revived Capitalism might very easily and quickly grow.

Lenin himself described the system introduced by the NEP as
a " transitional mixed system ", and to this mixed system as a whole
he gave the name of State Capitalism: a term he had earlier used
in the first part of 1918 to describe the economic policy of those
months, when he had spoken of it as " an advance on the present
state of affairs ", and as " economically immeasurably superior "
to the existing system.   Its introduction within " approximately six
months' time " could be accounted " a great success ".[1]   By State
Capitalism he meant control by the State *over* small-commodity
production ; and the existing form of it differed from other forms
in the fact that the working class held political power, and the
Soviet State held, politically and economically, " the commanding
heights " from which it could control the movements in the surrounding plain.[2]   By the term " mixed system " he meant simply
that the existing economy was a fusion—largely an unstable and
transitory fusion—of different elements : not only " pieces of both
socialism and capitalism ", but of individualist " small commodity
production " as represented by the peasantry producing for a
market, and even of the more primitive economic form of " patri-
archal, i.e. to a considerable extent natural, self-sufficient peasant
economy ".[3]   By the term " transitional " he meant that this
" intermingling " of elements could not be regarded as stable and
enduring.   It contained within itself the possibility either of a
recrudescence of Capitalism, if *kulak* and Nepmen and other
elements of Capitalism (or of Capitalism-in-embryo) were allowed
to grow too strong and to beget their kind, or of a development
towards Socialism, if a correct economic policy were pursued by
the State.   The leading rôle of the working class in the worker-
peasant alliance, and the use of the political power it possessed,
was the guarantee that this latter development could be converted

[1] *Selected Works*, vol. IX, 165, 168.
[2] By contrast, Bukharin, who had opposed this conception as spokesman of the
" Left Communists " of 1918, denied that State Capitalism could exist outside a
capitalist State : "There can be no talk of ' State Capitalism ' under the dictatorship of the proletariat . . . State Capitalism presupposes the capitalist State."
(*Economika Perekhodnovo Perioda*, chap. 7, *passim*).
[3] Lenin, *op. cit.*, vol. IX, 165–6.

from a possibility into a probability. The first prerequisite of such a development was the extension of agricultural co-operation ; the second the industrialisation of the country, towards which the first steps had already been taken by the electrification plan adopted at the Eighth Soviet Congress in December, 1920. This would strengthen and extend those socialist " islands " within the mixed economy and would lay the technical basis for large-scale production without which Socialism was inconceivable.

In 1918 he had written : " At present, petty-bourgeois Capitalism prevails in Russia, and it is *one and the same road* that leads from it to large-scale State Capitalism *and* to Socialism, through *one and the same* intermediate station called ' national accounting and control of production and distribution '. . . . It is not State Capitalism that is at war with Socialism ; it is the petty bourgeoisie plus private Capitalism fighting against both State Capitalism and Socialism. The petty bourgeoisie oppose *every kind* of State interference, regulation and control, whether it be State Capitalist or Socialist. . . . Either we subordinate this petty bourgeoisie to *our* control and accounting, or they will overthrow our workers' government as surely and as inevitably as the revolution was overthrown by the Napoleons and Cavaignacs who sprang from this very soil of small ownership." To this he added that " for the next few years we must learn to think of the intermediary links that can facilitate the transition from patriarchalism, from small production, to Socialism. . . . Inasmuch as we are as yet unable to pass directly from small production to Socialism, Capitalism is inevitable to a certain degree as the elemental product of small production and exchange, and we must utilise Capitalism as the intermediary link between small production and Socialism. . . . Not to try to prohibit, or lock up, the development of Capitalism, but to try to direct it into the channels of *State Capitalism*. . . . The whole problem, both theoretical and practical, is to find the correct methods of directing what is to a certain degree and for a certain time the inevitable development of Capitalism into the channels of State Capitalism." [1]

From these passages it is clear that the mixed economy which emerged under NEP was no sudden novelty, invented overnight or forced upon intentions quite alien to it by the failure of a " direct

---

[1] *Ibid.*, 167, 170, 180–1. The last two sentences of the above were added in 1921. The rest had been written and published in 1918 and was *requoted* by Lenin in April, 1921, to stress the continuity between the policies of the first half of 1918 and the policies of 1921 : that " the fundamental features of our economics in 1921 are the same as those existing in 1918." (*Ibid.*, 194.)

assault " upon the old régime.   It fitted completely, where War
Communism had not, into the conception which Lenin had
always held of " a definite transition period . . . for a whole
historical era " lying " between Capitalism and Communism " :
a transitional era which " cannot but combine the features and
properties of both these systems of social enterprise ".   After the
death of Lenin a controversy was to develop as to whether a
prior condition for further development beyond this transitional
economy towards a socialist one was the extension of the revolution
to other, and more advanced, countries of central and western
Europe : whether, it was " possible to build socialism in one
country ", backward as this country was in productivity and consequently poor, and isolated amidst a suspicious and hostile capitalist
world.   That such isolation would make such a further development
several times more difficult than it otherwise might have been is
fairly clear ; if only because it imposed the necessity of a high
degree of economic self-sufficiency and, as events were to show,
extensive diversion of resources towards the defence industries, and
a strained *tempo* of development both in their case and in the case
of industries upon which they rested.   About this there was never
any dispute.   But there is not much doubt that Lenin would have
considered this further development, not only an historical possibility, but an historical necessity if the Soviet régime were to
survive.   In transitional periods of history especially, policy cannot mark time for long : if the navigator does not set his course
boldly, he may well be carried backwards by the latent force of
those surviving elements of the old order that remain unmastered.

By a socialist economy, to which the mixed economy of the
NEP was regarded as a preparatory stage, Lenin meant a system
in which collective forms of production predominated, based on
collective, instead of individual, ownership of the means of production.   " Socialism," he said, " means the abolition of classes " ;
adding that " classes remain and will remain in the era of the
dictatorship of the proletariat : when classes disappear, the dictatorship will become unnecessary ; without the dictatorship of
the proletariat they will not disappear ".   In such an economy
some measure of economic inequality would still survive.   Property
incomes derived from ownership of land and capital would have
come to an end (or dwindled to insignificance), and with their
banishment would have gone both the class division and the
inequalities specifically attendant on them.   But according to the
well-known contention of Marx in his *Critique of the Gotha*

Programme, differences in work-incomes, according to the character and amount of work, would remain, until that happier period had been reached when " mastery of the productive forces " had progressed sufficiently to enable economic scarcity as a paramount problem of human society to be banished, and the ideal equality to a communist order to become an economic possibility. Lenin's vision of a socialist society and his attitude to the tortuous problems of a transitional economy in 1921 were shot through with a vibrant realism. This attitude sternly echoed the familiar saying of Marx that principles of " justice can never rise superior to the economic conditions of the time ".

CHAPTER SEVEN

THE FIRST YEARS OF ECONOMIC RECOVERY AND THE " SCISSORS " CRISIS OF 1923

I

During the civil war period engineering factories had been living on reserves of pig-iron, and by the middle of 1920 these had dwindled to half a million poods. The industry was only saved from complete stoppage by the discovery of considerable reserves in the Urals when this area passed back into the hands of the Soviet Government during that year.[1] Reserves of iron ore amounted to some 100 million poods ; and smelting difficulties arose, not from lack of ore, but from scarcity of fuel. Stocks of copper were also estimated at some 40 million poods.[2] Reserves of raw cotton in 1920 were actually quite large, equivalent to about four months' pre-war supplies and sufficient at the existing level of production for at least a year. But these reserves were mainly in Turkestan, whence they could not be moved for lack of rolling stock, even after the area had been cleared of bandits, and reserves at the factories were small, while cotton-dressing factories were closed for lack of fuel. Flax and wool stocks were in a somewhat better position ; but reserves of hides were scanty.[3] The fuel crisis which grew particularly acute in the early months of 1921 accordingly threatened a paralysis of industry ; and a solution of it was a crucial preliminary to economic recovery. In the second quarter of the year cotton mills received no more than 7 per cent. of their scheduled requirements of fuel, and linen factories only 44 per cent.[4] In August 35 out of 56 woollen mills were idle, largely for lack of fuel ; and of 64 cotton factories 51 were idle. The cement industry was producing only a mere 1 per cent. of its pre-war output for lack of fuel[5] The fuel situation, in turn, was aggravated by an extensive migration of hewers from the Donbas mines to the villages in the summer, owing to the non-arrival of food supplies for rations ; and a similar

---

[1] Larin and Kritsman, *op. cit.*, 65.
[2] Prof. Dolgov in *Manchester Guardian Commercial Reconstruction Supplement*, July 6, 1922, 218.
[3] Kritsman, *op. cit.*, 184-5.   [4] *Narodnoe Khoziaistvo Rossii*, 1921, 18.
[5] *Russian Economist*, vol. II, No. 5, 1616.

food shortage was responsible for a reduction in the output of Grozny oil.[1] Labour generally was exhausted and demoralised by the underfeeding and strain of the hunger years. The shortage of skilled labour was acute, and the administrative system was in such disorder as to be incapable in many cases of efficiently planning the distribution and utilisation of fuel and materials, even where supplies of these were to hand.

Few countries in such a plight are likely to find a means of breaking this vicious circle without resort to foreign loans. With the aid of short-term credits and loans, or of more long-period investments, working capital can be supplied to industry and the deficiency of fuel or food or materials repaired by imports from abroad. In this way Austria in 1922 was saved from wholesale starvation ; Germany in 1924 started her phenomenal recovery with the aid of the Dawes Loan ; and within more recent memory devastated countries have been rallied with the help of UNRRA supplies. But Soviet Russia in 1921 could expect no more than very minor help in this way. The wolves of armed intervention had but recently departed. There was little chance that the wolves would now return and feed their former victim. Ordinary business credits were virtually unobtainable until 1924, and then only in comparatively small quantities. The policy of granting " concessions " to foreign firms to undertake certain trading and industrial ventures was unsuccessful in yielding more than about 10 million roubles (gold) of foreign capital in the first years of the concessions policy. Certain sums (amounting to about £21 million) flowed in during 1921–2 in relief of the famine sufferers ; but these sums were small compared with the added results of the appalling disaster of the 1921 famine. Long-term loans were sought at Genoa, and then in London, in 1922 and 1923 ; but the quest was in vain. A part of the dwindled gold reserve could be shipped abroad in payment for imported goods ; but this reserve also soon reached its limits. These methods combined sufficed to finance an import surplus equivalent to about £20 million in 1921 and about £37 million in 1922, three quarters of this consisting of food. But that was all. In 1923 and 1924 the demands of currency and exchange stabilisation exacted a rigorous reduction of imports below the 1921 level and the conversion of an import into an export surplus. How very small were the figures of external aid compared with the magnitude of Russia's problem at the time may be judged if we set them beside estimates that were made in 1922 of the sum

---

[1] *Narodnoe Khoziaistvo*, 1921, 7, 12 ; Benediktov, *op. cit.*, 107.

required to reconstruct the country's transport system alone. These estimates mentioned a figure of £75 million as the minimum expenditure necessary to restore the main railway lines to working order, and £100 million to restore the secondary lines and the principal seaports as well.[1] For the major part, therefore, the means for reconstruction had in Russia's case to come from her own efforts and resources ; and the process of reconstruction had to be correspondingly more painful.

The most urgent task was a liquidation of the fuel crisis. This step, by solving some of the transport difficulties, would quicken the movement of raw materials and foodstuffs to the industrial towns ; and this in turn, by prompting some recovery of output of essential manufactured goods to be placed upon the village market, could induce the peasant to increase his sales of raw material and grain, and ease the famine in the towns and in the stricken Volga region and the paralysis of factory production. All this required an initial effort from tired muscles and jaded nerves and a further squeezing of the consumption of certain sections of the population, in advance of any relief to the situation that these measures could later afford. The immediate problem consisted in mobilising existing supplies of food and fuel and concentrating them on the strategic points ; and this could not fail to be at the expense of cutting down supplies to persons and institutions that were for the moment of secondary importance. Railwaymen and Donbas miners had to be given preference in the allocation of supplies over teachers and office workers. Fuel had to be supplied to the railways to quicken the movement of grain from the Urals, of coal from the Donetz, and of raw cotton from Turkestan, even though this might mean a temporary closing down of cotton mills in Moscow and Ivanovo-Vosnesensk for lack of fuel and a reduction in output of yarn and cloth.

Among the measures adopted to this end was a drastic reduction in the number of persons and institutions directly supplied with food by the State. The yield of the new agricultural tax had at first been estimated at 200 million poods. But as a result of the famine this figure was reduced to 140 million, which was no more than a half of what had been collected by requisitioning in the previous year. The reduction of State obligations to supply industrial enterprises left only 150 enterprises, covering 140,000 workers, completely dependent on State supplies at the end of 1921 ; while

[1] *Manchester Guardian Commercial Reconstruction Supplement*, July 6, 1922, 224.

workers in enterprises partly covered by State supplies were reduced from 1·5 million in October, 1921, to 1 million in the following February and to under half a million in the summer of 1922.[1] The result was actually to compel a number of factories to close down and others to reduce the numbers they employed ; which was reflected in a lowering of the level of production in several light industries, such as wool, linen, hemp and paper, in 1921 as compared with 1920. Administrative reorganisation resulted in a drastic reduction of the numbers employed on the railways ; the number of administrative workers in the textile industry was reduced by a third, and the number of productive workers per 1000 spindles in operation was halved ; while a special Commission for the Reduction of Staffs under the chairmanship of Larin made proposals to reduce the employees of State departments by 50 per cent. The first accompaniment of reconstruction was, accordingly, an increase in unemployment ; the number of registered unemployed standing at half a million towards the end of 1922. At the same time the real wages of those employed, which had risen a little in 1920 over 1919, were lower again as an average for 1921 ; and in the summer months, when the fuel crisis was at its height, fell to an extremely low figure, real wages in Moscow in these months being less than a half what they had been in December of the previous year. By the end of 1921 they had risen again with sudden steepness, only to fall once more in the early months of 1922. Life was often only sustained by petty thieving of property or peddling in the streets ; and the death-rate in that grim famine year reached the figure of 60 per thousand.[2]

To deal with the fuel crisis the whole energies of the Party personnel were mobilised. Propaganda by printed and spoken word called for a turn from the military to the industrial front. A new system of wage-payment was introduced, under which, in essential industries still supplied by the State, the wages fund paid to an enterprise was adjusted to the ratio of its output to the minimum number of labour units required in the circumstances to produce a standard output ; while a new scale of seventeen gradations of wages was introduced, which widened the differences of remuneration between skilled and unskilled. The central fuel administra-

---

[1] *Narodnoe Khoziaistvo*, 1921, 17 ; I.L.O., *Organisation of Industry and Labour Conditions in S.R.*, 54–6.

[2] *Narodnoe Khoziaistvo*, 1921, 6–7 ; Strumilin, *Na Khoziaistvennom Fronte*, 7–8, 86 ; L. K. in *Na Novikh Putiakh*, vol. III, 14. Strumilin estimates that additional income of the above kind amounted to about 40 per cent. of workers' wages at this time. The practice had been common throughout the civil war period.

tion was subjected to drastic reorganisation; and to deal with the
key situation of the Donbas a special Commission was despatched
by STO to reorganise mining in that area. Such supplies of food
as the State could mobilise were concentrated on the Donbas, and
distributed among the various mines according to the new system
of collective payment by results, in an attempt to combat the
summer migration of hewers back to the village. A ruthless concentration of production and a closing of the less efficient mines
was undertaken; with the result that by the end of 1921 mining
had been concentrated in 471 mines, instead of the 920 that had
been working in January. The number of mines operated by the
coal trust, Donugol, was reduced at first to 360 and then to 202
by October, 1922, and finally to 179 in October, 1923.[1] Numerous
small "peasant" outcrop-mines were leased out, and other mines
were placed under the control of other institutions such as the
Chemical Trust or certain State and municipal departments. At
the same time the number of workers in the mines increased towards
the end of the year, and the output per hewer was doubled. In the
final quarter of the year a marked improvement was registered ; the
coal output rising to 183 million poods against 130 million in the first
quarter of the year and leading to an accumulation of pithead
stocks.[2]

   The improvement of coal production was quickly reflected in
an easing of the transport situation. Trotsky was succeeded in 1921
by Dzherzhinsky as head of Narcomput ; and the latter proceeded
to decentralise the administration by grouping the railways into
regional administrations with fairly extensive powers of independent initiative, each line being placed in the hands of a line superin-
tendent. Orders for a large number of new railway engines had
been placed in Germany and Sweden ; and the work of railway
repair shops was improved by the application of special "shock"
methods to them. In the fourth quarter of the year railway activity
measured in pood-versts per month rose to 90,000 as against 35,000
at the beginning of 1920, and existing rolling stock began to be
more intensively used. In the course of 1922 the output of coal
rose by more than a quarter over 1920 to about one third of the
pre-war level ; while at the same time in June, 1922, the movement
of coal from the Donbas on the railways reached 26 million poods
compared with 10 million in February ; and pithead stocks which

[1] Benediktov, *op. cit.*, 96, 105, 107–8.
[2] *Narodnoe Khoziaistvo*, 1921 ; Smilga in *Econ. Zhizn.*, Nov. 6, 1921 ; P.
Bogdanov's report to the 9th Soviet Congress.

had mounted to 121 million in April had been reduced to 90 million by August, after which the movement of coal kept pace with current production.[1]

By the autumn of 1922 the economic position had sufficiently improved for the textile industry, whose production had been drastically restricted in 1921, to show a marked leap forward. The cotton industry in November began for the first time to report adequate supplies of fuel, and in December reported six months' stocks of fuel in 40 per cent. of the factories.[2] Cotton-spinning increased three times over 1921 to a fifth of the pre-war level, and woollen and linen yarn rose respectively to 27 and 36 per cent. of 1913.[3] The more favourable harvest of 1922, which yielded between 60 and 70 per cent. of the pre-war crop, eased the food situation of the towns sufficiently for real wages to show a marked advance in the course of the year : in Petrograd in October they were double the previous November, and in Moscow by December they had reached 76 per cent. of the pre-war level.[4] It was now raw materials, and not fuel and transport, that were the limiting factor upon the further recovery of light industry producing consumer goods. The cotton industry had always relied for half its supplies on imports. These were for the moment unobtainable in any adequate quantities and cotton-cultivation in Turkestan during the civil war had shown the most catastrophic shrinkage of any agricultural product, the acreage in 1921–2 being only 7 per cent. of 1916 and the yield per acre less than one half. The crop for 1922 was no more than 11,000, and the plans of the cotton com-mittee for increased cotton-growing, which involved considerable capital expenditure on irrigation work, were not likely to show much result in the immediate future. In the meantime available stocks in Turkestan were being rapidly depleted. Flax and hemp had not suffered so severely ; but the cultivation of tobacco and sugar-beet had suffered a reduction of crop in 1921 to under 5 per cent. of pre-war ; while the supply of hides was deficient owing to the reduction of cattle and horses by 40 per cent. By the middle of 1923 defi-ciency of raw materials had spread even to the languishing metal industry ; and the south was complaining of a famine of iron ore and Yugostal of a shortage of pig-iron.[5]

[1] *Industrial and Labour Information*, Sept. 1, 1922 ; Sept. 29, 1922 ; Dec. 8, 1922.
[2] *Ibid.*, March 16, 1923.
[3] P. Bogdanov in *Russkaia Promishlennost*, 1922, vol. VI.
[4] *Industrial and Labour Information*, March 16, 1923 ; July 13, 1923.
[5] Istomin and Ivanov in *Econ. Zhizn.*, Sept. 25, 1923.

II

This shortage of raw materials underlay a curious phenomenon which developed in the course of 1922, and which was in a sense the prelude to the famous " scissors crisis " of the following year, although in certain respects the situation in 1922 was quite opposite to that of 1923. We have seen that when industry was cut adrift from centralised supplies and allowed to fend for itself in the market, the new industrial trusts immediately found themselves faced with a shortage of working capital. At first this difficulty appeared as a marketing difficulty : as consisting in the absence of a marketing apparatus adequate to sell the products of industry and to purchase for it raw material. The initial efforts of the new trusts were accordingly turned to the hasty improvisation of a marketing apparatus of their own. Such an improvisation could hardly fail to be limited in range and primitive in character ; and the result was what came to be known as the *rasbazarivania* of the end of 1921 and the early months of 1922 : the hasty selling off of industrial stocks in local markets at such prices as these would fetch, which resulted in a squandering of industrial resources. To secure the means they lacked for continuing production, the trusts opened small shops or set up stalls in the streets in the locality of the factories, or employed itinerant pedlars to barter their products directly with the peasants in the village for materials and food. Sometimes they even paid wages in industrial products, leaving to the worker the task of reselling the products to obtain food. Inability to reach a wide market and eagerness to sell quickly caused industry to accept a much lower figure than it would ordinarily have done for the sale. In centres like Moscow, where several trusts opened shops in the same line, there was acute cut-throat competition which depressed selling prices still further and aggravated the financial plight of the trusts. Much of this trade still had a barter character. The Sugar Trust, for instance, produced in 1921–2 over 3 million poods of sugar, of which a substantial part was bartered directly with the peasants in the beet-growing areas in order to secure supplies of beet. Sometimes products were sold by direct goods exchange for things which the trust itself did not want and which it had to resell in another market before it could procure the materials it so sorely needed.[1] In the Donetz area

[1] L. K. in *Na Novikh Putiakh*, vol. III, 20.

certain trusts put on sale various products such as window glass in boxes and textile goods in the piece, and found these goods quite unsaleable, until the Gubsovnarhoz opened a trading department to set up numerous booths where the goods could be sold in much smaller units to the peasants.[1] The Glass and Pottery Board, which in the spring of 1922 was in the process of reorganising its industry on a trust basis, negotiated with Centrosoyus a direct barter of its products against food ; and, when Centrosoyus failed to supply more than 20 per cent. of the agreed amount, it opened a series of shops in Moscow and placed in them shop managers to whom it supplied goods on commission.[2] It was often in such cases that the private trader stepped in and purchased the goods for resale in another area at a handsome profit.

But the real cause of the plight of industry in the first three quarters of 1922 went deeper. It was not simply a matter of deficient marketing apparatus, even if this was an aggravating circumstance. The central State departments, the co-operatives and the trusts were all lacking in stocks of food and raw materials ; and all alike were desperately seeking to market such industrial goods as they could lay their hands upon in order to procure agricultural products from the village in return. Fundamentally it was the old problem of the economic relations between the town and the village, which we have seen as having such pivotal importance in 1916 and in 1918 and throughout the civil war years. Industry found itself faced with a " sales crisis "—with an almost inelastic market—because as a result of the famine of 1921 there were not the agricultural goods to be given in exchange. This was the reality behind the deficiency of working capital. As a result of the efforts of industry to procure more foodstuffs and raw materials, the terms of exchange between manufactures and agricultural produce moved violently to the disadvantage of the town ; the relative prices of the latter rising and of the former falling, until the extreme point of the movement was reached in the spring and early summer of 1922. One arshin of cotton piece-goods, which had exchanged in 1913 for 4·33 lb. (Russian) of rye flour, now exchanged in May, 1922, for no more than 1·68 lb.; while a pair of boots, which in 1913 had been worth 283 lb. of rye flour, was worth in May, 1922, no more than 133 lb. On the average a unit of industrial goods could procure no more than 65 per cent. of the

[1] Dolgov, loc. cit., 27–8.
[2] Cit. Industrial and Labour Information, May 26, 1922.

pre-war equivalent in agricultural produce.[1] Hence the paradox of industries unable to find buyers even though industrial production was less than a quarter of the pre-war, while currency inflation was still proceeding at a rapid rate : a paradox which caused such alarm to the leaders of industry, and prompted writers abroad to announce triumphantly " the breakdown of NEP ".[2] The fact was that the prevailing high prices for agricultural goods did not spell increased, but rather decreased, incomes for the peasants because they were associated with agricultural shortage ; and the income which the urban worker had available to buy manufactured goods had drastically shrunk because of the increased amount he had to spend on food. In other words, the " sales crisis " was an expression of a disproportion between agriculture and industry, under which the marketed surplus of the village was insufficient to supply the requisites of expanded production in the towns.

The acuteness of the crisis first became apparent in March ; and Lomov in *Economicheskaia Zhizn* of March 30th stressed the extreme gravity of the position and advocated a contraction of production and the export of surplus stocks. The question of the proper policy to pursue to alleviate the plight of industry became a matter of some controversy. There were many who argued that a contraction of production was wrong; and a report of the State Economic Planning Commission (*Gosplan*) expressed the view that the solution lay, not in output reduction, but in more liberal grants

[1] Rozenfeld, *op. cit.*, 428 ; Strumilin, *Na Khoziaistvennom Fronte*, 212, where the following index of industrial and agricultural prices is given :

					Agricultural	Industrial
1913	.	.	.	.	100	100
January,	11,	1922	.	.	104	92
February	1,	,,	.	.	105	90
March	1,	,,	.	.	109	82
April	1,	,,	.	.	111	77
May	1,	,,	.	.	113	74
June	1,	,,	.	.	106	89
July	1,	,,	.	.	104	92
August	1,	,,	.	.	100·5	99
September 1,		,,	.	.	94	112

It had been usual in the past few years for the inflationary price-rise to meet with a check between June and September, owing to the expectation of the harvest and the accumulation of currency funds for grain purchase. This year this seasonal break in the price index occurred two months earlier, in April, presumably on account of the quickened flow of industrial goods on to the market in the *rasbazarivania* period. (N. D. Kondratiev in *Na Novikh Putyakh*, vol. I, 7–8.)

[2] E.g. M. K. Braikevich in *Russian Economist*, vol. III, No. 9, 3195 : " The policy has broken down. . . . Russia is bound very soon to discard her present Communist oligarchy and establish a democratic regime." Again : " Russia is doomed to economic stagnation, local famines, and the actual dying out of the population of whole regions and to terrible misery." (A. Orlov, *ibid.*, 3140.)

to industry from the State Budget to supplement the working capital of the trusts and in the more prompt payment by State departments for goods purchased from the trusts. Vesenkha, however, in the course of April and May reduced the output programme for a number of industries : a policy which as a temporary expedient would seem to have been the correct one in the circumstances, since the root of the trouble was a lack of raw materials sufficient to support an expanded output programme. Clearly, it was much better that the lighter finishing industries should suffer some contraction in order that such resources as were available might be devoted to maintaining the activity of fuel and transport, than that the latter should be starved of resources by attempts to maintain the output of consumer goods at a higher level. At any rate these measures both eased the fuel situation towards the end of the summer (an improvement which reacted favourably upon the light industries towards the end of the year) and also led to a recovery of the ratio of industrial to agricultural prices after May. This recovery was further strengthened when the new harvest began to come upon the market in the summer and autumn ; and before the end of the year, as we shall see, the " price-scissors " were to open in the opposite direction.

It was to avoid any further cut-throat competition such as had characterised this " sales crisis ", and also as a logical step beyond the improvised marketing methods which had characterised the period of *rasbazarivania*, that in the spring and summer of 1922 the trusts began the formation of commercial syndicates. This represented the first serious attempt to deal with the problem of a commercial apparatus for industry under the new organisation ; and it has a particular interest as being the spontaneous creation of the trusts themselves. Once formed, the syndicates had to be legally registered, and to receive the sanction of Vesenkha for their commercial activities. But their formation represented an independent initiative on the part of industry, not a plan of organisation imposed from above.

In their constitution these syndicates were similar to any ordinary syndicate or cartel, being founded with a share capital subscribed by the various trusts that joined in their formation, and being charged with such commercial functions on behalf of the member bodies as these latter chose to give them. The precise function of the syndicates varied. In a few cases they were merely industrial bureaux partitioning the market among the trusts and agreeing upon minimum prices to avoid cut-throat competition. In other cases they combined this with the function of purchasing-

societies for material and fuel supplies. But in the majority of
cases they were definite commercial organisations, purchasing
supplies and marketing at least an agreed minimum proportion of
the output of the constituent trusts ; while in one or two instances
they inherited much of the property and some of the apparatus
and personnel of the old Glavki.[1]   Only in two cases did a syndicate
have a complete monopoly of the market in its product : namely,
the Salt Syndicate and the Oil Syndicate, the latter uniting Azneft,
Grozneft and Embaneft, and being legally endowed with a monopoly in the marketing of oil.   In other cases there were usually a
certain number of trusts and enterprises outside the syndicates,
marketing their goods independently ; and in a few cases different
syndicates themselves competed in certain lines.   But although
they resembled capitalist cartels in exercising considerable powers
over the fixation of market prices, there was a crucial respect in
which they differed from ordinary cartels : the syndicates had no
power to regulate output by *quota* arrangements, since the fixing
of the industrial programmes of enterprises was vested in Vesenkha.
Moreover, even in the matter of prices the State had powers—and
later exercised them extensively—to override the syndicates' prices
with official maxima of its own.

The first syndicate to be formed was the Textile Syndicate,
which was legally registered with Vesenkha as early as February
28th, 1922.   It had a capital of 20 million pre-war roubles, divided
into 10,000 shares which were allocated among the participating
trusts or autonomous factories ; and among the objects listed in
its statute of incorporation were : " (*a*) the co-ordination of trade
activity ; (*b*) the unification of storage and purchases ; (*c*) the
co-ordination of financial activities, especially by organising credit
for the members of the syndicate and by taking measures to facilitate
the settlement of mutual accounts among the members of the
syndicate."   The governing body was a six-monthly delegate
meeting of shareholders, which elected a Managing Board and a
President.   This meeting had authority over the admission of new
members and the fixing of the minimum proportion of their output
which member firms must hand over to the syndicate for disposal ;
while the Board had charge of all current business and the fixing of
sale prices.   Among the bodies eligible for membership of the
syndicate were : " (1) all textile federations, autonomous enterprises, raw material societies, companies and committees, expressing the desire to enter the Syndicate at its establishment, or afterwards, on condition of submission to the Statute and of buying the

[1] Rozenfeld, *op. cit.*, 230.

necessary number of shares in conformity with the Statute ; (2) those joint stock companies and State undertakings which by the nature of their activities are connected with the textile industry and are accepted as members by the delegate meeting of the Syndicate." Later the Syndicate entered the foreign market as a purchaser of raw cotton and wool, and established agencies in U.S.A. and Britain. By 1924–5 it had 50 shareholding members, covering 146 cotton, 86 woollen, 56 linen, 20 silk, 23 hemp and 11 hosiery mills, with a total of 535 thousand workers, some 8 million spindles and 240 thousand looms ; and it possessed 127 wholesale trading branches at home and abroad.[1]

In the metal industry there were, at the outset, three separate syndicates, the Yugometal of the southern area, the Uralmetal of the Urals area and the Agricultural Machinery Syndicate. These conducted sales on a commission basis, paying the trusts partly in cash and partly in materials purchased and supplied to them in return. The agreement in the case of Uralmetal was for the constituent trusts to hand over to it 50 per cent. of their output ; but actual practice varied, some marketing as much as 100 per cent. of their output through the syndicate and others failing to deliver the agreed proportion.[2] Owing to the existence of vertical metal trusts, however, which were self-sufficient in materials and fuel and did their own marketing, and owing to the prevalence of orders from central State departments, only about a half of the trusts in the metal industry were members of syndicates, the remainder working directly to State order or conducting their marketing independently. In the majority of industries by the end of the year at least half of the trusts belonged to syndicates. By the end of 1922 seventeen syndicates were in existence, federating 176 trusts and covering 54 per cent. of the total workers employed in trusts. At the end of 1923 189 out of 360 industrial trusts were syndicated and nearly 80 per cent. of the workers employed in State industry were in syndicated concerns.[3]

---

[1] *The All-Union Textile Syndicate* (Vesenkha, Moscow), 4 seq., 11, 15.

[2] Benediktov, *op. cit.*, 120 seq. In 1923 the three metal syndicates set up a joint bureau ; and two years after this a congress of the industry decided to reorganise into two syndicates, one for iron and steel and one for engineering.

[3] *Russkaia Promishlenost*, 1922, xii ; *Narodnoe Khoziaistvo S.S.S.R.*, 1922–3, 136. About the only failure among the syndicates was the coal syndicate, which laboured under special difficulties owing to delays in payment by its chief customer, the railways. Coming under severe criticism as a " bad, dragging commission-office, of no use to anybody ", it was liquidated in 1923, and the various coal trusts proceeded to form trading organs of their own. Donugol organised a network of some 300 commission-agencies for the disposal of coal. (Benediktov, *op. cit.*, 117–18.)

Indeed, this initiative of industry even went so far as to produce a certain tendency to a new kind of " syndicalism ". At a Congress of Industrial Bureaux in July, 1922, an influential body of opinion from the side of industry proposed the creation of a Council of Syndicates, to which the existing functions of Vesenkha in controlling production programmes, sales, finance and economic legislation should be transferred ; and some criticism was levelled at Vesenkha as a " bureaucratic interference ". Needless to say, this sweeping proposal was not accepted. But the State went sufficiently to meet the views of trusts and syndicates to institute regular joint congresses of representatives of industry and trade and representatives of Vesenkha, to create a permanent advisory council, attached to Vesenkha and representing trusts and syndicates, and to reduce the regulative functions of Vesenkha so as to give it in practice the status of a Commissariat of Industry and Trade.[1]

III

The recovery of industry proceeded from the level of about a quarter of pre-war production at the start of 1922 to about a third of pre-war production a year later. According to official estimates industrial production, which had stood at about 18 per cent. of the pre-war level in 1920–1, rose to 27 per cent. in the following year and to 35 per cent. of pre-war in 1922–3. The fuel industry, which had shown a large advance in the previous year, registered a proportionately smaller increase in 1922–3 : namely an increase of respectively 10 and 14 per cent. in the case of coal and oil. The metal industry showed the large percentage improvement of 70 per cent., but remained at a level of only 10 to 12 per cent. of the pre-war level. The lighter industries, profiting from the earlier improvement in the fuel and transport situation, showed a larger measure of recovery ; linen attaining to about three quarters of its pre-war level, other textiles to between 30 and 35 per cent., and the paper industry to rather more than 40 per cent.[2] Meanwhile agriculture in its recovery had reached a level much nearer to the pre-war than had industry. In 1923 the area sown to grain had recovered to about 80 per cent. of the area of 1916 (within the 1923 frontiers of the U.S.S.R.) and the gross production of grain to more than 70 per cent. of 1916. The quantity of agricultural produce placed upon the market, since it represented a surplus

[1] Cit. *Ind. and Lab. Information*, Sept. 29, 1922.
[2] V. Groman in *Narod. Khoz.*, 1922–3, xii-xiii.

over peasant home-consumption, remained further below the normal level than did the total crop. In pre-war days this marketable surplus (according to the estimate of Professor Prokopovitch) amounted to just over 30 per cent. of total agricultural production. In 1923 it reached less than a quarter of the total production, and amounted in quantity to rather less than 60 per cent. of the pre-war marketed surplus.[1] Thus, the flow of agricultural supplies on to the market was nearer to its pre-war volume than was the flow of industrial goods : compared with their respective pre-war levels agricultural produce was more plentiful than manufactures by about 70 per cent. Accordingly one might have expected *some* rise in the ratio of industrial prices to agricultural prices, compared with the pre-war ratio, to have been normal to the stage of economic recovery that had been reached in the second complete year of NEP. As a matter of fact, Strumilin (using cost in labour-time as a basis) made a rough estimate that each unit of manufactures represented an 80 per cent. greater real cost than a unit of agricultural produce, compared with the pre-war position of each.[2] A difference in the price ratio of this order of magnitude might, therefore, be held to have been warranted by changes in the real-cost situation.

What occurred, however, in the course of 1923 was a movement of the price ratio in favour of industry to a much greater extent than this. Reversing the situation in the first half of 1922, industrial prices in the winter of 1922–3 started to rise relatively to agricultural prices, and continued to rise until in the late summer of 1923 the change in relative prices was not merely to a 2 : 1 but to a 3 : 1 ratio in favour of industry. The terms of trade moved very much further in favour of industrial goods than they had moved in favour of agriculture in the spring of the previous year. This widening of the " price-scissors " was clearly much greater than could be attributed to the disproportion between industrial and agricultural recovery. Although this disproportion remained an important underlying factor, it was not the sole cause, and probably not the main cause, of the price movement ; and an explanation for the " scissors ", at least for the full extent of its widening in the summer and autumn of the year, has to be sought elsewhere.

The unravelling of the " scissors " phenomenon was for some

---

[1] *Khoziastvennie Itogy, 1922–3*, 8–12 ; *Abrégé des Données Statistiques de U.S.S.R.* (Admin. Cent. Stat., 1924), 54–69. In the case of grain all the above proportions were lower than for agricultural production as a whole. See below, page 217.

[2] Strumilin, *op. cit.*, 209, 220 seq. ; also cf. Rozenfeld, *op. cit.*, 431 seq.

time retarded by the overshadowing problem of the rapid rise of the *general* price-level over the year ; and discussion of the latter for some time obscured any discussion of the former. Rapid increase in the price-level had become, of course, a commonplace of many years' standing. But in the past two years, as we have already seen, the rate of depreciation of the paper rouble relatively to the rate of currency emission had actually slowed down ; and with an increase in the total goods turnover and in the volume of goods transactions against which money was used and held the total real value of the currency in circulation had increased. Moreover, as a first step towards monetary stabilisation, a Sovnarcom decree of October 11th, 1922, had authorised the State Bank to issue bank-notes in a new denomination, called the *chervonetz* ; and the issue of the new chervontsi notes began at the end of 1922. The year 1923 accordingly became notable in monetary history for the interesting experience of two unrated paper currencies, the one of strictly limited issue and prized as a means for holding values in stable form, the other still subject to inflationary depreciation.[1] The attention of economists in the first part of 1923 was, accordingly, focused rather naturally on the results of this new monetary experiment.

The fact which began to attract discussion in the first half of 1923 was that, not only did the rate of depreciation of the old paper rouble proceed at a greatly accelerated pace, but the purchasing power of the new chervonetz itself began to depreciate. The aggregate value of the rouble currency in circulation, which had risen to 95 million pre-war roubles in January, 1923, rapidly fell to 76 million in July and to as low as 34 million in October ; while the rise of prices in terms of paper roubles rapidly increased from 23 per cent. per month in the first quarter of the year until it reached 104 per cent. per month during the last three months of the year. Once again the depreciation of the rouble was proceeding faster than the rate of emission. The chervonetz, which at the beginning of the year had exceeded the pre-war purchasing power of 10 gold roubles,[2] depreciated until by October it had lost more than 25 per cent. of its January value.[3] Once disentangled, the causes of this

---

[1] Cf. Yurovsky, *op. cit.*, 86 seq. ; Katzenellenbaum, *op. cit.*, 101 seq.

[2] Presumably because it acquired a premium equivalent to the saving of losses from depreciation of holding wealth in the form of old paper roubles as a result of changing the latter into the new chervontsi.

[3] According to the Gosplan Wholesale Index Number its purchasing power on January 1st was equal to that of 11·08 pre-war gold roubles, by October 1st only 7·47. The latter was no lower than the *existing* value of the gold in 10 pre-war roubles (owing to the fall in the world value of gold in terms of goods). But in terms of

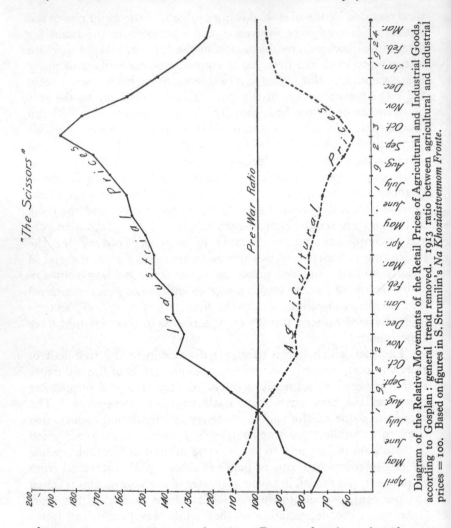

Diagram of the Relative Movements of the Retail Prices of Agricultural and Industrial Goods, according to Gosplan: general trend removed. 1913 ratio between agricultural and industrial prices = 100. Based on figures in S. Strumilin's *Na Khoziaistvennom Fronte*.

phenomenon are not very obscure. But at the time the pheno-menon came as a surprise ; and it is hardly to be wondered at that the explanation should at first have seemed difficult. At any rate, it afforded the principal discussion among economists in the late summer and autumn of the year ; and almost daily for several weeks the *Economicheskaia Zhizn* published the views on the matter of some economic or financial expert or of some leader in

retail prices, the purchasing power of the chervonetz was nearly 20 per cent. lower than this (owing to a widened gap between wholesale and retail prices since the war). (Cf. Yurovsky, *op. cit.*, 94–6.)

the trading and industrial sphere. Not until late in the discussion did the specific problem of the " scissors" secure any appreciable amount of attention ; and even when *Economicheskaia Zhizn* had pointed to the significance of this problem by running a symposium under the title of " Why Industrial Prices are Rising ", many of the contributors to the discussion failed to disentangle this issue from the more general monetary question.

In analysing the problem of the movement in the general price level two main tendencies of interpretation appeared. The first, represented principally by Professor Falkner, assigned chief importance to monetary factors as causes of the price phenomena of 1923, and the second placed emphasis on changes in the goods turnover. Professor Falkner expressed the view that the unexpectedly rapid rise of prices during the second quarter of the year, when usually there was a seasonal slackening of this rise due to the accumulation of money funds in anticipation of grain purchase after the harvest, was too large to be explained in anything but monetary terms. The rise between January and July was correlated fairly closely with an increase of currency in circulation : an increase due to a more liberal financing of trade and industry in order to supplement inadequate turnover capital. Since this had enabled industry to hold larger stocks of finished goods, it had exerted the larger influence on the prices of industrial products.[1]

Monetary factors were certainly the main part of the explanation of the rapid rise of general prices in 1923 ; but it scarcely sufficed to explain the rise of prices in terms of chervontsi roubles as well, and still less to explain the " scissors " rise of industrial prices at a more rapid rate than agricultural. It is clear that the initial effect of introducing the chervonetz was to depress the value of the old paper rouble still further, since by affording a new hoarding medium it tended to cause existing rouble balances to be disposed of rapidly in order to acquire the new currency, and from thenceforth the old depreciated rouble was only likely to be held for the minimum interval of time necessary to effect an exchange transaction. To this extent Gresham's Law was reversed, and good money drove out bad. This was no doubt an important cause of the enhanced rate of depreciation of the paper rouble after April. But its effect on the chervonetz should have been (as we have already seen) to raise rather than to lower its value. Possibly

[1] *Econ. Zhizn*, 1923, 179, 181, 182 ; also *Sots. Khoz.*, Nov.–Dec., 1923, 33–52. Tamarin, of the Salt Syndicate, expressed a similar view in *Econ. Zhizn*, Sept. 15, 1923 ; and Groman in *Nar. Khoz.*, 1922–3, referred to the price rise in the summer as revealing " the effect of credit inflation " (xxxviii).

by the summer chervontsi had been issued in sufficient quantities to satiate the hoarding-demand for stable currency ; and so far as this was the case, one might have expected the special premium placed upon it (compared with its pre-war equivalent) in the early months of the year to disappear. By August chervontsi constituted one half of the real money values in circulation, and there actually developed in that month a small-change famine and a minor tendency to exchange chervontsi holdings for old paper roubles (which formed the smaller denominatinos). But if this is to be taken as a sign that the demand for the new currency unit was strictly limited (owing to its large denominations) and was not extending as fast as its supply, the situation at any rate could hardly have been more than a temporary one. The new unit was only just beginning to penetrate into the countryside, and its use was still expanding quite rapidly. It is true that in June and July there was an increased rate of issue, consequent upon an abnormally liberal crediting of industry. But this was quickly checked, and the issue, even in these two months, can only be regarded as excessive in relation to a goods turnover which had meanwhile declined unexpectedly.[1]

The rival interpretation placed the main emphasis, accordingly, on changes in the goods turnover as an explanation of the novel and peculiar features of the price situation in 1923. Among those who inclined towards this view some placed emphasis on the rise of raw material costs, due to the growing raw material shortage, especially as the reason for the rise in price of industrial goods.[2] The most forceful exponent of this view was Professor Kondratiev who, while stating that price movements throughout the year were a joint result of an " unfavourable conjunction of changes in money circulation, in the level of goods turnover and in the speed of circulation of money ", contended that the principal cause of the changed rate of rouble-depreciation since April was due to a decline in the supply of goods coming on to the market for exchange against money. Prior to March this turnover had been growing. In March the turnover on the Moscow Goods Exchange reached 172 million gold roubles and the turnover of Moscow trusts reached 287 million. By April these figures had fallen to 106 and 140 million respectively—in the latter case a fall of as much as 50 per cent. A similar fall was reflected in the volume of railway loadings. In June there was some recovery, which was correlated with a

---

[1] Cf. N. D. Kondratiev in *Econ. Zhizn*, Sept. 26, 1923, and Scheinman, *ibid.*, Sept. 9, 1923.
[2] E.g. Birbraer in *Econ. Zhizn*, Sept. 6, 1923 ; Prof. Kalinikov, *ibid.*, Sept. 18 1923 ; N. Kutler, *ibid.*, Sept. 12, 1923 ; Prof. Dolgov, *ibid.*, Sept. 14, 1923.

slackened rate of rouble depreciation in that month ; but in July and August a fall in the goods turnover again occurred. Accordingly, a rate of issue of chervontsi which would not have been excessive if the goods turnover of the early months of the year had persisted caused a depreciation in their value in face of a goods turnover which, on the contrary to showing the expansion that could have been reasonably expected, suffered an abrupt shrinkage. The depreciation once started tended to cause industrial and trading institutions to reduce their holdings of chervontsi, which further aggravated the depreciation.[1]

The reason for this foreshortened goods turnover which was advanced by Professor Kondratiev directed attention to the problem of the " scissors ". " The basic cause of the depression of the goods turnover " lay in the fall of agricultural prices and the consequent narrowing of the village market.   In the spring peasant purchasing power normally declined. This year, in view of the low prices of grain which had ruled since the previous October, it had fallen more than usual. The remedy which he accordingly advocated was a raising of agricultural prices and a reduction of industrial costs.

The position was that the existence of terms of trade favourable to the village in 1922 had induced the peasant to expand his sowings and to increase his offers of grain ; and this had had the further result of expanding the market for industrial goods. But in 1923 the terms of trade had swung violently back in favour of the town and against the village ; and this, combined with the usual seasonal influences in the spring, had begun from April onwards, not only to narrow the market for industrial goods in the village, but also to reduce the peasant's willingness to bring his produce to market. If the situation continued, it might lead the peasant to restrict his sowings once again for lack of adequate incentive, or at any rate to refrain from further effort to extend and intensify his cultivation. This prospect, indeed, seemed very likely ; since the terms of exchange between town and village were coming to be as bad as they had been during War Communism. Retail prices for industrial goods in the village often showed a much greater rise than retail prices in the towns. The exchange value of salt and of textile goods had risen more than four times over 1913, but in the villages by much more, sometimes by as much as ten times.[2] A peasant often had to give " nearly the whole harvest of seven or eight dessiatines to buy a pair of boots ", while " a pood of salt

[1] *Ibid.*, Sept. 26, 1923 ; also Sept. 13, 1923.
[2] Kondratiev, *loc. cit.*, Sept. 26, 1923.

costs as much as a pood of meat ".[1] Moreover, it was probably the peasantry (at least the more well-to-do among them) who bore the main burden of inflation, owing to the fact that after selling their crop they tended to hold the proceeds in money form, for a considerably longer period at least than the town worker or an industrial or trading institution. By the autumn of 1923 there were signs that the peasantry were fully aware of this fact ; and in October cotton-growers in Turkestan were refusing to part with their crop except against the new chervontsi notes.[2]

There is, however, a difficulty attaching to Professor Kondratiev's diagnosis, so far as this explained the situation exclusively or mainly in terms of a contraction of village demand. If this factor had operated alone, one might have expected the initial check to the transactions between town and village to have brought its own remedy fairly quickly. One might have expected that trading organs, faced with a slackened market and accumulating stocks of unsold goods, would have reduced their prices, and agricultural prices have shown a recovery (or at least have ceased their fall) as soon as offers of agricultural produce on the market began to be affected by the unfavourable price ratio. A slight break in the " scissors " movement actually did show itself in wholesale prices in May and June, but did not appear at all in retail prices ; and after July the " scissors " (both wholesale and retail) continued to widen at an accelerated speed. The curious feature in the situation that calls for explanation is the continued steep rise of industrial prices in face of what, according to Professor Kondratiev's explanation, was a decline in demand owing to deficient peasant purchasing power. Actually it was after the harvest, when village purchasing power normally showed a seasonal recovery, that signs of a decline in peasant buying were most in evidence. In September, which was nearly the climax of the " scissors ", industrial prices had advanced so far as to cause a general " sales crisis " in industry, bearing many of the signs of crises of over-production so familiar to the capitalist world. Cries were then heard from all sides—and in most cases heard then for the first time—of insufficiency of markets, and of goods accumulating in store unsold and unsaleable. In Baku there was talk of closing down oil refineries because of accumulated reserves sufficient to exhaust the tankage accommodation.[3] In the Ukraine,

---

[1] Editorial in *Econ. Zhizn*, Sept. 20, 1923.   [2] Yurovsky, *op. cit.*, 91.
[3] *Econ. Zhizn*, Sept. 20, 1923. In August these reserves had already reached double the pre-war amount.

Chemugol and Yugosol (salt) were experiencing a depression of sales, and were complaining of " tightness " of credits ; while the Ukrainian Agricultural Machinery Trust reported stocks in the warehouses to the value of 3 million roubles.[1] Sales difficulties were also reported in the case of tobacco ; and Centrosoyus on October 1st had both a large debit balance and undisposable stocks of goods to the amount of three and a half million chervontsi roubles.[2] For large-scale industry in general Dzherzhinsky estimated the total unsold stocks in October to have amounted to some 400 million roubles, or 40 per cent. of annual industrial production.[3]

The principal cause, both of the decline in goods turnover in April, which had been mainly responsible for the summer depreciation of the chervonetz, and also of the extreme spread between industrial and agricultural prices in the summer of 1923, was undoubtedly the monopoly position in the market which State industry now occupied, since the growth of the syndicates, and the extent to which that monopoly power was being used in an attempt to repair their deficiency of working capital which had been so much accentuated during the *rasbazarivania* period in the previous year. In the first twelve to eighteen months of NEP competition had been fairly free. The monopoly given to the co-operatives as purchasers of agricultural produce had broken down in practice and in October, 1921, had been abolished. The trusts in their new-found independence seem in the majority of cases to have refused to deal through Centrosoyus, despite the preference clause in their charters, and to have preferred to purchase their supplies from private merchants or through their own agents ; and in 1923 Centrosoyus relegated dealings in agricultural produce to the background. Of the total sales of State industry in 1922–3 the co-operatives handled only 16 per cent., and of its total commercial turnover only 9 per cent.[4] At the end of 1921 Vesenkha had set up a central commercial department to act as a wholesale intermediary between various State organs ; and this went into the market as purchaser of supplies for industry. Provincial governments proceeded to set up trading companies ; and various central government departments, such as Narcomprod and the Commissariats of

---

[1] *Econ. Zhizn*, Sept. 21, 1923.
[2] *Ibid.*, Sept. 19, 1923 ; I.L.O., *Co-operative Movement in S.R.*, 169.
[3] *Promishlennost S.S.S.R.*, 13–14.
[4] I.L.O., *op. cit.*, 153, 157, 163, 167, 255. Of the supply of manufactured goods to the peasantry the rural co-operatives in 1922–3 supplied no more than 16 per cent.

Health and of Agriculture instituted their own buying departments. These various bodies tended to compete with one another on the market, at the same time as each of them clamoured for monopoly rights in its own particular sphere ; while in the *rasbazarivania* period industrial trusts launched out on the market on their own. But already by the summer of 1922 this situation was beginning to change. Measures had begun to be taken to limit competition between industrial organs and to give State industry a greater degree of control over the market. Although the new syndicates seldom had a complete monopoly, and were subject to the competition of trusts which remained outside the syndicates or of private bodies, they generally controlled a sufficient proportion of the transaction on the market to exercise a large measure of control over price. In the matter of grain and raw material purchases, a conference on the regulation of grain prices in September, 1922, had discussed measures for co-ordinating the work of the various purchasing organisations, and certain tentative agreements were reached which had the effect of limiting competition between them.

As a result, by the beginning of 1923 State industry was in a position to face the peasant buyer and the peasant seller across the market as more or less of a monopolist, and hence to turn the terms of exchange with the village in its favour. This, however, it could only do to any large extent by restricting its own sales on the village market : like any monopolist it could secure more favourable terms of exchange by restricting the supplies which it offered for sale. The result was apparent in the slackened flow of industrial goods on to the market after April, and in the resulting increase both of the general price index in terms of chervontsi and of the spread between industrial and agricultural prices—the " scissors ". To the resulting accumulation of stocks the trusts and syndicates were not particularly averse : many of them welcomed an opportunity of replenishing stocks that had been so sorely depleted a year ago. They anticipated that there would be larger village sales after the harvest ; and they were provided with the means of holding larger stocks by the fairly generous crediting of industry in the spring to meet those insistent complaints from industry of deficient working capital, which had been voiced particularly at the 10th Soviet Congress in the previous December.[1] But this accumulation of stocks necessarily had an upper limit ; and when, partly in alarm at the depreciation of the chervonetz and partly because of the

---

[1] E.g. in the Report on Industry by P. Bogdanov, who prophesied a repetition of the 1922 spring crisis unless credit advances to industry were expanded.

seasonal need to transfer credit into the channels of grain purchase, credits to industry began to be restricted again in August,[1] loud complaints of acute financial difficulties came from industry. It then began to be realised that at existing prices current sales did not suffice to cover current production, let alone to clear accumulated stocks. " Portfolios of undiscountable bills " and warehouses full to overflowing became the general order of the day. That the root of the matter lay in the use by industry of its monopoly power to turn the terms of trade with the village to its own advantage is indicated by the profit situation of industry at the time. The Odessa Leather Trust, for example, was reported to have made a profit of nearly 30 per cent. on its turnover for 1922–3, and the Moscow Silk Trust the enormous figure of 175 per cent. on its capital.[2] For the first time industry during this year showed a profit instead of a deficit ; net industrial profits growing from 52 million roubles (gold) in the first quarter of 1922–3 to 100 million in the second quarter and to 110 and 116 million in the third and fourth quarters of the year.

As soon as this explanation of the crisis was advanced,[3] the representatives of industry began to defend the maintenance of the existing level of industrial prices ; and opinion soon began to be grouped around the two camps of those who favoured a strengthening of the position of industry and of those who advocated that the monopoly of industry over the market should be curbed and the gap between industrial and agricultural prices narrowed by direct State intervention. The advocates of industry claimed that the level of industrial prices was no higher than was warranted by the existing level of costs :[4] a claim that was hard to square with the figures of industrial profits which have been cited above. Professor Strumilin of Gosplan strongly attacked Kondratiev's proposal to raise grain prices on the ground that the relation between agri-

[1] Although credits to industry were restricted at this time ; there was no *general* credit restriction at this time ; discounts by the State Bank actually rising from 83 to 103 million chervontsi roubles between August and October. (*Econ. Zhizn*, Jan. 8, 1924.)

[2] Chubar in *Econ. Zhizn*, Sept. 11, 1923 ; and report in *Econ. Zhizn*, Sept. 2, 1923.

[3] Several of the contributors to the discussion had previously stressed this point, but few had given it the prominence it deserved. Prof. Kondratiev had mentioned it among several causes of the relative depression of agricultural prices (*ibid.*, Sept. 26, 1923), and Prof. Weinstein of Narcomfin had referred to the use of their monopoly power by the syndicates to replenish their turnover capital from the proceeds of higher prices (*ibid.*, Sept. 12, 1923). A representative of Narcomfin at an Economic Conference of the Ukraine in September had also blamed the trusts for holding back goods and raising prices unduly (this was in answer to complaints of credit shortage : *ibid.*, Sept. 21, 1923). Cf. also Vladimirov, *ibid.*, Sept. 13, 1923.   [4] E.g. Prof. Kalinikov of Gosplan in *Econ. Zhizn*, Sept. 15, 1923.

cultural and industrial prices corresponded to the existing relation between the productivity of labour in agriculture and industry.[1] Nogin of the Textile Syndicate actually denied that a real sales crisis existed, and attributed the financial difficulties of the trusts entirely to the sudden restriction of credit by the State Bank.[2] Criticisms of the State Bank and of Narcomfin for their restrictive policy with regard both to credit and to State expenditure became numerous ; and there was an influential body of opinion which urged that the needs of industry would be better served if the Industrial Bank (Prombank), which had been established in October 1922, were strengthened so as to become the leading institution for long- and short-term credits to industry, in place of the State Bank.[3] Connected with this issue was the question of currency stabilisation ; many of the representatives of the " industrial tendency " regarding this policy as premature, and as being the root of the credit stringency which was weakening the financial position of industry.

IV

The policy which was finally adopted by the Government to meet the autumn crisis of 1923 showed little sympathy for the view that the weakness of industry was the root of present difficulties. On the contrary, the monopoly position of State industry in the market was singled out as the principal cause of the trouble. The medicine prescribed, designed to exert pressure on industrial organs to reduce prices, could hardly fail to be unpalatable to the heads of trusts and syndicates ; and there was a certain amount of opposition to the policy among industrialists. In addition to measures designed to reduce industrial prices, efforts were made to raise agricultural prices from their existing low level, partly by an altered price policy in grain purchase and by more liberal credits to grain-purchasing organs, and partly by a development of grain export. By a direct attack on the problem from both sides it was hoped that the blades of the " scissors " could gradually be closed. If industrial prices were reduced while at the same time village purchasing power was increased, the sales crisis in industry

---

[1] *Op. cit.*, 208–9.   [2] *Econ. Zhizn*, Sept. 29, 1923.

[3] The major parts of the capital of Prombank had been subscribed by trusts and syndicates and by Vesenkha, and accordingly industrial interests had predominant control over it. The State Bank had subscribed a small part, but no more than a small part, of its share capital. (Cf. Levin in *Econ. Oboz.*, Nov., 1925, 142–3.)

would inevitably be abated and the trade turnover between industry and agriculture be extended.

The pressure on trusts and syndicates to secure a lowering of their prices was exerted in three ways. First, and probably the most important, was a drastic rationing of credit to industry by the State Bank. This forced industrial and trading organs to unload their stocks on the market, in order to realise the working capital in money form which they could no longer secure by borrowing. Secondly, regulative measures were taken in the form of maximum selling prices through a newly instituted Committee for Internal Trade (*Comvnutorg*). Thirdly, in a few special cases, as a temporary expedient, the policy, known as "goods intervention", of importing manufactured goods at the lower world prices and using them to undercut the prices of industrial syndicates was adopted. But this was confined to a few stubborn cases, and was not adopted as a general policy. The possibility of importing finished goods and so extending this policy of " goods intervention " was limited for two reasons : firstly, by the need to curtail imports and create a favourable trade balance in the interests of currency stabilisation, and secondly by the need to import machinery and essential raw materials, such as cotton, on a considerable scale. There were, indeed, some among those who regarded the under-development of industry as the main cause of the " scissors " who advocated that " goods intervention " should be adopted on a much larger scale to meet the shortage of manufactured goods; and they brought the further accusation against the policy of currency stabilisation that it made any large-scale import impossible.[1]

Although in many cases large profits had been made by industry in the preceding months, it was true that in some cases price reductions could not be carried very far without turning profit into loss ; and on the face of it this seemed to be a vindication of those who saw the root of the trouble in the under-development of industry and not in its monopoly position in the market. But closer examination was to show that the level of industrial costs was abnormally high ; and one result of the policy of lowering industrial prices was to force industry to pay attention to the possibilities of cost-reduction. In some cases an increase in labour costs over pre-war (amounting to 60 per cent. in textiles and to as much as 200 per cent. in the case of iron) was a major factor ; and in one or two cases an increase in fuel costs. But the largest and most general

[1] E.g. Ossinsky in a resolution submitted to a meeting of Party Groups of the Moscow District, Dec. 29, 1923.

rise was in " general " and administrative expenses.[1] Part of this rise in overhead expenses was due to inefficiencies in the administrative apparatus. But the larger part was due to the fact that industry was still operating at a small proportion of its full capacity, so that fixed costs of administration, etc., represented a heavier burden per unit of the reduced output. The remedy for this was to expand output ; and until the bottlenecks in the supply of fuel and materials which retarded this had been overcome, to concentrate production on the more efficient plants. By contrast, a monopoly policy of high prices for industry, by restricting the volume of output which could find a market, was calculated to augment the burden of overhead costs measured per unit of output.

Already in the spring of 1923 the need for concentration of production had been stressed at the Twelfth Party Congress, and a Commission for the Concentration of Industry had been set up (which was later transformed into a Commission for the Revision of Trusts). After the autumn sales-crisis the policy was pushed forward with fresh vigour ; and the policy of concentrating output on the more efficient plants and economising in administrative expenses was the principal motive behind the reorganisation of trusts and the reduction in their number. At the beginning of the year the production " load " in the Leningrad Machinery Trust was as low as 12 per cent., in the Gomza only 20 per cent. In the Ukrainian Agricultural Machinery Trust it was actually only 6 per cent. and at the Putilov works in Leningrad under 5 per cent. These were extreme cases ; and heavy industry was in a worse position in this respect than light industry. But although the textile industry showed a nearer approach to full capacity working, the percentage for the cotton industry as a whole was only 46, while the active factories of the nine chief cotton trusts in February had only 38 per cent. of their spindles in operation. In the glass industry the equivalent figure was 42, in sugar and rubber 33 and 40 respectively, in paper 60, and in leather 69. Tobacco and chemicals were the only industries to approach a 75 per cent. " load ".[2] Even by the end of the year a great deal remained to be done.

But by the beginning of 1924 the policy of concentration had begun to achieve quite considerable results. In face of the autumn crisis the number of active cotton mills was reduced from 131 to 104, and in the case of woollen mills from 64 to 55. In the leather

[1] Cf. Dolgov in *Sots. Khoz.*, March, 1923, 29–30 ; Kaktyn in *Econ. Zhizn* March 31, 1923.   [2] Rozenfeld, *op. cit.*, 222, 225–6.

industry the number of active factories was halved, and in the metal industry the number was reduced from 69 to 39. In the case of cotton and leather this was accompanied by a small reduction in the number of workers, in wool and metal by an actual increase. As a result an appreciable fall in average costs was recorded. In the case of salt there was an economy in overhead costs amounting to 35 per cent., in coal 21 per cent., in iron 24 per cent. and in cotton spinning 18 per cent. Considerable economies in labour costs resulted as well : 21 per cent. in Donugol, 12 per cent. in oil, 29 per cent. in tobacco, 6 per cent. in cotton spinning and 12 per cent. in salt. By the end of 1924 a general fall of industrial costs, amounting to nearly 20 per cent. on the average, had been achieved.[1]

The Thirteenth Party Conference in January, 1924, endorsed the policy of lowering industrial prices, despite some influential opposition, of which more will be said in the next chapter. In March the currency reform was introduced, and the career of the depreciated paper rouble was brought to a close. The issue of the old rouble was discontinued, and in its place the new treasury note, convertible at a fixed rate into chervontsi, was issued by Narcomfin; with the old rouble redeemable until May 10th at the rate of 50,000 paper roubles of 1923 denomination for one rouble of the new denomination. Meanwhile the " scissors " had begun rapidly to close. The over-valuation of industrial goods against agricultural, as compared with pre-war, which had reached a ratio of more than 3 : 1 on the wholesale market at the beginning of October, had fallen to 2 : 1 by the end of 1923, and by October, 1924, had fallen to less than 1·5 : 1.[2] The index number of agricultural prices had risen in the former period from 0·56 to 0·74, while the industrial index had fallen from 1·72 to 1·47.[3] In the course of 1924 the closing of the " scissors " continued. Rye, which in August, 1923, had been priced at 49 kopecks a pood, by August, 1924, sold for 100, and wheat in the same twelve months rose from 92 kopecks to 164.[4] By February 1st, 1924, industrial prices on the average had fallen by some 14 per cent., and by October 1st, 1924, they showed a reduction of 29 per cent. over the peak of the previous October ; this reduction varying from about 40 per cent. in textiles, 35 per

[1] F. Dzherzhinsky, op. cit., 43, 44 ; Rozenfeld, op. cit., 443-4 ; Economic Review, Dec. 14, 1923.
[2] A. K. in Econ. Zhizn, Jan. 9, 1924 ; Krumin in Econ. Oboz., Dec., 1924, 8-9.
[3] Econ. Zhizn, Jan. 16, 1924. In both cases 1913 = 1.
[4] Econ. Review, Nov. 7, 1924. Rozenfeld gives different figures for retail uyezd prices in Oct., 1923, and Oct., 1924 : namely 37 and 80 for rye, 62 and 113 for wheat ; also 35 and 74 for oats, and 29 and 89 for barley. (Op. cit., 449.)

cent. in the food industry and 28 per cent. in mining to 15 per cent. in metal and 6 per cent. in woodworking. At the same time this reduction of costs was accompanied by an increase in output of some 30 per cent.[1] To the extent of about two thirds the price reduction in industry was covered by economy of costs. For the rest, it was at the expense of lowered profits to trusts and syndicates; industrial profits for 1923–4 being substantially lower than the previous year, although when expressed in terms of goods the decrease disappeared. The " scissors " continued to persist, but on a much reduced scale ; and its acute stage, when it threatened a crisis for industry and a swelling wave of peasant discontent, had passed.

This complex issue of policy, in which rival interpretations of the " scissors ", questions of currency stabilisation and credit policy, departmental questions of the State Bank *versus* Prombank and of Gosplan *versus* Narcomfin were interlaced, had already become the dominant question of economic policy by the beginning of 1924. In the discussion before and during the Thirteenth Party Conference it held the forestage. It caused the appearance of a definite minority opposition within the leading organs of the Government and of the Party. It proved to be the most important issue since the Tenth Congress ; it evoked a contest more bitter than that of the spring of 1918 ; and from it stemmed the political tendency known as " the dictatorship of industry ", about which more will later be said. To the historian of the period it has a special interest, since it marked a parting of the ways between two fundamentally different conceptions of NEP and of the whole transition period. Had its outcome been different, Russia would have travelled down a different road in the late 1920's, probably into territory very far distant from where she now is.

---

[1] A. Grintser in *Econ. Oboz.*, May, 1926, 50–1 ; *Econ. Review*, Nov. 7, 1924.

CHAPTER EIGHT

THE PROBLEM OF INDUSTRIALISATION

I

The divergencies of standpoint revealed by the discussion on the " scissors " crisis foreshadowed much more fundamental differences about long-term policy which were to crystallise over the next f₀ w years and eventually to form the basis for serious political antag₀nisms. These differences touched the question of the road that Russian economy was to travel once the immediate task of restoring industry and agriculture after the ravages of war had been completed. Russia presented a situation unique in world history. A country of weakly developed industry and primitive agriculture had been the scene of a Soviet Government, resting on a working class and peasant *bloc*, which had carried into effect the expropriation of its capitalist and landlord class and the socialisation of large-scale industry. If the economy represented by NEP was no more than a transitional halting-place—a " mixed system " combining elements of Socialism and Capitalism and also of primitive subsistence economy and petty production, in Lenin's description of it—the question at once arose as to the direction in which it was to develop. We have seen that Lenin clearly envisaged that " out of the NEP would come Socialism ". But on what kind of time-scale was this development of NEP into Socialism to be envisaged? Manifestly the precondition of it was an expansion of large-scale industry, resting on modern technique and an extensive adoption of co-operative methods by the peasantry. But in a country of undeveloped industry and a backward peasantry, could the completion of any such development be regarded as possible at all, unless the revolution were to spread to other countries and political support and economic assistance were to be forthcoming from the West? Moreover, if to advance was difficult, would not a mere "marking time" prove impossible for long and the very compromise upon which NEP was built involve a recrudescence of Capitalism and a gradual sapping of the socialist key positions that had been already won? The greater such a danger and the quicker the maturing of such retrograde tendencies, the more urgent was

177

the problem of industrialisation, if only as a counter-movement, and the smaller the chance that a slow *tempo* of industrialisation could appear on the agenda at all. There were indeed those who held that there was no solution to this whole problem in a backward country, isolated and alone. Trotsky in particular denied " the possibility of socialism in a single country ", and stated that " the contradiction inherent in the position of a workers' government, functioning in a backward country where the large majority of the population is composed of peasants, can only be liquidated on an international scale in the arena of a world-wide proletarian revolution ", and that " the real growth of the socialist economy in Russia can take place only after the victory of the proletariat in the more important countries of Europe ". From such a standpcint it inevitably followed that opportunism must replace any consistent economic policy : it was a matter of seizing such expedients as the situation offered, alternating between desperate sorties and retreats until such time as the spread of world revolution could bring sufficient reinforcement to one's side.

With the necessity for measures of industrialisation there was general agreement, in order to strengthen the socialist islands in the mixed transitional economy and to furnish the means for fulfilling the promise of the revolution to afford a higher standard of life to the urban working class and to furnish more commodities for the peasantry to buy. Concerning this there was little debate ; and by the Bolshevik Party at least this was regarded as axiomatic. The year 1925–6 was announced as marking the end of the period of restoration—of expanding production on the basis of existing technical methods and equipment—and as ushering in the period of reconstruction—of new investment and construction. In that year industrial production had reached the level of pre-war, while both the agricultural sown area and the gross production of agriculture exceeded nine tenths of the pre-war amount (in the case of grain somewhat lower). The Party Congress in December, 1925, went on record in support of the principle of industrialisation as keynote of the period which lay ahead. This was to state the problem, not to solve it. First and foremost was the question as to the source from which the resources for investment in new construction could be mobilised. This was not primarily a question of labour-power, since here there was an untapped reserve both in the margin of unemployment in the towns and, more important, in the hidden labour reserve of the surplus population in the countryside, which, although reduced by the agrarian reform compared with the

chronic rural over-population of Tsarist days, still existed.   But
the question as to the source from which the means for industrial
construction could be provided remained a serious question as
regards raw materials and sources of fuel and power and as regards
the supply of foodstuffs available to maintain a larger army of
industrial workers employed in factories or on construction work.[1]
The rate of industrial construction was itself conditioned by the
capacity of heavy industry to supply metal for structural steel and
machinery to install in newly built factories; and heavy industry,
particularly engineering, was weakly developed in Russia, while its
recovery had lagged behind that of most other industries after the
deterioration it had suffered during the years of civil war (iron and
steel production was still less than 60 per cent. of the 1913 level).
If the output of Russian heavy industry was to be supplemented
by import of machinery from abroad, then this raised the question
of reviving the pre-war grain export, and brought one round the
circle again to the problem of how to increase the available flow of
agricultural goods from a backward and slow-moving peasant agriculture.   On the answer to this riddle depended the decision as to
whether the rate of industrialisation was to be fast or slow—whether
plans to build up industry by a given amount were to be spread
over a long period or concentrated within the span of a few years.
The latter would place the greater strain upon resources in the near
future, but would the sooner yield the increased productivity out
of which new resources could be found.   The former would involve
a smaller annual investment problem, but at the expense of making
future years less rich in productivity than under the alternative and
more heroic method they could have been.

One aspect of this question was whether priority should be
given in the construction programme to heavy industry, which by
tackling the crucial bottle-neck would the sooner permit the rate of
total construction to be stepped-up, or whether priority should be
given to light industry, which would yield its fruit more quickly in
a larger supply of consumers' goods, with which to raise the urban
standard of life or to tempt more agricultural supplies from the
peasantry and expand the trade turnover between town and
village.[2]   Particular facets of the basic problem were such questions
as whether to place the chief emphasis on the expansion of agri-

[1] See above, pages 24–5, Chap. I.
[2] In technical language, the problem of investment has three dimensions :
there is the question of the amount of labour power and resources to be invested
per unit of time, and there is the time for which those resources are locked up
before they yield their results in final output.   See below, pages 234–5.

culture as the essential foundation for any growth of industry, or the converse ; how far it was safe to give rein to the *kulak*, with the attendant danger of a revived Capitalism in the village, in order to stimulate a larger agricultural surplus ; or whether alternatively to make concessions to foreign capital to aid the development of industry and to give credits for the import of machinery or of commodities which could repair the deficiency of urban and rural markets. In the early '20's an attempt had been made to invite the aid of foreign capital on a limited scale in the form of concession-grants. But we have seen that the policy did not meet with any great success, even at a time when Russia was in much need of economic assistance and was in a mood to pay a specially favourable price to obtain it. With the progress of economic recovery the mood changed. Russia was less in the position of a distress buyer of foreign capital and less willing to bid up the price. Moreover, it had become clear that little short of political capitulation by the Soviet Government, or the concession of control over whole areas to foreign representatives, would suffice to attract long-term capital from abroad in any large amounts. The negotiation of credits to finance current purchases of goods from other countries met with serious obstacles, and at various times was confronted with something like a boycott in foreign financial centres. The possibility of financing an import surplus for a limited number of years by purchases on credit, even at a high rate of interest, seemed to be a very limited one. Even to expand exports with which to pay for additional imports was apt to provoke a political boycott campaign, as with the Press campaigns against Soviet timber and oil and Siberian butter and Soviet " dumping " generally. Evidently Russia had little to hope in existing circumstances from external aid. Unlike other countries which had been suddenly transformed from backward agricultural economies to countries of modern large-scale industry, virtually no assistance could be relied upon from foreign borrowing. The transformation had to be financed from internal resources.

As regards concessions internally to embryo-capitalist elements, the year 1925 had seen the giving of a significant amount of rein to the *kulak*. In that year, the period over which land could be leased, which had previously been limited to six years, was extended to twelve years. The significance of this extension was that it was generally the more well-to-do peasant who leased land allotted to his poor neighbour which the latter was unable himself to work owing to insufficient implements or animals or man-power in his family. Such leasing was also one of the ways in which the peasant who lacked capital could hire implements of tillage, exchanging a portion of his land for a plough-team and for carting facilities with which to cultivate and harvest the remainder. An official enquiry in 1924, for instance, showed that the average holdings of lessors of land was about eight acres, and of lessees about twenty, and that the latter were about seven times as well equipped with livestock as were the former. Further, in the same year the employment of wage-labour on peasant farms, as a regular practice as distinct from occasional assistance at harvest time, was legalised. Doubtless there was no intention of these concessions being more than temporary. Even so we shall see that they were to rouse a good deal of criticism over the next few years, on the ground that they were placing the village and the future development of agriculture under the dominance of a newly revived class of small capitalist farmers. Any extension of these concessions would unquestionably have revived those pre-war economic and social tendencies in the village, an emergence of which might have contributed as much to undermine the position of the Soviet Government and to baulk its socialist policies as extensive concessions to foreign capital would have done.

II

Close on the heels of the measures which had terminated the " scissors " crisis, a trend of opinion became vocal which urged the need to shift the emphasis of policy from the development of agriculture to the strengthening of industry, and the attachment to industry of reserves which would enable an accelerated *tempo* of industrial expansion. Later this was to take the more systematic form of an opposition fraction within the Bolshevik Party, grouping itself round the personality of Trotsky. As early as October, 1923, a document signed by Piatakov, Preobrazhensky, Sosnovsky, Sapronov, Serebriakov, Rosengoltz, and others, called " The Declaration of the Forty-six ", had voiced criticism of the official policy then being pursued to liquidate the disparity between industrial and agricultural prices. A little later Ossinsky, in a statement on " The Immediate Tasks of Economic Policy ",[1] laid the blame for the events of the past year on " the lack of a plan uniting the work of all the branches of State economy ", and " the attempt,

[1] A resolution submitted to a meeting of Moscow Party Groups on Dec. 29, 1923.

instead of aiming at a general economic plan, to regulate economy from the financial centre ". Here he was evidently tilting at the position of influence enjoyed by the Commissariat of Finance and the State Bank and the policy of stricter crediting of industry which they had pursued in the autumn in order to exert a downward pressure on industrial prices. By implication it was a plea for strengthening the hand of Gosplan and subordinating financial policy to an economic policy in which the expansion of industry should have pride of place. From this he proceeded to argue that the leaders of the Party had postulated " a totally incorrect task " in directing that the price policy of industry should be so governed as to leave to industry only " the necessary minimum profit ". Instead, industry should be allowed to retain the profits resulting from cost-reduction ; a stable price being fixed and industry encouraged to obtain " the maximum profit . . . by means of enlarging and perfecting working capacity ". In addition, the official policy was criticised for underestimating the danger of the economic strengthening of private capital, which was in the possession of " 14 per cent. of the wholesale trade, 15 per cent. of the wholesale-retail and 80 per cent. of the small trade ", and had " accumulated large sums in goods and stable values ". Attention should be given to " the fight against private commercial capital, and more financial support should be given to the co-operatives as rivals to private trade ". Finally, with regard to foreign trade Ossinsky advocated a policy of " goods intervention " : of " partial importation from abroad of goods that we lack instead of the official aim of creating a positive trade balance " as a basis for the monetary reform. This " goods intervention " was to apply to consumer goods in deficit supply. As regards the import of capital goods, this would have to be financed by foreign borrowing to permit a " negative trade balance ".

In the same month Trotsky in articles in *Pravda* (subsequently printed as a brochure) had been more explicit on certain of the points that the Ossinsky memorandum had raised. If nationalisation was not to become " an obstacle to economic development " rather than an aid, and if private capital was not " to undermine the foundations of Socialism ", there must be a comprehensive economic plan in the application of which Gosplan must become the dominant organ. " In the struggle of State industry for conquest of the market, the plan is our principal weapon . . . Gosplan should control all the fundamental factors of State economy, to co-ordintate them with one another and with peasant economy. Its central work should be to develop State industry. Precisely in this sense I have had occasion to say that ' dictatorship ' ought to belong, not to finance, but to industry. . . . In other words, not only foreign trade, but also the re-establishment of a stable currency ought to be strictly subordinated to the interests of State industry."[1] At the Thirteenth Party Conference which opened on January 16th, 1924, the discussion was carried a stage further. Both Piatakov and Preobrazhensky followed Ossinsky in emphasising the large rôle played by the private trader, especially in village retail trade, and the need to counter his growth. Preobrazhensky estimated that between one third and one half of the net profits of trade and industry in the previous year had gone into the hands of Nepmen or capitalists, and claimed that the question of whether the Nepman would strengthen his influence with the peasant and form an economic alliance to stem the drift to Socialism, or whether the Workers' State would be strong enough to break such an alliance and convert the private trader into a dependent agent of State industry, was a pressing one. Piatakov attributed the " scissors " crisis of the previous year to the under-production of industry, and the relative surplus of grain, and declared that " the basic method of struggle with the ' scissors ' is an expansion of production ", which required generous State grants and credits to industry. Of the " active trade balance " policy of the Commissariat of Finance, he was particularly scornful : " We need, not gold, but the quickening of our industry and this we cannot do by piling up gold in the hands of Comrades Sokolnikov and Scheinmann."[2]

The so-called " dictatorship of industry " which the group around Trotsky was pressing at the Thirteenth Party Conference turned out to represent more than a temporary coincidence of opinion on certain *ad hoc* proposals. It represented a consistent line of policy, having a connection with certain fundamental assumptions that were only to be fully revealed at a later date. Substantially it conceived of further development as only possible in the existing situation in Russia if industry were to expand at the *expense* of the peasantry ; and this conception, implicitly at least, was to become the basis of the tendency known as the Left-wing opposition. It had its fullest and clearest formulation in a theory expounded at the time by Preobrazhensky in a paper communicated to the Communist Academy. The fundamental economic question

[1] *Novy Kurs*, 71.
[2] *Econ. Zhizn*, Jan. 17, 1924, Jan. 18, 1924 ; *Pravda*, Jan. 18, 1924, Jan. 19, 1924. Sokolnikov was Commissar for Finance at the time, and Scheinmann was Chairman of the State Bank.

of Socialism in the existing state of Russia was concerned with the
sources and methods of what he termed "primitive socialist
accumulation " by analogy with the " primitive accumulation " of
Marx, which had prepared the stage for the maturing of industrial
Capitalism.   The growth of State industry depended upon the
accumulation of capital in the hands of the State ;   and, apart
from loans from abroad, the only two sources from which such
accumulations could be derived were the surplus production of
State industry itself, due to its own inherent productivity (i.e. the
difference between the value of its production and what it paid out
in wages and salaries), and what it could derive from the " exploitation " of small-scale private economy by extracting from the latter
a greater sum of values than was given to it of industrial products
in exchange.   The less advanced was a country in its industrial
development, the greater the need of industry for capital accumulation to strengthen its position, and at the same time the greater the
reliance it would necessarily have to place on the second in the
absence of the first source of accumulation.

It was to this second source, which in contemporary conditions
he argued must be the essential source, that he gave the name of
primitive socialist accumulation.   This he defined as " the accumulation in the hands of the State of material means obtained
chiefly from sources lying outside the State economic system ".
" In a backward agrarian country this accumulation is bound to
play a very great rôle.   Primitive accumulation predominates con-
spicuously during this [transition] period ;   and we must therefore
designate this whole stage as the period of primitive or preparatory
socialist accumulation. "   These outside spheres of economy he
termed " colonies " ;   and the necessary economic basis of the
transition period was a relation of " exploitation " between the
" metropolis " of State industry and its surrounding " colonies " ;
the former drawing in " surplus value " from the latter, whereby it
expanded the basis of industry, its productivity and the possibility
of living on its own surplus, until finally petty private economy
was crushed out and " engulfed " in socialist economy, as the rise
of capitalism had crushed out the peasant and the small craftsman
and turned them into proletarians.[1]

The methods of this accumulation were two in number.   First,

[1] E. Preobrazhensky, "The Fundamental Law of Socialist Accumulation" in
Viestnik Komm. Akademia, vol. VIII, 59 seq., 69–70, 78 seq.   It seems distinctly
misleading for Prof. Karlgren to imply that this theory of "colonies" was the
official theory of the Government in its dealings with the peasantry. (*Bolshevist
Russia*, 163.)

the " colonial " areas might be subjected to direct taxation. But this had very definite limits : it might be evaded ; it was more easily felt and more likely to cause political complications. Second, and more important, was the method of market exchange between State industry and the " colonies ". Through the monopoly position of State industry on the market and by measures of " Socialist Protectionism ", adopted by the State for the express purpose of encouraging socialist industry, the rate of interchange between State economy and its " colonies " could be turned to the advantage of the former. Since this would operate by " altering and partly cancelling the law of [labour] value "—that is, by causing the product of a unit of labour or effort in State economy to exchange for the product of several units of labour in the colonies—it involved an " exploitation " of the latter by the former, and the creation of " surplus value " for the benefit of socialist accumulation. In other words, the " law of socialist accumulation " implied for Russia a monopoly price policy for State industry ;[1] and Socialism would develop according as the monopoly position of State industry and measures of State Protectionism succeeded in turning the rate of exchange between town and village in the former's favour. The only limit to this policy was the necessity for State industry, because of its backwardness, to make use of private capital for the time being and the necessity not to kill the goose so long as gold eggs were essential to socialist accumulation. " Monopoly capitalism," wrote Preobrazhensky, " leads to the creation of monopoly prices for the products of industry in the home market, gains a surplus profit in consequence of the exploitation of the small producers, and thus prepares the ground for the price policy of the period of primitive socialist accumulation. But the concentration of the whole of the big industries of the country in the hands of a single trust, that is in the hands of the Workers' State, increases to an extraordinary extent the possibility of carrying out such a price policy on the basis of monopoly, a price policy signifying another form of taxation of private production."[2] The economic " dictatorship of industry " over the peasantry was to become the Appian Way to Socialism.

This whole conception was open to a number of obvious objections. Firstly, if operated at all on the scale that Preobrazhensky's

[1] Preobrazhensky wrote : " I deliberately avoid saying ' increased prices ' since taxation in combination with sinking prices is not only possible but would in our case certainly attend sinking or unaltered prices. This is possible for the reason that when the cost price of goods is reduced the selling price is not reduced by the whole amount of the reduction of cost price, the difference being added to the funds of socialist accumulation." (*Op. cit.*, 80.)

[2] *Ibid.*, 78 seq. ; also cf. Preobrazhensky, *Novaia Economika*, 203 seq.

theory implied, it was calculated to rupture that *smytchka* between working class and peasantry that had lain at the basis of Lenin's conception of social development and had formed the corner-stone of NEP as a transition between Capitalism and Socialism. Politically it would have estranged the peasantry and even have run the risk of provoking an eventual *Vendée*. Economically it might well have had the effect of reducing rather than increasing the total volume of real resources which agriculture supplied to industry. The experience of War Communism had shown that the possibility of squeezing the peasant was a limited one outside a short period, and that even if he were subjected to compulsion as regards the amount he sold, he very soon reacted by reducing the amount he sowed. In this case the exploitation policy would have defeated its object of increasing (in real terms) the accumulated resources at the disposal of the State ; and the logic of the policy was progressively to apply measures of open coercion upon the peasantry and to return to the requisitioning policy of War Communism, with all the perils which this entailed. Secondly, it seems to have underestimated the latent sources of productivity that could be mobilised within State industry and trade in the shape of the more intensive use of under-employed labour and rationalised organisation and working methods ; although admittedly in the circumstances of the middle '20's these possibilities were strictly limited ones. Finally, it did not envisage the possibility of developing collective forms of agriculture on any considerable scale ; but neither did the majority of proposals which were canvassed prior to 1928.

It was on the first of these criticisms that the opponents of the policy of the " dictatorship of industry " chiefly concentrated. Bukharin and Rykov, who were at this time spokesmen of the official policy, both reiterated that the unfavourable terms of exchange between industrial and agricultural products were at the root of the " scissors " crisis, and that to turn the ratio of industrial and agricultural prices to the peasants' disadvantage as a deliberate act of policy would bring a return of this crisis, if not of an actual " grain strike " on the part of the village. Bukharin, in a reply to Preobrazhensky, appealed to Lenin's principle of the *smytchka* and denounced the theory of " primitive capital accumulation " as " completely trade unionist[1] and guild-like in character ", and underlined the danger that a monopolist policy for industry would lead to " parasitic decay ". " It would be nonsense on our part," he wrote, " to renounce the advantages of our monopolist position. But while

[1] He was evidently referring here to the sectional exclusiveness of craft unions.

utilising these advantages, we must take care not to diminish the powers of absorption of the home market, but to increase these powers. This is the most important point. The next is that we must utilise every advantage gained in such a manner that it leads to an extension of the field of production and the cheapening of production, to the reduction of cost prices, and consequently to ever cheaper prices in each successive cycle of production."[1] Rykov, in replying to Ossinsky, stated that reliance must be placed on an expanded trade turnover between industry and agriculture to provide the means for the expansion of industry. " There are many capital outlays," he said, " which must be postponed until such time as industry has won the possibility of increasing its revenues on the basis of an extended peasant market and increased mass production. . . . Every kopeck which can be supplied for the reconstruction of industry must be expended for this purpose without the slightest delay. But this must be done by forming an alliance with the peasantry, and not by fixing prices which the peasantry could not possibly pay. The conquest and satisfying of the peasant market will bring about socialist accumulation." Regarding private trade, he decried alarmist estimates of the situation. While it was true that private enterprise controlled four fifths of retail trade, the reverse proportions held of wholesale trade, where the State and co-operatives were firmly entrenched. Hitherto the State had been unable to afford the capital to engage in trade on an ambitious scale, and the private trader had accordingly performed a service to State industry which weighed more heavily in the balance than any profit he secured out of it. In some rural districts " the conditions obtaining are so Asiatic that there are not only no retail shops but not even pedlars. Where such a state of affairs obtains, the private retail business is naturally a step forward in comparison with present conditions, and it is manifestly impossible that State Capitalism should set itself the task, after only three years of NEP, of attaining a state of affairs where only a small number of State organs are required, forming an immediate connexion between the factory and the consumer."[2]

A subordinate but associated matter which came to the forefront in the following year was the wage policy of industry. What relation was there to be between rises in money wages and in industrial output ? And how was any gain in the productivity of industry to

---

[1] Printed in *International Press Correspondence*, vol. V, No. 5, 40, 45.

[2] Speech at meeting of Moscow Party Groups, Dec. 29, 1923, reported in *Econ. Zhizn*, Jan. 2, 1924. Cf. also Rykov's reply to the discussion at the Thirteenth Party Conference, *Pravda*, Jan. 19, 1924.

be shared between improving the standard of life of industrial wage earners, the demands of capital accumulation and the peasantry ? As a consumer of industrial goods the wage earner would gain from a lowering of industrial prices, which was the official policy, even if his money earnings remained constant. But as a consumer of foodstuffs (which bulked very large in his expenditure) he would only stand to gain if agricultural prices were reduced as well ; and the recent tendency had been in the contrary direction. It was on the relation between changes in wages and changes in output per worker that Dzherzhinsky forced a decision when he succeeded to the Presidency of Vesenkha in 1924. Revising the estimates previously made of the relation between wages and labour productivity, he pointed out that up to the end of the economic year 1923–4 money wages had risen more rapidly than output per worker; the former having doubled between October 1922 and October 1924, while the latter had increased by only 45 per cent.[1] Productivity still remained appreciably below pre-war ; and an announcement of Vesenkha had recently pointed out that to produce a pood of cotton goods now required 3·2 man-days as against 2·14 before the war. It was to the resulting rise of labour costs that Dzherzhinsky attributed a large part of the high industrial costs, of which there had been complaint, and the financial difficulties of industry. This matter of industrial costs was of crucial importance for the problem of capital accumulation. As soon as the industrial " load " had reached a normal figure and factories were working to full capacity with their existing equipment, the question of reconstructing and extending fixed capital would arise ; and unless industry could find the resources with which to do so out of the margin between its product and its outlay, there would result "a failure of industrial output to meet demand or to swallow up the surplus population of the village ".[2] A special commission established by Vesenkha to study the matter revealed a conflict of opinion about the causes of low productivity between representatives of industrial trusts and of the trade unions. The report was a compromise document which attributed the low productivity to a series of factors including the deterioration of plant, the swollen number of auxiliary employees, reduced skill and intensity of work on the side of the workers and a relaxation of discipline. But the report had focused attention on the importance of improving productivity, and Dzherzhinsky had squarely posed the question of the relation between changes in productivity and changes in

[1] Rozenfeld, op. cit., 352.   [2] Dzherzhinsky, Promishlennost S.S.R., 8, 11.

wages. At the beginning of 1925 a campaign for the rationalisation of production was launched, stress being laid equally upon economies of management and upon improvement of working methods. Already in the last quarter of 1924 the labour costs as a percentage of the total cost had registered a slight fall, and in the course of the next half-year productivity per worker achieved an appreciable advance while real wages remained constant.[1] A year later the position was further complicated by a rise in food prices in the spring of 1926 (for reasons which we shall presently consider), which had the effect of reducing *real* wages by 10 to 15 per cent.[2] This raised the sharp issue for discussion as to whether in such circumstances money wages should be raised or kept stable.

Another problem affecting the urban standard of life was the problem of unemployment. In the middle and late '20's unemployment was large and was tending to increase in the two years prior to the Five Year Plan ; and the total of those seeking employment in the towns, registered and unregistered, may well have reached a figure of two million. True, only part of this represented unemployment among the regular army of industrial workers who had been in regular industrial employment in the past. Much of it consisted of newcomers from the village and of seasonal workers who remained in the towns in the "off" season, instead of returning to their villages as formerly. In other words, it represented the seepage into the towns of part of the chronic rural over-population which had for decades been a symptom of Russia's economic backwardness—agrarian overpopulation which Strumilin estimated as standing in 1927–8 at between 8 and 9 million.[3] Only a large and rapid expansion of industry would suffice to make any appreciable inroad upon this large reservoir of surplus labour.

Nevertheless, the unemployment situation was a serious one, which continually exercised trade union circles in these years, and together with the slowness of wages to rise (since Dzherzhinsky had emphasised the need to relate wage increases to productivity) it was responsible in these years for a large amount of criticism in trade union circles against the management of industry and against official

[1] Rozenfeld, *op. cit.*, 361. This progress was checked, however, after the summer of 1925, and in Oct., 1925, labour cost as a percentage of total cost again slightly exceeded the figure of Oct., 1924. In his report to the Fourteenth Party Congress in Dec., 1925, Stalin also pointed out that " the development of our industry in existing circumstances can only take place if we accumulate the amount of surplus profits necessary for the financing of industry. If we were to raise the wages of labour unduly, no such accumulationu of surplus profits would be possible." (*Leninism*, 1928, Eng. ed., 386.)
[2] Statement of Tomsky at the Seventh Congress of Trade Unions.
[3] S. G. Strumilin, *Sotsialnie Problemi Piatiletka, 1928–9—1932–3*, 8.

policy. The Seventh Trade Union Congress in December, 1926, had drawn serious attention to the fact that unemployment was on the increase ; pointing out that, although industry had absorbed nearly half a million workers in the past year (excluding seasonal workers), yet the number of registered unemployed had increased by 100,000 and now exceeded the figure of a million. Since registration at employment exchanges of the Commissariat of Labour was voluntary, and since half the registered unemployed were trade unionists while the trade unions themselves had records of a million unemployed among their own members, the total of all unemployed, registered and unregistered, was estimated by Schmidt, the Commissar of Labour, in his report as probably reaching 2 million. Of these one half was "accounted for by the agricultural or urban excess population" ; 21 per cent. was classified as skilled workers, 18 per cent. as intellectual workers and 51 per cent. as unskilled. Unemployment among young persons was also described in the report as " deplorable ", 14 per cent. of those registered being under 18 years of age. Nearly two years later, in June, 1928, the Central Council of Trade Unions was reporting an increase in the number of trade unionists unemployed of from one and a half to two million in the course of the past winter. Even excluding seasonal workers, the figure stood at a million, of whom 25 per cent. were skilled workers, and a similar proportion had been unemployed for more than one year.[1] It was largely with the intention of meeting this situation that the announcement of October 25, 1927, was made to introduce the 7-hour working day in the course of the following year (without reduction in wages), the shorter working shift being combined with an extended working of multiple shifts. In this way it was hoped that greater employment and production would be obtained on the basis of the existing limited stock of industrial equipment—that existing machinery and buildings would be more continuously utilised so that a larger volume of employment and output would become possible. But the new system of shift-working was cautiously introduced and met some serious difficulties, sometimes coming up against the bottle-

---

[1] *Trud*, June 13, 1928, June 14, 1928. An enquiry among their own unemployed members was undertaken by the trade unions and showed that the average age of the unemployed was 31 years and the average duration of unemployment was nine months. Unemployment was proportionately much higher among women workers than among men. To qualify for unemployment benefit (which was administered through the trade unions) required that an applicant should have had a certain minimum term in employment ; and the benefit varied in amount between a fifth and a third of the normal wage, according to the category of the worker. New entrants into the labour market and seasonal workers with only a small record of previous employment were not eligible.

neck of limited supplies of skilled workers and of technical and supervisory staff, sometimes of inelastic supplies of raw materials (there being a fairly general complaint in these years of " shortage of working capital ").[1] At any rate, its effect in expanding the demand for labour did little immediately to reduce the dimensions of the unemployment problem, which was only to disappear and to give way to labour scarcity as a result of the large constructional activity of the first two years of the First Five Year Plan.[2]

III

The rejection of the opposition proposals at the Thirteenth Party Conference and the endorsement of the official policy of expanding exchange between town and village by lowering industrial prices proved to be only the first round of the fight. At the Fourteenth Party Conference and Congress in 1925 the opposition returned to the attack ; and this time Zinoviev and Kamenev, who had previously attacked the line of Trotsky, Ossinsky, Radek and Preobrazhensky, now joined forces with them. By this time the opposition had closed and organised its ranks considerably. It conducted independent propaganda of its own and its members were to face the charge of breaking the unity of the Party in action by forming a separate fractional organisation within the Party.[3] A new note of bitterness had crept into the discussions, surpassing any such note that there had been in the discussions of 1923. The new opposition did not constitute an entirely homogeneous grouping ; probably less now than formerly. But they had in common now as then an emphasis on the priority to be given to the rapid development of industry, if need be at the

---

[1] Cf. Report of Kiubyshev at the Seventh Congress of Trade Unions : " Lack of working capital " was the " real evil from which almost all branches of industry are suffering " (*Trud*, Dec. 14, 1926). Because of the difficulties mentioned above there was later an abandonment of the attempt at a universal continuous working week and a reversion in many cases to two-shift working. Cf. Engineer Ts. Kunikov in *Plan. Khoz.*, 1940, No. 9, 29 seq., who speaks of technical difficulties regarding repairs, etc., and low output on the night-shift.

[2] Even in the first year of the First Five Year Plan registered unemployment grew by 14·5 per cent. over the previous year, and the " strictly unemployed " (i.e. those who had previously been in industrial employment) by 8·4 per cent. Trade union figures showed a stabilisation of the position in this year ; and the growth in this year was largely due to the influx of persons seeking employment for the first time. But it was really only with the drastic stepping-up of the rate of industrial construction in the 1929–30 control figures that the reverse movement set in. Cf. *Kontrolnie Tsifri Nar. Khoz. na 1929–30*, 239–40.

[3] This charge resulted in the removal of Kamenev from his post as Commissar for Trade and Zinoviev from his position among the inner Political Bureau of the Party.

expense of agriculture ; an unwillingness to countenance any concessions to the peasantry ; and a distrust of the possibility of solving
the problem of socialist accumulation in Russia except by heroic
and extraordinary means.

At the Fourteenth Congress in December of the year the general
report on economic policy was presented by Stalin, and on his
report the principle of industrialisation met with fairly widespread
agreement. Moreover, it was to be industrialisation placing primary
emphasis on heavy industry.[1] The resolution (which was adopted
by 559 votes against 65 with 41 abstentions) enunciated as the
leading principle governing economic construction " that the Soviet
Union be converted from a country which imports machines to a
country which produces machines, in order that by this means the
Soviet Union in the midst of capitalist encirclement should not
become an economic appendage of the capitalist world economy,
but an independent economic unit which is building Socialism " ;
and it called for " a fight against disbelief in the construction of
Socialism in one country, as well as against attempts to regard our
industrial undertakings as State capitalist undertakings ". It was
on the policy towards the village that opposition criticism at this
time chiefly focused, and Zinoviev lamented the strengthening of
the *kulak* and denounced the recent concessions in the village as a
" retreat ". With this he coupled a critical appraisement of NEP
as a system which was far from being socialist, and which had never
been intended to continue as a stable system for any considerable
time, but only as an expedient to be pursued for a short time.
Perhaps this betrayed a certain hankering after the methods of
War Communism. At any rate, the reply made by Bukharin was
that NEP was not only a retreat, but represented a " regrouping
of forces and an advance upon a reorganised front line ", and that
the urgent need of the present lay in " the extermination of the last
remnants of War Communism ", especially in policy towards the
village.

Earlier in the year, a popular slogan had been issued by the
Party, " The Face to the Village " ; and the Fourteenth Party
Conference (which had preceded the full Congress) had called for

---

[1] In a draft plan of industrialisation for 1925–30, drawn up in 1925 in Vesenkha
under the initiative of members of the opposition (generally known as the OSVOK
Plan), very high rates of investment in industry had been provided for in the immediate future (though falling in later years) ; but no provision had been made for
expanding the specific weight of heavy industry relatively to light industry. In
fact, the plan was apparently based on the assumption that the existing proportion
between these two groups of industry should remain approximately constant ; and
the textile industry was to receive one sixth of all industrial investment.

" the elimination of the remnants of War Communism in the village ". Soviet officials in the country districts, still carrying over the traditions of the civil war period, too frequently adopted sergeant-major methods to get things done, ordering things by command and bullying those who would not be regimented. Village officials were often of inferior calibre, particularly in out-lying areas, tending to be stupid and inflexible, and sometimes petty tyrants and bribe-takers. " Our comrades in the country," said one Communist writer of the time, " are still too much inclined to command, to give orders, still strive too much to become the village ' boss '." Said another : " Some have become bureaucrats and ' command ' in their district in a most arrogant fashion, whilst a small section have become positively corrupt."[1] Arbitrary ap-pointments from above, which had been in force in the special circumstances of civil war, continued in many cases ; so that village Soviets, often lacking democratic character and influence, became dead wood and of little interest to the peasantry, in some cases being boycotted by them. A story was told of a peasant remarking at a Congress : " If they ordered us to elect a horse to the village Soviet, we should be compelled to do so."[2] In yet other cases a handful of rich peasants were able, by means of personal influence or bribery, to dominate the Soviets for their own ends. Stalin summed up the situation with characteristic bluntness. " Up to the present, in a number of districts the elections to the Soviets in the countryside have not been real elections but empty bureaucratic procedures, dragging in ' deputies ' by means of various kinds of artfulness and pressure on the part of a narrow group of rulers, fearful of losing their power. As a result, the Soviets risk being transformed from organs near and dear to the masses into organs foreign to the masses. . . . The old electoral practice in a number of districts is a relic of ' War Communism ', which must be abolished as a harmful practice, a practice rotten through and through."[3]

Following the decisions of the Fourteenth Conference, instruc-tions were issued by the Central Committee of the Party to its members in the villages to abolish forms of pressure on Soviet elections and of appointment from above, to restore the responsi-bility of Soviet delegates to their electors and to attract non-party

---

[1] A. Martinov in *Communist International* (N.S.) No. 9, 55 ; and article on " Tasks in the Rural Districts of U.S.S.R.", *ibid.*, No. 12, 19.

[2] Karlgren, *Bolshevist Russia*, 14.

[3] Address at Sverdlov University, June 9, 1925 ; published originally as *Bolshevism : Some Questions Answered* ,37, and later reprinted in *Leninism*, Eng. ed. 1928, 318.

peasants into active work in the co-operatives, in peasant mutual-aid committees, village libraries and club-rooms, etc. At the same time a certain "purge" of Party members in the countryside and of officials was undertaken, eliminating corrupt elements,[1] drawing in new blood and developing the constructive side of their activities in the direction of educational and economic work and activities among the village youth. Fresh elections were ordered in some 40 per cent. of the local Soviets which had previously been elected by a small minority of the village population. Directions were given that administrative measures for combating the *kulak* and the attempt to regiment the middle peasant must be abandoned, and emphasis was placed on "economic" measures instead, by which reference was chiefly intended to the strengthening and extension of agricultural co-operation.

The opposition feared these concessions to the village, and not only the concessions on leases and hired labour granted to the *kulak*. They feared that the peasantry as a whole was being given too large a share of the cake, and that the town proletariat and industrialisation would alike suffer in consequence. These fears were encouraged by certain difficulties in the grain collections in 1925, and by the appearance of what came to be known as a "goods famine"—the now familiar symptoms of industrial goods being in short supply relative to the demand. In the previous spring, at the Fourteenth Party Conference, Kamenev had actually joined with those who had stressed the danger of "rekindling the class struggle in the village", and declared that such a suggestion, based on "overestimation of the *kulak* danger", was more harmful in the conditions of the moment than the opposite error of "under-estimating the *kulak* danger" and wishing to give still more leash.[2] In his opening speech to the Fourteenth Conference he had

---

[1] Cf. Maurice Hindus, *Broken Earth*, 106–8, where the conversation of villagers is reported about chairmen and treasurers of neighbouring Soviets and other officials who were imprisoned, and some shot for corruption; Communists always being treated much more severely for such offences than non-party persons. One of the peasant grumbles was the number of new offences for which the new authorities inflicted punishment: "If you give someone in the Soviet a gift, no matter how small, maybe just to be nice to him, they put you in gaol. If you whip your child, they send an agent down to investigate you and threaten to lock you up. If you go to the woods, far, far away for a load of wood in summer, they put you in gaol." (*Ibid*, 193.)

[2] In his report in December, Stalin referred to these two deviations as equally "bad", but added that in existing circumstances it was more important that the Party in its struggle against these two deviations "should concentrate its fire upon the second deviation" because the tendency among Communists was to take the easier road of going for the *kulaks* root and branch instead of following the far more complicated plan of isolating the *kulaks* by entering into an alliance with the middle peasant. (*Leninism*, 1928 ed., 413.)

stated : " The removal of all obstacles in the way of the development of productive forces in the countryside, the disappearance of every vestige of ' War Communism ' from the village, the abandonment of those administrative methods which are inconsistent with the development of the productive forces in the rural districts, and finally the finding of honest Soviet officials for the village administrative apparatus—these are the concrete tasks now confronting us." Even Zinoviev had denied that the new proposals on agrarian policy represented " a swing to the Right " : " there is no swing to the Right ; it is the Leninist continuation of the policy pursued by our Party since 1917 and before this " ; and he proceeded to quote from a draft made by Lenin for an article in 1921 : " Ten to twenty years of the right relations with the peasantry and we have won on an international scale, even though international revolution should follow a slow pace." But in December they were declaring that concessions to the peasantry had gone too far, and that the consequential strengthening of the *kulaks*, who had now secured a dominant position in rural markets, was responsible for the decline in grain collections and the curtailment of grain supplies to the towns and for export, which was endangering the further expansion of industry. The *kulak*, it was now said, had shown himself sufficiently strong to defeat the State grain-purchase policy by holding back his supplies for a higher price ; and the benefits of the high price of grain had gone to enrich the *kulak* still further and had benefited the poor and middle peasants scarcely at all. The industrial goods famine was adduced as evidence of the lagging of industrial development and of the tendency for non-socialist elements in the transitional " mixed system " of NEP to develop faster than the socialist elements—of the danger that private accumulation might outdistance socialist accumulation. Proposals were made for doubling the capital allocation to industry for the coming year by means of a raising of the agricultural tax and a raising of the factory price of industrial goods. Said Smilga : " If the tax is not to play a stimulating rôle in encouraging peasant offers of grain, then the only means of attracting a surplus of grain from the peasants is the satisfaction of his needs in town goods."[1] Early in 1926, Trotsky said : " All reports indicate that our industry will meet the harvests of 1926 without any stocks of goods, which may mean a repetition of present difficulties on a larger scale. In these circumstances a good harvest may become a factor which does not accelerate the rate of economic development in the direction

[1] *Plan. Khoz.*, 1925, No. 9, 10-14.

of Socialism, but on the contrary will disorganise industry and exacerbate the relation between town and country, and in the town itself between consumers and the State."[1] There were even murmurings to be heard about an approaching Russian Thermidor, and of the State power becoming the instrument of an unholy alliance between bureaucracy and a reviving *kulak* class.

The official reply to the opposition consisted in a denial that the growth of the private trader and of the *kulak* was anything like as great as the opposition sought to portray. Stalin quoted figures to show that in internal trade " the share of the private capitalists is diminishing and the share of the State and co-operatives is increasing : for the year 1924–5, the share of the State was 50 per cent., that of the co-operatives 24·7 per cent. and that of private traders 24·9 per cent." In the following year Rykov quoted figures of the Central Statistical Department covering 35 provinces to show that, while it was true that the more well-to-do peasant with over ten dessiatines of land and four head of cattle had increased in the past three years, at the same time the numbers both of landless peasants and of those with less than two dessiatines (between five and six acres) and with less than two head of cattle had decreased. Moreover, nearly two thirds of all peasants possessed between six acres (approximately) and thirty acres, as compared with less than half three years before. What therefore had been occurring was a raising of the level of the whole village, including the village poor, and not a dichotomy of the village along class lines.[2]

At the time of the Fifteenth Party *Congress* two years later the opposition, led by Trotsky, Kamenev and Zinoviev, returned to the attack in two trenchantly worded " Counter-Theses ". Rich peasant farms, it was declared, now constituted 15 per cent. to 25 per cent. of the total number (varying according to region) and covered between 25 to 45 per cent. of the cultivated area and possessed 40 to 60 per cent. of the machinery. The easier terms of land-leases introduced in 1925 had benefited predominantly the *kulak* class : three quarters of land leased was concentrated in the hands of 16 per cent. of the richer farms, and in the past two years the cultivated areas in the hands of the richer peasant had more than doubled. Even the co-operatives were becoming perverted by *kulak* influence. At the same time there had been an appreciable increase in the number of landless persons in the village who were forced to undertake wage-labour to meet their subsistence needs.

[1] Cit. in Rykov's report to Fifteenth Party Conference.
[2] In report to Fifteenth Party Conference.

Moreover, the enrichment of the *kulak* had enabled him to hoard large stocks of grain : stocks which the Counter-Theses estimated at 800 to 900 million poods—a quantity appreciably greater than before the war—of which between a half and two thirds was in the hands of one sixth of the richer farms. These stocks placed the *kulak* in a dominant position in the grain market. But this was not all. The holding back of grain from the market threatened a crisis in the exchange between town and village, reduced the amount of grain available for export and hence the possibility of importing machinery for industrial construction, and lowered the urban workers' real wage by enhancing the price of food. It was this that was responsible for the slow rise in the workers' standard of life, of which the opposition made particular complaint, and for the rate of industrial construction provided for in the draft Five Year Plan being, in the opinion of the opposition, much too small. This in turn by retarding the growth of industrial production accentuated the shortage of manufactured goods, including the shortage of goods available to village markets, and so aggravated the crisis in the turnover between town and village in a vicious spiral. The lowering of industrial prices, to which official policy had given priority, could only properly follow as a result of increased capital accumulation and the re-equipment of industry ; whereas at present it simply reduced capital accumulation by lowering industrial profits. To strike at the root of this situation, the opposition proposed a sharp turn of policy towards an offensive against the *kulak*, of which the first instalment should be a compulsory grain loan of 200 million poods[1] levied on the richest 10 per cent. of peasant farms. With the proceeds of this loan grain exports could be increased and the import of industrial equipment in return be augmented (possibly doubled) in order to increase the rate of industrial construction. " Those who reject this way are left with the sole alternative of abandoning the foreign trade monopoly, of resorting to foreign capital for export and import, and of importing foreign goods for the village in exchange for the export of the accumulated reserves of grain."[2]

As we shall see in the following chapter, there was a good deal in this diagnosis which corresponded to the facts of the existing

[1] This amounted to between one third and two fifths of the annual pre-war grain export and to more than the average annual grain export for 1925–6 and 1926–7.
[2] Counter-Theses of the Opposition on the Five Year Plan and on Work in the Village, published in Discussion Supplements Nos. 3 and 5 of *Pravda*, Nov. 5, 1927, and Nov. 17, 1927. The signatories to these Theses were Trotsky, Zinoviev, Kamenev, Smilga, Rakovsky, Yevdokimov, Peterson and Muralov.

situation ; and there was not much inclination (except among the
" Rights ", of whom we shall speak presently) to dispute the suggestion that the time had come for an attack on the *kulak* to be
made. Molotov in his reply at the Fifteenth Congress stated that
" the question is not whether it is necessary or not to make a
' sharper attack ' on the *kulak*. It is obvious that we must, and
there is nothing to dispute about here. What we are concerned
with is the best method of conducting this attack. The Party
must find a new answer to it."[1] Here the Counter-Theses offered
no solution : merely an emergency expedient of dubious practicability. According to the estimates of the Central Statistical Office,
the figure of peasant grain reserves was not 800 to 900 million
poods as stated in the Counter-Theses, but 700 million : a difference approximately equal to the proposed compulsory loan. Moreover, it was denied that these reserves, although admittedly large
and recently on the increase, were predominantly in the hands of the
kulaks. Their geographical distribution, it was stated, suggested
that they were " for the most part safety reserves, predominantly
stored up in districts subject to drought ", and there was no correlation in the various districts between the size of grain reserves per
head and the preponderance of rich farmers.[2] While it was
admitted that the *kulak* influence had grown, the picture drawn by
the opposition was accused of being both exaggerated and one-
sided. The picture of *kulak* domination was obtained by the
unjustifiable device of including all peasants with holdings of more
than six dessiatines in the *kulak* category, whereas farms up to eight
or even ten dessiatines usually employed wage-labour only as
supplementary labour at certain seasons of the year, and could not
be classed as regular employers of labour. What could be properly
classed as *kulak* farms still only covered (according to one writer,
Yakovlev) little more than 10 per cent. of the arable area, and some
15 per cent. of the grain surplus. Molotov stated that the percentage of farms which both leased additional land and employed

[1] Report to Fifteenth Party Congress, *Econ. Zhizn*, Dec. 22, 1927, and *Rabochaia
Gazeta*, Dec. 23, 1927. In the summer of the following year M. Molotov pointed
out that " the unavoidable difficulties arising from the rapid rate of industrialisation, from the increased income of the agricultural population, especially of the
well-to-do *kulaks*, and from the mistakes of our planned economy have undoubtedly
created advantageous conditions for the *kulak* at the present time. . . . The rise of
the village during the last few years and especially the rapid growth of the *kulaks*
have gradually increased the demand for industrial products in the rural districts.
. . . The peculiar difficulties of our economic situation are therefore enhanced at
the present moment by . . . a disparity between the demand and supply of industrial
products and the increased activity of the *kulaks* against our grain supply policy."
(Speech at the Plenum of the Moscow Committee of the Party on Jan. 30, 1928.)
[2] Goldenburg in *Pravda*, Nov. 17, 1927.

hired labour was under 5 per cent. ; the amount of leased land amounted to no more than 7 per cent. of the total area ; and most of the leasing was done by middle peasants. "Capitalist elements", he said, "are making very slow progress indeed in the village at the present time. Still, it must be observed that the process has been noticeably more rapid during the last few years " ; and " on the whole the process of the growth of the capitalist elements in the village has been strengthened of late years", in some districts such as the North Caucasus the percentage of *kulaks* having doubled since 1923 (although still constituting less than 6 per cent. of all farms). At the same time, however, socialist elements in the village had " grown to a much greater extent " ; one half of the goods supplied to the village, for example, being in the hands of co-operatives and two thirds of all agricultural products which reached the market passing through State trading organs or co-operatives.[1]

IV

The other tendency to treat the situation as one where increasing concessions to Capitalism would have to be made, both inside and outside the country, also developed early in the 1920's, although it was not to crystallise in the form of the Right Opposition, grouped round Bukharin, Rykov and the trade union leader Tomsky, until the end of the decade, when the programme of industrialisation was drastically accelerated and a renewed assault on the *kulak* danger was made. In 1923 Krassin had urged a much more liberal concessions policy to attract foreign capital and the floating of a foreign loan of 300 to 500 million gold roubles ; and at one time he had even advocated a relaxation of the State monopoly of foreign trade to facilitate a more rapid import of goods. This view was one which certain economists of the old régime, who were working as " experts " in the Commissariat of Finance, had been pressing. For example, Professor Haensel wrote at the end of 1923 that " the transformation of industry demands a swift and grandiose flow of new capital ", and that the " voluntary flow of [foreign] capital, even at the price of sacrifice and the yielding of privileges is easier than the achievement of a large excess of exports over imports ",

---

[1] Yakovlev in *Pravda*, Nov. 5, 1927 ; Molotov in Report to the Fifteenth Party Congress. The Counter-Theses had made considerable use of an investigation undertaken by Gaister for the Communist Academy into a sample of 1200 peasant farms. Gaister subsequently wrote disclaiming the interpretation placed upon his figures. (*Econ. Zhizn*, Dec. 5, 1927, Dec. 6, 1927.)

involving the " pumping out of every ounce of surplus over bare
necessaries " :[1] a proposal that was described by another writer
as amounting to " an auction sale of Russia to foreign capital ".[2]
The view that the economic situation was so serious that " an
auction sale " was the least of evils was reinforced by a pronounce-
ment of the so-called " Baku Group " which created some stir at the
time.   This group was headed by Medvediev and Shliapnikov,
who in 1921 had figured predominantly in the Workers' Opposition ; and at the end of 1924 there appeared a sharply worded
criticism of Soviet policy in the shape of a " Letter to Baku " over
the signature of Medvediev.   According to Medvediev, it was
inevitable in the conditions of NEP that the old class differentiation
in the village should reappear.   The only way to restrain it, and to
meet the relative overpopulation in the village that it occasioned,
was a rapid industrialisation of the country to absorb the surplus
population.   " To conclude that we should be able to extract
enough capital for the development of our extinct industry from
taxation would be to console ourselves with hollow illusions.   To
flatter ourselves that we could raise this capital ' out of pennies '
would be to add to the old delusion another. . . .   The Government
should take energetic steps to raise the necessary means by foreign
and internal State loans and by granting concessions with greater
loss and greater sacrifice than the State is prepared to take on itself
for granting credits.   Great material sacrifices to international
capital, which is prepared to build up our industry, would be a
lesser evil than the condition into which we might drift in the next
few years."

Cousin to this viewpoint was the opinion that since industrial
growth was limited by agriculture, the stimulation of peasant agriculture by extensive concessions must have priority, even if this
should result in giving rein to the revival of petty capitalism in the
countryside.   From time to time between the " scissors " crisis and
the end of 1925, a policy of so-called " goods intervention " had
been canvassed : a large-scale import of consumers' goods from
abroad to supplement the deficient supplies that home industry
was able to furnish, and by placing them on village markets in
particular to coax more products from the peasantry and thereby

---

[1] *Sots. Khoz.*, Nov.-Dec., 1923, 70, 75.   Presumably Prof. Haensel, in speaking
of an " excess of exports ", must have been referring to an excess over the import
of *consumers'* goods in order to enable an import of capital goods.

[2] Bronsky, *ibid.*, 28–9.

increase the trade turnover between village and town.[1] Here there was no very clear-cut division between the two wings of the opposition tendency, and at various times this proposal was included in the policy advanced by supporters of Trotsky : for example, it was advanced by Ossinsky at the end of 1923 and again by Smilga in 1925. Its advocacy was particularly associated with the name of Sokolnikov, at one time Commissar for Finance, who undoubtedly represented at the time the Right tendency although he later joined forces with the Zinoviev-Kamenev-Trotsky *bloc*. At the Fourteenth Party Congress in 1925 he advocated that the programme of industrialisation should give priority to the expansion of light industry and hence should rest on the continued import of capital goods from abroad : a proposal which was sharply criticised by Stalin on the ground that " if we remain at this stage of development in which we do not ourselves manufacture the means of production, but have to import them from abroad, we cannot have any safeguard against the transformation of our country into an appendage of the capitalist system ".[2] Another spokesman of this view was Shanin, who wrote that " the supposition that in the immediate future our industry can develop at the same pace as agriculture is essentially wrong. As a matter of fact this problem is insoluble, or at least cannot be solved without a large import of capital or a sudden forcible arrest of the development of agriculture."[3] The implication of this view, presumably, was that, on the contrary to what the advocates of " dictatorship of industry " were urging, priority must be given to the development of agriculture, since Russian industry could only expand on the basis of imported equipment (not merely for the time being, but for a long period), and this import of machinery would only become possible on the basis of an enlarged surplus of agricultural produce for export. The logical outcome of this was the policy being advanced by Professor Kondratiev, who in 1924 was the author of a five year plan for 1923–8 issued by the Com-

---

[1] One school of thought among certain agrarian economists in State institutions, especially among those associated with Prof. Kondratiev's Conjuncture Institute, was in favour of relaxing the foreign trade monopoly so as to encourage a revival of the export trade in agricultural products. Cf. the remarks of Prof. L. Litochenko on the need for an export market to provide a higher standard of life for the village and afford both the inducement and the means to increase production for the market, especially of more intensive crops. (*La Situation Économique de l'Union Sovietique*, 44–5.)

[2] Reply to discussion at Fourteenth Congress, published in Stalin, *Leninism*, 1928, Eng. ed., 427.

[3] Shanin in *Bolshevik*, 1926, No. 2, 70; also Shanin in *Econ. Obozrenie*, Nov., 1925, 25–32.

missariat of Agriculture of the Russian Republic. In this he stressed that " at the centre of attention stands everywhere the creation of a rationalised agriculture ", and advocated generous financial assistance to peasant economy and greater freedom for land leases and the hiring of labour by well-to-do peasants—in other words, an accelerated revival of *kulak* farming.

About the same time[1] Bukharin in an unguarded moment pronounced the slogan, addressed to the peasantry, of " enrich yourself ". This was widely taken to imply that the official policy (of which Bukharin was then a spokesman) rested on the encouragement of private accumulation of capital and the enrichment of a *kulak* class, and was seized upon by critics of the Left as a sign that Soviet policy was treading the pre-war Stolypin road. The slogan was quickly denounced by the Central Committee of the Party,[2] and the interpretation placed upon it was disowned by Bukharin. Later events were to show, however, that the phrase was not entirely accidental, and that it was a foretaste of a tendency which was to harden into a distinctive line of policy. In the course of the next three years there were a number of statements made both by Bukharin and by Rykov which implied the conception that it was possible for the transition from the " mixed system " of the NEP, with its economic backwardness and low level of technique, to Socialism, based on developed industry and collective forms of production, to occur without any break in essential continuity. Bukharin in a pamphlet entitled *Building Socialism* spoke simply of strengthening and using State industry " as a commanding height, and without undue haste proceed[ing] to round up the seething, unorganised economy under socialist influence ". Peasant agriculture and State industry would develop along parallel lines, the growth of each aiding the growth of the other. In the progressively expanding turnover of trade between agriculture and industry there was no " objective necessity " for a crisis to occur, provided only that economic planning was successful in maintaining a proper " equilibrium " of growth—maintaining certain essential proportions in the growth of industry and agriculture. Even the *kulak*, it seemed, had a constructive part to play in this smoothly continuous transition, so long as his relative weight in the whole, and hence his influence, was reduced as a result of his " encirclement " by a network of agricultural co-operatives which were to expand progressively at the same time. Peasant agriculture, with all its individualist tendencies and its germs of revived capitalism, would

[1] In a speech in April, 1925.   [2] Cf. Stalin, *op. cit.*, 449–51.

grow into Socialism through interpenetration with an all-embracing system of co-operative credit and co-operative trade.

Events were to show that a necessary corollary of this notion of development was that the rate of industrialisation should be a low rather than a high one ; since in the interests of the postulated conditions of equilibrium, the rate of investment and construction must always be adapted to the existing condition of agriculture and its surplus product. The re-emergence of sharp symptoms of crisis in the trade relations between town and village in the course of 1927–8 (which will be described in the next chapter) seemed to belie the practicability of a smooth and gradual development within the confines of the NEP. As in 1923, the debate started in earnest on the question of diagnosis. Was the trouble due to the strength of the *kulak*, against whom an offensive would have to be waged before further progress was possible ? Or was it a sign that industrialisation was straining at the short leash which the existing state of agriculture allowed it ; and if so, had the answer to be that industrialisation must toe the line, or that novel and exceptional measures must be taken to transcend the present limits of agriculture ? At first the tendency was to stress the mistakes in planning, and in particular in State policy towards the grain market, which had undoubtedly aggravated the difficulties. But when in 1928 the difficulties of 1927 were repeated in an even graver form, it was clear that something more fundamental was wrong.

In 1928–9 the decision was taken to accelerate the pace of industrialisation and to put renewed restrictions on the *kulak*. The growing inclination of those adhering to the " Right tendency " was to attribute the prevailing difficulties to the fact that the *tempo* of industrialisation had been forced to an inadmissible degree and to distrust the new measures against the *kulaks* as having deleterious effects on agricultural production. Shanin, whose views on the relationship between agricultural and industrial development we have already quoted, spoke of the proposed *tempo* of industrialisation as resting on " inflationary financing ".[1] Bukharin in a series of articles entitled " Observations of an Economist ", written in the autumn of 1928,[2] took as his starting point the view that " the essential part of the task of working out a plan of national economy " is the determination of " the conditions for the correct co-ordination of the various spheres of production, or in other words the condi-

---

[1] L. Shanin in *Plan. Khoz.*, 1928, No. 10 ; and some remarks of S. G. Strumilin in reply, *Plan. Khoz.*, 1929, No. 1, 106–7.

[2] Published in *International Press Correspondence*, Oct. 19, 1928, Oct. 26, 1928, Nov. 2, 1928.

tions of *dynamic economic equilibrium* ", and that any " crisis-like factors disturbing the process of reproduction . . . can only arise from a failure to observe the conditions of economic equilibrium ". Under the guise of an attack on the " super-industrialisation " proposals of Trotsky, he proceeded to show that the real cause of present difficulties was that industrial construction was increasing too fast for the conditions of agricultural production (or at least would not bear any further increase), as witnessed by the fact that foodstuffs, consumption goods, and building materials were all alike in deficit supply, compared to the demand. This did not mean that industry was backward compared with the growth of agriculture : on the contrary it meant that the plans of industrial construction were higher than the existing supply of raw materials and of foodstuffs would permit. Further, the high rate of investment itself " created a record demand for industrial goods " which industry was unable to satisfy : " industry in its development encounters the limits of this development ". " The failure of industry to satisfy the demand of the village " was not evidence of a too slow rate of development of industry. Quite the contrary was true : " Whilst industry develops at a tremendous pace, whilst the population increases rapidly and the needs of this population increase steadily, the amount of grain remains unaltered ", and any "further acceleration of the speed of development of industry depends to a considerable extent on agricultural raw material production and agricultural export", and any further capital investment " must be effected with due consideration for all those factors which guarantee a ' more or less crisis-free development ' and better co-ordination". " Any overstraining of capital expenditure will lead in time to the stoppage of enterprises already begun ; it will react unfavourably on other branches in every direction, and it will finally *retard the speed of development.* . . . Our bow is at a very high tension. To increase this tension still further, and to increase the ' goods famine ' still more, is impossible. . . . The acuteness of the goods shortage must certainly be alleviated. . . . The first steps in this direction must be made at once."

The implications of this document were plain, if cautiously expressed. In form it did no more than underline a passage in the resolution of the Fifteenth Congress which had said : " It is incorrect to take as a starting point the demand for a maximum pumping over of means from the sphere of agriculture into the sphere of industry ; for this demand would mean a political rupture with the peasantry as well as an undermining of the home market, an undermining of export and an upsetting of the equilibrium of the whole economic system."[1] But the whole tenor of the argument was a warning against a rapid *tempo* of industrialisation and an emphasis on the need to adapt industrialisation to the demands of the peasant market. In two letters to the central committee of the Party in July and November, 1928, Frumkin, however, was more explicit. The position in the village was deteriorating, the village being hostile to the government and " the main mass of the middle peasantry being left without any hope or any prospects ". His advice was that " we should not hinder the *kulak* undertakings in their production ", that " the State farms should not be extended over-hastily ", and that in the coming year a smaller sum should be invested in industry than the 800 million roubles officially proposed.[2] At the same time Stalin was speaking against " the Right deviation " as " leading to the development of conditions which are requisite to the restoration of capitalism in this country "; and in the following April he was delivering a more forthright attack on Bukharin and the " new opposition " as the main danger to be combated. " This new period of reconstruction of the whole national economy on the basis of Socialism," he declared, " gives rise to new class changes . . . it demands new methods of struggle, the regrouping of our forces. . . . The misfortune of Bukharin's group is that it is living in the past, that it fails to see specific features of this new period and does not understand that new methods of struggle are needed. Hence its blindness, its bewilderment, its panic in the face of difficulties."[3]

In a situation that was standing still, with historical forces frozen into immobility until this or that economic programme could be drafted, discussed and implemented, such differences as were debated in that quinquennium of controversy prior to the First Five Year Plan might have seemed to be academic issues, with no very decisive criterion by which one viewpoint could be declared more right than the others. Was it not all a surprising amount of smoke and noise over the difference of a few hundred million roubles of capital investment, or about whether a rich peasant

---

[1] The resolution had, however, gone on to say that " it would be incorrect to renounce altogether the use of means drawn from agriculture for the furtherance of industry ", since " at the present time this would mean a retardation of the speed of development, to the detriment of the industrialisation of the country ".

[2] Cf. Stalin's Report at the November Plenum of the Central Committee of the Party.

[3] Speech to Plenum of Moscow Party Committee, Oct. 19, 1928, and speech to Plenum of Party Central Committee, April, 1929. Bukharin and Rykov were members of the Political Bureau at this time but represented a minority viewpoint.

should sign a lease for twelve years or only six ? What heated the debate and gave these differences in policy a more crucial significance than on first inspection they might seem to have had was the fact that the situation was a rapidly moving one. The situation was still unstable, even if less so than in the first eight months between the Soviet Revolution and the Civil War. This meant, not only that what was practicable and what impracticable to do depended upon a fine diagnosis of the existing situation, but that an apparently small difference of emphasis in policy might make all the difference to the direction in which the economic system actually moved. If one failed to notice the strength of a current, or swam too weakly against it, one might be carried in a direction quite opposite to that in which one intended to go, to a distance that might make eventual return many times more difficult or for a lengthy season impossible. A decision between a low and a high rate of industrialisation was not a matter simply of temperament or of relative " preference " between the present and the future, nor was it only a matter of the limits set by the peasant market. It was a matter of the strength of contrary tendencies at work which were making for a revival of Capitalism, and the rate at which State industry would have to be strengthened if these tendencies were to be counteracted. This implied as a special corollary that the question of *dating* a particular answer was of prime importance. As is the case with problems of military strategy, the same answer could be wrong at one time and correct at another. Many have been puzzled by the fact that those who sponsored a renewed offensive against the *kulaks* and a hastened *tempo* of industrialisation in 1928 were largely the same persons as had condemned this when it had been the policy of the opposition in 1925. If it was wrong in 1925, was it not wrong also three years later ; and if right in 1928 was not its condemnation in 1925 thereby proved to have been a mistake ?[1] But it does not follow that what may have been practic-

---

[1] This view is expressed, for example, in E. Strauss' *Soviet Russia*, 156–7, 160–1 ; where it is stated that if the offensive against the *kulak* had come earlier, in 1924 or 1925, the path of industrialisation would have been enormously easier and smoother. " The policy of *laissez-faire* in the village and of benevolent neutrality towards the *kulaks* as proprietors had landed the Soviet Power in a first-class crisis [in 1927–8] . . . had permitted the *kulaks* to become powerful enough to challenge the Soviet Power. . . . Delay of this task [of dealing with the *kulak* problem] for two or three precious years . . . increased its difficulties and reduced its beneficial results." (*Ibid.*, 160–1.) Against this view Stalin argued in a speech in Oct., 1928, that at the earlier date the peasants were not experienced enough or in a mood to take to collective farming, nor were the members of the Party capable of organising it successfully. Moreover the State did not possess the material resources necessary to make this counter-weight to the *kulaks* a success, while industry was insufficiently developed to supply the new farms with machinery and tractors. (Cf.

able in 1928 or 1929 was necessarily practicable at an earlier date when both industry and agriculture were weaker, or that what circumstances may have made imperative in 1928 was demanded also at a time when the *kulak* influence over the village and the grain market was smaller. When we add to such considerations as this the uncertainties of a changing international situation and the estimated probability that the intervention-years of 1918–21, with foreign armies standing on Russian soil, would return again, the unleisured note of tension in these discussions and the belief that there was one correct solution to the problem of industrialisation, and that all other answers were dangerously mistaken, is more easily appreciated.

Leninism, 1940, Eng. ed., 272–3 ; also cf. 323–5.) In 1925 Stalin had said : " We introduced NEP knowing perfectly well that this involved the reinvigoration of capitalism, the reinvigoration of the *kulaks*. . . . Yet directly the *kulaks* so much as poke their noses round the corner, many comrades turn pale with fear and shout ' Help ! Murder ! Police ! ' So pitiable is their panic that they quite forget the middle peasant. Yet our main task in the village at the present time is to win over the middle peasant . . . to isolate the *kulak* by entering into a firm alliance with the middle peasant." (Report to Fourteenth Congress, Dec., 1925.)

CHAPTER NINE

THE AGRARIAN SITUATION ON THE EVE OF THE FIRST FIVE-YEAR PLAN

I

The rate at which agricultural production could expand and afford a growing supply of raw materials for industry and foodstuffs for industrial workers appeared as the crucial question in economic discussion in the second half of the decade : an issue upon which all other hopes and possibilities depended. An important fact, affecting agricultural productivity, was that the Land Reform of 1917–18 had achieved, not only the break-up of the large estates, but an equalisation of peasant holdings themselves and also a considerable increase in the number of peasant farms. The proportion of cultivated land in peasant hands had risen from 70 per cent. to 96 per cent. But the number of peasant households between 1914 and 1928 had risen by more than a third, so that the average size of a peasant farm was little if any larger than before.[1] Largely owing to the strength of Left S.R. influence in the villages at the time of the carrying out of the Land Decree, only a small proportion of the land was reserved for large-scale State farms.[2] The 4000 to 5000 State farms (*Sovkhozy*) that existed during the civil war period covered no more than about 5 million acres. But they apparently leased as much as a half of this land to individual peasants ; and a considerable number of these farms were abandoned in the early '20's. A further 3 to 4 million acres was (in the spring of 1921) in the hands of some 14,000 collective farms (*Kolkhozy*). These were generally no larger than about 100 to 120 acres (and in the Ukraine smaller even than this), and often included no more than 10 to 15 families. The majority were not very successful, a considerable proportion of them dissolving

---

[1] In 1914 it was estimated that the number of peasant households was between 18 and 19 millions ; in 1928 there were more than 25 million. Meantime the rural population had increased by less than 15 per cent., so that the increase of farms was mainly due to a larger number of persons successfully claiming the right to hold land (including land grants to previously landless families).

[2] See above, pages 80–1.

annually and a high proportion of their members leaving; and in the early '20's the number of these collective farms also declined. Later there was some improvement; and in 1927 their number was about as large as it had been at the end of the civil war, and they covered an area of 5 to 6 million acres (with a crop area of about 2 million). State farms at this date numbered some 3000, and covered between 3 and 4 millions of crop acreage. But on the eve of the First Five Year Plan State and collective farms together supplied less than 2 per cent. of the total grain crop and covered little more than 1 per cent. of the cultivated area.[1] Agriculture was overwhelmingly small-scale individualist peasant agriculture; and it was upon this type of economy that the government and industry depended throughout this period for raw materials and for foodstuffs.

The equalisation of peasant holdings themselves was shown in an increase in the importance of the *seredniak*, or middle peasant, type of holding, with a corresponding decrease in the importance alike of the large holding and of the smallest type of holding (of the *bedniak*) that was insufficient to furnish the means of livelihood for a family. Holdings of more than about 27 acres had fallen from some two thirds of the total area of peasant land to about two fifths by the middle '20's; while farms of between 15 and 27 acres embraced nearly one half of all peasant land, instead of one third before the war, and they constituted one half of all peasant holdings.[2] In the black-earth region the larger type of holding covered only 10 per cent. of the cultivated area as against 25 per cent. at the time of the 1905 revolution; while many who had previously been landless were now in possession of allotments of land and had even risen into the ranks of the middle peasantry. In 1927 in the chief grain areas only 6 per cent. of peasant families were altogether lacking in crops, against 15 to 16 per cent. in 1917 in Russia proper and 20 per cent. in the Ukraine. With regard to livestock and agricultural equipment, however, the equalisation was less marked. Here considerable inequalities remained. More than a quarter of peasant families possessed no working animals and had to work their land with rented teams; and an investigation undertaken by Gosplan in 1929 revealed that in the main grain-producing regions the richest 10 per cent. of the peasantry owned between 35 and 45 per cent. of the agricultural means of production and some

---

[1] V. P. Timoshenko, *Agricultural Russia and the Wheat Problem*, 107, 127.

[2] Expressed as a proportion of the rural population, Chernomordik speaks of the *seredniaki* as composing 66 per cent. in 1926–7, and the *bedniaki* 20 per cent. the former constituting " the central figure of agriculture ". (*Op. cit.*, 115.)

30 per cent. of the draught animals.[1] It was on this inequality of equipment that the *kulak* was still able to fatten, despite the agrarian reform of 1917.

A report made by Yakovlev of a tour of investigation undertaken in the course of 1924 furnishes some illuminating details of the situation in the village during the period of NEP, and at the time attracted a good deal of attention. His description of a typical *volost* in the Tambov *gubernia* affords a vivid close-up picture of that embryo of a reviving class differentiation which survived in the village of the NEP period, despite the equalising tendencies of the 1917 land reform. One peasant in the *volost* of Znamenka had owned before the war some 150 acres, traded in timber and owned a bakehouse. In 1924 he no longer had the bakehouse, but trading remained his chief means of support, and he advanced credits to his clients to the sum of 150 roubles monthly. Another trader, Yefimov, who kept a private shop, had added to his own 30 acres another 30 from his poorer neighbours. Another owner of 150 acres had built a mill, employing in it a man who worked 12 to 14 hours a day for a wage of 15 poods of rye flour a month. A certain Skorotchkin was a trader in horses and spent most of his time in riding to neighbouring towns and villages in pursuit of his trade. To these persons the poorer peasantry presented a sharp contrast. A certain Denisov, in return for the loan of a plough and horses to plough two thirds of a dessiatine, gave a quarter of a dessiatine to his richer neighbour. Another after he had hired a horse for ploughing and carting retained only 13 out of a harvest of 35 poods per dessiatine, and of this remainder the agricultural tax took a half. A widow, Vieselova, with no means of cultivating the land allotted to her, had to pay 3 poods of grain and 35 quarts of milk to another to plough her two dessiatines for her ; for the sowing of it she had to pay 8 poods, and for the reaping of the harvest she had to part with another pood of grain. In addition she had to pay 21 poods in tax ; so that by April she was herself destitute of food and was forced to sell her only calf. Her son who worked for a rich peasant received a bottle of lamp-oil in payment for two days' work.[2]

In a second village, Voronsov, conditions were considerably different : a difference which the investigator attributed to the

[1] M. M. Wolf, *Puti Rekonstructsii Selskovo Khoziaistva v Piatiletie*, 11. This author hastens to add that not all of these upper ten were to be identified with *kulaks*, and that the latter probably composed only 4 per cent. of the farms. At the other end of the village 30 per cent. of the households in the main grain regions had only between 5 and 7 per cent. of agricultural means of production.

[2] Y. Yakovlev, *Nasha Derevnia*, 19–25.

existence here of a small but flourishing co-operative society, organised on the initiative of the local teacher. This society not only performed functions which made a Yefimov or a Skorotchkin superfluous, but gave special aid to the poorer peasants and spared them the need of resorting to the money-lender and of hiring their land and their labour to the *kulak*. In three months alone the society had given loans amounting to more than 5000 roubles to 34 peasants to purchase seed and horses and stock. It had a store which sold more cheaply than the private trader ; it loaned horses to its members ; and it gave subsidies from its profits to a number of poor widows. The majority of those who benefited from its credits were poor peasants, the remainder being middle peasants: of the 34 obtaining credit for seed a half had originally had no horses, but 10 of these had managed to buy horses with the aid of its credits since the formation of the society.[1]

This type of rural economy remained moulded in the traditions of the pre-1917 Russian village : individualistic, primitive in its methods of tillage and rootedly conservative. Its productivity was still low and seemed destined to remain so. The spread of agricultural co-operation and the efforts of the Commissariat of Agriculture were responsible for some improvement. In numerous cases a consolidation of scattered strips in the open-field system was achieved ; and redistribution of land was generally prevented from occurring more frequently than once every nine years. Some departure from the old three-field system to improved systems of rotation was in progress. This was the case particularly in the western Ukraine, with an introduction into the rotation of potatoes and beet and the extension of hay on crop land ; while winter wheat (which usually has a higher yield unless it suffers from " winter killing ") was being increasingly introduced along with winter rye in the rotation. In 1926 the Commissariat of Agriculture was able to claim that in the course of the past four years some 600,000 farms, covering nearly 10 million acres, had transferred to improved crop rotation ; over 400 villages in the province of Kaluga having transferred *en bloc* in 1924 and in the county (*uyezd*) of Volokolamsk only 83 villages retaining the traditional three-field rotation.[2] The agrarian expert Professor Oganovsky estimated that by 1927 some 10 per cent. of peasant farms in the western districts had introduced improved rotation, and that by 1932 this proportion could

---

[1] Y. Yakovlev, *Nasha Derevnia*, 48–9.
[2] L. Kamenev in *Plan. Khoz.*, 1925, No. 1, 8. Cf. also Tcherchinsky in *International Review of Agricultural Economics*, Oct.-Dec., 1924, 501, 536 seq. ; Rykov to Plenum of Central Committee of Party, Nov. 25, 1928.

be expected to have increased to 20 or 25 per cent. In the grain-deficiency region north of the black-soil belt hay was being increasingly introduced into the rotation and the dairy industry was being developed, together with the growing of potatoes and flax. Generally in the north and north-west the movement towards diversified farming was more pronounced than in the black-earth zone. Even in the south, however, there was some extension of maize, sunflower, tobacco and the sowing of leguminous hay. But in the central black-soil region in 1926 early ploughing of fallow was only practised on some two fifths of the fallow,[1] and in the Ukraine on little more than a half. Although in the middle Volga from 80 to 90 per cent. of the land under spring wheat was ploughed in the previous autumn, in the southern steppes of the lower Volga and in the north Caucasus the proportion was less than half. Double ploughing remained uncommon, except in Siberia, the Urals and Central Asia, where natural conditions had given it something of a tradition. Most sowing was by hand, and only in the extreme south and south-east were seed-drills at all common. Nearly a half of all harvesting and over a third even of all threshing was still done by hand.[2]

Progress was occurring and was likely to continue ; but the rate of progress seemed destined to be slow : too slow to increase the yield of agriculture at a speed at all commensurate with the needs of a growing urban population and a growing industry. If industry had to march in step with peasant agriculture, no more than a very low rate of industrialisation could be placed upon the agenda. Professors Oganovsky and Weinstein in 1927-8 hazarded the estimate that yield per acre might increase in the near future at a rate of 2 per cent. per annum, or at twice the pre-revolutionary

---

[1] Owing to lack of meadows it was customary to use fallow as pasture, and therefore to postpone ploughing as late as possible.

[2] Timoshenko, op. cit., 200-4, 263-5. Migration outside the village commune was permitted, and indeed encouraged by special loans, especially if the migration was of a group character ; and new farm colonies formed in this way usually consisted of concentrated enclosed farmsteads. Yakovlev mentions a colony of this type which went out from the village of Pavlovka in the Tambov *gubernia*. As a result of the migration, even though a transfer to enclosed farmsteads was not made, the number of pieces of land per family was reduced from 20 to 8, and the maximum distance of land from their homes was reduced from 7 versts to 2. Previously in the village " all their day was spent in riding from piece to piece, harnessing and unharnessing ; they never had time to plough ". The colonists were mainly poor and middle peasants, the majority young men who had served in the Red Army. The land assigned to them had previously formed part of a nobleman's estate, and since it had not been ploughed for twenty years, it needed two or three horses to plough it, so that communal sharing of plough-teams became the custom from the beginning. (Yakovlev, op. cit., 71-2.)

rate ; and although this was regarded in some quarters as unduly conservative, there seemed to be no sure ground for expecting a substantially higher rate. A fact of some importance is that (according to the estimates of another agrarian economist of the time, Professor Litochenko) the net revenue of peasant holdings (unlike the position in Western and Central Europe) was appreciably smaller per unit of labour on small than on large holdings (and in very small holdings it was apparently somewhat smaller even per unit of area than on middle farms) : evidence of the poorer equipment of the former and of an uneconomically high ratio of labour to both land and to capital.[1] In general, on middle and poor farms the margin for any accumulation of capital to rectify this situation was remarkably small, and in many cases non-existent. To effect any considerable improvement in the material equipment of agriculture would have required a very large investment of capital in agriculture by the State ; and without this the potentialities of co-operative credit were bound to be straitly limited. Until the end of the '20's the ability of Russian industry to supply agriculture with modern machinery, let alone with tractors, was small ; and until a chemical industry had been developed, the supply of artificial fertilisers (apart from imported supplies) was deficient. Attempts were made after 1925 to supply agriculture with tractors on a more generous scale. In 1924-5 some 5000 had been imported and supplied mainly to village Soviets for co-operative use. In 1925-6 it was planned to import 17,500 and to manufacture another 1800 at home : figures which by the end of the decade had grown to an annual importation of 23,000 and a home production of some 10,000.[2] But as long as they continued to be employed on small peasant holdings, their utilisation was bound to be inefficiently low ; and the majority of them seem in fact to have been employed on collective or State farms.

II

After 1925, however, it was to become increasingly clear that there was another effect of the 1917 Land Reform which presented

[1] Prof. L. Litochenko in *La Situation Économique de l'Union Soviétique* (1926), 34-7.
[2] *Narodnoe Khoziaistvo, 1924-5*, 14 ; G. Krumin, *v Borbye za Sotsialism*, 23. The commonly accepted figure of tractors in use before the war is 600. They were in use, however, on the large estates and were usually the large 30-50 h.p. German tractor ; whereas those in use in the '20's were mostly the smaller Fordson-type tractor.

a more serious barrier than the backwardness of peasant economy in productive technique. The summer and autumn of 1925 was a time of optimism and high expectations. The harvest had been a good one, the gross harvest of grain exceeding that of 1916 by a substantial margin. In the following year the harvest was even better ; and there was a surplus for export, large enough to enable the peak of post-war grain export to be attained. The period of " restoration " had closed ; the monetary reform had been satisfactorily completed ; and the era of new construction was opening with flying colours. It is hardly surprising that what was to prove the crucial limit on development should not have been appreciated sufficiently to occupy the forestage in discussion at the time when the decision was taken in principle to embark on a programme of industrialisation. It was the experience over the next two years of trying to accelerate the rate of new construction within the narrow margin of available resources that focused attention upon the essential limiting factor.

When one examines the details of the agricultural situation in the optimistic year 1925–6, a remarkable fact soon arrests one's attention : the failure of the *marketed surplus* of agriculture to recover to the pre-war level, despite the recovery both of the cultivated area and of the gross harvest. While the total agricultural area in that year stood at 95 per cent. of the pre-war normal, and the gross harvest had surpassed it, the surplus placed on the market outside the village stood at no more than 70 per cent. of the pre-war amount. With grain the position was much worse. Its gross production was nearly nine tenths of 1913 ; but the marketed surplus of grain was less than one half of the pre-war amount. The fact was that only 17 per cent. of the total yield was being sent away to market by the peasantry.[1] In the case of grain in the following year only 13 to 14 per cent. of the total harvest was marketed, compared with 26 per cent. in the pre-war period. The apparent gap in urban consumption which this shrinkage of marketed grain supplies occasioned was met by reducing the export of grain, which even in the peak year of the post-war period did not exceed a third of the pre-war quantity. As soon as the question arose of importing machinery extensively to further plans of large-scale industrial construction, the dilemma became acute between reducing urban food consumption and cutting the import plan because agriculture

[1] *Kontrolnie Tsifri Nar. Khoz. S.S.S.R., 1927–8* ; Prof. Weinstein in *Econ. Bulletin Koniunkturnovo Instituta*, 1927, Nos. 11–12.

could not support a corresponding volume of exports. Hopes for
a time were placed on filling the gap in exports by developing the
export of timber and oil. But the hard fact remained that the
margin of possible import, either for construction purposes or to
meet the deficit in manufactured goods, was an extremely narrow
one. The opposition had maintained that "the slow development
of industry retards the development of agriculture". The situation seemed rather to be that the decline in the marketed surplus
of agriculture was a fundamental barrier to the further advance
either of an expanded foreign trade turnover or of the urban
standard of life. So long as industry remained undeveloped, it
could supply neither the means of industrial construction nor
finished commodities for village or foreign markets in adequate
amount; and until the flow of agricultural products on to the
market was increased, there was no possibility (short of starving
the towns) of finding the exports with which the means for the
expansion of industry could be purchased from abroad.

The deficiency in the marketable surplus could evidently not
be wholly or even mainly attributed to the *kulak*, since as much as
85 per cent. of the total grain production now fell to middle and
poor peasants, as against some 50 per cent. before the war; although
it is true that the influence of the *kulak* as a *middleman* in the grain
market had a good deal to do with the increasing difficulties of the
next five years. Many, especially from the camp of those who
favoured additional concessions to agriculture, suggested that the
remnants of the "scissors" were to blame; with the corollary that
industrial prices must be lowered still further and consumers' goods
imported (instead of machinery) and thrown on village markets—
the "goods intervention" of which there was revived talk in 1927.
While success had very largely attended the policy of closing the
"scissors", we have seen that some element of them remained;
and the peasantry as a whole still suffered worse terms of trade
between his produce and manufactured goods than in pre-war days,
even in terms of wholesale prices, while in terms of retail prices the
exchange was even less to his advantage. This relative undervaluation of agricultural produce no doubt exercised some influence,
the extent of which is impossible to measure. But to attribute the
whole of the shrinkage in the amount marketed to a decline in the
inducement to sell is scarcely even plausible. If this had been
mainly responsible, one would have expected it to have had more
effect than was apparent upon the sown area and upon the amount

harvested (as was the case during the war and the civil war years) ;[1] whereas it was the shrinkage of the marketed surplus even in face of a restoration of the sown area that was the crucial phenomenon to be explained. It looked rather as though the situation was such that the peasantry would need to be given more manufactured goods for each pood of grain—that it would be necessary for the "scissors" not merely to close but to open in the opposite direction—to persuade him to market as much as formerly. It was possible even that there might be *no* rate of exchange, however favourable, that would induce the village to part voluntarily with as large a proportion of its harvest as it had done before the war.

With his strong instinct for essentials, Stalin early in 1928 emphasised that the fundamental reason was to be sought in the very character of the agrarian revolution of 1917. In pre-war days it had been the large estate and the *kulak* farm that had been the mainstay of production for the market. The estates had marketed nearly one half of their grain crop, and *kulak* farms about a third. Together they accounted for nearly three quarters of all marketed grain. The poor and middle peasants were primarily subsistence farmers. The holdings of the majority of them had been too small even to supply the food needs of the family, and they had supplied labour to enlarge the production of the estates and the *kulak* farms. They had marketed on the average less than one sixth of their grain, and accounted for little more than one quarter of all the marketed grain. Now since 1917 the estates were no more ; while State and collective farms (as we have seen) replaced them to the extent of no more than a sixth of their former area and production. The number and size of *kulak* farms had likewise declined, and as producers of grain they retained only a third of their pre-war importance. Land was more equally distributed ; there were fewer very small sub-subsistence holdings ; and the poorer and middle peasants now not only accounted for 85 per cent. of the grain production, but were themselves consuming more of what they harvested from their fields. The village was eating more of what it grew, and selling less, because it was more egalitarian than formerly.[2]

---

[1] True, there was a decline in sown area in 1928, which some quoted as evidence of agricultural regression, due to lack of economic inducement to the peasantry. But this fall seems to have been largely, if not wholly, due to a failure of winter crops as a result of weather conditions in the southern steppe region.

[2] Speech of Stalin to a joint meeting of students of the Communist Academy, Sverdlov University and Institute of Red Professors, published in *International Press Correspondence*, June 14, 1928, and in *Leninism* (1940, Eng. ed.), 205 seq. ; also Molotov's report, *Econ. Zhizn*, Dec. 22, 1927, and *Rabochaia Gazeta*, Dec. 23,

Some support seems to be lent to this view by a geographical shift in grain surpluses. Figures for long-distance shipment of grain by rail between grain-surplus and grain-deficiency regions indicate that there was a sharp fall in such shipments from the Volga region, and to a less extent from the southern steppe region, especially in the case of wheat, the decline in which was balanced only to a very small extent by increased shipments of rye. These areas had previously been ones where wheat production had been specially stimulated by the export trade; but they had also been regions of extensive estates and large *kulak* farms, which had been the main producers for export. By contrast, transport of grain from Siberia had markedly increased. Here large estates had not previously prevailed and holdings remained larger than elsewhere after the agrarian reform of 1917. One estimate even suggests that between 1926 and 1929 well over a third of all wheat surpluses for the deficiency areas came from beyond the Urals as against less than 10 per cent. in 1913.[1] An important consequence of this regional shift was to increase the average distance which a pood of grain supplied to the deficiency areas had to travel; and if the total surplus had recovered to the pre-war level,

1927. The following figures, compiled by the Central Statistical Department, were quoted by Stalin:

	Total grain production (m. poods)	Per cent. of total	Grain placed on market outside village (m. poods)	Per cent. of total	Percentage of total harvest which is marketed
Before the war:					
Landowners . .	600	12	281	21·6	47
Kulaks . .	1,900	38	650	50	34
Poor and middle peasants . .	2,500	50	369	28·4	14·7
	5,000	100	1,300	100	26
1926–7:					
State and collective farms . .	80	1·7	37·8	6	47·2
Kulaks . .	617	13	126	20	20
Poor and middle peasants . .	4,052	85·3	466·2	74	11·2
Total . .	4,749	100	630	100	13·3

[1] Timoshenko, *op. cit.*, 421–9. The central black-earth zone showed a decline in shipments of wheat but an approximately equal rise of rye. This author estimates that the distance over which wheat was hauled in the '20's was about *double* the pre-war, partly owing to the decline of wheat export and the diversion of wheat from the southern steppe northwards to the consuming areas. In 1925–6 11–15 per cent. of grain was hauled more than 2,000 kilometres, against 6 per cent. in 1913. Cost of transport, which amounted to one seventh to one sixth of the price paid to the producer of wheat before the war, rose to one quarter in 1926–7. (*Ibid.*, 332–3.)

the strain on railway transport would have been very greatly increased over pre-war.

It was fresh difficulties in the grain market in the course of 1927 and 1928 that brought this question of the marketable surplus to the forefront. Grain prices in the Russian village had always shown a seasonal variation between autumn and spring ; this difference being a powerful factor in the enrichment of the *kulak* and the impoverishment of the *bedniak*.[1] After the harvest the poorer families were keen to sell, in order to get cash to pay the debts incurred at seed-time and harvest and to pay taxes. It was a buyers' market, and the richer peasant with some capital, who could afford to wait, purchased grain cheaply in order to hold it speculatively for a rise later in the year. In the spring and early summer when stocks were becoming low, both in the towns and among the majority of village households, the price was apt to rise again. Both in 1924 and 1925 this seasonal fluctuation had been of great amplitude : in 1924 the March price in many areas had been more than 80 per cent. above the price of the previous October, and in 1925 nearly 40 per cent. greater than in the autumn of the previous year. In an organised attempt to break this seasonal price-rise efforts were made in 1926 by the government to limit competition among grain-purchasing organs, and to restrict the participation of private capital in the grain trade. Private traders were required to register, and registration was refused to those for whom grain trading was not a primary occupation. Credits to private grain traders were curtailed, and transport priority and milling priority in State mills were reserved for State and co-operative organisations. In the early '20's there had been as many as 18 major State collecting organisations, and in addition certain other organisations which bought and sold grain as a side-line.[2] By 1926 these had been reduced to 9 (of which the chief were Khleboprodukt, which was in 1927 to take over the grain elevator system ; the trading company called Gostorg ; and Centrosoyus, the co-operative wholesale organisation) ;[3] and their activities were

[1] See above, page 44.

[2] For example, up to 1927 the State Bank continued to engage in the trade in grain.

[3] Khleboprodukt was registered as a company, with its share capital held by various Government departments such as Narcomtorg and Narcomfin. Later it became Soiuskhleb, when it took over a number of parallel regional organisations such as Ukrkhleb. At first Centrosoyus occupied a more prominent place than the agricultural co-operatives. Later these latter became the collecting organisations in all areas distant from railways and waterways, and State organisations made their purchases at rail depots and river ports. At the end of the decade the grain-collecting activities of Centrosoyus were discontinued. (Cf. Timoshenko, *op. cit.*, 441.)

co-ordinated by means of upper and lower "price limits" issued by the central economic organs of the government to define the price range within which State and co-operative bodies could enter into purchase-contracts. The position was that in the year following these measures about a half of the total trade in agricultural products was handled by the co-operatives, 28 per cent. by State trading companies, and only 23 per cent. by private traders.

The policy of price stabilisation proved to be remarkably successful. Between October, 1926, and March, 1927, agricultural wholesale prices rose by no more than 2 per cent. But the following autumn was to show that success had been purchased only at a price. By the end of 1927 there was a grave deficiency in grain collections. In November and December collections had dropped to less than a half of the level of the same month of the previous year. The situation seriously threatened both the food supply of the towns and the export plan, and with the latter the import plan and the programme of capital construction for the year. In the first two months of the new economic year grain exports were less than a half the monthly average for 1926–7, and in the remaining months of 1927–8 monthly grain export fell to a few thousand tons. Attempts were made to rectify the position by special measures. Manufactured goods were directed in larger quantities to the grain regions to tempt more sales of grain for cash. Certain emergency measures were even taken (which were terminated, however, in the spring), including a new article of the criminal law to control speculation in produce by providing that surplus stocks above a certain figure were liable to confiscation and the offender to a fine. Despite these measures, grain collections for the whole economic year from October, 1927, to October, 1928, were smaller by some 14 per cent. than in the previous year, although the harvest was smaller by no more than 7 or 8 per cent.; and stocks in the hands of grain-collecting organs by the end of the agricultural year were lower by about a third than a year previously. The month of July, 1928, on the eve of the new harvest, actually witnessed a purchase of grain abroad to the amount of some 12 million poods, or about two thirds of the total amount exported since the previous October: a fact which aroused excited comment in the foreign press at the time. Combined with this grain shortage went an accentuation of the "industrial goods famine": a "break in the equilibrium between supply and demand" which Mikoyan, the Commissar for Trade, estimated to amount at prevailing prices to a deficit in supply of 300 million roubles.[1] The collection difficulties represented, however, primarily a crisis of the grain market, and did not affect most other agricultural products, in particular so-called technical crops. The prices of these, such as oil seeds, flax, hemp, mahorka and butter, had recently been raised as compared with grain prices (in an attempt to correct a previous undervaluation) and were relatively favourable. Indeed, while this price ratio of different products sustained the supply of " technical crops ", it no doubt helped to worsen the position of grain.[2]

Speaking in the summer of 1928, Stalin described the situation very bluntly as follows : " On January 1st of this year there was a deficit of 128 million poods of grain as compared with last year. . . . What was to be done in order to make up the lost ground ? It was necessary first of all to strike hard at the *kulaks* and speculators. . . . Secondly, it was necessary to pour the maximum amount of goods into the grain regions. . . . The measures taken were effective, and by the end of March we had collected 275 million poods of grain. . . . [But] from April to June we were unable even to collect 100 million poods. . . . Hence the second relapse into emergency measures, administrative arbitrariness, violation of revolutionary laws, raids on peasant houses, illegal searches, and so forth, which affected the political conditions of the country and created a menace to the *smytchka* between the workers and the peasants."[3] Although prices for grain were raised in the autumn of 1928,[4] the market position failed to improve, but on the contrary continued to deteriorate. The amount of grain collected in the economic year 1928–9 turned out to be still lower than the previous year and no more than two thirds of the amount collected in the relatively good year of 1926–7. This was partly due to destruction of winter-sown crops and a

---

[1] *Economicheskaia Zhizn* estimated that between July and December of 1927 the purchasing power of the country had grown by 11·6 per cent. and the supply of finished industrial goods by only 3·2 per cent. The increased purchasing power was evidently a result of a rise in constructional activity in the autumn and winter, which had been financed partly by trusts drawing upon accumulated reserves and partly by an extension of long and short-term credits from the banks.

[2] Zalkind in *Econ. Obozrenie*, May, 1928, 143 seq. ; Prof. Pervushin, *ibid.*, 115 seq., and in *Econ. Zhizn*, Oct. 1, 1927 ; *Econ. Zhizn*, Feb. 2, 1928 ; Mikoyan's report in *Econ. Zhizn*, Dec. 20, 1927 ; Zalkind in *Econ. Zhizn*, Dec. 23, 1927 ; and editorials in *Econ. Jhizn*, Dec. 13, 1927, Jan. 5, 1928.

[3] Speech at meeting of active members of the Leningrad organisation of the Party on July 13, 1928, published in *Leninism*, vol. II (Eng. ed., 1933), 128–9. Stalin went on to speak of the necessity of discontinuing emergency measures such as searches and of increasing the price of grain.

[4] By amounts varying between 14 and 29 per cent. according to the district. In the Ukraine " bazaar prices" for rye and wheat increased two and a half times between October, 1927 and October, 1928, being more than double the planned State collection prices. (Averbukh and Briukhanov in *Plan. Khoz.*, 1929, No. 10, 91, 94, 100–1.)

subsequent drought in the north Caucasus and the Ukraine in 1928; but the deficiency could not wholly be attributed to this cause. As a result, in issuing the Control Figures for 1928-9 in September, 1928, Vesenkha was constrained to point out that "the demands raised by individual industries [for capital investment] must be diminished rather than increased", in view of the "limited amount of imported machinery which we are in a position to buy, and of the [limited] amount of building materials available". Such was the gravity of the situation in the very year that the First Five Year Plan was to be launched. Few programmes of extensive construction can ever have been launched under less favourable auspices.

The marketable surplus of grain was significant in another connection than the needs of the towns and of export: namely in connection with the supply of grain to those areas which specialised in the production of other crops, whether foodstuffs or industrial raw materials. The regions of the west and north-west, where dairy-farming and the cultivation of flax and sugar-beet prevailed, and the cotton-growing areas of Turkestan and Trans-Caucasia had been traditionally grain-deficiency regions which needed to import grain on an extensive scale. One of the requirements of industrialisation was that the areas most suitable for "technical crops" should specialise upon them to a greater extent than formerly. Attempts were now being made, for example, to expand the cotton area of Turkestan at the expense of grain, and to supply the grain needs of this area instead with Siberian wheat carried over the new Turksib railway. The size of the marketed surplus from the main grain regions acted as the limiting factor upon such developments. In the words of Krzhizhanovsky to the Fifth Soviet Congress on the eve of the First Five Year Plan: "The grain question is the most basic question of agriculture. Clearly, only when we have decided the grain question can we proceed to the solution of other questions of agricultural economy. Our special regions in which animal breeding or technical cultures ought to predominate can develop only when they are assured that there is a firm grain basis beneath them: when they are assured that their needs in grain can be satisfied."[1]

[1] G. M. Krzhizhanovsky, *Piatiletnii Plan Narodno-Khoziaistvennovo Stroitelstva S.S.S.R.*, 2nd ed., 59-60.

III

It was in this atmosphere that the epoch-making decision was taken at the Fifteenth Party Congress to build the industrialisation programme upon the introduction of large-scale farming on co-operative lines as its corner-stone. This transformation of the age-old basis of Russian agriculture was adopted as the " missing answer " for which the country was seeking : as the only solution to the riddle of how to industrialise on the basis of NEP without reverting to the pre-war Stolypin road ; the only release from that closed circle of interdependent limiting factors within which the discussions of the past four years had revolved. In his report to the Fifteenth Congress in which this policy was enunciated Stalin had spoken as follows: " The way out is to turn the small and scattered peasant farms into large united farms based on the common cultivation of the soil, to introduce collective cultivation of the soil on the basis of new and higher technique. The way out is to unite the small and dwarf peasant farms gradually and surely, not by pressure but by example and persuasion, into large farms based on common, co-operative cultivation of the soil, with the use of agricultural machines and tractors and scientific methods of intensive agriculture. There is no other way out."

In a sense this was a continuation and development of the policy of extending agricultural co-operation which had been emphasised by Lenin as the means by which the socialist element could master the individualist tendencies in NEP economy, and which had been relied upon throughout the decade as the chief instrument for keeping the economic influence of the *kulak* within bounds. But co-operation hitherto had been predominantly in the sphere of trade and of credit. Co-operative production, as we have seen, had been of meagre proportions to date and not markedly successful. The step from co-operative trade and credit to co-operative production in agriculture raised problems of a magnitude that had not previously been tackled, and involved a transformation in the economic basis of the Russian village which held a deeper significance than previous developments in agricultural co-operation had done. Yet without the more elementary and less dramatic progress in co-operation over the past years the new departure would have been unthinkable except as a purely alien and hot-house growth. This progress had been slow but far from negligible during the middle '20's. In 1924 the membership of agricultural co-operatives was officially given as between 2 and 3 million, or about 10 per cent. of all peasant households.[1] By 1928 the figure had reached 10 million, or nearly a half of all peasant households. Of these nearly two thirds were attached to some 10,000 trading societies and another 800,000 to various producing societies such as dairy co-operatives and societies for joint use of machinery.[2] A considerable part was played in this expansion by the Agricultural Bank, founded in 1924 with the aim of financing agricultural credit associations (and followed subsequently by three separate agricultural banks of different republics); this bank being the recipient of grants from the Budget to augment its long-term credit fund.

The principle of continuity of the new development towards co-operative production with these earlier developments lay at the heart of the new policy. It was emphasised that there was no intention of breaking with Lenin's principle of the *smytchka* and of the firm alliance with the middle peasantry. The intention was that the bulk of the peasantry, schooled by their experience of co-operative methods in sale and purchase and in the hire of machinery, should be won to collective farming by a demonstration of its patent advantages to their interests, and that the new system should not be implanted on the village as an alien growth, arousing deep-seated peasant hostility towards importations from the town. This intention, as we shall see, was not always adhered to in the execution of the new policy in the hectic year of 1929. But the design was clearly revealed in the choice of the type of co-operative farming that was to receive official encouragement in the propaganda " drive " towards the new goal of policy. Previously co-operative farming had taken three forms. First there was the commune, under which the members not only farmed collectively, but lived together in a communal establishment. Secondly, there was the *artel*, under which members kept their own dwellings and gardens, but had their agricultural land and implements in common, farmed collectively and shared out the crop. Thirdly, there was the more elementary form (the society for joint cultivation, or TOZ) where each peasant household retained his separate holding

---

[1] The proportion of the population served by *consumers'* co-operation in that year was estimated as about 16–17 per cent. : in the towns 44 per cent. and in the countryside 8–9 per cent. (I.L.O., *Co-operation in Soviet Russia*, 245.)

[2] *Soviet Union Yearbook, 1930,* 217. Some of the societies here listed as credit societies apparently combined trading activities with credit functions (like that in the village of Voronsov, mentioned above). Cf. also G. Ratner, *Agricultural Co-operation in the Soviet Union*, who gives a higher figure of 12·5 million as the total membership of all agricultural co-operatives, including numerous small village co-operatives not affiliated to a co-operative union or main credit society (*ibid.*, 5–6).

of land and even his own implements and draught animals, but the households co-operated to work the land and shared out the crop according to the size of their several holdings. Many, if not most, of the collective farms of the early '20's had been of the first type ; and the fact that these represented such a radical break with village traditions (together with the fact that their members were often townsmen taking to agriculture, rather than peasants proper) contributed much to the high percentage of failures. It was now decided that the second type combined the advantages of involving the least break with the traditional mode of life of the peasantry and at the same time of affording an adequate basis for the use of modern mechanised methods of cultivation. The *artel* form, as the most suitable " bridge " for the mass of the peasantry from individual to collective production, accordingly became the model according to which the collective farm movement was built. At the same time a system of " forward contracts " with individual peasant farms over wide areas was introduced, by which credit facilities and supply of manufactured goods were coupled with a guarantee of certain minimum supplies of grain.

These new farms would possess the advantage of improved cultivation by mechanised methods, which were difficult if not impossible to develop on small holdings, and of providing a larger proportion of their produce for the market—some 30 per cent.[1] as compared with 11 or 12 per cent. on poor and middle peasant farms. Experience was to show the latter—the contribution of these farms to the marketable surplus—to be more important, in the immediate future at any rate, than the results they achieved in raising the crop yield per unit of area. In other words, the effect of the new methods was primarily labour-saving ; releasing labour-time in the village either for cultivation of market-garden produce on the collective farmers' garden-allotments to supplement their own diet or for sale in local markets, or for supplying labour to industry (e.g. by certain members of the peasant household taking seasonal building or construction jobs or moving off to find employment in a factory).[2]

But it was not estimated at first that collective farming would develop at more than a relatively slow pace ; and the First Five Year Plan only budgeted for the new system to embrace some 6 million peasant households (or about a quarter of all peasant

[1] According to figures cited by Stalin, collective farms in 1927 marketed 35 million poods out of a production of 80 million. (*Leninism*, 1940 ed., 324.) Many of these farms were, however, more specialised in type of crop than the ordinary run of peasant farms.   [2] See below, pages 252-3.

households) and about 15 per cent. of the cultivated area by 1933. The draft of the First Five Year Plan cautiously admitted that " the fact must be faced frankly that in this field we are still feeling our way, that the fundamental technical principles of collective farming have not as yet been clearly formulated ". Collective farming was a middling-long-term expedient for solving the difficulty of supply-ing agricultural produce to an expanding industry and an expand-ing population ; and the short-term problem, urgent and insistent, of filling the gap in the grain supply remained. It was mainly to meet this short-term problem—to exert an effect on the marketed surplus of grain within the next few years—that, in addition to the " drive " for the formation of collective farms, a programme of building large-scale State farms was launched. The function of these " grain factories " was to extend the area of grain cultivation (chiefly wheat) by ploughing up new land, mainly land in the more arid regions of the north Caucasus or east of the Volga, in Siberia and in Kazakhstan, which was suitable only for extensive cultivation. These farms had the special advantage that over 60 per cent. of their produce constituted a marketable surplus. The intention was to treble the area covered by these *Sovkhozy* in the course of a few years, so as to enable them to supply about a million and a half tons of grain for the market, or nearly one fifth of the State and co-operative grain collections in the year 1928–9. A grain trust (Zernotrest) was instituted and about 150 large grain farms, often of several hundred thousand acres, were planned.[1] As a result of these measures the Five Year Plan provided that by the summer of 1933 one fifth of the grain crop and two fifths of the marketed surplus of grain should be provided jointly by State and collective farms. The results in the first few years were to exceed expectations. In 1929–30 the supply of marketed grain from State farms already exceeded the 1933 target of one and a half million tons ; and in that year a resolution of the Party called for a doubling of the original target for 1933 so as to raise the area covered by them to nearly eight times their 1928 acreage. The magnitude of this task can be judged from the fact that in his report to the Sixteenth Party Congress on June 27th, 1930, Stalin was able to claim that by the end of the First Five Year Plan the Grain Trust would have " as large an area under grain as the whole of Argentine to-day ", and that State farms altogether would embrace " one million hectares more under grain than the whole of Canada has to-day ".

[1] J. Stalin and L. Kaganovich, *Otchet Tsentralnovo Komiteta XVI Siezdu V.K.P.*, 34.

To exploit the possibilities of the new large-scale farming to the full required large capital investments, especially in the provision of tractors for ploughing, without which the tough soil of virgin steppe land could not be tamed on any sufficient scale, and in the provision of combine harvesters which alone could enable the effective harvesting of these large areas to be undertaken. As we shall see, the Five Year Plan provided for very large investments in agriculture, especially in the so-called " socialised sector ".[1] This, in turn, depended on a rapid expansion of the machinery industry, and on the completion of new tractor-building plants projected at Stalingrad and Kharkov and Cheliabinsk. In the allocation of these tractors the new farms would have priority ; the State farms owning machinery as part of their capital equipment, but collective farms being serviced in this respect by the newly invented Machine Tractor Stations—tractor garages, to supply tractor-teams to collective farms over an area, together with their servicing and their personnel, in return for the payment of a certain fraction of the harvest. A special advantage claimed for these Machine Tractor Stations (which were a development from a pioneering scheme by Markevitch in the neighbourhood of the Shevchenko State Farm in the western Ukraine) was the considerable saving of capital in the mechanisation of agriculture which resulted from an increase in the degree of tractor utilisation[2] and from economies of machines, buildings and repair services. A good deal of discussion took place as to the amount of capital investment that the new methods would require. Zernotrest had calculated that, in order to organise a mechanised economy on its grain farms, investment would have to be at the rate of about 80 roubles per hectare of arable (a figure corresponding fairly closely to the estimates of the American agriculturist, Campbell, for rather similar American conditions of extensive grain farming), or, with the inclusion of working capital, a figure of 150 roubles per hectare of sown area. Marke-vitch, however, claimed that, in his experience with Machine

[1] The Control Figures for 1929–30, for example, which represented an increase on the original provisions of the Five Year Plan, provided for an increase of investment in agriculture by more than two and a half times the level of the previous year. Two thirds of this was to be in State farms, a tenth in collective farms and only a quarter in the private sector. (Cf. E. I. Kviring in *Plan. Khoz.*, 1929, No. 9, 42–3.)

[2] The Commissariat of Agriculture made the claim in 1930 that the degree of tractor utilisation on collective farms had reached 2500 hours per year, or more than four times what was usual on American farms and about 60 per cent. more than on large American mechanised farms. The figure represented nearly a doubling of the figure for 1928 before Machine Tractor Stations had been widely adopted. (Cit. Joan Beauchamp, *Agriculture in Soviet Russia*, 95–6.)

Tractor Stations in the western Ukraine, the necessary capital investment did not exceed a quarter of this figure.[1]

But although the new policy was intended to represent no break in the attitude of the government to the mass of the peasantry—merely to offer intensified inducements to them to step upon that "bridge" to socialised agriculture which the *artel* form of collective farming was designed to provide—it inevitably involved a greatly sharpened antagonism with that richer stratum of the peasantry who had hitherto occupied a dominant position in the grain market. The Gosplan report which we have already quoted showed that in the main grain-producing regions the upper 10 per cent. of peasant households owning more than a third of the agricultural means of production accounted for one third of the sown area and two-fifths of the marketable surplus of grain.[2] It was the holding back of their grain in the hope of better prices by this well-to-do group that was regarded as having been chiefly responsible for the difficulties in the grain market in 1927 and 1928. It was to their interest that trade in grain should be as free as possible and the urban and export demand extensive; and they resented the control over grain purchase prices exerted by the growing dominance of a few large State buying organisations, competition between which was restricted by demarcation agreements and the system of official "price limits". For them the growth of a new category of large-scale farms, preferentially treated with regard to credits, machinery and forward purchase contracts, represented a most unwelcome form of competition. It was the original intention that within five years' time the new collective and State farms combined should occupy virtually the same proportionate weight in the grain market as the well-to-do upper 10 per cent. of peasant farms had previously done: namely, that they should account for nearly 40 per cent. of the marketed surplus of grain.[3] This new contribution to grain supplies was not intended necessarily to *supplant* the well-to-do individual peasant farms in the market, but in the main to supplement them, and in so doing simultaneously to strengthen the influence of the State over the grain market and to guarantee an adequate grain supply to the towns. But it was inevitable that the new mode of production would elbow out the economy of the richer individual

---

[1] M. M. Wolf, *op cit.*, 20–1.   [2] *Ibid.*, 12–13.

[3] *Ibid.*, 34–6. Kolkhoze alone, as we have seen, were planned to account for rather more than 20 per cent. of marketed grain. In terms of *all* agricultural products, however, the proportions were smaller; and the combined contribution of Kolkhoze and Sovkhoze in 1933 was estimated to amount to only a fifth or less of the marketed surplus.

peasantry to some extent, and at any rate preclude its expansion ; and this heightened rivalry between the two was the ground of that " sharpened class struggle in the village " which occupied discussion in 1928 and 1929.

The opposition of the *kulaks* and those who supported them among the more well-to-do middle peasantry began to be increasingly pronounced. It ranged from passive resistance and boycott, through spontaneous or concerted slaughtering of cattle rather than consign them to the new collective farms, to acts of arson and violence against the new farms and their personnel. At first the official attitude towards the *kulaks* was a fairly cautious one. After the Fifteenth Party Congress even the special concessions to the *kulaks* of 1925, regarding leases and hired labour, were not revoked. Stress was laid in the summer of 1928 on repealing the emergency measures adopted during the months of the grain crisis to search out and requisition surplus hoards of grain. But in the second year of the Five Year Plan—" the spinal year of the Piatiletka " as it was once called[1]—the policy towards the *kulak* was abruptly changed from one of " encircling the *kulak* " and limiting his influence to one of " eliminating as a class " the upper 5 or 6 per cent. of labour-employing, land-leasing, grain-trading and money-lending stratum of petty-capitalist farmers. This new " offensive against the *kulaks* " took the form, not only of repealing the concessions made to them with regard to leasing land and hiring labour, but of granting powers to village Soviets forcibly to expropriate the machinery, working cattle and other farm property (above a certain minimum standard) belonging to *kulaks* for the benefit of collective farms. This new legislation was in form no more than permissive. But it was rapidly and widely acted upon ; and the statement was subsequently made by Yakovlev, the Commissar for Agriculture, that by the summer of 1930 some 15 per cent. of the capital of collective farms consisted of such expropriated property.[2] The winter of 1929–30, in particular, witnessed the now notorious "excesses" and wholesale departures from the voluntary principle.[3] Against those who resisted or retaliated rigorous police measures were taken, including the large-scale deportations of *kulaks* from the areas of keenest resistance in the south-east about which has been written so much in other countries. The winter and spring of that "spinal year" of 1929–30 was to witness those tense months of turmoil

---

[1] Title of an article by Krzhizhanovsky in *Plan. Khoz.*, 1929, No. 12.
[2] Statement at Sixteenth Party Congress; cit. by Timoshenko, *op. cit.*, 115, who estimates that this figure probably amounted to about one third of the former means of production of the *kulaks*.   [3] See further below, page 247.

in the village which are depicted in the novels of Sholokhov about this period and from which the new type of Soviet village was to be born. The birth-pangs were sharp; the attendant midwifery was rough, indeed brutal. But those few months may well come to be regarded as a turning-point in the economic history both of Europe and of Asia in the twentieth century.

CHAPTER TEN

THE FIRST FIVE-YEAR PLAN

I

As far back as 1926, the year of the first " Control Figures ", Gosplan had been charged with the duty of drafting a Five Year Plan.   The preparatory work for this was centred in the economic-statistical section of this organisation, and a special commission was set up in Gosplan to coordinate and direct the work, called the Central Commission for Perspective Planning, under the chairmanship of Professor (now Academician) Strumilin.   The very first draft, covering the period of 1925–6 to 1929–30, was made the subject of discussion at a congress of planning workers drawn from various parts of the country in March, 1926.   In March of the following year a revised draft, entitled " Perspectives of Development of the Economy of the U.S.S.R. for 1926–7 to 1930–1 ", was submitted to a second congress of planning workers for discussion. In the two years that followed, this became the subject of animated discussion and was to undergo further modification and successive redrafting before the Five Year Plan emerged in its definitive form.

The year 1926–7 had been designated as the first complete year of the so-called " reconstruction period ", when the work of restoring production on the basis of existing capital equipment had been completed, and the question of enlarging the capital equipment of industry by new construction appeared at the head of the agenda of economic policy.   In December of the previous year the Fourteenth Party Congress had resolved on the industrialisation of the country, including the independent development of heavy industry as a firm foundation for future building.   In November, 1926, the Fifteenth Party Conference had amplified this resolution with the statement that every effort must be directed in the coming period towards an enlargement of the country's stock of capital equipment and the " reconstruction of the whole economy on a higher technical basis ". " One of the distinguishing features," it was stated, " and at the same time one of the chief difficulties of the first period of industrialisation, is that expenditure on capital construction will require considerable effort from the economic system of the country, while the results of this new construction will only come upon the market after a considerable interval of time, often amounting to several years". In this new period it was inevitable that the volume and the form of capital development would assume a dominating influence over all branches of economic life. The plan of capital development was bound to become the backbone of economic policy; and decisions regarding it could evidently no longer be left uncoordinated in a period when innovation and change had begun to take precedence over routine adaptation to a familiar situation. Investment decisions in any one sector of the economy or at any one date needed to be related to a consistent picture of development sketched over a considerable period of time. Five years was initially chosen to be this period for an initial "perspective plan", on the ground that this was likely to be the construction-period of the more ambitious technical projects to be undertaken in the years ahead. The need for a perspective of development over an even longer period of 10 or 15 years was urged by some, and a draft of "a general plan for 15 years" was actually prepared;[1] but uncertainties in the situation were likely to multiply sufficiently as the horizon of vision was extended to endow anything much longer than a five-year scheme of development with too many imponderables for it to have much practical value.

The intention was that the Perspective Plan should in the first instance constitute a kind of dummy or skeleton framework around which various economic bodies and various industries should prepare their detailed sectional programmes, both for the five-year period and for the initial year of the quinquennium. When these latter had been received, the draft was to be reworked into a definitive Five Year Plan, to which for the future the annual "Control Figures" and the annual plans of departments and industries would be closely geared. The initial draft was described as affording "lines of direction", which, although lacking "the precision and abundance of data desirable for the general [i.e. the final] plan", postulated certain key quantities and relationships around which the remainder would need to be moulded, such as "the speed of development of the main branches of the economy and their interdependence, as well as the general *tempo* of socialist accumulation [of capital] over the period in question". But the programme

---

[1] Cf., for example, A. M. Sabsovitch in *Plan. Khoz.*, 1929, No. 1, 54 seq. The original draft of this so-called *genplan* had been drawn up by Professors Osadchy and Oganovsky, and had provided for a doubling of the *per capita* national income by 1941 and for a "descending curve" of rates of industrial development over the period.

of programme-making did not go according to schedule. By the summer of 1927 very few of the sectional programmes that were to have been drafted on the basis of the Perspective Plan had in fact been received ; and on June 9th *Economicheskaia Zhizn* was complaining roundly of " a violation of an explicit directive " and declaring that a planned economy was impossible " if strict time-keeping and reliability fail to be maintained ". The two largest republics, Russia and Ukraine, failed to supply either any comments on Gosplan's project or their own programmes ; while other republics submitted their programmes only for particular sections of the plan. Several of the leading economic departments of the Union government, including Vesenkha and the Commissariat of Trade, were silent and made no constructive contribution to the confection of the plan ; while even those departments which made a contribution " submitted material of a very desultory character which reached Gosplan so late as to be virtually unusable ".[1] Centrifugal tendencies in the economy were still sufficiently strong to cause most of the constituent elements of the annual plan for 1927-8 to be constructed without much reference to Gosplan's " lines of direction ", even if in a number of respects they were a considerable improvement on their predecessors in having greater concreteness and a closer relationship with the situation in the localities. Moreover, Vesenkha had actually produced a draft Five Year Plan for industry of its own in January, 1927 (under the inspiration of Kuibyshev), without waiting for the Perspective Plan of Gosplan : a plan that was calculated on a different set of prices and based on a different definition of industry.[2] This draft was actually to exercise more influence on the Control Figures for 1927-8 than the Perspective Plan of Gosplan did ; and since it gave much greater prominence to heavy industry than previous proposals had done, it was also to have a seminal influence of no small importance on the reconstructed Plan that emerged from Gosplan towards the end of the following year.

But the fundamental factor obstructing the concoction of a general plan at this time was the dispute that raged, and had still to be settled, about first principles of economic policy, such as those

[1] I. Gladkov, " Towards a History of the First Five Year Plan ", in *Plan. Khoz.* 1935, No. 4, 122.
[2] The Perspective Plan had calculated in gold roubles ; Vesenkha adopted the method of valuation in terms of chervonetz roubles at 1926-7 prices. It was also Vesenkha that inaugurated the classification of industries into Group A (producing capital goods, or means of production) and Group B (producing consumption goods). Cf. F. Pollock, *Die Planwirtschaftlichen Versuche in der Sowjetunion,* 276-7 ; I. Gladkov, *loc. cit.*, 126-7.

which the last two chapters have described. Discussions of principle took place among the experts of the planning commission itself (about which more will be said in a later chapter) ; and the Perspective Plan subsequently came under criticism for underestimating the possibilities of development and being tinged with the defeatism of " Right wing " conceptions.[1] In particular, this Perspective Plan was bounded by the notion that the existing basis of agriculture would remain substantially unchanged throughout the quinquennium, and that, while primary emphasis was to be laid on the development of industry, the pace at which industry could develop was fairly straitly limited by the conditions of agriculture, and by the meagre ability and readiness of peasant economy to supply produce to the market. The authors of the first draft of the Plan had spoken as follows : " The time for a decisive reconstruction of rural economy does not fall within this quinquennium : it still lies ahead. Our chief efforts must centre on the industrial front, without forgetting, however, the huge significance of the agricultural sector. This situation requires us in this Plan to extrapolate those tendencies in peasant agricultural economy of which there is sufficiently clear evidence at the present time." And in their introduction to their second variant, the authors had postulated that " the production of State and collective farms plays so insignificant a rôle in the whole of rural economy, that its change of weight over the quinquennium is of a quite insignificant order of magnitude ".[2] Proceeding on these assumptions, it is hardly surprising that many of the Gosplan economists (including the head of its industrial section) should have greeted the rival and more ambitious project of Vesenkha as " unreal " and as building " castles in the air ". It was only after disputes about fundamental premises such as these had been resolved that the preparation of a coherent and agreed Plan became possible ; and it was not until two years after the first appearance of the Perspective Plan, and then only after a further series of directives, drafts and re-drafts in the course

[1] The original Perspective Plan for 1926–7 to 1930–1 had provided for a growth of industrial production of 77 per cent. (in census industry), and the second draft, covering the period 1927–8 to 1931–2, provided for a 78 per cent. increase according to its lower variant and 103 per cent. according to its higher variant, and for a rate of investment of about half that of the final Plan. (S. G. Strumilin in *Plan. Khoz.*, 1929, No. 1, 104, 115.)

[2] At the second congress of planning workers in 1927 an agrarian economist of Right tendency (Prof. Oganovsky) had spoken in warning tones as follows : " Mr. Harvest, Comrade Harvest, Citizen Harvest—he is the master of the country. On him manifestly depends the *tempo* of industrial development, of the development of transport, of foreign trade, or of whatever you please. Thus it is and thus it must be in our agrarian-industrial country " (cit. I. Gladkov, *loc. cit.* 119–20).

of 1928, that the Five Year Plan in its final form was adopted. In August, 1928, Gosplan issued a new "preliminary model" of a Five Year Plan (which came to be known as the "August version") covering the period from the autumn of 1928 to the autumn of 1933. This was drawn up in two variants: the one an "initial" or "minimum variant", resting on a cautious estimate of a number of uncertain factors in the situation; the other, the "optimal" or "maximum variant", built upon more optimistic assumptions. It was the latter that was finally approved in the spring of 1929 by the government as the definitive First Five Year Plan.[1]

In its introduction to the project Gosplan explained that this optimal variant rested on the following premises: "(a) that there will be no serious failure of the harvest in the course of five years; (b) that a considerably wider expansion of intercourse will be obtained with world economy, both as a result of the substantial export resources available (due to a full realisation of the directives of the Central Executive Committee on the raising of the crop yield) and in addition, and more especially, as a result of a much greater increase in long-term credits from abroad in the opening years of the Five Year Plan; (c) that a sharp increase will take place in the qualitative indices of national economic construction within the next two years (e.g. cost of production, crop yield, etc.); and (d) that there will be a fall in the proportionate weight of expenditure on national defence in the general economic system."[2] Its keynote was set by the high rate of investment for which it provided and by the large proportion of this investment that was devoted to heavy industry. Over the five years the amount to be invested (net) in the economy as a whole was set at the surprising figure of between a quarter and a third of the national income[3] (a proportion two and a half times that in pre-1914 Russia and about twice that in pre-1914 Britain); and of the amount of it to be invested in industry (about a third of the whole) three quarters was assigned to heavy industry. Investment is to be measured not only according to the quantity of labour and resources which are assigned to work of construction, but also according to an additonal dimen-

[1] F. Pollock, op. cit., 263–78, 291–325; I. Gladkov, loc. cit., 112–39; also S. G. Strumilin in Plan. Khoz., 1929, No. 1, 104 seq. The Control Figures for 1928-9, the first year of the Piatiletka, were actually worked out by Vesenkha in August, 1928, at the time of Gosplan's "August Version" of the final Plan, and were confirmed and put into operation before the final version of the Five Year Plan (which was reworked in the course of the winter by Gosplan and Vesenkha) had been completed.

[2] Piatiletnii Plan Nar. Khoz. Stroitelstva S.S.S.R., 2nd ed., vol. I, 11.

[3] Cf. S. G. Strumilin, Sotsialnie Problemi Piatiletki, 2nd ed., 42–53; Memorandum No. 3 of the Russian Department of Birmingham University.

sion : the length of the construction period during which labour
has to continue to be applied to this purpose, or the length of time
over which the labour and resources initially invested have to be
" stored up " before they eventuate in an addition to final output.
In assigning so much of its investment to heavy industry, the Five
Year Plan was embodying labour and resources in a form in which
a particularly long interval was likely to elapse between the original
locking-up of those resources and the emergence of an additional
product of finished goods as a final consequence of the new steel
mills and power stations that were rising in the open steppe.
Between seed-time and harvest Soviet economy had an unusually
long time to wait before the fruit of its labours were ripe to be
enjoyed. Measured by both dimensions, the investment programme
which formed the backbone of the Five Year Plan was an ambitious
one.

It is often supposed that this high rate of investment was
designed at the expense of an absolute fall in consumption. But
this is a misconception so far as the original design was concerned.
Nothing of the kind, at least, was contemplated when the Plan was
originally made. The optimal variant of the Plan provided that,
while the share of consumption in the total national income was to
fall from 77·4 per cent. to 66·4 per cent. over the quinquennium,
its absolute amount was to increase by about 40 per cent. when
expressed in current values of each year or (since a fall of retail
prices of about 20 per cent. was budgeted for) an increase of consumption in real terms by as much as 75 per cent. Annual net
investment meanwhile was to increase by three times when expressed in the current prices of each year, and by appreciably more
when expressed in real terms. This is shown in the table on the
adjoining page 236, which is expressed in milliards of roubles in the
current prices of each year, and which includes the figures of both
variants of the Plan.[3] Nor is it even true that, comparing the
two variants of the Plan, the higher rate of investment in the optimal
variant was to be purchased at the expense of a smaller increase of
consumption than in the minimal variant ; although this appears
at first sight to be the case when values are expressed in the current
prices of each year. But since the former variant budgeted for a
larger price reduction over the quinquennium than the latter, as
one of the architects of the plan, Professor Strumilin, pointed out,
" if consumption in the year 1932–3 is expressed in the prices of

---

[1] Taken from S. G. Strumilin, *op. cit.*, 52. Cf. also *Piatiletnii Plan*, vol. I.,
20–75, 83.

Variants of the Plan and Years	National Income	Non-productive Consumption		Gross Investment	Amortisation	Accumulation in both Fixed and Working Capital		Growth of Fixed Capital	
			In % of Col. 2				In % of Col. 2		In % of Col. 2
1	2	3	4	5	6	7	8	9	10
1927–8 .	24·7	20·0	80·1	7·99	3·33	4·66	18·9	3·72	15·1
Minimal variant :									
1928–9 .	27·5	21·3	77·4	9·70	3·48	6·22	22·6	4·64	16·9
1929–30 .	30·5	22·8	74·9	11·37	3·70	7·67	25·1	5·84	19·1
1930–1 .	33·5	24·5	73·0	13·04	4·00	9·04	27·0	6·87	20·5
1931–2 .	36·9	26·7	72·4	14·58	4·38	10·20	27·6	7·68	20·8
1932–3 .	40·6	29·6	73·0	15·76	4·81	10·95	27·0	8·54	21·0
For the five years	169·0	124·9	73·9	64·45	20·37	44·08	26·1	33·57	19·9
Optimal variant :									
1928–9 .	27·5	21·3	77·4	9·70	3·48	6·22	22·6	4·64	16·9
1929–30 .	30·9	22·2	71·8	12·41	3·70	8·71	28·2	6·47	20·9
1930–1 .	34·8	23·6	67·9	15·22	4·04	11·18	32·1	8·23	23·6
1931–2 .	38·7	25·8	66·8	17·34	4·49	12·85	33·2	9·39	24·3
1932–3 .	43·3	28·8	66·4	19·55	5·01	14·54	33·6	10·96	25·3
For the five years	175·2	121·7	69·5	74·22	20·72	53·50	30·5	36·69	20·9

1927–8 we reach a figure of 35·5 milliard for the minimal variant and 37 milliard for the optimal variant, i.e. significantly more . . . (and we have) a rise in *per capita* consumption over the five years of 58 per cent. for the minimal variant and 66 per cent. for the optimal ".[1]

So far as consumption at least was concerned, things did not work out according to these preliminary estimates. This was largely because of the occurrence of certain unfavourable factors which could scarcely have been foreseen when the Plan was originally designed, chief of which were the large-scale slaughter of livestock as a reaction of the peasantry (and particularly of the *kulak* elements among them) to the collectivisation campaign—an event which had disastrous effects for a number of years on the supply of meat and dairy products as well as on the manuring of land and on the animal power available to agriculture—and the unfavourable movement in the country's terms of foreign trade as a result of price movements on world markets, consequent on the world economic crisis, which sharply narrowed her import capacity. Moreover, the increasing sense of danger of war in the East, following the publication of the notorious Tanaka Memorandum, in which Japanese schemes of expansion on the mainland were cynically outlined, encouraged an appreciable acceleration of the *tempo* of investment, and a stepping-up of the targets for heavy industry, under the slogan of " Piatiletka v Chetire Goda " (The Five Year Plan in Four Years), that was manifestly unrealistic. When adjustments were needed not merely to maintain top priority for investment-projects in heavy industry in face of adverse circumstances, but even to raise it, the output targets for the consumption-goods industries were the ones that suffered a reduction.

In the case of all four of these key assumptions on which Gosplan had built its higher version of the Plan, conditions were to turn out less favourable than was postulated, and in the case of at least one of them conditions were to be distinctly less favourable than a " normal " expectation, let alone a frankly optimistic expectation, would have forecast. In other words, conditions were to turn out less favourable, not merely than the assumptions of the optimal variant of the Plan, but less favourable than the estimates on which the minimal variant had been built. It is true that the harvest of 1930 yielded a bumper crop, which provided a surplus for export greater than in any year since the revolution and equal in quantity to about one third of the pre-1914 level. But 1931 witnessed a

[1] *Op. cit.*, 53 ; *Piatiletnii Plan*, vol. I, 20, 103–7.

partial failure of crops in the eastern black-earth region, and the repercussions of this caused the 1932 crop to be again below normal. In the sphere of foreign trade there was no improvement in the long-term-credit position, but rather a worsening ; while the " scissors " movement of agricultural and industrial prices on world markets in 1930 and 1931—the much greater fall of agricultural prices, and particularly grain prices, than of industrial prices—had a particularly unfavourable impact on Soviet economy as an exporter of raw products and an importer to a large extent of finished manufactures. Between 1929 and 1931 the prices of raw produce on world markets fell between 20 and 30 per cent., while the prices of manufactured goods fell by only between 10 and 20 per cent. Between 1928 and 1931 wheat and rye lost some 60 per cent. of their value.[1] The foreign trade position of the U.S.S.R. might have been even worse had not an important part of her imports in 1931 consisted of metals and raw materials whose prices had fallen more than those of finished manufactures. As it was, Russia's export prices in the first half of 1931 had fallen by something of the order of magnitude of 30 per cent. and her import prices by only 20 per cent. over the level of the first half of the previous year.[2] In order not to curtail her imports of constructional materials, of which she had been relying on an actual increase in these years, resort was had to pruning of imports of lower priority, including raw materials for certain consumption goods industries (e.g. textiles, where output in consequence actually fell in certain years of the quinquennium ; imports of raw cotton in 1931 being cut to one third of the 1928 figure) and to the export of a number of goods which were in short supply in the home market (tobacco and matches, sweetmeats, linen, and dairy produce) at the expense of home consumption. So far as defence-expenditure was concerned, where the Gosplan estimates had relied on a reduction, an actual increase was to take place in the later years of the Plan. " In view of the growing danger of war, the U.S.S.R. was obliged

[1] League of Nations Report on *The Course and Phases of the World Economic Depression*, 1931, 167 seq.

[2] The index of physical quantities of imports and exports given in Dr. Baykov's *Development of the Soviet Econ. System*, 265, which at first sight seems to imply that the terms of trade moved *in favour* of the U.S.S.R. in these years, is to be explained by the fact that the index is of total imports and exports and that in 1929 the U.S.S.R. had a favourable balance of trade, while between 1930 and 1932 she ran an unfavourable balance. In other words, what economists refer to as the " *gross* barter terms of trade " did go slightly in favour of the U.S.S.R. in 1930–2, while the " *net* barter terms " moved against her. This meant that such foreign credits as the country was able to obtain in those years were used up in offsetting the unfavourable movement in net terms of trade.

to increase its defence programme for the purpose of improving the defensive capacity of the country."[1]

Regarding the increase in the productivity of labour, events were to show that the Plan had embodied a serious miscalculation. This was something that cannot be attributed in the main to the intervention of incalculable "accidental" factors like a war danger or the impact of economic crisis abroad. The expected improvement in labour productivity had been based on the joint result of the new plant and equipment, which a high rate of investment was to bring to birth, and of more rationalised methods of work and of industrial organisation. Here there had evidently been excessive optimism as to the speed with which many of the new plants could be brought into full and successful operation and yield their fruits in heightened productivity, and as to the speed with which rationalised methods, particularly in building operations, could be achieved. Instead of the doubling of productivity per worker which had been envisaged, the actual increase by the end of 1932 was no more than 41 per cent. (in heavy industry the increase was 53 per cent.).[2] It had been on this rise of productivity that the expected fall of costs and of industrial wholesale prices by some 20 to 25 per cent. had been based; while the construction programme had been built on an expected fall in building costs of as much as 40 per cent. over the whole period. It was this lagging of labour productivity behind the expected improvement that caused Stalin in January 1933 to issue his famous slogan, "Fervour for new construction . . . now is not enough; we must supplement it with enthusiasm and fervour for *mastering* the new factories and the new technique",[3] which was to bear fruit during the period of the Second Plan.

A crucial consequence of this miscalculation was that the fulfilment of the output-programme required a much larger expansion of the labour-force of industry than had been budgeted for. The original Plan had envisaged an increase of workers in industry by a third (in industry and building combined by 58 per cent.), and of all wage- and salary-earners by just under 40 per cent.[4] Actually by the end of 1932 both the number of workers in industry and the total number of wage- and salary-earners had almost

---

[1] *Summary of the Fulfilment of the First Five Year Plan* (Gosplan), 8.

[2] *Ibid*, 27, 190. In an immediate sense it might appear that this was due to the large influx of raw labour from the village. But at the same time the failure of the output per head of the *existing* labour-force to rise as much as had been expected was the reason, fundamentally, why the intake of *new* labour had to be as large as it was.

[3] In Report to Joint Plenum of C.C. and Control Comm. of C.P.S.U., Jan. 7, 1933.   [4] Cf. Strumilin, *op. cit.*, 20–1; *Piatiletnii Plan*, vol. I, 94.

doubled ; while the number employed in building and construction was more than four times what it had been in 1928.[1] So far as the employment situation was concerned this was wholly beneficial. It was rapidly to transform the situation from one of surplus labour (which we have seen existed at the beginning of the Plan) to one where jobs competed for men and women to fill them: shortage of skilled labour that was to become increasingly acute after 1930. But it was a factor in swelling the wage-bill of industry which not only kept industrial costs at a higher level than costs as planned, but also inflated demand in urban retail markets and accentuated the " goods famine ", with the upward pressure on prices (outside the sphere of ration prices) that this entailed. To this expansion of the wage-bill (and hence of demand on urban markets) a rise in the level of money wages in excess of the Plan's estimates also made its contribution. Whereas the original Plan had budgeted for an increase of money-wages by 50 per cent., average annual wages in fact doubled ; and instead of the rise of productivity being double the rise of wage-rates, as had been intended, the increase of money-wages was two and a half times the rise of productivity. The reasons for so large a rise in wage-rates were complex, and were in part due to a too elastic system of credit facilities for industry in the early years of the quinquennium, about which more will be said in a later chapter. But, as a combined result of a higher wage-level and an increase of numbers, the total wage- and salary-bill of the country quadrupled, or double what had been estimated.[2] As additional consequences of the unanticipated increase in the ranks of the industrial army went a high labour turnover (due to the plethora of jobs and the influx of raw recruits for industry from the village), with its disorganising effects on

[1] *Trud v. S.S.S.R. : Statisticheskii Spravochnik* (Ed. A. S. Popov, 1936), 24 ; *Summary of the Fulfilment of the First Five Year Plan*, 286.

[2] *Ibid.*, 287 ; Strumilin, *op. cit.*, 59. The increase in the annual wage and salary fund was from 8,158 million roubles in 1928 to 32,737 million in 1932. In building alone the increase was from 720 million to 4,715 million. (*Trud v. S.S.S.R. : Statisticheskii Spravochnik*, 20–1.) Strumilin's estimate for the income of the urban proletariat had been 6·7 milliard roubles in 1927–8 and 12·8 in 1932–3 (according to the optimal variant of the Plan), and for the expenditure of this income he gave the following figures :

	1927–8	Per cent.	1932–3	Per cent.
Purchase of agricultural products	2,891	43·5	5,009	39·0
Purchase of industrial goods	2,288	34·2	4,174	32·5
House-room and communal services	582	8·7	1,220	9·5
Cultural-educational and social-political expenditures	355	5·3	1,053	8·2
Taxes	20	0·3	52	0·4
Miscellaneous	236	3·5	565	4·4
Savings	334	5·0	773	6·0

industrial production, and an accentuation of the housing shortage in the towns.

II

During the first two years of the Plan the process of reconstruction proceeded smoothly enough: more smoothly, perhaps, than had been envisaged. True, the "disequilibrium between demand and supply" in the market for consumers' goods, which Bukharin and his fellow "Rights" denounced, was accentuated; and throughout 1929 the grain situation continued to be a serious one, with grain collections by the State slightly below the average of the two preceding years. The supply of certain technical crops had increased (flax and cotton by 13 to 14 per cent.), largely due to an upward revision of the official purchase-prices; but the rise in grain prices proved to be appreciably more than had been anticipated.[1] In 1930, however, there was to be a bumper harvest which provided a surplus for export, capable of repairing in that year the effect of the fall in export-prices. Moreover, the progress of the collective farm movement was surpassing expectations. In the first year of the Plan the number of peasant farms that had been organised in collective farms had more than doubled, and the sown area of collective farms had trebled, at the same time as the total agricultural area of sown land had risen by 5 per cent. Professor Strumilin of Gosplan could proudly claim that "in this most important and decisive sector we emerge stronger than the Plan presupposed".[2] The opening of the calendar year 1930 was to see a figure of 4 million peasant households as the number in collective farms; which represented about one fifth of all peasant households and already two thirds of the target which the Plan had set for 1933. Moreover, in the concluding months of 1929, following the harvest, grain collections by the State had shown a very marked upward movement on the figure for the same period of the preceding year. On the basis of the enlarged crop area of State and collective farms during the first year of the Plan, it was confidently expected that in the following year State and collective farms would be able to supply some 6 or 7 million tons of grain for the market, which was about half of the total of marketed grain, or more than

---

[1] S. Turetsky in *Planovoe Khoziaistvo*, 1929, No. 11, 139; A. Averbukh and A. Briukhanov, *ibid.*, 84 seq.; A. Mendelson, *Plan. Khoz.*, 1929, No. 5, 54–76. Of the earlier part of the year "a counter-attack of *kulak* elements in the village" had been remarked upon, "expressing itself in a check to grain deliveries and a very significant accumulation of private capital" (*ibid.*, 70).

[2] "Control Figures for 1929–30", *Plan. Khoz.*, 1929, No. 9, 18.

the Five Year Plan had intended to be reached by 1933; and that the total marketable surplus of grain would be restored to three quarters of the pre-war level as against less than 40 per cent. two years before.[1] As regards industry, the increase of output for 1928-9 had amounted to nearly 24 per cent., as compared with the $21\frac{1}{2}$ per cent. that the Five Year Plan had stipulated: a rate of increase that was to be maintained and even slightly exceeded in the second Plan year. At the same time the rise in the productivity of labour in 1928-9 had almost reached the target-figure of an annual increase of 17 per cent.

It was in this optimistic atmosphere that the decision was taken to accelerate the *tempo* of development above the level of the original Five Year Plan. A start was made in this direction in the Control Figures for 1929-30. For the year 1929-30 the Control Figures raised the estimates for investment, both in industry and in the economic system at large, by about a third over the figure for that year in the original Plan. The figure of industrial production was advanced by one eighth, so as to raise the rate of increase in production substantially above the figure of 21 per cent. which had been set as the annual rate of increase for the whole quinquennium. But the most drastic revisions were in the sown area and production of State and Collective farms, which were advanced by more than twice.[2] This precedent was followed in subsequent years; and the official date for the termination of the First Plan was eventually set at the end of the calendar year 1932, or three quarters of a year earlier than had been originally designed.[3] The target rate of increase of industrial production for 1931 was nearly double that which the original Plan had assigned to this year. According to the latter the target for coal production in the final year of the Plan was to have been 75 million tons; yet the Control Figures for 1931 were already setting a figure of 83 million tons, while the coal target for 1932 was as much as doubled. The 1931 target for pig-iron was similarly stepped-up from 6·2 to 8 million and for 1932 from 10 to 17 million tons.[4] Several important new construction projects were started in these years which had not

[1] *Otchet Tsentralnovo Komiteta XVI Sezdu V.K.P.* (Stalin and Kaganovich), 29.
[2] *Ibid.*, 23–6; E. I. Kviring, *loc. cit.*, 41–66; G. M. Krzhizhanovsky in *Plan. Khoz.*, 1929, No. 11, 8–13; *Kontrolnie Tsifri na 1929–30 g.*, 48–9. The 1930 target for the sown area of these farms was two thirds of the original target for 1933.
[3] In 1930 a transition was made from the agricultural year to the calendar year as the period for all plans and economic estimates. To balance up the agricultural year of 1929–30 with the calendar year 1930, a "special quarter" was inserted at *the end of 1930.*
[4] *Narodnoe Khoziaistvo S.S.S.R. na Porogo Tretievo Goda Piatiletki i Kontrolnie Tsifri na 1931*, 43.

been upon the original agenda of the first quinquennium of construction. These included a new tractor plant at Kharkov, and the initial production of combine-harvesters as well as tractors ; a start with the production of synthetic rubber and the opening-up of the new Karaganda coalfield in Kazakhstan. In addition, the date for completion of certain construction projects already on the agenda was advanced : the Stalingrad tractor plant, for example, was to be completed in " two building seasons " instead of in three or four, and the " forced construction " of the Magnitogorsk, Kusnetsk and Zaporozhe metallurgical plants was called for.[1] Over the whole period of four and a quarter years from October, 1928, to December, 1932, actual investment in industry (valued at current prices[2]) turned out to be higher by nearly a third, and in heavy industry alone by nearly a half, compared with the original estimates for the whole five-year period. This increase in investment in heavy industry was at the expense, not only of investment in the lighter industries, producing consumption goods, where development programmes were curtailed, but also in some cases of current output in these trades (e.g. in the case of textiles owing to a reduction of imports of raw materials). Morever, the increased investment in industry as a whole was partly at the expense of investment in other directions : for example, while total investment in the socialised sector showed an increase of 12 per cent., total investment in the economic system at large turned out to be somewhat less than the Five Year Plan had envisaged, owing to the drastic shrinkage of the sector of private enterprise.[3]

That " spinal year " 1929–30, the second of the quinquennium, when the accelerated *tempo* of construction was first set in motion, was certainly a turning-point in more respects than one. It was to be the year of the mobilisation of forces for the crucial battle of the collectivisation campaign, which included the despatch of special detachments of young Communists from the towns into the villages as part-organisers, part-propagandists to storm the citadel

[1] Cf. resolution of Sixteenth Party Congress, June 26–July 14, 1930. (*Rezolutsii i Postanovlenia XVI Sezda V.K.P.*, 36, 39.)

[2] The correction to be made here for the rise of prices is probably not as great as is sometimes assumed, since heavy industry continued to be subsidised at this period, with the aim of stabilising prices, and the cost of investment largely reflected the prices of products of heavy industry. Higher wage costs on construction-sites, however, must have been an important factor in inflating the cost of investment from 1930 onwards.

[3] *Summary of the Fulfilment of the First Five Year Plan*, 270. Investments in the private sector for the 4¼ years turned out to be only 43 per cent. of the figure originally set for the 5 years. Of investment in industry 86 per cent. was in heavy industry and only 14 per cent. in light.

of age-long peasant traditions under the banner of a radically new way of life for the village. It was to be the year of the crucial battle with the Right opposition and the capitulation of its leaders. It was to be the year both of the final offensive against the *kulaks* and of serious " excesses " and departures from the voluntary principle in the formation of collective farms which Stalin had postulated at the Fifteenth Party Congress two years before. To a large extent the acute economic difficulties of the next two to three years, such as the acute shortages of supply on the retail market, the unanticipated enlargement of the industrial labour force and of the urban population, can be attributed to this forcing of the pace : at least, to the impact of this accelerated *tempo* of industrial investment on that sharp deterioration of a number of factors in the economic environment which were to cloud the concluding half of the quinquennium. But if we are to appreciate the atmosphere of those years, in which epoch-making decisions of economic policy were to be taken, one thing that is generally omitted has to be borne in mind. The situation that Soviet economy had reached was regarded as being one of those crucial stages in the process of history where, if progress along a certain line of development is to be made with any rapidity at all, it has to be made under the impetus of an initial rush ; where the inertia-forces that have accumulated and crystallised over a whole preceding epoch of history have to be overborne by the momentum of this sudden move, if they are not to retard and deflect the course of movement over several decades ; where the process of sapping and infiltration must needs give way before the simultaneous and abrupt assault. There is no doubt that in those crucial years the situation was conceived, as in 1917 Lenin had conceived it, in terms very similar to military strategy, with its single-minded concentration on a strategic objective, on a crucial timing and a crucial line of thrust. In such a situation the rules and habits of normal continuity in development are rudely broken ; and economic targets lose their character of cold prediction (if they can ever be that entirely) and assume an evocative rôle. When we add to this the sense of urgency aroused by the sudden recrudescence of the war-danger, we can appreciate better the temper of the years when Soviet economy seemed to stake all on beating the clock, and to take risks which seemed to defy the dictates of reason. We may even feel that what the onlooker at the time may have seen as unreasoning lack of caution, in retrospect is to be appreciated as one of those acts of faith and courage without which history is not made.

We have seen that the upward revision of targets which started at the end of 1929 was not entirely ungrounded in the evidence of successful achievement to-date. The plans for transforming agriculture had previously been regarded as the weakest link in the chain. Of these the original Plan had spoken cautiously, in these words : " Unusual difficulties are involved in the problem of reorganising farming on a collective basis and of devising such forms of collective organisation as will guarantee the maximum effectiveness of the capital invested. The fact must be frankly faced that in this field we are still feeling our way, that the fundamental technical principles of collective farming have not as yet been clearly formulated."[1] Events to date seemed to show that in estimating the progress of the collective farm movement the original Plan had so far proved over- and not under-cautious. This unexpected break-through on the crucial sector of the front not only required altered provision in other directions—for example, an acceleration of the production-plans for tractors to feed equipment to the new farms—but opened up new possibilities for the advance of industry. Hailing the first year of the Piatiletka as " a year of great change ", Stalin in November, 1929, had spoken of the situation in these confident terms : " We are advancing," he said, " full steam ahead along the path of industrialisation to Socialism, leaving behind the age-long ' Russian ' backwardness. We are becoming a country of metal, a country of automobiles, a country of tractors. And when we have put the U.S.S.R. in a motor-car and the *mouzhik* upon a tractor . . . we shall see which countries may then be ' classified ' as backward and which as advanced."[2] Moreover, even though it was true that the pace of construction was at the moment straitly limited by the shortage of building materials, there was at least some weight in the argument that, since metals generally were in scarce supply, the right course was to shift the investment-priority still further in favour of heavy industry, so as to reinforce this weak point on the economic front, to remove this brake on the rate of progress at the earliest possible date.[3]

---

[1] *The Soviet Union Looks Ahead*, 85.
[2] In *Pravda* on the occasion of the twelfth anniversary of the October Revolution.
[3] The returns showed that in 1928–9 there was a deficiency of bricks and timber (as a percentage of the demand) of 17 to 18 per cent., of glass 23 per cent., and of cement 4 per cent. At the same time, of " black " metal there was a deficiency of supplies to the extent of nearly 30 per cent. ; even a top priority like transport only receiving 87 per cent. of its demand (and handicraft production only a half). " White " metals, despite a substantial import of them, were in short supply to the extent of 25 per cent. (I. G. Turovsky in *Plan. Khoz.*, 1929, No. 12, 35–6.)

The gravest loss suffered by Soviet economy in the battle for the village was the widespread slaughter of livestock which so drastically reduced the number of draught animals and cattle. The *kulaks* had struck a damaging counter-blow against those who had decreed their " elimination as a class ", and had won a considerable section of the " middle peasantry " to their side in doing so, if only by virtue of deep-rooted peasant instinct which had no further use for property that was to be no longer in their own individual ownership. By 1931 the number of cattle had fallen by nearly a third (and by 1932 more than a third) of the 1929 level ; sheep and goats had fallen by a half ; and horses by a quarter. Moreover, the fall in the animal population continued of its own momentum until 1933 ; and it was only after that year that the process of recovery began.[1] It took the remainder of the decade to make good the loss and to regain the *status quo ante*. By the end of 1939 the 1929 level had scarcely been reached in the case of cattle and had not yet been reached in the case of sheep and goats. Only pigs were substantially above it ; and they had made a quick recovery and had topped even the 1928 peak by 1936. Horses, on the other hand, were little more than half the 1929 figure.

One result of this, in addition to its effect on the supplies of meat and hides and dairy produce, was that it caused a larger gap in animal power for cultivation than could be filled by the supply of tractors to agriculture for several years. If one assumes that one tractor horse-power is the equivalent of two live horses in working capacity, the total tractive-power in agriculture, both animal and mechanical, in 1932 apparently works out at less than the 1929 level by about one sixth : a leeway which was only fully made up after 1935.[2] This was no doubt a powerful contributory factor in the poor results which the majority of collective farms were to show in their early years, and in the failure of crop-yield to improve in these years as the Plan had intended. The Plan had budgeted for an improvement of yield by as much as 35 per cent. in the case of grain between 1928 and 1932. The actual grain yield failed to improve, and for the average of the years 1929–32 it was even slightly lower than the average of 1925–8. This average for the four harvests which fell within the foreshortened term of the First Plan was, of course, depressed by the two bad harvests of 1931 and 1932 (both of which

[1] Except in the case of pigs, which reached their low point in 1932 at a little more than half the 1929 level.
[2] Cf. V. P. Timoshenko on " Soviet Agricultural Reorganisation " in *Stanford Wheat Studies*, 1936–7, 311.

were smaller than in any year since 1924). But even if we take 1933, with its grain harvest larger than 1928 by about a fifth, it remains true that increase of area had contributed about as much to the increase since 1928 as had higher yield per acre ; and it was only from that year onward that any appreciable improvement of grain-yield became evident. The main contribution that collective forms of agriculture made in these hard years of the first quin-quennium to the progress of industrialisation was the substantial increase they afforded in the marketable surplus of agricultural produce, which in the harvest year 1932–3 was almost double what it had been six years before in the case of grain and potatoes, and more than double in the case of cotton, flax and wool.[1]

How much of the destruction of livestock was a result of the exaggerated pace to which the collectivisation campaign was carried in the winter of 1929–30 we cannot tell. It has now become fairly clear that Stalin himself was responsible both for shortening the time-table of 'mass collectivisation' and, in part at least, for the measures of 'pressure from above', including violent and arbitrary police measures, at this time.[2] But it was evidently the urgent desire to put a stop to the alienation of the middle peasantry, with its dire political and economic repercussions, that called forth Stalin's famous letter of March 2nd, 1930, in which he blamed the lower levels of the Party for offending against the voluntary principle in the forma-tion of collective farms. In this letter, entitled "Dizzy with Successes", he denounced the violation "in a number of districts" of "the voluntary principle and the principle of allowing for local peculiarities". He referred to efforts, made "not infrequently", to "*substitute* for preparatory work in organising collective farms the bureaucratic decreeing of a collective farm movement from above,[3] the formation of collective farms on paper—of farms which do not yet exist". He spoke of "unseemly threats against the peas-ants" (including in Turkestan threats "to resort to military force" and "to deprive peasants who do not as yet want to join the collective farms of irrigation water and of manufactured goods"); of "the distortions of so-called 'Lefts'" which serve merely to "strengthen

[1] Cf. figures in A. Baykov, *Development of the Soviet Economic System*, 325–6.
[2] In discussion of a report by a special commission presided over by Y. A. Yakovlev in the Politburo on 22 Dec. 1929 amendments had been pressed by Stalin and Riskulov which, *inter alia*, removed the report's emphasis on adhering to the principle of "voluntariness" (cf. *Voprosi Istorii K.P.S.S.*, 1964, No. 1, 32–43).
[3] It is true that some warning had been given against "'decreeing' of the collec-tive farm movement from above" in a directive of the Central Committee of the Party published in *Pravda* on Jan. 6. (Cf. *Osnovnie Directivi Partii i Pravitelstva po Khoziaistvennomu Stroitelstvu, 1931–1934*, 2nd ed., 48–50.)

our enemies", and of "blockhead exercises in 'socialisation'" of every calf and hen, which were "disintegrating and discrediting" the collective farm movement. He added a jeer at "revolutionaries" who begin the work of organising an *artel* by removing the church bells. "Methods of collective farm organisation in developed districts cannot be mechanically transplanted to backward districts": the grain-deficient regions of the north or districts of backward nationalities such as Turkestan must be treated differently from the wheat-growing districts of the steppe. Adaptation to local conditions, "coupled with the voluntary principle, is one of the most important prerequisites"; while the agricultural *artel*, where the main means of production and farm buildings are in the collective ownership of the group, but dwelling houses and gardens, "a certain part of the dairy cattle, small livestock, poultry, etc" are individual possessions, must be "the main link in the collective farm movement".[1]

From this time onward the focus of attention was shifted towards a consolidation of what had been achieved rather than extension of the size or number of collective farms : to enlisting non-party "middle peasants" for leading positions in the farm and solving the practical problems involved in farming along the new lines.[2] But any attempt to assimilate the régime on a collective farm to that of a State farm, or even to create joint "combines" of the two types of farm, was officially frowned upon.[3] At first there was a large drop in the number of peasants in collective farms in consequence of the reassertion of the voluntary principle. From a figure of 14 million on March 1st, 1930, the membership in terms of peasant households fell to 5 million by May. It was not many months, however, before the upward curve was resumed. While official pressure on peasants to join was thenceforth proscribed, some substantial economic preferences were granted to the collective farm by comparison with the individual farmer. These preferences included an exemption of all animals and livestock from tax for two years, whether these were the property of the Kolkhoz or of its individual members, favourable terms of credit and priority in allocation of manufactured goods in scarce supply. A form of contract between the State and the collective farm was introduced under which its land was granted to the latter in perpetual user-

---

[1] This letter was published in *Pravda* on March 2, 1930, and is reproduced in the 1940 English edition of Stalin's *Leninism*, 333–8.

[2] Cf. Stalin's article in *Pravda*, "Reply to Collective Farm Comrades", April 3, 1930, reproduced *ibid.*, 339–58.

[3] Cf. Decree of Sixth Soviet Congress, *Osnovnie Direktivi, 1931–1934*, 44.

right and could not be alienated.[1] In the spring of 1932 permission
was granted to these farms to sell any of their surplus produce that
they might choose on the free market—the so-called " Kolkhoz
market " : a permission that was subsequently extended to produce
from the private allotments of individual collective farmers[2]. About
the same time a directive of the Central Committee of the Party
expressly repudiated any coercive appropriation of cows and small
animals belonging to individual members of collective farms ; and
there followed a series of measures to facilitate the acquisition of
minor livestock by collective farmers for their own use.[3] By the
end of 1932 the membership of collective farms (in terms of the
number of peasant households) had again passed the 14 million
mark. This figure represented more than 60 per cent. of the
peasantry. These 200,000-odd farms embraced two thirds of the
total sown area, compared with a percentage of one seventh which
the original Five Year Plan had set as the achievement of its final
year. The number of tractors had increased six or seven times
and the current annual output of tractors had grown to be a third
of the total stock. State and collective farms between them now
supplied 84 per cent. of the marketed surplus of grain and 83 per
cent. of that of cotton ; so that the new forms of agriculture could
justly be said to occupy " a decisive rôle in the food supply of the
country " and " in the creation of a raw material base for industry
and export ".[4]

In 1928 State farms had received a great deal of emphasis and
attention as an immediate contribution to the problem of supplying
grain to the towns or for export. Giant mechanised " grain

---

[1] Cf. also the decree of TSIK and Sovnarcom of Sept. 3, 1932, which " prohibited any re-allotment of land in the working use of Kolkhozy " ; " prohibited
regional organs of government from cutting off land from one Kolkhoz for transfer
to the use of others " and laid down that " a change in the boundaries of Kolkhozy
in connection with their fusion or separation is allowed only with the agreement of
not less than three quarters of the members of the Kolkhozy " in question. Land
Commissions were set up in each region to arbitrate in disputes about land-
boundaries of collective farms. (*Osnovnie Direktivi, 1931–4,* 82–3.) Two months
later all movable property of Kolkhozy was protected from arbitrary disposal or
seizure by any organ of government (Decree of Nov. 10, 1932, cit. *Spravochnik
Sovetskovo Rabotnika,* 475).

[2] In January of the following year a revision was made in the mode of assessment of the " obligatory deliveries " of produce by collective farms, so that the
delivery quota should be fixed early in each winter for the next crop year. Its
obligation was then known by a farm in advance, and any surplus it had at its own
disposal.

[3] *Osnovnie Direktivi, 1931–4,* 92–5. Even members of agricultural " communes "
(as well as of *artels*) were allowed and encouraged to have their own livestock.

[4] *Summary of the Fulfilment of the First Five Year Plan,* 147, 285 ; *Osnovnie
Direktivi, 1931–4,* 52 ; A. Gaister on " Agriculture in the Last Year of the Piatiletka ", *Plan. Khoz.,* 1932, No. 1, 148 seq.

factories " were planned, to bring relief to the grain market over the next two or three years while the more slow-moving campaign to induce individual peasants to become collective farmers was getting into its stride.   In 1928 there were some 3000 of such farms with a crop-acreage of some $3\frac{1}{2}$ million.   The intention of the Five Year Plan had been to develop them to cover an area three times as large and to yield about $1\frac{1}{2}$ million tons of marketable grain, or some 17 per cent. of the total marketable grain surplus.   A special Grain Trust was formed, and plans were launched for the institution of huge extensive grain farms of 100,000 acres or more, chiefly in the more arid regions east of the Volga and in the North Caucasus, and later in West Siberia and in Kazakhstan.   In the first year of the Plan about 120 of these new Grain Trust farms were launched, having an average size of 140,000 acres ; and in the autumn of 1929 a revised target for State farms of 25 million acres of grain was instituted, which was nearly eight times (instead of three times) the 1928 area.   By the end of 1931 it was reported in *Pravda* that the number of giant farms of the Grain Trust had grown to 207, having an equipment of 16,000 tractors and 5,000 combine-harvesters and covering a crop-acreage of 12 to 13 million acres.   It was these farms, breaking the virgin soil of the steppe, that had been responsible for most of the expansion of the total area under grain in these years.[1]   By the end of 1932 the sown area under State farms had increased about eight times over the 1928 level and embraced one tenth of the total sown area of the country ; while their supply of grain to the State was four times as great as in 1928. They employed about a million workers (or rather less than 2,000 per farm) ; they possessed more than a half of all the tractors ; their average size was about 6,000 acres.[2]

Compared with the amount that had been invested in them, the results of these State farms were less impressive than at first sight appears.   While they had performed an essential rôle in extending the area of cultivation in the lean years, as regards yield and total production they had fallen short of expectations.   This was pro-

---

[1] The State farms were chiefly growers of wheat, so that one result of their expansion was an increase of the wheat area (mainly winter wheat) between 1928 and 1931 by about a third.   From 1931 there was a tendency for the total area under rye (which made up some 46 per cent. of the total area under bread grains in 1928) to fall.   Over the period 1928–32 there was a rather greater expansion in the area under bread grains than of the total grain area, owing to a change-over from fodder grains to bread grains. (Cf. Timoshenko, *op. cit.*, 327, 334.)

[2] The grain farms were comparatively few in number (under 500 or an eighth of the total), and organised on a very much larger scale.   In addition to them there was a much larger number of much smaller State farms cultivating special crops like beet, tea or tobacco, or rearing livestock.

bably due in part to deficiency of experienced personnel and the difficulties of successful management and supervision of farming operations in such large units. But it may have been attributable more largely to an initial over-estimation of the possibilities, by deeper ploughing, of extracting larger yields from the land in the regions of deficient rainfall in the south-east. In November, 1931, sharp criticism of the working of many State farms was voiced in a statement issued over the signatures of Stalin and Molotov. Commissions of investigation had reported cases of " crying inefficiency and mismanagement ". " The land cultivation on State grain farms," it was said, " was quite unsatisfactory, and they have failed to utilise the ample technical equipment available to them for the improvement of yields."[1] Subsequently at the Seventeenth Party Congress at the beginning of 1934 Stalin complained of State farms that " they still fail to cope with their tasks ". " I do not in the least underestimate the great revolutionising rôle of our State farms," he said, " but if we compare the enormous sums the State has invested in them with the actual results they have achieved to date, we shall find an enormous balance against the State farms. The principal reason for this discrepancy is that our State grain farms are too unwieldy ; the directors cannot manage such huge farms. The farms are also too specialised : they have no rotation of crops and fallow land ; they do not engage in livestock breeding." After 1931 " giant mania " and talk of " grain factories " quickly went out of fashion ; and in the following year a number of State grain farms in the more arid south-eastern districts of low yield were abandoned. Now that the period of acute emergency was passed, when quick returns were a dominant consideration, the personnel and equipment of such farms were better transferred to areas of greater humidity whose land held better promise of crop-improvement. Steps were simultaneously taken to reduce the size of the larger grain farms and to decentralise their administration. The Grain Trust was split up into a number of regional trusts (some 20 in number) at the same time as a special Commissariat for State Farms was instituted in Moscow.[2] Not only did State grain farms become smaller, but they were subdivided into a number of departments, each of them under its own management like the main sections of a large industrial concern. Subsequently

---

[1] *Izvestia*, No. 28, 1931.
[2] In 1935 there was a further change, the regional trusts being abandoned in favour of the division of the country into five main territorial regions, each covered by a special regional division of the Commissariat. At the same time the authority of the director of a State farm was strengthened.

a maximum of between 50,000 and 60,000 acres was set to the size of a farm, with each constituent department or division of it occupying a crop area of 5,000 to 6,000 acres. Moreover, the extreme specialisation of the early years tended to be abandoned, at any rate in grain farming, in favour of greater diversification of crops, with greater emphasis on crop rotation and the inclusion of livestock ; at the same time as separate houses and market-garden allotments for employees were introduced, to bring their condition of life into closer accord with that of collective farmers and to reduce labour-turnover. Emphasis was in general shifted from enlargement of crop area to improvement of yield ; with a corresponding regional shift of weight towards more intensive methods of cultivation in the northern parts of the black-earth zone, in the west and north-west, as well as to development of wheat cultivation in Siberia. In the final years of the Second Plan there was even a slight reduction of the total acreage of these farms and some transfer of grain lands from State farms to collective farms.

Although the new system of mechanised, large-scale farming was slower to bring an increased yield than had been anticipated it must be borne in mind that this was not the essential function which, as a short-term expedient at least, it was required to perform. There can be little doubt that, given time for adaptation to the new system and its adequate equipment (which was lacking in the first half of the thirties), it opened the way to a more rapid and substantial improvement of production[1] than the old system could have done (short of a revival of *kulak* farming, at least). What it essentially did was to raise productivity per man-hour of labour, owing to the labour-saving effects of mechanisation. An important result has been to release much of the labour-time of collec-

---

[1] Such data as existed at the time suggested that the yield per acre tended to be at least some 15 to 20 per cent. greater than on an individual peasant farm. The Kolkhoz Experimental Institute, on the basis of an examination of comparative results in three main grain districts, produced figures to show that gross income per family was about double that on individual holdings in the Middle Volga, more than three times in the Lower Volga and some 80 per cent. higher in the North Caucasus. But there is no indication as to how selective this samples was; and the disparity between the results for the three districts is large. It was also found that the man-power required on the Lower Volga was one person per 4·7 hectares on collective farms as against one person per 2·6 hectares on an individual farm. (Cit. League of Nations, *Report on the Agricultural Crisis*, vol. II.) Towards the end of the decade, results for the Ukraine indicated a fall in expenditure of labour per hectare on collective farms of about one sixth compared with 1933, and a halving of this expenditure compared with individual peasant economy in the middle 1920's. Per centner of grain the expenditure of labour in 1937 was said to be only 60 per cent. of what it had been in 1933, and a third of what it had been in the 1920's. But 1937 was a good crop year. (A. Mkrtumov in *Plan. Khoz.*, 1940, No. 2, 69.)

tive farm members for cultivation of their own market-garden
allotments and care of minor livestock,[1] as contributions to their
own subsistence, as well as to release man-power for migration
from agriculture into industry. Moreover, mechanised cultivation is capable of reducing the very large seasonal fluctuation in
the labour-needs of peasant farming, which was formerly responsible for maintaining on the land a very large reserve of labour
more or less idle for all but certain seasons of the year when the
need for working hands was at its peak. In 1928 it had been
estimated that there was a seasonal labour surplus in winter of
about 16 million persons, or a quarter of the labour-force of the
village, whereas in August during the harvest season there was
an actual deficiency of labour amounting to $1\frac{1}{2}$ million persons,
which had to be met by bringing old men and children to work in
the fields. The degree of mechanisation that had been planned for
1932-3, if it succeeded in relieving the pressure of work at the peak
and in supplanting labour equivalent to $2\frac{1}{2}$ million worker-years for
the one or two months of the harvest season, would " denote a total
economy of labour power over this pair of months of not less than
15 million persons ".[2] Over the period between the two census
years of 1926 and 1939 the density of the farm population relatively
to sown land area has been estimated to have declined by 25 to
29 per cent.[3] This suggests that productivity per head in agriculture may have risen by 60 per cent. or more between 1928 and
the end of the 1930's.

There was also considerably more likelihood that the new type of
farming could be weaned from age-long tradition in methods of
cultivation and educated to improvement. This became the main
emphasis both in State and collective farms in the years of " consolidation " in the middle '30's which were quickly to succeed the
rough and ready methods of the pioneering years. Increasing
attention was paid to improved rotation, the introduction of fodder-
crops into the rotation, and the early ploughing of fallow. Russian
soil had always been deficient in manure, owing to the paucity of
animals on the majority of peasant farms ; and this deficiency could

[1] While these allotments represent only a small fraction of the total area of
collective farms (under 5 per cent.), they are the most intensively cultivated, being
mainly devoted to market gardening, and represent a substantially larger proportion
of the value of total production. The number of working days put in by an average
collective farmer on collective work in the farm fields is very far from being a full
working year.
[2] S. G. Strumilin, op. cit., 10. This rural surplus population, partly seasonal,
partly absolute, is, of course, a familiar feature of other peasant countries of
Europe, as we have remarked above (chap. I).
[3] F. Lorimer, The Population of the Soviet Union, 110.

only be repaired by an enlargement of the number of animals on the collective farms. Here there was much leeway to be made up before any advance on the old position could be made. Artificial fertilisers act powerfully upon the yield in the northern *podzol* zone : more powerfully than they do on the richer black soil of the steppe region, so that their influence is an equalising one.[1] On the poorer soils of the former region with their greater rainfall (especially in the north-west) they give promise of something like a doubling of yields.[2] But without a development of the chemical industry to a level several times the size that it had reached by the end of the decade, the supply of fertilisers was insufficient for more than a small fraction of the cultivated area of the whole country.[3] For the present, accordingly, chemical manuring had in the main to be confined to land under " industrial crops ", especially beet and cotton, which react strongly to the application of artificial manures ; and this policy was largely responsible for the impressive increase of yield of such crops in the course of the 1930's. In other districts reliance was placed on a rapid enlargement of the area under clover and lucerne (which make a substantial contribution of nitrogen to the soil). The Second Five Year Plan, as we shall see, made no provision for an enlargement of the cultivated area, as its predecessor had done (in fact, its figure for 1937 was even slightly lower than the original target-figure for 1932 had been) ; but concentrated instead on calling for a substantial increase of yield as the result of qualitative improvements in methods of farming : a percentage increase approximately the same as that which the First Plan had hoped for but had not achieved.

III

We have seen that over the period of 4¼ years, which was to become the official term of the First Plan, the rate of investment in

[1] Potash has very little effect at all on the latter, except in the case of beet and most vegetables. But nitrogen and phosphates have a powerful effect on *most* types of soil, even though a smaller effect on yield of black-earth soil than on *podzol*. On the chestnut soils of the Black Sea–Azov region phosphates, however, have very little effect.

[2] Cf. Academician Prianishnikov and Prof. Lebediantsev in *Plan. Khoz.*, 1935, No. 3, 67–96.

[3] It was estimated that to raise the level of artificial manuring on the 70 million hectares of cultivated land which respond most strongly to chemical fertilisation up to the Dutch level would require a quantity of fertilisers equal to the whole world production of fertilisers in 1929, or more than six times the output of the whole Soviet chemical industry at the end of the Second Five Year Plan. To raise the level of manuring up to that of the German level would require half this amount. (*Ibid.*, 79.)

heavy industry was considerably increased over the original estimates, mainly at the expense of investment in light industry ; while investment in factory industry at large and in State and collective farming and Machine Tractor Stations was increased at the expense of investment in other directions,[1] especially in small-scale handicraft production and in the private sector of agriculture. In the iron and steel industry new blast furnaces[2] brought into operation during these years represented a quarter of the total number of blast furnaces in operation at the beginning of the period, and nearly two thirds of their output capacity. In the engineering industry nearly a half of the machine-tools in operation in 1932 had been installed during the period of the Five Year Plan ; and in certain branches such as motor-cars, tractors and machine-tool construction the proportion of new equipment rose to 80 per cent. and more. In the coal industry about a quarter of total output came from new pits put into operation during the Five Year Plan : a proportion which in 1933 was expected to rise to 35 per cent. In the oil industry the number of wells in operation had risen by a quarter since 1928 ; while two thirds of the plant in primary refining and practically all of the cracking plant was created during the years of the Plan. The total capacity of electric power stations had more than doubled. The chemical industry was mainly a new industry, as was a large part of the food-processing industry. Even the cotton industry had seen one million new spindles, or one-seventh of the former spindle-equipment, installed. In agriculture the net increase in the stock of agricultural machinery (after allowing for " normal " depreciation) was estimated at round 100 per cent. ; while in industry the coefficient of mechanical power per man-hour of human labour was estimated to have risen by 33 per cent., and that of electrical power supplied to industry by 88 per cent.[3]

Looked at in the round, one can say that the Plan attained its primary objective, construction of heavy industry on a firm basis, with brilliant success, even reaching some of its main targets ahead of schedule. The capital goods industries, making means of production (classified as " Group A industries "), registered an increase in gross output (valued in prices of 1926–7) of two and a half times, or slightly more than the original Plan figure for 1932–3. The output of machinery of all kinds increased four times, con-

---

[1] One direction (significant as being a large consumer of metal) in which investment fell somewhat short of the original estimates was the construction of new railway track.   [2] This excludes " reconstructed " furnaces.
[3] *Summary of the Fulfilment of the First Five Year Plan*, 49–52, 270, 275, 282.

siderably exceeding the original target.[1] Oil slightly exceeded the Plan, nearly doubling its output ; and the output of electrical power increased more than two and a half times, although this fell short of the planned rate of increase. The production of large-scale industry as a whole registered an increase of 118 per cent., which was somewhat short of the 133 per cent. planned for the final year of the quinquennium.

Curiously enough iron and steel were laggards, falling substantially behind the Plan ; although the tonnage of pig-iron nearly doubled, while steel output grew by the more modest percentage of 40. Both pig-iron and steel had been intended to reach an output-level of 10 million tons by the fifth year, whereas in fact they only attained 6·2 million and 5·9 million respectively. Coal, again, was about 10 million tons short of the 75 million set as the target for 1932–3. The reason for this lagging of iron and steel was that, despite the impressive achievements in construction in this industry, there had been unexpected delays in getting many of the new plants into effective use : a failure which caused foreign critics at the time to say that, while the Soviets could build they could not handle modern technique, and that " giant mania " in Soviet industry had spawned a race of white elephants. Already *The Times* of October 7th, 1930, had stated editorially that " the Plan has begun to show signs of breaking down " ; and the *New York Times* two years later dismissed the Plan as " really not a plan " but a " gamble ". Early in 1930 the *émigré* Professor Prokopovitch was prophesying that " the Five Year Plan is unrealisable ; . . . industry will soon be faced by a crisis and an arrest in its development ; the decline of agriculture will be markedly accelerated ".[2] But while there was delay in mastering the problems of normal operation, and much of the construction work had been inefficient, events were to prove that in the main the foundations had been soundly laid ; and it was to be the task of the first few years of the Second Plan to surmount these initial difficulties, following Stalin's injunction in January, 1933, to " master the new technique ". Those difficult four and a quarter years had at any rate to their credit in this industry the construction of 17 new blast furnaces and the bringing into use of another 20 by reconstruction and modernisation ; thereby increasing the total number in use from 69 to 102 ; the installation of 45 new open-hearth

---

[1] See Note on Industrial Statistics at end of the chapter.
[2] In *Annals of Collective Economy* (Ed. E. Milhaud, Geneva), Jan.–Aug. 1930, 86–7.

furnaces, in addition to the reconstruction and modernisation of 21 more, and 15 new rolling mills *plus* 12 reconstructed ones. The foundations had been laid for two new iron and steel centres, Magnitogorsk and Kuznetsk, which between them in the years of the Second World War were to take the place of the Dnieper and Donbas. In addition these years had brought to birth a series of new industries, such as synthetic rubber, plastics, artificial silk and aeroplanes.

The poorest showing came from some of the consumer goods trades, whose investment plans, as we have seen, were pruned in favour of heavy industry in the difficult years. Certain of the consumer goods industries, indeed, registered substantial progress, most notably boots and shoes, the output of which increased nearly three times and passed their target ; and the total output of consumer goods industries showed the considerable increase of 87 per cent. True, as Dr. Baykov has reminded us,[1] this cannot be taken as a true measure of the consumption fund of the country, since part of the increase in factory industry was at the expense of a (temporary) curtailment of small-scale handicraft production ; but it remains true that the factory-output of consumption goods as a whole had undergone a substantial enlargement over this period, despite its position of secondary priority. This advance was not, however, shared by the textile industry, where the output both of cotton and woollen goods, for reasons already mentioned, was somewhat below the 1928 level, and was to remain so for another three years. On the other hand, a development which made an appreciable contribution to the working-class standard of life was the considerable growth in the number of canteens and dining-rooms attached to factories and enterprises of all kinds. In total the network of public catering establishments increased so that by 1932 it was estimated that in the main industries they were capable of supplying a daily meal to between two thirds and three quarters of the workers.[2]

In addition to the problems created in these years by the rapid enlargement of the labour-force of industry and the influx of

[1] *Op. cit.*, 165–6.
[2] The number of dishes per day served in urban catering establishments run by the co-operatives (Centrosoyus) or by the Commissariat of Supply in 1932 was given as 29 million as against 2 million in 1928 (*Summary of Fulfilment*, 289.) There was a parallel development in the '30's of large " kitchen depots " for the supply of cooked meals to a circle of feeding establishments in an area, with some development of a " cash and carry " system to individual consumers. (Cf. a privately circulated memorandum by F. Le Gros Clark on *Soviet Forms in Communal Feeding*, June, 1942.)

untrained labour from the village, unfamiliar with and still un-adapted to the conditions of industrial life, there was a huge problem to be solved in the supply to industry of a growing techni-cally equipped personnel. Even at the beginning of the First Five Year Plan there was an acute shortage of trained personnel, and nearly a half of the posts at the higher managerial level were held by persons who lacked any specialised technical training. The proportion of skilled manual workers in industry was only two thirds of that in German industry. To bridge the gap in the first few years considerable reliance was placed on foreign engineers and technical workers—American, German and some English. But at the same time a campaign was launched to increase the number both of higher technical schools of university and secondary school standing and also of factory schools for the training of skilled workers. By the closing year of the Plan there were reported to be some 200,000 students in higher technical colleges of university standing and some 900,000 receiving education in secondary techni-cal schools (*technicums*) ; while there existed factory schools and courses capable of handling a million workers per year. The number of " specialists " in industry and other branches of econo-mic life who were equipped with technical education of a university or secondary-school standard were said to have increased two and a half times since 1927-8 and to number between a quarter and half a million.[1] The original Plan, with its more cautious provisions for expansion than were ultimately attempted, had called for 40,000 new engineers of university education in industry alone, for nearly 20,000 civil engineers and 20,000 agricultural experts. Quite apart from this there were the demands of scientific research, on the one hand, and of the teaching and medical professions, on the other hand, upon the products of higher education. This acute shortage of trained personnel at all levels, and the fact that so large a proportion of such personnel as was available was newly (and sometimes inadequately) trained and young in experience, must be taken into account in assessing the difficulties and the deficiencies of these years of great change.

To give encouragement to the growth both in quantity and quality of the higher technical grades, as well as to improve their morale and win their whole-hearted co-operation, serious measures

---

[1] *Summary of Fulfilment of First Five Year Plan*, 229-33, 295 ; *Trud Pervoip Piatiletke* (Komakademia, 1934), 79, 82, 91-3 ; J. G. Crowther, *Industvry an Education in Soviet Russia*. For industry alone the increase of numbers for those with higher education is given as from 13,700 to 49,200 and of those with secondary education from 10,500 to 70,300.

were taken in the early '30's to improve their terms of employment and their living conditions. Enterprises were encouraged to assign them special dining-rooms and living quarters. A government order of March 25, 1932, instructed Gosplan to arrange for the provision of special housing facilities for engineers and technicians over the next two years, in addition to those that were already being provided on new industrial sites. For example, it was stipulated in some detail that there should be ten blocks of flats, each containing 300 apartments, in Moscow, five in Leningrad, and two each in Kharkov and Stalingrad ; the standard to be three or four rooms in each flat, in addition to kitchen and bathroom. Smaller blocks, having 100 flats a piece, were also to be built in 27 other towns, and blocks of 50 flats in a further 67 towns.[1] In all negotiations about wages and working conditions the special sections formed by engineering and technical staffs in the trade unions (the E.T.S.) were accorded the right of separate representation. Generally, with regard to remuneration, there was a reaction against the " wage-levelling " tendencies of the second half of the '20's (which had been pursued as an intentional policy by the trade union leadership under Tomsky), and a widening of the wage-differentials between grades, with the deliberate intention of stimulating a high rate of increase in the ranks of skilled workers and technicians.[2] This new emphasis was largely a response to Stalin's famous Six Point Speech of June 23rd, 1931, in which he called for a new attitude towards the technical staff and inveighed against notions about wage-levelling. In this speech he noted " definite signs of a change of attitude towards the Soviet Government on the part of a certain section of the intelligentsia who formerly sympathised with the wreckers ", which imposed upon the government and the working class the need " to change our attitude towards engineers and technicians of the old school, to show them greater attention and solicitude, to display more boldness in enlisting their co-operation ", while at the same time striving to enlarge their ranks by creating a quite new industrial and technical intelligentsia from among the working class itself.

Of the financial policy of these years, and in particular of the changes in the credit system which took place between 1930 and 1933, more will be said in a later chapter. The increased investment programme of the period had been financed largely by allocations from the Budget : more largely than had been intended in

---

[1] Cf. V. V. Prokofiev, *Industrial and Technical Intelligentsia in the U.S.S.R.*, 67–8.
[2] See below, page 422.

the original Plan, where the main source of the funds for investment was designed to be the reserves accumulated by industry itself from the results of economies in cost which were anticipated but were not in fact to be realised. To some extent this increased expenditure for capital purposes out of the Budget was met by an increase in the revenue from industrial profits taxed into the Budget and from the issue of State loans to individuals and to institutions. But from 1930 onwards the main contribution to mounting expenditure on " financing the national economy " and on defence came from the Turnover Tax (equivalent to the British war-time purchase tax), which had succeeded an older industrial licence duty (levied in proportion to normal turnover) in the taxation reform of 1930. The supply of currency had increased in very much the same proportion as the total wage and salary bill had grown : a correlation that one would naturally expect, since in a planned economy the principal determinant of the volume of cash in circulation (given the factors which determine the average interval between receipt of income and its expenditure) will necessarily be the total of wages. Mainly as a result of this expansion in the volume of money incomes, the " goods famine " was to survive into the second year of the Second Five Year Plan ; and with the shortage of goods continued the special measures taken to meet it, such as rationing and the system of " closed shops " for the preferential allocation of supplies to particular categories of consumers (e.g. special factory co-operatives for supplying workers in essential industries) and the system of differential prices in the various grades of market. But with the passing of the bad harvest years of 1931 and 1932 and of the immediate danger of war in the Far East (which had undoubtedly contributed to a worsening of conditions in 1932 by occasioning an emergency accumulation of supplies of grain and oil, etc., by the government), the tense atmosphere of the hard years, when the foundations were being laid, was to be relieved a little. Although life was to remain hard and the effort of construction unrelenting, something of the grand design lying behind the cold figures of the Plan was beginning to take visible shape in the new economic life that was so rapidly appearing on every side.

NOTE TO CHAPTER TEN ON SOVIET
INDUSTRIAL STATISTICS

Mr. Colin Clark in his *Critique of Russian Statistics* attempted an independent estimate, on rather sketchy data, of the increase in output over this period, valuing certain leading commodities in terms of their dollar prices in U.S.A. in 1928 (and in the case of certain consumption góods at their English prices in 1928) and reached a figure of increase that was only about a half of the official figure: namely a 132 per cent. increase in the output of investment goods, over the six years 1928 to 1934. It is possible to hold that the Soviet method of valuation in terms of 1926–7 values tended to exaggerate the increase by giving unduly heavy weight to newer commodities (e.g. tractors or machine tools) whose cost in 1926–7 were relatively high and which subsequently showed large rates of increase. But it is hard to believe that the effect of this is as large as Mr. Clark makes out, or that the dollar valuations chosen by him are to be regarded as any more "normal" than Russian prices in 1926–7. As a matter of fact a second set of estimates by Mr. Clark for 1934–7 (calculated "at 1934 values in gold francs") very closely confirms the Soviet official figure of increase for those years.

It is undeniable, of course, that measurement of the change in an output-total will be very different when conducted in the different price-structures of various years (the problem being well-known to statisticians under the name of the Paasche-Laspeyres discrepancy—the discrepancy between valuing a change according to the prices at the end-year or the beginning-year of the period in question—and a problem by no means confined to Soviet statistics.[1]) It stands to reason, therefore, that a valuation in 1926–7 prices will probably show a larger rise than other estimates using the price-weights of a later year (or of more developed countries).

What the controversy started by Mr. Colin Clark has, however, tended to conceal is that, even when allowance has been made for such a discrepancy, the qualification involved is probably not very great compared with the rate of growth that is in question: it probably does not amount to more than some 25 or 30 per cent for the period of the First and Second Five Year Plans (to which criticism has mainly applied). An American economist in the '50's tried to construct an index of his own of Soviet industrial output, using as weights the wages and salaries prevailing in the year 1934 instead of selling prices of seven years before. The result was to show an annual rate of growth of industrial output from 1928 to 1937 of about 14 per cent., or for the decade as a whole a little less than a fourfold increase, compared with an increase of five-and-a-half times shown by the official index. An estimate by Dr. F. Seton, of Oxford, by a different

---

[1] An American calculation of the output of items of machinery in U.S.A. has shown that a valuation in prices of 1899 yields a *fifteen*-fold increase between 1899 and 1939, but no more than a *two*-fold increase when valued in prices of 1939 (A. Gerschenkron, *A Dollar Index of Soviet Machinery Output, 1927–8 to 1937*, California, 1951, 52).

method, reaches a closely similar result.[1]   At anyrate, when one looks at
the kind of quantity-increases that one finds in the Table on page 326, it
might seem to the plain man rather trivial to spend time arguing whether
an order of magnitude of 15 or 20 times, or of 20 or 30 times, is properly to
be regarded as the 'true' increase of the aggregate.

Another and distinct ground for criticism, chiefly by American writers,
is that the official index was inflated by the introduction into the index of
new products at the (higher) prices of later years.   This criticism would
seem to have much less weight than has commonly been given to it, since
producers' goods (where growth and innovation were chiefly in evidence)
were apt to be stabilised in price (*e.g.* by subsidy) in the early '30's and many
of them seem actually to have fallen in price owing to cost-reductions; while
from 1936 onwards the method of dealing with new products was changed.[2]

There has, indeed, been a good deal of discussion in Soviet literature
about the problems connected with measuring the volume of output in
terms of "constant prices of 1926–7"; and a number of writers have
pointed out its unsuitability in some respects (cf. D. I. Chernomordik
in *Narodny Dokhod S.S.S.R.* (1939), 27, who points out that the prices of
another base year need to be adopted instead in the case of lines of production subject to technical reconstruction or of new products; A. L.
Rothstein, *Problemi Promishlennoi Statistiki S.S.S.R.* (1936), 242–4).
The method adopted was to value all output which had a prototype in
1926–7 in terms of the prices of that year (this year being chosen as the first
complete year after the end of the "restoration process" when prices
might be considered to have returned to a "normal" level).   All enterprises were instructed annually to enter both planned and actual output in
their returns, and also their main expenditures, *both* in current prices of
the year in question *and* in the prices of 1926–7.   The difficulties introduced by new commodities, whose costs in the first few years of their
introduction may be "abnormal", have been particularly stressed in
discussions of the matter.   At first the practice was adopted of valuing
any new product in terms of its price in the year in which it was fully put
into production; and in 1934 part of the output of the engineering
industry (where new products composed nearly two thirds of the total
output in the middle '30's) was calculated in revised prices which differed

---

[1] D. R. Hodgman, *Soviet Industrial Production 1928–1951* (Cambridge, Mass.,
1954); F. Seton, "Tempo of Soviet Industrial Expansion", Manchester Statistical
Society, 9 Jan. 1957.   This rate of increase comes remarkably close to the results of
a calculation of the unweighted average of quantity-increases of basic metal-fuel-
power output made by the present writer (an article in *Soviet Studies*, April 1953,
reprinted in *On Economic Theory and Socialism* (London, 1955), 118–128).   For the
period between 1937 and 1951 Prof. Hodgman's index shows a somewhat larger
discrepancy from the official figure than for 1928–37 (but then his data for this
period are more scanty): his index shows a doubling of output between 1937 and
1951 as against an increase of three times according to the official index.   Another
American, G. Grossman, has made an estimate for national income as a whole (*i.e.*
including agriculture) and reaches a figure of 6·5–7 per cent. as the annual rate of
increase between 1929 and 1950 (*Soviet Economic Growth*, ed. A. Bergson, Evanston
and N.Y., 1953, 9).   In this case the discrepancy from the official estimate was much
greater, the latter being more than double the former.

[2] Cf. A. Bergson, *Real National Income of Soviet Russia since 1928* (Harvard
1961), 182–6; and the present writer in *Review of Economics and Statistics*, Feb.
1948, and *op. cit.*, 118–19.

from those which had been used in drawing up the plan for that year (*The Second Five-year Plan*, Gosplan 1936, 575 footnote). This procedure was criticised on the ground that "being an expression of the relative significance of this or that aspect of production in different periods, 'constant' prices lose the notion of an internally linked system of weights in the base period", and there results "an inevitable distortion of the weights of heterogeneous articles in a general total of production constructed on the calculation of individual articles according to prices of various years" (A. I. Rothstein, *op. cit.*, 244). In 1936 a new method of calculation was adopted for all commodities newly introduced since 1926–7. According to this method they were to be valued in terms of their 1935 prices, and then reduced to the level of 1926–7 by means either of some standard coefficient for that branch of industry (i.e. an index of the change in prices between 1926–7 and 1935) or else by reference to "a type of product close to it in structure and quality" (*Ibid.*, 248–9). In the case of industrial co-operatives production is measured in "unchanged prices of 1932", and these are then reduced to the level of 1926–7 by the co-operative centre before being submitted to Gosplan. (Cf. "Instructions for the Composition of the Economic Plan for 1937" in *Plan*, 1936, No. 18, 29.)

Calculations in terms of constant prices of 1926–7 have been criticised as unsuitable in particular for measuring investment and fixed capital, owing to the considerable changes in building costs over the intervening period. (Cf. M. Gutstein and M. Persitz in *Plan. Khoz.*, 1939, No. 8, 42–3.) In the post-war (Fourth) Five-Year Plan all investment was calculated in terms of 1945 prices; and is accordingly not comparable directly with figures of total production and national income or with investment figures in previous Five-Year Plans. Previously to this, the practice had been adopted in the Second Plan of valuing investment in 1933 prices, and in the Third Plan in prices of December, 1936.

The parallel valuation of output and costs which industrial enterprises are required to make in terms of *current prices* of the year in question constitutes an essential basis of the Financial Plan, of the comparison of planned costs with actual costs and the calculation of the profit or loss position of an enterprise (see below, Chapter Fifteen). The Budget as a constituent of the Financial Plan is for obvious reasons expressed in terms of current values of the year in question.

Discussion of pre-war valuation in 1926–7 prices, however, is to-day of historical interest only, since this method of valuation was terminated with the Fourth Plan. From 1950 industrial output has been calculated in the prices of a particular month or year of the quinquennium in question:[1] during the Fifth Plan in the prices of 1 January 1952 (new products of subsequent years and "that part of production which is not reckoned in natural units" being reduced to the basis of 1 January 1952 by an index of the average price-changes of the remaining output of the enterprise or industry in question);[2] and for the Sixth Plan in terms of the prices pre-

---

[1] *I.e.* of wholesale (*optovie*) prices, *without* turnover tax.

[2] *Planovoe Khoziaistvo*, 1952, No. 1, 77–9; cf. also G. I. Baklanov, *Promishlennaia Statistika* (Moscow, 1953), 123, where the defects of measurement in 1926–7 prices are explicitly mentioned, including the difficulty of valuing new products, but without any indication of the net effect of these defects.

vailing on 1 July 1955.[1] The method of valuing output in up-to-date (but 'constant') prices has accordingly been assimilated to the method previously adopted for valuing investment at the prices prevailing in a given year of the relevant quinquennium.

In Soviet industrial statistics four main types of aggregate are distinguished, together with certain important subdivisions.

Firstly, there is what is known as *Gross Turnover of Production*, which is the total of all the finished production of enterprises together with the total of all semi-manufactured products worked up in any of the workshops or departments of an enterprise in the given accounting period. (A. I. Rothstein, *op. cit.*, 122-3; N. S. Burmistrov, *Ocherki Tekniko-Ekonomicheskovo Planirovania Promishlennosti*, 37.)

Secondly, there is *Gross Production*, which is equal to the above total *minus* the value of that part of the semi-manufactured products *of each enterprise in question*, which was worked up during the accounting period in succeeding stages of production of *that enterprise*. For example, in an enterprise which combines a tannery and a shoe factory, this total will consist of the output of leather by the tannery *plus* the output of shoes by the shoe factory *minus* the quantity of leather that has entered into finished shoe-production in the period. If the quantity of partly finished boots in the boot factory or of leather in the tannery has altered, this change of "goods in process of production" ought also to be allowed for. In Soviet industry an annual inventory is made of such "uncompleted work in progress"; and a complete definition of Gross Production reads accordingly as follows: the quantity of products, whether finished or semi-finished, turned out by any factory during the year, *less* the quantity of any such semi-finished products from the constituent factories of an enterprise which has been embodied in the output of other constituent factories of that enterprise during the year, *plus* or *minus* the change in quantity of unfinished goods in process of production inside a factory over the year. Actually this latter quantity is only allowed for in four industries (including engineering) where the amount of such unfinished work is likely to be considerable as a proportion of annual output. (A. I. Rothstein, *op. cit.*, 129-30, 144-5; N. S. Burmistrov, *op. cit.*, 37-9; "Instructions for the Composition of the Economic Plan" in *Plan*, 1936, No. 18, 29.) It will be clear that this total will differ according to the nature of the manufacturing unit on the basis of which it is reckoned, e.g. whether the enterprise is taken as being one factory or several factories, and embracing only one stage of production or vertically combining several; since in the example just given the leather used to produce boots would *not* have been deducted from the total if the tannery and the boot factory had been *separate* enterprises. In a few cases materials purchased from outside are deducted: for example in the printing industry "the cost of basic materials (paper), both its own and that supplied by a customer, is not included in the general value of production". ("Instructions" in *Plan*, 1936, No. 18, 31.) But this is a rather special case and is not typical. To this question we shall return in a moment.

---

[1] *Voprosi Ekonomiki*, 1955, No. 8, 74-5. Output in 1955 was to be valued both at January 1952 prices and in July 1955 prices so as to link the index-series relating to the past quinquennium with the new one.

Thirdly, there is the *Traded Product*, which is simply equal to the total of finished output of all enterprises, *minus* that part of it which is used by an enterprise internally instead of being sold to another organisation. (Rothstein, *op. cit.*, 175.)

Fourthly, there is *Net Production*, in the usual economic sense of this term, which is used for purposes of calculating the National Income. One writer has defined it as follows: "One can arrive at the total of net production of industry by subtracting from the total of gross production (with increment of goods in process) the expenditure on materials used up (including that on materials used in the increase of goods). This quantity should consequently include that net product which is included in the increment of goods in process and of partly finished products." (A. I. Pashkov in *Narodny Dokhod S.S.S.R.*, 58.) As we shall see below, not only used-up materials but also depreciation of fixed capital is deducted to arrive at net production for the purpose of estimating National Income.

If we return to the second of these aggregates, there are three distinct subdivisions of it which are distinguished by A. I. Rothstein in his illuminating analysis of industrial statistics:

(*a*) There is Gross Production calculated according to "the factory method", with the factory or trust taken as the unit (according to whichever is treated as the independent accounting unit for making returns in connection with the plan). This is a quantity analogous to what is called "national production" in the statistics of some other countries; and, as Rothstein points out, as a magnitude it is "very conditional . . . and dependent on the degree of differentiation of productive processes, on specialisation of industrial undertakings, on the quantity and weight of semi-finished products entering into commodities, etc." (*Ibid.*, 273.)

(*b*) There is Gross Production calculated, not on the basis of a single enterprise, but for the economy as a whole, with a deduction of all materials entering into final production, whether these are products of some branch of the enterprise responsible for the final product or whether they come from outside. It is "a sum of the gross factory production of enterprises entering into the national economy, with the elimination of double counting of materials entering into the production of individual enterprises" to which (*a*), the so-called "factory method" of calculation, is subject. (*Ibid.*, 274.)

(*c*) There is Gross Production as the result of the *production of the particular period* in question. This is analogous to the conception of national income in other countries, and in Britain to the category "net produced value". It is defined as Gross Production calculated according to method (*b*) "with correction for the used-up part of the residue of semi-finished or partly finished production carried over from the preceding accounting period".

Net Production is distinguished from (*c*) by the fact that, to arrive at the former, "amortisation of means of production and other elements of fixed capital entering into the productive process at the beginning of the given accounting period" is deducted. (*Ibid.*, 274.)

In attempts to reduce Net Production to a basis of "constant prices of 1926–7" there were greater difficulties than in the case of Gross Production. The principal difficulty was the considerable change since 1926–7 in the relative prices of elements entering respectively into cost and finished production, mainly due to changes of technique and of productivity. A. I. Rothstein cites an interesting example of a nonsense-result of trying to measure net production in the prices of a much earlier year. A certain Leningrad enterprise, which had unusually complete pre-revolution records of costs and prices, attempted to estimate its net production in some year in the middle '20's in terms of 1913 prices, and reached a *negative* figure. The reason was that in the course of recent years the enterprise had reorganised its technique on the basis of using electrical power, which was then relatively cheap compared with the price of the product, whereas in 1913 electricity had been relatively expensive, for which reason it had not been used. To value the *quantity* of electricity used in the 1920's in terms of the 1913 *price* resulted accordingly in an inflation of the cost-figure relatively to the value-figure of the final product. Hence the method of direct valuation in terms of constant prices of an earlier year is not employed in estimates of Net Production. Two methods of avoiding this difficulty and of reducing the Net Production as calculated in the current values of any year to the constant level of a base year have been used.

Firstly, there was the method employed by Prof. Strumilin in preparing the Control Figures for 1929–30. According to this the relationship of Net Production to Gross Production in the base year, 1926–7, is calculated, in terms of the prices of that year. This provides a coefficient of the share of Net in Gross Output. In subsequent years the Gross Production valued in 1926–7 prices is then multiplied by this coefficient to give the size of "Net Production in constant prices of 1926–7". The defects of this method are evident enough. It makes no allowance for changes in subsequent years in the proportion of net to gross production: changes which are likely to occur as a result of technical change and of the rise of new industries or of shifts between industries. "Calculation of the dynamic of net production carries over the dynamic of gross expressed in constant prices, i.e. to net production is imputed the tempo of movement of gross." (*Ibid.*, 307.)

Secondly, there is a method suggested by a statistician writing in the monthly organ of Gosplan in 1934 (V. Katz, "Basic Questions of Methodology and Method in Calculating National Income" in *Plan. Khoz.*, 1934, No. 7, 143.) This avoids the difficulty of assuming a constant ratio between the *magnitudes* of gross and net output. But since it rests on an assumption that the *price movements* of gross and net production can be identified, it still involves the difficulty of ignoring changes in the ratio between the two totals which may result from changes in the relative weight of different industries having different ratios of net to gross output. This Katz method is as follows. Net production in any year is calculated in terms of the current prices of that year. It is then translated into terms of 1926–7 prices by means of the price index (showing the price-change since 1926–7) appropriate to gross production; i.e. according to the ratio of gross production calculated in current prices to gross production calculated in constant prices of 1926–7. For this calculation, three figures are used: (i) gross production in current prices, (ii) gross production in constant prices of 1926–7, (iii) net production calculated in current prices.

The coefficient derived from the comparison of (i) and (ii) is then used to reduce (iii) to the final result, "net production expressed in constant prices." A. I. Rothstein expresses the view that the movement of gross production calculated according to the "factory method" may show a significant divergence over time from the true movement of net production: which remains a defect of this second form of calculation. It should be noted that Turnover Tax was included in the estimate of net product at current prices: i.e. the latter was a valuation in terms of *market prices*. (Cf. A. I. Pashkov, *op. cit.*, 84–8; A. I. Rothstein, *op. cit.*, 302.)

In principle National Income in the U.S.S.R. is confined to so-called "material production" and excludes services; although this principle has not gone undisputed among Soviet economists (cf. A. I. Pashkov in *Narodny Dokhod S.S.S.R.*, 75; S. Turetsky in *Planovoe Khoziaistvo*, 1939, No. 10, 92–3).

In practice services supplied directly to a consumer and unconnected with the supply of a material commodity are not classed as part of current production, and their value is not included in estimates of the national income (either directly or *via* the incomes of those who supply them). Some services, however, *do* qualify for inclusion: medical services attached to industry are apparently counted, and other social services for workers financed from supplements added to the wages-bill of enterprises; film stars' salaries are presumably included in the net value created by the cinema industry and similarly the services of public catering personnel. On the other hand, services that do not fall within such 'industrial' categories as these are not included: for example, incomes of professional workers from private practice, or workers in the health and educational services, the armed forces, living accommodation and *passenger* transport. While the services of administrative personnel in industry at the level of enterprises and of trusts are included, the higher administrative personnel (of ministries and glavki) are not included (cf. *Slovar-Spravochnik po Sotsialno-Ekonomicheskoi Statistiki*, 2nd ed. 1948, 82–3). How important quantitatively these excluded services are is difficult to estimate: a Soviet source has suggested that they may amount to about 10 per cent. of personal incomes. (In the U.S.A. these excluded services might well account for 30 per cent. of the total; cf. M. Kolganov in *Planovoe Khoziaistvo*, 1955, No. 11.) In conclusion it may be noted that national income estimates include seven main categories. According to *Slovar-Spravochnik po Sotsialno-Ekonomicheskoi Statiski* (1948) these seven categories are as follows: (1) industry, (2) building, (3) agriculture, (4) transport (goods), (5) communications (that part which serves productive sectors), (6) trade, (7) other branches (including forestry, publishing, and hunting and fishing, fuel-collection and fruit-picking carried on as individual occupations).

Statistics of industrial production have, finally, to be distinguished according to the spheres which they cover. Here three main categories are found. Firstly, there is the output of *all* industry, including handicraft co-operatives, etc. Secondly, there is the output of all *large-scale* (or factory) industry, which includes all establishments with not less than sixteen workers where mechanical power is used and not less than thirty workers where no mechanical power is used. Thirdly, to make the above figure comparable with pre-1914 data, the total output of large-scale industry excluding timber and fisheries and railway repair shops is often published separately. This is commonly called *census industry*. Since 1932 the category of census industry in industrial returns has been understood to mean "in general all industrial enterprises, state, communal [i.e. municipal] and co-operative, i.e. all enterprises whose activity is planned on a national scale" and whose activity is included in the Promfinplan (industrial-financial plan). The older definition was, however, preserved "for the comparison of indices in the construction of dynamic series, showing the activity of industry in past years". (A. I. Rothstein, *op. cit.*, 71–2.) This was used, for example, in the 1936 statistical abstract entitled *Socialist Construction in the U.S.S.R.* (cf. footnotes to pages 41 and 47.)

CHAPTER ELEVEN

THE SECOND FIVE-YEAR PLAN

I

The Second Five Year Plan, extending from 1933 to the end of 1937, was able to build upon the experience of its predecessor and to learn from some of the latter's mistakes. Under the slogan of " master technique " and " consolidate the gains already won ", it paid more attention to qualitative improvement both in the work of collective farms and in that of the new plants and industries recently brought into existence, and it set more modest targets for the increase of labour productivity and the reduction of costs than the first Plan had done. Both a high rate of investment and the priority assigned to heavy industry in the plans for construction were maintained. But the rate of investment, while it increased absolutely, was slightly eased as a proportion of the total national income, and a good deal more space was assigned to the development of the light industries than these had occupied originally in the First Plan. The proportion of the national income devoted to investment was to fall from 24 per cent. in the final year of the First Plan to $19\frac{1}{2}$ per cent. in the last year of the Second ; and the amount of capital invested in the consumer goods industries (Group B) was increased proportionately by very much more than investment in the capital goods industries (Group A).[1] The

[1] In the Second Plan all investment and construction and changes in fixed capital are calculated in terms of 1933 prices ; whereas the investment figures for the First Plan had been calculated in terms of the prices of each year, which makes comparisons between the totals for the two Plans difficult. In the figures as given the value of construction work in Group B industries during the Second Plan was to be $4\frac{1}{2}$ times as large as in the First Plan, and in the case of Group A industries $2\frac{1}{2}$ times as large.

There is this caution, however, to be attached to comparisons between investment in the First and Second Plans as a proportion of the National Income. The above figure of 24 per cent. for 1932 (*The Second Five Year Plan*, 545) contrasts surprisingly with Strumilin's figure of 33·6 per cent. for 1932–3, cited on page 236 above. Yet the absolute figures of actual investments under the First Plan accord pretty closely with Strumilin's figure of what had been planned for the quinquennium. Owing to the operation of subsidies to heavy industry at that time, it seems probable that the current prices of capital goods over these years showed a much smaller rise than consumer goods. A *possible* explanation of the above discrepancy may be, therefore, that the different price-movements of capital goods and of others had the effect of lowering the weight of capital goods (and hence of investment) when valued in the current prices of later years.

successes previously achieved in constructing an industry of machine-building could now begin to be utilised in turning out equipment for the lighter industries : spindles and looms for the textile industry, lasting machines for boot and shoe manufacture and mechanical equipment for paper mills, sugar refineries and food-canning works. The output of cotton-spinning machines and looms was to be increased by more than ten times, so as to increase the total spindleage capacity of the industry by some 40 per cent. and the number of looms by about 25 per cent. ; machinery for the leather and the boot and shoe industry by four times and equipment for food-processing plants by two and a half times. In consequence the rate of increase of output of consumption goods was designed to be a higher one than in the case of capital goods : an annual rate of increase of $18\frac{1}{2}$ per cent. for the former, or a growth of about 133 per cent. over the quinquennium, against an annual rate of increase for all industry of $16\frac{1}{2}$ per cent. and for the capital goods industries of $14\frac{1}{2}$ per cent.[1] The output of cotton fabrics was to be doubled, that of woollen fabrics and boots and shoes more than doubled, that of office and school supplies to be trebled, that of linen goods and hosiery, of bicycles and of watches and of musical instruments was to increase more than four times. On the basis of this a twofold increase was anticipated in the urban workers' consumption of food products and of manufactures. In addition developments in urban building and municipal economy were planned so as to expand dwelling accommodation by one third, the number of hospital beds in towns by 44 per cent. (and in the countryside by nearly double), to give tramway systems to an additional 20 towns and bus services to 80, and to provide all cities of more than 50,000 inhabitants with a sewerage system and all places of more than 10,000 inhabitants with a piped water-supply. But despite this more generous provision for the industries catering for the consumer, about three quarters of the total investment in industry was still to be devoted to the industries producing capital goods.[2]

The " fundamental and decisive economic task " of the Second Plan was defined by its authors as being " the completion of technical reconstruction in the whole of national economy ", so

---

[1] These are the figures as finally confirmed in a joint decree of TSIK and Sovnarcom dated Nov. 17, 1934. The original draft of the Plan prepared by Gosplan contained somewhat higher estimates of growth in all three cases.

[2] *The Second Five Year Plan* (Gosplan, 1936), 31-2, 68, 83-8, 94, 246-7, 545-6, 580-5, 615. The proportion of industrial investment devoted to light industry was approximately the same as in the original First Five Year Plan, but considerably more than had actually been invested in light industry over the period 1928-32 (which was only about one seventh).

that on its termination some four fifths of all industrial output would come from " new enterprises built or completely reconstructed during the First or the Second Five Year Plan period ". As a condition of this the task was set of " mastering all aspects of the operation of the new enterprises and the new technique ", and with it " considerable improvement in the productivity of labour, the lowering of production-costs and a decided improvement in the quality of output ".[1] The draft of the Plan was only finally confirmed by the government after the experience of an interim one-year plan for the first year of the new quinquennium. This year proved to be the least successful of any of the whole decade, and the increase of production fell short even of the moderated pace (compared with those of the previous four years) that the annual plan had set.[2] As a result, the Second Plan, unlike the First, emerged in its final form with targets that were lower, and not higher, than those in the preliminary draft ; and the stress was laid upon solidity rather than mere magnitude of achievement. In particular, it was emphasised that the lagging of iron and steel production must be overcome, and " one of the principal tasks " for this industry was defined as being " the mastery in the shortest possible time of the new equipment already in operation as well as of that to be installed during the period ". Part of the trouble in getting new plant into operation in the past few years had been a lack of balance between different stages of production (due, for example, to different plants or different sections of a complex plant being completed at different dates) ; and special attention was now directed towards the improvement of vertical balance within the industry, as well as to such matters as a raising of the coefficient of efficiency of furnaces and maximum fuel economy. At the same time an impressive volume of new construction, which included 45 new blast furnaces, 164 open-hearth furnaces, and 107 rolling mills, was to be put into operation over this second quinquennium ; and the 1937 targets for pig-iron and for steel were set respectively at 16 and 17 million tons, which in each case represented an increase of more than two and a half times the 1932 figure. The " mastering of technique " on which so much emphasis was placed implied also that some of the improvement in labour-

---

[1] *The Second Five Year Plan* (Gosplan, 1936), 93.

[2] The rate of increase for 1933 was only 6 per cent. In 1934, however, it was to recover to 18 per cent. and in 1935 to 20 per cent., so that the interruption of growth was to prove no more than temporary. However, in 1933 labour turnover was lower, and the increase of labour productivity was greater than in the two preceding years and for the first time was slightly in excess of the increase in wage rates. (Cf. B. Marcus in *Plan. Khoz.*, 1934, Nos. 5–6, 148 seq.)

productivity which had been anticipated but only very partially realised in the first quinquennium should be achieved in the second. The rise in productivity that was called for by 1937 was set at 63 per cent. : a figure that was only two thirds of what the First Plan had initially stipulated, but was half as much again as the actual increase that the First Plan had been successful in achieving. On the basis of this it was estimated that costs of production would be lowered by 26 per cent. ; while the total labour force in industry would grow by 28 per cent. (as against almost a twofold increase between 1928 and 1932) and in the economic system at large by 26 per cent.

Linked with the tasks set for iron and steel were two further ones affecting heavy industry. The first of these was to extend the range of machine-tool production, the foundations of which had been already laid under the First Plan ; the second was to develop the production of a considerable range of non-ferrous metals, which had previously been deficit commodities needing to be imported. It was stated that " the Second Five Year Plan envisages the mastery of the production of up to 200 new sizes and types of machine-tools " ; and this task was spoken of as " the main link in the plan of machinery production, the link which ensures the production of machines to make machines ", which must be strengthened " so that the machine-tool requirements of national economy can be met and the Soviet Union be made technically and economically independent in this field as well ". In other words, a leading objective of the Second Plan in this field was to make the pressure to import machinery, which had so augmented the stringencies of the First Plan, a thing of the past. Development in these years was to be concerned particularly with the more complex types of machine-tools such as milling and grinding and gear-cutting machines and automatic and semi-automatic machines. Machine-tool production as a whole was planned to increase nearly two and three quarter times in the number of units being manufactured, and, since special emphasis in development was laid on complex types, by more than five times in value.

In non-ferrous metallurgy there was to be special concentration on developing the production of copper, zinc, tin, nickel and aluminium. Such metals were in growing demand by the electrical industry, including all branches of radio work, and by the defence industries, and their production had been comparatively small hitherto. Copper was to be developed in the Urals and near Lake

Balkhash in Kazakhstan ; lead at Chimkent in Kazakhstan, in the Altai region, in the North Caucasus and in the Far East ; zinc in the Urals and at Kemerovo in Siberia. At the beginning of the second quinquennium aluminium production was already being carried on at two main centres, both of them located close to sources of cheap and plentiful hydro-electricity : on the lower Dnieper in the south and on the river Volkhov in the north, just east of Leningrad. In addition to erecting a supplementary plant for the supply of alumina at Tikhvin on the Volkhov, a start was to be made at the end of the period of the Second Plan with the construction of a third centre of aluminium production in the middle Urals, at Kamensk. This was destined to have a crucial significance for the future, in the years of war, as a centre of production beyond the reach of the German invasion. It was also to have an enduring importance since the Urals bauxite deposits are superior both in their richness and their quality to those of Tikhvin, and are comparable in quality to the best French bauxites.[1] The immediate limitation on the progress of this third centre was the deficient supplies of electrical power for the electrolysis process, until the projected hydro-electric scheme on the river Kama, to the west of the Urals, had reached a more advanced stage of development. The inauguration of aluminium production had been an achievement of the first quinquennium (the first production of aluminium was in 1932) : to the second quinquennium fell the task of extending it and of founding a third and more easterly centre. The production of nickel, tin and magnesium, however, had to be started *de novo* under the Second Plan : nickel in the Urals, tin in the trans-Baikal region and in Kazakhstan, magnesium on the Dnieper and in the northern Urals.[2]

The industrial development which the Second Plan inherited from the First was beginning already in the first few years of the 1930's to place a serious strain on the transport system. By 1934 transport was being spoken of as a bottleneck, barring the way to further expansion. It was becoming clear that a considerable increase in the amount of capital invested in an extension of transport facilities was a *conditio sine qua non* of further industrial advance.[3] The road-network remained in a quite primitive condi-

---

[1] Cf. *Plan. Khoz.*, 1936, No. 7, 164–5 ; Academician Archangelsky and E. Rozhkova in *Plan. Khoz.*, 1935, No. 4, 38. The Urals deposits were discovered in 1928.

[2] The nickel combine at Ufalei near Cheliabinsk was due to start production in 1934, and the first mill for the concentration of trans-Baikal tin ore in 1933.

[3] Cf. I. Smirnov in *Plan. Khoz.*, 1934, Nos. 5–6, 26 ; N. Breus and A. Shleifman in *Plan. Khoz.*, 1935, No. 8, 72 seq.

tion outside the boundaries of the larger towns. River transport, although extensively used, was for the most part very poorly equipped as regards harbour-facilities and river-port equipment. The freight-capacity of railroads was limited by the fact that lines were often single track over long distances, while ballasting and gradients were such as seriously to reduce train-speeds and the tractive capacity of locomotives, compared with railways in western countries. Terminal facilities were inadequate, and signalling arrangements were backward.[1] Between 1932 and 1937 the amount of goods traffic on the railways was to increase by nearly three quarters, so that by the latter date the total volume of freight carried was actually five times what it had been in 1913. Meanwhile the actual length of track had risen by no more than some 50 per cent. since pre-revolutionary times, so that the load of goods traffic per mile of railway reached the amazing figure of three times what it had formerly been in Tsarist times. In 1939 an official estimate placed " the annual traffic per mile of track "—the " traffic coefficient " of Soviet railways—at more than double the figure for U.S.A.[2]

This enhanced strain on the transport system was largely a natural consequence of industrialisation in its early stages. The shift of population from village to town involved a movement of foodstuffs from their districts of origin to urban consumers on a larger scale. The growth of new industrial centres, such as Magnitogorsk in the southern Urals, the Kuznetsk basin in Siberia, Karaganda in Kazakhstan, involved, at least initially, the transport over long distances of building materials, of components and semi-finished products as well as of the final product. The first effect of industrialisation, in other words, was to increase considerably the volume of interchange of products between different regions of the country. The Ural-Kuznetsk combine of which so much was talked in the early '30's, based on the exchange of Ural ores for Kuznetsk coal between two metallurgical centres which were respectively deficient in coal and ore, involved a greatly increased strain on the section of the trans-Siberian line lying between them. At the start the new industrial regions were apt to lack balance, and hence to rely on importing semi-finished products from other regions, or to export some of their products elsewhere in a semi-

---

[1] At the end of the First Plan less than one fifth of the loading and unloading of freight was handled mechanically, and automatic block signalling systems existed only over some 300 or 400 miles of line. (Cf. *The Second Five Year Plan*, 343.)

[2] V. Molotov, *The Third Five Year Plan for the National Economic Development of the U.S.S.R.* (Report to Eighteenth Party Congress, March, 1939), 35.

finished state. As late as the close of the decade one finds the Kramatorsk heavy engineering works in the Donbas obtaining iron from Magnitogorsk in the Urals, while at the same time the Tagil railway wagon works in the Urals relied for two thirds of its metal on the Donbas or on the central industrial region to the west. One hears of electrical engineering factories in Moscow, Leningrad and Kharkov transporting semi-finished metal from as far as 1300 miles to the east and of Urals iron and steel works drawing their manganese from the Caucasus. It was estimated that nearly one third of the coal mined was transported over distances of more than 500 miles to its final destination.[1]

But a further contributory cause was the much greater distance over which grain, and especially wheat, had to be transported as compared with pre-revolutionary days. This was partly due to the decline in export of grain, which meant that grain from the previously exporting districts near the Black Sea ports was now diverted inland towards the grain-deficiency areas of the centre and north. But it was also largely due to the increased rôle of Siberia and northern Kazakhstan as a grain surplus area. Siberian grain now flowed not only westward across the Urals in increasing quantities to supplement the supplies of marketed grain in the more thickly populated region of European Russia, but it was also transported south along the new Turksib railway to Soviet Central Asia, which had been encouraged to extend its cultivation of cotton at the expense of the area sown to grain, under the promise of the new grain supplies which the new railway-link with Siberia would bring. At the end of the '20's it had been estimated that of the wheat supplies transported long distances from wheat surplus regions about 40 per cent. came from east of the Urals, as compared with less than 10 per cent. in Tsarist times ; and between 11 and 15 per cent. of the country's grain was transported distances of more than 2000 kilometres, as compared with only 6 per cent. in 1913.[2]

Until the output-capacity of the country's iron industry had been expanded considerably, the possibility of any large-scale reconstruction of the transport system was very slender. Railway construction is a voracious consumer of metal, and during the First Five Year Plan the demands of industrial construction and of railways upon the scarce supplies of iron and steel available were

[1] Cf. Voznesensky, *Khoziaistvennie Itogi 1940 Goda i Plan Razvitia Nar. Khoz. S.S.S.R. na 1941 god.*, 24–5.
[2] Cf. V. P. Timoshenko, *Russia and the Wheat Problem*, 332–3, 421, 429.

sharply competitive ; and it was the latter demand that was made to yield place to the former. During the Second Plan, however, it became possible to include more ambitious projects of transport improvement upon the agenda, although still only on a limited scale, despite the increases in blast-furnace capacity which the First Plan had succeeded (if after some delay) in achieving. While three times as much metal was assigned to railway construction in the Second Plan as had been assigned during the First, greater emphasis was laid on the improvement of existing lines than on the construction of new lines. To the latter only about one seventh of the capital invested in railway development was directed. There was to be a good deal of double-tracking of existing lines, including some 2000 to 3000 miles of the Trans-Siberian and of stretches of the railway network connecting the Donbas with Leningrad, Moscow and the Volga region. Gradient-reduction work was to be undertaken on a number of other lines, including the Turksib and Murmansk and the lines connecting Moscow with the Urals. Provision was made for an extensive mechanisation of terminal facilities, so as to raise the proportion of freight that was handled mechanically from 20 to nearly 60 per cent. Reference was made to " a shift on a number of lines from the use of steam engines to that of electric and Diesel locomotives, the introduction of powerful locomotives, large-capacity freight cars, automatic brakes, automatic couplings and automatic block signals, the laying of heavy rails, change from sand to crushed stone or gravel ballast ". There was even an ambitious plan for electrifying some 3000 miles of line (or more than was in operation in U.S.A. in 1931), chiefly in hilly districts such as the Caucasus and the Urals, in parts of the Donbas and Kuzbas and also suburban lines in some of the larger cities ;[1] but as events were to turn out most of this programme of electrification had to be postponed and was not in fact undertaken during the second quinquennium. As regards water-transport the Second Plan provided for the construction of the Moscow-Volga canal, linking the river Moskva with the upper Volga and converting Moscow itself into an important inland river port ; the widening of the worst section of the old Mariinsky canal system in the north (linking Lake Onega and hence the Neva and the Baltic with the Volga) ; and improvements of river-port facilities and the river fleet. At the same time a beginning was to be made with the con-

---

[1] At the beginning of the Second Plan there were only about 100 miles of electrified railways in existence in the country. (D. I. Chernomordik, *Ekonomicheskaia Politika S.S.S.R.*, 302).

struction of arterial motor highways linking Moscow with Leningrad, Minsk, Kharkov, the Crimea, the Caucasus and the Urals and linking Leningrad directly with Kiev and Odessa.[1]

This situation of strain upon the transport system—a strain which for a number of years was likely to increase, in view of the slowness with which capital reconstruction of the transport system could be accomplished—imposed the necessity of choosing the location of new industrial plants so as to economise the use of transport to the maximum possible extent. In the case of " weight-losing " forms of production (of which metallurgical industry is the leading example) this transport-economy was achieved by a shift in the location of production towards its raw materials. In view of the rich mineral resources towards the east, which in Tsarist times had previously lain for the most part undeveloped and even in many cases uncharted, this requirement of the economic situation dictated that eastward shift of the centre of gravity of industrial development which it had been one of the aims of the nationality policy of the Soviet Government to achieve : namely, to accelerate the economic development, and in particular the industrialisation, of what had previously been the most backward, " colonial " areas of the Russian Empire. The Second Five Year Plan laid special emphasis on " continuing the shifts in the geographic distribution of the forces of production which have taken definite shape as a result of construction under the First Five Year Plan," such as " the creation of a second coal and iron base in the East—the Ural-Kuznetsk Combination—and the great strides made in the industrial development of the national districts : achievements the importance of which cannot be overestimated ". Reference was made to a " new geographic distribution of productive forces which will ensure a more even allocation of industry in the U.S.S.R. and will bring industry into closer proximity to the sources of raw materials and power, the specialisation of the principal districts on specific crops or branches of agriculture, the overcoming of the economic and cultural backwardness of the national republics and regions and the great progress in the direction of eliminating the contrast between town and country " as constituting a " principal objective of the construction plan for the second five year period ".[2] But in addition to a movement of heavy industry towards its sources of fuel and raw materials, the

---

[1] *The Second Five Year Plan*, 338–48, 350–6, 360–1. For the position regarding railways at the end of the period of the second plan cf. I. Liebin in *Plan*, 1937, No. 9, 12–17, and No. 15, 10–15 ; also L. Wolfson *et al.*, *Razvitie Zheleznik Dorog S.S.S.R.* (1939), 165–8.   [2] *Second Five Year Plan*, 373–4.

principle of transport-economy also required that as far as possible a balance should be achieved between the main stages of production in each of the main regions. In the opening stages of industrial reconstruction such a balance was far from being achieved, as we have seen. In fact at the outset of industrial construction in new areas the strain on the transport network was considerably increased ; and one finds it hard to see how the initial effect could have been other than this. Even in the third and fourth years of the Third Plan serious complaint was still being made of " excessive long-distance hauls and cross-hauls ", especially in the case of coal and timber, and insistence was being officially laid by the chairman of Gosplan on the need to improve this situation by an improved vertical balance in each industry in each region and by a greater utilisation of local supplies of materials for building purposes and for light industries.[1]

II

Once the difficulties of its initial year were passed, the progress of the Second Plan was in general much smoother than that of the First. The special difficulties and miscalculations which had marked its predecessor, and had made the first three years of the '30's a period of strain and sacrifice, had now been left behind. In particular, the grain supply to the towns, which had earlier constituted the weakest link, the snapping of which would have dislocated the whole Plan, was no longer a cause for serious anxiety. The battle over collective farming had been won ; and emphasis had shifted from an extension of collective farms to a consolidation and improvement of the work of those already existing. This work in many cases left much room for improvement. Old peasant habits and attitudes and methods of work were inevitably carried over into the new economic form ; and there was still leeway to make up in adequate equipment of the new farming with machinery and with technical advice and knowledge, as well as with a system of incentives fitting their situation. By 1935 the food position in the towns had shown sufficient improvement for the rationing system to be abolished. The extension of productive capacity in heavy industry had laid the material basis for a higher rate of constructional activity. And although the shortage of building materials of all kinds, which had so narrowly limited development-plans in the first quinquennium, had still in 1935 to be treated

---

[1] Voznesensky, *op. cit.*, 24–5.

as one of the leading bottleneck factors, a distinct easing of this shortage was apparent in the last two years of this second quinquennium.[1] After the experiences of the First Plan both the mechanism of planning and its methods had been considerably improved, as we shall see in a later chapter. So also was the mechanism of financial control. Moreover, the productivity of labour, instead of disappointing expectations as it had previously done, during the second half of the Second Plan exceeded expectations, largely owing to the rise of the Stakhanov movement of which we shall later speak. As a result the Second Plan, unlike its predecessor, was carried through with only a comparatively small increase of the labour force : namely an increase of 18 per cent. Nevertheless the expansion of the total wage-bill, again, greatly exceeded the provisions of the Plan—the expansion being 150 per cent. instead of 55 per cent.—as a result of unanticipated increases of money wages.

Yet one disruptive and largely incalculable factor actually bulked larger than previously. This was the darkening of the international horizon, with the aggressive designs of German Fascism and the gathering clouds of rearmament and the threat of war. Again the original development plans for the consumption goods industries had to be pruned, and likewise some of the projects for railway development, especially those for the electrification of suburban lines, in favour of allocations of man-power and materials for armament industries and of greater emphasis on heavy industry than had been originally designed. This revision of the plan *in media re* was underlined with disarming frankness by M. Molotov in his Report on the results of the Second Plan and the intentions of the Third to the Eighteenth Party Congress at the beginning of 1939. " During the Second Five Year Plan period," he said, " the growth of heavy industry was considerably more rapid than that of industry manufacturing consumers' goods. This was mainly due

---

[1] A special drive for rationalising the production of building materials had been given a high place on the agenda in 1933. But even in 1934 there were still complaints that improvement was very slow and that very little reduction in costs had been achieved. Cement production in 1935 was larger by no more than 13 per cent. than in 1932. There was no Stakhanovite movement as yet in the industry. Brick factories still retained the most primitive equipment. The annual plan for 1936, however, budgeted for a 41 per cent. increase in production of cement and a 47 per cent. increase of bricks. (V. Chubar on " The Building Materials Industry " of *Plan. Khoz.*, 1936, No. 6, 13 seq.) Between 1934 and 1937 the actual output in cement was increased by some 50 per cent. But in the summer of 1937 complaints continued to be heard about inadequacies of the building materials industry, of the " quality of building materials extraordinarily low and their prime cost high ", acting as a negative influence upon the tempo of capital building work (I. Saulov in *Plan*, 1937, No. 15, 24).

to the circumstance that in the course of the fulfilment of the Second Five Year Plan it became necessary for us to introduce major corrections into the plan for the development of industry. As had been the case under the First Five Year Plan, the international situation compelled us to increase the rates of development that had been laid down for the defence industry . . . (and this) made it imperative to accelerate considerably the expansion of heavy industry at the cost of reducing to a certain extent the rate of growth of light industry."[1]   In particular textiles once again fell a long way behind the Plan in their rates of increase, the output of cotton and woollen goods growing by only 40 per cent. and 22 per cent. respectively over the five years, compared with the approximate doubling of output which the original Plan had intended.   Nevertheless light industry as a whole was claimed to have doubled its output over the period,[2] as compared with the increase by two and a half that had been originally designed.   If true, this was no mean achievement.   In the case of leather goods and of sugar the original targets were very nearly reached, with a doubling and a trebling respectively of the output of these two industries.

In the case of heavy industry, the production of pig-iron showed a marked improvement ; the 1937 output being more than double that of 1932.   But it still somewhat lagged behind the Plan, even if this lag was much smaller than during the first quinquennium. Steel, however, slightly surpassed its target ; registering an impressive advance from 6 million tons in 1932 to 17·6 million in 1937. Rolled steel also succeeded in trebling its output.   This time oil was one of the chief laggards, attaining only 30·5 million tons instead of the Plan figure of 46·8 million.   Coal, with a doubling of the 1932 output to 128 million tons in 1937, also fell noticeably behind the goal of 152 million which had been assigned to it.   On the other hand, the achievements of the machine-making industry were once more outstanding.   The industry as a whole registered a threefold rise of output, as against the twofold increase which had been its target.   The motor-car industry was exemplary in exactly fulfilling its bold target of an eightfold increase.   Mainly as a result of these

[1] V. Molotov, *The Third Five Year Plan for the National Economic Development of the U.S.S.R.* (Moscow, 1939), 11.

[2] I.e. in values calculated according to prices prevailing in 1926–7. Light industry, and textiles in particular, came in for a good deal of criticism at the end of the Second Five Year Plan, on the ground that they had hitherto failed in "mastering new technical standards", despite the fact that the successes of recent years in agriculture had " given the possibility of deciding the raw material problem of light industry, and in particular the problem of cotton " (L. Friedlander in *Plan*, 1937, No. 3, 19).

successes in engineering (an industry whose products had a large weight in a summation of the total value of industrial output), the gross production of large-scale industry slightly exceeded the Plan, increasing by 121 per cent. over the five-year period compared with the stipulated 114 per cent. Another measure of the progress achieved is that over the single quinquennium the coefficient of electrical power per worker in industry had more than doubled ; while over the decade as a whole the amount of mechanical power per worker had grown at a mean annual rate that was more than double the annual rate of growth of power per worker in the industry of U.S.A. between 1899 and 1929. During the period of the Second Plan the " tractor park " of the country had been doubled, and its " motor-car park " increased eightfold. In 1937 four fifths of industrial output came from plants that were newly built or else had been radically reconstructed since 1928. Two new metallurgical plants alone, Magnitogorsk in the Urals and Stalinsk in Kuzbas, had a productive capacity equal to that of the pre-1914 iron and steel industry. More than one half of all the machine tools in use on January 1st, 1938, had been produced during the period of the two Five Year Plans and nearly nine tenths of the tractors and combine-harvesters.[1]

If we survey the changes wrought in the economy at large by this decade of grand construction, we must inevitably be impressed by the extent to which the transformation had been qualitative as well as quantitative. The quantitative growth of industry can be epitomized in such indices as these : that the output capacity of the iron and steel industry had been expanded by four times over the decade between 1928 and 1938, of coal by three and a half times, oil nearly three times, and of electrical power by some seven times ; while at the same time a whole range of new industries had been established, such as aeroplanes, heavy chemicals, including plastics and artificial rubber, aluminium, copper, nickel, tin. The U.S.S.R. had become the largest producer of tractors and railway locomotives in the world, and the second largest producer of oil and gold and phosphates. This expansion of industry, marching as it had done with the transformation of agriculture, represented a radical change in that " transitional mixed system " of the period of the NEP in the middle '20's. Not only had the " islands " of socialist industry grown, both absolutely and in the specific weight which

---

[1] Molotov, *op. cit.*, 10–12 ; *Itogi Vipolnenia Vtorovo Piatiletnevo Plana Razvitia Narodnovo Khoziaistva S.S.S.R.*, 19–22, 61, 70 ; B. Sukharevsky in *Plan. Khoz.*, 1940, No. 6, 14.

they represented in the economy at large, but collectivist forms of production by the end of the Second Plan overwhelmingly preponderated, while the individualist sector of the economy (including individual forms in retail trade) had dwindled to insignificance. In the middle 1920's some four fifths of the occupied population had been peasant producers or individual handicraft workers; while private traders had been responsible for the major part of the retail trade and a substantial part of the wholesale trade of the country. By 1938 the number of wage and salary earners, employed in industry and in other branches of the economy and of government service, had grown from one tenth to form more than one third of the occupied population. More numerous than these were co-operative producers—working members of collective farms in agriculture or of various kinds of industrial co-operatives in handicraft and small-scale local industry[1]—who in 1938 composed 55 per cent. of the occupied population. Those classified as "individual workers", consisting of the remnants of the old individual peasantry and individual artisans in the handicraft trades, amounted to no more than 6 per cent. of the occupied population: a percentage curiously close to that of a similar category, "workers on own account", in the British census returns.

The decade of the First and Second Plans embraced, accordingly, the crucial watershed between the State Capitalism of the early and middle '20's, with its complex admixture of economic forms, and the predominantly collectivist or socialist economy that had emerged by the closing years of the '30's. It was to set the seal of legal form upon this transformation that the new Constitution of 1936 was prefaced by a section entitled " The Structure of Society ",[2] in which the forms of property and enterprise existing in this new stage of development were explicitly defined. Here, in Article 4, " the economic foundation of the U.S.S.R." is declared to consist of "the socialist economic system and the socialist ownership of the tools and means of production ", which have now

---

[1] These are the Incops of Mr. and Mrs. Webb (*Soviet Communism*, 219 seq.), some 20,000 in numbers and embracing some two or three million working members in various trades such as wood-working, sports goods and musical instruments, toymaking, artistic products, some types of pottery, rug-making, household equipment and food products, and repair work. Fishermen and artists, and also trappers and hunters in the extreme north, are sometimes organised in bodies of this kind, which are regulated under Statutes not dissimilar to those of the Kolkhoz or agricultural *artel*.

[2] This is the translation offered by the Webbs (*Ibid.*, 528[1]). Elsewhere it has been translated as " Social Organisation " or " The Organisation of Society ". Stalin described this new Constitution as " the registration and legislative embodiment of what has already been achieved and won in actual fact ". (*Leninism*, 1940 ed., 570.)

become " firmly established as a result of the liquidation of the capitalist economic system, the abolition of private ownership of the tools and means of production, and the abolition of the exploitation of man by man ". Article 5, however, proceeds to define socialist property as having two forms : " either the form of State property (the wealth of the whole people) or the form of co-operative or collective property (the property of separate collective farms or of co-operative associations) ". The two Articles which follow expand this definition of the two forms by declaring, firstly, that " the land, its deposits, waters, forests, mills, factories, mines, railways, water and air transport, banks, means of communication, large State-organised farm enterprises (State farms, machine tractor stations, etc.) and also the basic housing facilities in cities and industrial localities are State property, i.e. the wealth of the whole people " ; secondly, that " public enterprises in collective farms and co-operative organisations, with their livestock and equipment, products raised or manufactured by the collective farms and co-operative organisations, together with their public structures, constitute the public, socialist property of the collective farms and co-operative organisations ".[1] But, in addition to socialist property, explicit recognition is awarded to two categories of individual or personal property : the one category applying to ownership of means of production and a form of private enterprise corresponding thereto, the other to durable means of consumption, or articles of personal use, and to saved personal income. Article 9 contains the declaration that " alongside the socialist system of economy, which is the dominant form of economy in the U.S.S.R., the law allows small-scale private enterprise of individual peasants and handicraftsmen based on their personal labour, provided that there is no exploitation of the labour of others ". Here reference is clearly intended to individual enterprise of the worker-owner or non-capitalist type. Article 10 declares that " the right of personal property of citizens in their income from work and in their savings, in their dwelling-house and auxiliary husbandry, in household articles for personal use and comfort, as well as the right of inheritance of personal property of citizens, is protected by law ".

Corresponding to these economic changes of the crucial decade

---

[1] It is added in Article 7 that " every collective farm household shall have for personal use a plot of land attached to the house and, as personal property, the subsidiary husbandry on the plot, the house, productive livestock, poultry and small farm tools, according to the Statutes of the agricultural *artel* " ; and in Article 8 that " the land occupied by collective farms is secured to them without payment and without time limit, i.e. in perpetuity ".

of construction went those changes in the social composition of the population of which mention has been made. In this connection M. Molotov stated, in the report to the Eighteenth Party Congress from which we have already quoted : " Though we have purged the U.S.S.R. of hostile classes, we have not yet abolished classes altogether. There remain the working class and the peasantry. But they are no longer the former working class nor are they the former peasantry. Their rôle in society and in the State has changed. Their mode of life, their culture and morals have changed in many respects." This contention he proceeded to expand as follows : " Having eliminated the remnants of the exploiting classes, we have established a society of two mutually friendly classes, the working class and the peasantry. This society has given rise to an intelligentsia of its own, which is no longer bourgeois or bourgeois-democratic, but is, in the main, a socialist intelligentsia. This intelligentsia, linked with ties of blood to the working people and to Socialism, plays a great part in the work of directing the development and consolidation of the new society and State. The antagonism that used to exist between town and country has largely been uprooted ; but a substantial difference between the above two classes still exists. This difference exists, primarily, because the workers are employed in establishments which are the possession of the whole people, are socialist-State in character, while the peasants work in collective farms, which are socialist-co-operative in character. Both of these classes, the working class and the collective-farm peasantry, are already classes of socialist society."[1] Two and a half years earlier Stalin had claimed that " the working class of the U.S.S.R. is an entirely new working class " and " the Soviet peasantry is an entirely new peasantry ", " the like of which the history of mankind has never known before ".[2]

---

[1] *Op. cit.*, 15. As regards the intelligentsia, Stalin, in his report on the Draft Constitution to the Eighth Congress of Soviets, Nov. 25, 1936, had defined them as " a stratum and not a class ". " The intelligentsia has never been a class, and never can be a class—it was and remains a stratum, which recruits its members from among all classes of society. . . . In our day, under the Soviets, the intelligentsia recruits its members mainly from the ranks of the workers and peasants." Of collective farmers he said : " The fact that the majority of peasants have started collective farming does not mean that they have already ceased to be peasants, that they no longer have their personal economy, their own households, etc." Hence they could not be identified with workers in State industry in one homogeneous class. (*Leninism*, 1940 ed., 581–2.)   [2] *Ibid.*, 566.

III

A crucial economic link between agriculture and industry, which had grown with the growth of collective farming, illustrates one of the ways in which the relationship between agriculture and industry had been transformed. Previously the relationship between agriculture and industry had been predominantly a market one—a relationship of simple commodity exchange. The supply of agricultural produce forthcoming depended in the main on the structure of prices (although it was capable also of being influenced by such things as taxation policy) ; with the resulting instabilities and incalculable movements, seriously restrictive of economic planning, which an earlier chapter has described. With the campaign for collectivisation went a system of " forward contracts " with collective farms (as also with individual peasant economies), in an attempt to secure firm guarantees of supply upon which the production plans of industry for the coming year could be built. These supply-quotas, contracted for in advance and originally voluntary in form, became obligatory in fact ; and were recognised as such by a decree of January 19th, 1933.[1] Varying according to the area of sown land and the qualities of the soil on the basis of standard averages laid down in the decree for each region,[2] these delivery quotas were to be paid for at fixed official buying prices ; and therefore had the character of a requisition rather than a tax. But since these buying prices were a long way below the market price, they represented substantially a form of tax in kind, which, since it varied in some rough relation to the yield of land, can perhaps be regarded as an instrument for skimming part of the differential rent of land which would otherwise have been retained by the more favourably situated farms. (In addition to these obligatory deliveries at " delivery prices ", there were so-called " decentralised collections ", which were the result of voluntary sales-contracts to the State at " State purchase prices " which were considerably higher than the former.) At the same time the burden of these quotas in relation to the gross produce began to

---

[1] Cf. *Osnovnie Direktivi Partii i Pravitelstva, 1931–4*, 103.

[2] These standard averages for 1933 ranged from 3·3 centners per hectare of autumn-sown grain in the Crimea and 3·1 in the Ukraine to 0·8 centner in the Leningrad and northern regions and White Russia. These figures were for Kolkhozy not served by Machine Tractor Stations. In the case of those served by such stations the figure was somewhat lower : 2·7 centners in the Crimea and 0·6 in the north. (*Ibid.*, 103.)

be eased,[1] and collective farms were granted the right of free trade in any part of their produce in excess of their deliveries to the State : a right which was extended to the produce of the homesteads of individual collective farmers. This right was the basis of the so-called Kolkhoz market—the sale of collective farm produce from stalls or shops in local urban markets or by direct contract with various types of institution—which remains virtually the only surviving type of open competitive market in the Soviet economic system of to-day. The system of obligatory deliveries, as we have said, afforded to industry and to the towns a guarantee of a certain minimum supply of agricultural produce, on the basis of which industrial plans and forecasts could be built for at any rate a limited period ahead. These quotas, being fixed in advance, and independent of the actual gross output of the farm, also acted as a stimulus to the farmers to maximise the size of their crop. But since, as we have also seen, the effect of the new method of farming was highly labour-saving, the transformation of agriculture had the effect of simultaneously releasing labour from the land in favour of industry and of reducing the number of mouths in the village that needed to be fed out of the produce of the local soil. As a consequence, the marketable surplus of agriculture, available to supply the expanding towns and industry, considerably increased, and in the case of grain was in 1938 some two and a half times what this surplus had been ten years previously.[2] Between the censuses of 1926 and of 1939 the rural population had declined by 5 per cent. (and the actual farm population by considerably more), despite a natural increase for the whole country of 15·9 per cent. ; while the urban population had doubled. The fact that of this increase in the urban population some 20 million was accounted for by migration from the village affords a measure of the contribution which the revolution in agriculture had made to the growth of industry.

The improvement in the food position and the increase in the supply of consumer goods, although they took second place to the expansion of heavy industry, had been, nevertheless, considerable ; and had resulted in an improvement during the second half

---

[1] According to figures cited by Dr. A. Baykov (*op. cit.*, 203), deliveries by collective farms to the State (presumably including both the obligatory deliveries and the so-called " decentralised collections ") as a percentage of gross yields averaged 32 per cent. in 1931 and 1932 and 20·5 per cent. in 1933 and 1934.

[2] In 1940 the quantity of grain marketed outside the village was 38 million tons, compared with 21·6 million tons in 1913. (A. Zelenovsky in *Plan. Khoz.*, 1946, No. 1, 31.) The 1940 figure represents just over 31 per cent. of the gross product as against 26 per cent. in 1913 and under 14 per cent. in 1926–7.

of the '30's in the standard of life of the population compared with the hard years at the conclusion of the First Five Year Plan, and probably also (though some western writers have disputed this) compared with 1927 or 1928, before the high rates of investment of the Five Year Plans had begun. The absence of a retail index number (which was discontinued in 1930 simultaneously with the extension of rationing and the system of multiple prices for the same commodity in different categories of market) makes any simple measurement of real wage movements impossible for this period.[1] Official data concerning urban workers' budgets indicated a large increase in consumption of certain leading foodstuffs between 1934 and 1937. But there is some evidence that during the middle and late '30's the average standard of life of the village in most regions improved relatively to that of the towns. Official surveys of a sample of collective farm villages in the Middle Volga and the Kuban and parts of the Ukraine in 1937 indicated that, compared with the bad year of 1932, the annual dividend accruing to the average collective farmer, both his dividend in kind and his dividend in money, had increased between two and three times, and that members of peasant families were on the average consuming 50 per cent. more bread and milk and several times as much meat and lard as in pre-1914 days.[2] The increase of housing accommodation in the towns seems to have lagged behind the very rapid growth of urban population.[3] At the same time, with the amount and character of new building, the qualitative standard on the average of housing accommodation available must have improved;

[1] Some writers have attempted to compare the movement of average money earnings of workers with price movements between 1928 and 1938 and have claimed that average real wage-earnings fell (e.g. S. N. Prokopovicz, *Russlands Volkwirtschaft unter den Sowjets*; L. E. Hubbard, *Soviet Labour and Industry*). Mr. Yugoff calculates that the average wage of industrial workers would only buy in 1935 rather less than one half as much of a given "food basket" in Moscow as in 1928, and in 1939 about three quarters. (*Russia's Economic Front*, 297-9.) More recent estimates by Dr. Janet Chapman are quoted below, page 315. What seems to have happened during this period is that real wages of industrial workers *fell*, while *per capita* consumption on the average *rose* for the population as a whole. owing to the considerable increase in industrial employment, with a resulting shift of population from countryside to towns (*i.e.* from lower-paid to higher-paid occupations). Dr. Chapman finds a substantial discrepancy between results measured in terms of 1928 price-weights and in terms of 1937 price-weights.

[2] Cit. A. Yugoff, *op. cit.*, 216. Mr. Yugoff actually gives a figure of eight times as the increase in meat and fats: a figure which seems unbelievably high, despite the fact that average peasant consumption of meat was formerly very small. Official figures quoted in an article in *Soviet War News* (Feb. 16, 1944) spoke of peasant meat and butter consumption as being double pre-1917, of sugar seven times and of a range of manufactured goods such as cloth and footwear three times.

[3] Apparently between 1923 and the end of the '30's urban dwelling accommodation had grown by about 80 per cent. (cf. A. Sharov in *Plan. Khoz.*, 1945, No. 3, 42). Meanwhile the urban population had more than doubled.

and of the improvement of civic amenities in many towns, such as sewage and water and tramway systems, which were designed to fall within the period of the Second Plan, we have already spoken. The factories in which the urban worker spent his working life were better built, much better lit and ventilated and equipped with welfare facilities than in former days ; and his working hours were shorter. With regard to rural housing it seems clear that there was a fairly general and considerable improvement. Of this improvement an *émigré* writer has spoken in these terms. "The old hut, built of clay, without a chimney, with its sleeping bunks and tiny windows, has disappeared. New houses with more light and space have been built in large numbers. The interior of the house has become cleaner; furniture, crockery and linen have appeared for the first time."[1]

With the large influx of population from agriculture to industry, a substantial " upgrading " of the population had occurred so far as earnings-levels were concerned. A larger proportion of the population were earning at the level of earnings appropriate to industry (which had traditionally been higher than in agriculture by a substantial amount) ; while full employment had enlarged the earnings-opportunities of the existing urban population. Regarding the *per capita* food consumption of the population as a whole, Mr. Colin Clark, who estimated that between 1928 and the hard year of 1932 this may have fallen by as much as 20 per cent., has concluded that by 1934, the final year of rationing, this had been almost restored to the 1928 level ; while his estimate of the output of consumption goods and services other than food (including public services but excluding dwelling accommodation) was that these had risen by as much as 45 per cent. Between 1934 and 1937 he calculated that food consumption per head rose by 9 per cent. and urban food consumption (excluding bread) by 20 per cent. per worker's family. This seems likely to be a conservative rather than a generous estimate (for one thing Mr. Clark over-estimates the population increase, using a figure of 17 per cent. as the increase between 1928 and 1937 instead of 10 per cent.). In the case of non-foodstuffs the increase was no doubt greater ; and estimates by the same writer for " other goods sold at retail " suggest a per head increase for the whole country of something in the

---

[1] Yugoff, *op. cit.*, 218. This author adds that " in many regions the villages have electric light, a pump and paved streets . . . a hut reading-room and frequently a club, a day nursery and a hospital ".

neighbourhood of 30 per cent. over the years 1934 to 1937 alone.[1]

Examination of figures of production of particular foodstuffs gives a somewhat uneven picture. The grain crop in 1940 was larger than 1928 by 30 per cent. and larger than 1913 by 25 per cent.[2] Allowing for the increase in population between 1928 and 1940 (amounting to about 12 per cent.), and for larger territory by 1940 (adding a further 12 per cent. of population), this represents a grain output per head in 1940 about 5 per cent. higher than in 1928. Since in pre-1914 times a large proportion of the crop (about one third) had been exported, whereas in the middle and late '30's this proportion was almost insignificant (well below 5 per cent.), it seems likely that the grain available for consumption per head in 1940 was appreciably greater than at the earlier date. Moreover a larger proportion of the bread-grain consumed was now wheat (owing to some growth relatively of wheat over rye, and owing to the fact that wheat had previously been the main export crop). It has to be borne in mind, however, that the 1940 crop was exceptional, and the position was less favourable for the average of 1938–40 and grain output per head was *below* 1928. While the *per capita* production of animal products was no doubt smaller in 1937 than it had been in 1928 (owing to the decline of livestock), the *per capita* production of sugar had nearly doubled and of potatoes and other vegetables had probably risen by about a fifth or a quarter, and may well have been as much as double the level of twenty-five years before.[3]

But to combat any tendency to complacency with the results achieved, emphasis was being laid in the final years of the decade on the fact that output figures, when measured *per capita* of the population, remained a long way below those of western countries, even if in absolute output many branches of Soviet industry had attained their objective of " catching up and overtaking the economically and technically advanced countries of the west ". With the exception of grain the *per capita* supply of foodstuffs remained well below the standards of most west-European countries and of America: in the case of meat, the equivalent figure cannot have been more than a third that of England (i.e. in pre-war days)

[1] Colin Clark, *Critique of Russian Statistics*, 24–5, 63, 68.

[2] While the 1940 crop, it is true (and is shown below), was an exceptional one, so also was 1913 a favourable year to take for comparison with the pre-revolutionary period, since it showed the highest figure for any year of the pre-1914 quinquennium.

[3] Yugoff, *op. cit.*, 200.

or U.S.A., and was about two thirds that of Czechoslovakia, of milk not more than a half that of England and two thirds that of France, and even of sugar no more than a half the German, English or North American level. This is hardly to be wondered at when we remember that a major part of the territory of the U.S.S.R. lies in Asia and that her population includes a variety of Asiatic peoples whose standards of life were traditionally akin to those of China or of India and not to those of European nations. As M. Molotov was concerned to stress in his report on the Third Plan, *per capita* production of textile goods was no more than a quarter or a third that of Britain or U.S.A., and even in the case of leather footwear—an industry that had made such impressive strides in the course of the decade—it had not yet reached the level of half the British or the American (i.e. it was capable of giving every member of the population on the average about one new pair of boots or shoes annually). Much the same applied to heavy industry, which had previously been so backward and had recently made such dramatic progress. Changes beyond recognition had occurred since a quarter of a century ago when Russia's *per capita* output of electrical power had been only about one seventh that of U.S.A., of steel about one eleventh that of U.S.A. and one sixth that of Great Britain, of coal only 4 per cent. that of U.S.A. and little more than 3 per cent. that of Great Britain. Yet even in 1937 the *per capita* output of electrical power remained at only one third the British or German level and one fifth the American ; of steel at between one third and one half the British or German level and between one quarter and one third the American ; and of coal less than one sixth the British and between one fifth and one quarter the American and German. " In some quarters," said M. Molotov, " people have begun to forget that we are still behind some capitalist countries economically, that is in industrial output per head of the population. . . . They have begun to forget that the lag which we must make good in order to catch up with other countries is the result of more than a century of backwardness in Russia before the revolution. We must be sure not to forget this, and cannot possibly rest content with what we have achieved."[1] To overcome this lag—" to overtake and surpass the most highly developed capitalist countries of Europe and the U.S.A." in *per capita* output as well as in absolute output levels—was the task which crowned the economic agenda in the years immediately preceding the war.

[1] Molotov, *op. cit.*, 17–19 ; also Stalin's report to the same congress in *Leninism*, 1940 ed., 633–4.

CHAPTER TWELVE

THE THIRD FIVE-YEAR PLAN AND THE WAR AND THE FIVE-YEAR PLAN FOR POST-WAR REHABILITATION AND DEVELOPMENT

I

In its drafting, and still more in its execution, the Third Five Year Plan was dominated by the lengthening shadows of war. This third quinquennium opened with the inglorious year of Munich. Its penultimate year was to witness Hitler's unprovoked and unannounced assault upon the U.S.S.R. It remains for history only as a design : as a vessel shattered by barbarian hands before it could be completed.

We do not know the proportion of investment or of industrial output which armament production constituted under this Third Plan. But that this was much larger than anything attempted prior to 1938 is certain. In 1940 the allocations for defence from the budget were double the 1938 figure and equal to the allocations made from the budget for capital investment in the economic system as a whole ; and investment and defence combined probably swallowed about a half of the national income in the year before the U.S.S.R. entered the war. For the following year the budget estimates raised defence expenditure yet further to a level three times that of 1938. Barely had the fruit of his labours in the lean years begun to ripen for the ordinary citizen than they were to be snatched from his grasp, at first by the insistent hand of rearmament and all too soon by the cruel and relentless blight of war. Scarcely more than twenty years after the wars of intervention had been terminated, the Russian land, the fair new towns, the new mills and factories and collective farms, were to be ravaged by an invader more ruthless than any since the days of the Tartars.

Preoccupation with considerations of defence was evident in the main emphasis of the Plan : on transport improvement, on non-ferrous metals and special steels and on the chemical industry. One of the central slogans of the Plan was " Make the Third Plan a Chemistry Plan ", and M. Molotov in his report to the Eighteenth Party Congress called for a " forcing of the pace " of machine-building in general—the development of " an up-to-date machine-building industry fully on a par with the principal achievements in world engineering "—and of the production of aluminium, zinc, lead and nickel in particular. In expectation of a further increase in freight traffic on the railways by the end of 1942, it was intended that railway construction should add some 7,000 miles of new track to the railway network, as compared with only some 2,500 miles built under the Second Plan ;[1] that some 5,000 miles should be double-tracked and about 1,200 miles electrified. Water and road transport were also to receive special attention. Emphasis on the development of new industrial districts in the east, which we have noticed in the two previous quinquennia, was continued, and was even more heavily underlined. This was particularly the case with reference to certain of the non-ferrous metals, whose production was located near their sources of raw materials, which for the most part were in the Urals or further east. An example was the development of the third centre of aluminium production at Kamensk, near Cheliabinsk, in the Urals, close to new bauxite deposits of considerable richness. Another example was the rapid development of new and rich oil deposits between the Volga and the Urals—the so-called Second Baku—which were designed by 1942 to yield some 7 million tons of oil, or nearly as much as the whole Baku output in 1913, and approaching a quarter of the 1940 output of the Caucasian oilfields. This occupied a place of special prominence in the Plan, not only for what were presumably important strategic reasons, but in view of the fact that the expansion of fuel and power supplies had begun to lag behind the needs of industry and transport, despite the impressive growth of electricity and also of coal during the previous decade.[2]

Had it not been for the clamant needs of rearmament, it seems likely that this Third Plan would have seen a considerable shift in priority to the consumer goods industries, so that the greatly enlarged capacity of heavy industry could be utilised to achieve an equivalent expansion in the capital equipment of the lighter industries and by the end of the quinquennium in the flow of consumer

---

[1] The Second Plan had actually *intended* to start the construction of 9,000 miles of new line and to open to traffic during the period about 7,000 miles.

[2] Molotov, *op. cit.*, 29. The plan of power-station construction, however, under the Second Plan had only been half-fulfilled. (*Ibid.*, 25.) It has to be remembered that some of the lagging of output behind the Plan in certain sections of heavy industry in the course of 1937 and 1938 was probably attributable to the "purges" of those years, which drastically affected the personnel of industrial management. But by 1940 new personnel had probably acquired sufficient experience to repair some part, at any rate, of the loss of efficiency that the purges had cost.

goods on to the market; yielding thereby a substantial rise in the standard of life both of the urban and the rural population. But once again the chance of any rapid expansion of these industries had to be sacrificed to the needs of heavy industry and to investment in armaments and in armament factories. Of gross capital investment in industry no more than 15 per cent. was assigned to the consumption goods industries : equal to the proportion assigned under the First Plan. Once again the rate of increase of heavy industry was to be substantially greater than that of light industry : the increase in output over the period being placed at 103 per cent. for the former and only 69 per cent. for the latter. Although textile production was scheduled for an increase of between 50 and 60 per cent., the absolute figure (in million metres) set for 1942 was actually lower than the target-figure originally set (but not reached) for 1937 in the Second Plan ; and the leather and sugar industries were scheduled only for a 43 and 44 per cent. increase respectively. The output of tinned goods was to be doubled and of paper to rise by 56 per cent. By the end of the new quinquennium the production of capital goods was to have a value-weight in the output of all industry of more than 60 per cent. ; and Soviet machine-tool production was to surpass the 1929 output level of U.S.A.

The proportion of these capital goods, however, which consisted of equipment for the consumer goods industries was to rise. Between 1914 and 1939 the spindleage-capacity of the cotton industry had increased by no more than 12 per cent. : a striking contrast to the expansion of productive capacity in many other industries, and especially in heavy industry. At the end of the Second Plan the current *output* of spindles, measured per head of the population, was less than 10 per cent. of the equivalent figure for U.S.A., and the output of looms about 17 per cent. By the end of 1942 it was intended that the production of spinning-frames and of looms should be increased respectively by six and four times, so as to raise the output of them per head of the population to between a third and a half of the U.S.A. level in the case of spindles and to nearly two thirds of the U.S.A. level in the case of looms.[1] As regards the *stock* of capital equipment (the so-called " equipment park "), estimates were current on the eve of the war that, if the level of production designed for 1942 were to be maintained, this stock of equipment, measured per head of the population, would

---

[1] D. Erlich, " The Cotton Industry and Basic Economic Problems in U.S.S.R.", in *Plan. Khoz.*, 1940, No. 9, 83–5. Figures given in an earlier article by Sukharevsky, referred to below, differ slightly from those mentioned by Erlich.

reach the U.S.A. level of 1937 round about the year 1952 in the case of spindle-capacity as well as in the case of such things as turbines, generators and electric motors.[1] Such were the heartening perspectives of economic progress over a further decade of peaceful construction which were to be interrupted so soon by the smoke and thunder of battle along a front of 2000 miles.

The annual rate of increase of industrial output under the Third Plan was a relatively modest one (14 per cent.), compared with the *tempo* of growth demanded by the First and Second Plans. During the first three years of the quinquennium this intended rate of progress was almost maintained. The available figures indicate an increase in the gross output of industry over the three years of 44 per cent. ; with the capital goods industries showing a 50 per cent. increase and the consumption goods industries a growth 'of 33 per cent. The total national income over the three years showed a rise of 30 per cent. This was achieved despite a serious lagging behind during the first half of 1940 (partly, no doubt, owing to the Finnish war), and a failure on the part of a number of important industries including oil and iron and steel, to reach the planned level of output over the year as a whole. In the latter part of the year a substantial improvement was reported. But the 1940 output figures for pig-iron and oil showed scarcely any advance on 1938 ; and steel production stood at only 18·3 million tons as compared with 18 million in 1938 and 17·7 million in 1937. The output of coal was some 28 per cent. higher than in 1937, and the output of electricity was higher by a third. For 1941 substantially larger rates of increase were planned than the original plan for the quinquennium had envisaged : an increase in total industrial output of 17 to 18 per cent., in iron and steel of 21, in machine-tools of 28, in cement of 38, in aluminium of as much as 66, in cotton and leather goods of 11, in tinned foodstuffs of 24, and in sugar of 27.[2]

---

[1] B. Sukharevsky, " Machine Construction and Basic Economic Problems in U.S.S.R." in *Plan. Khoz.*, 1940, No. 6, 18–19. This writer points out that " in *per capita* standards of production of machines as a result of the Third Five Year Plan, Soviet industry will approach the U.S.A. more closely than in *per capita* output of the things produced with the park of those machines". (17.)

[2] N. Voznesensky, *Economic Results of the U.S.S.R. in 1940 and the Plan of National Economic Development for 1941*, 8–10, 14.

II

According to most of the standards by which economists have tried to measure the economic war potential of a country, the U.S.S.R. was still economically weaker than Germany in 1941, despite the advances of recent years, and was substantially weaker than the whole of German-occupied Europe. If we take the 1938 output figures (which are the latest available for Germany) for key products such as coal, pig-iron and steel, we find that Germany (including Austria and the Saar) possessed a substantial margin of superiority over the U.S.S.R. German coal output reached some 186 million tons against 133 million in the U.S.S.R. (a figure which by 1940 had only risen to 166 million) ; pig-iron was 18 million against 14·6 (and 15 by 1940) ; steel was 23 million against 18 (and still under 19 by 1940). If there is added to the German figure the production of countries occupied by or in alliance with Germany, whose industries at the time were subject to the German Reich, the level of German-controlled output in each case is raised to a level almost double that of U.S.S.R. : coal to over 280 million, pig-iron to over 30 million and steel to nearly 40 million. On the other hand, the U.S.S.R. had plentiful supplies of iron ore (producing in 1938 a fifth of world supplies, measured in terms of their metal content), and her oil output exceeded by nearly four times the supply available to Germany, including Roumanian production. In the production of copper she had a substantial lead over Germany, although not over the combined output of Germany and German-occupied countries. If we take the national income per head as an index of economic potential, we find that Germany possessed an even more marked superiority. In absolute figures it seems probable that the national income of the U.S.S.R. was somewhat greater than that of Germany, although very much less than that of Germany and German-occupied countries combined. But measured per head of the population it was probably less than half the German ; being about double that of Poland and approximately on a level with that of Austria or Czechoslovakia.[1] In this sense the years of peace had been all too short for the U.S.S.R. : a consideration which no doubt played an important part in the timing

---

[1] These statements (which must not be regarded as anything more pretentious than rough guesses at what, from the nature of the case, is incapable of precise measurement and comparison) are based on figures given by Mr. R. W. B. Clarke in his *Economic Effort of War*, 224, and adjusted for probable changes over the three subsequent years.

of Hitler's attack in the east. It was also the consciousness of German economic superiority in certain crucial respects that no doubt influenced the Soviet Government in attaching paramount importance to the strategy of the long-delayed second front in the west, and in " buying time with space " while they were building the war potential further east that was to drive the *Wehrmacht* fifteen hundred miles from the Volga to beyond the Oder.

All such simple measures of war potential are, however, seriously inadequate ; and if we take their evidence alone, the halting of the German army at Stalingrad and the arming and launching of the counter-offensive which liberated the Ukraine and Belorussia must be counted among the miracles of modern times. Such measures allow neither for the proportion of resources which can be swiftly and easily adapted to the ends of war production, nor for the difference between the long and the short period view— between what are elements of strength in waging a *blitzkrieg* (where existing stocks rather than productive capacity may be the paramount consideration) and what are elements of strength in a war of attrition. They do not allow for the spirit of the people, which the war of liberation showed to be so crucial a factor in the stamina of a nation in accepting sacrifices and additional strain, as well as in the extent and efficiency of war-time improvisation and creation. Moreover, they take no count of the fact that war potential is a matter of qualitative balance of a number of essential constituents as much as of the overall magnitude of war production as a whole. As in the case of human nutrition, a number of elements need to be present in certain minimum quantities, and a deficiency in any one of them cannot necessarily be repaired from the surplus productive capacity of some other element. This aspect of economic potential is incapable of expression in simple numerical form. It is obvious enough that a country cannot fight a war without iron-ore or oil. But it is also true that a number of other materials, for which there are no adequate substitutes, such as manganese, aluminium, nickel, chrome and various metal alloys, are crucial to that country's war effort. Even though a relatively small quantity of each of them may suffice, the absence of any one may prove the Achilles' heel by which a nation strong in other signs of economic potential may be brought down.

In these respects the U.S.S.R. was rather more favourably situated. Certain sections of industry, which had expanded most rapidly in the pre-war decade, such as the production of motor vehicles and tractors, were quickly adaptable to the ends of war production. Her economic system, with its experience of planning over a decade and a half, was much more suited to rapid improvisation and adjustment and to implementing plans and allocations of resources efficiently than German economy proved to be. The morale of her people proved to be remarkably high. In materials such as manganese and phosphates she was well supplied ; and she was fairly well placed with regard to chrome ore and bauxite, potash, asbestos, zinc and lead.[1] Although she was deficient in natural rubber, her production of synthetic rubber started,[2] if anything, a little earlier than Germany's and probably climbed ahead of it. Judging by the consumption of pre-war years, her main deficiencies were in copper (despite large increases in production and a lead over German production), probably in nickel, in tin and in such things as magnesite, molybdenum, tungsten, vanadium and antimony. Her total stock of machine tools probably did not exceed half a million, against 1·3 million in Germany and 0·7 million in Britain ; and she was also deficient in certain types ; her industry still being insufficiently equipped for the production both of large machine tools (e.g. of as large as 1000 tons) and of small precision machine tools. Germany's conquests had probably repaired (at least, to a large extent) her previous deficiencies in iron ore and timber, and in pyrites, lead, chrome, magnesite, zinc and bauxite. But German production seems to have remained seriously deficient in oil, copper and manganese, nickel and tin, wolfram and antimony, molybdenum and vanadium, tungsten, rubber, asbestos and phosphates. Of a number of these Germany was known to have built up large stocks. But for a long war her position with regard to many of them was probably weaker than that of the U.S.S.R.

More serious, however, for Soviet economy than any initial weaknesses in her war potential was the blow she suffered from the extent and swiftness of the German invasion in the autumn and winter of 1941 and in the summer offensive of 1942. Utilising the advantages of surprise and of initial superiority in field-experience

---

[1] On the eve of the war about 87 per cent. of her needs for aluminium were met from home production, in the case of lead 77 per cent. and of zinc 99 per cent.

[2] In 1931, when a Russian variety of Buna, called Sovprene, was put into production. This was derived at first from grain and potato alcohol, and later from acetylene and petroleum and coal by-products. The pre-war output has been estimated at between 50,000 and 60,000 tons, and already in 1937 75 per cent. of Soviet needs were said to be satisfied from home production. Three of the largest plants were apparently in Armenia, at Voronezh and at Magnitogorsk in the southern Urals. (Cf. U.S.S.R.: Album of Scientific Publishing Institute of Pictorial Statistics (Moscow) ; H. L. Fisher, Rubber and its Uses, 107–8 ; Statistical Year-book of League of Nations, 1940–1, 126.)

and equipment, the momentum of the German assault carried the invader into what had been until recently the industrial nerve-centres of the country, and over some of her richest agricultural lands. While in the north and centre the attack was halted at the approaches to Leningrad (which was, however, surrounded and for months isolated from the rest of the country) and to Moscow, in the south the whole of the rich Ukraine, the Crimea, the Donetz and the Don and the North Caucasus region were absorbed, and the rising industrial centre of Stalingrad on the banks of the southern Volga, where the advancing flood was stemmed and turned back, was left a smoking and empty shell. Despite the rapid development of the new centres of heavy industry towards the east, the region of the lower Dnieper and the Donbas retained its pre-eminence as a centre of iron and steel production ; and, as engineering centres, Leningrad, Moscow and Kharkov still held pride of place—Moscow as a centre of electrical engineering and machine-tools, Leningrad of shipbuilding and engineering, and Kharkov of heavy engineering. In the immediate pre-war years the Ukraine still accounted for more than a half of the coal, iron-ore and iron and steel production of the country. As a result of invasion Soviet economy accordingly lost between a half and two thirds of her pre-war output of coal, about 60 per cent. of her production of iron ore and about a half of the pre-war productive capacity in steel. She lost between a third and a half of her grain lands, some nine tenths of her sugar-beet and a half of her pig population. Two out of three of her centres of aluminium production (at Tikhvin on the Volkhov and at Zaporozhe on the Dnieper) were within the area of German occupation. It was estimated at the time that during the winter of 1941–2 " about 20 to 25 per cent. of the productive capacity of the engineering industry was lost in occupied territory ",[1] despite the evacuation of part of it. The food industry of the country lost 40 per cent. of its capital equipment.[2] Oil production was more fortunate, since the German invasion of the Caucasus was halted on the Terek before the main Caucasian oil centres, which still accounted in 1940 for almost nine tenths of Soviet oil supplies, had been reached. But places such as Maikop in the north Caucasus, which were occupied, were centres of high-grade fuel-extraction, and their occupation represented an appreciable qualitative loss ; for a time the passage of oil-tankers up the Volga, from the Caspian into central Russia, was interrupted ; and owing to

[1] Dr. A. Baykov in London-Cambridge Economic Service Memo. No. 89 April, 1942.   [2] V. Zotov in Plan. Khoz., 1945, No. 5, 16.

the cessation of boring and the evacuation of personnel, production in the Caucasian oil-fields as a whole fell at one time by nearly a half.[1]

The full story of the eastward evacuation of Soviet industry from the threatened industrial districts of the west has still to be told. But we know sufficient of the scale on which it was conducted to appreciate that it made a major contribution to the recovery of Soviet war production after the summer of 1942. Before the war a beginning had been made with the construction of parallel plants, in a number of cases, in the eastern regions. As the German wave advanced, whole plants, or a substantial part of them, were evacuated (such of their equipment as could be dismantled and moved, their staffs with their families) to new sites beyond the Volga, in the Urals or further east still in Siberia. On these new sites temporary structures, often of wood, were hastily erected, local labour was recruited to fill the gaps made by withdrawals into the forces, and in a remarkably short space of time production was resumed. In many cases claims were made to have passed their former output within the space of six months of arrival or even less. In these new centres life was hard, especially amid the rigours of a Siberian climate, and the strain of improvisation was enormous. Housing accommodation was inadequate and in some cases non-existent. Building materials were scarce and the transport system congested. Local labour had to be trained anew ; new sources of materials and components had frequently to be developed. Lighter industries seem mostly to have gone to the Volga region : for example factories in the Moscow district making shells and grenades. Tank, aircraft and artillery plants were largely despatched to the Urals. Much of the machine-tool production came to be located as far east as the Kuznetsk basin, which became an important centre of production of armament steel and had plentiful supplies of coal. Some idea of the extent of this evacuation can be gained from the fact that more than half the population of Kiev and Kharkov, between 800,000 and a million persons, are said to have been evacuated in this way ; and that more than 70 per cent. of the total capital equipment (other than building structures) of Leningrad industry was evacuated to the east in the course of 1941–2.[2] There is some reason to think that evacuation from the areas occupied by the Germans in 1941 amounted to as much as a half of the urban

---

[1] M. Mkrtchian in *Plan. Khoz.*, 1947, No. I, 39–40; A. D. Perejda in *American Review on the Soviet Union*, Aug. 1946, 6–7.
[2] L. Volodarsky in *Plan. Khoz.*, 1945, No. 5, 64.

population of this area, and that the number evacuated into unoccupied territory may have reached or even exceeded 12 million.[1]

At the same time existing plants and industries of these eastern regions were expanded at an impressive speed. In particular, it is clear that investment in steel capacity continued on a large scale. Magnitogorsk completed what was claimed to be the largest blast-furnace in the world during the war years ; altogether in the eastern regions 10 new blast-furnaces, with an annual output capacity of two and a half million tons, were brought into operation between 1941 and 1945, and 45 marten ovens, 14 rolling mills and 13 coking ovens ; and between 1941 and the summer of 1945 the steel capacity of the new regions was expanded by more than 50 per cent.[2] A new tractor plant was built in the Altai region, a new plant for producing combine-harvesters at Krasnoyarsk on the Yenisei and agricultural machinery factories in the Urals and in Kazakhstan. So rapid was the advance of armament production in the east that already in the summer of 1942 it could be officially stated that " at the opening of the second year of war our industries are able to provide a larger quantity of arms and ammunition than before the war, despite the difficulties brought about by the war."[3] In the early months of the following year it was stated in an Order of the Day by Generalissimo Stalin that the previous superiority of German war production in tanks and aircraft was on the point of being overcome ;[4] and by the summer of 1943 Soviet production of tanks and aeroplanes surpassed that of Germany. In the course of the war years the capacity of electrical power stations in the Urals, Siberia, Central Asia and the Volga region was doubled; the output of Kuzbas coal increased 35 per cent. and the extraction of Kuzbas coking coal was doubled ; and the coal output of the whole country was enabled to reach the pre-war level two years after the end of the war, despite the devastation of the Donbas. One result of these developments was very greatly to increase the congestion on the railway network of the Urals region and on the lines connecting the Urals with Kuzbas and the Urals with the west. On

[1] Cf. F. Lorimer, *The Population of the Soviet Union*, 195–7.

[2] B. Sukharevsky in *Plan. Khoz.*, 1945, No. 3, 11 ; N. Eremenko in *Plan. Khoz.*, 1946, No. 2, 89–90 ; A. Korobov, *Plan. Khoz.*, 1946, No. 3, 22. The output of coke was doubled and that of iron tubes was almost trebled.

[3] *Pravda*, July 19, 1942.

[4] Order of the Day on Red Army Day, Feb. 23, 1943. His actual statement was : " Hitlerite Germany, which forces the war industry of Europe to work for her, until recently enjoyed superiority in equipment over the Soviet Union, above all in tanks and aircraft. . . . But in twenty months of war the situation has changed."

some of these lines the burden of freight traffic grew by 50 per cent. and more during the war years.[1]

But the war-time slogan of " all for the front " involved a big contraction in the consumer goods industries (many of which were in the west and did not have priority in evacuation) and a cutting to the bone of the supply of all but the bare essentials for civilian consumers. The fall of civilian consumption was evidently much greater than anything experienced in this country or in France. When the Germans retreated the deliberate devastation was extraordinarily thorough. Mine-shafts were not only flooded but systematically wrecked; iron works, steel furnaces and factories demolished; and railway tracks so extensively destroyed by means of special devices as to be unusable without extensive relaying. The countryside in the path of the German retreat for hundreds of miles was made a wasteland, devoid of livestock and buildings and often of inhabitants. Nearly 2000 towns, 70,000 villages and factories employing 4 million persons were partially or wholly destroyed, according to official calculations, and 25 million persons were rendered homeless. Contemporary Soviet estimates placed the sum of this appalling devastation at half the material devastation in Europe.

III

After destruction of such a magnitude, restoration of economic life in the western regions was a task that inevitably required for its completion the labours of several years. Already in 1943, in the wake of the advancing Red Army, a first beginning was made in the revival of cultivation, of the main arteries of the transport network and of the most essential industrial enterprises. In the summer of 1943 a very detailed plan was prepared and issued as a directive of the central government for the return of livestock and machinery and the grant of loans for seed and for dwelling-houses. Arrangements were also outlined for railway workers in these liberated districts to be given special privileges such as the grant of small land-allotments (similar to those of collective farm members) and loans for the erection of dwelling-houses, repayable over a period of seven years.[2] In the Ukraine alone in the two

[1] On the line between Akmolinsk and the Karaganda coalfield the increase was 58 per cent., and on one of the chief lines from the Urals to the west it was 75 per cent. (I. Kovalev in *Plan. Khoz.*, 1945, No. 5, 5.)

[2] Decree of Sovnarcom on Urgent Measures relating to Economic Reconstruction in the Districts liberated from German Occupation, *Sovhoznoe Proizvodstvo*, 1943, No. 8, 5–26.

years after her liberation, 26,000 collective farms and over a thousand machine tractor' stations were re-established.[1]   At the same time strenuous attempts were made during the war years to extend the cultivated area in the east, in substitution for the losses in the west.   The task was not an easy one, since mobilisation for the Red Army had deprived collective farms on the average of a quarter of their total labour force (measured in working days), and of more than 40 per cent. of the labour force devoted to field work on the farm fields : a gap which had to be repaired by increasing the amount of field work performed by women and juveniles.[2]   Particular attention was paid to the cultivation of sugar beet in Kazakhstan, to replace the loss of the main regions of beet cultivation in the west (part of the equipment of sugar refineries having been successfully evacuated and transferred).   The expansion of wheat was undertaken in the trans-Volga region and Siberia (where special emphasis was placed on winter wheat).   In 1942 the crop-acreage in the unoccupied regions had been expanded by some 5 million acres and in 1943 further increases of acreage of a similar magnitude were undertaken in these regions.[3]   In the neighbourhood of all the large towns there was an expansion of market-garden allotments (both of farmers in the vicinity and of urban citizens and institutions), which increased the supply of potatoes and other vegetables in Moscow by about a sixth and in some other cities by as much as a third—and in the swollen Urals town of Sverdlovsk by more than a half.[4]   For the country as a whole in 1944 vegetable production was 14 per cent. higher than in 1940.[5]

A small beginning had also been made in the war years with a revival of certain of the light industries ; although so long as the war continued they inevitably occupied a place of relatively low priority, even when they were largely working on supplies for the army.   Thus the textile industry in 1944 claimed a modest output increase of some 12 per cent., and a rise in the productivity of labour, although its output-targets for the year had not been ful-

[1] B. Sukharevsky, loc. cit., 13.
[2] I. Slatin in Sotsialisticheskoe Selskoe Khoziaistvo, 1944, No. 4, 36.
[3] Cf. S. Demidov in Sots. Sels. Khoz., 1943, Nos. 3–4, 5 ; 1944, No. 4, 11 seq. In 1943 some of the largest targets for increase in grain crop area were in Central Asia (Uzbekistan 28 per cent., Turkmenistan 49 per cent.), where it seems clear that the previous specialisation on cotton-growing was relaxed in favour of a return to larger cultivation of grain.
[4] Ibid., 16. In the spring of 1945 sales on collective farm markets in the main towns were reported as being about a third larger than twelve months previously in the case of potatoes and vegetables, more than a third in eggs and butter, and greater by a half in meat. 1944 had itself shown larger increases of potatoes and meat over 1943. (A. Liubimov in Plan. Khoz., 1945, No. 4, 27.)
[5] S. Demidov in Plan. Khoz., 1945, No. 2, 46.

filled ; and more substantial increases were designed for the ensuing year.[1] Already in the same year, 1944, the boot and shoe industry was beginning to devote some attention to the putting into production of new designs of men's and women's shoes for civilian wear, and certain branches of the hosiery industry (chiefly in the Moscow district) were claiming substantial increases in labour productivity and a shortening of the production-cycle as a consequence of the introduction of conveyor methods of production.[2] The commodity turnover on the ordinary market during the first half of 1945 already showed a substantial increase of nearly 30 per cent. on the corresponding period of the previous year.[3] In the twelve months following the cessation of hostilities a transfer of war-plants to production for the civilian market began to be undertaken on a considerable scale. The clothing industry, which had been engaged on army supplies during the war, seems to have taken the lead in supplying the civilian market once more ; the boot and shoe industry apparently being not very far below the pre-war level of production six or nine months after the end of the war. Supplies for the civilian market also began to appear during this immediate post-war period from a number of plants producing such things as radio sets, watches, household utensils and utility furniture.

But at the conclusion of the war, and even by the end of 1945, no more than a fraction of the former productive capacity of the devastated regions had been restored. Despite the restocking of collective farms in these areas by the return of evacuated livestock and machinery, only a minor proportion of the machinery and livestock destroyed or taken away by the Germans can have been replaced.[4] In the autumn of 1945 it was officially stated that three quarters of the pre-war arable area of the Ukraine had been put under cultivation and that the equipment of Machine Tractor Stations in the Ukraine was already adequate to undertake four fifths of the ploughing of fallow and spring ploughing and a half of the winter ploughing.[5] But since the yield must still have been

---

[1] I. N. Akimov in *Tekstilnaia Promishlennost*, 1944, Nos. 11–12.

[2] Cf. *Legkaia Promishlennost*, 1944, Nos. 7–8, esp. A. F. Shchegolev, 4.

[3] A. Liubimov, *loc. cit.*, 22.

[4] The number of horses removed to Germany from these areas is stated to have been 7 million and the number of horned cattle 17 million.

[5] Statement of N. S. Khrushchev at Kiev on Oct. 13, 1945. In the occupied regions as a whole some 3,000 machine-tractor stations and 85,000 collective farms had been reconstituted. (A. Korobov, *Plan. Khoz.*, 1946, No. 3, 22.) By the end of 1946 all the pre-war machine-tractor stations, three quarters of the pre-war sown area and more than half of the livestock owned by collective farms and by collective farm members individually had been restored in the liberated regions (S. Demidov in *Plan. Khoz.*, 1947, No. 1, 3–4).

lower than normal by a substantial amount, the level of production in this region for the agricultural year 1945–6 could hardly have been more than half the normal, even if weather conditions had been favourable.[1] But to add to the effects of war, the Ukraine and the Volga region were to be smitten in 1946 by what has been described as " the worst drought in our country for the last 50 years " ;[2] as a result of which the de-rationing of bread and cereals, announced for the end of 1946, had to be postponed for a further year. In the mines of the Donbas restoration work by the end of the war was said to have been completed so far as one third of pre-war coal capacity was concerned, and preliminary drainage completed in mines responsible for one half of pre-war output. Six months later the mines of the Rostov coal combine (which had been liberated somewhat earlier) actually reported that they had reached their 1940 output-level. In the autumn of 1945 the Ukrainian section of the Donbas was even said to be producing as much as 38 per cent. of its pre-war average daily coal output ; and in the Ukraine as a whole nearly 100 engineering plants were stated to be in production again, including the Mariupol steel-works and the Voroshilovgrad locomotive works.[3] By the end of the year coal output in the Donbas had reached a half of its pre-war level.[4] The food industry by the beginning of 1945 had exceeded its reconstruction target·and had already restarted nearly 2000 enterprises in the liberated areas ; or about one third of those located in these areas before the war. Of the damaged railway track some 50,000 kilometres or more of railroad track were said to have been restored by the end of 1945 as well as half that distance beyond the western frontiers of the U.S.S.R.[5] Of damaged waterway systems not only the Svir lock system, linking Leningrad with the upper Volga *via* the Mariinsky canal, had been reopened by the midsummer of 1946, but also the northern half of the waterway from the Baltic to the White Sea

[1] Certain statements in the West were nevertheless claiming that the U.S.S.R. had an export surplus on which claims ought to be made to make good the grain deficiency in central and south-eastern Europe. Actually in the course of 1945–6 the U.S.S.R. from her scanty supplies made some substantial contributions to the needs of neighbouring countries (to Rumania, Poland, Finland and Czechoslovakia as well as to France), totalling more than a million tons. Up to the summer of 1946 (when opposition in the U.S. Senate and House of Representatives secured its termination) the Ukraine and Belorussia were in receipt of some UNRRA supplies.   [2] S. Demidov, *loc. cit.*, 4.

[3] N. S. Khruschev, *loc. cit.*   [4] A. Panov in *Plan. Khoz.*, 1946, No. 2, 101.

[5] In an address by I. Kovalev, reported in *Trud*, June 15, 1945, a total of more than 100,000 kilometres was mentioned as the length of " trunk lines restored and constructed during the war years " (at home and beyond the frontiers), and in addition nearly 700,000 kilometres of telegraph and telephone lines. It is expected that the railway system of the Ukraine will be fully restored by 1948. (A. Galitsky in *Plan. Khoz.*, 1946, No. 2, 115.)

which had been within the sphere of military operations and had been systematically damaged by the Germans. So also had the Dnieper-Bug canal, linking the Dnieper through the Pripet marshes and the forests of Brest with the Vistula. But twelve months after the end of the war through traffic along the Dnieper was still impossible ; and it was not until 1947 that work on the great Dnieper dam and its lock-system was completed, and its power plant and also one of three blast furnaces of the adjoining Zaporozhe iron and steel works were restarted. The task of rebuilding the shattered towns and rehousing their populations was a gigantic one : inevitably a matter of several years, despite the large amount of attention devoted to the use of new types of building materials and the development of prefabrication and assembly of standard completed parts on the site. On January 1st, 1946, the transfer to-date of two and a half million from dugouts to dwellings was reported, and the restoration of 70,000 schools and 6,000 hospitals in the devastated areas. Yet impressive as this figure of rehousing was, it covered only one tenth of the total rendered homeless by the war. In Stalingrad about the same date one sixth of the dwellings had been rendered habitable, but two thirds of the former inhabitants were back in the town.

As long-term targets, requiring " perhaps three new Five Year Plans, if not more ", Stalin at the beginning of 1946 projected a trebling of the pre-war steel output and coal output to 60 million and 500 million tons respectively. This steel target for " three five year plans or possibly even more " was higher than the U.S.A. output for the two pre-war peaks of 1928 and 1937 and double the U.S.A. output in 1938 ; but it was below the wartime peak of U.S.A. production in 1944, which was 81 million. The coal target was rather more than double the pre-war British output figure, but was again slightly below the U.S.A. war-time peak. Both targets were in fact achieved by 1960. For oil production the figure was 60 million, or slightly less than double the pre-war output, and no more than a third of the U.S.A. output in 1940. These targets were presumably intended to be no more than rough and tentative indicators of the magnitude of the economic tasks that lay ahead. But it is of interest to note that the suggested rates of growth were substantially lower than those provided for under the first three plans and actually maintained prior to the war; even after allowance for at least the first three of the fifteen being devoted to making up the leeway of the war years. At first sight they seemed to indicate that a much more prominent place was envisaged for investment in the consumer goods industries over these three post-war quinquennia than in the pre-war period, so long as the international situation proved favourable to peaceful construction.

The project for the post-war and fourth Five Year Plan, which was presented to a session of the Supreme Soviet and adopted by it on March 18th, 1946, indicated that at least for the first post-war quinquennium investment priority was to remain with heavy industry. This was hardly surprising in view of the large amount of building and re-equipment, with its demands on supplies of building materials of all kinds, structural steel and machinery, which had inevitably to take pride of place during three or four out of the five post-war years. In this new Plan the task of restoration in the devastated regions necessarily bulked large: so large as to exert a preponderating influence over its whole shape. Moreover, so long as the international horizon remained clouded, and an enduring structure of Great Power co-operation for the maintenance of peace had not emerged, the Soviet Government would evidently wish to expand its armament industry (or, at least, the economic roots from which such an industry could quickly grow) towards the American level. In a country that is still not rich in capital equipment, even if it is rich in natural resources, this, again, must straitly condition the system of priorities assigned to different branches of industry in future growth.

Neither the proportion of the national income assigned to capital investment[1] nor the proportion of capital investment to be assigned to heavy industry was explicitly stated in the published draft of the Plan. Figures were given to show that of the sums devoted to capital construction in industry about 35 per cent. were designed to fall within the spheres of the three Ministries for Construction in the fuel industry, in heavy industry and in enterprises serving the army and navy. But it is not clear how far this figure is comparable with figures of the share of investment going to the capital goods industries in pre-war Plans. If it is at all comparable, then the share of the latter was much smaller than formerly. The output targets, however, for the industries producing capital goods were relatively high. For iron and steel they were set at 35 per cent.

---

[1] Unfortunately the figures for the national income given in the draft Plan are expressed in terms of 1926–7 prices, whereas the figures for capital investment are "in 1945 estimated prices", and the two sets of figures are therefore not comparable. But for the final year of the Plan (1950) the amount of net investment has been stated as being 21 per cent. of the national income, together with an additional 6 per cent. of the national income devoted to "the building up of reserves". This compares with "rather more than a quarter of the national income" devoted to net investment "including reserves" on the average of the period from 1928 up to the war (A. Petrov in *Plan. Khoz.*, 1947, No. 2, 64).

above pre-war, for coal at 51 per cent. (with special emphasis on coking coal and on the development of the concentration and briquetting of coal), for the chemical industry at 50 per cent. (with the production of synthetic rubber to be doubled), and the output of electricity at 70 per cent. above 1940 (and the output capacity of power stations by rather more). The figure for steel in 1950, namely 25½ million tons, represented a doubling of output over the five years, and that for coal, 250 million, an increase over 1945 of two thirds. By contrast, the target for oil was only set at 35 million tons, a mere 14 per cent. above the pre-war level; and the contribution of the "eastern districts" (i.e. east of the Volga and including the "second Baku") to this output was set to rise from 12 per cent. in 1944 to 36 per cent. in 1950: a remarkable shift of weight away from the traditional districts. The reason no doubt was the difficulties caused by the cessation of borings in the Baku oilfields under stress of wartime conditions. (Total oil production had fallen by 1945 to less than 20 million tons.) The rates of advance assigned to the engineering industry were outstanding, amounting to a doubling of the pre-war output level for machinery. Over the five years the output of tractors and motors was to be stepped up three and a half times, no doubt by reconverting certain plants engaged in war-time on tank production. The output of electrical equipment by 1950 was to be two and a half times the pre-war. Special attention was given to expanding the number and range of types of machine tools, with the output of forge and press equipment raised by 1950 to two and a half times the pre-war. A figure of 74,000 was mentioned for the production of machine tools in 1950, of which 12,300 should consist of "multi-purpose and special-purpose machine tools". Similar high rates of expansion were assigned to non-ferrous metals such as aluminium, nickel, lead, zinc, magnesium, molybdenum and tungsten.[1]

[1] The increases mentioned for aluminium, nickel and molybdenum were a doubling of output, for lead, zinc, magnesium two and a half times, for tungsten concentrates four times. The draft of the Plan referred to these as increases "during the five-year period". Since absolute output figures in their case are available neither for 1945 nor 1950, it is impossible to express the 1950 targets as increases over the pre-war level.

It has to be borne in mind, of course, that present-day territory and population are larger than prior to 1939. The population added by these new territories amounted to an increase of about 12 per cent. Military and civilian losses suffered by the U.S.S.R. during the war (which approached 20 million) more than offset this increase. The new territories moreover are ones whose industries and agriculture were among the most devastated during the war. Making allowance for increase of territory and war losses and also for the rate of natural increase, it has been estimated in a recent study by the Economic Department of the League of Nations that the 1945 population may have been 188 million, compared with just under 174 million in 1940. (F. Lorimer, *The Population of the Soviet Union*, 181–90.) This, however, turns out to have been an overestimate.

A substantial proportion of the increase of engineering production was intended to consist of equipment for consumer goods industries. The output of textile machinery was designed to rise to four times the pre-war level, with special emphasis on ring-spinning frames and automatic looms. As a result the capacity of spinning mills was to be increased by nearly 3 million spindles over the five years. The targets for consumer goods industry were less precise and less detailed than those for heavy industry, and in the event a number of them were not fulfilled. It was stated that "the output of foodstuffs and consumer goods" by 1950 would "surpass the pre-war level", as a result of "an annual increase of 17 per cent.". In the course of the discussion of the draft plan the Minister for Trade added that "the marketable supplies of food commodities would increase by 50 per cent. and of industrial consumer goods by 36 per cent." over the five years.[1] The 1950 target for cotton cloth was some 18 per cent. higher than 1940, for woollen cloth 32 per cent., for leather footwear 13 per cent., and rubber footwear 25 per cent. The output of artificial silk was designed to increase to four and a half times the pre-war level, of the paper industry by 84 per cent. and of the fishing industry by 50 per cent. above pre-war. Mention was also made of the putting into production of such things as electron microscopes and television sets, and the mass production of cinema projectors and cine-cameras, cameras, cheap motor cycles and bicycles, radio sets, clocks, watches, gramophones and refrigerators.[2] The rates of increase here mentioned are substantial ones, even if they were considerably lower than those planned for some branches of heavy industry. But while the increases above the pre-war level were smaller than in the case of heavy industry, and the 1950 output-figures for cotton and woollen textiles were actually lower than the targets set in both the original First and Second Five Year Plans for 1932 and 1937 respectively (though not in fact attained), it has to be remembered that the consumer goods industries had considerably more leeway to make up, as a result of the war, than heavy industry, which had enjoyed priority of expansion in the new regions during the war years.

[1] This statement apparently referred to values at *current* prices of each year, and allowed for a fall in prices, whereas the quantities referred to in the Plan itself were expressed in *unchanged* prices (mostly in terms of 1926–7 prices; although investment expenditure, as we have seen above, had been calculated in terms of 1945 prices, presumably due to the large changes in building costs over the past ten years).

[2] A detail of some small interest is that the proportion of Moscow's heating to be supplied centrally from district heat and power stations through a network of transmission pipes was to be raised to 36 per cent. by 1950, according to the municipal plan. Previously only about one eighth of Moscow's buildings had their heating supplied in this way.

For agriculture, compared with industry, the targets were in most cases considerably more modest than those for industry. The grain harvest by 1950 was designed to show no more than a 7 per cent. increase over 1940.[1] For the so-called industrial crops somewhat larger increases were planned: 22 per cent. for beet, 25 per cent. for cotton, and 39 per cent. for flax. Increases in the cattle population of 39 per cent., in sheep and goats of 75 per cent., and in pigs of 200 per cent. *over 1945* are mentioned. But the animal population suffered gravely in the war years, despite the evacuation of some from the western regions towards the east.

War-time movements of industries and population, of armies and their equipment, placed a very great strain on the transport system especially in the Urals and Siberia. The work of restoration and new construction in the post-war period inevitably involved a similar strain. It was estimated that over the post-war quinquennium the total freight to be carried by railway, water and road would rise by more than a third above the level of 1940.[2] A place of special importance had, accordingly, to be given to an extension of the transport system: to the restoration of existing arterial roadways and the building of between 7000 and 8000 miles of new motor roads; the restoration of the canal system and of river-port facilities and the extension of navigable inland waterways by some 80,000 miles; the construction of some 4,500 miles of new railway line, half of them in the Urals, in addition to the restoration of existing lines. Among the new lines to be built in the five-year period (but not in fact completed until much later) was one parallel to the west Siberian section of the Trans-Siberian some 150 miles south of it, and connecting the steel town of Magnitogorsk in the southern Urals directly with Stalinsk in the Kuznetsk basin (and continued in the west to Kuibyshev on the Volga and in the east to Abakan near Minusinsk and to Taishet). The line from Akmolinsk to Karaganda and Lake Balkhash was also planned to be joined to the Turksib railway to the east.

Special emphasis was laid in the Plan upon the restoration of industry in the older industrial centres of the west and south-west. In the majority of cases the output in these centres was set somewhat above pre-war: industrial production as a whole in the former occupied areas was intended to be 15 per cent. above the pre-war level. But since the larger rates of growth above the pre-war level were in

[1] See, however, the note about grain figures attached to the Table on page 311.
[2] On the eve of the war nine tenths of all goods traffic was still carried by railway, 8 per cent. by water, and only 2 per cent. by motor transport by road.

the unoccupied regions, the result was to carry the pre-war tendency towards an eastward shift in the economic centre of gravity an important stage further. For example, it was intended that the coal production of the Donbas should be raised slightly above its pre-war level to 88 million tons. But this implied a fall in the proportion of the country's coal mined in the Donbas to 35 per cent., compared with 60 per cent. in 1937 and 78 per cent. in 1928. Similarly in iron and steel production, the pre-war level of production in the south was to be restored; but in view of big developments in the wartime centres in the Urals and Siberia, and to a smaller extent in the Far East, in Transcaucasia and in Kazakhstan, the relative importance of the new centres would be considerably increased. Much of the new non-ferrous metal production was in the Urals, Siberia and Central Asia. Similarly in the textile industry a substantial part of the new mills to be constructed were apparently to be in Siberia and Central Asia. In Kazakhstan during the war years the output of electricity rose to a milliard kilowatt hours (or about one half of the total output of electricity for the whole of the pre-1939 territory of the U.S.S.R. in 1913). Under the new Five Year Plan this output was to be nearly doubled by 1950. Yet on the eve of the war the total capacity of power stations in Kazakhstan had been only one quarter of a million kilowatts and at the opening of the Second Five Year Plan eight years before a mere 60,000.

The Plan as a whole can be summed up in the estimate that the output of industry as a whole would be raised by 1950 to 48 per cent. above the pre-war level. This necessitated the restoration of over 3,000 medium and large industrial plants, and the new construction of a further 2,700: a total which included 45 blast furnaces, 165 open hearth furnaces, 90 electric furnaces, 104 rolling mills and 63 coke batteries rehabilitated or newly built, in addition to the opening of about 250 new collieries and new iron-ore mines with an aggregate annual output of 35 million tons. A rise of labour productivity of 36 per cent. over pre-war was anticipated, on the basis of an increase in "the amount of capital equipment per worker by approximately 50 per cent." The fixed capital of the economic system as a whole in 1950 (including agriculture, transport and communal building, as well as industry) was projected as being 8 per cent. above the pre-war level.

The following table presents in summary form the output of certain leading products, giving the Plan-targets and the actual level achieved in 1950, and comparing these with pre-war figures and also with those of 1913 (where these exist) and of 1928.

Product	Unit	1913[1]	1928	1940	1950 planned	1950 actual
Pig-iron . . .	m. tons	4·2	3·3	15·0	19·5	19·2
Steel . . .	m. tons	4·2	4·3	18·3	25·4	27·3
Rolled steel . .	m. tons	3·5	3·4	—	17·8	20·9
Coal . . .	m. tons	29·1	35·5	166	250	261
Oil . . .	m. tons	9·2	11·7	31	35·4	38
Electricity . .	md. kwh.	2	5	48	82	91·2
Copper . . .	th. tons	—	19·1	161	—	255
Aluminium . .	th. tons	—	—	74·4	—	—
Cement . . .	m. tons	1·5	1·8	5·8	10·5	10·2
Railway locomotives	conventional units	418	478	928	2720	1212
Goods wagons . .	thousands	14·8	10·6	31	146	51
Tractors . . .	thousands	—	1·2	31	112	116
Motor vehicles .	thousands	—	·7	145	500	363
Grain . . .	m. tons	80–82	73	95·5	127·2[2]	81
Sugar . . .	th. tons	1290	1283	2150	2400	2500
Paper . . .	th. tons	205	284	812	1340	1200
Cotton cloth . .	m. linear metres	2227	2678	3954	4686	3899
Woollen cloth . .	m. linear metres	95	87	120	159	155
Leather footwear .	m. pairs	60	58	211	240	203
Rubber footwear .	m. pairs	28	36	70	88·6	111

[1] 1913 figures are for Russia with the pre-1939 territory of the U.S.S.R.
[2] This is presumably the inflated "biological yield" figure (on which basis, presumably, the 1940 figure was given at the time as 119): figures which were subsequently (after the death of Stalin) revised downward to a "barn yield". The revised figure for 1950 (actual) is given here.

Twice within a quarter of a century, twice since the inauguration of the Soviet régime, the people of that country had seen their land ravaged by wars far more deadly than anything that has visited our own island within modern times. Twice, weakened and overwrought by the years of famine and carnage, they had painfully to bend already aching backs to rebuild their shattered economic system, in many respects from its foundations. Having rebuilt, they then set themselves further tasks, which at the inception of the planning era strained the imagination of the world and were dismissed abroad as brittle dreams. Many have marvelled that men and women could possess the endurance to do such things. Revolution, however, is a strange fire which not only consumes but also produces new elements with unfamiliar qualities. Only a rare spirit forged in a people by its history, a boundless faith in their own ability to wring achievement from the future, is capable of inspiring men and women to endure and to strive as the Russian people have done. Least of all people on earth could they wish to see another war in our time.

CHAPTER THIRTEEN

THE TWO POST-WAR DECADES

I

The reconstruction years, following the ravages of war and military occupation, were neither easy nor untroubled; and the first two years, in particular, of the Fourth Plan were ones of acute difficulties and of intense hardship. 1946 was overshadowed by a crop-failure due to what was officially described as "the worst drought in our country for the last fifty years"; and it was also a year of reconversion of industry from a war-time to a peace-time basis, as a result of which industrial production fell below the pre-war level by about a quarter (and consumer goods production by considerably more than this—probably by as much as a third or even two-fifths).[1] It seems likely that the grain harvest in 1946 was only about a half of the pre-war level; and since fodder-grains were particularly affected, there was a serious setback to the recovery of livestock (and especially pigs) from devastating war-time losses.[2] In reporting six years later to the 19th Party Congress Malenkov was to state that "the war retarded our industrial development for eight or nine years, that is, approximately two five-year plans."[3]

The following year 1947, however, witnessed considerable improvement. Firstly there was a large improvement in the harvest. Secondly, industry had surmounted most of the dislocations attendant upon reconversion and re-tooling; and industrial production as a whole was said to have recovered to 90 per cent. of the pre-war level (heavy industry to just above it; but consumer goods production was still some 20 per cent. below it). In 1948 it was announced that for the first time industrial production had passed the pre-war level in the course of that year; although it was not until the end of

---

[1] Cf. G. Malenkov, *Report to the Nineteenth Party Congress* (Moscow, 1952), 53. The production indices (1940=100) for 1945 and 1946 were here given as 92 and 77 respectively for "All Industry", and 112 and 82 respectively for "Production of Means of Production". Also cf. A. Bergson, J. H. Blackman and A. Erlich, "Post-war Economic Reconstruction and Development in the U.S.S.R." in *Annals of the American Academy of Political and Social Science*, May 1949, 59, 62.

[2] *Ibid.*, 62–3.

[3] G. Malenkov, *op. cit.*, 52.

1949 that industrial output in the devastated western areas (where the bulk of consumer goods industries were located) was restored to pre-war.

In view of the improvement in the situation in 1947, derationing of foodstuffs was undertaken in December of that year, and coupled with it a monetary reform designed to reduce the amount of money in circulation (expanded by some two and a half times during the war),[1] by the issue of new money to replace the depreciated war-time rouble. The official decree of December 11 announcing the change contained this explanation : " During the years of the Patriotic War the expenditure of the Soviet State on maintenance of the Army and on the development of the war industry rose sharply. The enormous war expenditure demanded the issue for circulation of large amounts of money . . . At present, when the transfer to open trade at unified prices has become the task of the day, the great amount of money issued during the war hampers the abolition of the rationing system, since the surplus money in circulation inflates market prices, creates an exaggerated demand for goods, and increases the opportunities for speculation."

A leading object of the change was, no doubt, to tax hoarded stocks of money accumulated (largely, though not entirely, in the countryside) by war-time sales of scarce foodstuffs at greatly inflated prices (e.g. on the collective farm markets and by private specula-tion). A central feature of the monetary reform was that the new money was exchangeable for the old at parities that varied according to different categories. *Cash* holdings were exchangeable on the basis of ten old notes to one new ; whereas savings bank deposits under 3,000 roubles were exchangeable on a one-one basis (with deposits of over 3,000 at progressively less favourable ratios). State bonds of recent loan issues were exchangeable for a new conversion loan (carrying 2 per cent. interest) at a ratio of one rouble of the new loan for three of the old ; the reason for this dis-crimination as officially given being that " a considerable part of the State Loans were created during the war, when the purchasing power of money fell, whereas after the currency reform the State will redeem that debt with full-value roubles ".[2] But while the main burden of the change was borne by hoarders of cash, the level of wage and salary payments remained unaffected (except for a raising of the very lowest wage categories). The new uniform retail

[1] N. Voznesenky, *War Economy of the U.S.S.R. in the period of the Patriotic War* (Moscow, 1948), 111.
[2] Decree of Dec. 11, 1947.

prices were fixed at a level intermediate between the former ration prices and the higher ' commercial prices ' at which off-ration purchases could be made in the State shops. It seems probable that the result was to reduce the urban cost of living by approximately a half compared with what it had been in the years prior to the monetary reform.[1] Thereafter the policy was adopted of making successive price-reductions (while keeping money wages more or less stable) as increased supplies of consumers' goods became available; the result of this series of price-reductions being to bring the retail price-level by the end of 1954 to about 20 per cent. above the immediate pre-war level (i.e. 1940) and the level of real wages (excluding the value of free services) to about 65 per cent. above pre-war (i.e. 1940).[2] It seems probable that the average real income of the collective farm peasantry rose during this period by rather more than that of industrial and other workers.

The progress of reconstruction in the course of 1948 was sufficient to justify the hopes on which the monetary reform was based ; and of the agricultural situation at the end of that year the Central Statistical Administration was able to report that " despite unfavourable weather conditions in most of the Volga regions, the gross grain harvest practically reached the pre-war level of 1940, while average grain yields per hectare exceeded the pre-war level."[3] Industrial output showed the remarkably large rise of 27 per cent. over the previous year. Altogether during these first three years of the Five Year Plan some 4,000 industrial plants had been put into

[1] M. C. Kaser, "Soviet Statistics of Wages and Prices", in *Soviet Studies* (University of Glasgow), Vol. VII, No. 1, 39. On the eve of the monetary reform retail prices were about three times the level of 1940; while the average level of money wages was less than double pre-war.

[2] *Ibid.*, 42–3; *Politicheskaia Ekonomia: Uchebnik* (Moscow, 1954), 462. An article in *Planovoe Khoziaistvo*, 1955, No. 4, 8, claimed that by 1955 real wages had reached a level of 90 per cent. above 1950. S. Figurnov (in *Sotsialisticheskii Trud*, 1959, No. 5) gave a figure of 74 per cent. as the increase in 1954 over 1940. *Narodnoe Khoziaistvo S.S.S.R.* (Moscow, 1956) gave for 1955 an index number of retail prices in State shops of 138 (1940 = 100) and for prices in Kolkhoz markets of 111 (1940 = 100). It is to be noted that prices in 1940 were appreciably above the level of 1937 and real wages lower. A comparison with 1937 instead of 1940 would therefore yield a smaller increase than the above mentioned. According to the estimates of Dr. Janet Chapman real wages in 1954 were around 40 per cent. above 1937, but per capita household purchases of goods for the country as a whole had risen by substantially more than this (*urban* per capita purchases by rather *less* than 40 per cent.). Her estimate of real wages at the end of the war is barely two thirds of 1937, and in 1937 something between 17 and 43 per cent. below 1928– although per capita consumption for the country as a whole had risen between those two dates. (*Real Wages in Soviet Russia since 1928*, Harvard 1963, 166, 170.)

[3] Report on the Fulfilment of the State Plan for 1948. According to the revised figures published subsequently (on the basis of barn yield), this claim was true for the mean of the years 1938–40 but not for 1940 itself which was an above-average year.

operation, of which about a half were completed in the course of 1948.

The main targets of the Five Year Plan were actually attained ahead of time, and it was claimed that the overall industrial target set for 1950 was exceeded by 17 per cent. The Report on the Fulfilment of the Fourth Five Year Plan, issued by Gosplan and the Central Statistical Board in April 1951, announced that the plan had indeed been completed in four years and a quarter.[1] Industrial output in 1950, the last year of the plan, stood at 73 per cent. above 1940, with capital goods about double but consumer goods no more than 23 per cent. above pre-war. Ferrous metals exceeded the pre-war level by 45 per cent., coal by 57, oil by 22 and electricity by 87, but textiles, clothing, footwear and other light industries only by 17 per cent. Grain output, although short of the plan-target, was somewhat above the average of the three pre-war years. More surprisingly it was announced that "the total head of productive live-stock, sharply reduced during the war, was restored, and in 1950 increased by 4 per cent. compared with 1940 in all categories of farming."[2] However, while cattle and sheep and goats were above the pre-war level, cows and pigs were still below (horses were also very substantially below), as is shown in the table below on page 319. As was to transpire in the course of the next few years, the failure of grain and livestock to recover as rapidly as industrial production was to be the crucial limiting factor upon the rise in the standard of life in the course of the 1950's.

II

Details of the Fifth Plan were not publicly announced until just before the 19th Party Congress in October, 1952.[3] Its' two main features were: (1) a rate of increase of industrial production of 72 per cent. over the quinquennium, which was lower than that of previous plans (even somewhat lower than in the unfinished Third Plan);[4] (2) a narrowing of the divergence between the rates of growth of the two main departments or sectors of industry pro-ducing capital goods and consumer goods: output of the former was

---

[1] See *Planovoe Khoziaistvo*, 1951, No. 2, 3–13.

[2] Report of Gosplan and Central Statistical Board on "Results of the Fulfilment of the Fourth Five-Year Plan.'.

[3] See "Directives of the Plan" in *Planovoe Khoziaistvo*, 1952, No. 4, 4–25.

[4] A quinquennial increase of 72 per cent. represents an annual (compound) rate of 12 per cent., which is to be compared with 18·3 per cent. between 1928 and 1940 according to the official index (on which see above, 261–2) and 20 per cent. in the concluding three years of the Fourth Plan.

to grow by 80 per cent, and of the latter by 65 per cent., whereas, by contrast, between 1928 and 1940 the former grew about double as fast as the latter. The result was accordingly to place more emphasis on raising the level of consumption.

It may be noted that special emphasis was placed on a rise in labour productivity (of approximately 50 per cent) as a factor in the growth of output. The rise in the number of 'factory and office workers' over the quinquennium was set at the comparatively low proportion of 15 per cent. (actuality was to exceed the forecast). In this connection Malenkov in his report to the 19th Party Congress claimed that "labour productivity in industry increased 50 per cent between 1940 and 1951", and that this accounted for two thirds of the rise of industrial output over that period. The days when growth of output could depend on extensive widening of employment by drawing upon a rural surplus of labour were evidently drawing to a close.

Investment in house-building was to be raised, and urban housing financed by the State was to be higher by about a fifth (measured in floor-space provided) than in the previous quinquennium of reconstruction. During the period of the Fourth Plan about 100 million square metres of floor-space were built by "State enterprises, institutions and local Soviets, and also by the population of towns and workers' settlements with the aid of State credits".[1] This was equivalent to about 2½ million small flat-dwellings of 2 rooms *plus* kitchen and bathroom. In addition, about 2,700,000 rural houses were built. The new Plan mentioned a figure of 105 million square metres for urban building by State organisations alone (i.e. excluding building "by the population of towns and workers' settlements with the aid of State credits", which had previously accounted for some 12 per cent. of the whole); but it was silent about the volume of rural building.[2]

The successive price-cuts and the rise in the standard of life from 1949 onwards have been mentioned in the previous section. On the course of 1953 a new emphasis on raising living-standards came into official pronouncements and policy. The price-reductions announced in the spring of that year were larger than usual, and had the effect of increasing consumers' purchasing power probably by a sixth. Retail turnover, measured in constant prices, was at any rate greater by 15 per cent. in the first half of the year compared with the corresponding period of the previous year, and State Loan issues during the year were reduced by more than a half. In the autumn

[1] *Planovoe Khoziaistvo*, 1951, No. 2, 13.
[2] *Planovoe Khoziaistvo*, 1952, No. 4, 21; U.N. Economic Commission for Europe, *Economic Survey of Europe since the War* (Geneva, 1953), 49.

a series of Ministerial Decrees were issued to improve the previously low incentives to agricultural production (by tax revisions and price-adjustments), to increase the supply of foodstuffs to the towns and to raise the targets for the output of consumer goods in the two concluding years of the Fifth Plan. This was the first occasion on which revision of a Plan in the middle of a quinquennium had been in favour of consumer goods industries (in the pre-war period such a revision had invariably been at the expense of this sector of industry and in favour of heavy industry under the pressure of rearmament). In the second half of 1953 the output of consumers' goods increased by 14 per cent. over the same period of the previous year, or by more than the increase of industrial output in general.[1] There was talk of giving priority to light industries in the supply of personnel, of materials, of power and of equipment and repairs; and in the course of the year about 300 new industrial enterprises producing consumer goods were brought into operation and some 6,000 new shops were opened; while a decree of October 23 outlined a programme for building 40,000 new shops and 11,000 new restaurants in the course of the next three years. At the same time there was some adjustment in the import-programme to provide more room for the import of consumer goods.

It was to transpire, however, that the position in agriculture during the early years of the '50's had in crucial respects actually deteriorated. The head of cattle declined between 1950 and 1953 (the fall being among those privately owned, which was not compensated by the incresed number in the ownership of State and collective farms), and the number of cows remained below, not only the 1928 level, but also the (lower) 1940–41 level. Supplies of meat and milk to the towns remained practically stationary over the years 1950, 1951 and 1952. Sheep and goats (which are mainly owned by State or collective farms) increased by only 15 per cent. over the three years and even pigs by only 21 per cent. over pre-war. A leading reason was shortage of fodder. Grain output in these years showed no improvement, being on the average of 1951–53 only 3 to 4 per cent. above 1950, which as we have seen was very little above the pre-war level.[2] Sugar-beet and raw cotton did only a little better, and the output of flax declined drastically. This was the reason for renewed attention to agriculture, to overcome this grave 'agri-

---

[1] Indeed from 1951 to 1954 the growth-rates of capital-goods and consumer-goods industries were identical. 1937 was the only year previously when consumer goods had incresed faster than capital goods.

[2] The 1950 figure of 81·2 million tons was *below* that of 1940 (according to the subsequently revised figures), but slightly *above* the average of 1938–40 (*cf. Narodnoe Khoziaistvo v 1963 g.*, 273).

cultural lag'; which took the form, not only of increased investments in agriculture in the next two years and improved procurement-prices to farmers for grain, vegetables and livestock, but a
campaign to encourage the extension of maize cultivation and the
'virgin lands campaign' to bring under the plough over the next
three years some 70 million acres (30 million hectares) of steppe-
land in Siberia and Kazakhstan, thereby increasing the sown area
of the country by about a sixth (of which by the end of 1954 rather
more than half had already been ploughed-up).

In the second half of the decade these measures were to bear fruit
in a surprisingly steep rise of grain production—by as much as 50 per
cent. above the level of the early '50's. Already by 1955 grain production had exceeded the 100 million ton level, compared with 81
million for 1950 (and a similar figure for the average of 1949–53); and
by 1960 it was to rise further to 125 million (124·7 being the average for
1959–63). Some technical crops such as sugar-beet and flax showed
an even more remarkable advance: sugar-beet more than doubling
and flax increasing by some 70 per cent. or more over the decade.
Already by 1955 the number of cows had recovered to above the
pre-war level and of all cattle to above even the 1928 level; while the
number of pigs had doubled over the quinquennium and the number
of sheep and goats had grown by more than 40 per cent. The data on
livestock at various dates are summarised in the following table:[1]

LIVESTOCK NUMBERS

(million head, on present territory)

	1 Jan. 1929	1 Jan. 1941	1 Jan. 1946	1 Jan. 1951	1 Jan. 1954	1 Oct. 1955	1 Jan. 1960	1 Jan. 1964
Cattle . .	66·8	54·5	47·6	57·1	55·8	67·1	74·2	85·4
of which Cows .	33·2	27·8	22·9	24·3	25·2	29·2	33·9	38·3
Pigs . .	27·4	27·5	10·6	24·4	33·3	52·1	53·4	40·9
Sheep and Goats .	114·6	91·6	70·0	99·0	115·5	142·6	144·0	139·5
Horses .	36·1	21	10·7	13·8	15·3	14·2	11·0	8·5

[1] Report of N. S. Khrushchov to the 20th Party Congress, Feb. 14, 1956;
Results of the Fulfilment of the Fifth Five-Year Plan; U.N. Economic Commission
for Europe, *Economic Survey of Europe in 1953* (Geneva, 1954), 52: *Narodnoe
Khoziaistvo S.S.S.R. v 1958 godu*, 445–6; *Narodnoe Khoziaistvo S.S.S.R. v 1963
g.*, 311.

As regards industrial output, the first half of the decade witnessed a rather greater increase both in total output and in consumer goods than had been set in the plan-targets. The total increase from 1950 to 1955 was 85 per cent. as against a planned increase of 72; while the increase in the consumer goods sector was 76 per cent. compared with a planned increase of 65. The capital goods industries still held the lead (although not a large one) with a 91 per cent. increase, compared with a plan-target of 80. The result was to raise the level of industrial output to roughly double the pre-war level, and even industrial consumer goods to double pre-war. The rise of national income over 1940 was officially stated as being 80 per cent., and "the turnover in State and Cooperative retail trade during the same period more than doubled".[1] House-building in towns (*including* building on private account with the aid of State credits) amounted to about 154 million square metres of floor-space, or some 50 per cent. more than in the previous quinquennium; while rural house-building, at 2·3 million houses, was smaller by about half a million houses than it had been during the period of the Fourth Plan.[2]

The Sixth Plan, covering the years from 1956 to 1960, which was presented to the historic 20th Congress of the Party in February 1956, did not differ very much from its predecessor. The overall growth of industrial output was set at 65 per cent., with a 70 per cent. increase as the target for means of production and a 60 per cent. increase for consumer goods (as against percentages of 72, 80 and 65 respectively in the plan for the previous quinquennium). The national income as a whole was to rise by 60 per cent., with a 30 per cent. rise "in the real wages of factory, office and other workers over the five-year period", and a 40 per cent. increase in "the incomes of collective farmers in cash and in kind". The "volume of State capital investments in the national economy" was to show a 67 per cent. advance on that of the Fifth Plan. The target increase in labour productivity in industry was again set at 50 per cent. (a little higher than the 44 per cent. achieved in the previous quinquennium). Total employment of wage- and salary-earners in the economy at large was to grow by no more than 13–14 per cent., and in industry alone by only 10 per cent.[3] The Draft Directives on the Plan (as published in the Moscow press on January 15th for submission to the Congress) stated

---

[1] Report on the Results of the Fulfilment of the Fifth Five Year Plan, Gosplan.

[2] *Planovoe Khoziaistvo*, 1956, No. 2, 7.

[3] The increase in total employment was in fact to be some 7 million more than this, or about double the planned increase. Between 1950 and 1955 the total labour force in the economy had grown from 39 to 48·4 million and in industry alone from 14 to 17·4 million, an increase of 23 to 24 per cent. in each case (*Narodnoe Khoziaistvo S.S.S.R.*, Moscow 1956).

that "the present level of social production enables the Soviet state to develop rapidly not only the production of the means of production, which has been and remains the unshakeable foundation of the national economy as a whole, but also the production of consumer goods, to increase considerably social wealth, and thence progress towards the building of a communist society in our country". Malenkov in his speech at the Congress claimed that in output of electricity the Soviet Union already "firmly holds second place in the world", and Bulganin in presenting the Plan claimed that she would produce by 1960 "more steel, power, cement and fuel than is now produced by Britain, France and Western Germany combined". State-financed housing (both urban and rural) was to amount over the five years to some 205 million square metres, the equivalent of about 5 million small flat-dwellings of 2 rooms *plus* kitchen and bathroom.[1]

For agriculture the unrealistically high target of 180 million tons of grain was set for 1960 (largely on the basis of the anticipated results of the 'virgin lands campaign').[2] Very little, however, was to be heard of this figure thereafter; and in his famous speech of 15 December 1958 Khrushchov was to denounce the previous inflation of the grain-production figures (in terms of so-called 'biological yield'); whereafter the figures for all previous years as well as current were to be expressed in terms of 'barn yield' (*ambarnii urozhai*).[3]

In general the results of the second half of the decade attained the plan-targets, although the increase of consumer goods production fell somewhat behind (just over 50 per cent. instead of the planned 60 per cent.); and the general rate of growth was somewhat smaller in the second half of the decade than it had been in the first half.[4] The output at various dates of particular products, expressed in physical

[1] Directives of the 20th Party Congress on the Sixth Plan, § VIII, para. 8. It was claimed that this figure was "nearly double the figure for the Fifth Five Year Plan".
[2] On the basis of the *old* figures, this would seem to have represented an increase of about 40 per cent.
[3] He blamed primarily Malenkov for this. But the statistical inflation had evidently originated in the time of Stalin, probably as early as 1938 at least. Malenkov was accused in particular of representing the 1952 grain harvest as being 8,000 million poods, or nearly 130 million tons, when the true figure was 6,000 million poods, or about 97 million tons.
[4] The rate of growth of *net material product* is given in *Some Factors in Economic Growth in Europe during the 1950's* (U.N., E.C.E., Geneva 1964, Tables 3 and 5, Chapt. II, 9 and 15) for 1950 to 1959 as being 10·5 per cent. annually: 11·3 per cent. for the first half of the decade and 9·5 per cent. for the second half (up to 1959 only). *Planovoe Khoziaistvo* in 1961 (No. 9, p. 9) gave 10·6 per cent. as the mean annual growth-rate of industrial production over the past sixteen years, and claimed that Soviet industrial production in 1960 was 60 per cent. of American.

units, is given in the Table on page 326. Expressed in terms of annual (compound) growth-rates, the overall industrial performance during this quinquennium can be expressed as follows:

Annual Percentage Increase of:	1956	1957	1958	1959	1960
Gross Industrial Output	11	10	10	11·4	9·5
of which:					
{ Group A (means of production)	11·4	11	11	12	11
{ Group B (consumer's goods)	9·4	8	7	10·3	7
Labour Productivity	7	7	6	7	5
National Income	12	6	9	8	8

In one sense, however, this Sixth Plan was never completed, in that it was overlaid and superseded at the end of 1958 by a new *Seven*-Year Plan, designed to cover the period of 1959 to 1965. This was duly adopted by the 21st Party Congress on February 5th, 1959. The main reason for the supersession of the old plan by the new before the period of the former was terminated was to make provision for special emphasis on development of the chemical industry, with a view to the substitution of plastics for traditional materials and of synthetic fibres for natural fibres in the clothing industry as well as to increase the supply of fertilisers for agriculture. Among other structural changes envisaged were a more rapid replacement of coal by oil and gas in the fuel balance; a concentration in the engineering industry upon the development of automation-instruments; and renewed emphasis upon developing the resources of the eastern regions, especially East Siberia and Kazakhstan.

The rate of progress envisaged in the new Seven-Year Plan was slightly less ambitious than previously: an overall increase of industrial output of 80 per cent. (or 8·6 per cent. annually), with 85–8 per cent. for producers' goods and 62–5 per cent. for consumers' goods (respectively 9·3 and 7·3 per cent. annually). The national income was to rise by 62–5 per cent.; the total number of persons employed by 21 per cent., and the real incomes of wage- and salary-earners and of collective farmers alike by 40 per cent. Productivity of labour in industry was scheduled to increase by 45 to 50 per cent. (a somewhat lower annual rate than previously).[1] The output of the chemical industry was to be increased three times,[2] as was the supply of mineral fertilisers. In addition, special attention was to be paid, as regards investment, to agriculture and to housing (and in connection with this, building materials industries). In what was in effect a housing 'drive', provision was made ("through State capital investment together with the people's own funds, aided by State credits") for the building of "a total of 650 to 660 million square metres of housing, or nearly 15 million flats, which is 130 per cent. more than the number completed in the previous seven-year period"; in addition "7 million dwellings will be put up in rural areas by the collective farmers and village technicians themselves". If these targets are achieved, it has been estimated that as a result "nearly one household in two will have obtained new accommodation by 1965".[3]

Coupled with these economic objectives there were also some social ones. Already at the 20th Congress in 1956 Bulganin, in the course of introducing the Sixth Plan, had announced the intention of introducing during the quinquennium the following measures: (a) a reduction in working hours from eight to seven per day (with six hours in mining and dangerous occupations and for young persons between 16 and 18 years of age[4]), "or in some branches to a five-day week with an eight-hour working day, and two days off"; (b) a reduction of Saturday working (and on the eve of holidays) by two hours as from 1956; (c) a raising of the minimum wages of the lowest income categories, and a removal of some existing disparities in wages; (d) radical improvement of the pensions system, raising in particular the minimum level of old age and disablement pensions (the latter being implemented forthwith by a new pensions law, raising this minimum to 300 roubles monthly, which was adopted by the Supreme Soviet

[1] A prospective shortening of working hours was, no doubt, partly responsible for this as well as for the larger increase in employment that was allowed for. Over the '50's the annual rise of labour productivity had been more than 8 per cent. in productive sectors (*Some Factors in Economic Growth in Europe during the 1950's*, U.N., E.C.E., Geneva 1964, Table 5, Chap. II, 15), but it was somewhat lower in the second half of the decade. In industry labour productivity doubled over the decade (*Narodnoe Khoziaistvo S.S.S.R. v 1963 g.*, 62). The increase in the number of industrial workers over the decade had been 64 per cent. – substantially more than had been planned.

[2] It was stipulated that "about half of all the allocations for the development of the chemical industry will go to construct enterprises for manufacturing plastics, artificial and synthetic fibres, synthetic rubber and alcohol".

[3] *Economic Survey of Europe in 1959*, U.N., E.C.E., Geneva 1960, Chapt. IV, p. 1. According to *The Times* of 5 August 1963, the U.S.S.R. came highest in Europe (with a figure of 11·8) in the average annual number of new dwellings per 1,000 inhabitants in 1961–2.

[4] A six-hour day for young persons was introduced in 1956 (by a decree of May 26th of the Presidium of the Supreme Soviet) to operate from July 1st.

in July).   About the same time (in April of the year) came a final repeal of the 1940 Labour Decrees restricting labour movement (further described below on pages 491–2).

Among the targets for the Seven-Year Plan, provision was made, firstly for a completion in 1960 of "the transfer of factory and office workers to a 7-hour working day" and of underground workers in mining to a 6-hour day;[1] secondly for raising the minimum wage in two stages, between 1959 and 1962 to 400–450 roubles a month "in all branches of the national economy", and between 1963 and 1965 to 500–600 roubles;[2] thirdly, for raising the minimum old age and disablement pensions to 400 roubles by 1963 (with 340 roubles in rural areas) and by 1966 to between 450 and 500 roubles.[2]   In July 1964 the Supreme Soviet decided to extend the State system of old age pensions to collective farmers (at lower rates than for wage-earners) as from January 1965, also maternity benefits for women collective farmers and grants for orphans.   (Previously collective farmers could rely only on pension-schemes provided by the *Kolkhoz* itself.)

Since 1960 the actual growth-rates have been lower than in the previous decade, and in 1963 and 1964 there has been some sign of a further slackening—whether temporary or more lasting it is too early at the time of writing to see.   Up to 1963, at any rate, it could be claimed that the industrial results of the first five years of the seven slightly exceeded the planned targets; with production of consumers' goods again falling somewhat below it (an average annual increase of 6·4 per cent. instead of the planned 7·3) and that of producers' goods (Group A) somewhat exceeding it (with just over 10 per cent. annually compared with a planned 9·3).   But the 1964 result fell definitely below the planned trend (although the first half of 1965 showed a recovery to 9·3 per cent); and agriculture over the period, particularly in view of the bad crop of 1963, failed to fulfil expectations.   The following gives a summary picture of the announced results since 1960:

[1] As a further outlook, 1964 was mentioned as the start of "a gradual transfer to a 35-hour week" (with 30 for underground workers and those engaged on work "involving harmful labour conditions"), and the intention was indicated of eventually introducing a "five-day working week".

In a speech of 5 May 1960 to the Supreme Soviet Khrushchov claimed that since April 1st "about 16 million have been working a shorter seven- and six-hour working day", and that "the changeover of all factory and office workers to the seven- and six-hour day will be completed this year".

[2] These figures refer, of course, to *old* roubles prior to the rouble-revaluation of 1961, when all rouble-prices and rouble-payments were revalued at the equivalent of 1 new rouble = 10 old roubles, with equivalent changes in the gold and foreign-exchange values of the rouble.

Annual Percentage Increase of:	1961	1962	1963	1964	1965
Gross Industrial Output	9·2	9·7	8·5	7·1	·8·6
of which: Group A (means of production)	10	10	10	7·8	8·7
Group B (consumers' goods)	6·6	7	5	6·5	8·5
Labour Productivity	3·6	6·2	4·9	4	5
National Income	7	6	4	7^1	6

It may serve to place such growth-rates in perspective (as well as the increases for particular products which follow) if we put them in a comparative setting. Since the end of the period of post-war reconstruction up to the last year or two (at the time of writing) annual compound growth-rates, as we have seen, have averaged about 10 per cent. This is appreciably less than in the pre-war period. But it is higher than that attained by capitalist economies in the past during exceptional boom periods (e.g. Japan between 1907 and 1913, U.S.A. between 1885 and 1889 and the United Kingdom in the immediate post-war years), it is more than double the average rate of growth of total output in U.S.A. between 1871 and 1913 and more than three times the U.S.A. rate of growth of total output in the 1950's.

It was on the assumption of a continuance of such growth-rates (or even of something between this and the somewhat lower level envisaged in the Seven-Year Plan) that the longer-term (twenty-year) targets were based which were embodied in the new Party Programme (envisaging "the transition to Communism") presented to the 22nd Party Congress of October 1961. These long-term projections anticipated a rise in industrial output of 150 per cent. over the decade of the '60's (an annual compound rate of just over 9 per cent), and a surpassing of the U.S. level both of total output and of output *per capita* by 1970 (on the assumption that the latter continued to grow in the '60's at the same rate as it had done in the '50's).

---

[1] This is the figure given in the Report of the Central Statistical Department on the Results of the State Plan for 1964. An earlier, and presumably provisional, report in *Planovoe Khoziaistvo* (1965, No. 1, 1–2) had given a higher figure (of 7·8) for the growth of industrial production and a lower figure (only 5) for growth of national income. The above figures for Group A and Group B in 1964 are taken from the *Planovoe Khoziaistvo* article.

COMPARATIVE OUTPUTS of MAIN PRODUCTS at VARIOUS DATES

	Unit	1928	1940	1950	1960	1965
Coal	million tons	35·5	165·9	261·1	513·2	578
Oil	million tons	11·6	31·1	37·9	147·9	243
Electricity	milliard kWh	5·0	48·3	91·2	292·3	507
Gas	milliard cub. metres	·3	3·4	6·2	47·2	129
Pig Iron	million tons	3·3	14·9	19·2	46·8	66·2
Steel	million tons	4·3	18·3	27·3	65·3	91
Rolled Steel	million tons	3·4	13·1	20·9	51·0	70·9
Iron Ore	million tons	6·1	29·9	39·7	105·9	153
Cement	million tons	1·5	5·7	10·2	45·5	72·4
Bricks	milliard units	2·9	7·5	10·2	35·5	34
Mineral Fertilisers	million tons (in conventional units)	·1	3·2	5·5	13·9	31·3
Caustic Soda	thousand tons	—	190	325	765	1303
Artificial Fibres	thousand tons	·2	11·1	24·2	211·2	407
Synthetic Resin and Plastics	thousand tons	—	14·9	74·5	331·7	821
Metal-cutting Machine Tools	thousand units	2·0	58·4	70·6	155·9	185
Steam Locomotives	units	479	914	985	—	—
Main-line Diesel Locomotives	in sections	—	5	125	1303	1485
Main-line Electric Locomotives . .	in sections	—	9	102	396	641
Goods Wagons . .	thousand units	7·9	30·9	50·8	36·4	37·2[4]
Passenger Wagons .	units	387	1051	912	1656	1986[4]
Motor Vehicles .	thousands	·8	145	363	523	616
Motor Cycles and Scooters . .	thousands	—	6·8	123	552	721
Bicycles and Mopeds .	thousands	10·8	255	649	2950[5]	3900
Tractors . . .	thousands (natural units)	1·3	31·6	116	238	355
Grain-harvesting Combines . .	thousands		12·8	46·3	59·0	85·8
Paper . . .	million tons	·3	·8	1·2	2·4	3·4
Cotton Fabrics . {	million linear metres	2678	3954	3899	6387	—
{	million square metres	—	2704	2745	4838	5504
Woollen Fabrics {	million linear metres	86·8	119·7	155·2	341·8	—
{	million square metres	—	152·1	193·2	438·5	466
Linen Fabrics . {	million linear metres	174·4	285·5	282·2	559·2	—
{	million square metres	—	268·3	257·4	516·1	547
Silk Fabrics . {	million linear metres	9·6	77·3	129·7	809·7	—
{	million square metres	—	64·2	105·9	675·2	796
Knitted Wear .	million garments	8·3	18·3	197·5	583·9	907
Leather footwear .	million pairs	58	211	203	419	486
Rubber footwear .	million pairs	36	70	111	n.a.	n.a.
Clocks and Watches .	million units	·9	2·8	7·6	26·0	30·6
Radio and Television Sets . . .	million units	—	·16	1·07	5·88	8·9
Soap[1] . . .	million tons	·3	·7	·8	1·5	1·9
Granulated Sugar .	million tons	1·3	2·1	2·5	6·3	11·0
Butter[2] . . .	thousand tons	82	226	336	737	1070[3]
Vegetable Oil[3] . .	million tons	·45	·79	·82	1·58	2·7
Meat[3] . . .	million tons	·67	1·50	1·55	4·40	5·2
Fish . . .	million tons	·84	1·40	1·75	3·54	5·7
Confectionery .	million tons	·09	·79	·99	1·7	2·3
Tinned Foods . .	milliard tins	·1	1·1	1·5	4·8	7·0
Grain . . . {	million tons	73 (av. 1928–32)	95·5 (av. 1938–40)	81·2 (av. 1949–53)	125·5 (av. 1959–63)	(av. 1964–5)
{		73·6	77·9	80·9	124·7	135·8

[1] In terms of 40 per cent. content of fatty acids.
[2] Does not include production in individual (peasant) households.
[3] Does not include production in individual (peasant) households or collective farm production. (The larger total is nearly double that given above in the case of Meat.)
[4] For 1963.
[5] For 1961.   n.a. = not available.

SOURCES: *Narodnoe Khoziaistvo S.S.S.R. v. 1958 g.*, 158 seq; *Narodnoe Khoziaistvo S.S.S.R. v. 1962 g.*, 124–6; *Narodnoe Khoziaistvo S.S.S.R. v. 1963 g.*, 117–20, 273; Ts.S.U. Reports on Results of Fulfilment of State Plan, for the relevant years; U.N., E.C.E., *Economic Survey of Europe in 1955*, Table XXX; *Economic Survey of Europe in 1960*, Table XIII; *Economic Survey of Europe in 1964*, App. to Chap. I.

On similar assumptions, a six-fold output-increase for industry was envisaged by 1980, a five-fold increase for national income and an increase in real income *per capita* of the population by more than two-and-a-half times. Targets of somewhat smaller but comparable size were also set for agriculture; but these seem to be much less firmly based than those for industry.

In the course of making these projections, emphasis was again laid upon the importance of "ensuring a rapid increase in the output of consumer goods" and "an accelerated development of all branches of light and food industry" (while "the share of consumer goods in the output of heavy industry will also increase"). The enunciation of principle was unqualified: "The growing resources of industry must be used more and more to meet fully all the requirements of Soviet people and to build and equip enterprises and establishments catering for the household and cultural needs of the population. . . . Output of consumer goods must meet the growing consumer demand in full, and must conform to its changes."

III

The 20th Party Congress of 1956, in so many respects a watershed between periods, if not epochs, was to usher in a number of quite crucial changes within the field of economic and social policy. First, there were some important changes regarding agriculture. Secondly, there followed a sweeping decentralisation of industrial management on geographical lines in 1957. Thirdly, there were reforms with regard to payment and conditions of labour and social insurance.

We have mentioned the concessions made to agriculture during the first half of the decade in the shape of improved procurement-prices to farmers. This was followed by tax concessions and by simplified planning methods in agriculture (previously there had often been 200 or more targets for a collective farm in the annual plan), with a decentralisation to the provincial administration of responsibility for working out detailed plans for farms, and greater discretion to the farm management to decide questions about production on the basis of appropriate financial incentives: for example in 1955 the previous crop plans and schedules for livestock breeding were abolished. In 1958 came two significant changes in principle in the relation between collective farms and the State: the abolition of the compulsory delivery-quotas which had existed since the early '30's and the grant to collective farms for the first time of the right to own their own machinery (indeed, encouragement to them to do so). The abolition of compulsory deliveries[1] was proposed by Khrushchov in a report to the Central Committee of the Party on June 17th, 1958. In their place were to be uniform procurement-prices, differentiated according to zones, at which the State would buy all produce contracted for between State buying organs and the farms in any given year (these prices to be subject to some variation according to the state of the harvest in the year in question).[2] The change was duly confirmed by a decision of the Council of Ministers, together with new uniform zonal procurement-prices; and its general effect was undoubtedly to increase substantially the incomes of collective farmers.[3] The re-organisation of the State Machine and Tractor Stations (i.e. their translation from machine-hire into repair and service stations) and the transfer (by purchase spread over several years)[4] of their machinery to collective farms, had been proposed by Khrushchov five months earlier to the Central Committee of the Party at the end of February and officially adopted by the Supreme Soviet on March 31st.

In the course of outlining his proposal Khrushchov had stated that "as a result of amalgamation there are now some 78,000 collective farms in the country in place of more than a quarter of a million in 1949", and that "last year the collective farms each had on an average 1,954 hectares, or in other words over three times as much as before amalgamation"; thus it was claimed that the farms, being larger and having larger reserve funds, were now in a position to purchase and to own their own machinery.[5] That there was some reluctance on doctrinal grounds to accept the change, at least initially, is shown by the fact that, in the course of discussion of it, reference was made (e.g. by Ostrovitianov) to "the incorrect view of those who believe that concentration of the basic means of production in the collective

---

[1] Together with payments in kind for the services of the State Machine and Tractor Stations, through which "a goodly portion of agricultural products was received" by the State.

[2] Apart from the damaging effect of very low procurement prices before 1953 and frequently inequitable variations in these prices, the complaint was made that the previous system had discouraged regional specialisation. The example was given of the Baltic republics, "where the natural and economic conditions made it profitable for the national economy to develop animal husbandry and potatoes and industrial crops", and "collective farms have been under obligation to deliver grain to the State as compulsory deliveries and payments in kind". (Khrushchov's speech to C.C. of C.P.S.U., 17 June 1958).

[3] Cf. *Economic Survey of Europe in 1958*, U.N., E.C.E., Geneva 1959, Chap. I, p. 19.

[4] Sale by instalment and on credit was explicitly provided for; and it was stated: "there must be no haste in this matter".

[5] It was further stated, (a) that a half of the 660,000 lorries working in agriculture were already in the possession of collective farms, (b) that the cash income of collective farms had increased threefold between 1950 and 1956.

farms will weaken public ownership"; against which it was insisted that "it is theoretically incorrect and harmful in practice to set the two forms of socialist property one against the other",[1] and that "the advance towards communism will proceed" *both* through "the perfection of State property" *and* "the rapid development of cooperative and collective farm property".

The drastic changes of 1957 in the administration of industry involved the abolition of the 30-odd Ministries which had previously (through their industrial sub-departments, or *Glavki*) governed the main branches of industry from a single all-Union centre, and the subordination of industrial enterprises instead to more than a hundred (at that time) regional economic councils (*Sovnarkhoze*). To some extent the change may, perhaps, be regarded as having been as much political as economic in intention, since these Ministries had grown to be highly centralised bureaucratic structures, often remote from the individual production plants which they administered—having something of the nature of powerful industrial empires, with research institutes, supply and sales organs and constructional companies of their own. The new regional councils were both more numerous (each accordingly having less to administer) and also in closer touch, geographically at least, with the enterprises over which they held sway. As we shall see later, in Chapter Fourteen (where we shall return to this and subsequent changes), this did not necessarily bring greater independence to the individual enterprise and its management, whose powers were little greater, at any rate *de jure*, than they had been before. Theoretically at least they were still subject to the authority of *glavki* (if now at the regional level not the centre) as regards their operative plans, their supply-allocations and the disposal of their output. If only a first step in decentralisation, however, the reorganisation was manifestly welcome, since the previous system had accumulated some serious defects, as we shall see, and had come to constitute a hypertrophy of centralisation. The main defect of the new regional form of organisation was a tendency to local autarky, or at least of what was called 'parochialism' (*mestnichestvo*). A region tended to give priority to local needs over demands outside the region that might be more urgent from a national standpoint, and similarly to give preference to local sources of supply in meeting the demands of its own industries and consumers. It was no doubt as an offset to this that in May 1961 a partial regrouping of *Sovnarkhoze* took place into 17 larger economic regions each with a coordinating council to mediate between the several *Sovnarkhoze* within its area;

[1] *I.e.*, State property and collective farm property.

and the total number of regional *Sovnarkhoze* was reduced to about half their previous number (namely 47 in 1964).

In September 1965 it was announced (in Kosygin's report to the C.C. of the Party on 27 September) that these regional councils would be terminated, and a return be made to the control and direction of industry by 20 central Ministries, simultaneously with measures for giving increased autonomy to industrial enterprises (of which more will be said later). Of the new Ministries nine were to be all-Union Ministries, covering various branches of machine-building, the remaining eleven were to be so-called Union-Republican Ministries.

IV

In some ways of greater importance from a long-term point of view were several critical reconsiderations of points of theory and doctrine that followed the criticism of Stalin voiced at the famous 20th Congress—criticism that was renewed after the defeat of the 'conservative' group of Malenkov, Kaganovitch and Molotov in 1957 and was sharpened yet again at the 22nd Congress of 1961, when Sino-Soviet differences were on the point of deepening.[1] We have already mentioned the new formulation with regard to 'the two forms of socialist property' in connection with the transfer of agricultural machinery to collective farms. This itself was an implied criticism of a standpoint adopted by Stalin in his *Economic Problems of Socialism in the U.S.S.R.* of 1952, to the effect that at some stage (before "the transition to communism" was possible) collective farm property must be transformed into State property. No less important were two other formulations in the same booklet that were subjected to reconsideration, concerning the relative growth-rates of heavy and light industry and the rôle of market relations and of 'economic law' in a socialist economy.

In this booklet of 1952 Stalin had affirmed the traditional priority of heavy industry (Marx's Department I, producing means of production) as a continuing and essential principle of development ("in order to pave the way for a real, and not declaratory, transition

---

[1] Mikoyan in addressing the 22nd Congress on 20 October 1961 spoke of "the conservative dogmatic group", and said that disagreements with them "were not differences on limited organisational or specific political questions", but "concerned the definition of the entire policy of the party at the new stage in its historical development, its general line"; these disagreements dating back to before the 20th Congress when "they repudiated all that was new and opposed the propositions advanced later at the 20th Congress of the C.P.S.U." It has now become clear that the Chinese disagreements also go back to the 20th Congress.

to communism"). He spoke of "a continuous expansion of all social production, with a relatively higher rate of expansion of the production of means of production". At the same time he defined the "basic economic law of socialism" as being "to secure the maximum satisfaction of the constantly rising material and cultural requirements of the whole of society". In the course of 1953 and 1954 a number of economists advanced the thesis that past achievements in building heavy industry had laid the basis for a reversal of the traditional priority, and that in the period ahead expansion of consumer goods production should take the lead.[1] But at this time the official view continued to affirm the need for maintaining the traditional priority, on the ground that if the consumer goods industries were expanded at a faster rate over a period, their further progress would very soon be retarded by insufficient productive capacity in the capital goods industries to provide the means for both capital replacement and new investment in the former. As we have seen, the rates of growth of the two main sectors of industry (Groups A and B) were brought much closer together during the '50's than in the pre-war decade. Nonetheless Group A has continued to expand at a faster rate, both in plan-intention and in actual fulfilment—although how much significance (in the context of Marx's analytical distinction between two departments) is to be assigned to this remains doubtful, in view of the fact that some industries belonging to Group A have taken to producing durable consumer goods and in view of substantial shifts of investment towards both agriculture and housing. Although the official view has never repudiated the previous doctrine, some recent statements certainly seem to have qualified it almost out of existence; and even as early as 1956 Khrushchov in his report to the Congress of that year seemed to assign equal place to the promotion of both categories of output when he declared: "Now that we possess a powerful heavy industry developed in every respect, we are in a position to promote rapidly the production of both the means of production and consumer goods; the Party is doing, and will continue to do its utmost, to ensure that the requirements of the Soviet people will be satisfied more fully and better; it considers this its prime duty to the people."

Among the more outspoken of recent authoritative statements on the matter was one by the late Academician Arzumanian in *Pravda* of February 24th and 25th, 1964. In this he explicitly rejected a

[1] E.g. P. Mstislavsky in *Novy Mir*, 1953, No. 11; I. Vekua in *Voprosi Ekonomiki*, 1954, No. 9; and E. Kazimovsky cited in *Voprosi Ekonomiki*, 1955, No. 1, 20. For the contrary opinion cf. S. G. Strumilin in *Voprosi Ekonomiki*, No. 11, 22–39, and K. V. Ostrovitianov in *Pravda*, March 27, 1955.

denial made by Molotov that socialism could be described as "production for consumption"; and, with regard to "the dynamics of Department 1 and Department 2", he declared that "up to now the task of defining the correct proportions between them has been hampered by certain theoretical vestiges engendered by Stalin's erroneous dogmas", leading to "an inadequate development of the production of consumer goods" and to "priority growth of the output of means of production becoming an end in itself".   After indicating that since 1953 the increase of output of means of production had exceeded that of consumer goods "by only 20 per cent" (compared with "70 per cent in the period of the pre-war Five Year Plans"), he concluded that "at the present time life sets us the task of bringing the rates of growth of Departments 1 and 2 still closer together".[1] The concluding part of the article was concerned to show that in the U.S.A. as well as in the U.S.S.R. the capital-output ratio had tended in recent decades to *fall* as a result of technical progress; consequentially the nature of technical progress could not be adduced as a reason for a necessary and continuing "increase in the share of output of Department 1".   While making a formal bow to the principle of giving "preference to the output of means of production", the article concluded: "the proportions between Departments 1 and 2 may fluctuate" according to a number of factors, and "dogmatic arguments and a biassed unfounded approach are particularly harmful in establishing the proportions".   It stands to reason, as reflection will easily show, that to pursue an increase in the future growth-rate of consumption by enlarging the relative size of the capital goods industry can only be a policy for a limited period, and not indefinitely: a truth of which that original theorist Feldman was well aware.[2]

The rôle of commodity production (or market relations) was referred to also in Stalin's 1952 booklet. His contention was that commodity-production and hence the law of value, on the contrary to "withering away", still prevailed under socialism; but he attributed this (at least mainly) to the existence of the "two forms of socialist property", characterising respectively industry and agriculture, between which commodity (*i.e.* market-exchange) relations prevailed—this rather than the existence of a market for consumers'

---

[1] A. Kosygin in his speech on the 1965 plan to the Supreme Soviet in December 1964 also spoke of "an approximation of the rates of growth in consumer goods production to the rates of growth in production of means of production" as one of its main tasks.

[2] On Feldman see further below, page 360–1; and cf. an article by the present writer in a forthcoming volume of essays in honour of Paul Baran, edited by Bernard Haley.

goods as concomitant of a system of money wage-payments and of the use of money-wage-differentials as production-incentives. Intermittently the question had been debated since the 1920's; and to begin with it was commonly denied that the law of value operated under socialism. Since this applied essentially to conditions of commodity production and exchange, it would cease to serve as an economic regulator as soon as planning came to rule the production and distribution of goods. Later the view gained ground that in the transitional state in which Soviet economy then was the law of value continued to operate, but was in process of being "merged" into the principle of "planned guidance" as the "active principle" of socialism; and that while planning for the time-being utilised the law of value, "in so far as the planning principle is gaining strength, the law of value is transformed directly into the law of labour expenditure".[1]

Preoccupation with practical tasks of construction and development in the '30's tended to push the whole issue into the background and to assert the primacy of the "active planning principle". But during the war the issue was revived by an unsigned article in the journal *Pod Znamenem Marksizma* (No. 7-8, 1943), which denied that the law of value was "abrogated in the socialist system of national economy": "on the contrary, it functions under socialism, but it functions in a transformed manner." Soon after the war, Voznesensky, then chairman of Gosplan, in his *Voennaia Ekonomika S.S.S.R.* (Moscow, 1948) answered affirmatively the question as to whether planning had to reckon with economic laws, and stated (pp. 145-6) that "in socialist economy the law of value means the necessity of conducting a monetary, not merely a physical, registration and planning of the costs of production. . . : The State plan in socialist economy makes use of the law of value to achieve the requisite proportions in producing the social product and in distributiong social labour." This in itself was not very illuminating; and the Stalin booklet of 1952 did little to make abstract generalisation more concrete by indicating the specific planning or pricing principles that "use of the law of value" implied. He contented himself with the statement merely that "laws of planning under socialism are objective laws, which reflect the fact that the processes of economic life are law-governed and operate independently of our will", and with emphatic denial that planning can "abolish existing economic laws

---

[1] I. Lapidus and K. Ostrovitianov, *An Outline of Political Economy*, (English ed., London 1929), 471. A useful summary of and commentary upon the whole discussion is contained in R. L. Meek, *Studies in the Labour Theory of Value* (London 1956), 256 *et seq.*

and create new ones", or that such laws "have been 'transformed' on the basis of planned economy".

The economists' debate, however, which started in 1956, was quick to interpret the question in terms of price-policy: namely, that an end should be made to "arbitrary" price-fixing as an instrument of planning policy (this being denounced as "subjectivism" in planning). Instead, prices should be more closely related to value, in the sense that they should more closely reflect the 'normal' expenditure of social labour in the course of production: in particular, this should be done with regard to the relationship between the prices of capital goods (products of Group A industries) and the prices of consumers' goods (products of Group B industries). But once the issue had been formulated in this way, the advocates of price-reform immediately divided (for the most part) into two broad camps, according as they interpreted this to mean that relative prices should accord with 'values' (in the sense of Volume I of Marx's *Capital*) or with 'prices of production' as the 'transformed form of value' (in the sense of Marx's Volume III).[1]

In so far as discussion has still taken the old form in recent years, this has had the effect of extending the category of 'commodity production' so as to embrace the production of means of production as well as of consumers' goods, and of emphasising the importance of commodity-production and of market categories (and with this the use of economic instruments and incentives in production), and their continuation, even intensification, during the coming period. In contrast to Stalin's opinion that commodity-relations (depending as he thought upon the existence of collective farm property) were already "beginning to hamper the development of our productive forces since they create obstacles to the full extension of government planning", the new Programme of 1961 spoke of the need in this period "to make full use of commodity-money relations in keeping with their new meaning in the socialist period". It went on to refer to the importance of combining planning of "key targets" and "coordinating and dovetailing plans drawn up locally" with an "extension of operative independence and *initiative* of enterprises". Mikoyan in addressing the 22nd Congress (on October 20th, 1961) rejected the proposition[1] that "problems of distribution and exchange are solved by introducing a [directly State-organised] exchange of

---

[1] Some account of this discussion in its first stage was given by the present writer in *Science and Society*, Fall 1960, 289–311, reprinted in H. G. Shaffer, *The Soviet Economy: A Collection of Western and Soviet Views*, (New York 1963), 378 seq.

[1] Mentioned in the Stalin booklet of 1952.

products between town and country". He went on: "There are still individual comrades who propose the abolition of commodity-money relations at once. Letters to this effect have been addressed to the central committee of the C.P.S.U. in connection with the discussion of the draft programme. The experience of our construction shows that the commodity-money relations native to socialism will survive throughout the period of transition to communism."

Formulations of this latter type have created the setting in which concrete discussion has taken place in recent years of new decentralised economic forms, or 'models', of a socialist economy, such as are described towards the end of Chapter 14—innovations which ten years previously would have been denounced as a dangerous intrusion of "market autonomism" into the citadel of the "planning principle". The kernel of these new forms, which are in process of being actualised (if no more than experimentally at present), is the right of the enterprise to contract directly for its product and its supplies with other enterprises (or trading organisations), combined with the use of the net income of the enterprise[1] as a collective incentive to its personnel in the conduct of their productive operations. In one sense this may be regarded as a reversion, after the years of hyper-centralisation (when emphasis was upon quantitative growth and upon a fairly limited number of 'key objectives'), to the position occupied by the industrial enterprise in the early days of *Khozraschot* in the '20's. At the same time there is an important difference: those were the days of the 'mixed economy' of the NEP when planning was in its infancy, whereas to-day this (partial) enterprise-autonomy is set within the framework of a developed and matured planning system, operating with centrally-coordinated short-term and long-term plans: moreover, within the framework of a controlled price-structure, even if prices are likely to be given more flexibility than formerly, especially in the case of new products or special qualities.

It happens to be a Czech economist (Professor Ota Šik, himself the initiator of a comparable measure of economic reform for his own country) who has most clearly epitomised these new trends in terms of the traditional discussion. After referring to "progress made in the social sciences, including political economy, since the late 'fifties in all the socialist countries", and in particular "a deeper theoretical examination of economic relationships under socialism", he wrote as follows: "Until recently, the connection between planning

---

[1] Either treated as a ratio to its capital for incentive (i.e. bonus) purposes, or after deduction, *inter alia*, of a charge (or tax) proportioned to the total of basic and turn-over funds (capital) employed.

and the market was incorrectly understood and the concept of the market was applied to the socialist economy in a sort of shamefaced way. It was held, wrongly, that planned social coordination, planned management of production, was the absolute antipode of orientation on the market, of utilising market levers. Planning was assumed to be an attribute of socialism alone and production for the market a feature solely of capitalism. These tenacious theoretical premises brought much harm; because of them a system of planning and management was adhered to which meant that production could not be adequately geared to its proper aim . . . and consumers could not exert any direct influence on the producers. . . . In the light of this the difference between capitalist and socialist economy was not accurately defined. For the difference does not consist in production under capitalism being necessarily geared to the market whereas under socialism the market plays no rôle whatever. Socialist planned production should consistently seek to satisfy market demand." He concludes by saying: "Means of production should also be regarded as commodities, bought and sold by socialist enterprises, with only minor quantities of goods in short supply being directly distributed in exceptional cases to meet priority needs. The market they enter is a specific type of market—a market of socialist enterprises."[1]

Time will show whether this is an extreme view or whether it sounds the keynote of the future.

[1] *World Marxist Review* (Eng. ed. of "Problems of Peace and Socialism"), London, March 1965 (Vol. 8, No. 3), 17; c.f. also W. Brus, *Ogólne Problemy Funkcjonowania Gospodarki Socjalistycznej*, Warszawa 1961.

PART THREE

CHAPTER FOURTEEN

THE PLANNING SYSTEM

I

The system of economic planning in the U.S.S.R. did not spring full-grown from the head of Lenin, as some people seem to have assumed. It had a history of growth and change over two decades, at some stages of tortuous growth ; and certain historical pre-requisites were needed before economic planning could be anything more than partial and tentative—a fitful hand upon the reins rather than a curbing and steering of the team. In the early years of the revolution planning was more in evidence in speeches and on paper than it was in actuality. It was a propaganda phrase rather than an economic force. For some years even after the creation of central planning machinery, neither the objective situation con-fronting it nor its own subjective fitness for the task enabled it successfully to bring to birth a realistic unitary plan for the integra-tion of the economy as a whole. Important developments both in the economy at large and in the methods and the machinery of planning had to occur before these limitations could be overcome. It was, indeed, the achievements of the First Five Year Plan that prepared the ground over which global planning of production could operate successfully and at the same time afforded the exact-ing school of experience in which alone the capacity for effective planning could be developed.

During the early months of the Soviet régime we have seen that indirect control over economic life, by methods familiar enough in the war economies of various countries in recent years, reinforced by a partial nationalisation of key enterprises, was all that appeared on the economic order of the day. During the period of War Communism nationalisation and direct State operation of production became much more sweeping. But the measures taken for the direction of industry and the distribution of supplies were of a diffuse and patchwork character, among which " shock tactics " for clearing up this or that breakdown on the economic front occupied a prominent place. Such tactics, inspired by the imme-

337

diate urgencies of a critical military and economic situation, could have little regard for more long-term considerations or for their effect on other sectors of economic life which at the moment lacked top priority. There was frequent talk at the time of the need for introducing some unified economic plan which could co-ordinate sectional efforts with a vision having a wider perspective both in space and time. For instance, the Party programme of March, 1919, postulated as an urgent task " the greatest possible concentration of the whole economic activity of the country in a unified plan worked out for the whole State " ; and in the latter days of the civil war the Ninth Party Congress declared that " the fundamental condition for the renewal of economic progress in the country is an unswerving execution of a unified economic plan designed for the coming historical epoch ". The Supreme Economic Council (*Vesenkha*) had, in fact, been given the task of " working out a unified production plan for the whole of Russia and of the Soviet Republics friendly to Russia " ; and the Second Congress of Economic Councils in December, 1918, passed a resolution calling for the preparation of " a single economic plan " for the coming year. But this body had little possibility at the time of doing more than co-ordinate in a crude and improvised fashion the work of the main branches of industry ; and in view of the large number of quite small enterprises that had been hurriedly swept into the net of nationalisation, such co-ordination (as we saw in Chapter Five) even within industry itself was often more conspicuous by its absence than its presence. Capacity to co-ordinate industry with other branches of economic life was lacking ; and the departments concerned respectively with industry, with transport and with the collection and distribution of supplies were to a large extent separate economic sovereignties. Not until the Council of Defence (which became the Council of Labour and Defence (STO)), to which the Eighth Soviet Congress was to give supreme co-ordinating authority in the economic sphere, could be relieved of exclusive concentration on military requirements, did the possibility exist of subordinating these sovereignties to a larger policy. As Dr. Friedrich Pollock has said of the civil war period, " there were, it is true, many plans, but there was no Plan ".[1]

Planning machinery, as a specialised and permanent arm of the State, had its beginnings in the foundation of the famous GOELRO, or State Commission for Electrification, mainly on the

---

[1] Cf. F. Pollock, *op. cit.*, 233–5. Kritsman, the historian of war communism, makes a similar remark. (*Geroicheski Period*, 115.)

initiative of Lenin, in March, 1920, before the end of the civil war.
Its immediate task was the preparation of an Electrification Plan
for the R.S.F.S.R., for presentation to the forthcoming Eighth
Soviet Congress. The precedence given to electrification at this
time conformed to Lenin's principle that in an undeveloped country
the transformation of its power base was essential as a prior condition of its modernisation and of the building of Socialism : a
principle which was summed up in his well-known aphorism that
" Soviets *plus* Electrification equals Communism ". Its staff consisted of engineers, and its President was himself an engineer,
Krzhizhanovsky, a colleague of Lenin since the days of the Emancipation of Labour groups in Petersburg in the '90's. Its work resulted
in the Plan for a system of 30 central power stations of $1\frac{1}{2}$ million
kilowatt capacity in the aggregate, some based on water power, some
coal or oil burning : a plan which was intended to guide the power-
development of the country over the next 10 to 15 years and was
in actuality to be accomplished within a decade.[1] The Eighth
Soviet Congress in December, after the conclusion of the war with
Poland, ratified this Electrification Plan, while at the same time
instructing STO to undertake the co-ordination and direction of
the economy as a whole. Of this GOELRO plan Krzhizhanovsky,
its chief architect, has spoken as follows : " Our country was still
in the midst of the calamity of war ; we were still continuing to roll
into the abyss of deepest economic disorder. And then, according
to directives of the Party, there was created the first perspective
economic plan. We proceeded to collect a handful of people,
scientific and technical workers, and under the immediate guidance
of Vladimir Ilyitch [Lenin], we tried to pick our way among the
economic chaos surrounding us, tried to harness to the conquest
of science and technique those active elements among the workers
and peasants whose creative power we perceived and recognised
in the midst of ruin and war. In this plan we daringly sketched an
impression of our future, a design of that building which we can
and must convert into reality. Very soon we were assailed with
banter : people said that it was not a plan of electrification but of
' electric-fiction ' ; they said it was poetry, an imaginative creation,
far from reality."[2]

Two months later, in February, 1921, the GOELRO was
merged in a larger body, the even more famous *Gosplan*, or State

---

[1] *Electric Power Development in U.S.S.R.* (ed. B. I. Weitz), 10-12.
[2] G. Krzhizhanovsky's report to Fifth Congress of Soviets of the U.S.S.R., *Plan.
Khoz.*, 1929, No. 5, 9. Ten years was set as the *minimum* period for the fulfilment
of this plan. Lenin called it " the second programme of the Party ".

Planning Commission. This new commission was not endowed with executive powers ; but like its parent and predecessor was an advisory body attached to STO. Its task was to draft plans and to pass judgment on departmental plans submitted to it. But STO and not Gosplan had the power to endow any of these plans with operative force. The decree of February 22nd, 1921 (signed by Lenin), under which Gosplan was founded, defined the function of the new body as being " to work out a unified economic plan for the whole economy on the basis of the Electrification Plan approved by the Eighth Soviet Congress " and " to exercise a general supervision over the operation of this Plan ". As an immediate task it was to start an examination of the various departmental plans for the coming year. Krzhizhanovsky who had been President of GOELRO became its President. Its total personnel at first numbered only 40, chiefly economists and engineers. But by 1923, after further reorganisation, its staff had been enlarged to 300. In 1925 for the first time branches of Gosplan were set up in the various republics, regions and provinces, linked with and subordinated to the parent body. By the following year the Gosplan of the Russian Republic alone (as distinct from that of the Union government) had a personnel of more than 900, and had a dozen regional commissions and forty-three commissions for smaller districts subordinate to it, as well as a legion of planning bureaux or agencies in individual enterprises and industrial plants.[1]

But the activities of Gosplan in the early years fell below current expectations and cannot be regarded as highly successful, if we judge them according to the terms of reference of the new body. Its work had been divided into six sections covering the main branches of economic life, and ten sub-commissions had been formed, each of them attached to (and subordinated to) one of the Commissariats (or Ministries) concerned with economic functions. But there proved to be little synthesis or co-ordination of the work of these various sections, and the sub-commissions attached to the Commis-

---

[1] Cf. F. Pollock, *op. cit.*, 245–7, 263 ; C. Bettelheim, *La Planification Soviétique*, 11 ; A. Zelenovsky on " Twenty-five Years of Gosplan " and I. Gladkov on " Lenin and the Organisation of Gosplan " in *Plan. Khoz.*, 1946, No. 1, 25 seq., 37 seq. Even after the setting up of these planning bodies in the republics and regions, for some time complaints continued to be heard that the republican Gosplans " lacked sufficient knowledge and data about local concrete conditions and the possibilities of individual enterprises ". (Cf. A. Anikst on " Ten Years of the Gosplan of R.S.F.S.R." in *Plan. Khoz.*, 1935, No. 3, 19.) Even as late as 1937 complaints were heard in a meeting of active members of the Gosplan of the Russian republic that this body " had no close links with its periphery" (*Plan*, 1937, No. 8, 30).

sariats tended to take a purely departmental view. This division into sections according to what was called the " operational " principle was later condemned, and reorganisation (which at first was apparently very incomplete) was undertaken so as to divide the work according to function. Krzhizhanovsky wrote at the time of the need to eliminate " every tendency to separatism " ; and it seems clear that a struggle against departmental separatism was the essence of the problems of these early years and the main reason for the reorganisation which took place in its third year. A difficult process of curbing centrifugal forces was to characterise the next few years and was essential before planning could have any chance of success. The idea of a unified Plan for 1921 was soon abandoned ; and instead the attention of Gosplan was concentrated on a series of partial plans, dealing with those sectors of the economy that had suffered most from the disorganisation of the war years or most urgently demanded attention in view of immediate needs : for example, partial plans for fuel (in particular for the reconstruction of the Donbas), for transport, for food, for metal, and for foreign trade. These were comparable, perhaps, to the reports of Royal Commissions or Departmental Committees in this country, rather than to the concrete plans of operation which developed later. They criticised, for example, the Chief Administration for Fuel Production for having no real knowledge about existing stocks of fuel, about the consumers of fuel and the conditions of production in the localities, and hence indulging in purely paper planning of fuel allocation. They criticised the crop and consumption estimates of the Commissariat of Supply as containing serious errors. They criticised the transport department for constructing its transport programme " without any exact reference to stocks of fuel on the one hand or the utilisation of rolling stock on the other ", and for ordering abroad three or four times as many petrol containers as it could transport. In September, 1921, Gosplan was responsible for a report on the restoration of agriculture in the famine area.[1] It also undertook a larger and more comprehensive report on the economic regionalisation of the country (November, 1921). This method of approach to its work, from particular studies to the more general, seems to have been largely on the advice of Lenin, who in an early instruction to the new body (dated May 16, 1921) stated that he could see no trace of any unifying principle in their plan-making, and that their method seemed to

[1] This was published in an English translation (by Eden and Cedar Paul) for the Information Department of the Russian Trade Delegation in London.

be one of perfecting everything simultaneously without establishing the order of dependence of various factors on one another, and thereby constructing a priority list of reconstruction tasks. He urged the need for a more rigorous and methodical procedure, based on the selection of " leading links " in the chain of economic causation and the use of " minimum conditions " and of several variants ; and he suggested that the first task should be to examine the food supply as a basic factor, and from this foundation to proceed to draft a provisional general plan for the economy over the next two years. In view of the large element of uncertainty attaching to this basic factor, any plan that was built upon it should be prepared in three variants according as the supplies proved to be equal to, below or above the current estimate.[1] Connected with this, another elementary task was still to be accomplished : namely to work out a comprehensive system of priorities to be uniformly applied in the allocation of all types of supplies and productive resources, and a system of co-ordinating links between the allocation of one type of supply and the allocation of another type where the needs for the two were closely related (i.e. constituted a " joint demand "). One observer wrote at the time that " it often happened in Germany, and it now often happens in Russia, that a factory has to remain temporarily idle because some among the ten authorities who allocate the items necessary to its production have failed to produce them ".[2]

In these early years the attempts of Gosplan at co-ordination seem to have reached little further than a rather peremptory dovetailing of sectional programmes, chiefly by way of arbitrating between rival departmental claims (not unlike the activities of the Production Executive in British war economy in the early years of the Second World War). The tendency seems to have been to start from the estimates submitted by various industries and departments as to what they could produce and what they required, and then to aggregate these several plans into a general one after a series of incidental adjustments effected by interdepartmental negotiation and rough-and-ready compromises.[3] This was, of course, better than nothing, but it was hardly as yet planning in the full sense of the word. The opposite procedure does not seem to have been applied

---

[1] Cf. I. Gladkov, *loc. cit.*, 46–7.

[2] E. Varga in *Russische Korrespondenz*, 1921, 65, cit. Pollock, *op. cit.*, 113.

[3] Even fifteen years later we still find criticism being voiced that differences arising between the planning bodies and government departments were too often settled " by the method of unprincipled mutual compromises " and that planning workers were too uncritical towards departmental projects. (*Plan*, April 25, 1937, 27.)

(or was only tardily adopted) of starting from the supplies available of the main " production factors " (labour, materials, food and fuel supplies, transport facilities, etc.) and then allotting these according to a priority-scale. At the base of this weakness lay, not only the stubborn sectionalism of departments, each jealously nursing its autonomy, of which we have spoken—a sectionalism which needed time to overcome—but also the divorce of Gosplan from the lower levels of economic life—the localities and the individual enterprises. This divorce meant that Gosplan lacked the detailed information concerning resources available and conditions of production, on which alone a central plan of allocations could be firmly built. Until in 1925 a beginning had been made with forging the necessary links with the localities by instituting subordinate branches of the planning machinery at these lower levels, this weakness could not be overcome.

At the time of the first reorganisation in 1923 there was a good deal of discussion concerning the precise powers and functions of what was frequently referred to as the Economic General Staff. Trotsky pressed for Gosplan to be given executive powers. But this was opposed by Lenin, who, though he had personally urged the formation of Gosplan, stressed the danger of confusing the functions of a specialist body (staffed as it was mainly by bourgeois experts) with those of a political organ—with the functions of a supreme organ of State that was executive and policy-making at the same time. The power of taking decisions about policy and issuing statutory orders continued, accordingly, to be vested in STO. A Party resolution of the Twelfth Party Congress in 1923, however, clearly stipulated that " it must be established as an unshakable principle that no economic question of State of general importance can be decided by the higher authorities until it has passed through Gosplan. All attempts by the various economic bodies to circumvent Gosplan when putting decisions into execution must be condemned as a manifestation of economic short-sightedness and as a most harmful relic of administrative sectionalism. ' The resolution of this Congress also made clear that successful planning of the interrelations between different branches of industry and between industry and agriculture could only come from practical experience over a considerable length of time, and that for some time to come the work of Gosplan was bound to be preparatory and experimental. A few years later, a suggestion was made that Gosplan should be given the status of a People's Commissariat (or Ministry) in the Union government, and that at the same time all governmental departments in the various republics should be placed under obligation to prepare and submit their departmental plans according to lines laid down by Gosplan. But while the latter proposal was adopted, the former was not.[1]

We have said something in a previous chapter[2] of the difficulties and of the discussions which took place in the course of the preparation of successive drafts of a Five Year Plan, with which Gosplan was so largely occupied between the end of 1925 and the end of 1928. Closely parallel to these discussions went controversies about the annual Control Figures, which were first drafted by Gosplan in 1925, the same year in which instructions were received to begin work on a Perspective Five Year Plan. The intention was that these Control Figures should ultimately become the blueprint of a fully integrated operative annual plan, by which the work of all branches of the economy should be steered in the coming year. When a Five Year Plan had been finally perfected, these Control Figures would be fitted to its larger framework, as in military operations tactical orders are moulded to the design of a general strategical plan. Work at the two levels was, accordingly, to proceed along parallel lines ; the experience of each enriching both its own and the other's technical accomplishment. But at the start these Control Figures were no more than tentative and provisional. The modest little volume of less than 100 pages, of which the first Control Figures in 1925–6 consisted, constituted a landmark in that they represented the first attempt to draft an annual plan on the basis of a comprehensive view of economic interrelationships and movements, instead of from departmental programmes already constructed in the light of sectional needs and thrown into some kind of general shape in purely empirical fashion. In words used by the Presidium of Gosplan, " the Control Figures from the very beginning linked yearly plans with the problems of perspective plans ". But they did not claim as yet to constitute an operational blue-print, still less the final programme into the procrustean bed of which departments had to fit. They were intended to be guiding lines, in the light of which the operational programmes of the various Commissariats were to be constructed, but not positive directives.[3] They were scaffolding round the building rather

---

[1] The proposal came from the Department for Workers' and Peasants' Inspection (Rabkrin), which had undertaken an investigation of the work of the planning organisation, and had emphasised the need for uniformity in all branches of planning work. (Cf. Pollock, op. cit., 274.)   [2] Chapter Ten.

[3] The word used to describe them was the untranslatable term "orientirovka", which is contrasted with " a directive plan ". Perhaps " lines of orientation " is closer to the original than " guiding lines ". But the less cumbrous, if less arresting, phrase has been used in the text.

than the limbs of the structure itself. In the words of a writer in the monthly organ of Gosplan, they were " the framework of a plan ; the levels around which actuality can fluctuate, and within the limits of which scope is afforded for operational manœuvring ". The same writer has described the subsequent " evolution of the idea of control figures " as being " from non-obligatory guiding lines[1] into a plan ", to which " there corresponded also an evolution in their composition and form from summaries, initially very mechanical, to more systematic summaries, and from these to a synthetic, directive plan ".[2]

The reception accorded to these first Control Figures was a varied one, and much of the comment was highly critical. On the one hand, Trotsky greeted the Control Figures with extravagant eulogy : they were " the glorious historical music of growing socialism " ; they were joined by " unbreakable threads backward to the Communist Manifesto of Marx and Engels in 1848 and forward to the socialist destiny of mankind " ; " the day of their inauguration should be marked in red on the Soviet calendar ". Prematurely as it turned out, he declared that " each figure is not only a photograph but also an order ". Their authors had not claimed as much ; although perhaps there was here some ambiguity, since the economic departments were exhorted by Gosplan to build their plans on the basis of the Control Figures at the same time as the latter were described as no more than tentative and provisional guiding lines.[3] They were described by Gosplan, on their official presentation to STO, as no more than " *approximate* directives for the work of formulating actual operational plans ", to be used by the responsible authorities with caution as merely first steps towards the creation of an economic plan ; and the President of STO, while

[1] The word used here is " orientirovka ", mentioned in the previous footnote.
[2] M. Persitz on " Five Years of the Control Figures " in *Plan. Khoz.*, 1929, No. 11, 167–8. This statement he proceeds to expand as follows : " The transition from summaries to formulation of synthetic problems, from analysis to synthesis, from imperfectly thought-out organisation of work to system, expresses the degree of mature methodology achieved in the composition of plans and is a criterion of this maturity. From the planning of sectors we proceed to the planning of the economy as a whole, and this contributes to a strengthening of the planning of particular sectors. The transition from sectors to embrace the economic complex can only be accomplished by means of a synthetic perspective upon a series of individual portions of the plan. Direct synthesis from sectors to economic totality is not possible."
[3] Cf. M. Persitz, *loc. cit.*, 168. Speaking of the Control Figures of the following year in retrospect several years later, another writer said that they " were not a directive plan ", and that " their task was to give the general orientation lines and a characterisation of the coming year as a whole, in order that the Commissariats and economic organs could compose their sectional economic plans on the basis of these orientation lines." (A. Anikst, *loc. cit.*, 17.)

recognising their value as a first rehearsal, refused to recognise them as affording the governing principles for constructing departmental programmes in the coming year.[1] The intention of Gosplan had been that the Figures should be submitted to the various economic Commissariats, including industry, both at the Union and the republican levels, after which the latter were to submit their own departmental programmes to Gosplan by mid-September, together with such criticisms as they might have of the Control Figures. Within a further month Gosplan would issue its comments on, and amendments to, these departmental plans ; and in the light of this interchange of projects the definitive economic plan for the coming year would be sanctioned by STO. As it turned out, however, most of the separate authorities apparently ignored the Control Figures ; and before long these had been seriously discredited as containing serious errors. What chiefly contributed to their discredit was the faultiness of the crop estimates on which they rested. Their authors, on their part, had in advance blamed the statistical data supplied to them by the economic departments as being " more than imperfect : they are tendentious and on most occasions express, not the objective situation in actuality, but some compromise between this and the specific interests of this or that office ".[2] In the light of this, some mistakes in their composition were to be expected. In the following year the complaint was repeated that " the main obstacle in the work of composing the control figures is the extremely unsatisfactory state of statistics in the U.S.S.R. Information on the sown area and harvest estimates are unsatisfactory and chaotic. The most important question of our future—the character of social stratification in the village and its *tempo*—cannot be illuminated in our work for lack of data."[3]

In this respect their successors in subsequent years began to be more fortunate. With the setting up of planning organs at the lower levels of economic activity, and an improvement both in its own direct knowledge of the situation and in the quality of the statistics generally available, Gosplan's estimates began to gain in realism. For one thing, once Gosplan had its " eyes and ears " closer to the ground, it could collect data relevant to the kind of questions that its experience of planning showed that it needed to ask, and closer touch with reality could assist it to discover the correct questions to ask and the correct manner in which they should

[1] Cit. Pollock, *op. cit.*, 258–60.
[2] *Kontrolnie Tsifri Nar. Khoz. na 1925–6*, 11–12.
[3] *Kontrolnie Tsifri na 1926–7 g.*, 9.

be formulated. In the second year the claim was made that " the control figures for 1926-7 appear as a synthesis of conclusions flowing both from objective tendencies of development of the economy and from economic policy posited by the government ", and that they are simultaneously a forecast of objective tendencies and a directive which steers events.[1] In this year an important step was taken towards official recognition of the Control Figures. It was laid down by the government that if the operational plans of any department corresponded to the Control Figures as confirmed by STO, no further confirmation of these plans by higher authority was necessary. Disputes, however, developed as to the rate of industrial development that it was correct to provide for ; there were several changes in this figure in the discussions which preceded final confirmation ; and the actual rate of increase both of production in large-scale industry and of building for the year was eventually higher than the Control Figures had originally estimated.[2] One of their critics maintained that " they still have nothing in common with reality on fundamental and important questions : on the one side is the plan and on the other is reality " ; while their claim to be directives as well as estimates had been nullified by the fact that, after their publication and " absolutely independently of them, the government had drafted a series of directives, which were put into practice ".[3] By 1927-8 the published Control Figures had grown in size to a large volume of over 500 pages. Their compilation had been more thorough and they had been more firmly rooted in actual possibilities on the basis of closer co-operation between central and local planning organs. They had been prepared in the light of a specific resolution of the central committee of the Party (in August, 1927), which had called for a radical change in their character, so that they might afford " not only general guiding lines, but also concrete directives and limits for the drawing up of all operative plans and of the State budget ".[4] They were subsequently described as " already a step in their own transformation from a summary into an economic plan ".[5] Those for 1928-9, geared as they were to the Five Year Plan which was then in the final stages of preparation, succeeded in becoming, in fact as well as in theory, the actual model upon which the definitive operational plans for the year were constructed.

---

[1] *Kontrolnie Tsifri na 1926-7 g.*, 3, 9.
[2] M. Persitz, *loc. cit.*, 174. The increase of production was 18 per cent. against an estimate of 14—nearer than in the previous year ; but the equivalent figures for building were 26 per cent. and 17.   [3] Birbraer, cit. Pollock, *op. cit.*, 269.
[4] I. Gladkov in *Plan. Khoz.*, 1935, No. 4, 122.   [5] M. Persitz *loc. cit.* 168.

From thenceforth the practice of ratifying the Control Figures as the operative annual plan was adopted, instead of ratifying separately a series of departmental plans.[1]

II

In the course of the discussion of these early Control Figures a controversy over the methodology of planning developed which was to run parallel with those controversies over larger questions of policy that attended the preparation of the Five Year Plan during these years.[2] The Preface to the 1925–6 Control Figures had briefly indicated the three main methods used in their construction. These were the methods of so-called " static and dynamic coefficients ", of " expert estimates " and of comparative study of pre-war data.[3] The last of these was described as playing a reserve rôle as a final check on results arrived at by the other two. The first was an attempt to formulate certain governing equations, or laws of equilibrium relationships, on the basis of the experience of recent years. The static coefficients were an attempt to define " structural relations, so to speak, as coefficients of proportionality ", and " dynamic coefficients were the change in those relations over time, the translation of some particular proportion on to another level ".[4] The second method consisted of the use of technical reports on the productive capacity of various industries obtained from engineers and technicians on the spot.

These might seem to be harmless enough components of any economic calculation. But around them strenuous and embittered discussion was to rage over the next few years. This discussion took initially a very abstract form, and at first glance might seem to have been a verbal battle devoid of substantial meaning. But on a closer view it is evident enough that the discussion was occupied with very substantial matters concerning the *use* to which these methods were put—the particular emphasis and interpretation laid upon them in the complex art of compiling plans. It might seem idle to discuss in the abstract what place comparisons with pre-war data could have in the assessment of future trends. The information afforded by such comparison was evidently not negligible ; yet no one could reasonably suggest that it should be relied upon alone. But as to the precise emphasis to be placed in any particular

---

[1] From 1931 the Control Figures came to be officially spoken of as the Annual Plan.   [2] See above, Chapter Ten.   [3] *Kontrolnie Tsifri na 1925–6*, 13–17.   [4] M. Persitz, *loc. cit.*, 169.

instance on such analogies, in contrast to other considerations, there was plenty of room, of course, for differences of opinion. The method of static and dynamic coefficients essentially rested upon the extrapolation of observed trends of past years into the future ; and about the validity of this—whether the estimates derived from it were helpful or misleading as first approximations— a great deal could be said. Even the results obtained from the " expert estimates ", and the significance to be given to them, depended on the way in which the questions were framed on which the technicians were invited to express their opinion. A question such as " what is the maximum production of which industry A is capable in the coming year ? " is not capable of a simple answer, until the premises are defined upon which the answer is to rest. Even " the productive capacity of existing equipment " (apart from any possibility of expanding or renewing that equipment) is not an unambiguous notion : it may mean one thing if the plant can count on acquiring any quantity of materials or skilled labour it may desire, and quite another if the materials and labour available to it are more straitly defined. One of the criticisms of the first version of the Five Year Plan was that it was " composed by sections of Gosplan on the basis of extremely questionable expert estimates on the state of industrial equipment and the possibility of development of particular branches, in which the experts chiefly occupied themselves with searching for ' bottlenecks ' and not with surmounting them."[1]

Issues of this kind concerning the interpretation of the three methods were closely associated with the question whether the Control Figures in particular, and how far economic plans in general, were to be regarded as scientific forecasts or as policy-programmes—as prognosis or command. Discussion as to whether the early Control Figures were merely " guiding lines " or " directives " was not concerned with the purely administrative question as to the exact place they were to have in the confection of plans. At any rate, the discussion was not long confined to the purely administrative issue. It quickly became an issue concerning the essential nature of any economic plan, whatever its stage of maturity ; behind which there loomed the more fundamental question as to the part which " economic law " could be conceived to play in the complex transitional " mixed economy " of the NEP. Ought the goal of economic planning to be to steer the economy in whatever direction, and at whatever speed, the pro-

[1] Gladkov, *loc. cit.*, 118.

gramme of the Soviet Government dictated ? Or should it, from the very nature of the situation, confine itself to enunciating the laws and tendencies which must inexorably be followed if economic crises and breakdown were not to result ? Put abruptly in this form, the antithesis is clearly seen, of course, to be unreal and absurd. To answer the first question with an unqualified affirmative would be to claim for the State divine omnipotence, and to assert the complete dethronement of economic law. To answer the second question in the affirmative would be to identify Soviet economy with an anarchic *laissez-faire* economy, ruled by atomistic competition, and would be virtually equivalent to a complete negation of planning as an influence on the long-term trend of events. Any plan must in some form be a synthesis of forecast and directive. Like the process of history itself, it must necessarily be a blend of subjective and objective elements. Strumilin at one stage tried to resolve the difficulty by emphasising the greater part that determinism must play in short-term plans and the greater scope for policy in plans which possessed a wider time-horizon (a matter to which we have already referred in our first chapter). " The annual plan," he wrote in the introduction to the Perspective Plan, " is above all affected by objective circumstances, which are not dependent on our planned interference. Capital investments of previous years and the previous harvest determine in advance almost 100 per cent. of the economy of the coming year in the field of production, import and export, the budget, credit, etc. The possibility of a new arrangement of the existent productive powers so as to attain a more effective combination of them is very limited indeed within one year. They are already much bigger for a period of five years ; for a period of ten to fifteen years, with a high rate of accumulation, they are even enormous. And if each plan constitutes a blend of elements of forecast as to what is objectively unavoidable with planning of what is desirable, forecast takes first place in annual plans and planned direction in the several-year plans." This distinction was, doubtless, true and important ; and might be held to be a reason for the adoption of different methods of compilation in plans covering different periods of time. The grouping of factors into the dependent and independent variables of the problem might properly differ in the two cases ; and in the longer-term plan the number of quantities capable of being treated as independent would probably be larger. But this, again, affords no more than a formal answer. We are still no wiser as to the precise emphasis that should be given, in any given type of plan, to the extrapolation of past trends into the future, as limiting factors on development, and to the effort to steer and to mould future development by the infusion into it of novel elements—by giving the plan an evocative character as a policy-making document.

Two economists in Gosplan, Groman and Bazarov, were the chief exponents and defenders of the three methods of plan-making to which we have referred. What brought them under the fire of criticism was their attempt with the aid of the " static and dynamic coefficients " to construct a rigid system of limiting conditions on development—" laws " of equilibrium development which government policy could only ignore at its peril. The chief of these concerned equilibrium relations between the rate of growth of industrial production and the rate of growth of agricultural production. By an extravagant over-simplification Groman used the method of extrapolation to propound his notorious 37–63 relation : the proposition that an equilibrated and crisis-free development must rest on a value-relationship of this order of magnitude between the marketed surplus of agricultural and of industrial products. The relationship between marketed supplies was in turn derived from an exchange-ratio which was held to constitute an " exchange of equivalents " between industry and agriculture : a notion which at first was accepted as a reasonable corollary of rejecting Preobrazhensky's theory about the necessity for deliberately establishing " non-equivalent " terms of exchange. Here, again, in estimating the proper ratio of equivalence, generalisation from the pre-war position had a leading influence. This 37–63 relation was apparently treated as one of the crucial constants to which changes in other magnitudes must be subordinated. The conception led its adherents to propound a rigid order of determination of different factors, and hence an irreversible order of determinism in the manner in which the various sections of the plan were constructed and adapted to one another. Bazarov himself referred to this theory as providing a " genetic " foundation for planning, and contrasted it with " teleology " in planning.

What gave this " theory of equilibrium " its peculiar significance in the discussions of those years was, again, not the truth or fallacy of the equations it propounded as a formal scheme, but a more substantial assumption inserted into the foundations of the theory : a premise upon which rested the particular one-way order of determinism that was its practical corollary for plan-making. This was the assumption that, in the existing situation of the country under the NEP, agriculture represented a sector where the laws of an individualist economy essentially held sway. Here objective factors ruled, in the main outside the reach of planned directives and conscious steering. All one could do here was to enquire as an impartial scientist what were the objective tendencies defining the rate of growth that was *probable*. Here it was that extrapolation on the basis of the trend in past years and comparisons with the pre-war period had their principal uses. Given an answer to this enquiry, as a basic *datum*, and given certain other data such as the probable rate of increase of the population and the consumption-needs of the urban population, most of the remaining magnitudes in any plan of economic development were determined within fairly narrow limits—the exportable surplus, and hence the volume of foreign trade, the amount of resources available for investment in the development of industry, and hence both the rate of growth of industrial production and the relative growth of industries pro-ducing consumer goods and capital goods (the latter being defined jointly by the 37–63 relation between agricultural and industrial commodities on the market and by the amount of resources avail-able for investment as a whole). The order of determination essentially ran from agriculture to industry, and in particular to consumers' goods industry ; and from the latter to heavy industry producing the capital goods on which the expansion of light industry was built.

The practical implication of this was to give preponderant weight to the element of forecast or prognosis in planning method and to give to policy-elements and conscious steering of events a correspondingly minor place. Above all, the theory was denounced as being " pessimistic " and " minimalist " regarding the possibili-ties of rapid industrialisation ; and its " theory of equilibrium ", with its corollaries as to the dire consequences of maintaining too high a rate of investment, became a butt for attack as the theoretical foundation of the Right-wing opposition during the discussions which accompanied the launching of the First Five Year Plan. Bazarov had insisted that " the type and style of our economy is predetermined by the actual state of our productive possibilities, their disposition and the interrelationship of social forces determin-ing the path of our ultimate economic development " ; and he spoke of the " unapproachable fortress in which, despite all the counter-currents in our planned economy, hides the *mouzhik* (peasant), like a snail in his shell, easily and simply escaping beyond all attempts of planning to reach him ". Groman con-tended that " the methods and the forms of society are dictated by the objective conditions of society and the objective trends of its development inherent in it ". For this reason " pre-war relations, in which the conditions of economic equilibrium were expressed, provide to a large extent regulative standards, in the objective sense, for present-day economic movements ". From this the conclusion was drawn that a subordination of planning to the policy of transforming the economy into a socialist economy, rather than to strictly " economic " criteria, would run the danger of " an arrest of production and of commodity-turnover, and a paralysis of the productive forces ". Another economist, who wished to subordinate industry to agriculture, Kondratiev, went so far as to say that " planning work must avoid the fetishism of precise calculations ; it must bow before an understanding of those processes which are in actual motion in the economy ; we must grasp those basic processes which confront us ". In other words, the function of a planning body was in a fundamental sense passive and not active : its function was to study the economic forces around it and to provide the responsive instruments through which the " laws " and tendencies immanent in those forces could be put into operation and be given a smooth and frictionless effect.[1]

A particular corollary drawn by Bazarov and others, which played a considerable part in the discussions of those years, was the inevitability that rates of growth in economic development would follow a " descending curve ". This implied that, once the " restoration period " was over, and existing equipment was being used to full capacity, the rate of increase of industrial production must slacken from year to year ; and it seems to have been derived from an application of some kind of notion of " diminishing returns " as an historical tendency in economic development. This view was reflected in a statement of the 1926–7 Control Figures that, owing to the end of the " restoration process ", the *tempo* of growth provided for in that year represented a marked retardation, and that further retardation was to be anticipated in the following year.[2]

As we have seen in a previous chapter, it was quite true that in the conditions which confronted planning in the middle 1920's the limitations imposed on socialist industry by its dependence on the market, which formed the life-line connecting it with agriculture, narrowly circumscribed the rate at which industry could advance and the amount that planning could achieve. It was quite true

---

[1] Cf. I. Gladkov, *loc. cit.*, 119–20, 129 ; V. Groman in *Plan. Khoz.*, 1925, No. 1, 88 ; I. A. Bialii in *Plan. Khoz.*, 1929, No. 9 ; also Pollock, *op. cit.*, 282 seq. ; Obolensky-Ossinsky in *Socialist Planned Economy in the Soviet Union*, 43.

[2] *Kontrolnie Tsifri, 1926–7*, 217.

that, with a weakly developed industry surrounded by a predominantly peasant economy in the countryside, the relatively inelastic marketable surplus of agricultural produce formed a crucial bottleneck. A deterministic theory which made planning chiefly a matter of prognosis and emphasised the dependence of industry upon agriculture confirmed for many people in those years the baffling sense of a closed circle of interdependent limiting factors to which all economic discussion seemed to lead. Once, however, the transformation of peasant agriculture on to an entirely new basis had been placed on the agenda, and had justified its claim to be regarded as a practicable solution, the situation was radically changed. A new qualitative element had been introduced, providing a break in the closed circle and altering the pattern of " causal-genetic " determination. There was now no more reason to assert the one-way dependence of industrial growth on the growth of agriculture than to assert the contrary (for example, the dependence of agricultural production on the supply of tractors and of chemical manures). Between the two there was a more complex relationship of interdependence, which certainly could not be summarised in any simple arithmetic relationship between the supply of industrial and of agricultural goods. Moreover, once the real resources available to provide a margin for capital investment had been appreciably enlarged (i.e. the supply of raw materials for industry or for export and of marketed foodstuffs to support a larger industrial population), there was a much larger scope for policy-questions concerning the rate of investment and the form and destination of invested capital (e.g. between light and heavy industry) to exercise a dominant influence over the shape of economic plans. The larger the investment-programme, the larger would be the proportion of economic resources and of the economic decisions affecting their allocation which had no immediate relationship to a market or to the determining influence of such " automatic " objective processes as a market contains. Hence the principles and methods which had bulked so large in the composition of the early Control Figures fell into disuse, not only because of the discredit attaching to them from their association with a rejected theory, but because extrapolation of tendencies observed in a previous period had little relevance to the changed situation of the 1930's ; while at the same time " expert estimates " had been transmuted into something different : an interpenetration of the planning apparatus with the productive apparatus at various levels, and the preparation of plans, not as the product of ratiocination at some high bureaucratic level, but by hands that were constantly on the pulse of events.

The method which survived as the leading method in Soviet planning was called the method of balances, which has been described by a leading worker in Gosplan as " the most important means for the establishment of inter-economic and inter-branch links in our economy ",[1] and as " the most important method of preventing disproportions in the economy ".[2]   This was no more than the use of a complex system of equations between the various magnitudes in a plan as the tests of internal consistency or coherence between its various elements.   It is obvious enough that any programme must observe some rules of co-ordination between the parts of which it is composed ; although the compilation and application of such balances in their actual detail may be a complicated task.   It was only in the course of the 1930's that the system of balances became at all comprehensive (previously it had applied only to certain key-spheres such as the supply of and demand for building materials) ; and even at the end of the Second Five Year Plan they left much room for improvement with regard to the amount of detail concerning qualities and lines of products into which they entered, and the extent to which they took account of the complications introduced by jointness or complementarity in production or in demand.[3]

This method of balances differed from their predecessors, the " static and dynamic coefficients ", both in being less pretentious and in the manner in which they were derived.   They did not attempt to define an overall structure of relations to which all plans must conform, deriving these relations from observed correlations in past events.   They constituted a much more flexible system of detailed links, and were derived from actual knowledge of the requirements of the productive process : for example, they rested on a knowledge of the actual requirements of a building programme and hence of the relation that must prevail between this and the available output of building materials, or on

[1] S. Turetsky on " Balance Problems in Economic Planning " in *Plan. Khoz.*, 1936, No. 2, 157.   The term " branch " here refers to a particular branch of industry ;   the reference being to the relations between various branches inside industry itself, as distinct from the relations between industry as a whole and other sectors of the economy.   [2] G. Kosiachenko in *Plan. Khoz.*, 1946, No. 4, 11.
[3] Cf. B. Sukharevsky in *Plan. Khoz.*, 1937, Nos. 11–12, 27 seq. ; cit. Bettelheim, *op. cit.*, 100 seq. ; also A. Baykov, *op. cit.*, 444 seq. It was only in July, 1934, that an order of Sovnarcom introduced a uniform procedure and system of classification and nomenclature for the preparation by industry of balances of supplies of materials and equipment. (Cf. N. S. Burmistrov, *Ocherki Tekhniko-Ekonomicheskovo Planirovania Promishlennosti*, 72 seq.)

knowledge of the actual raw material and labour requirements of a given production programme in an industry under given conditions. In this sense they constituted what may be termed " technical coefficients of production "[1] and not inductive statistical generalisations. At the heart of this method lies the detailed *costing* of output-programmes, about which more will later be said :[2] that is, a costing initially in real terms—in terms of the actual input of resources required at each stage of production to yield a given output. Without a firm knowledge of such coefficients, the necessary links will be missing : a consideration which again underlines the fact that economic planning could not rest content with mere generalised statistical data, submitted in the traditional forms, and that it had to strike roots into individual enterprises and plants in order to be in continuous and close touch with the particular situations on which its system of balances depended. An example of progress in this direction was the introduction in the course of the Third Plan of more detailed technical indices, such as utilisation of machinery expressed in machine-hours and as a percentage of potential time, the amount of metal used in particular products, the extraction-rate of metal from ores, as well as qualitative indices defining the standard of finished products.[3] Closely linked with this was the practical problem of systematising the various categories that were used in the compilation of data in the preparation of plans and in the formulation of input- and output-programmes for individual industries, so that the various sections of the plan could be related to one another and synthesised : a problem with which thought and discussion was very largely preoccupied in the middle '30's. When a satisfactory classificatory system had been worked out, its translating into simplified and standardised forms for reporting and submitting plans was a compelling necessity.

One might conclude that the discussion of the earlier planning methods had been largely negative in its results : that in discarding the more clear-cut " genetic " determinism of these methods it had put nothing in their place. Does this not leave important *lacunae* in the theory of planning, where empirical groping or the play of bureaucratic fancy must take the place of scientific method ? To a large extent it is true that those early discussions ended on a note

---

[1] Not all the equations which constitute the system of balances have this form. Some of them have a money form; and we shall see later that a balance of crucial importance for the Financial Plan is concerned with aggregate sales and purchases. But in an important sense the technical equations can be said to be the foundation of the structure.   [2] See Chapter Fifteen.   [3] Cf. *Plan*, 1937, No. 11, 44–5.

of negation. But on reflection it is not easy to see how they could have done otherwise ; and it must be remembered that in introducing the method of balances they shifted enquiry and discussion to a different and more fruitful plane—the detailed inter-relationships and needs of particular production processes. These relationships appear to be analogous to those which the experimental physicist or chemist discloses, defining the characteristics of the material with which he works. Would it not be as absurd to expect a theory of planning to include the operations of the planning body itself in a closed circle of determined relationships, as to expect a law of physics or of chemistry to include the scientist himself and his experiments (the active, planning element) as one of its terms ? Certainly this new method does not of itself afford any rule as to the *order of determination* of the various quantities of which the series of balances consist. If there were never any choice in the matter, as we have said, planning could play no rôle as an economic force, save as a possible way of achieving a short-cut to a path of development which would in any case emerge under an unplanned market economy, and of smoothing out the oscillations through which in the latter the 'equilibrium' movement would be approached.

At the same time it is possible to hold that in the construction of plans having a fairly limited time-horizon, the range of such choices (for reasons at which we hinted in our first chapter) can be defined within relatively narrow limits (as in navigation, for example, can the performance of a vessel or a machine of a particular type under a particular set of conditions); and that although the character of these limits will change with every substantial change in the economic situation (e.g. with the stock of capital equipment, relatively to natural resources and labour, and the state of technique) it should be possible to arrive at certain generalisations about them which will hold for a considerable range of such situations.

There is, however, a notable respect in which the question of the structural interdependence of the economy, as represented by a system of balances, failed to be advanced from promising beginnings, and where the polemics against the Gosplan economists proved to have a negative and inhibiting effect. No attempt was made (so far as one is aware) to generalise the system of input-output relationships, or even to contemplate mathematical techniques for doing so, in the way that this was done outside the country by Wassily Leontief. A single balance by itself is, of course, simply a single supply-demand equation for a product, and a collection of them is no more than a set of such separate equations. The problem of consistency of such a set involves taking into account all the interdependencies between them, which means, mathematically speaking, treating them as a system of simultaneous equations and considering the conditions for solution of the whole system.   In more concrete terms, in so far as a particular output becomes an input that enters into another balance-equation, the quantities of one balance cannot be adjusted (*e.g.* by stepping-up its output-target) without having repercussions upon a whole series of other balance-equations.   And it is this kind of repercussion—the precise pattern of the cross-connections between the individual balances—that determines what is possible and what impossible within the limits of certain constraints or conditioning factors (which include the technical coefficients, supply of labour and natural resources—and in the short-run the productive capacities of installed equipment in various sectors and industries).

This neglect is the more surprising in view of the pioneer work of economists like P. I. Popov and L. Litoshenko and M. Barenholz in the '20's in (building on Quesnay's *Tableau* and Marx's reproduction-schema) devising the notion of a "national economic balance" conceived as a complex of input-output relationships, and the marrying of this with the notion of input-output coefficients (so necessary to give it operative significance for constructing a plan).[1]   It is further surprising in view of the historical fact that Leontief himself at the time reviewed these pioneer essays in the Gosplan organ and showed appreciation of their path-breaking character.[2]

Empirically Gosplan can hardly have failed to explore these inter-relationships and to have taken them into account.   But there were practical reasons why empirical pursuit of them in the course of plan-making could never be carried very far; and this may well explain (in part at least) why they were content to make do without inventing more sophisticated methods—as well as itself constituting a defect in planning, in the sense that the balance-method as used could in practice entail lack of precision.   When in the final stages of preparing a plan balances had to be recalculated (as some at least inevitably had to be), the planning time-table[3] permitted no more than a re-

---

[1] The relevant sources are: P. I. Popov in *Balans Narodnogo Khoziaistva Soiuza S.S.S.R. 1923–4 goda*, ed. P. I. Popov (Moscow 1926), 282 seq.; L. Litoshenko, *ibid.*, 56 seq.; M. Barenholz in *Planovoe Khoziaistvo*, July 1928, 325 seq. An English translation of these is in N. Spulber, *Foundations of Soviet Strategy for Economic Growth* (Bloomington, Indiana, 1964), 20–87, 99–123.

[2] In *Planovoe Khoziaistvo*, 1925, No. 12, 254 seq.; also trans. in Spulber, *op. cit.*, 88.

[3] This is not entirely arbitrary, of course.   Work on the preliminary draft outline plan ("control figures") for the coming year generally starts in the spring or early summer of the previous year, on the basis of current data about performance during the first half of the year in question; and for obvious reasons it can hardly

calculation of so-called 'first order' and possibly at most 'second order linkages', or effects, of an initial change, but no more than this. In other words, the full repercussions on other output-targets of a change at one point could not, for practical reasons, be explored. Consequently, the calculated inter-relationships on which the final set of plan-targets was based could be no more than an approximation. At the global level the orders of magnitude involved in what the approximation ignored might be quite small. But at the level of particular enterprises, and in the case of particular products, they could be considerable—large enough on occasions to be the cause of dislocation and serious bottlenecks. Such lack of precision may not be any greater, of course, than what is unavoidably present in the information coming up from below and forming the basis of planning calculations; nor may it in fact be any greater than the *actual* flexibility present in any set of input-norms or coefficients (*i.e.* the actual possibilities at the operational level of economising on particular inputs, if pressed, or of resorting to substitution). Moreover, the cruder 'partial equilibrium' method (as one may call it) of operating with a series of separate balances step-by-step may have certain advantages of flexibility in practice over more sophisticated methods for finding a 'general equilibrium' solution (*e.g.* flexibility in allowing for variation in coefficients instead of operating with fixed coefficients).[1] The fact remains, however, that when plan-targets are adjusted upwards, there is no guarantee that available supplies of essential inputs, on

---

start earlier than this. The intensive period of re-calculating balances and co-ordinating data, in connection with supplemented or revised targets coming up from lower levels, is apt to be the autumn; the definitive plan, with its appropriate supply-allocations, must be handed down before the end of the year if localities and enterprises are to base upon it their operational programmes and arrangements for the coming year. It was in view of serious and often disorganising delays in the completion of plans that a definite time-table was imposed by decree in 1946, mainly with a view, apparently, to bringing the various Ministries into line (Decree of 29 August, 1946).

[1] There is also the relevant consideration that if the particular inter-relationships of an input-output table have what is called either a 'quasi-diagonal' or a 'quasi-triangular' form, they may be capable of being handled by relatively simple and 'partial' methods. In the former case the production-plan is capable of being split into a number of more or less independent parts, each treated separately; in the latter case plans for various industry-groups exhibit a unilateral dependence and can be handled separately provided they are handled in a certain sequence—in other words, in this latter case there are no complicated feed-back relationships, or if these exist they are comparatively unimportant (cf. Oskar Lange, *Introduction to Econometrics* (Warsaw 1962) 2nd ed., 233–9). A "conclusion of great significance for planning" drawn from the Soviet 1959 input-output table was that "a comparatively small group of productive links have decisive importance in the system of inter-branch links". The table exhibited more than 4,000 inter-industry (or inter-product) linkages; of these about 500 only included more than 95 per cent. of all material expenditures (L. Berri, Klotzvog and Shatalin in *Planovoe Khoziaistvo*, 1962, No. 2, 55).

which achievement of the targets depends, will always be adjusted, or *can* in the circumstances be adjusted to match.

Probably a more important reason, however, why theoretical refinement of the balance method was not followed up was the disfavour into which this type of analysis fell during the early '30's, as a by-product of polemic against the Gosplan economists of the Groman-Bazarov school. Such attempts were apt to be denounced as 'mathematical formalism', and as 'bourgeois formalism' to boot; and in a period ruled by dogmatism, especially in the social sciences, such as was to develop as the decade advanced, this kind of slur, once pronounced, was sufficient to inhibit initiative in this direction and at any rate to preclude it in published form. On one occasion, indeed, at the time the head of Gosplan (Kuibyshev) explicitly condemned what he chose to term "the statistical-arithmetical deviation in planning", and in particular the use in planning of "abstract models".[1] A contributory factor was the growing wall that came to be erected between planning as a practical pursuit and 'theoretical' political economy (as exemplified in Stalin's statement in the 1952 booklet that "the rational organisation of the productive forces, economic planning, etc., are not problems of political economy, but problems of the economic policy of the directing bodies"[2]). While this served to render political economy an abstract and rather arid repetition of accepted doctrines, it probably helped to confine planning and planners firmly to the path of empiricism. At any rate, the result was that it was not until the revival of discussion and re-thinking from 1956 onwards that there was renewed interest in input-output analysis and in the possibilities of using Leontief-methods in planning (along with attendant interest in the use of computers and in cybernetics).

Another unfortunate casualty of this reaction against "mathematical formalism" was the use of dynamic growth-models as a tool of long-term planning. Here one has in mind particularly that original thinker, G. A. Feldman, whose work fell into oblivion and had no sequel, despite the fact that it was he who furnished theoretical justification for the "investment-priority for heavy industry" which we have seen came to form the policy-keynote of the pre-war decade. Feldman's analysis also derived from Marx's famous 'schema of reproduction'; although he sought to adapt this for his own purpose by converting Department 1 entirely into a 'growth sector' (*i.e.*

---

[1] Cf. G. Sorokin in *Planovoe Khoziaistvo*, 1956, No. 1, 43, who cited this approvingly—even as late as 1956.
[2] *Economic Problems of Socialism in the U.S.S.R.* (Moscow 1952), 81. He went on to speak of these as being "two different provinces which must not be confused".

concerned with *new* investment), which he designated the *u*-sector, and by leaving in the second sector all stages of production of consumers' goods, including such raw material and replacement of equipment as were required to produce "the consumer goods necessary for satisfying an existing level of needs". On the size of the *u*-sector depended the size of total net investment, and hence the rate of growth of productive capacity and of output at any given date. His crucial equation expressed the growth-rate as a product of the proportionate size of this *u*-sector and the "effectiveness of capital". In his own notation this crucial equation was written

$$D' = S.\frac{D_u}{D}$$

where S stands for the effectiveness of capital (or ratio of output to capital), D_u for the output-capacity of the *u*-sector, D for total output (with D' for the rate of increment of output, or the growth-rate of the economy as a whole). An interesting feature of this method of analysis was that, by contrast with traditional investment-theories, it did not stress the antithesis between growth and consumption, but on the contrary represented the building-up of productive capacity in the capital goods sector as the necessary condition for achieving a higher growth-rate of consumption in future years. To every desired growth-rate of consumption in the future, postulated as a long-term planning objective, there corresponded a certain relative size of the capital goods sector (and hence a certain investment-allocation to it in the intervening years to build it up to the required size).[1]

In the second half of the '30's a half-hearted attempt was, indeed, made (prompted, it has been said, by Stalin[2]) to revive a discussion about a synthetic "balance of the national economy". Strumilin tried to develop some kind of analysis on the basis of Marx's 'schema'; and he was in turn criticised, in no very constructive fashion, by Notkin and Tsagolov.[3] The discussion scarcely got beyond questions of classification (*i.e.* a listing of the actual relationships of which account must be taken); it was soon to be dismissed by authority as unsatisfactory and was rather abruptly adjourned. After that for two decades silence reigned.

[1] G. A. Feldman in *Planovoe Khoziaistvo*, 1928, No. 11, 146 seq., and 1929, No. 12, 100 seq.

[2] It has been said that the question was posed by him to a conference of "Marxist agronomists" as far back as 1929. (V. Sobol, "On a Scheme for a Balance of the National Economy" in *Plan. Khoz.*, 1940, No. 6, 3 seq.) But this was probably the pretext, merely, for reviving the question.

[3] Strumilin in *Plan. Khoz.*, 1936, Nos. 9–10, 86 seq.; A. Notkin and I. Tsagolov in *Plan. Khoz.*, 1937, No. 4, 78 *seq.*, and in *Plan. Khoz.*, 1936, No. 7, 132 seq. Also cf. Strumilin, *K Perestroike Sovetskogo Ucheta*.

III

The activities of the planning system are not confined to the preparation of plans. Since the start of the planning era an increasing amount of attention has been paid to what is known as "plan fulfilment." This is not intended to mean simply a *post facto* audit or inspection to allot praise or blame for achieving or falling short of the target. Nor is its meaning exhausted by saying that it is concerned with keeping industry on the rails of the plan. Stalin once spoke of a Five Year Plan as "a first approximation", which had to be improved and rendered more precise on the basis of local experience of working of the Plan." Molotov when speaking on the Third Plan said: "We have not devoted enough attention to supervising plan fulfilment."[1] In other words, putting of a plan into operation is itself part of the process of fitting it to actual data and of testing-out its correspondence with reality. Such a process cannot be confined to the stage when the Plan is being put on paper for the first time. To start to act upon the Plan is to put questions to reality (as a scientist does in his laboratory) which could not be answered in any other way. The way that programmes shape when translated into practice gives fresh experience and new data to the planning organs, which need to be continually alert, not only to receive and sift these new data, but to adjust the shape of the Plan as it proceeds in whatever way this closer acquaintance with reality shows to be required. Thus the Plan, like a living organism, can be made to grow and modify its shape as part of its activity.

Clearly this task of controlling the Plan-in-operation no less abounds in problems and difficulties than the task of preparing plans in the first instance. If the requirements of the Plan are adhered to with too much rigidity, serious hitches and dislocations are bound to develop as unforeseen eventualities crop up : dislocations which are likely to extend the area of their influence and do more damage the longer their repair is delayed. If, on the other hand, in the interests of flexibility, the hand of control is too lenient and executive organs are encouraged to treat the programmes allotted to them, not as instructions, but only as advice, then evasions of the Plan are likely to be multiplied for no sufficient

---

[1] Molotov, *op. cit.*, 25. An example of this emphasis was the reorganisation in 1932, in the case of the Gosplan of the Russian republic, of the former " conjuncture bureau " as a department for the fulfilment of economic plans. (Cf. *Spravochnik Sovetskovo Rabotnika*, 102–3 : Decree of Sovnarcom, June 7, 1932.)

reason ; and these evasions will themselves introduce new unforeseen elements, with their consequential hitches and maladjustments affecting other parts of the Plan. The planning authorities must therefore be in a position to judge, and to judge quickly, whether a failure to observe the provisions of the Plan is justified by circumstances or whether it is unjustified. If it is unjustified, measures need to be taken to ensure that the failure is quickly corrected. If it is justified by the course of events, then the necessary revisions required by the situation must be worked out in such a way that the resulting chain of adjustments shall cause a minimum of disturbance to other parts of the economy. It may be that, because a particular plant is behind with its output-programme, a second plant which relies upon the first for materials or components is prevented from working to full capacity. An urgent question will then arise in this form : is it more economical to allow the second plant to maintain its output by tapping some higher-cost source of local material supplies or some inferior substitute which will increase its own difficulties in production and possibly affect the quality of its product ; or alternatively to divert supplies to it from other industries, cutting down the allocations and the output-programmes of the latter ; or again seek to remedy the lag of the first plant by allowing it to draw upon supplies of skilled labour that is in short supply, at the risk of starving other industries of labour and adversely affecting their fulfilment of the Plan ? Sometimes important and far-reaching policy-questions will be involved, as under the First Five Year Plan, when metal and building materials were in short supply, and a decision had to be made between a pruning of the construction programme of heavy industry, cutting the allocations of metal for railway development, or exporting raw cotton (at the expense of a reduced output of cotton goods) in order to import metals and machinery. Unless such decisions can be taken quickly, and the consequential revisions worked out and sanctioned, the adjustments which follow in the wake of events will be haphazard and may be the reverse of what is desirable. Skilful and frictionless revision in face of unforeseen events requires a developed machinery and technique of observation and of analysis of the current situation at every point, as well as a machinery and technique of control. It will also, of course, be greatly facilitated by the possession of certain reserves (e.g. of key raw materials and mobile equipment) to give elbow-room to manœuvre. From this continual, almost day-to-day, process of observation and analysis of the current situation there will be collected the information necessary for preparing the shorter-term plans which have to be adapted both to the framework of the longer-term perspective plans and to the changing situation—the annual plans within the Five Year Plans, and the quarterly plans within the annual plans themselves. Thus the act of planning can be said to consist of moving towards a successful blend of policy with reality, of subjective design with the objective situation, of directives with prognosis, by a *succession of approximations* ; but a succession of approximations written, not simply on paper, but in action.

In this steering of the Plan-in-operation the lower units of the planning mechanism act as the eyes and ears of Gosplan. In many cases, where no more than local adjustments are required, they will play the operative rôle in initiating or sanctioning any revisions that have to be made. They will be the " progress officers " of the Plan. These tentacles of the planning octopus, which feel out the ground over which it moves, came to form a double series of limbs reaching down to the operational units in the economic field. One series reaches down through the apparatus of economic administration, through the Commissariat and the trust to the individual factory. The other reaches down geographically through the republic and the region to the *rayon* or local district. At each of these levels there is a planning section attached to the relevant administrative body ; this section being directly connected with, and subordinated to, the one immediately above it.[1]

For example, according to the reorganisation decree of 1935, in all autonomous republics of Russia there were to be planning boards of from 15 to 30 persons at each of the levels of the *Krai* or territory, the *Oblast* or region, and the *Okrug* or canton. These boards were to be appointed by the governments of the regions or districts to which they were attached, and were to be divided into a number of subsections concerned with such matters as local industry and industrial co-operatives, agriculture, trade and road transport. To town governments were to be attached planning boards of 10 to 20 persons, appointed by the presidium of the town soviet, on the

---

[1] Cf., however, the following statement by Mr. J. Miller : " No Planning Commission . . . has executive authority over those below. . . . But if necessary a Planning Commission or planning-economic department may advise its Soviet Government, Commissary or Director to make the necessary orders or recommendations downwards, which will reach the planners below, through the Soviet or Director to whom they are responsible. By now, however, the direct authority of Gosplan U.S.S.R. over other planning organs, on matters of planning technique and procedure, is considerable, and defined in law as well as in practice." (" Soviet Planning Organisations " in *Slavonic Review*, April, 1938, 11.)

nomination of the planning committee's chairman, from among persons in leading positions in municipal economic organisations. Below them were to be smaller planning boards, of from 7 to 12 persons, attached to the *rayon*, or district, of the town.[1] Again in the larger pre-war Commissariats, such as the Commissariat of Heavy Industry, there were planning sections for the main branches of industry (e.g. metals) with a personnel of about 30 persons, who were in direct liaison with a corresponding section in Gosplan itself of some 4 to 5 persons, and also with planning sections attached to industrial enterprises within their field. Each of these bodies in the process of planning handles a two-way traffic. At first, there come down " preliminary directives " and " preliminary orientating data " on certain crucial matters such as capital investment, labour supply, average wages. These initial directives are sometimes spoken of as " control limits ". At each stage these directives and data will be expanded and particularised before being handed further down. Then the movement begins in the reverse direction According to uniform schemes of presentation, the responsible body at each level then submits its own draft detailed proposals for embodiment in the final plan.[2] These travel up and back, and submitted to preliminary adjustment and integration at each stage they finally reach Gosplan at the all-Union level, where the final work of synthesis has to be performed.[3] The completed system of particular programmes, when it has been finally ratified by the government, then returns as the operative plan with binding force on all branches of State activity.

The machinery of Gosplan itself was the subject of two major reorganisations during the decade of the '30's. The first of these was in April, 1935, and was primarily concerned with giving a greater

---

[1] *Spravochnik Sovetskovo Rabotnika*, 99–100.

[2] Cf. *ibid.*, 101 ; also the instructions drawn up by Gosplan for drawing up the " limits " for the plan for the first year of the third quinquennium (1938) in *Plan*, 1937, June 25, 38. A particular example in the sphere of foreign trade is the following : " The Commissariat of Foreign Trade communicates the control limits to the Export Corporations and the Agents of the Commissariat. On the basis of the control limits, the Export Corporations and Agents draw up their preliminary annual plans and submit them to the Commissariat of Foreign Trade. On the basis of these draft plans the Commissariat draws up its annual plan which it submits to the government for approval." (M. Zhirmunski, *Soviet Export*, 76–7.) Obolensky-Ossinsky says that " the plans of the departments and republics sometimes differ considerably from the original limits ". (*Op. cit.*, 45.)

[3] Since 1936 the Republics and the Commissariats of the Union Government submit their plans directly to the Union Sovnarcom (and not via Gosplan) - Gosplan being asked to report on them as a whole. As Mr. J. Miller has remarked : " In recent years, as the experience of the province and republic Planning Com; missions . . . has increased, Gosplan U.S.S.R. has tended to occupy itself less with local and industrial detail, and more with the general co-ordinating work." (*Loc. cit.*, 10.)

emphasis to what was called "synthetic planning". Special departments of synthetic planning, five in number, were instituted. Apart from these there were to be sixteen departments corresponding to the main branches of economic activity (fuel and power, mining and metallurgy, etc.) to concentrate on the planning of these particular branches, and seven sections dealing with a variety of special subjects such as labour, public health and defence. The directing body of Gosplan was a president and a central council of 70 persons, appointed by Sovnarcom. In commenting on the reorganisation the head of Gosplan stated that "the fact that, notwithstanding the instructions of Stalin, already issued in 1929, we have not up to now worked out a balance for the whole economy, is to be explained by the absence of synthetic organs in Gosplan to occupy themselves with this work". The work of "checking the fulfilment of the plan is laid on all departments and sections, both synthetic departments and departments for branches of the economy" and "must become an organic part of the work of every department and section, since without a deep knowledge of actual conditions in the course of carrying out the plan, neither its fulfilment can be guaranteed nor a perspective plan of economic development be constructed ".[1] Two years later, however, there continued to be complaints from planning workers themselves of unsatisfactory control of plan fulfilment and the insufficiency of " balancing links between various projects in a plan ".[2]

The reorganisation of February, 1938, had a double importance. In the first place it confirmed the status of Gosplan as a permanent commission directly attached to Sovnarcom (which it seems to have become de facto a few years previously). At its head were to be a President and a Board of 11 persons, appointed by Sovnarcom from among departmental chiefs in planning work or " scientific workers and eminent specialists ", in addition to a wider council of 90 members of Gosplan and other planning workers. While it remained an advisory body, not an executive department of State, it fulfilled the very important rôle of co-ordinator-in-the-first-instance of the programmes of the various commissariats, and its chairman was a member of Sovnarcom itself. Secondly, Gosplan was empowered to institute authorised representatives to supervise

---

[1] V. Mezhlauk in Plan. Khoz., 1935, No. 4, 3–6 ; cf. also Bettelheim, op. cit., 72–3.
[2] Cf. Plan, 1937, No. 8, 28–9, 33, 35. Another complaint was that " it was no secret that quarterly plans often reach enterprises at the end of the quarter " and are so much waste paper. (Ibid., 29.)

the fulfilment of plans in the various republics and regions. Such representatives were to act independently of the planning boards attached to republics and regions, and the appointment was to be made by Sovnarcom of the Union on the nomination of the President of Gosplan. Gosplan was granted the right to require any governmental body to present it with " documents, materials and necessary explanations relevant to controlling the fulfilment of economic plans " ; and its " principal task " was expressly defined in the reorganisation decree as being " to ensure that correct proportions are observed in the development of different branches of the economy and to take the requisite measures to prevent disproportions from developing ". The number of departments of synthetic planning was reduced to four, dealing with the general economic plan, capital construction, finance, and regional distribution of production ; and the number of sections handling special branches of economic activity was increased to twenty-six.[1]

But although the duty of Gosplan to control the fulfilment of plans as well as to draft plans received special emphasis, there remained a clear line of distinction between economic planning and economic administration, and between the machinery and personnel of each. The planning apparatus, as we have seen, is not executive, even if at each level of administration it is associated in intimate liaison with executive bodies. It does not give orders regarding the conduct of economic life, even if the plans it draws up, when they have received official sanction from the supreme executive organs of state, have the obligatory character of economic orders of the day. Even in its supervision of the carrying out of plans, its concern is with certain quantitative indices, defining the central objectives of industrial policy, and not with the particular methods by which those objectives are attained. An analogy can, again, be suggested of the difference in an army between the work of the staff, concerned with first the drafting and then the coordinated operation of the general strategic plan, and the unit commanders concerned in conducting the tactics by which the main objectives laid down in the strategical design are reached.

Along with the changes in planning methods and machinery, the administration of industry itself underwent certain changes in the decade before the war, although for reasons that were different in the main. The pattern of organisation was far from uniform for all industries or even for all branches of the same industry ; and

[1] Cf. Bettelheim, op. cit., 74–8; Industrial and Labour Information, vol. LXIX No. 4, 99 ; J. Miller, loc. cit., 8–13.

any generalisation made about it is inevitably incomplete and is apt
quickly to become out-of-date. Yet there are certain main direction-
lines of movement that can be summarised in general terms without damage to the general picture, which is one of considerable
variety. But in case this variety should be overlooked, and an
impression gained of too great uniformity of administrative pattern,
it should be borne in mind that, as regards types of administration,
Soviet industry in the first place divides into three main categories. Heavy industry is the most centralised of all, both by
reason of the extent to which production and management are
concentrated, for the most part, in large units, and because, as a
producer of capital goods, it works to government order and not
for the market, and its activity is governed by the Investment or
Construction Plan for the country at large : a section of the plan
which forms the main artery on which all other branches of the
plan depend. Up to 1957 this branch of industry was directly
administered by Commissariats (later called Ministries) of the Union
Government. Light industry, however, concerned with the output
of consumers' goods has always been more decentralised, being
subordinated in the first instance to appropriate Commissariats or
Ministries in the various republics, subject to general supervision by
Commissariats of the appropriate branches of industry (textile industry,[1] light industry, the food industry, as also agriculture and the
fishing industry) at the Union level. Finally there is local industry,
concerned predominately with serving the local market and drawing
its raw materials from local sources in the main, which is administered by the local bodies within whose sphere of competence they
fall, whether it be region, province or municipality, subject to the
general supervision of special Commissariats or Ministries of Local
Industry in each republic.[2] Much of this local industry is organised
as industrial co-operatives, having their own federations and associations for common purposes; and in the years before the war, as
well as during the war and after, a good deal of emphasis was
placed on the rapid development of such industries and the encouragement of them to show the maximum initiative in adapt-

---

[1] The administration of the textile industry is nowadays separated from other
branches of light industry; and the Commissariat of Light Industry since this
separation was mainly concerned with the leather and footwear industry; also with
such things as knitted goods production, porcelain and hardware, radio sets and
bicycles.   Timber and certain building materials also come within this category.
[2] What is called "municipal economy" (e.g. local transport services, repair
shops, etc.) is also subordinated to a special Commissariat of Municipal Economy
at the republican level; and the same is true of road transport.

ing their production to local conditions of demand and of supply.[1] A few months before the outbreak of war a significant step was taken in the direction of greater freedom of action for local industry by a grant (by Sovnarcom decree of January 7th, 1941) of considerable latitude to local soviets to draw upon certain funds and supplementary credits for the financing of capital development in local industry " beyond the limits established for capital work by the Plan ".[2] In this sphere a very large measure of decentralisation operates ; and both in making plans for the amount and character of production and in carrying out those plans the initiative apparently rests predominantly with local bodies.

In the first two of these three main categories of industry there existed in the early '30's a hierarchy of several stages between the factory at the bottom and Vesenkha at the top. Vesenkha itself had as sub-departments what were called Chief Administrations for particular spheres of industry. Under them were groups of allied industries organised in Combines, each of which might cover an industry, such as cotton, or else a branch of an industry, such as a homogeneous branch of engineering.[3] These Combines were financially autonomous bodies, engaged primarily in the supply of materials and the sale of the final product and in exercising a general supervision over the industrial policy of their respective branches of industry. They were also responsible for the appointment of managerial personnel in the constituent enterprises and for organising the training and supply of labour. Beneath them were a number of Trusts, each with its Trust Board ; these being groupings of related or contiguous factories. Throughout this hierarchy what was known as the principle of " functionalism " applied to management and direction : i.e. a particular person (or department) would be responsible for a particular function or

[1] Already at the Seventeenth Party Congress Stalin had stressed the importance of developing local industry and giving it the chance of " showing initiative in producing goods of general consumption ". In the Second Plan the expansion of local industry occupied an important place ; this expansion amounting to nearly three times between 1932 and 1937. But its development at this time remained patchy, half of it being in the neighbourhood of Moscow and Leningrad and two thirds of the districts of the country lacking any local industry at all ; while facilities for capital expenditure were still deficient. (Cf. N. Gavrilov in *Plan*, 1937, No. 11, 12–16.)

[2] Cf. N. N. Rovinsky, *Gosudarstvennii Biudjet S.S.S.R.*, 332–3. This latitude for supplementary investments by local bodies was subject to the limit of a maximum figure.

[3] These Combines had been formed in 1930 primarily to take over the functions of the Syndicates (see above, pages 158–60), and later came to exercise powers of supervision over their several branches of industry.

aspect only (e.g. labour or raw materials or finance) of the industry or of the factory which he controlled.

The tendency of subsequent change was, firstly to simplify this multi-link system and to abolish altogether some stages in the hierarchy, and secondly to banish " functionalism " in favour of individual responsibility of one man for all the operations within a particular sphere, any functional specialists or sections being directly subordinated to him as assistants.   In 1934 the Combines were abolished,[1] and at the same time the number of separate Trusts was reduced. At the top the work of Vesenkha was divided between a number of newly created Commissariats for special spheres of industry.   Food had already been detached from its purview in 1930; and two years later Vesenkha yielded place to three separate Commissariats for Heavy Industry, for Light Industry and for Timber.   Subsequently these were further divided.   By an order of Sovnarcom of August 22, 1937, machine-building was separated from the Commissariat of Heavy Industry and placed under a separate Commissariat, to have charge of motors, tractors, machine-tools, railway locomotives, agricultural machinery and electrical machinery, and in addition rubber and glass.   Previously to this, defence industry had been placed under a separate Commissariat.   There was also a drastic simplification of the system of leading departments within each Commissariat, and the establishment of direct links between the plant and the central body, with an increasing tendency for operative decisions to rest with the former, including supply-arrangements within a general scheme of allocations laid down by the latter.[2]   In the first two months of 1939 came a more drastic splitting up of the main industrial Commissariats.   The Heavy Industry Commissariat was divided into Fuel, Electricity, Iron and Steel, Non-ferrous Metals, Chemicals and Building Materials.   The recently formed Com-

---

[1] There remained a few special exceptions.   For example, the coal industry had regional combines for each of the main coal regions, Donbas, Kuzbas, Urals, Karaganda, Moscow district, Central Asia and Transcaucasia ; and these regional combines had respectively twenty-two, eleven, five, three and four Trusts subordinated to them.   (Granovsky and Marcus, *Economika Sotsialisticheskoe Promishlennosti*, 577.)

[2] In the case of heavy industry in 1937, before the disappearance of the single Heavy Industry Commissariat, these chief administrations covered such branches as iron and steel, oil, chemicals, non-ferrous metals, power, mining, building materials, nickel and zinc ; and numbered thirty-three in all.   Cf. M. Kaganovitch in *Plan. Khoz.*, 1935, No. 3, where these changes were hailed as having scored " heavy successes in organising production " in heavy industry and having dealt an important blow against " armchair bureaucratic methods of directing industry " by simplifying the number of links and transferring engineers from offices to the enterprises themselves.

missariat for Machine-building branched out into Heavy Engineering (machine-tools and locomotives), Medium Engineering (motor-cars, etc.) and General Engineering (instruments, etc.). In the case of food, fisheries, meat and dairy produce were brought under Commissariats separate from the Commissariat of Food ; in the case of light industry, textiles were placed under a Commissariat of their own ; and in the case of the defence industries there took place a subdivision into Aircraft, Shipbuilding, Munitions and Armaments. By these changes the number of separate industrial Commissariats was increased to the remarkably high figure of twenty-one. Chief Administrations still apparently continued to exist as subsections of each Commissariat ; although their importance had no doubt been reduced with the multiplication in the number of Commissariats. These had taken over from the old Combines the right of appointing managerial personnel and the commercial functions of supply and sale. They also had charge of those scientific research institutes which, organised on fairly specialised lines, are attached to the various industrial Commissariats. In industries where the unit of production was large the factory generally had a direct link with this Chief Administration of the Commissariat, the director of the latter and the manager of the former being in personal touch with one another. Where the unit of production was small, however, or where the industry was complex in structure, factories remained grouped into Trusts, as the responsible financial units, and it was the Trust that had direct connection with the Chief Administration.[1]

This tendency was continued immediately after the war; the number of Commissariats being increased still further. An example was the formation of a special Commissariat to undertake the designing and manufacture of all railway rolling stock (taking over among other things the war-time tank-producing plants controlled by the Commissariat of the Tank Industry which was to be liquidated), of another to have charge of agricultural engineering (i.e. producing agricultural machinery and equipment), and the formation of special Commissariats to have charge of all construction work in a certain sphere of industry; for example, all construction work for heavy industry or for the fuel industry. At the same time emphasis was laid on local industries to handle the supply of such things as furniture and household utensils.

---

[1] Granovsky and Marcus, *op. cit.*, 566 seq.; Bettelheim, *op. cit.*, 46–7; *Industrial and Labour Information*, vol. LXIV, 65, 274 ; vol. LIX, No. 5, 174 ; vol. LXIX, No. 6, 226.

IV

Description of the administrative structure of a planned economy affords no direct guidance to its actual functioning; and the post-war period was to show that, at any rate in relation to the conditions and tasks of a new situation, the planning system had come to exhibit defects of over-centralisation. Moreover, certain of the methods used to harness the operative independence of the enterprise to the purposes and stipulations of the plan both cramped initiative at lower levels and placed a premium on purely quantitative fulfilment. Although the principle of *Khozraschot*, as enunciated in the '20's,[1] still governed the rôle of enterprises and their relation to administrative bodies, at least in theory, their autonomy had come to be progressively hemmed-in by various plan-limits (restricting, *e.g.*, the size of their wage-bill and their material-inputs) and by the multiplication of target-norms laid down for them in the annual (operative) plan. The growing tendency (not an unnatural one) in the '30's, and still more in the years of war and post-war reconstruction, was for the planning authorities to resort to more detailed directives whenever things failed to go according to plan. (In the terminology of later criticism, they resorted increasingly to 'administrative measures', in dealing with defects of fulfilment, not to 'economic measures'.) When, for example, the stipulation of an output target in general terms (whether in value, or in terms of some physical unit such as weight or number of standard units) resulted in concentration by enterprises on certain lines or types or grades to the exclusion of others, the reaction was to add detailed stipulations about the 'assortment' of the output-target (*e.g.* by stipulating minimum quantities of such lines or types as tended to be ignored and accordingly to be in short supply). When output-targets tended to be fulfilled but without the requisite cost-reduction, a number of detailed 'qualitative norms', affecting inputs and productivity, were added to the targets laid down in the plan.

In the pre-war years of the 'big push' and of industrialising 'against the clock' under the lengthening shadows of war, these centralising tendencies were not inappropriate, and may even be regarded as inevitable. The problem was one of constructing heavy industry (including, as the decade advanced, a defence industry) at as

---

[1] At the start of the First Five Year Plan the principle was, indeed, reaffirmed by resolution of the 16th Party Congress in May 1929; and what had previously been the rights of Trusts were now extended to industrial enterprises generally (Cf. S. Mawrizki, *L'Industrie Lourde en Union Soviétique* (Geneva and Paris, 1961), 55-6.)

high a rate of growth as was consistent with maintaining certain consumption-standards for a growing industrial labour-force; of concentrating resources upon certain key sectors, industries and plants. The situation was not unlike that which confronts every economy in wartime. To maximise growth subject to certain insurmountable constraints was more important than counting the cost and economising on every rouble—except, of course, where failure to do so reduced the rate of growth achievable in the priority sectors. Not only was the system of priorities fairly easy, but the network of decisions to be taken was still a fairly simple one, at least by comparison with what it was to become two decades later. True, this complexity increased rapidly as the pre-war decade advanced, and problems of controlling plan-fulfilment became an increasing preoccupation. For example, the number of technical norms handled by the Second Five Year Plan, although showing an advance on anything handled previously, was little more than 300.[1] Yet in 1952 the annual plan mentioned as many as 5,000 products and their targets, and even as late as 1958 about 2,450;[2] while the method of balances had come to cover about 1,000 items[3] (compared with about half that number as the highest number reached in pre-war days). Meanwhile the number of separate enterprises by the '50's exceeded 200,000, and the number of items included in the official list of industrial nomenclature of 1960 reached 15,000 products; while the so-called organs of material-technical supply and sale handled the distribution of more than 10,000 items.[4]

Thus in the post-war period both the complexity of the decisions embraced by planning had greatly increased (by reason both of the growth of industry itself and the enhanced degree of detail which planning had taken under its wing) and also the nature of the situation with its attendant problems had changed. It had changed with the increasing emphasis laid on growth of consumption and on satisfying the needs of consumers (in the words of the 1961 Party Programme, "the growing resources of industry must be used more and more to meet fully all the requirements of Soviet people and to build and equip enterprises and establishments catering for the household and cultural needs of the population"). While growth was still a leading objective, it was now increasingly growth for con-

[1] Cf. S. Mawrizki, op. cit., 67. The number of plan-indices in the 1953 plan had doubled over 1940 (ibid., 77).
[2] Ibid., 110; I. A. Yevenko, Planning in the U.S.S.R. (Moscow, no date), 93.
[3] A figure of 1,600 for the Gosplans both of the Union and the Republics is given by V. Nemchinov, Ekonomiko-Matematicheskie Metodi i Modeli (Moscow, 1962), 69.
[4] Ibid., 69.

sumption within current planning horizons, and much less exclusively a circular process of expansion within the capital goods sector alone. The production of new products and innovation in quality and design became of equal importance to multiplication of the output of a given list of existing products; and for the former the over-centralised system of the immediate pre-war and post-war years was proving itself increasing unsuitable.

There was another and different respect in which the situation was changing. At the start of the industrialisation drive there were still plentiful reserves of labour in the countryside (and in the late '20's even some unemployed reserves in the towns). Industry could expand by drawing upon such surplus labour, attracted by employment opportunities and higher earnings into the rising industrial centres: a process that we have seen was helped by the mechanisation of agriculture. Two decades later, such reserves, if they still existed at all after staggering war-time losses of manpower, were very much smaller; and expansion of output had to come increasingly from increased production per man employed instead of from an increase in total employment (as we have seen that post-war plans have tried to budget for). Even more than before is a premium placed, accordingly, on technical innovation and economic efficiency; and while technical progress can be greatly aided by centralised research and design and pressure from above, it essentially depends upon constant initiative at the operational level, at the place of production.

To the defects of overcentralisation, particularly as regards the allocation of supplies of the most important 'funded' materials, was added certain distorting effects of the indices whereby quantitative fulfilment of plan-targets was expressed. In any case there was strong pressure upon any management to fulfil such quantitative indices as a so-called "success indicator". But to this influence was added that of substantial bonuses paid for plan fulfilment; the influence of which came to swamp that of the so-called Director's Fund which was financed out of profit[1] (especially as the latter was hedged about with conditions, such as the need for the plan-targets first to be fulfilled before payments could be made into the Fund, and bonus-payments from it were subject to a ceiling of five per cent of the total wage-bill). How various ways of measuring plan-targets could exercise a distorting effect is now a familiar story: when the target was expressed in weight, the plan was more easy to fulfil if things were made fewer but heavier than if made in larger quantities but light (stock examples being nails and bedsteads). If the

[1] See below, page 391 and note.

target were in length, this prompted the weaving of narrow cloth of simplest pattern; if it were in gross value (as was the common practice) it encouraged the production of 'material intensive' products: that is products whose final value was composed of a high proportion of materials or components purchased from other enterprises or industries compared to the value added within the enterprise in question (*e.g.* clothing made of expensive materials in preference to cheaper lines, tools made of high-grade steels, completely assembled motors or tractors rather than the separate sale of spare parts).[1] It was largely due to such distorting influences that planning in this period met with so great difficulty as it did in getting its 'assortment plan' fulfilled, and why certain types of shortage (e.g. of spare parts) were so stubborn and resistant to attempts at remedy.

To some extent these defects could be, and were, removed without any radical change in the structure of administration and planning. Nonetheless the question of how to regulate incentives to the enterprise and preservation of the old centralised structure of administration and planning were closely connected, and to change the answer to one question inevitably implied some change in the other. But there were defects of the highly centralised system that were more fundamental that those that have just been mentioned. First, it is clear that for its basic information about technical norms and productive capacity the planning authorities inevitably relied, in the main, upon enterprise managements themselves. The former might have ways of checking the data supplied to them by the latter (e.g. by comparison of various estimates and of these with results, comparison between similarly-situated enterprises, or by special *ad hoc* investigation); but such checks could be no more than partial, and the greater grew the complexity of the system the less capable was an overstrained planning personnel of checking the data supplied by 200,000 and more enterprises. Thus to some extent at least, and in many cases to a large extent, enterprises could influence the output-targets and norms that were set for themselves, and accordingly the amount and type of materials and equipment assigned to them. The traditional emphasis on quantitative fulfilment of output-targets engendered an atmosphere in which any management was under strong temptation to belittle the productive capacity of its enterprise,

---

[1] A contributor to *Pravda* in the 1962 discussion used these strong words of the gross production index: "We know many examples when enterprises in pursuit of plan fulfilment in gross terms worsen quality, turn out products in an assortment not corresponding to the needs of industry and the population. In pursuit of plan-production in gross production, unfinished production is frequently magnified." (V. Cherniavsky in *Pravda*, 19 October, 1962.)

to 'keep something in reserve' and to acquire for itself lenient 'norms' that were easy to fulfil. Whence the saying that "a wise director fulfils his plan perhaps 105 per cent. but never by 125 per cent.". It became customary, it seems, for the planning authorities, suspecting that data about norms and estimates of requirements coming up to them from below would err on the 'soft' side, to overcompensate for this by so-called 'tight' planning, which often became 'over-tight' planning. The result was not only to penalise the conscientious by imposing on them tasks that were beyond their ability to fulfil, but also to cause supply-bottlenecks and failures in deliveries, which disrupted the production-flow in the enterprises and industries depending on punctual delivery of the supplies in question; sometimes starting a chain-reaction of defaults all down the line. Stalin, indeed, at one time afforded a general justification for this situation and this practice by enunciating the view that under socialism it was proper that demand should always run ahead of supply.

Secondly, emphasis on purely quantitative achievement tends to conflict with improvement of quality and with the introduction of new products. Introduction of a new product is apt to involve time and trouble for a management—it involves experimentation and trial runs, possibly some re-tooling. A manager under pressure to fulfil an output-target as the prime consideration will grudge such delays and be likely to concentrate on uninterrupted production of the old and familiar product. By encouraging myopic concentration on short-term results at the expense of long-term (one symptom of which has been the characteristic *shturmovshchina*, or 'storming', in the final stages of a planning period), it may also bias managements against new and more efficient methods of production, since the process of introducing them is likely for a time to disrupt the current production-flow.

Thirdly, experience has shown that under the previous system there was too little economy of plant and equipment and too little concern at the enterprise level to maintain it adequately and to put it to the best use. Indeed, in later years there was increasing complaint about actual misuse of expensive plant and the keeping by enterprises of needless excess capacity. This is mainly because the size of so-called 'basic funds' (fixed capital) does not affect output-costs and has not been made to impinge upon the enterprise financially;[1] the provision of new equipment having been the subject of a

---

[1] Cf. R. G. Karagedov, "Pribyl kak ekonomicheskaia kategoria" in *Problemi Politicheskoi Ekonomii Sotsialisma* (Moscow 1960) ed. Y. A. Kronrod, 86, on "the great insufficiency of existing indices of profit turns out to be its extremely weak link with the utilised productive funds of enterprises".

free grant to the enterprise by the State. To this extent it may be regarded as a defect of the price-system rather than of centralisation *per se*. In fact the two things can scarcely be separated, since it is characteristic for a highly centralised system to rely on securing conformity with its designs by means of administrative orders rather than by 'economic measures' such as price-inducements. This is in fact what in the past has occurred.

Among the first public complaints of overcentralisation to be heard was in the joint resolution from the Central Committee of the Party and the Council of Ministers of 14 October 1954, which spoke of "exaggerated centralisation", chiefly with reference to the structural confusion, methods and swollen personnel of the administrative apparatus, rather than to planning methods.[1] After that date, however, steps began to be taken to reduce the number of output-targets written into the central plan, and to devolve responsibility for a large number of supply-allocations to the republican Gosplans. By 1958 the number of targets included in the central plan for major industrial products had been reduced to little more than 1000, compared with nearly 5000 six years before.[2] But this represented mainly a spreading of the load at top levels, and enhancing the importance of planning-work at republican levels as compared with the all-Union summit. It did not substantially affect the relationship between plan and enterprise, or between enterprises and their immediate administrative superiors, the Chief Administrations or Glavki of the appropriate Ministries. It remained an attempt to deal with problems of economic *functioning* by means of purely administrative re-shuffles.[3] The same is even true of the drastic decentralisation scheme of 1957 to which reference was made in the last chapter,[4] and to which the slogan of "bringing administration closer to production" was attached. This involved the abolition of nearly all the old industrial Ministries at the centre; in their stead responsibility for industrial administration was devolved to economic councils, or *Sovnarkhoze*, in each region (initially more than 100 in number), and the administrative departments, or *Glavki*, responsible for a particular branch of industry, were transferred to the regions to

---

[1] Cf. Mawrizki, *op. cit.*, 75–6. Subsequently to this resolution some 200 Ministerial *glavki* and 900 supply organisations were suppressed.

[2] *Ibid.*, 110; Yevenko, *op. cit.*, 93.

[3] The inclination to adopt this approach was still present some six or seven years later, to judge from a statement in *Pravda* of 1 November 1964: "It must be pointed out that among us the idea still exists that it is possible to solve complicated economic problems by administrative measures: all one has to do is to reorganise the apparatus, to merge two administrations into one, or on the contrary to divide one trust into two, and everything will be lovely. This is a most fallacious approach."

[4] Page 329 above.

become industrial sub-departments of the *Sovnarkhoz*.[1]   Meanwhile, the organisations responsible for organising supplies or sales for a branch of industry (the *glavsnab* and *glavsbyt*) were retained at the national or republican level, being subordinated to Gosplan of either the Union or the Republic (later to the Republic), with branches of these organisations at the regional *Sovnarkhoze*. As an exception to this in the case of consumers' goods, the selling organisations were subordinated about the same time to the republican Ministries of Trade (with the intention thereby of submitting them to consumers' influence and to the needs of the retail network instead of subjecting them to the influence of producers' interests as had too often happened previously).

Yet the situation of the individual enterprise was little affected by these administrative changes, except possible *de facto*. Their discretion with regard to investment expenditure was slightly, but only slightly, increased (by raising somewhat the ceiling on the size of small investment expenditures they could incur on their own responsibility and out of their own funds). The system of centralised supply-allocations remained substantially unchanged, although in the case of consumers' goods the list of things falling within the category of 'decentralised supplies', open to distribution by direct contract between enterprises or between an enterprise and a trading organisation, was somewhat widened. Certain changes were also made, in the case of light industry and consumers' goods, with regard to the form in which output targets were expressed. Gross output was changed to net output, or 'value added' (*normativnaia stoimost obrabotki*), as the basis for estimating plan-fulfilment over a large part of Soviet light industry in 1957, and later (in 1964 and 1965) this change was extended to the whole of textiles, shoes, printing, artificial leather and fruit-canning, and more widely adopted by a number of Sovnarkhoze such as the Middle Volga and Donbas.[2] Moreover, from July 1959 onwards gross output was generally abandoned, with the exception of a few industries, as the basis of premiums to managerial or technical staffs.[3]

[1] The decree of the Supreme Soviet of February 1957 in its preamble declared: "It is impossible to direct production in concrete fashion and efficaciously from a few Ministries and specialised Administrations on an all-Union scale.   The centre of gravity of effective direction of enterprises and workshops must be transferred down to administrations in the economic regions."   The two economic Ministries preserved from liquidation at the national level were the Union Ministry of Central Electrical Stations and that of the Defence Industries.   The operative date for the changeover was to be 1 July 1957.

[2] *Planovoe Khoziaistvo*, March 1964, 93.

[3] Cf. A. Bachurin in *Voprosi Ekonomiki*, 1959, No. 11, 82.   Fulfilment of so-called "qualitative targets" (e.g. cost-reduction) was substituted.

The subsequent, and in many ways more interesting, stage in discussion and reform opened in *Pravda* on 9 September 1962 with a much-quoted article by Professor E. Liberman, entitled "Plan, Profit, Premia", in which there was outlined a radically new measure of independence for the enterprise, coupled with a new incentive system for the enterprise. "The proposed system will free central planning from petty tutelage over enterprises, from costly attempts to influence production, not economically but by administrative measures. The enterprise itself knows best and can discover its potentialities." The article had opened by declaring that "it is essential to find a sufficiently simple and at the same time soundly-based solution to one of the most important problems posed by the Programme of the C.P.S.U.: to construct a system of planning and estimating the work of enterprises so that they shall have a lively interest in fulfilling the plan-targets to the maximum, in introducing new technique and best-quality products, in a word in the maximum effectiveness of production". Firstly, it was proposed that the plan for an enterprise should stipulate only the general volume of production and time-limits for delivery. Secondly, there should be the maximum use of direct links between suppliers and consumers; and on the basis of this (and of the global plan-target) "all remaining indices", or targets and coefficients (labour productivity, number of workers, wage-bill, investments and new technique), should be left to the enterprise to determine. Thirdly, a single incentive fund, for payment of premia to its personnel, should be established on the basis of payments into this fund in proportion to its net income, or "balance-sheet profit": moreover, in proportion to profit as a ratio to the size of its "basic and turnover funds" (capital). Thus net income, or profit, would become a "synthetic index" of enterprise-achievement, replacing the previous multiplicity of indices, while at the same time, by relating this to the size of capital employed, it would provide the inducement previously lacking for economical use of plant and equipment and circulating capital.

There followed a series of vigorous discussion-articles in the columns of *Pravda* in the course of the ensuing weeks, with a considerable measure of support for the proposed scheme from those with practical experience of industry. At the same time it met with some doubts and opposition from professional economists of the older school. The immediate upshot was a period of experimentation with the proposed measures. In particular, two associations (*obedinenie*, or *firmi*) of enterprises in the clothing industry, called *Bolshevichka* and *Mayak* in Moscow and Gorki respectively, adopted the practice of devising their own production plans on the basis of direct advance-contracts with retail shops. Within limits selling-prices could be varied by agreement between factory and retailer; and bonuses on wages were payable out of profits. This experiment was deemed a success, at any rate in leading to production of improved quality that found favour with consumers; and the concerns in question received a good deal of favourable publicity.

The next stage came two years later when the discussion was re-opened in the columns of *Pravda*, this time by an academician and automation-expert V. Trapeznikov on 17 August 1964. "It is time," he wrote, "to abandon obsolete forms of economic direction, resting on indices and directives, and to transfer to a more simple, efficacious and cheaper form of regulating the work of enterprises. This regulation should be such that the personnel of enterprises are economically interested in developing their work in a direction that is advantageous to the national economy." The index that best achieved this end was, in his opinion, profit: to choose this as the main index of achievement by an enterprise would greatly simplify the problem of economic regulation; and its adoption should be combined with more flexibility of price, especially in the case of new products or those of superior quality, and also with the adoption of an interest-rate on capital.[1] Writing in support a month later (on 20 September) Liberman returned to his own proposals and stressed that what was at issue was "not a reform of indices, but a reform of the relations between enterprises and the national economy".[2]

This time there was an extension of the *Bolshevichka* and *Mayak* experiment to some 400 textile, clothing, leather and boot and shoe factories in ten or more leading cities of the Union. These were said to include all, or at least a major proportion of, clothing, textile and boot and shoe enterprises in Moscow, Leningrad, Gorki, Kiev,

[1] The scale of incentive-payments originally proposed by Liberman related these to the *rate* of profit on capital. But his suggested scale, as it stood, was defective (for example, of two enterprises with the same *total* profit the one with the larger capital would receive the larger incentive-payment). It would rather look as though in the later schemes the method had been adopted of levying a charge or tax proportioned to capital, and relating incentive to profit *net* of such a tax. This is the method adopted in the Czechoslovak and East German schemes, also in Poland. However, in his later discussion-contribution of 1964 Liberman still refers to his scheme for bonus (e.g. in the form of a percentage addition to wages) as related to the profit-*rate*, and rising with it.

[2] With reference to foreign comments on "the profit motive", he wrote: "Our profit, if one starts from the fact that prices correctly express average expenses of production for the branch [of industry], is nothing else than the result of increase in the productivity of social labour concretised in money form. That is why we are able, in basing ourselves on profitability, to encourage real effectiveness of production. But with that said, encouragement is not enrichment. . . ."

Kharkov, Odessa, Minsk, Lvov, Riga, Talinn and Vilnius, as well as some associations and factories in Central Asia and Transcaucasia.[1] This remains a small sample of all the industry of the country. But unless some dramatic reversal of present trends occurs, the signs are that this is a model of the future that will be extended further, even beyond the boundaries of consumer goods industries.[2] In some neighbouring countries changes in the same direction are already being introduced on a more general scale: for example, the scheme of Professor Ota Šik in Czechoslovakia, in some ways even bolder (since the enterprise will plan its production only within the framework of a long-term plan), and changes in contemplation or in being in East Germany and in Poland. Their experience, if it is successful, will surely not be without influence on Soviet practice.

Towards the end of September 1965, in a report to the Central Committee of the Party, the Chairman of the Council of Ministers (Kosygin) announced the introduction of new measures for extending the independence of enterprises and changing the system of economic incentives along 'Liberman'-lines. This was to be done simultaneously with a reversion to supervision by 20 central Ministries. Enterprises were to be given merely a general production target expressed in terms of *marketed* output (with limits on their total wage-funds and stipulated payments from and to the State Budget). Given this, they were to have full responsibility for working out their detailed output-plan and other indices. Profitability was to be established as the main index or criterion of efficient performance, and an incentive-fund, financed by proportionate deductions from profit, was to be made the primary source for bonus-payments to workers in each enterprise. No mention was yet made, however, of superseding or curtailing the system of centralised supply-allocation; although an increase of direct contractual relations between enterprises would seem to be the logical accompaniment of greater independence of enterprises regarding their output-programmes.

There remains to mention the increasing vogue since 1956 of various mathematical methods, in economic theory and practice,

[1] Cf. *Ekon. Gazeta*, 28 Oct. 1964.

[2] Several engineering plants were mentioned as subjects of experimental introduction of new methods involving an "enlarged rôle for profit in the system of indices for judging the work of enterprises" (moreover "balance-sheet profit related to total fixed and circulating capital") in a Report of the Commission on Economic Experimentation adopted by a meeting of Scientific Councils of the Academy of Sciences in February 1965 (*Ekonomicheskaia Gazeta*, 3 March 1965). Elsewhere in the report reference was made to experimentation with "new indices of production that reflect utility-characteristics of products", i.e. quality-indices related to use-value.

which we have seen had been for some time under a cloud. This was associated, of course, with the increasing use of electronic computers and computer-programming techniques, in both planning and administration. It took a number of forms. First, one should mention in this connection the official sanction accorded, after long-drawn-out discussion, to the use of a standard 'coefficient of effectiveness' of investment (or what is its inverse, a 'period of recoupment') in choosing between alternative technical variants in investment projects. These had been used for some time in the practice of 'project-making' departments in railway transport and in electrification. But in 1960 their general usage was sanctioned (indeed encouraged) by the issue of a booklet of standard methods by Gosplan and the Academy of Sciences jointly.[1]   Secondly, there was the increasing attention paid to linear programming techniques along the lines pioneered by Kantorovitch in 1939 (but for many years ignored, with the possible exception, again, of transport problems) with his "method of decisive multipliers".   It is well-known that the search for 'optimal' methods of production is associated with sets of 'shadow prices' which when used show the 'optimal' method as the least-cost, or most profitable, result.   Accordingly the discussion and use of such techniques has had implications for the inconclusive discussion about price-policy and the need for price-reform (which most participants have agreed to be urgently necessary, even if they have been unable to agree about the correct solution).   Thus Kantorovitch has himself drawn conclusions for price-policy, as has also Novozhilov.[2]   Thirdly, there is the renewed interest, at the theoretical level, in the use of dynamic economic models, as witnessed by the publication in 1962 of a work on mathematical methods and models by the late Academician Nemchinov,[3] in which explicit reference was made to the early attempts in the '20's to build an "inter-branch balance of productive links", or input-output table, to

[1] *Tipovaia Metodika Opredelenia Ekonomicheskoi Effectivnosti Kapitalnikh Vlozhenii i Novoi Tekhniki v Narodnom Khoziaistve S.S.S.R.* (Gosplanizdat 1960). Cf. a description of this by the present writer in "Notes on Recent Economic Discussion", *Soviet Studies*, Vol. XII, No. 4, April 1961, 342 seq.   There was to be no uniform coefficient, however: it was to be allowed to vary somewhat as between sectors.   In Poland and in Hungary, *per contra*, a uniform coefficient has been adopted.

[2] Cf. A. V. Kantorovitch, *Ekonomicheskii Raschot Nailushchego Ispolzovania Resursov* (Moscow 1960), esp. 142 seq.; V. V. Novozhilov, "Zakon Stoimosti i Planovoe Tsenoobrazovanie" in *Problemi Primenenia Matematiki v Sotsialisticheskoi Ekonomike*, sbornik II (Leningrad University, 1965), 9–55; V. V. Novozhilov "Teoria Trudovoi Stoimosti i Matematika" in *Voprosi Ekonomiki*, 1964, No. 12, 96–110.

[3] V. S. Nemchinov, *Ekonomiko-Matematicheskie Metodi i Modeli* (Moscow 1962), 410.   The edition was one of 6,000 copies, and was published by Sotsekgiz.

its influence upon Leontief and to the pioneering work of Barenholz that we have mentioned above.

Fourthly, increasing use has been made of more mathematically refined input-output techniques in conjunction with the traditional method of material balances, of which something has again been said above. In 1959 there was constructed an input-output table by the Central Statistical Office, covering 83 industrial branches (in value terms) and 157 product-items (in both physical units and in mean realisation prices). In 1961 came the first all-Union planning input-output table, designed in connection with the annual plan for 1962.[1] It is too early to say what part these methods can play in the methodology of planning and to what extent precisely they can assist in any of its essential problems. One difficulty in the use of these more sophisticated methods (apart from the question of technical coefficients touched on above) is the difficulty of information and of aggregation: namely, that information does not necessarily reach planners in a form suitable for using such techniques in the process of plan-construction. This should not be irremediable, but reform may take some time. It is obvious that the complexity of an input-output matrix tends to increase as the square of the number of its items; which is a reason why a fairly high degree of aggregation may be necessary in defining product-groups or industries for this purpose. Yet the basic production-data at the level of industries and enterprises will have a high degree of particularity (or of *dis*aggregation in the current phraseology); this applying both to the crucial input-output coefficients *and* to the destination of the product (*i.e.* to what other plants or industries it is supplied and for what purposes). At some higher level (*e.g.* of the industrial branch or the *Sovnarkhoz*) these data will be aggregated in some form (*e.g.* into product groups), and in this form passed on to the higher planning authorities. But it may be that this form of aggregation is not of the precise form, either as regards coefficients or product-destinations, as is required for an input-output table.[2] And if the higher level is not itself in possession of the detailed data from the lower level, it cannot re-work the raw material of the latter to its own specification (*e.g.* when targets are changed). The fact that the information was not available to Gosplan in suitable forms was certainly an obstacle to the use of matrix techniques for some time. But the difficulty should be remediable, in large part at least; and measures have been subsequently in train to

[1] V. S. Nemchinov, *op. cit.*, 70.
[2] Moreover, there is the crucial difficulty again that the "averaged" coefficient will be relative to the product-assortment at the level at which the averaging is done.

refashion the forms of classification of data from the enterprise upwards so as to suit it to the requirements of such methods.[1]

This relates to the choice of a self-consistent plan. But there are numerous possible self-consistent plans; and there remains the problem of selecting the plan that is (in some sense) 'optimal' from among the range of available consistent plans. This is, of course, a distinct problem in its own right and one to which increasing attention is being paid—much greater attention than was possible, or perhaps relevant, at an earlier stage when growth was the ruling preoccupation. But at present one cannot say that, apart from the application of linear programming techniques to particular problems, much progress has been made towards it solution.

[1] A mathematical economist has recently stated the requirements, in general terms, as follows: "The elaboration of a system of interconnected economic-mathematical models, the mathematical means for their processing and the optimum solution of economic planning problems is one of the most important tasks now facing Soviet economic science. . . . The drawing up of a unified system of economic planning information is one of the top-priority tasks among the broad range of problems involved in improving economic administration and planning. This field reveals acute conflicts between the requirements of exact administration and planning and the outdated forms of document-handling and communication." (N. Fedorenko in *Pravda*, 17 January 1965.)

CHAPTER FIFTEEN

THE FINANCIAL PLAN AND THE FINANCIAL SYSTEM

I

We have seen that the economic plans with which the planning system is concerned essentially consist of production programmes and the crucial equations or balances which mediate between policy-objectives and real data in the course of planning are material balances, expressing a quantitative relationship between real things, whether these be commodities or factors of production. Hence the kernel of any plan is the Production Plan, which is a complex of output-programmes for all the main products of the economic system, embracing real expenditure and real product, input and output in each case. Far from being just an incidental collection of programmes, this forms an integrated system in the sense that the individual output-quotas have been dovetailed into one another by the crucial method of material balances that we have described. As backbone to this part of the plan is the Plan of Capital Construction : the programme of construction of new factory buildings and extensions and large-scale renewals. But the plans do not consist only of a Production Plan, even if this is in a genetic sense primary. Nor is the method by which plans are integrated and tested for consistency concerned only with material balances. Alongside the Production Plan stands the Financial Plan, within whose sphere falls a number of crucial equations or balances which need to be expressed in terms of money-prices (as do also many of the aggregates in the Production Plan, when dissimilar material things are to be added together). Moreover, several of these balances expressed in terms of money are crucial ones for the purposes of that " synthetic planning " of which we spoke in the previous chapter. Within this sphere falls the formation of prices. Included in it are such constituents as a Credit Plan and a Cash Plan and also the Budget.

An immediate question which here arises in some people's minds is why so elaborate a Financial Plan should be necessary. If Soviet economy has gone so far as to plan production directly—to attempt to co-ordinate the movements of various parts of the economy by establishing direct production-links, independently of a market, as though the economy were a single enterprise—why should it be necessary for planning to concern itself with a financial superstructure as well? It can be admitted that some unit of account will be needed in order to equate heterogeneous things, and that accordingly aggregates will have to be expressed in a money-form, without accepting the necessity for such pieces of financial apparatus as credit and balanced budgets, or for the emergence of a specific " financial problem " as something distinct from real problems concerning relations of production. Is not the appearance of such things in Soviet economy a surprising carry-over from capitalist conditions into a situation where they are so much useless baggage? Among Soviet economists themselves there were some in the early '30's who spoke of the approaching decease of money, and the early possibility of organising directly the exchange of commodities as a corollary of the direct planning of production.[1] There were those who declared that " planning is a method for the complete abolition of credit ".[2] There are, again, others who, approaching the matter from an opposite direction, expect that a solution of financial problems must in some sense take precedence over the successful allocation of productive resources, and that certain financial principles, conditioning expenditure to revenue raised, will need to be observed as much in a socialist as in a capitalist economy, if economic chaos is not to intervene.[3]

This latter point of view ignores the very simple fact that, when the allocation of productive resources is controlled directly by a planning authority, it is not necessary to mobilise financial resources (e.g. by taxation or savings) as a *pre-condition* of mobilising and allocating the real resources required. The question whether the community can afford to build a Dnieper dam or another trans-Siberian railway is simply a question as to whether the manpower and resources required for doing so exist and can be spared from

[1] Stalin in his report to the Seventeenth Party Congress tartly dismissed these views as " leftist petit-bourgeois chatter " : the talk of Don Quixotes lacking "the most elementary sense of reality", who do not realise what "a complicated and difficult business " is " a direct exchange of products " about which they talk. (*Leninism*, 1940 ed., 512.) Cf. also *Economika Sovetskoi Torgovli* (1934), 17-23, 389-94.

[2] Kozlov in *Problemi Economiki*, 1930, No. 2, 84-5, cit. A. Z. Arnold, *Banks, Credit and Money in Soviet Russia*, 362.

[3] A naïve example of this view is the question that is sometimes asked as to the sources from which so much money was raised to make the large investment expenditures of the Five Year Plans possible ; the implication being that the mobilising of the money was the prior condition of mobilising the real resources for construction work under the Plans.

other uses and are mobile enough to be transferred. It is only in a capitalist economy, under which production is governed by "automatic" responses to price-movements on a market, that there is truth in the contention that financial resources have to be raised and spent as a prior condition of influencing production. But in a planned economy the notion that financial problems have priority over problems of production clearly has the cart standing in front of the horse.

The opposite view, that in a planned economy there need be no financial problem at all, ignores the fact that the payment of incomes in the form of money, with the free disposal of this income[1] as its corollary, requires the existence of a retail market for consumer goods, in which commodities are sold against money without discrimination to consumers who are free to pick and choose what they will buy and to distribute their money as they please. The existence of a market of this kind obviously precludes any centralised and direct organisation of the distribution of consumer goods to the final consumer (e.g. by systems of rationed supplies). From the consumers' angle the retail market remains a "free market". On this depends a very important consideration : namely that the state of this market—the relation between the volume of purchases at any given set of retail prices and the supplies available—will be powerfully affected by the circumstances attending the circulation of money income : by the size of the flow of incomes in the first place and by what happens to those incomes after they have been received. Any acceleration of this flow, unless it is in some way intercepted and diverted before it reaches the retail market, will increase the pressure on that market from the side of demand. Unless this increased flow is closely geared either to an increased flow of consumer goods from the factories into the shops or else to measures for intercepting this income flow (e.g. by direct taxes, savings deposits and savings loans[2]) before it reaches the market, the stability of the retail market will be disturbed. From the experience of wartime and post-war conditions most of us to-day have become familiar with the consequences for the market of such heightened pressure : consequences which express themselves as shop-shortages, patchy distribution of short-supplies and queues. It is the problems attending this circular flow of money income—a

---

[1] So far as purchase of consumer goods is concerned.
[2] Or alternatively by an upward adjustment of retail prices : a matter to which we shall return later.

flow which starts with payments from the State to individual citizens and then returns (unless it be hoarded) by a variety of routes to the State once more—which form the kernel of the financial problem ; and it is the fact that the volume of this flow and the precise route by which it eventually returns to the State are not matters of indifference to the production and distribution of goods which gives this problem the importance it continues to have. Evidently any fundamental change in the Production Plan is likely to affect this flow : it may change the amounts paid out in wages or the amount of consumers' goods passing from the factories into the shops, or both ; and these changes will require that certain financial adjustments are made to enable the monetary flow to fit in with the structure of production. In other words, the Financial Plan will need to be appropriately geared to the Production Plan and the gearing altered to conform with any fundamental alteration in the latter.

The question may still be asked why the payment of incomes in money, with a flexible retail market as its corollary, should be regarded as a necessary accompaniment of a planned economy. If it be true that the financial problem with its complexities hinges upon this feature of the economic system, why should not the latter be dispensed with as a source of needless complication ? Why not introduce instead that direct exchange and distribution of consumer goods of which some Soviet economists at one time spoke ? The answer which I think would be given in the U.S.S.R. to this question is that under the conditions which Marx described as the first stage of Socialism, although the profit-motive as a regulator of production and investment has been banished and the inequalities dependent on property incomes have been abolished, the existence of wage-differences according to the kind and amount of work performed necessarily plays a rôle in production : a rôle in work-incentives and in regulating the supply of labour to different grades and industries. If wage-payments are to play this rôle, it is in practice essential that a system of wage-payments in money (with its corollary of freedom in spending) should prevail, in order to give wage-differences for various categories of work the maximum of uniformity. It might be argued that wage-differences could quite well co-exist with a system of paying wages in kind : income differences taking the form of different allocations of some standard ration. But in practice such a system would have the very strong disadvantage that, in view of variations in individual tastes, such differences would have a widely unequal significance for different workers, while the absence of any freedom of choice in spending would seriously diminish the strength of the incentive which a wage-income offered. This was a conclusion which the experience both of War Communism and of the rationing period in the early '30's would seem to have established beyond dispute.

But while the financial problem can be said to have its roots in this crucial feature of Soviet economy—the part played by wage-differences among the incentives to production—this is not the whole of the matter. We shall see that money and its attendant problems of money-costing and pricing play an important part in economic accounting, and hence, in the relation between planning and the enterprise *qua* operational unit. The importance of this aspect of the financial problem is expressed in the frequency with which reference is made in Soviet planning literature to the necessity for the famous *Khozraschet* (economic accounting) and its attendant " discipline of the rouble ". Yet it remains true that what is termed " the balance of income and expenditure of the population " and its relation to the current saleable supply of consumers' goods and services form the crux of the problem of financial planning in Soviet economy ; and, as Soviet writers have indicated, this relation constitutes one of the essential balances with which " the synthetic method of planning the economy " is concerned.[1]

II

The crucial point at which the Financial Plan is geared to the Production Plan is the translation of the basic costing-data about production programmes into money terms. Such costing, as we have seen, is initially in real or material terms : a calculation of the input of various productive factors (labour-power, raw materials, wear and tear of machinery) involved in a given output. When this is translated into money, in terms of prices of these productive factors, we have the familiar statement of cost in the generalised form that a certain output-programme y will involve the expenditure of x roubles, xa of this going in wages, xb in raw materials, etc. This constitutes the basic " planned cost " of a given output (after

---

[1] Margolin on " The Balance of Money Income and Expenditure of the Population " in *Plan. Khoz.*, 1937, No. 11–12, 103, 114 ; cit. Bettelheim, *op. cit.*, 116, 125. This crucial balance, says this writer, " serves as a method of verifying the extent to which the planning of the volume of money-wage funds corresponds to the funds of commodities for individual consumption."

due allowance has been included for depreciation of plant[1], and certain overheads such as administration have been included). From this basis there is built up the system of prices of output, on the one hand, and a Credit Plan and a Cash Plan, on the other hand, governing the relations between the banking system and productive organisations. Every industrial enterprise has to draw up a financial statement of its activities in this generalised form as well as the detailed items of its production programme expressed in material terms.

The addition to this " planned cost " of a small margin of profit, known as the " planned profit " and reckoned at varying rates as a percentage of the " planned cost "[2], produces a figure which constitutes the selling price of the product of the enterprise.[3] This latter[4] is the price at which the enterprise is credited for its output when this has been completed and delivered to the whole-sale-distributive organisation. A similar procedure is then in turn

[1] Cf. " Part of the value of fixed capital expended in the production process is restored out of the value of the finished product in repair of amortisation. In calculating the prime cost of production there is included a determined percentage of the value of fixed capital depending on the term of service of that capital. When the product is sold, these percentages of the value of fixed capital are accumulated and form an amortisation fund." (Prof. N. N. Rovinsky, Gosudarstvennii Biudjet S.S.S.R. (1944), 64.) Some figures for 1932 show that in heavy industry the percentages of prime costs which consisted of wages, raw materials and amortisation were respectively 43·5, 37·4 and 6 per cent. In the food-processing industries the corresponding percentages were 15·5, 69·9 and 1·9 per cent. In mining wages composed about 68 per cent. (D. I. Chernomordik, Ekonomicheskaia Politika S.S.S.R., 224.) For industry as a whole the proportion of " administrative-management and other non-productive expenses " in prime costs were stated as being 11·8 per cent. in 1932 and 8·3 per cent. in 1936. (S. Turetsky in Plan., Nov. 22, 1936, 38.) Cf. also for the method of reckoning prime cost, Materiali k Postroeniu Systemi Pokazatalei Ucheta Nar. Khoz. S.S.S.R. (1932), 26, 37–8.

[2] The variations of the percentage are apparently to a large extent influenced by the rate of turnover.

[3] When factories are grouped in Trusts, the Trust is generally the unit for assessing this " planned cost ". This means that the figure will be some kind of average for the different factories controlled by the Trust. It is then left to the discretion of the Trust how to reallocate this planned cost (and any resulting profit) among the different factories under its control according to the special circum-stances of each. (Cf. Bettelheim, op. cit., 204–5 ; W. B. Reddaway in The Banker, Oct., 1941, 51.) In other words, individual plants are not generally allowed to retain any differential rent arising from superior location or equipment.

[4] Actually what is known as the wholesale price at which the product passes from the industrial enterprise includes the Turnover Tax (about which something will be said below). This wholesale price includes planned cost + planned profit + Turnover Tax ; the latter being paid by the industrial enterprise. To be complete the statement above should be qualified in this sense. For simplicity it has been left in the text without this qualification.

As regards transport costs, in the case of some commodities these are included and of others excluded (being carried to the account of the buyer). The latter applies to the majority of things bought and consumed by industry itself (oil and cement being exceptions) ; while almost all goods of " individual consumption have selling-prices ' free of station of consignment ' ". (S. Turetsky in Plan. Khoz., 1939, No. 12, 107.)

applied to the distributive organisation, which receives goods for which it is debited, and after incurring certain costs of handling and storing eventually sells them again at whatever is the pre-determined selling-price at that stage in the journey of the goods towards the consumer.

It will be clear that the consequence of this system will be to make the actual profit which the enterprise finally receives vary inversely with the level of the *actual cost* it has incurred relatively to the planned cost. In this respect the situation has some analogy with a war-time contract between a government department and a con-tractor in our own country of the type known as the " target cost contract ", based on pre-costing of the order. If the enterprise manages to carry out its production-programme with a greater economy of means than the plan has budgeted for, and hence to reduce its actual expenditure below the planned cost, it will be left with a margin greater than the planned profit.[1] If, on the other hand, it carries out its programme with less efficiency than the Plan had stipulated, its actual cost will come out higher than the planned cost, and it will not succeed in realising its profit-margin as planned, and it may even make a loss. The result of this will be to provide the enterprise with an incentive to maximum efficiency, and to penalise it for being less efficient than it had been expected to be. The use of such profit as it retains is carefully regulated ; part of it being taxed into the Budget (which means in fact that part of the benefit of any economy it makes accrues to the community as a whole for purposes that are financed out of the Budget), part being placed to reserve with the Industrial Bank (Prombank) for purposes of capital development within the industry, and the remaining part paid into what was formerly known as "the Director's Fund", for use at the discretion of the enterprise for certain named purposes, which include bonuses to the staff, and welfare facilities and housing for its employees.[2] It is significant that a much larger proportion of any extra profit (over the planned profit) may be devoted to this latter purpose, beneficial to the members of the enterprise itself,

---

[1] Cf. N. N. Rovinsky, *op. cit.* 65–6.

[2] One half of the Director's Fund was required by law to be spent on workers' housing. Other objects listed in the decree (of April 19, 1936) under which the Fund was established were: "improvements in other aspects of cultural-living services for workers, engineer-technical workers' and office workers in the given enterprise (crêches, kindergartens, clubs, dining-rooms, etc.)", "individual pre-miums for workers in the establishment who have distinguished themselves", "supplementary capital works", and on "supplementary rationalisation measures and technical propaganda". The expenditure of monies in the fund was to be decided in consultation with the factory committee of the trade union. (*Spravochnik Sovetskovo Rabotnika*, 746–7.) After the war this was renamed the Enterprise Fund.

than in the case of the minimum planned profit.[1] The retention of extra profit, as reward of efficiency, accordingly plays the rôle of a collective incentive to the personnel of each factory and each enterprise " to beat the Plan ". It should be emphasised, however, that as a financial incentive this has a very restricted and special character. With both its output and the sale-price of that output fixed in advance by the Plan, the enterprise can do nothing to improve its financial position by restricting output : on the contrary, to restrict output will reduce its receipts and hence any profit to be left in its hands. Here the enterprise is harnessed firmly within the shafts of the Plan.[2] The sole way in which it can improve its financial position, and hence the sole direction in which profit can operate as an incentive, is by an economy in its consumption of productive resources. In the language of economists, it has no inducement to " act monopolistically ", even if it would for long be permitted to reduce its output : it can only make the best of its financial position by " acting quasi-competitively " (as some economists have used this term).[3]

If industrial enterprises lacked any financial resources of their own, and all their debit and credit payments took the form of bank-book entries in a system of universal overdrafts from the banks to industry, the deterrent of suffering a loss if they were inefficient would obviously lose its sting. If an enterprise made a loss, this would be equivalent merely to a piling up of book-debits against it in the bank : the loss would figure as an increased indebtedness to the banks ; and in the degree that these debts became frozen, all industrial losses would be met by a virtual subsidy *via* the banks. This is in fact what tended to happen on a fairly large scale in

---

[1] Just prior to the war these proportions were respectively 2 per cent. and 50 per cent. During the war payments into the Director's Fund were discontinued. (M. l. Bogolepov, *The Soviet Financial System*, 12–13.)

[2] Enterprises have been able, however, in some cases to increase their profits by altering the proportions in which they produced different "lines" of a commodity, in so far as some yielded more profit than others. This problem was one that received a good deal of attention in the later '30's; and led in particular to a greater emphasis on definitions of quality in plans and on plan-fulfilment as regards quality and assortment.

[3] Mr. J. Marschak in an introduction to *Management in Russian Industry and Agriculture* makes the surprising assertion that this system operates monopolistically and that cost-economies are "withheld from consumers" (xxi, xxiv). Needless to say, the sharing of economies between State and enterprise operates only within the planning period of one year. If, on the other hand, Mr. Marschak intends this assertion to refer to the size of the revenue which accrues to the Budget from the Turnover Tax, he is ignoring the fact that the relation between cost and retail price is necessarily determined by the rate of investment (and hence need have no connection at all with any "monopoly policy") for reasons which are discussed below.

certain industries for a time during the First Five Year Plan.[1] Moreover, if industry had no funds at all over the use of which it had some discretion, the opportunities for it to display any initiative would be much reduced. The system has accordingly been developed since the early '30's whereby each enterprise finances its " normal " level of expenditure on current production out of its own working capital ; and only expenditure needs in excess of this normal are allowed to be the occasion of credit from the State Bank. Under this arrangement industries subject to seasonal fluctuations either of productive activity or of expenditures on raw materials are most reliant on credit for meeting their current out- lays, and there is a large variation between industries in this respect ; food industries, for example, meeting nearly a half of their annual needs for working capital out of credits, and heavy industry only 5 or 6 per cent.[2]

When the annual plan budgets for an increased output programme for an enterprise, and hence an increased rate of current expendi- ture, an addition to its working capital is allowed for as part of the plan of capital investments : an addition based on a calculation of what is known as its " normative ". This " normative " is reckoned in units of a day's production of the enterprise ; and the essential determinant of its size (apart from such things as the dates and intervals of delivery of raw materials and of despatch and pay- ment for finished production) is the " period of production ", or length of the productive cycle, between the input of materials and of labour and the emergence of the final product. The longer this is, and the larger the proportion of materials and labour expended which have to be used at a relatively early stage of production, the higher the " normative " of working capital needed (measured in

[1] Since 1936 subsidies have been terminated for all branches of industries. Up to that date some subsidies continued to be given to certain plants in heavy industry, largely as a legacy of the position in the 1920's when heavy industry was backward and the cost of production at any rate in older plants was uneconomically high. But so long as subsidies continued, it meant that the price at which other industries used their products did not even cover prime costs in the marginal plants.

[2] Cf. V. Sitnin and Z. Sitkin in *Plan. Khoz.*, 1940, No. 2, 23. The complaint was made, in the case of heavy industry, that the smallness of its reliance on bank credit reduced the possibility of the State Bank exercising a control over the industry's expenditure and hence over the detailed implementation of the Plan, thereby weakening the " discipline of the rouble ". Accordingly in 1939 certain engineering enterprises were transferred on to a new system of credit which rendered bank credits a larger source of working capital for them. The intention was thereby to enforce measures to reduce the abnormal stocks of semi-finished products in the hands of engineering firms. To this end it was arranged that 20 per cent. of the value of unfinished stocks and 50 per cent. of the value of finished products in stock should be covered by bank-credit. (*Ibid.*, 23, 25–7 ; N. N. Rovinsky, *op. cit.*, 111.)

production-days, or relatively to current production) will be.[1] These funds of working capital in the possession of an enterprise are supplemented by a proportion of any profit accruing to it ; and the bank keeps the loan account of an enterprise separately from the account in which the latter's own capital is entered. Sums may not be transferred from this second account to meet indebtedness to the bank except with the consent of the industrial undertaking concerned : a provision which has been described as being " of great importance for strengthening *khozraschet* and the creation of an interest for an undertaking in the accumulation of its own means ".[2]

The additional need of an enterprise for working capital in the quarter or quarters of the year when its volume of production or its expenditures under the Plan are relatively high[3] is met by what are known as " planned credits ", which compose the Credit Plan of the State Bank. These credits are not only confined to financing purposes provided for in the Production Plan, but they are earmarked for specific expenditures involved in the planned costing of the output programme ; and the bank is charged with the duty of controlling the use of such credits to ensure that they are not used for purposes other than those for which they have been

[1] Cf. N. N. Rovinsky, *op. cit.*, 102–9 ; also S. G. Strumilin, *K Perestroike Sovetskovo Ucheta*, 22–6. The essentials of this system were introduced by a decree of STO of July 23, 1931. Prof. Rovinsky illustrates this calculation by the following example of two sorts of production A and B. (*Ibid.*, 105) :

Days of Productive Cycle	Daily Expenditures A	B	Value of a Unit of the Commodity					
			Beginning of Day A	B	End of Day A	B	Mean of Day A	B
1	20	4	0	0	20	4	10	2
2	4	6	20	4	24	10	22	7
3	4	8	24	10	28	18	26	14
4	2	12	28	18	30	30	29	24
	30	30	—	—	—	—	21·8	11·8

In A the coefficient of growth is 73 per cent., and for B 39 per cent. Hence the normative is $\frac{73}{100} \times 4$ for A and $\frac{39}{100} \times 4$ for B.

[2] N. S. Burmistrov, *Ocherki Tekhniko-Ekonomicheskovo Planirovania Promishlennosti*, 169. Under what was known as the " contocorrenta " system, which existed for a short time prior to the decree of June 23, 1931 (which separated these two accounts), such transfers could be made.

[3] " In branches with seasonal fluctuations in output, the need for working capital of its own is determined according to the scale of production of the quarter with the minimum programme. Seasonal increases in working capital in other quarters are covered by a credit from Gosbank." (*Ibid.*, 109.)

assigned. A similar control over the use of credits applies to long-term credits or capital grants or expenditures from reserves for capital repairs and extensions in the case of the Industrial Bank, which is now the bank for financing all capital construction projects. So close is this control over the use of monies assigned for capital purposes in these forms that on a large construction site the Industrial Bank will often have its own office and a representative who directly checks all expenditures in connection with the construction work. There is a further respect in which this system provides a supplementary instrument for controlling the execution of production plans by means of the credit system. This depends upon the fact that the credit advances made to industry (which figure to industry as debts) will be automatically liquidated[1] as industry completes its Production Plan. As enterprises fulfil their output-quotas, they will be credited in the books of the State Bank with the value of the commodities which they have delivered to the commercial organisation ; and this will automatically cancel the debit items which these enterprises have previously incurred in the course of paying out wages and consuming raw material. By observing the rate at which this process of liquidation is taking place in its books, the Bank possesses an easy generalised index of the degree of success with which the Production Plan is being carried out : of quickly observing where hitches and delays and inefficiencies are occurring and of reporting these accordingly.[2] Thus the much-talked-of " discipline of the rouble " acts, not just as an end-of-the-year audit *post facto*, but as a continual week-to-week, almost day-to-day, check on results.

In principle the banking system can only grant credits within the limits of the Credit Plan. Some flexibility, however, is allowed for by the provision of certain " unplanned credits ", to meet unforeseen delays or breakdowns in the flow of production and supplies. These, as their name implies, can be made outside the limits of the Credit Plan, at the discretion of the Bank on special occasions. For example, there is a special type of credit, loans against bills of lading, designed to bridge the gap between the

[1] Subject, however (since 1931), to the right of the purchaser to refuse to allow permission to the bank to debit its account if he considers that the supplier has not fulfilled the terms of the supply-contract. Debiting of the buyer's account (with the buyer's permission) has to *precede* the crediting of the supplier's account. This was one of the principles laid down in the 1931 changes : the second phase of the Credit Reform.

[2] Cf. Prof. M. Bogolepov : " The *raschotnii* account of industry in the bank accordingly becomes a barometer of the financial situation of industry and a pledge of normal relations between it and the bank." (*Plan. Khoz.*, 1936, No. 5, 87.)

dispatch of commodities by a factory and their arrival at their destination and the receipt of payment for them.[1]   Credits of this type are quite commonly included among the " planned credits ". But transport delays or failure of a purchaser to accept invoices on goods delivered (thereby delaying payment for them) is a leading cause of the demand for credits beyond the plan.   " Unplanned credits " can, however, only be granted for strictly limited periods, the maximum being one month.   A further category of credit consists of supplementary credits which the Bank can open in favour of an enterprise when for any reason some revision of the Plan has been sanctioned, and additional finance is needed to meet the adaptations that have to be made.   A minor example of this, which was publicised[2] as an exemplary piece of initiative on the part of the Bank, was when the Leningrad branch of the State Bank, having discovered the existence of excess stocks of unused timber in a local wagon-building works, offered a special nine-month credit to finance the formation of a furniture workshop to utilise this timber, in view of urgent demands at that time for an increased supply of household goods.

Parallel with the Credit Plan, the Cash Plan regulates the amount of currency that the State Bank is authorised to issue. Since transactions between organisations are effected simply by book-keeping entries at the Bank, cash only plays a rôle (with compara-tively rare exceptions) in payments of incomes to individuals, in transactions between individuals, or back again in payments from individuals as taxes, tram-fares or purchases in State shops, etc. As far as industry is concerned the basis of the Cash Plan will be the wage- and salary-bill for a certain period. For agriculture the relevant factor will be the purchase-price paid to collective farmers for the aggregate of the so-called " centralised " and " decen-tralised " collections, together with wages paid out on State farms. The amount of cash issued, therefore, in Soviet economy plays no independent causal rôle : it is itself contingent upon other elements in the Plan, such as the wage- and salary-bill, which are in fact the decisive factors in determining the income of the population.   In constructing the Cash Plan, however, it is not sufficient to ascertain the amount to be paid out in wages and salaries in a given period. The period within which this money returns once again to the State, whether as taxes or savings or over a shop-counter, also has

---

[1] This type of loan was specially important in the case of heavy industry, of whose credits half consisted of loans of this type. (V. Sitnin and Z. Sitkin, *loc. cit.*, 23–4.)   [2] *Finansovaia Gazeta*, Oct. 14, 1938 ; cit. Bettelheim, *op. cit.*, 197.

to be calculated. Moreover, this calculation is apparently made, not only on an all-Union scale, but separately for each region ; and this for a double reason. In the first place, such data will enable the bank " to calculate in advance whether its stock of notes will be sufficient, whether it will have to draw additional supplies from the head office or will be able to withdraw currency from circulation ". Secondly, it plays a part in determining the regional plan of distribution for consumers' goods. " Every regional financial organ, either the local office of the Commissariat of Finance or the local branch of the Gosbank, makes an analysis of the estimated cash situation in its territory for the coming period. The primary object of the analysis is to determine the total value of consumers' goods that should be made available, and this in turn is a guide to the amount of credit that should be distributed to the various retail organisations supplying the wants of the population."[1]

The planned costs of production and of distribution are the foundation from which is built the final retail price at which commodities pass into the hands of consumers. But they do not compose the whole of that final price. In fact, throughout the ten or fifteen pre-war years there was always a substantial gap between the level of costs and the level of retail prices. This gap is bridged by a Turnover Tax (analogous to the British Purchase Tax), which diverts the difference[2] between these two sets of prices into the Budget, instead of allowing it to accrue as profit either to the distributive organisation or to the industrial enterprise. In fact, in the case of certain things, like goods with seasonal price-variations or with a range of lines and qualities too complicated to be separately rated to a tax, yet varying in their prime costs (e.g. certain textile and hosiery products), a uniform rate of tax is replaced by what is frankly an appropriation by the taxation authorities of whatever happens to be the difference between wholesale price and retail price (less retail discount) in the form of a so-called " budget margin ".[3] Alternatively one could speak of the Turnover Tax as an instrument for building up planned costs of production and distribution (after the addition of the planned profit margins for the industrial and the distributive enterprises) into retail prices. The rates of this tax are high, and the extent to which they have the effect of stepping-up selling-prices to retail prices is accordingly

---

[1] L. E. Hubbard, *Soviet Money and Finance* (1936), 69–70.
[2] I.e. all of it except the comparatively small part that is left as profit to industrial and distributive enterprises.
[3] Cf. A. K. Suchkov (Ed.), *Dokhodi Gosudarstvennovo Biudjeta S.S.S.R.*, 14–17, 44–50.

considerable. Throughout the '30's the size of the revenue from this tax had been increasing, and in 1940 it accounted for as much as 70 per cent. of the revenue of the Union Budget.[1] An explanation as to the rôle that this tax plays in the financial relations of Soviet economy, and the reason why the gap between costs and retail price is as large as it is, provides an important key to understanding that crucial " balance of income and expenditure of the population " and its relation to the current supply of consumption goods, which we have seen lies at the heart of the financial problem.

Let us for the moment adopt the simplification of assuming that all income received by the population in wages and salaries (and by collective farmers and co-operative workers as net money income for the production they have sold) over a given period of time is spent by them on consumption goods. This is equivalent to saying that they do not on balance save any part of their money income, either by adding to their holdings of cash or by increasing their deposits at the State Savings Bank or by subscribing to State Loans (also that they do not *dis*-save), and that no part of their income has to go in direct taxation to the State.[2] The total of incomes paid out as wages, salaries, etc., will depend upon the total amount of production in the economy as a whole (in a closed economy) valued in terms of costs. If the whole of this production consisted of consumption goods, destined to appear in the retail market for consumers to buy, or of materials, components and instruments of production concerned in the production of those consumption goods, and no net investment (or dis-investment) was taking place—i.e. no alteration in the quantity of capital goods or of stocks of " goods in process "—then we should clearly have the very simple situation where the expenditure of citizens exactly equalled the current supply of consumers' goods valued at their cost (= amount of money paid out to workers concerned in their production, directly or indirectly, at all stages of production). If we write the average wage level as w and the total number of workers as x, then it follows that the total wage-bill wx will equal (on the highly simplified assumptions we are making) *both* the

---

[1] Of the combined budgets of the Union and the republics it composed only 58 per cent., since the tax plays a much smaller part in budgets of the republic than it does in that of the Union.

[2] Or alternatively, if we assume that *some* salaries are those of civil servants engaged in providing services to the population free of charge, that direct taxation (levied on those deriving their incomes from some form of production and on civil servants providing free services) is no more than sufficient to pay the salaries of these civil servants.

total costs of the goods produced and made available over the period *and* the total expenditure of citizens in the retail market (since their expenditure = their income = wx).

If, however, we suppose that net investment is taking place, and that a certain proportion of the labour force, say $\frac{1}{y}$, is being employed on building new power stations and new factories and adding to the stocks of semi-finished goods or means of production, then the above equality between the total supply of finished consumers' goods at cost and the expenditure of the population will no longer hold. The latter will be larger than the former by an amount equal to $\frac{wx}{y}$; since the total expenditure of citizens in the retail market will still equal the total wage-bill wx, but the costs incurred in producing the consumers' goods which have issued from the production line during the period will only equal that part of the total wage-bill represented by $wx . \frac{y-1}{y}$, and $wx - wx . \frac{y-1}{y} = \frac{wx}{y}$. In other words, the gap between total consumers' expenditure and the supply-at-cost of goods coming on to the retail market will be proportional to the amount of investment expenditure (in relation to the wage-cost of consumer goods) that is being undertaken.[1] What applies to investment expenditure will apply to any other expenditure, such as that on armaments, which does not enter into the costs of the current output of consumption goods. This is a simple and obvious relationship as soon as it is stated ; but it is deserving of emphasis since it constitutes a quite fundamental equation in the financial problem of a socialist economy.

There will be two ways in which this lack of equality between the expenditure of consumers and the supply of consumers' goods can be rectified. Firstly, the retail prices of consumer goods can be raised above their costs by an amount equal to $\frac{wx}{y}$: namely, by an amount equal to that part of the wage-bill that is being incurred in constructing new capital equipment and in making armaments and in adding to the stocks of unfinished goods in the consumption goods industries and in lines of production ancillary

---

[1] It is to be noticed that this relationship holds, *ceteris paribus*, irrespective of productivity. An increased productivity of labour, increasing the flow of consumer goods, will enable retail prices to be lowered. But it will at the same time reduce the prime cost of output ; and the *relation* between prime cost and retail price will not necessarily be affected.

thereto. The gap will then appear, not as a lack of balance in the retail market, but as a margin between two sets of prices : retail prices and costs. The function of the Turnover Tax in the Soviet financial system is to divert this price-margin directly into the Budget ; and in this sense it is, as Professor Bogolepov has said, " not a price-determining factor, but follows from the prices fixed by plan ".[1] Without any more than an apparent shift of substantial emphasis, one might alternatively say that this tax serves as an easy device for adjusting retail prices of consumers' goods so that the requisite balance of the retail market can be preserved.

Secondly, the excess spending power of the population, which had grown faster than the value-at-cost of consumers' goods, could be reduced by drawing off a proportion of money income in the form of taxation or by the sale of State bonds or by encouraging income receivers continually to add to their savings bank deposits. If the additional income from all these sources was equal to the amount that was being spent on new investment and on armaments and the like, then neither the balance of the retail market need be disturbed nor need any gap appear between retail prices and costs. If we write as z the amount by which the income of citizens is reduced in any of the above ways before it is spent, so that $wx - z$ is the amount of current expenditure by citizens ; then the necessary condition[2] is that z should $= \dfrac{wx}{y}$

III

We have seen earlier that as soon as the rate of investment began to be increased at all appreciably during the last three years of the 1920's the symptoms of an acute " goods famine " began to appear. This was the expression of that surplus expenditure in retail markets $\left(= \dfrac{wx}{y}\right)$ which the above equation would lead one to expect in a situation of rising investment. Both industrial and agricultural prices were subject to control, so that this situation was only to a small extent offset by a rise in industrial profits (and hence in the revenue flowing into the Budget from taxation of profits),

[1] *Op. cit.*, 11.

[2] It should be noted that this is *not* necessarily the same thing (although it may in some circumstances be *approximately* the same thing) as saying that, if the Budget expenditure of the State is balanced in the orthodox sense by revenue from direct taxes and loans, the necessary balance in the retail market is secured. Saving or dis-saving may take place in the form of a change in bank deposits of private individuals or in private money hoards of individuals.

and in the purchase of State loan by trading and industrial organisations out of their reserves. By 1930 investment expenditure financed out of the Budget had increased four times and by 1932 more than ten times, compared with the financial year 1927–8. While there was some increase in these years in State loans and in direct taxes, in 1932 the total revenue from direct taxation and loans combined amounted to no more than one fifth of the budget expenditure on " financing the national economy ". From 1930 onwards the chief source of increased revenue, balancing the increased investment-expenditure, was the Turnover Tax. In 1932 it contributed some $17\frac{1}{2}$ milliard out of a revenue total of 30 milliard roubles ; by 1935 it was contributing more than 50 milliard out of a revenue total of 67 milliard. Indeed we can trace a fairly close correlation, as one might expect, between the mounting curve of expenditure on investment and defence over the decade and the mounting revenue from the Turnover Tax. In 1932 revenue from this tax, as we have seen, was just over 17 milliard. The combined figure for expenditure out of the budget for defence and for financing the national economy was 25 milliard. In 1934 the two figures were respectively 37 and 37 ; in 1938 they were 80 and 75 ; in 1939 they were 92 and 100 ; in 1940 they were 106 and 113 ; and in the 1941 estimates they were 124 and 144 (the widened gap in this year being approximately covered by an increase in taxed profits).

This " goods famine " which became so particularly acute in the years of the First Five Year Plan has, of course, its now-familiar analogy in the conditions of short supplies and unsatisfied demands which have characterised the economic situation in Britain and other countries during the war and immediate post-war years. At the time it was common among observers outside the country to attribute the situation in U.S.S.R. to " inflation " ; some explaining that this was a reason why the Plan was likely to suffer shipwreck (since the necessary equilibrium between goods and money was not being preserved), others claiming that this was the secret source (" forced saving " resulting from the inflation) by means of which the constructional successes of the Plan were being achieved. But the phenomena of these years had nothing to do (except for a particular qualification to be mentioned presently) with " inflation " in the sense of an incautious monetary policy which, if changed, could have yielded an altered situation in the retail market. While it is true that the amount of money in circulation increased during this period, this was simply the consequence, an inevitable consequence, of a larger total wage-bill. The increase in money was approximately the same proportion as the increase in the total wages-bill; and larger supplies of cash to pay this larger wages-bill would have been required in any circumstances[1] to finance a larger volume of employment, by whatever financial policy the employ-ment-creating expenditure had been financed. As we have already seen, money does not play an independent causal rôle in the Soviet system of financial planning, being itself determined by the level of employment and the average level of money wage ; and between 1928 and 1932 the essential fact was that the employment of wage-earners in industry had doubled.

It is, of course, true that the results of expanded money income would have been different if either private savings or direct taxation of incomes had been increased. To this extent the result was affected by the source of revenue upon which the Budget relied to finance its investment-expenditure. But while subscriptions to State loans to some extent increased with the rise of incomes, this accounted for only a minor proportion of that increase in income ; and little attempt was made to step-up the rates of income taxation. A little reflection will, I think, show that in the circumstances of Soviet economy neither of these two sources could have been expected to furnish additional revenue of the required amount. In a society with large income inequalities, an increase of income accruing to the rich is likely very largely to be saved, since in their case satiety in consumption has been so nearly approached. But in a society without the large income inequalities characteristic of a capitalist society the major part of any increased income is likely to be directed towards consumption, and only a small part of it be saved ; and this is the more likely to be the case, the lower the average standard of life has previously been. Again, in a capitalist society, income taxation can be increased by progressively graduat-ing the rates of taxation levied on large incomes ; and since these large incomes are predominantly derived from property-rights and not from work, these high rates of tax will exercise little or no adverse effect upon productive activity. But in a society where incomes are work-incomes (other than such things as pensions and small amounts received as interest or premiums on State loans or

---

[1] Subject, however, to the 'qualification that, if the increased wage-payments had all been deposited in the Savings Bank immediately they had been received, and not drawn upon, the total of cash out in circulation would not have needed to be increased, since cash would have been returning to the Savings Bank as fast as more cash was being issued by the State Bank to industries to meet their larger wage-bills But cash *plus* deposits would have increased.

savings bank deposits), high rates of income-taxation would tend to have discouraging effects on productive activity.[1] It is hardly conceivable that during the First Five Year Plan, when so much attention was being directed towards encouraging improved work and the acquisition of skill by means of widened wage-differentials and the extended use of payment by results, the incentives which the State was offering with one hand should have been simultaneously blunted by the other hand through increased tax-deductions. In the circumstances of Soviet economy it was clearly impossible that increased investment expenditure of this magnitude could be financed to any more than a minor extent out of increases in income-taxation or in subscriptions to State loans.

In the first few years there was one respect in which financial policy (or the lack of it) can be said to have contributed to an accentuation of the " goods famine ". During the first year and a half of the First Five Year Plan a certain amount of unplanned credit expansion took place : credit expansion undertaken on the initiative of subordinate bodies in excess of any that had been allowed for in the Plan. Between October, 1928, and October, 1930, the total of short-term loans and discounts of the State Bank had doubled.[2] At this time the Bank still exercised a certain amount of discretion in granting credits, and one industrial or trading enterprise could grant credit to another by means of bills of exchange which were discountable. In addition to capital expenditure financed out of the Budget, there was investment financed out of that part of industrial profits which was left at the disposal of enterprises themselves and by means of loans from the Industrial Bank ; the latter being found from the deposited reserves of industrial trusts and other State bodies. The main form that unplanned investment seems to have taken in the early years of the First Five Year Plan was investment in stocks of materials (or sometimes a reserve staff of skilled labour) financed by means of short-term credit from a bank or from some other organisation. Often this investment in stocks was prompted by an industrial manager's desire to guard himself against possible shortage at a

---

[1] The question may be asked whether taxation would tend to have any more adverse effects than the reduced purchasing power of a given money wage owing to the scarcity of goods in the retail market. The answer is clearly an affirmative one : (1) since it is common knowledge that, except at times of very rapid monetary depreciation, people customarily think in terms of money earnings rather than of real earnings ; (2) the recipient of a money income always has the chance of saving it, even if there is little attraction in spending it in the present : he is influenced in obtaining that money income by expectations about its future purchasing power as well as by its present purchasing power. [2] Arnold, *op. cit.*, 371.

later date. The effect of what in some directions had become a competitive scramble to acquire and to hold materials in short supply was to aggravate the shortage and to dislocate the Plan. It must also have been to a considerable extent responsible for bidding up the prices both of raw materials and of skilled labour, and hence of raising the level of money-incomes and the money expenditure of consumers beyond what these would otherwise have been.

It was to meet this situation that the Credit Reforms of 1930 to 1932 were introduced. By a joint decree of TSIK and Sovnarcom of January 30th, 1930, the granting of credit by any State body, co-operative society or " mixed joint stock company without the participation of foreign capital " to another was prohibited, and the only form of credit permitted to these bodies from thenceforth was to be bank credit, which could only be granted by the State Bank within the limits of the Credit Plan. This was supplemented by the decrees of January 14th and March 20th, 1931, which further defined the limits within which credit could be given by the Bank, and the procedure according to which enterprises must enter into agreements for delivery of goods to purchasing bodies and must lodge the resulting documents with the State Bank as a condition of receiving the credit advances required to finance the conclusion of these supply-agreements. According to this revised procedure the bank could only debit the purchasers' account on the delivery of goods with the purchaser's consent. This gave the purchaser the opportunity of objecting if the order had not been fulfilled according to the terms of the agreement. It was also provided that the supplier's account was not to be credited until the purchaser's had been debited. Further decrees of STO of June 16th and June 23rd, 1931, established the procedure for crediting economic enterprises in greater detail, and laid down regulations governing the working capital of State undertakings. The main purpose of the decree of March 20th, 1931, was to remove certain deficiencies in the system which had immediately followed the decree of fourteen months before. These deficiencies were described as being " direct indiscriminate crediting under the plan " and "automatism in crediting, which excluded the possibility of control from the side of the bank over the process of fulfilment of the plan " ; " weakened responsibility on the' part of economic organs in their profit and their working capital, which led to a weakened interest in the results of their activities " ; and " non-observance of the principle of contractual relations between undertakings and societies (suppliers and purchasers), which weakened control by the consumer over the supplier in questions of quality and assortment of products and conditions of payment ".[1]   Finally, in 1932 the Industrial Bank itself was reorganised.   Henceforth it could only make long-term grants to industry for a purpose and to an amount that had already been authorised in the general plan.   As a result of this important series of changes, credit institutions could no longer exert an independent influence on production and prices, as they had previously been able to do by virtue of the limited autonomy they had possessed with regard to credit-advances.

During the years when the " goods famine " was particularly acute, and when it applied to prime necessities of life as well as to comforts and luxuries, the situation was met by the introduction of rationing, in order to secure that available supplies were distributed equitably.   Already in 1929 rationing was introduced for bread on the initiative of the larger towns, beginning with Leningrad and Moscow.   Later this was extended until it embraced virtually the whole urban population ; and rationing was also introduced for sugar, tea, vegetable oil and butter, potatoes, eggs, meat, jam and macaroni.   In 1931 and 1932 a large number of other consumers' goods, such as textiles and soap, were included, until rationing covered nearly a half of all manufactured consumers' goods that were sold through the co-operative network and about 70 million persons.   Peasants, being self-suppliers of grain, etc., were not usually included in the scheme of food rationing, except in regions which specialised on industrial raw materials, such as the cotton-growing regions.   In their case industrial goods in short supply were supplied (since an order of the Commissariat of Internal Trade in June, 1929) in proportion to their fulfilment of their delivery-quotas of agricultural produce to the State buying organs.

This rationing system was marked by two main features. Firstly, the ration was graded according to categories, preference being given to manual workers and later to workers in the most essential enterprises ; while at the same time, in the case of deficit-commodities other than foodstuffs, factory canteens and the so-called " closed co-operatives ", which catered for special categories of workers, received the pick of the available supplies.   Secondly, the ration had the form, not of a maximum but of a guaranteed minimum at a certain fixed ration-price.   As such it provided a kind of " iron ration ".   Extra quantities, when they were available,

---

[1] *Spravochnik Sovetskovo Rabotnika*, 761-4 ; N. S. Burmistrov, *op. cit.*, 165-6. For a full and lucid account of the Credit Reform and its early defects cf. Arnold, *op. cit.*, 351-74.

could be purchased " off " the ration. These " off-ration " purchases, however, were at substantially higher prices. This formed
a basis for the novel system of differential prices for the same
commodity which characterised these years. The same commodity had a different price according to the market in which
it was purchased : it had a different price in a " closed co-operative " according to whether it was purchased " on " or " off " the
ration ; it had a different price " off " the ration in a " closed
co-operative " from what it had in the so-called " commercial
stores ", which were conducted by various State and municipal
bodies as ordinary open shops ; and it had a different price in the
latter from what it might have (if it were obtainable there) in the
private market. Hence there was no single price-level and money
had no unique purchasing-power. The purchasing-power of one's
money income depended on the type of market in which one was
able to spend it, and how the expenditure of it was distributed
between these different markets. The result was a partial, but not
complete, divorce between income and consumption ; and the
system accordingly represented a compromise between controlling
the distribution of scarce supplies so as to guarantee an iron ration
of essentials to everyone, with a preferential ration to essential
workers, and maintaining free spending-outlets to consumers so
that differences of money income would continue to exert an
influence as incentives to productive activity. Had there been no
opportunity for additional purchases " off " the ration and in open
shops, the attraction of earning additional money income would
have been greatly reduced. As it was, the rewards of extra work or
of promotion to a higher level had some chance of being realised in
additional purchases, even if at a much enhanced price.

But this compromise, though satisfactory enough for a period,
was an uneasy one ; and as time went on, and the complications of
the system grew, its disadvantages became increasingly marked.
The divorce between income and consumption, even if it was no
more than partial, was bound to exert some blunting effect on wage-
incentives ; and the system of multiple prices and markets robbed
money-wage differentials of any precise and uniform significance.
The consumption of any individual depended only partly on the
income he earned. It might depend even more on his ration-
category, on whether or not he was a member of a " closed co-
operative ", and on whether the co-operative to which he belonged
was in a high or a low priority-classification for receiving supplies.
It became clear before very long that the system of privileged

categories had come to stand in contradiction with the system of incentives that the structure of money-wages was designed to afford. This contradiction became specially marked in the course of 1932 and 1933 when a decentralised system of self-supply (through the so-called O.R.S.) for individual factory stores and canteens was developed. Under this system (which was expanded again in the war years) the closed co-operative of a factory was encouraged to contract for its food supplies directly with a collective farm or even to run its own allotment or farm. Hence the factory a worker belonged to, and the efficiency of its self-supply service, often became considerably more important than the money-wage he received. Wage-differentials lost much of their meaning ; and the operation of any consistent money-wage-policy became impossible. This was no doubt the principal reason for the abolition of rationing in 1935, the reintroduction of a single market price for all categories of shops and the restoration of a normal retail market.[1] This step had meanwhile been made possible by an increase in the supply of necessities such as bread, sugar, meat and fats and tea, which had followed the consolidation of collective farming in the first two years of the Second Five Year Plan.[2]

Prior to 1935 the Turnover Tax had played the rôle of equalising the price-differences in the system of differential prices so far as the receipts of distributive organisations were concerned. In other words it skimmed off the surplus in the price at which goods in the commercial shops could be sold. Over the preceding two years the sphere of these " commercial shops " had widened at the expense of " closed supplies " ; and the sums accruing as Turnover Tax had correspondingly increased. After rationing had been lifted and the unrestricted right of consumers' expenditure had been restored, the new uniform market prices evidently had to be set at an appreciably higher level than the old prices at which rations and privileged supplies could be obtained. Otherwise the expenditure of consumers would have been in excess of the supplies

---

[1] There were other criticisms levelled against the previous system : a tendency to encourage graft and to give opportunities for peculation, and a tendency to encourage inefficiency and poor service to the consumer in the absence of retail competition. For example an article in *Bolshevik* (Sept. 30, 1934) declared that it had given the co-operatives " an undeserved monopoly on the market, with a neglect of the consumer and a poor quality of service as the result ".

[2] Bread and other cereals were de-rationed on Jan. 1, 1935, and by the end of the year ration cards were also abolished for meat, butter, vegetable oils, fish, sugar and potatoes. The *Torgsin* shops where goods were sold against precious metals or foreign valuta (mainly used by foreigners) were closed by Feb. 1, 1936.

available, and the " goods famine " would have been accentuated. Actually the new price-schedules at which goods were to be sold in State shops and co-operatives were substantially higher than the old ration-prices but lower than the prices prevailing in the " commercial shops ".[1] At the same time the Turnover Tax was extended to all commodities destined for the retail market ; and it became the exclusive instrument by which the amounts available for sale and the current demand were equated in the case of each commodity by adjustments of its retail price.

During the period of the Second Five Year Plan the rate of investment as a proportion of the national income was relaxed a little ; rather more of current investment was directed to the consumers' goods industries ; and the flow of consumers' goods on to the market increased considerably. The problem of the gap between cost and retail price was accordingly stabilised, and in the course of 1936 and 1937 the prices of many things were lowered.[2] But before the Second Five Year Plan had been completed a new form of expenditure, that on rearmament, was to come into prominence, and by the end of the decade was to challenge comparison with investment expenditure from the Budget. Prior to 1935 this had been of relatively minor importance. In that year it represented rather less than a quarter of the sums spent on financing the national economy. By 1938 it had risen to nearly a half of the sum devoted to the national economy, or about 20 per cent. of the total budget expenditure, as compared with only 5 per cent. in 1932. The problem of the gap was accordingly to grow rather than to diminish as the war years were approached, and with it the significance of the Turnover Tax. In 1935 receipts from the Turnover Tax composed about 65 per cent. of the gross retail turnover of State and co-operative trade. By 1937 this percentage had fallen a little to 60 per cent. : a relative level at which it remained in 1940.[3]

[1] To compensate workers who had previously relied to a very large extent on rationed goods (e.g. because they were in the lower-paid categories and industries or had a large number of dependants in the family or alternatively had been in essential plants with special opportunities for obtaining privileged-category supplies) money-wage rates were raised by 10 per cent.
[2] E.g. the government order of June 1, 1937, effecting a price-reduction of 15 or 16 per cent. for most consumer goods.
[3] Cf. Baykov, op. cit., 260. The rating of this tax varies for different commodities from 1 and 2 per cent. (a purely nominal rate for most capital goods which since they enter into costs are maintained as far as possible at stable prices) up to nearly 100 per cent. The higher rates of tax are apt to be on luxury goods, since these tend to be in particularly scarce supply. The general effect of the differential rating apparently is, therefore, to cause the price structure to discriminate against non-essentials (and hence to make *real* differences of income smaller

Some foreign commentators have described the Turnover Tax (together with taxed Profits and Loans—although their inclusion has not always been explicit) as the measure or embodiment of the " savings " of the community involved in State investment ; and at least one writer has devoted several pages to an analysis in this sense.[1] It is to be doubted, however, whether much meaning can be given to such a description, which may prove more misleading than illuminating. The expression can of course be rendered quite harmless if one is careful to make clear that the word " savings " is being defined merely as the difference between total output and that part of output which consists of consumption goods, and if one is careful explicitly to rid the statement of misleading causal implications. But if it is defined in this way, nothing is added to what we have said above about the necessary correspondence between price-relationships and the distribution of productive resources by identifying the Turnover Tax with " savings " in this sense. The pitfalls that beset any careless use of " savings " in this context become apparent when one realises that the size of the tax required will depend on the particular definition of costs that is adopted for fixing " planned cost " (and hence the size of the gap between cost and retail price). If amortisation-allowances for depreciation of plant were not included in costs (as we have seen that in fact they are) the Turnover Tax would need to be equivalently higher, since the gap to be bridged between cost and retail price would *ipso facto* be larger. In this case the meaning of the term " savings " would have to be stretched to make it correspond to *gross* investment instead of *net* investment. The same applies to the overhead expense of industrial administra-

than an inspection of *money* differences would lead one at first sight to suppose). That this is so has been denied by a reviewer of the present writer's *Soviet Planning and Labour in Peace and War* (M. Florinsky in *Journal of Political Economy*, March, 1945, 92). But the appearance to the contrary seems mainly due to the high rates levied on agricultural foodstuffs. In their case, however, the significance of the rate is not so much to *raise* their market price as to bridge the gap between the exceptionally low collection-prices (having the effect of a tax) and the market price, and hence may be regarded as mainly that of skimming off into the Budget the " differential rent " of land (see above, page 284). Actually the Turnover Tax on grain comprises as much as 20 per cent. of the whole revenue from this tax. Undertakings producing goods of mass consumption from local materials were exempted from Turnover Tax by a decree of Jan. 7, 1941, and industrial co-operatives (since their costs are apt to be relatively high owing to their lower technical equipment and sometimes inferior supply-facilities) are generally given the concession of a lower rate of tax on their products. (Cf. A. K. Suchkov, etc., *Dokhodi Gosudarstvennovo Biudjeta S.S.S.R.*, 27, 31, 40–1.)

[1] L. E. Hubbard, *Soviet Money and Finance*, 185–97. Elsewhere Mr. Hubbard refers to it as " a monopoly profit accruing to the Government as sole supplier of consumption goods to the people ". (*Ibid.*, 322.)

tion (e.g. of the higher economic bodies) : the Turnover Tax, and hence the definition of " savings ", would have to be adjusted according to where the line was drawn between administrative overheads which were and which were not included in the costing of industrial goods. The word " savings " is a product of individualist conditions where new capital is provided out of the incomes of private capitalists—incomes which they have had in their personal possession to dispose of by a conscious act of choice between various possible destinations ; and the implication that a decision to refrain from spending it immediately on consumption involves a sacrifice or " abstinence " on the individual's part has been used by economists as a justification of the payment of interest. Even under Capitalism in modern times, in view of the increasing importance of new investment provided out of company reserves, the old concept of " saving ", even if it is shorn of any residue of the notion of abstinence, has become full of difficulties. In speaking of a socialist economy the term is better avoided altogether.

The Turnover Tax, as we have seen, is the immediate instrument by means of which the prices of different commodities on the retail market are adjusted, both as a whole and relatively to one another, according to the degrees in which they are in short supply relative to the current demand. But, given consumers' expenditure, it is the supply of these commodities as established by the Production Plan that, in a more fundamental sense, determines the relative prices of different commodities, and hence the rates of tax necessary to build up their cost-prices to the requisite retail level. In choosing between the things that are available for them to buy, consumers in the U.S.S.R. (since 1935, and apart from wartime rationing) have complete freedom of choice. But a question commonly asked by economists is the extent to which the Production Plan, in fixing the proportions in which different sorts of consumer goods will be turned out, is influenced by the demand of consumers for different articles as registered on the retail market : how far does consumers' choice between what is placed in front of them govern what is produced ? In the varying rates of Turnover Tax (and hence ratios of retail price to prime cost) the planning authorities evidently possess a simple and direct index of the varying degrees to which different things are in short supply compared with the current demand. This index does not of itself afford an automatic criterion as to the relative advantage, from a social point of view, of augmenting the supply of different things. A certain commodity A, which has a higher ratio of price to prime cost than B, may require for its production a proportionately much heavier outlay in buildings and mechanical equipment than is required for the production of B ; and when building materials and machine-tools and metal (and capital goods generally) are scarce, it may be more advantageous to increase the production of B which requires few of such things, even though (according to the index afforded by relative rates of Turnover Tax) it is less in short supply than A. Moreover, various social priorities may affect the decision, such as the desirability of giving bicycles a preference because they enable people to live further from work and at week-ends to enjoy the countryside, or of giving books and music a priority over vodka. Again, the production of certain commodities may involve the use of certain resources which are in specially scarce supply, either temporarily or permanently, and are in urgent demand in the capital goods industries or in armaments. Accordingly an increase in the supply of these may be more difficult to arrange, without damaging consequences in other directions, than the supply of other things for which, on first inspection, the need appears to be less urgent. Nevertheless, the ratio of retail prices to prime cost affords *an* index, which is relevant to decisions about the planning of production, even if this index has to be balanced against other criteria (some, but not all, of which can be reduced to simple quantitative form) ;[1] and presumably it is an index which is taken into account in Soviet planning.

In the latter half of the pre-war decade a good deal of attention was coming to be paid to the question of the links between industry and the consumer, and to the necessity for less dictation by industry of the types and quantities of consumer goods and for a greater measure of adaptation of industrial plans to the requirements of consumers as registered in the market or in other ways. Previously to this the economic situation had been dominated by problems of investment and of guaranteeing a minimum of essential goods to the population ; and there was little on the economic agenda which immediately involved any very subtle considerations about consumers' tastes. But at the end of the period of rationing the complaint began to be common that under the prevailing system of " closed " shops and restricted purchases the producer could

---

[1] So far as the amount of capital involved in the increased output of a commodity is the main consideration, this is capable of simple quantitative comparison with the ratio of prime cost to retail price (roughly = rate of Turnover Tax). All that is here required is a knowledge of the ratio of capital to output in various lines of production ; and the allocation of available capital could be decided by direct comparison of this ratio with the ratio of cost to price. Cf. the reference to the notion of *net productivity* in Chapter One page 14.

make the consumer accept whatever he cared to produce, and that he took little trouble to adapt production to what the consumer wanted. A greater decentralisation of consumer goods industries, of which we have spoken, and in particular a growing emphasis in the later '30's on local industries, geared to local markets, was largely motivated by the desire to make production more responsive to the consumer. An article in the Gosplan organ in the year when rationing was terminated quoted a recent study of the supply-orders of universal stores (*Univermags*) in different districts, which revealed a much larger variation in these orders than could be explained by differences in consumers' demands in the several districts. "Study of demand", said this writer, "finds itself still in an unsatisfactory condition".[1] A year later another writer was still complaining that "up to the present time both in whole-sale and in retail trade we have still employed, to a significant degree, the old methods of planning inherited from the period of the ration-card system. In wholesale trade we are far from having liquidated conservatism and armchair-bureaucratic methods of direction ". Not only were the more subtle variations of taste among individual consumers neglected, but " the supply-plans only weakly take account of the structure and seasonal fluctuations of demand according to regions " ; and in many outlying regions in the past year supplies had fallen considerably short of the spending power of the population, while in centres like Moscow and Leningrad supplies had exceeded the current demand. " From a cursory analysis of the total trade turnover for 1935 flows as an indubitable conclusion the necessity for deeper and more concrete planning of trade turnover . . . in relation to the effective demand of the population in individual regions." Distributive organisa-tions were firmly reminded that " the consumer demands attention to himself and consideration ; he does not like to stand in queues ; he demands swift and cultured service ".[2] In 1936 the Commis-sariat of Trade issued special " instructions on the preparation of materials about the purchasing power of the population ". But in the summer of 1937 a writer in the Gosplan fortnightly *Plan* was reporting examples from districts in western Siberia where local economic organs could not produce the most elementary information concerning local purchasing power, and was proposing the institution of a special commission at a Union level for the study

[1] Y. Shnirlin, " Study of Consumers' Demand and Advance Orders " in *Plan. Khoz.*, 1935, No. 7, 78–9.
[2] Z. Bolotin in *Plan. Khoz.*, 1936, No. 6, 90–2, 95–6 ; also U. Cherniavsky and S. Krivetsky, *ibid.*, 114 seq.

of demand in the localities.[1] If wholesale and retail distribution still paid such scanty attention to demand, the influence which the latter could exert upon industry in constructing its production plans must have been very weak. It is not without significance that the year following the end of rationing saw the publication of a work which was referred to as " the first work of scientific investigation devoted to supply and demand in the U.S.S.R." and contained a chapter devoted to methods of studying consumers' demand.[2] In the last few years of the decade a number of industrial departments and trusts were endeavouring to apply new methods of testing-out the desires of consumers by means of questionnaires and sample surveys in shops, and, in advance of new designs, by means of travelling exhibits about which consumers were invited to record their preferences.

However, in 1937 complaints are still heard, this time of " a hypertrophy of planning of trade funds ", and " a planning of wholesale trade which has not been built in harmony with the liquidation of the rationing system ".[3] An important step towards decentralisation was taken in that year, when an arrangement was introduced whereby supply-allocations were only to continue to be carried out centrally as heretofore in the case of cotton textiles, footwear, hosiery and ready-made clothing. The allocation of all other consumer goods was to devolve on each region separately. There was also to be a category of so-called " regulated " goods,[4] including such things as household accessories, standard foodstuffs, " cultural articles ", and silk and linen goods, the allocation of which was to be controlled only so far as a broad allocation between State trading concerns and Co-operatives was concerned, and for the rest was left to be governed by direct contracts between supply organisations and the distributive agencies in the various regions.

In our first chapter we made some reference to the discussion there has been among economists in the west concerning the so-called question of " consumers' sovereignty "in a planned economy ; and we gave some reasons for thinking that the problem of adapting production to demand is in some ways much simpler and in other

---

[1] N. Cheklin, " On the Extensive Study of Purchasing Power ", Plan, 1937, No. 6, 26 ; also M. Valkov in Plan. Khoz., 1935, Nos. 11–12, 175.

[2] Supply and Demand in U.S.S.R., edited by A. I. Malkis ; reviewed in Plan. Khoz., 1936, No. 7, 224 seq.

[3] N. Riauzov in Plan, 1937, No. 11, June 10, 1937. " Ration cards have been liquidated in retail, in wholesale they continue to reign, leading to bureaucracy and the freezing of trade turnover." (Ibid.)

[4] A distinction between " regulated " and " normed " supplies had already been introduced two years previously by a decree of January 1, 1935. (Cf. G. A. Neymann, Vnutrennia Torgovlia S.S.S.R. (1935), 314–16.)

ways much less simple than the abstract " models " of the problem which they have created have led most economists to suppose. In the first place, the problem of static adjustment to a given pattern of demand is matched in importance, if it is not dwarfed, by dynamic problems concerning the development of the economy as a whole : development which is likely to change many of the variables in the problem of static adjustment in ways which can only imperfectly be foreseen and allowed for until the changes occur. Secondly, the static problem of allocating resources between different lines of production will itself be confined within the framework of certain strategic decisions, concerning such things as the rate of investment (and hence the relative size of the capital goods industries and the form which new construction shall take), the location of industry, the relation between industry and agriculture, which by common admission constitute policy-questions that cannot be satisfactorily decided by any verdict of a market. Thirdly, even within these limits, it seems probable that actual discontinuities on the side both of production and of demand cause decisions about the proportions in which different consumer goods shall be produced to have a much narrower range of practicable alternatives between which to choose than economists, who tend to think in terms of smooth curves of continuous variation, have usually supposed. With regard to new commodities and varieties of a commodity catering for new wants, in no economic system can the market afford any automatic index to guide production. Here the initiative must necessarily rest with the producer : an initiative which will inevitably play an " educative " rôle in the development of individual tastes and conventional standards. The power of choice between standardisation combined with cheapness and dearer variety will generally be conditioned straitly by the level of economic development that has at any time been reached (since this will determine how much variety the economy can afford—how far existing resources will stretch) ; and, as we have earlier said,[1] the essence of rising standards of living, as fruit of economic progress, probably consists quite as much in multiplying variety (and hence developing " new wants ") as in augmenting the quantity of familiar commodities which are already woven into the pattern of pre-existent consumers' demand. At comparatively early stages of economic development, the problem of allocation of labour between different consumer goods will be fairly simple. The resources available will not permit the number

[1] See Chapter One, page 19.

of alternatives to be large (if the maximum productivity of labour is to be achieved by making fullest use of the advantages of specialisation and standardisation); and in the satisfaction of primary needs for food, clothing, house room there is no very complex problem of individual consumers' choice.   At more advanced stages of development, the range of alternatives is wider, and commodities concerning which consumers' tastes are more varied occupy a more prominent place.   At the same time, when this more advanced stage has been reached, the equipment of industry and the productivity of labour will have grown sufficiently for the need to husband resources with studied economy to become less urgent: more latitude can be given to varying tastes by allowing a generous margin in the varieties placed before consumers, and a failure to allocate resources in precisely "optimum" proportions will cost the community less than when productivity was smaller and primary needs were still unsatisfied.   Nonetheless, there remains here a problem, not to be neglected, as post-war experience shows.

If we view the matter in this larger setting, questions about the influence of demand upon production are seen in rather different perspective; and it is less surprising that the problem of demand and its influence over production should have bulked no larger among the problems of Soviet planning at an early stage of growth than it appears to have done.   Soviet planning had been preoccupied with major questions of economic development, concerning the relations between industry and agriculture, the rate of investment and the location of industry.   Such central strategic issues had necessarily to be decided as centralised policy-decisions, which once taken moulded the general shape of the economic plan.   Even within the sphere of consumer goods production the dominant problem in pre-war days was that of producing a comparatively narrow range of necessities of life in certain minimum quantities. Had not rearmament and then war intervened, the decade of the '40's would have already seen consumer goods production and problems of its adaptation to demand occupying a more dominating position.   To judge from pre-war trends that were already apparent, Soviet economy would probably have met these problems by an earlier movement towards decentralisation in the detailed operations of light industry, in order to bring the initiative in planning the production of this branch of industry much closer to the markets which it served.   As it was, such problems did not emerge as major ones until the 1950's.

IV

Certain things remain to be said about the structure of the banking system and the taxation system. During the period of NEP and after the monetary reform of 1924, the banking system was not greatly differentiated, either in its structure or its technique, from the banking system of other countries. Superficially at least, its relations with industry resembled those which prevail in the capitalist world. The State Bank, or Gosbank, was both a bank of issue and a deposit bank, primarily for State institutions; and like the Bank of England it was also to some extent a bankers' bank, although this aspect was on the wane in the 1920's, compared with pre-revolutionary times. Its credit operations were principally short-term, and it was chiefly concerned in granting short-term loans to industry and trade in the form of advances and bill-discounting. Alongside Gosbank were a number of specialised banks, including two (later reduced to one) engaged in the granting of long-term credits to industry. These latter were the Industrial Bank, or Prombank, and the Electrobank, which, as its name implied, had been instituted to finance projects under the Electrification Plan and which in 1928 was amalgamated with Prombank. In 1925 there was formed a Central Municipal and Housing Bank (Tsekombank) to finance housing construction and municipal development, and to co-ordinate some fifty-odd pre-existing municipal banks, of which the best known was the Moscow Municipal Bank. There was also a specialised Bank for Foreign Trade; and there was the Co-operative Bank which financed the co-operative movement. In the middle 1920's these leading six banks had nearly 2 milliard roubles of credit outstanding, of which about a half was to State industry, and a further third to State trading bodies and the consumers' co-operative movement. About a half of the whole consisted of long-term credit, and nearly a third took the form of bill-discounting.[1]

These banking institutions catered primarily for the socialised sector of the economy. Their capital had been obtained from various State organisations, and their deposits predominantly consisted of the balances of State institutions. In the sphere of agriculture there existed numerous mutual credit societies, formed on a co-operative basis among the peasantry to supply peasant needs

[1] Cf. L. E. Hubbard, *op. cit.*, 8–13. For pre-revolutionary banking cf. L. Epstein, *Les Banques de Commerce Russes* (1925).

individually or through various supply co-operatives. In the middle '20's they numbered nearly 200, but their deposit resources were slender, and the interest they were paying to attract funds from depositors was very much higher than that paid by any other bank. These, together with other types of co-operative society, drew most of their funds from the Central Agricultural Bank which had been formed in 1924. In 1929 a special agricultural bank was formed to finance the collective farm movement, known as the Selkhozbank, which in the following year absorbed the older Agricultural Bank. There also existed in the '20's a certain number of mutual credit associations engaged in financing private trade and production. But their activities were never on more than a very modest scale.[1]

On the eve of the First Five Year Plan an important step was taken towards the specialisation of the banking system by an order requiring State institutions to deal each with a single bank. At the same time a special banking committee was set up by the Commissariat of Finance to regulate all banking operations. As a result of these and subsequent developments Gosbank became the institution for short-term crediting of State industry and trade, of the co-operative movement and of other credit institutions. All State enterprises were required to keep their accounts with Gosbank, and by the end of 1928 it had acquired a virtual monopoly of short-term credit operations.[2] Private depositors were catered for by the State Savings Bank, which provides for individuals the ordinary deposit and cheque and transfer facilities with which we are familiar. The other large banks like Prombank became long-term credit institutions, each specialised to a particular sphere. Under the investment programmes of the Five Year Plans they became the organs for handling and allocating the grants for capital development made to industry and other branches of economic activity out of the Budget. As regards the major part of their activities, interest-free grants, of which they were merely intermediate agencies, replaced long-term credit advances of the traditional kind. But for a time these institutions retained some latitude in supplementing such grants at their discretion with advances out of the reserves deposited with them.

It should be explained that part of investment, varying during

---

[1] Hubbard, *op. cit.*, 11 ; A. A. Santalov and L. Segal, *Soviet Union Yearbook*, 1928, 434-6.
[2] Arnold says that Gosbank controlled some nine tenths of short-term credit after the Credit Reform. The municipal banks were responsible for most of the remainder. (*Ibid.*, 352.)

the '30's between a quarter and a third of the whole, is not financed by grants from the Budget in this way.[1] This part is financed out of the share of the profits of economic enterprises which is retained by these enterprises and deposited with Gosbank or with Prombank as a reserve. Amortisation allowances (which are entered, as we have seen, in prime costs) are now divided into two parts : the one earmarked for periodic expenditures on capital building and reconstruction (between which and completely new building the line is difficult, if not impossible, to draw), which is deposited with Prombank, and the other assigned to current repair and maintenance of plant, which is deposited with Gosbank.[2] Sanction has to be obtained for any expenditures out of such reserves by inclusion of the expenditure in the Financial Plan, as in the case of expenditures financed by budgetary grants. The distinction between reinvested profits which do and which do not pass through the Budget seems to be a relic of the pre-Five Year Plan period, when the rate of investment was much smaller, when the funds for investment were mainly derived from the reserves of industry itself (" internal accumulation "), and the distinction corresponded to profit that was transferred for investment in some *other* field of industry and profit that was ploughed back as investment in the *same* field. But the distinction evidently retains some importance; since in practice an enterprise or a branch of industry will be able to have a larger say in the disposal of a reserve existing in its own name than over the disposal of a grant to it from above ; and the leaving of part of its profit at the disposal of an enterprise will afford it a collective incentive to efficiency, by endowing it with funds in the use of which it is able to take the initiative.[3] It is apparently assumed at any rate that an industry will display a greater sense of responsibility for its investment projects if these are financed out of its own reserves than if they are financed out of the Budget.[4]

---

[1] In 1940, after an increase in the self-financing of investment by industry, 24·3 milliard out of 36 milliard roubles, or 67½ per cent. of gross investment, came from the Budget. (K. N. Plotnikov, *Biudjet Sovetskovo Gosudarstva*, 89)

[2] N. N. Rovinsky, *op. cit.*, 123. By a Sovnarcom decree in 1936, annual amortisation charges were fixed at between 5·5 and 6 per cent. of the value of the plant, equipment and buildings of an enterprise (valued in terms of original cost). Included in this is the charge assigned to current repairs, varying between 2·2 and 3·6 per cent.

[3] In the 1940 Plan, out of total planned profits of 33 milliard roubles some 22 milliard was taxable into the Budget and 11 milliard was retainable by industry.

[4] Cf. the expressed hope that the raising to 40 per cent. of the proportion of capital investments in heavy industry in 1937 to be financed out of the industry's own resources would result in " raising the sense of responsibility for fulfilling the plan of capital work " both quantitatively and qualitatively. (A. Shor in *Plan*, 1936, No. 24, 45.)

In the course of the first year of the First Five Year Plan it was found that the existing system of credit still gave too much latitude to industrial and trading enterprises to evade the directives of the Plan, to accumulate stocks of materials in short supply or to compete for scarce supplies of skilled labour and to fall behind with deliveries of finished goods, financing the lengthened production-period and the larger stocks by means of credit-advances. As a result, the Credit Reform (or series of reforms) was introduced which has been described above, and which virtually terminated both the bill of exchange[1] and other forms of commercial credit between enterprises and made bank-advances within the limits of the Credit Plan the sole form of credit to economic organisations. Thenceforth the Banks shed what remained of their character as credit-institutions of the traditional type, and virtually became book-keeping departments and financial watchmen of the planning system. While economic enterprises were left free to make their own supply and delivery arrangements on a contractual basis, the overall financial limits within which they could do so were subject to strict control, and the principle ruled that credit should (save in exceptional circumstances) be given to the buyer and not to the seller. But although it was stressed that, by virtue of these credits, the Banks should exercise a supervision over the uses to which they were put, it did not follow that this control was always as close in practice as it appeared to be on paper ; and even in 1940 we hear the complaint that banks sometimes give credit to enterprises in connection with the supply of goods which have not been covered by a written contract (which is required by law as a condition of a bank-advance being made) and in connection with the fulfilment of orders for which the terms of the contract regarding quality and date of delivery have not been observed.[2]

In the same year as the Credit Reform was initiated, a reform of the tax system abolished the majority of the taxes which had previously existed, and radically simplified the revenue system. Prior to this the tax system had retained much of its traditional form. There had been some seventy-odd taxes, including income[3] and inheritance taxes, the agricultural tax on peasant farms, customs and excise, a tax on excess profits, and various stamp duties. There

---

[1] What was actually terminated was the use of any kind of *buyers'* paper. Not all kinds of commercial paper were, therefore, banned, and the ban only applied to the socialised sector. But in practice nearly all such transactions came to an end, including promissory notes. (Cf. Arnold, *op. cit.*, 351.)

[2] Sitnin and Sitkin, *loc. cit.*, 25.

[3] The income tax was graded according to classes.

was also an industrial and trading licence duty, which was graded according to the size of the turnover of an enterprise : a tax of which the Turnover Tax in its subsequent form would seem to have been the lineal descendant. Revenues from direct and indirect taxation were about equal ; the former representing a much larger and the latter a much smaller proportion of total tax revenue than in Tsarist times. The taxation reform of 1930 abolished the old classification into tax and non-tax revenue, direct and indirect taxation, and for the seventy-odd existing taxes and duties substituted six main sources of revenue. Two broad revenue-categories were distinguished : " revenue from socialised economy " and " methods of mobilising the resources of the population ". The former included the Turnover Tax, a tax on co-operative enterprises of all kinds, including collective farms, and a tax on profits. Of these the Turnover Tax, for reasons which we have examined, turned out to be far the most important. It was substituted both for most of the old excise duties and for the old licence duty. The second category included subscriptions to State loan by individuals, direct taxes (which included income tax, inheritance tax, and a special agricultural tax) and certain minor licence and stamp duties and customs duties.

Income tax has accounted only for a small proportion of total revenue. But in making any comparison with the budgets of other countries it must be borne in mind that a central peculiarity of the Soviet Budget is the prominent place occupied in it by capital allocations to industry, agriculture and transport: an item which does not figure in the traditional form of budgets in capitalist countries, where most of the sums devoted to capital investment flow through the new issues market or else come directly from the accumulated reserves of private companies. The income tax rates are small compared with other countries, and not very steeply graduated; varying from $1\frac{1}{2}$ per cent. at the lower end of the scale up to 13 per cent. on incomes above 1000; with a minimum exemption limit of 260 roubles monthly (raised in 1960 to 500 roubles). These rates apply to all wage and salary earners. The basis of taxation for writers and artists is yearly income; $1\frac{1}{2}$ per cent. being taken from an income of 1800 roubles a year and 13 per cent. from incomes above 12,000 roubles. Persons in private practice (*e.g.* lawyers or doctors) are taxed at higher rates rising to 69 per cent. on incomes above 70,000.[1] Handicraftsmen of all kinds are taxed at rates which are 10 per cent. higher, and peasants, whether collective farmers or

[1] A. M. Alexandrov, *Finansi S.S.S.R.* (Moscow 1952), 330–1.

individual farmers, are subject to a special agricultural tax, which so far as possible is assessed according to their farming income, according to standard rates varying with area and type of crop; the rates for individual peasant farmers being double those levied on collective farmers, in the latter case tax being assessed on the income it is estimated that they will derive from their own allotments. Collective farms and other co-operative organisations are taxed on their net revenue or dividend.   In May 1960 the intention of gradually abolishing direct taxation of wages and salaries in future years was officially announced.

In addition to the Budget of the Union, there are Budgets of the Republic and also local Budgets, the revenue of these latter being raised either from a share of the yield of the main taxes (e.g. income tax and Turnover Tax) assigned to them from the Union Budget or by supplements to certain taxes which the republics and local governments are empowered to levy.   Taxed profits of industry of republican and local significance also accrue to the Budgets of the republican government and the local authority respectively.   The relative importance of various items of revenue in these budgets on the eve of the war (*i.e.* for 1941) is shown by the following figures[1] (in milliard roubles).

	Union	Republics	Local Bodies
Turnover Tax . . .	113·3	2·9	8·6
Taxed Profits . . .	19·2	6·3	6·2
State Loans . . .	9·5	·9	2·9
Taxes on Enterprises . .	1·3	—	3·9
Taxes on the Population .	7·4	—	5·1
Local Taxes and Duties .	—	—	2·5
Miscellaneous Duties . .	2·6	·3	1·4
Other Income . . .	6·5	·6	2·5
Social Insurance Contributions[2] . .	7·7	2·3	—
Customs Duties . . .	3·0	—	—
Total	170·5	13·3	33·1

In the case of the Union Budget the main items of income and expenditure are illustrated in the following table, giving figures for 1963.[3]

[1] Based on N. N. Rovinsky, *op. cit.*, 34, 48.
[2] After 1938 *all* social insurance income and expenditure (and not only that earmarked for health services) passed through the Budget.
[3] *Narodnoe Khoziaisto S.S.S.R. v 1963 g.* (Moscow, 1965), 654–5.

STATE BUDGET OF THE UNION.
1963
(*in milliard roubles*)

Income

Turnover Tax	34·5
Tax on Profits	25·7
Tax on Income of Co-operatives, Collective Farms and undertakings of social organisations	1·4
State loans	1·3
Taxes on the Population	6·3
Income of Social Insurance Funds	4·7
Miscellaneous	15·6
Total	89·5

Expenditure

Financing the National Economy	38·8
Education	13·7
Health and Physical Culture	5·3
Social Security	8·1
State Social Insurance	3·4
Defence	13·9
Administration	1·1
Miscellaneous	2·7
Total	87·0

At the summit of the Financial Plan stands a final *résumé* of all the financial transactions that fall within the frontiers of this Plan. This is called the Unified Financial Balance of the Financial Plan, and includes a number of transactions which do not appear in the State Budget, either of the Union, the Republics or the localities. For example, it includes the credit transactions between the banking system and economic institutions and the investment-expenditures of industry out of its own reserves. What it has not included to date is the expenditure of consumers in the retail market. It is, therefore, a balance of all the main payments within the economy other than those made against goods-in-process or against goods passing over the shop counter into the hands of the consumer. As such it is complementary to the Production Plan, which rests on a balance of supply and utilisation for all commodities and productive resources. It depends upon and is the price-expression of the relations which form the texture of the Production Plan; and it will reach a larger total, *ceteris paribus*, the larger the amount of labour and productive resources that are engaged on tasks other than current supply for the retail market. But while the Financial Balance has an important place in crowning the edifice of the Plan, it is a determined rather than a determining element in the closely fitted strucure. Its general shape and size are determined by decisions about the allocation of productive resources, which form the basis of the Production Plan; but the state of the Financial Balance does not condition the shifting of productive resources.

CHAPTER SIXTEEN

THE LOCATION OF INDUSTRY

I

To those acquainted with the theory of industrial location the distinction is a familiar one between industries which are attracted to sources of power or fuel, to sources of raw materials and to the markets which they serve. The famous weight-losing principle of Alfred Weber has provided a basis for classifying industries into these primary types, and has been widely used as a criterion of what is and what is not the most economic location for a particular process of production. Of itself it does not provide the means for an exhaustive classification of industries, since not all types of production approximate to a single-line process in which the weight of a fairly homogeneous input can be compared simply with the weight of output. Some industries represent assembly-processes to which heterogeneous components are drawn from widely scattered sources, each source composing too small a part of the total supply to exert a pull in any particular direction, even if in total the various components lose weight in the course of being worked up into a final product. Nor does it afford an invariable criterion of what is an economic situation, since it takes account only of costs of transport, and is framed in terms of minimum transport-cost alone. As Weber himself pointed out, other factors, such as the situation of auxiliary industries and of labour supply (not to mention socio-economic considerations such as the avoidance of congested or over-specialised areas) may quite properly dictate a different pattern of industrial location from that shown by the least-transport-cost map. Nevertheless, for a number of important industries, particularly heavy industries, the weight-losing principle retains pre-eminence. In copper production as much as 100 tons of ore are sometimes needed to yield one ton of copper ; in which case the economy of bringing the copper plant to the ore rather than transporting the ore to the copper plant is likely to prevail over rival considerations. On the other hand, the development of the processes of copper concentration on the ore-field reduces the need for the main process of copper production to hug the site of raw materials ; and it may be that instead a decisive consideration becomes the proximity of the consumers of a by-product such as sulphuric acid, which has been the reason for the location of a copper plant in the central Urals near Sverdlovsk (since sulphuric acid is less transportable than copper concentrates). Other examples can be drawn from modern types of production based on an electrolysis process. The manufacture of aluminium, for example, requires some 25,000 kilowatt hours of electrical energy to produce a ton, or the equivalent of about twenty times the coal needed to smelt a ton of iron. Being so highly electricity-using, its production can usually only be economically carried on in the neighbourhood of plentiful and cheap supplies of hydro-electricity. The attraction of basic iron and steel production to the vicinity of coal and ore (and if utilising low-grade ore to the latter rather than to the former) is sufficiently familiar. The fact that a modern integrated iron and steel plant is a large consumer of water, and hence cannot be easily located in arid regions, is perhaps less familiar.[1] The same need for water appears in copper refining ; and in the Balkhash copper district the refining plant has for this reason been located at Pribalkhash on the lake, and copper brought a distance of 25 miles from the mining centre.

When, however, instead of attempting to explain or to foretell the " natural tendencies " of industry in a *laissez-faire* capitalist economy, one is searching for some criterion of optimum location in a planned economy, the problem becomes more complicated, and easy principles of determination lose a good deal of their relevance. Many factors which were treated as constant magnitudes before become variables, and moreover dependent variables, in the problem for solution. The transport map may be adapted to the requirements of industry, as well as industry moved to the least-transport-cost location on an existing transport-map.[2] New

---

[1] Cf. *Electric Power Development in the U.S.S.R.*, ed. B. I. Weitz, 369, which points out that a modern iron and steel plant consumes around 4,000 cubic feet of water per ton of pig-iron, and that a plant with an annual output of a million tons annually may require 100 to 140 cubic feet of water per second for continuous-flow cooling. When it is combined with coking plant and nitrogen-fertiliser plant its requirements will be still higher, probably by 50 per cent. or more. This series of studies goes on to say that " an analysis of the location of projected iron and steel combines shows that most of metal production will actually be concentrated at the ore fields and water supply sources ; no more than 30 to 40 per cent. will be produced at plants located near the power bases." (*Ibid.*, 370.)

[2] This consideration will not, of course, affect the unambiguous character of the notion of least transport-cost location expressed in spatial terms. In other words, this notion will still be a valid criterion underlying decisions about building a new railway or moving an industry. But it may well affect a particular solution of the problem on the basis of a pre-existing transport-map of unevenly distributed transport facilities ; and in certain marginal cases, at least, a revision of the transport map may be a decisive influence.

power sources may be developed ; new mineral resources, previously unprospected or unexploited, may be worked and industry
moved to their vicinity, instead of development being confined to
resources or raw materials near the old centres of industry. In
conformity with a long-term plan, not only may whole industries
be moved to a new location as a unit, but a whole industrial complex,
embracing auxiliary industries and industries linked by the utilisation of by-products as well ; and where industry goes, there go
centres of population and consequently markets and labour supplies
also. According to a Soviet view, " at the present level of development of productive forces none of the natural factors of location
can alone be decisive, even if a narrow engineering-economic
approach to the solution of these problems is adopted. Modern
engineering is so powerful that it can effectively overcome the
most unfavourable natural conditions of production ". In particular " concentration of production, by introducing ·new factors in
location, weakens the localising effect of each factor. It decreases
the probability of their coinciding and makes possible greater
flexibility in location. . . . By the use of plant combination, ore
enrichment, the concentration of production and modification of
technological processes, we can obtain a number of variants of
location and combination of various industries that are equivalent
with respect to favourable natural conditions and engineering-
economic characteristics."[1]

In the old Russian Empire, as we have seen, industrial development was mainly in the west, and to a long-term view its location
was far from rational according to any of the usual criteria. Heavy
industry, for reasons that were obvious enough, was located in the
Donbas-Dnieper region between the rich coal deposits of the
Donbas and the ore deposits of Krivoi Rog some two hundred
miles to the west. Here were centred almost nine tenths of the
mining of coal in the whole Empire (apart from Poland), and three
quarters of the smelting of iron. Other centres, potentially suited
for ferrous metal production, were for the most part neglected.
Even the old traditional centre of iron mining and smelting in the
Urals had been rapidly eclipsed in the second half of the nineteenth
century with the obsolescence of charcoal smelting, and by reason
of the distance of this region from labour supplies and from
potential customers. On the eve of the First World War it smelted

---

[1] *Ibid.*, 355-6, 358. Mention is made of the vistas opened by the development
of synthetic production of raw materials, " increasing the number of raw material
bases ". (357.)

only one fifth of the country's pig-iron, and nearly all of this in old-fashioned furnaces within the forest regions of the north and centre. Concentration on the Dnieper-Donbas region was chiefly due to the attraction of finishing industries and railway demand (railways being dominant customers of the iron industry as well as direct consumers of coal), and these were in turn dominated by the few large western centres of population or by the attraction of export markets. Kharkov, Moscow and Petersburg were centres of engineering, and there was some shipbuilding in Black Sea ports in the south and in the capital in the north. But primary metal production remained firmly attached to the coal and ore of the region where it had developed so rapidly in the '70's and '80's ; and the central provinces round Moscow, where most of the metal-using industry was situated, smelted only one fifth of the country's pig-iron. Of oil production 97 per cent. came from the Caucasus, largely because this was accessible for export *via* the Black Sea. Electrical power production, being mainly for lighting and municipal services, was chiefly in the neighbourhood of large towns like Petersburg, Moscow and Baku, and largely relied on drawing fuel from a distance. Water-power was virtually unharnessed, and peat for power production scarcely used at all. Light industry clustered round the few large western urban centres. The textile industry was almost entirely located in the central and north-western districts (83 per cent. of the linen, 85 per cent. of the woollen and 99 per cent. of the cotton), to which the raw material (with the exception of flax) generally had to come by a 2000-mile railway haul.

In total two thirds of Russia's large-scale industry which in 1914 fell within the pre-1939 frontiers of U.S.S.R. was concentrated in a few large urban centres of the west : chiefly the St. Petersburg and Moscow and Dnieper-Donbas districts. To the east and south-east vast areas, despite their rich untapped mineral resources and considerable agricultural promise, remained thinly populated, and urban and industrial development in them remained at a very low level. In Siberia, Central Asia and Kazakhstan, composing three quarters of the whole territory of the country, there were only 6 per cent. of industrial plants classified as " large-scale " or factory in type. The Kuznetsk basin in western Siberia, which rivals the Donbas in its coal resources, produced less than a million tons of coal a year, or under 3 per cent. of the total output of the country, and this chiefly for fuelling the trans-Siberian railway. These Altai foot-hills, which are now thought to contain a third of the coal reserves of the Union, were then almost unknown as a coal centre (such attention as had been given to this area in the past having been mainly directed towards rare or precious metals). Siberian towns were mostly mean and sprawling garrison and trading and transhipment centres, strung out along the railway at points where it crossed a river artery, and possessing no industry of any consequence beyond spirit-distilling and flour-milling. Political influences, as well as absence of population-centres and markets and ill-favoured transport and credit facilities, retarded the economic development of these " colonial " regions. It was a constant complaint of the bourgeoisie of Siberian towns that, as a market (such as it was) for manufactured goods, Siberia was kept as an exclusive preserve for the industries of central European Russia, and her meat and dairy produce and wheat were siphoned out in return along the trans-Siberian railway (although here again they complained that the zoning of railway-rates was unfavourable to their chance of competing in the markets of western Russia and in the export trade). A proposal to develop the Yenisei water route as a means of import and export relations with Europe, which to be practicable would have required a lowering of customs duties, was defeated ; and Siberia, which had no more than eight members in the Duma, attributed the defeat to the influence on the government of Moscow industrialists.[1] Non-ferrous metallurgy, which now occupies so important a place in the eastern regions, was almost non-existent in the old Russia. At the same time ferrous metallurgy presented a picture of mineral resources unexploited, many of the lowest-cost locations for extraction and smelting unused, and finishing processes separated from pig-iron and steel-smelting, even though both had gravitated towards the west.

We have seen that one of the striking features of economic development since 1928 has been the eastward shift of industry, not in the sense of any decline or even lack of growth in the older centres, but of an eastward shift of relative weight by the development of new industrial centres. As a result, the share of the Donetz basin in total coal production had already in 1937 fallen to 60 per cent. instead of 87 per cent. in 1913. After the war it accounted for less than a half, and the Dnieper-Donbas region even after its restoration for no more than a half of total steel output. On the eve of the Second World War the Caucasian oil regions still accounted for 80 per cent. of the oil; but by 1950 they accounted for no more than 64 per cent., and by 1960 it was planned that 75 per cent. of all oil should come from the new Volga-Urals region.[2]

---

[1] M. Philips Price, *Siberia*, 259.   [2] Bulganin's report to 20th Congress.

In its long-term programme for the geographical distribution of industry Soviet planning has treated the fuel and power network as the foundation-plan of its structure. When the original Electrification Plan was drawn up, and a year later the Regionalisation Plan of Gosplan, the main emphasis had still to be given to the older regions. The traditional centres of population and of industry had for the time being to be treated as the crucial constants in the problem. The supply of electrical power to industry was a novelty; and the enlargement of the power base for the industries of the Ukraine, the Moscow and Petrograd regions had priority among the tasks of the coming decade. A beginning was to be made with power development in the Urals and the Caucasus; but the electrification of Siberia and Central Asia and the Baikal and trans-Baikal region remained for the agenda of a second or third stage. Among hydro-electric projects included in the Goelro plan were the Volkhov[1] and Svir stations near Leningrad, the Dnieper dam at Zaporozhe in the Ukraine, Caucasian stations on the Kuban river and near Vladikavkaz, and west of the Urals a station on the Kama near Perm. Stations near Moscow (e.g. the Kashira, Shatura and Stalinogorsk) and stations at Ivanovo-Voznesensk and Balakhna near Nizhni (now Gorky) were designed to be mainly coal- or peat-burning, as was also the Donbas network, and in the Urals a station at Cheliabinsk and another near the town that was subsequently known as Sverdlovsk.

In the First Five Year Plan the traditional industrial districts still had the main emphasis in electric power development. The capacity of the Moscow region was to be quadrupled, that of the Leningrad region rather more than doubled and that of the Ukraine increased ten times (mainly due to the coming into operation of Dnieprostroi: in the Donbas itself the capacity was only to be doubled). But there was a beginning of that shift of attention towards new regions which was to become more marked later. In the Urals which to date had an insignificant power capacity, the two main projects included for that region in the Goelro plan but not yet implemented were to be constructed: Cheliabinsk with a capacity of 120,000 kw. and the Kama station[2] with 150,000. In

---

[1] The Volkhov was the first of the Goelro stations to be completed: it was opened in 1926 with a capacity of 58,000 kw. The Dnieper station was opened in 1932 and was designed to have eventually a capacity of 558,000 kw. The lower Svir station followed in 1933 with 96,000 kw.

[2] The project for a station near Perm was actually postponed until the later years of the Second Plan, and was due for completion during the Third Plan. There also appeared in the First Plan another and more ambitious project for a hydro-electric station between the upper Kama and the Pechora, based on the

addition the new steel town of Magnitogorsk in the southern Urals was to have a power plant and also Nizhni-Tagil further north, utilising blast-furnace gas, while the existing Kizel plant near Solikamsk was to be extended. In Transcaucasia mountain rivers were to be harnessed to a number of stations (including the Riom plant near Kutais) so as to double the capacity of this region to a total of 200,000 kw. In Central Asia there were to be some small hydro-electric plants with an aggregate capacity of 50,000 kw. mainly to supply power for irrigation projects. But for the whole of Siberia beyond the Urals the programme remained a very modest one. What there was of it was concentrated on the Kuznetsk basin, which was awarded two stations with a capacity of some 40,000 kw. each. Similarly, with regard to coal production : the shift of relative weight towards newer regions was still very small. The Urals, which in 1928 produced less coal than Kuzbas, were scheduled to raise their position in the coal supply of the country from $5\frac{1}{2}$ to 8 per cent. ; while the Kuzbas was to take a first step, but still no more than a first step, towards becoming " a second Donbas ". These two regions, which for a time were treated as a single " combine " in the development of iron and steel production, were together intended to produce less than a quarter of the Donbas output and 16 per cent. of total output in the final year of the Plan.

By the end of the First Plan the growth of heavy industry in the two rising centres of the Urals and Kuznetsk was moving ahead of fuel and power capacity, at least in the case of the former, which was particularly poor in supplies of coal. The Second Plan declared that " just as at the end of the First Five Year Plan period the electric power supply of the first coal and metal base of the Union was decidedly reinforced, so during the Second Five Year Plan period an electric power base sufficiently powerful to meet the swiftly rising demand of Urals industry must be created ".[1] Chiefly by increasing the capacity of existing stations, the power capacity of the Urals network was to be augmented three times to 1,300,000 kw. by 1937, the whole network from Berezniki to Magnitogorsk linked in a single high-voltage transmission system, and the total electrical consumption of the region quintupled. For Kuzbas the plan was again more modest ; but it was to have two large inter-connected heat-and-power stations (Kemerovo and Kuznetsk)

creation of a large storage lake, diverting part of the waters of the Pechora and Vychegda into the Kama. But this was also postponed, and was not to come on the agenda until after the construction of the Perm station.
[1] *The Second Five Year Plan*, 165.

with a total capacity of over 150,000 kw.; and the new coal centre of Karaganda in Kazakhstan was to have a regional station of 48,000 kw. capacity. In coal production the end of the second quinquennium was to see a substantial shift of weight towards the new regions. By 1937 Siberia, Kazakhstan and the Urals combined accounted for 28 per cent. of the total output. Of iron and steel production the Urals and Siberia accounted for some 29 per cent., and Kuzbas produced as much as one third of the whole pre-1914 output of the country. The more ambitious power projects in Siberia still lay in the future on the eve of the war : they were scarcely regarded as likely to come upon the agenda before the middle or later '40's. First of these was a group of hydro-stations on the upper Irtysh near Semipalatinsk, with a total capacity of two million kw., to supply power to the rich mining region of the Altai and to form the basis for its development as a centre of electro-metallurgy, producing ferro-alloys and aluminium. No more than two or three of these stations, including the Shulba station near Semipalatinsk, were on the agenda for early construction in the first half of the '40's. These were intended to be earmarked to supply power to mining and ore concentration in the Altai region ; and it was said that " the Irtysh hydro-electric stations rank among the cheapest power resources of the Soviet Union ". Eventually it is hoped thereby to electrify the Turksib railway. Second was a scheme for eight large stations on the Angara river and four on the Yenisei in eastern Siberia, with a combined capacity of 13 million kw. When completed these would enable the Baikal region (which also has coking coal at Cheremkovo) to become one of the largest centres of electricity-consuming industries, such as aluminium, magnesium and other non-ferrous metal and ferro-alloy industries and synthetic chemical production, in the world. But before the war it had not been intended that more than one of the stations should be erected until the middle '40's. Of a parallel co-ordinated river scheme for the Volga—described by Molotov as " the biggest of its kind in the world ", and partly intended to irrigate large tracts of land east of the Volga—some beginnings had been made by the Third Plan ; but completion of the two largest stations on the lower Volga (at Kuibyshev and Kamyshin) was still regarded as a task for the next stage of development in the later '40's.[1]

[1] Cf. E. A. Russakovsky in *Electric Power Development in the U.S.S.R.*, 445–8, 466–73 ; Acad. I. Alexandrov on " Angara-Baikal Region " in *Plan. Khoz.*, 1933. Nos. 7–8, 67 ; Prof. N. Kolosovsky in *Plan. Khoz.*, 1940, No. 6, 87 ; I. Dobronravov on " Utilisation of the Energy of the Kuibyshev Hydro-Network " in *Plan Khoz.*, 1939, No. 8, 47 seq.

II

Despite the rise of electricity, coal together with mineral deposits remains a powerful magnet to industry. Electrical power development is not closely anchored to natural geography : the power map can be redrawn by human planning, as the Goelro plan made a preliminary attempt to do. Electricity itself is more transportable than coal ; and once coal has been converted into electrical power, industry has a longer leash and can move further afield in search of alternative locations. But suitable positions for hydro-electric development are comparatively rare (short of very large initial capital costs in raising the levels of rivers and forming storage lakes) except in mountainous regions ; and where these are not available, the production of electricity generally has to rest on coal.[1] Moreover coal is required for metallurgical production ; and although the modern tendency is for iron and steel making to move away from coal towards ore (and sometimes towards finishing plant), this movement cannot proceed very far distant from coal ; and regions that are rich in coal retain an advantage as centres of heavy industry which other regions lack. Chemical industries largely rest on the utilisation of by-products from the process of coking or of metal production, and will accordingly need to have their roots in the neighbourhood of coal and metal.

The prevailing tendency in the U.S.S.R. has been for the newer steel plants to be located near ore rather than near power and fuel, while at the same time districts have been chosen where the latter are to be found at no great distance from the former. Round these iron and steel locations have generally been grouped metal-using finishing industries ; although in two cases, as we shall see, there has been a tendency to reverse the order of determination in the case of old-established centres of engineering. Consequently " iron and steel combines, together with central (power) stations, fix the basic intra-regional contours of the location of productive forces ",[2] and the planning of new regions has generally started from these, closely linked as they are in turn with coal and mineral deposits as the primary and determining factors. Boundaries between the main industrial regions into which the country falls tend accordingly to follow the lines of the " divides " between the main coal basins.

[1] Sometimes on peat and oil, and also nowadays partly or even largely on blast furnace gas, which can free the power plant and metal works also, to some extent, from attachment to the site of coal.
[2] *Electrical Power Development in the U.S.S.R.*, 369.

Knowledge about Soviet coal resources, as of mineral resources generally, has been greatly extended over the past twenty years ; and the known coal resources of the country are now said to be five times greater than they were thought to be in 1913. At present the Donbas, Kuzbas in Siberia, and Karaganda in Kazakhstan remain the three main coal centres ; with the inferior deposits of the Urals and what is known as the sub-Moscow basin following in the second rank. To these have to be added the newly developed arctic Pechora coalfield at the northern end of the Urals, Cheremkovo to the west of Lake Baikal in eastern Siberia which since the war has been developed with the industrial growth of this region, and some coalfields of no more than minor importance at present in the Far East (where the Bureya basin in the Amur Valley has rich potentialities) and in southern Central Asia. To the future belong two areas, of which previously little or nothing was known, but which now are thought to possess coal reserves which may one day place them in the front rank : the Tungus basin east of the Yenisei, deep in the *taiga*, and the Yakut coal deposits in the distant middle reaches of the river Lena.

Among these coalfields the traditional centre of the Donbas, with its very rich and closely localised seams, at no very great distance from iron ore, still holds the lead. The coal is famed for its high calorific value and coking quality ; and there is anthracite at the eastern end of the basin, which in the years before the war was the area of most rapid development. Attracted originally to the coal and drawing ore by rail from Krivoi Rog, iron and steel plants have recently shown a tendency to move towards the ore: for example, a new plant at Krivoi Rog and plants at Mariupol and at the Kerch ores in the Crimea. Prior to the revolution metal-*using* industries were not much developed in the south, except at Ekaterinoslav on the Dnieper. Much of the metal went north to the central region and to Petersburg. But since the 1920's the Ukraine and the region to the east of it have become an important centre of heavy engineering : for example Kharkov, with its electrical engineering, machine-tool manufacture and its tractor plant ; agricultural machinery at Rostov-on-Don and Odessa ; and shipbuilding and marine-engineering at Nikolaiev and Odessa. Further to the east there was the engineering centre of Stalingrad on the river bend where the Volga comes nearest to the Don : a town which grew from sleepy dusty Tsaritsin of 20,000 inhabitants in the '20's to the modern industrial city of half a million which the Reichswehr sought to capture and reduced to a blackened shell.

In all these cases finishing industries have been attracted, if not into close proximity to coal and basic metal production, at least to the same region ; and in pre-war days there was much talk of the need to carry this process of balancing finished production in the region with primary metal production still further.

Kuznetsk in central Siberia, the *parvenu* rival to the Donbas, is now estimated to have coal reserves amounting to some 400 milliard tons, more than five times those of the Donbas and surpassed only by the Appalachian coalfield in U.S.A. Its coal is of very high calorific value, exceeding that of the Donbas, and has a smaller sulphur content. Before the war it took second place in output to the Donbas, although it still accounted for no more than a sixth of the country's output. During the war, however, it has undergone considerable development and its relative importance to-day must be much greater. The coal of this region makes good quality coking coal with a low ash content. The seams are at moderate depth and often very thick. In the course of the 1930's this district developed more rapidly as a centre of finishing industry than of primary iron and steel production ; at the end of the decade being a *consumer* of some 16 per cent. of the pig-iron output of the country, or about half as much as the whole Ukraine, but as a *producer* of iron and steel accounting for only 10 per cent. and falling behind the Urals.[1] The reason for this was that originally Kuzbas lacked iron ore while the Urals were deficient in coal ; and the intention was that Kuzbas coal should travel west to repair the coal-deficiency of the Urals metal industry and iron ore should return eastward to Kuznetsk. But as both centres grew with giant strides, the strain on the railway facilities of Western Siberia raised the question of feeding each with what it lacked from some nearer source of supply. On the weight-losing principle it was easier to send pig-iron than ore eastward from the Urals ; and accordingly for the time-being finished metal production developed in the Kuznetsk area at a more rapid pace than primary production. Later ore deposits (with a high metal content but containing a high proportion of sulphur) in the Altai foothills, at Gornaia Shoria some seventy miles from Kuznetsk, were opened up; and in the future will increasingly supply the needs of this area from a nearby source; although at the end of the war these local ores supplied only 35 per cent. of the needs of Kuzbas, which still had to draw 65 per

---

[1] Cf. A. Baykov in Birmingham Memorandum No. 12, on Second and Third Five Year Plans, 3.

cent. of its ore supplies from Magnitogorsk.[1] Further distant there is also ore near Minusinsk; and there is manganese near Achinsk on the trans-Siberian. At the same time the completion of the Kartaly-Akmolinsk railway in 1937 enabled coal for the Urals and especially for Magnitogorsk and the southern Urals, to be drawn from the new Karaganda coalfield by a much shortened railway haul.[2] In the decade before the war the growth of Kuznetsk and its neighbourhood as an industrial region was quite phenomenal. Novosibirsk, which at the beginning of the century was a townlet of 5000 inhabitants, by the 1939 census had become a city of nearly half a million. Kemerovo grew from a townlet of 4000 inhabitants at the time of the revolution and 22,000 in 1926 to 133,000 in 1939. Stalinsk, which is the main iron and steel centre, had less than 4000 inhabitants as late as the middle '30's and had been swollen to a town of 170,000 by the end of the decade. Altogether the main towns of the Kuzbas region before the war had a population of some two million. The area had become a centre of the production of machine tools and high-grade steel (during the war of armament steel), of railway locomotives and also of various light metal products. It was on its way to becoming a centre of heavy chemical production (e.g. at Kemerovo), using waste products from local coke manufacture and ores for the production of synthetic rubber, liquid fuel and analine dyes. Nearby Tomsk had become a centre of aeroplane manufacture.[3]

The Karaganda coalfield, to the north of Lake Balkhash, being of most recent development before the war still occupied a fairly low place as a coal producer, mining some 4 or 5 million tons. In potentiality it is far inferior to Kuznetsk, and its deposits are probably less than a quarter of the Donbas. On the other hand, they probably exceed the resources of the Urals by four or five times ; and this district is of rapidly rising importance as the source of supply of high-quality coking coal to the southern Urals,[4] and also a source of supply to the important copper centres of Kounrad and Pribalkhash to the south on Lake Balkhash. This coalfield is now spoken of as the future " fuel base for Ural metallurgy " ; and its target at the end of the Third Plan had been set at 13 million

[1] N. Eremenko in *Plan. Khoz.*, 1946, No. 2, 92.
[2] The distance from Kuzbas to Magnitogorsk is some 2,300 kilometres. After the new line had been opened Karaganda was nearer to Magnitogorsk by some 1,100 kilometres than Kuzbas.
[3] D. Bogorad on " The Kemerovo Power-Chemical Complex " in *Plan. Khoz.*, 1935, Nos. 11–12, 154 seq.
[4] In 1939, however, the Urals still only drew 25 per cent. of its coking coal from Karaganda and continued to rely fairly heavily on Kuzbas coal. (Cf. I. P. Sekt on " Karaganda Coal : Magnitogorsk Works " in *Plan. Khoz.*, 1940, No. 4, 96–103.

tons. At the same time there is iron-ore within 200 miles of the coal : a distance less than that of Krivoi Rog from Donbas. A defect, however, of the coal of this district is a high ash content and low phosphoric composition, which necessitate concentration, and the absence of water in this arid region is said to be a serious bottleneck on development. The town of Karaganda planted down in the desert steppe has also been a mushroom growth. In the middle '20's it scarcely existed. By the time of the census of 1939 it had a population of nearly 170,000;[1] in 1964 it had 477,000.

Of the Urals as a coalfield there is little to say. Rich in many kinds of metal, and with oil deposits (" the Second Baku ") to the west of it, this region only has some small deposits mostly consisting of rather inferior coal, which amount in quantity to no more than a tenth of those of the Donbas. Brown coal is mined east of Sverdlovsk and at Cheliabinsk. On the western slopes at Kizel there is some coal of better quality which can be used for coking ; but for most of her coking coal the region has to depend on imports from outside (from distant Kuzbas and now increasingly from Karaganda). Before the war the total coal output of the Urals was larger than Karaganda (some 8 million tons) ; but whereas Karaganda seemed destined for rapid expansion, the chances of future expansion of the Urals region were inferior to those of most other centres.[2] But its richness in high-grade iron ore (the Magnitnaya mountain beside which Magnitogorsk was built alone holding deposits of some 450 million tons with an iron content of 60 per cent.) has made it a centre of iron and steel production, which at the end of the 1930's produced twice as much steel as Kuzbas and one fifth of the steel output of the country. Closely associated with primary production are finishing metal industries : tractor production at Cheliabinsk, railway wagon building and heavy engineering at Nizhni Tagil and in the extreme south of the Urals at Orsk locomotive building, machine tools, and also heavy chemicals, which are also located in the extreme north-west at Solikamsk and Berezniki on the upper Kama. In addition the Urals are a centre of non-ferrous metal production, such as aluminium and nickel, of which we shall speak below.

---

[1] Cf. *Karaganda : Tretya Ugolnaia Baza Soiuza*, 14, 25, 7, 55, 111; cit. *Plan. Khoz.*, 1936, No. 8, 224. Recent discoveries have revealed rich iron ore deposits, which may eclipse those of Magnitogorsk, on the Ayat river in northern Kazakhstan, close to the Karaganda railway ; and also ore deposits of considerable importance in the valley of the Arys river five miles from the Turksib railway (Cf. V. G. Garkovetz in *Doklady Akademii Nauk*, 1946, vol. LIV, No. 4, 337–8).

[2] In the pre-war decade, however, its rate of expansion had been second only to Kuznetsk.

In the years just before the war a great deal of emphasis was being laid on the development of what is known as the sub-Moscow coal basin (south of the Oka river round Tula and south of Riazan) in combination with the ores of the so-called Kursk magnetic anomaly. The brown coal of this basin is of low quality, possessing only half the calorific value of Donbas coal and having a high ash and sulphur content. The reserves are estimated at about 14 to 15 milliard tons. In 1913 only 300,000 tons were mined ; and although by 1928 this had been increased to a million tons, it represented only some 3 per cent. of the total coal output of the country. The development of new methods of coal-dust burning, especially for power stations, gave it new importance as a basis for electrical power development in this region ; and both power stations and a chemical plant were erected in the neighbourhood of the coal. It is in this region that underground gasification of coal has been considered as an economic proposition and its development started before the war (also in one or two Donbas mines). The principle was adopted of converting the low-grade coal of this region (as with the low-grade coal of the Urals) into electrical power for industry, and thereby reserving the high-grade coal of the Donbas for metallurgical and chemical production. As a result, by the end of the '30's the sub-Moscow field was producing nearly as much coal as the Urals—about 8 million tons ; and on the eve of the war 10 millions. Meanwhile the Moscow region had continued to develop as an engineering centre ; and at the end of the Second Five Year Plan it was responsible for nearly a quarter of the machinery production and electric steel and accounted for nearly a sixth of the metal consumption of the country, of which 85 per cent. had to be imported from other regions, most of it from as far afield as Donbas and Magnitogorsk. Emphasis accordingly began to be laid on the development of primary metal production at Tula and Lipetsk, on the basis of the Kursk magnetic ores, local coal and peat, and the extensive use of metal scrap for steel, in order to reduce the reliance of the metal-using industries of the central industrial region on long-distance imports of metal.[1]

---

[1] Cf. E. Lemberg on " Questions of the Development of the Metallurgy of the Centre " in *Plan*, 1937, No. 12, 10–18. Reference is here made to successful experiments in the use of gas from peat, with an oxygen blast, for blast furnaces. Moscow brown coal had been previously considered unfit for coking. Recent laboratory experiments, however, had suggested that some Moscow coal could be successfully mixed with Donbas coal in a new type of furnace. Cf. also S. Guberman on " Economic Problems of the Moscow Region " in *Plan. Khoz.*, 1935, No. 3, 152–7 ; A. Baronenkov on " Kursk Magnetic Anomaly " in *Plan. Khoz.*, 1939, No. 11, 125 seq.

Leningrad with its general engineering and shipbuilding is also a metal-consuming centre which has previously had to rely on the primary production of other and distant areas. The opening up of iron ore in the Kola peninsula and near Lake Onega has raised the question here also of reducing its dependence on outside supplies by developing primary production in the district. To this end the Pechora coalfield at Vorkuta in the northern Urals, which was connected with the northern railway network by a new railway completed during the war, assumed special importance; the deposits of this field (where large outcrops were discovered by Professor Chernov in 1923) being thought to fall only a little short of those of the Donbas. The coal of Vorkuta has a low sulphur and phosphorus content and a moderate ash content, its calorific value is close to that of Donbas coal and it is suitable for coking.[1] Under the Fourth Five Year Plan a new metallurgical plant was to be built near Leningrad, to utilise Pechora coal and ore from the Kola peninsula.[2] This plan also provided for the building of a new metallurgical plant in Transcaucasia, based on Gruzinsky coal, with a capacity of half a million tons of steel " to cover the whole Transcaucasian consumption of metal " (also a tube factory in Azerbaizhan to supply the oil industry); and also a new metallurgical plant in Kazakhstan based on Karaganda coal and nearby ores, which together with the Uzbekistan plant " will satisfy the basic metal needs of all the republics of Central Asia ".[3]

The three other coalfields which remain as potential bases for industrial development in the future are the Cheremkovo basin in eastern Siberia (a few miles from the Trans-Siberian line) and the Tungus and Yakut. Of the potentialities of the first of these, in conjunction with long-term electricity developments on the Angara and Yenisei rivers, something has already been said. Cheremkovo coal is inferior in quality and quantity to that of Kuznetsk, and until recently was mined in a few million tons chiefly

[1] Cf. S. Slavin in *Plan. Khoz.*, 1935, No. 3, 136–40; also E. Steingauz on " Fuel-Power Balance of Leningrad and Ways of Reconstructing it " in *Plan. Khoz.*, 1935, No. 8, 109 seq.; L. Volodarsky on " Reconstruction and Development of Leningrad Industry " in *Plan. Khoz.*, 1945, No. 5.

[2] A report by a committee of the Academy of Sciences recommended three locations for steel plants : Cheropovetz west of Vologda, Lodeiny Pole on the Svir near Lake Ladoga, and Annensky Most. The report calculated that *pig-iron* transported from plants in the Ukraine or the Urals would work out cheaper in Leningrad than pig-iron of local manufacture (taking into account the transport of ore and coal), but that *steel* could be made more cheaply in this region owing to the plentifulness of available scrap (previously exported to other regions) and the large part played by scrap in the marten oven charge (Acad. I. Bardin, I. Probst, B. Rikman in *Plan. Khoz.*, 1946, No. 5, 46–7).

[3] N. Eremenko in *Plan. Khoz.*, 1946, No. 2, 93.

for railway and domestic purposes. Its calorific value is somewhat below that of Kuzbas, Donbas or Karaganda or even Kizel coal. But the seams are at small depth, and can be mined more cheaply even than those of Karaganda or Kuznetsk. Preliminary tests suggested that it could supply coking coal of fair quality. Total deposits are estimated at between 70 and 80 milliard tons and the brown coal deposits at Kansk further west nearer to Krasnoyarsk on the Yenisei at about 40 milliard.[1] This has some importance in view of the possibilities of this region in other respects (including its position astride the Trans-Siberian line), as a centre of metal, glass and chemical industries. There are deposits of iron and manganese on the western shores of Lake Baikal and iron deposits lower down the Angara valley. These deposits have been estimated at some 500 million tons and their metal composition is high. Irkutsk, with a population of a quarter of a million, already produces aeroplane engines, mining machinery and some machine tools.[2] If cheap hydro-electricity can be developed here in the future, this may well become the leading centre of electricity-consuming chemical-metallurgical industry.

The Tungus basin to the north-west, between three tributaries of the Yenisei, is potentially much richer, and some estimates (which remain no more than provisional, since it has not yet been fully prospected) place its deposits close to those of Kuzbas. But it is at present too far from transport lines (except by river) and centres of population to have early economic importance. At present no more than a very small amount of coal is mined in the lower Tungus valley mainly for supplying the local power plant at Igarka near the mouth of the Yenisei and for fuelling river steamers. In Yakutia along the Lena valley there are again coal deposits which it is thought may come close to those of the Tungus basin in quantity. A little of this coal is mined near Yakutsk, mainly to fuel the local power station ; and there are also some mines in the valley of the Vilui, a tributary of the Lena, where there is an iron works at the small town of Viluisk with an annual capacity of a quarter million tons of pig-iron ; there being iron ore in this valley and also in the Aldan valley and the upper Lena.[3]

Mention should finally be made of some locations of steel

---

[1] Cf. S. Kazmin on " Rational Utilisation of Cheremkovo Coal" in *Plan, Khoz.*, 1939, No. 11, 131 seq.

[2] N. Kolosovsky in *Plan. Khoz.*, 1935, No. 4, 143–53 ; also cf. G. B. Cressey, *The Basis of Soviet Strength*, 209.

[3] J. S. Gregory and D. W. Shave, *U.S.S.R. : a Geographical Survey*, 304. 320–1, 606.

plants in two regions remote from any of the familiar centres. At Konsomolsk in the Far Eastern Territory on the lower Amur a steel mill was constructed before the war which used coal from the rich Bureya coalfield further up the Amur valley and local ore. In 1942 a steel mill was opened at Tashkent in Central Asia. Both Trans-caucasia in the extreme south and the Kola Peninsula in the extreme north-west (which also has large nepheline deposits which it is thought may yield aluminium, and apatite deposits which are used for phosphatic fertiliser) have been seriously discussed in recent years as regions of iron and steel production.

When we come to consider non-ferrous metals we find the locational pull of raw materials operating very strongly in favour of new industrial regions : the Urals in particular and central Siberia ; also the Baikal and trans-Baikal region ; the Caucasus, Central Asia and the Kola Peninsula. Some of these, which are highly electricity-consuming, require the presence of cheap sources of power in the neighbourhood of their raw materials ; and in this case the limiting factor on their development tends to be the rate at which power-projects, involving large initial investments of capital, can be developed in the appropriate regions. Here the Caucasus, with its opportunities for hydro-electricity, has a manifest advantage ; and in the future the Urals when the large Kama river power-project can be completed, and the Irtysh and Baikal regions when their respective river-dam schemes can be translated from paper into reality. The production of other metals, again, will need to be carried on in fairly close association with ferrous metal-lurgical plants and finishing works.

At present the Urals occupy a leading position with regard to such industries, with their resources of nickel, bauxite, copper and chrome. The first centres of aluminium production in the pre-war decade were in the west, both located near hydro-electric plants : at Tikhvin on the Volkhov near Leningrad, using local deposits of bauxite discovered in 1930, and at Zaporozhe on the Dnieper, where it is economically advantageous to carry the bauxite to the source of power. Urals bauxites are, however, considerably richer and compare in quality with the best French bauxites ; and a third plant at Kamensk was producing substantial supplies of aluminium before the war. The limiting factor on its development was the availability of power, which was conditioned by the development of the Kama river schemes. Actually the Urals deposits were first discovered two years earlier than the Tikhvin, but their exploitation was not started until later. Bauxite was also discovered in 1933 in north-eastern Kazakhstan, near Akmolinsk and in the Bat-Bakharinsk district, and in the same year in the Angara valley : both of them regions which are scheduled for future hydro-electrical development.[1]

The Lake Balkhash district in Kazakhstan, as we have seen, has become a large centre of copper production. Also, further south, in Central Uzbekistan some fifty miles from Tashkent another copper centre was being developed under the Third Five Year Plan, utilising some rich local ore deposits and drawing power from the Chirchik hydro-electric plants, which at the same time provided a basis for a new nitrogenous fertiliser plant in the proximity of Tashkent. Central Asia also has lead and zinc at Chimkent. To the south of the Ferghana valley there are some large mercury mines ; and in the mountains there is some tin and platinum and radium. Tin deposits are also to be found in the Trans-Baikal region and are thought to exist in the Altai and in the far north-east in Yakutia and the valley of the Kolyma. Before the war the two main centres of nickel production were in the Urals, at Ufalei near Cheliabinsk and at Aktiubinsk in the south (where one half of the country's nickel reserves are said to be situated). But nickel ores are also found in the Kola Peninsula, in Kazakhstan, and inside the Arctic circle near the estuary of the Yenisei, at Norilsk, where mining was started before the war, the ore being refined in the town (which has 30,000 inhabitants), and shipped from the nearby river-port of Dudinka up the Yenisei to the Trans-Siberian railway. Lead and zinc are also mined in the Caucasus and in the Altai, as well as in the Urals and at Kuznetsk ; and copper is also found, apart from Central Asia, in Transcaucasia (in Armenia and Azerbaizhan) and north of Lake Baikal in eastern Siberia. Tungsten ores are, again, found in the Urals, in the trans-Baikal region (where one of the largest deposits in the world is being worked by a special Tungsten Combine in Buriat Mongolia) and in the Far East. Wolfram is found in the southern Urals and the trans-Baikal, and small deposits of molybdenum in the Far East, the Altai and Transcaucasia.[2]

Consumer goods industries, as one might expect, are much more dispersed, adapting themselves to the distribution of population

[1] Academician A. Archangelsky and E. Rozhkova on "Bauxite Deposits in U.S.S.R." in *Plan. Khoz.*, 1935, No. 4, 37–51; also cf. *Plan. Khoz.*, 1936, No. 7, 165. At the time in the case of the Angara deposits "the transport situation of these deposits is very unfavourable".

[2] Prof. D. Shcherbakov on "Problems of Geological Prospecting Work for Minor and Rare Metals" in *Plan. Khoz.*, 1936, No. 6, 56–63; J. S. Gregory and D. W. Shave, *op. cit.*, 241–2, 299, 304.

between various regions rather than shaping that distribution in any large degree. Moreover, as earlier chapters have shown, the official policy since the middle '30's has emphasised this dispersion, and the need to make each of the main regions as self-sufficient as possible in the supply of commodities which cater for consumers' needs. The textile industry is still mainly concentrated in its traditional centres to the north-east of Moscow and at Leningrad. But in the '30's a number of cotton mills were planned in the cotton-growing region of Central Asia, at Tashkent, Askhabad, Ferghana, Stalinabad and Khozhent, and also in Armenia, and a large hosiery mill at Tiflis. The mills constructed in these regions during the Second Five Year Plan were intended to have an eventual capacity equal to one fifth of total output, and to supply sufficient to meet the local demand ; but it is to be doubted whether this objective was near to being achieved by the outbreak of war. Western Siberia was also to have its cotton combine, drawing its raw cotton *via* the Turksib railway on the return journey of trains which carried Siberian timber and grain to Turkestan. The paper industry was another which remained attached to a limited number of locations ; but in this case not for reasons of tradition and history, but for the more solid economic reason of the need to be close to timber, as in Karelia and the upper Volga, the northern Urals and Siberia.[1] Food-processing industries are apt to be attracted to their respective sources of supply, such as fish-canning works to Astrakhan and meat-canning works to cattle-rearing districts such as Kazakhstan and the Volga and Eastern Siberia, sugar-refineries to the area of beet cultivation. The Second Five Year Plan had laid special emphasis on local industry, operating on a regional basis, " in close touch with local consumers' needs, with special local conditions ", as an increasingly important source of supply of " manufactured goods of general consumption " and as a means of meeting " the growing individual demands of the general consumer for better quality in the sewing of garments and shoes, in the manufacture of household goods and of objects of art produced by handicraft industry . . . of toys, musical instruments, sporting goods, and of radio, photographic and school supplies".[2] But the actual development of local industry usually seems to have fallen short of stated

---

[1] Prior to the revolution the paper industry was for the most part organised in small plants and was backward in technique : there were some 75 smallish factories of an average size of less than 100 workers, mostly in Poland, Latvia and Estonia. (Cf. V. Chuistov, " On the Development of the Paper Industry in U.S.S.R." in *Plan. Khoz.*, 1939, No. 10, 63 seq.)

[2] *Second Five Year Plan* (Gosplan), 274, 276.

intention. Molotov in 1939 spoke of the need to secure in each of the main economic regions "an all-round economic development, which means that in each of these regions we must organise a fuel industry and the production of commodities like cement, plaster of paris, chemical fertilisers and glass, as well as mass consumption goods of the light and food industries in sufficient quantity to meet the needs of these regions. Each republic and region must produce foodstuffs in general mass demand . . . also manufactures like fancy goods, needle trade goods, furniture, bricks, lime, etc." To this he added the interesting remark that "we must strictly forbid the construction of new plants in Moscow, Leningrad and a number of other major industrial centres".[1] Mention was also constantly made in the pre-war decade of the intention to "break down the contrast between town and country"; by which was intended presumably a design to build collective farm communities into hamlets possessing many of the amenities of urban life, linked with townships as district centres possessing processing plants for certain types of agricultural produce and secondary industries serving the needs of the neighbour-hood. In such centres collective farms and farmers would establish their "kolkhoz markets"; from them they would obtain various types of repair and servicing facilities; and from them they would draw their main requirements in manufactured goods.

The war, as we have seen, accentuated the shift of economic development towards the eastern regions, even if much of the evacuated population returned westward after the war had ended. It has been estimated that the population of the Urals, West and East Siberia and the Far East increased by nearly 10 million between 1939 and 1959, the greater part of this expansion occurring during and just after the war. The same estimate suggests that 20 per cent. of the total employed population was in Siberia and the Far East in 1956, and 34·5 per cent. if we add the Urals region, compared with 15·6 and 27·2 per cent. respectively in 1940.[2] A city like Novosibirsk had grown from a population of 400,000 in 1939 to over a million in 1964, Sverdlovsk in the Urals from 420,000 to nearly 900,000, and Alma-Ata at the southern end of the Turksib railway from 220,000 to over 600,000. The Seven-Year Plan of 1958 "proposed to make use of the natural resources which are richest in content and most advantageous as regards conditions of exploitation, particularly in the Eastern areas". Mention was again made of bringing industry "closer to the sources of raw materials and fuel"

---

[1] *Third Five Year Plan*, 39.
[2] J. A. Newth in *Soviet Studies*, January 1959, 269–78.

and of "the further specialisation and integrated development of . . .
large economic-geographical areas". Over 40 per cent. of capital
investments during the seven years were to go to the Urals, Siberia,
Far East, Kazakstan and Central Asia (*i.e.* to the *non*-European parts
of the Union); from which areas as a whole it was anticipated that
by the middle '60's nearly a half of all iron and steel, coal and electrical
power would come. Emphasis was also laid on the construction of
"the third iron and steel centre" of the U.S.S.R. in eastern Siberia
and completion of "the world's biggest hydro-electric station",
Bratsk (on the Angara near Lake Baikal), with the start of a comparable
giant at Krasnoyarsk on the Yenisei. Regarding transport, although
the proportions of total investment assigned to railway investment
seems to have fallen, these locational developments have been aided
by such work as the completion (and electrification) of what is known
as the South Siberian Railway, and extensive modernisation of the
railway system by the replacement of steam traction with diesel or
electric (the Seven Year Plan anticipating that by 1965 over 80 per
cent. of railway goods traffic would be hauled by electric or diesel
engines, compared with 26 per cent. in 1958).

The general picture that we seem to receive from the crowded,
quickly changing canvas of Soviet economic life is of eight or nine
main industrial regions each raised upon the foundation of its main
power-fuel-mineral situation. Within each region the order of
determination has generally been from mineral and power resources
to heavy industry, and from heavy industry to transport facilities,
the growth of towns and the founding of light industries which cater
for the consumer. According to the variety of conditions, particularly as regards fuel and minerals, there has been some specialisation between regions, as we have seen : regions of cheap electric
power being scheduled for modern electricity-consuming types
of industry and regions rich in high-grade coal for basic metallurgical production linked with chemical industries manufacturing synthetic products. Again, the specialisation of finishing
industries may be determined by the needs of the region : agricultural machinery in the black-earth belt of the south, mining
machinery in the Urals or Siberia. But this specialisation has, on
the whole, been subordinated to the aim of creating so far as possible
a " balanced economy " within each region. With regard to heavy
industry itself, this balance is far from being achieved as yet
between successive stages of production and between main branches
and auxiliary branches (utilising by-products or supplying components) ; and the volume of inter-regional exchange in the

products of various stages and branches of metal and chemical production is still very large. If there are economic advantages at all in regional specialisation, then some, perhaps a considerable measure of, inter-regional exchange must be expected to survive as a permanent feature.[1] But the principle that such exchange should be lessened (relatively even if not absolutely) as the development of the various regions proceeds has been seen in application in several cases in the years before the war—in the rapid development of engineering in the Ukraine and the attempts to develop primary metal production in the Moscow region and in Leningrad —and it will no doubt exert a further influence upon regional distribution of industries over the next two decades. But in achieving variety and dispersion of economic activities within each region the main rôle has been reserved for light and small-scale industries. While these will necessarily cluster to a large extent round the large centres of population where heavy industry is located, their presence will add variety to the types of employment in the neighbourhood of these focal points of urban development ; and so far as the planning of them is guided by the emphasis on dispersal and local orientation, they seem likely to serve as the basis of numerous more scattered and variegated small urban concentrations, further distant from the coalfields and mineral deposits.

---

[1] It is to be noted that in so far as labour and capital can be treated as mobile between regions (as to a large extent they can be in *long-term* planning), *comparative* cost differences lose most of their relevance as a basis of regional specialisation, and absolute cost differences (allowing for transport cost) become the main economic criterion.

CHAPTER SEVENTEEN

TRADE UNIONS, WAGES AND CONDITIONS OF LABOUR

I

Although it is often by implication denied, the human factor, in the shape of popular morale and initiative, has unquestionably played a greater, and not a smaller, part in the changes which this book has described than it plays in the working of other economic systems. No one who is acquainted with the character of those changes and with the processes from which they derived can seriously maintain that they were the product of a few planners and political executives at the top and that they did not in major degree depend upon activity and initiative at every level. Something much more than passive acquiescence was evidently needed to make collective farming a success, with its novel techniques and forms of labour, or to ensure that the multitudinous problems arising at the factory level in the day-to-day carrying out of industrial plans were solved instead of being evaded. It is inconceivable that economic changes, so ambitious in their character and extent, could have been effected without a fairly radical transformation of attitudes and relationships in industry and in economic life generally: in particular, a transformation in the attitude and relationship of workers to the productive unit of which they were part. Not only is it true that social change gave to life a quality it had not previously possessed ; but the changes that were occurring themselves demanded a new quality in economic life, since without it they could not possibly have endured.

Forms of organisation and also the psychology of incentives have here been factors of outstanding importance. As regards the latter, we shall presently see that full scope has been given to the play of individual incentives to work in the form of wage-payment systems according to results. While the profit-incentive as prime motive and governor of output and investment has been banished (the entrepreneur-decisions of economic textbooks being no longer in the hands of autonomous individuals but controlled by the plan), monetary incentives connected with wage-differentials have continued to be an economic force in Soviet economy so far as labour is concerned, as well as wage-premia related to the collective results of an industrial or trading enterprise.   At the same time every attempt has been made to weave these individual incentives into a pattern in which collective incentives and sentiments occupy an entirely novel position: to place them in a setting in which a sense of responsibility and of zeal for the collective achievement of the factory or the industry formerly was thought only capable of prevailing when an economic enterprise was yoked to an individual by bonds of private ownership.   As educators in these new attitudes, Soviet trade unions, since the early days of the revolution, have been cast in a leading rôle.   Since trade unions in the U.S.S.R. are not only industrial in structure, but are built upon the workshop as a basic unit of organisation (with its factory committee), they have exercised an influence at the factory level, not only over labour conditions, but over productive activity and economic morale, such as the trade unions of other countries can have seldom if ever exercised even under the most favourable conditions.

A unique characteristic of Soviet trade unionism, as singled out by Mr. and Mrs. Webb, is " the intense interest that it takes in increasing the productivity of the nation's industry ; in its inclusion within its own membership of the directors and managers who have taken the place of the capitalist employers, and in its persistent desire to reduce costs ".[1]   But this characteristic was not an immediate and spontaneous product of the revolution ; and it did not develop without some acute differences and struggles within the trade unions themselves over the position and functions of trade unionism within a socialised industry.   Linked with this is an organisational feature of which mention has already been made: the fact that the frontiers of a trade union are coterminous (approximately) with the industry in which its members work ; that it includes within the same union all crafts and grades within that industry from unskilled to technical and managerial personnel ;[2] and that its unit of organisation, instead of being the geographical branch, is the factory or place of work, with the factory committee (*Fabcom* or *Mestcom*) combining the rôles of branch committee and shop stewards' committee and the workers' side of a joint production committee in our own country.   Trade unions are elective bodies, independent of the State ; and in the later part

---

[1] *Soviet Communism*, 218.

[2] Scientific and technical personnel, however, have their own sections within the industrial unions, and these sections often meet in regional and national conferences of their own.

of the pre-war decade special emphasis was placed on activities conducted by elected voluntary members, instead of by paid officials, at the local and the factory level. A trade union is, however, only entitled to legal recognition as such if it is accepted for affiliation to the central body of the trade union world, the Central Council of Trade Unions : a body which (like the A.F. of L. in U.S.A. but unlike the T.U.C. in Great Britain) has the power to take decisions which are binding on the organisations affiliated to it : for example, on questions concerning demarcation and wage-policy. Like its British counterpart, a Soviet trade union " is based on optional individual membership and subscription "— trade union membership cannot legally be made a condition of employment, but trade unions can and do insert a " preference in employment " condition in their agreements ; " it appoints and pays its own officials and manages its business by its own elected committees ; it conducts, through its highest committees and its national officials, the collective bargaining by which the general scheme and standard rates of wages are fixed " and " it takes part, through its chosen representatives and appointed officials, in almost every organ of government ".[1]   In the course of the 1930's the links between the machinery of the State and trade unionism were drawn closer in two respects. The first of these could perhaps be more properly described as a devolution of what had previously been State functions upon the trade unions than as a more intimate linking of the two. In 1933 the former Commissariat of Labour was disbanded. This had always been very closely connected with and directly influenced by the trade unions (the Commissar being customarily appointed on the nomination of the trade union Central Council). Now its two main functions, the administration of social insurance (other than health insurance and old-age pensions)[2] and factory inspection, were transferred to the Central Council of Trade Unions. Secondly, it became the practice for a general wages policy, defining the general contours of the wage structure, to be agreed upon annually between the Central Council of Trade Unions and the highest organs of government in the economic sphere in the course of the drawing up of the annual economic plan. This centralised agreement on wage policy established the

---

[1] *Soviet Communism*, 218.
[2] Health insurance, in the form of general medical service, was administered by the Commissariat of Health, and old age pensions (together with relief of persons not employed on a contract of service and hence not within the range of ordinary social insurance) by the Commissariats of Social Welfare in the various republics.

" wage-limits ", which, according to a Sovnarcom decree of 21 February, 1933, " all economic organisations and enterprises " were enjoined " strictly to observe in concluding collective agreements " about wages in their several industries.[1]

That an arrangement of this latter kind is an almost essential ingredient of a socialist planned economy should be evident on reflection.   In the first place it is evident that, if the output of various industries is to be planned, measures must be taken to ensure that the labour is forthcoming in quantities and qualities necessary to produce the requisite output in each case ; and (short of compulsory direction of labour) these measures will need to include the arrangement of such a relationship of wages between occupations as will attract labour to various industries and localities in the desired quantities.[2]   Secondly, it will be impossible for any part of the Financial Plan, of which we have spoken above, to be firmly constructed (e.g. the provisions for crediting enterprises or the planning of costs and of prices) until the main structure of wages is known, at least within not very wide limits of possible variation.   Thirdly, once the production plan for the output of consumption goods has been determined, the level of *real* wages as a whole (as distinct from the distribution of a given total of consumption between different groups of workers) cannot be affected by any subsequent alterations of *money* wages.   All that the latter can do is either to alter the level of prices or else to create a condition of short supply in the retail market for consumers' goods.   If the concern of the trade unions is with the level of real wages, it is obvious that their intervention must take place in the course of drawing up the production plan at an early stage, and not in the form of subsequent bargains in terms of money wages.   For these reasons, it is scarcely conceivable that wages could be settled by a process of separate and autonomous collective bargaining, industry by industry, such as has been traditional in the capitalist world, and such as to a large extent continued to exist in the U.S.S.R. under NEP throughout the early and middle 1920's.

It was quite early and fairly generally recognised after the

---

[1] *Spravochnik Sovetskovo Rabotnika*, 268–9, clause 9.   The State Bank was obliged to confine any credits for wage-payments within these wage limits.

[2] It is, of course, conceivable that the planning body should take the wage structure, determined independently by " autonomous " collective bargaining in each industry, as part of its *datum* and adjust its production (and financial) plan accordingly.   But such an arrangement would drastically restrict its power to plan production according to particular policy-ends ; since the wage structure which emerged in this way would largely influence, and " arbitrarily " influence, the supply of labour in various industries and hence the production that was possible in those industries.

revolution that the functions of trade unions would be substantially different from what they had formerly been. But it was a matter of prolonged discussion as to what form this difference should take. While the variety of viewpoints in the early discussion which followed the revolution was considerable, opinions tended to fall between (and in varying degrees to combine) two clearly defined and contrasted notions. On the one hand was a syndicalist tendency which we have seen at work in the activities of factory committees in the early part of 1918 and again as inspiring the " workers' opposition " group in the trade union discussions of 1920–1. According to this view, the administration of industry must devolve in large measure upon the trade unions themselves. Thereby administrative decentralisation would be combined with direct democracy in industry : control over an industry and its policy by the workers in that industry. It is not easy to see how economic planning, of the kind that developed in the 1930's, could have risen on a foundation such as this. On the other hand, there were those who took the view that trade unions could have no independent function in a Soviet State, and that they must become merged in the State machinery as organs of State endowed with special functions in the sphere of wages and labour discipline. This latter view was termed " the nationalisation of the trade unions ". It secured some reinforcement from the pressure of events during civil war towards compulsory labour discipline and the formation of labour armies to carry out tasks of special urgency on the economic front. But against this view Lenin early threw the weight of his authority in addressing the trade union congress of January, 1919. As a result, the main resolution of this congress, while for-bidding factory committees to " carry on an existence separate and apart from the trade unions " (as a sequel to which the central committee of the factory committees was disbanded), and advocating that trade unions should " co-operate with the Soviet authori-ties ", " perform certain of the functions at present discharged by the Soviets " and " aid in setting up various State institutions ", pronounced against the transformation of unions into State organs.[1]

[1] The report of the Central Council of Trade Unions for 1919 spoke of three coequal tasks which " throughout the time of the proletarian revolution, and particularly during the past year, Russian trade unions have placed before the workers " : namely, " first, at each step to defend the socialist revolution from attempts at counter-revolution ; secondly, to aid the Workers' and Peasants' Government to organise the national economy ; and thirdly, to guarantee to the wide masses of the workers that material minimum which the Soviet State, in conditions of civil war and economic disorganisation, has at its disposal ". (I. Glebov in Introduction to *Otchet Vserossiskovo Tsentralnovo Sovieta Profes-sionalnikh Soiuzov za 1919 g.*, viii.)

As a matter of fact, on the contrary to trade unions becoming sub-ordinated to and absorbed into the State machinery, the trade unions already had considerable sway over numerous governmental bodies. In November, 1917, they were immediately given five seats on the Council which was set up to implement the Decree on Workers' Control ; they had been given six places on one of the principal committees of the new Commissariat of Labour and the right of nominating most of the regional and local labour commissaries ; and they were invited to send at first four and later as many as thirty-five to the Central Executive Committee of the Soviets (TSIK). Speaking at the Second Trade Union Congress, the Commissary of Labour had declared that his department regarded it as their duty to carry out the decisions of the Congress and that their policy was " to see that all sections of the Commissariat are largely composed of members of trade union institutions ". Moreover, with the aggravation of the supply situation as a result of deepening civil war, the unions carried out an increasing amount of the work of Narcomprod ; and when Rabkrin (Workers' and Peasants' Inspection) was instituted in February, 1920, they secured the right of nomination of its inspectors.[1] On the other hand, under war conditions internal democracy within the trade unions tended to fall into abeyance at the same time as working relationships in industry came to approximate to those in the army.

The same issue again arose in the controversy which started at the Fifth Trade Union Conference in November, 1920, as a result of the military measures adopted by Trotsky, as Commissar of Ways and Communications, towards labour in transport and towards the railway trade unions.[2] In the ensuing discussion within the Party the anarcho-syndicalist conception expressed itself in the views of the " workers' opposition ", with their advocacy of " committee management " in industry and " the transfer of the administrative functions of industry into the hands of the unions " and at the local level into the hands of " factory and shop committees ".[3] At

[1] Cf. I.L.O., *The Trade Union Movement in Soviet Russia* (1927), 32-6. This report apparently could see no distinction between the so-called " nationalisation of trade unions " and trade union representation on government bodies ; and it seems to quote the above examples as evidence of the *de facto* development of the former.   [2] See above, page 127.

[3] Alexandra Kollontai, *Workers' Opposition in Russia*, 48-9. The Theses of the Workers' Opposition had spoken of " the organisation of control over the social economy " as " a prerogative of the All-Russian Congress of Producers, who are united in the trade and industrial unions which elect the central body directing the whole economic life of the republic ". This policy Lenin referred to as one of " unionising the State " and " transferring the apparatus of the Supreme Council of the National Economy piecemeal to the corresponding trade unions ". (*Selected Works*, vol. IX, 35.)

the same time Trotsky, with his policy of " shaking up the trade unions " and the " progressive amalgamation " of the trade unions " with the economic organisations ", represented the conception that in a Soviet State trade unions had no longer any independent rôle to fill. To this Lenin opposed the idea of the trade unions as being " not State organisations, not organisations for coercion ", but " educational organisations that enlist and train " : " schools of administration, schools of management, schools of Communism ". Elsewhere he spoke of them as " transmission belts " and " cogwheels " between the governing Party and the non-political and backward masses, generating a new socialist morale or consciousness in the latter and new attitudes towards production, while at the same time protecting the workers against " bureau-cratic distortions " in " their own State" and providing the means whereby the politically conscious vanguard could " absorb into itself the revolutionary energy of the class ".[1]

One of the central contributions of Lenin to the theory of the proletarian revolution had been his idea of the special rôle to be played by the Party—" a Party of a new type ". This idea is not something that can be fitted into the accepted categories of political theory, derived as these so largely have been from the experience and the ideology of the bourgeois revolutions of the nineteenth century. It is not to be thought of in terms of formal constitutions, with their elaborated divisions of function and balance of power. It must essentially be placed in an historical setting : against a background of rapidly changing class relations and changing composition of a class, in an epoch of historical transition when the equilibrium of society is precarious and is easily shifted. A continuance of the guiding rôle of this Party was for Lenin an essential condition of progress through the eddies and maelstroms of this transition period towards Socialism. To surrender this leading rôle, and the political and moral integrating force which it enabled the Party to exercise, would be to run the danger of political and economic disintegration of this complex and unstable transitional society, and to invite the eventual rekindling of Capitalism upon its ruins. To accept the direct control of industry by the unions would

---

[1] *Selected Works*, vol. IX, 4–5, 9. Lenin adds : " They are not the ordinary type of school, for there are no teachers and pupils : what we have is an extremely peculiar combination of what capitalism has left us, and could not but leave us, and what the revolutionary advanced detachments, so to speak, the revolutionary vanguard of the proletariat, promotes from its own ranks." Elsewhere he speaks of them as " reservoirs of State power ", and of " the *main* thing " as being, " not administration, but *contacts between* the central administration . . . and the *broad masses* " (*Ibid.*, 70.)

be to replace the steering hand of the Party by the decentralised rule of politically inexperienced mass organisations.[1] Here every political demagogue or Utopian crank or reactionary charlatan could make hay. At the same time, the steering hand of the Party was not something which could operate in a void, divorced from the masses. It was not conceived by Lenin as a form of autocratic domination *over* the masses ; even if some have represented it as being this. Still less was the guiding rôle conceived by him as a monopoly of political and economic activity : as something that was a *substitute* for popular initiative at various levels from the bottom upwards. Quite the contrary : it was thought of as galvanising such action from below. Hence the need for those " driving belts " or " cogwheels " between the Party and the masses, through which the steering and educating influence of the Party on mass activity could be exercised. Hence the impossibility of any liquidation of trade unions and other organisations of popular initiative—the inadmissibility of any congealing of the live democracy (and it was the democracy of *action* of which Lenin always spoke, not the democracy of *consent*) by over-centralisation within such bodies or by too close identification of them with the State machine.

As we have earlier seen, what emerged as the official policy of the Party and of the Government pronounced both against any " State-isation " of the trade unions and against the placing of the control of industry in their hands. Trade unions were to regain their position as democratic bodies and as voluntary bodies which they had to a large extent lost during the civil war period ; their officials to be subject to election and not to appointment. Their chief task was to be the representation of their members' interests in dealing with the managing bodies of industry ; while at the same time participating in the control of industry by appointing representatives to the bodies concerned with economic administration.

This view of trade union status and function was embodied in the decisions of the Trade Union Congress of 1922, after which it became the basis of the Labour Code of the same year. A trade union was defined by the Code as being " an association of citizens working for gain in undertakings, establishments and enterprises,

---

[1] In 1918 Lenin had spoken of " the need to learn to combine the ' meeting ' democracy of the masses—turbulent, surging, overflowing its banks like a spring flood—with *iron* discipline while at work. . . . Large-scale machine industry— which is precisely the material productive source and foundation of socialism— calls for absolute and strict unity of will, which directs the joint labours of hundreds, thousands and tens of thousands of people." (*Selected Works*, vol. IX, 221–2.)

public or private " ; and its functions were defined as being " to appear before the various authorities on behalf of wage-earners as parties to collective agreements and to represent them in all matters affecting their work and their conditions of life " ; " to represent the interests of wage-earning and salaried employees in relations with the management of the undertaking, institution or enterprise " and " before governmental bodies and other public authorities " ; to supervise the enforcement of labour legislation and to " co-operate with the State authorities concerned in the protection of the workers ". The Code provided that a trade union could secure legal recognition by registration with the Central Council of Trade Unions ; but without such registration and without acceptance for affiliation by that Central Council it could not enjoy a legal status. In their relations with the managements of industry the trade unions were granted certain rights and at the same time assigned certain duties. Managements were forbidden to hinder the activities of factory committees or to dismiss their members ; and were obliged to provide the use of a room or office for these committees, to give " free access to all persons on the business of the committee " and to defray their expenses. These committees were given (in a supplement to the Code) the right of joint decision with the management over such things as the " rules of employment " (governing matters such as fines and rules of discipline), the working of overtime and the fixing of the output-standards in connection with wage-payment systems. They were granted the right of appeal in any case of dismissal of a worker ; and, to enable them to exercise this right, it was provided that two weeks' notice of any dismissal had to be given to the factory committee. At the special labour sessions of the local courts of first instance, the People's Courts, one of the three members of the bench was reserved for a trade union representative. On their side the factory committees were required to " co-operate in the regular carrying on of production in State undertakings, and (to) participate in the control and organisation of economic activities ".[1]

---

[1] Cf. extracts from the Code in App. II of *Trade Union Movement in Soviet Russia ; Spravochnik Sovetskovo Rabotnika*, 274 ; cf. also J. Freeman, *The Soviet Worker*, 137 seq. Among other matters affecting the terms of employment which the Labour Code included were : the stringent limitation of overtime beyond 8 hours a day (in 1930 reduced to 7 hours until just before the war) ; the provision of two weeks' holiday annually with pay ; the exclusion of women and young persons from night work and from " dangerous occupations " ; the prohibition of employment of children under 16 save in exceptional circumstances by permission of the factory inspectorate and then for no more than 4 hours a day ; and the limitation of hours of young persons between 16 and 18 to 6 hours, falling between 6 a.m. and 10 p.m.

Strike action by trade unions remained legal under the terms of Soviet labour legislation, and in the course of the early and middle '20's numerous strikes took place (in 1922–3 some 500 were officially recorded involving some 154,000 workers and 322,000 lost working days, and in 1925 some 200).   A strike conducted without the sanction of a trade union could, however, be made the occasion of a prosecution before the People's Court if this was done at the initiative of the trade union concerned.   The general policy of trade unions was to discourage resort to strike action, so that strikes officially sponsored by a union were extremely rare (of the 500 in 1922–3 no more than 11).   A trade union journal officially stated that " it would be absurd for trade unions to deny the possibility of labour disputes.   Conditions of labour are laid down, both in State and in private enterprises, by agreements between the parties concerned ; and the existence of an agreement implies the possibility of disagreement or dispute."[1]   But the Central Council of Trade Unions issued an instruction to its affiliated bodies that strike action must only be employed in the last resort after every attempt had been made to utilise the conciliation machinery for the settlement of disputes.   A resolution of the Eleventh Congress of the Party had stated : " In the case of friction and disagreement between any section of workers and the institutions of the workers' State it is incumbent on the trade unions to assist in terminating the dispute as quickly and effectively as possible by endeavouring to secure for their members such improvements as are compatible with the economic development of the workers' State and are without injury to other sections of workpeople."   In practice, a dispute that had reached an advanced stage was usually dealt with by the intervention of the Commissariat of Labour, which had been given powers to intervene at its discretion and to refer the matter compulsorily to arbitration in cases of dispute in a State enterprise. For the settlement of conflicts a whole series of dispute bodies had been set up : joint disputes committees in each enterprise, representing jointly the management and the factory committee ; the labour sessions of the local People's Court, which might *inter alia* sit in judgment on disputes, if these were referred to it, as well as hear charges of breaches of the labour law ; local conciliation boards constituted *ad hoc* by local organs of the Commissariat of Labour, and consisting of representatives of the parties to the dispute with an impartial chairman ; and finally arbitration courts,

---

[1] *Vestnik Truda*, 1922, Nos. 11–12 ;   cit. *Trade Union Movement in Soviet Russia*, 170.

constituted in a similar manner to the conciliation boards, but having powers to deliver a binding award.[1]

According to the terms of the Code, and of the supplementary regulations attached to it, membership of a trade union was to be voluntary, and membership of a union was not made a condition of employment. At the same time, certain privileges were attached to membership, such as higher rates of social insurance benefit and the right of having an individual complaint sponsored officially by the union before a disputes committee or a labour session of the local Court. It was, moreover, open to a trade union to include a clause in a collective agreement establishing preference in employment for trade union members : a right of which considerable advantage was in fact taken by trade unions in framing their collective agreements with industry. After the introduction of the NEP, membership of a trade union was thrown open without discrimination to all employed persons, including the technical and managerial staff in all except private undertakings and including casually employed seasonal workers (for example building workers coming into the towns from the villages during part of the summer). Exclusion and expulsion from membership, of which there was at one time considerable complaint in the early '20's, was officially discountenanced by the Sixth Trade Union Congress, save in the most extreme cases of misconduct.[2] Members of co-operative producing units, whether industrial co-operatives or collective farms, were not, however, eligible for membership ; nor were individual peasants or handicraftsmen working on their own. As a result of the reversion to voluntary membership following the introduction of NEP and of the exclusion of independent handicraftsmen and co-operative producers, the membership fell considerably until in 1924 it stood at less than 6 million, compared with over 8 million in 1921. In the former year the number of wage- and salary-earners was about 8 million, of whom some two thirds were members of a trade union. Between then and the beginning of the First Five Year Plan the number of employed persons grew relatively slowly ; and in 1928 wage- and salary-earners numbered no more than just under 9 million.[3] After that date the number of trade unionists grew rapidly, mainly as a result of the growth of

---

[1] Cf. *Spravochnik Sovetskovo Rabotnika*, 286–7.

[2] Cf. *Trade Union Movement in Soviet Russia*, 78–80.

[3] Of these no more than 3 million were employed in large-scale industry. Another 670,000 were in building. By 1935 the total number had nearly trebled ; those in large-scale industry had more than doubled to 7 million ; and those in building had increased three and a half times to 2·2 million. (*Trud v. S.S.S.R. : Statisticheskii Spravochnik*, Ed. A. S. Popov (1936), 24.)

the total number of wage- and salary-earners. By the end of the 1930's the number of the latter had grown to 30 million, of whom some 84 per cent. were members of a trade union.

Regarding the participation of trade unions in the management of industry, a joint circular was issued by the Central Council of Trade Unions and Vesenkha in November, 1923, which, after affirming the principle that " the directing economic organs have full authority in all matters connected with the management of the undertakings entrusted to them " and that " it is inadmissible for trade unions to interfere with the management of undertakings ", made the declaration that " when appointing the managing bodies of trusts or separate undertakings, economic organs must invite the trade unions to submit candidates, and provide them with a list of other candidates, and, although the final decision lies with these economic organs, nominations must be examined in consultation with the trade unions ". The trade unions must further " be represented on the commissions which prepare the plans of economic organs " and the bodies which decide " the undertakings which are to constitute a trust or to be leased " or which determine " the branches of industry in which mixed companies can be formed and the conditions under which private capital may be admitted into Russian industry ". The trade unions continued to be directly represented in the highest organs of state, for example in STO and Gosplan and Vesenkha and Rabkrin, as well as in a number of economic commissariats.

In the final years of the decade, in face of the new situation introduced by the launching of the First Five Year Plan, differences concerning the functions of the trade unions broke out anew. The context of the discussion had been narrowed considerably since the beginning of the decade. It was no longer a question either of placing industry in the hands of the trade unions—by common admission this would have scarcely been consistent with the system of economic planning which had developed—or of merging trade unions into the State machine. It was a matter of the relative emphasis to be given to the two main functions of trade unions, between which during the NEP period a somewhat uneasy balance had been struck : the functions of " representing the interests of wage-earning and salaried employees " and " co-operating in the regular carrying out of production in State enterprises ". It was clear that the tasks imposed by the Five Year Plan gave a new urgency to the latter. Moreover, complaints were abundant that labour discipline was often bad ; and with a big influx of raw labour from the village, which would be the consequence of industrial expansion, these conditions might deteriorate rather than improve, unless " a turn towards problems of production " on the part of the trade unions was successful in creating a new atmosphere in the workshops. Tomsky, who had been chairman of the Central Council of Trade Unions throughout most of the previous decade, had always been a champion of trade union independence ; and had been identified with a policy of giving precedence to the task of " representing the interests of wage-earners and salaried employees " over that of co-operating in the improvement of production. One result was a tendency in most of the years of the second half of the decade for money wage-rates to rise faster than the rise of labour-productivity : a tendency which at the beginning of the First Five Year Plan, when the demand for labour was expanding rapidly, threatened to undermine those estimates of cost reduction on which the financial sections of the plan had been built and to accentuate the pressure on the retail market. Moreover, the trade union movement under his leadership had pursued a deliberate policy of wage-equalisation,[1] not only by bringing formerly low-paid industries into line with traditionally better-paid ones, but by narrowing the differentials between skilled and unskilled grades.

In a period when the need was abnormally great for wage-differentials to stimulate a rapid increase in the supply of workers suitable for the skilled grades and for responsible posts, it was inevitable that such a policy would arouse criticism from the heads of industry. In a period of rapid change in the demand for labour, wage-differentials, if they are to have an influence as incentives to labour, will need to be abnormally wide, rather than the converse, since they have to be geared to a desired *rate of increase* (which in this case was an unusually rapid one) in the supplies of skilled labour, and not merely to the maintenance of a normal supply. Since Tomsky himself was connected with the " Right-wing tendency " which opposed a high rate of industrialisation, he was unlikely to be very responsive to the requirements of a policy which he distrusted. Already in 1926, in an address to the Seventh Trade Union Congress, Tomsky, in announcing the policy of wage-levelling, had made a surprising statement, which seems to have

---

[1] A decision to this effect had been taken at the 7th Trade Union Congress in Dec., 1926. Two years later a report of the Central Council (Oct., 1928) claimed definite results. At this time it was said that the ratio of wages in the most skilled category to those in the lowest was 3 : 1 ; that only 8·5 per cent. of workers earned less than half the average wage and 48 per cent. between a half and the average wage.

passed unchallenged at the time : a statement which does not accord with the available data about the distribution of wage-earnings in Soviet industry.   After a reference to the need for " a levelling of the increasingly incongruous gap between the wage of qualified labour and the wage of simple, unqualified labour ", he made the following international comparison.   " Indeed, when foreigners travel here they are surprised most of all by the circumstances that under the dictatorship of the proletariat in our revolutionary unions . . . the difference between the pay of qualified and unqualified labour is of such a colossal magnitude as does not exist in western Europe.   Of course, this is explained by the fact that we are too backward technically, that too large a rôle is still played by individual skill, handicraft practice, etc.   But the explanation is one thing and elementary class justice is another."[1]

In the course of 1928 and 1929 complaints began to multiply about a " slackening of labour discipline " in industry, about absenteeism and bad timekeeping and malingering while at work. The labour turnover was on the increase, and in 1930 had reached figures of over 100 per cent.   Various reasons were given to account for this state of affairs : the large influx of raw labour from the village, unused to the discipline of a modern industrial establishments, and increased consumption of alcohol and bad housing conditions.   But industrial managers complained that the unions did little or nothing in the matter, and that the local organs of Narcomtrud and labour appeal tribunals took altogether too complacent an attitude.   It was said that on appeal workers were reinstated when they had been dismissed for most serious offences, such as rowdyism in the factory or theft or assaults on the factory staff ; with the result that managers felt that their hands were tied.[2]   Even Tomsky himself, in his opening address to the Eighth Trade Union Congress in December, 1928, quoted cases of acts of violence against foremen, including a case at the Skorokhod

[1] Cit. A. Bergson, *The Structure of Soviet Wages*, 187.   Prof. Bergson's analysis of Soviet wages shows that the range of inequality was " closely proximate to that among American workers in 1904 " (which is the year he takes for purposes of comparison, in view of the similarity of technique in most American industries at that date to Soviet industries prior to the Five Year Plans).   The analysis of Soviet figures refers to 1928, after Tomsky's wage-levelling policy had been in operation for two years.   But the effect of this policy in those two years cannot have made *much* difference to the comparison, and what is said of 1928 must have been approximately true of 1926 as well.   Nor does it seem likely that the inequality of American wages grew smaller in any considerable degree, if at all, between 1904 and 1926 when Tomsky spoke.
[2] Cf. *Econ. Zhizn.*, 3 March, 1929 ; *Industrial and Labour Information* (I.L.O.), 1929, No. 30, 140 seq.; for estimates of labour turnover cf. *Narodnoe Khoziaistvo*, 1932, 449.   In 1930 the rate was as high as 176.

factory in Leningrad where a foreman had been killed by a worker, and spoke of the " necessity of preventing the formation of groups among the workers who do not understand that Soviet industry is a socialist industry . . . that it is his duty to make sacrifices, that he must put off till to-morrow the satisfaction of the most legitimate needs of the working class "[1]—a way of expressing the matter which was probably calculated neither to make successful propaganda among doubting workers in favour of improving production nor to reassure his critics.

Criticism was especially levelled at Tomsky for harbouring a " syndicalist " tendency in his policy ; and at the meeting of the Central Council of the Trade Unions at the end of May, 1929, Tomsky was relieved of his duties as President, although for a time the secretary of the Council, Dogadov, who had shared responsibility for the policy pursued hitherto, retained his post. Commenting on the change, an industrial journal made this comment on trade union policy : " Not long ago the leaders of the trade unions were inclined to omit from their list of daily tasks the campaign for strengthening discipline, increasing individual output and fulfilling the Plan. . . . Still more recently the trade unions considered that the making of collective agreements was the best means of extracting from the management of industry the maximum of concessions while imposing on the trade unions the minimum of concessions."[2] Later the changes in the leadership of the trade unions went further, since the old leaders were stated to be " incapable of appreciating the rôle of the unions during the period of economic construction ", and to have " opposed efforts to reorganise the unions so as to remove mistakes ". Said the report of the new Central Council to the Ninth Congress in 1932 : " The old leadership gave precedence to the ' defensive ' work of the trade unions, contrasted with their task of co-operating in socialist construction." The slogan was issued of " face towards production ". " We must stand at the head of the initiative of the working masses in the matter of struggling to raise the standard of technical literacy," said Shvernik. " We must devote particular attention to raising workers with low qualifications up to the highest level of qualifications."[3] The new Central Council proceeded to lay special emphasis on the encouragement of " socialist competition " between different sections of workers and between different factory committees ; on the organisation of *udarnichestvo* (shock

[1] *Trud*, Dec. 13, 1928.   [2] *Torgovo-Promishlennaia Gazeta*, June 4, 1929.
[3] N. M. Shvernik, *Sadachi Profsoiuzov v Rekonstruktivnii Period*, 38–9.

brigades) among workers, setting higher standards of work ; on the organisation and encouragement of ambitious schemes of technical training ; and the introduction of new incentive-systems of wage payment to encourage higher output. Among the instructions on the work of factory committees which were issued by the Central Council in 1932 were the following tasks : " to see that the greatest possible use is made of piecework and that payment for work done is made on the basis of progressive premiums " ; " to prevent waste or overspending which may occur from the employment of excessively large staffs, or of the use of overtime to any large extent " ; " to combat spoiled work and stoppages of work which disorganise production " and to draw " the broad masses of the workers into dealing with this most urgent problem " ; and "to strengthen the activities of workshops and factories (through conferences to discuss production and brigades) so that the conferences become practical schools of training of broad masses of workers in the management of production ". In 1931 came Stalin's famous " Six Point speech ", in which he gave a prominent place to a reversal of that wage-levelling policy that had been pursued in the latter half of the 1920's. Trade unions and industrial managers alike must combat " lack of responsibility towards machinery ", " leftist practices of wage equalisation ", lack of personal responsibility and the old hostile and suspicious attitude towards the old engineering and technical staff. They must strive to " master technique ", to increase the training of skilled workers and to enforce strict cost-accounting methods in industry. " We can no longer," he said, " tolerate the situation where an iron-founder is paid the same as a cleaner and an engine-driver no more than a copyist." " The consequence of wage equalisation is that the unskilled worker lacks the incentive to become a skilled worker and is thus deprived of the prospect of advancement ; as a result he feels himself a ' sojourner ' in the factory, working only temporarily so as to earn a little and then going off to ' seek his fortune ' elsewhere. . . . Hence the heavy turnover of labour power."[1]

This turn towards production was not accomplished without loss of attention to the other main function of trade unions, and also without a weakening of internal trade union democracy. In the middle '30's complaints became fairly common that insufficient attention was being paid by trade unions to improving the working conditions and the housing conditions of their members.

[1] Speech to Conference of Business Executives, June 23, 1931, in *Leninism*, Ed. 1940, 368 seq.

References were also made to cases of arbitrary action by officials in substituting appointment for election within the union and in some cases overriding elections.   The trade union journal *Trud* spoke of " flagrant abuses of trade union rights and a neglect of the needs of union members ".[1]   Cases were quoted where workers were illegally deprived of their " rest-day " by the management under pretext of " voluntary labour " without protest from the trade union, and factory committees were accused of giving " passive support to the management in such abuses ".[2]   To judge by an order of the Soviet Control Commission in 1936 on " the examination of workers' complaints ", forbidding certain practices, breaches of regulations concerning disciplinary penalties and the hearing of appeals and complaints had been frequent.[3]   Since 1928 and 1929 the pendulum had evidently swung some distance in the opposite direction.   At a meeting of the Central Council of Trade Unions in the spring of 1937 the secretary, Shvernik, cited in his report a number of instances of undemocratic practices and criti- cised the lack of attention in trade union work to safety measures and cultural work.   A resolution adopted by the Council, which was given considerable publicity, instructed all trade union bodies to terminate the practice of filling vacancies on committees by co-optation and of voting for officers on the basis of lists instead of by individual candidature.   New elections were called for within three months, on the basis of a secret ballot and the nomination from the floor of candidates who were to be open to public discus- sion and criticism.   Increased attention was to be paid to the work of the labour inspectorate ;   encouragement was to be given to the appointment of voluntary inspectors from among the trade union rank and file ;   and the administration of social insurance benefits was to be placed in the hands of an elected insurance council in each factory.[4]

Measures were at the same time taken to reduce both the rôle and the number of paid officials in the trade unions and to increase

---

[1] *Trud*, March 26, 1937 ;   cf. also Feb. 27, 1933 and April 24, 1934.
[2] *Ibid.*, April 27, 1935.
[3] *Izvestia*, May 30, 1936 ;   also *Spravochnik Sovetskovo Rabotnika*, 218–21. This order forbade " communications of a confidential character relating to workers transferred from one establishment to another " and the imposition of disciplinary penalties without the culprit being given a hearing.   It condemned " procrastination and a formal-bureaucratic attitude towards suggestions and complaints from workers " and dismissals of workers for " formal motives ", including " social origin of parents " ;   ordered that records of complaints should be kept, and a time limit fixed for an answer to them ;   and announced the setting up of a special Bureau of Complaints attached to the Commission of Soviet Control.
[4] Cf. *Industrial and Labour Information*, vol. LXII, 449–52 ;   also the present writer in *Organised Labour in Four Continents*, Ed. H. A. Marquand, 311–12.

the rôle of the voluntary rank and file member in trade union work ; and in 1936 a drastic reduction in the paid staffs of trade unions took place, a maximum being set upon the size of such staffs in the future.   A trade union leader declared at the time that the aim of the change was to make the voluntary worker " the central figure " in trade union work.[1]   Steps had been taken in the direction of decentralisation earlier in the decade by breaking up the larger unions and forming new ones.   In the '20's there had been 23 unions, each covering one of the main branches of industry.   One of them, the Metal Workers' Union, covered a whole congeries of kindred industries and had a membership of more than a million. By 1931 the number of separate unions had been increased to 44, and by 1937 to as many as 162 ; the Metal Workers, for example, being divided into seven independent unions covering industrial branches such as engineering, motors and aircraft and non-ferrous metals ; the Miners' Union being divided into four societies, covering respectively coal, iron, peat and other ores.[2]   The basic unit of organisation, as we have remarked, was the place of work. The meeting of the members of a given factory (sometimes of a particular shift) or mine or depot or office or laboratory in theory elected their committee by ballot for one year.[3]   In each locality the various enterprises in an industry combined to elect a district or regional committee, and there were periodically regional congresses of the industry.   At an all-Union level each trade union was headed by a central committee elected by a delegate conference of the trade union; while the Central Council of the whole trade union world (a large body of 170, which in turn appointed a smaller presidium and a secretariat) was subject to election at biennial trade union congresses, consisting of between one and two thousand delegates, elected not from the national committees but from provincial or regional congresses of the various unions.

II

Since the early days of the revolution, largely on the insistence of Lenin, and against the prejudices of many trade unionists, the principle of introducing payment by result had been adhered to in industry wherever circumstances favoured this mode of payment. This was justified, not only by expediency in the circumstances of

[1] Evreinov, *Trud*, Jan. 15, 1937.
[2] Cf. A. Losovsky, *Handbook on the Soviet Trade Unions* (Moscow, 1937), 19.
[3] The elected member was supposed to be subject to recall at the request of one third of the members, and the committee was required by the union constitution to meet at least once a week.

the moment, but by reference to the principle laid down by Marx in his *Critique of the Gotha Programme* that in " the first stage of socialism " incomes would be related to the quantity and quality of work performed ; if only because " socialism is the society which grows directly out of capitalism " and " capitalist society has left us such relics and habits as unco-ordinated labour, lack of confidence in social economy, the old habits of the small producer, which prevail in all peasant countries ".[1] But while to this extent individual incentives to production were to continue as an economic force, and the pricing of labour-power according to the conditions affecting its supply was to remain as the basic constituent of economic accounting, every opportunity was taken of stimulating a new spirit and a new attitude towards work. Of this new attitude Lenin cautiously hailed the first signs in the *subbotniks*, or voluntary weekend labour to meet urgent tasks on the economic front, in the dark days of the war-time winter of 1919. In 1930, amid the dust and sweat of the construction years, Stalin returned to this theme, and spoke of the campaign for what was known as " socialist competition " in reaching production-targets as the beginning of " a radical revolution in men's views of labour, transforming labour from an unworthy and painful burden, as it was formerly considered, into a matter of honour, a matter of glory, a matter of valour and of heroism ".[2] This did not prevent him from simultaneously calling for a maximum utilisation of incentive-methods of wage payment to increase production and to enhance skill. Following Stalin's Six Point speech of 1931, the sphere of payment by results was further extended, until by the later '30's something approaching three quarters of all workers were being paid according to some variation of this system. In coal-mining the percentage was as high as 80 per cent., with nine in every ten workers being employed on some form of piece-work. In building even bricklayers and painters had a form of group payment by results.[3]

A common form of piece-work at the time was the so-called "progressive piece-rate" system, under which earnings rise progressively as output increases above a certain rate. For example, a standard output per unit of time is fixed for various jobs: a standard which is determined in consultation between the factory committee and the management (the technical assessment of the various jobs being in the hands of a special rate-fixer) and which,

[1] Lenin, *Selected Works*, vol. VIII, 239.
[2] Speech to 16th Party Congress ; Stalin and Kaganovitch, *Otchet Tsentralnovo Komiteta 16 S'ezdu V.K.P.*, 52.
[3] *Industrial and Labour Information*, vol. XL, 113.

when fixed, plays a crucial part in costing as the basis for annual and quarterly plans. Output in excess of this standard is paid at a rate 50 per cent. above the normal piece-rate for the job. According to some variations a 10 per cent. increase on standard is paid at a 50 per cent. higher rate, a 20 per cent. increase at double the usual rate, and so forth. Workers who fall below the standard are paid at the standard rate. In the event of the slowness of his work being due to causes outside his control, his earnings are subject to a guaranteed minimum of two thirds of the normal earnings (i.e. of the earnings of a worker producing at the standard rate) : a minimum which does not apply if the lowness of output is held to be due to the fault of the worker himself.[1] In many industries the majority of piece-workers were paid by this method: for example, in the iron and steel industry in 1937 three quarters of all workers were on piece-work and of these over a half were working to progressive piece-rate scales. The effect of such methods of payment was, of course, to widen the dispersion of earnings between fast and slow workers in any grade, as well as to raise the average level of money earnings as a whole : a factor which was responsible for the continued tendency during the Second Plan that we noticed above for money wages to rise considerably more steeply than had been provided for in the original Plan. On grounds of incentive there was evidently a great deal to be said for allowing money earnings to rise in this way during an exceptional period, even if it was not possible immediately to expand the supply of consumption goods in like degree. Professor Bergson in his interesting analysis of Soviet wage statistics has shown that the dispersion of wage-earnings (plotted on a Lorenz curve) was smaller in 1928 than it had been in 1914, and that, although by 1934 the inequality had become greater again, as a result of the policy of widening wage-differentials which we have described, " in 1934 inequality of reward still was less than that which prevailed in 1914 ". The combined wage *and salary* bill displayed a larger inequality in its distribution than the wage bill alone ; although not so much larger as one might at first suppose. In 1934 the upper 20 per cent. of all earners in industry received 40·3 per cent. of the total wage and salary bill, while the upper 20 per cent. of *wage* earners received 37·3 per cent. of the *wage* bill.[2]

Unfortunately the year to which Professor Bergson's study relates was prior to the termination of rationing and prior to the

---

[1] L. Weinstein, *Zarobotnaia Plata* (1937), 24 seq. ; decree of March 17, 1934, cit. *Spravochnik Sovetskovo Rabotnika*. 268.   [2] A. Bergson, *op. cit.*, 120–7.

effects of the Stakhanov movement (of which we shall speak below). Rationing, of course, had the effect of making the inequality of *real* earnings smaller than the inequality of *money* earnings ; and derationing in 1935 tended to have the opposite effect. Certain adjustments were made, however, in money wages in compensation for the result of derationing which had the effect of reducing the inequality of money earnings in 1935 (so that " in 1935, apparently, money earnings were less unequal than in 1934, but perhaps somewhat more unequal than in 1928 "[1]), and this change may have counteracted, partly if not wholly, the effect of derationing on real earnings. The influence of Stakhanovism is more difficult to estimate ; and the absence of detailed earnings data for later years makes a similar analysis for these years at present impossible. This influence was no doubt in the direction of augmenting the spread of earnings once again, in view of the high rates of earnings which Stakhanovite workers, who achieved new output standards, were able to enjoy. On the other hand, it has to be remembered that, since Stakhanovites were chiefly found among manual workers, the effect of the movement would tend to be to raise the average earnings of wage earners relatively to those of salary earners, and *to this extent* reduce the total dispersion of the combined wage *and salaries* bill.

Later, in the post-war period, the system of progressive piece-rates and large bonuses for special performance increasingly fell into disfavour. From the worker's point of view it was a disadvantage that, having grown used to a level of earnings which included a large element of bonus, he should have to drop down onto the basic wage when output fell owing to circumstances beyond his control (*e.g.* some dislocation of the factory's production-flow). This could involve a considerable sacrifice of earnings. From the management's point of view it had the disadvantage, as we shall see, of tending to raise costs. In the course of the 1950's a movement developed towards reducing the steepness of progressive bonus-increases. Later the system as a whole was increasingly dropped, simultaneously with a tendency to reduce earnings-differentials by raising the bottom-grades. Whereas in 1956 some 40 per cent. of industrial workers had been covered by "progressive piece-rate" systems, by 1960 this system had almost disappeared from heavy industry and was being rapidly reduced elsewhere.[2]

---

[1] A. Bergson, *op. cit.*, 131.
[2] W. Galenson, "Wage Structure and Administration in Soviet Industry", in *Internal Wage Structure* (Amsterdam, 1964), 324–5.

At the end of the Second Five Year Plan the position regarding wage-scales was that these were graded into categories which varied in number from eight in heavy industry to some fifteen in textiles, with a relationship between the highest and the lowest categories of about one to three.[1] This applied to earnings of the various grades at the *standard* rate of output. The dispersion of actual earnings was of course greater than this; and when this has been taken into account, the earnings of higher-paid grades may well have been some five or six times that of the lower grades.[2] Stakhanovites regularly attaining standards of output and quality substantially ahead of the normal standards generally received a premium of 100 per cent. or more in addition to the normal wage of their grade; and this tended to bring their earnings to a level double or even in certain cases three or four times what non-Stakhanovite workers of similar grade would earn. Prior to 1940 it frequently happened that a foreman received less wages than the general run of skilled workers when Stakhanovites constituted a large proportion of his department. Accordingly from 1 June, 1940, the rates for foremen were raised to a scale which ranged between a lower limit of 500 to 550 roubles monthly and an upper limit of 950 to 1100 ; and it was provided that foremen were in future to share in bonuses for high output in the form of a bonus paid when production in their department was in excess of the planned quota. The average earnings of workers at this period were between 200 and 300 roubles monthly. Engineers and technicians with special qualifications were paid at special rates of remuneration ; and in 1935 their average monthly earnings were 436 roubles, or rather more than double the average for all wage- and salary-earners at that time.[3] The equivalent figure on the eve of the war was probably in the neighbourhood of 550 roubles. Teachers in secondary schools apparently received between 300 and 600, teachers in universities between 700 and 900, and professors from 1000 to 1500, with top-ranking scientists sometimes ranging above the latter figure as high as 2500.

[1] Lorwin and Abramson in *International Labour Review*, Jan., 1936, give a ratio of 1 : 3·13 for the metal industry, which is only very slightly higher than the ratio announced by the Central Council of Trade Unions in Oct., 1928, as a result of two years of their wage-levelling policy : namely 1 : 3.
[2] Prof. Bergson's figure of the ratio of the ninth decile to the first decile in Oct., 1934, was 4·15 : 1 for wage- and salary-earners combined and 3·74 : 1 for wage-earners alone.
[3] *Socialist Construction in U.S.S.R.*, 368, 385 ; *Trud v S.S.S.R. : Statisticheskii Spravochnik* (1936), 82. The figure for office workers was 234 roubles and for manual workers 185. In some industries the spread was greater, e.g. black metallurgy, with a figure of 608 for engineering and technical personnel, 270 for office workers and 209 for manual workers. (*Ibid.*, 147.)

It is clear from these figures that, while the range is large, the highest paid among the skilled workers overlap with office workers and professional workers ; their earnings being above those of all but the highest-paid sections of the latter.

Talk about a new attitude to production and new social incentives to labour was to bear fruit in the course of the third year of the Second Plan. When the Stakhanov movement began to develop, it was commonly discounted abroad as a propaganda-façade ; while some dismissed it as being simply Taylorism in Russian clothes. But subsequent events as well as closer enquiry into the movement show that it cannot be so lightly dismissed as this. The methods used in the main introduced no new principle, and it is true that few of them will surprise students of American Scientific Management. Many of them represented an extension of the division of labour in an elementary form. As Ordzhonikidze, Commissar for Heavy Industry, said at the time :[1] " There is nothing strange, nothing bewildering in all this. . . . Correct division of labour, correct organisation of the work-place, correct arrangement of the technical process—there you have the secret of the Stakhanov movement." What was novel about it was that it represented a movement to rationalise working methods that arose from the initiative of individual workers themselves ; and as such its achievements came as a definite surprise to the management of industry. What in other countries has generally been devised by functional foremen and efficiency engineers, often in the teeth of relentless hostility from ordinary workers, was now being initiated by workers themselves. Moreover, it was an emphasis on rationalising working methods or technique and not on greater effort on the worker's part as previous campaigns of shock-brigades and socialist competition had very largely been. It showed a concern with quality, and not an attention to quantity alone. It was a product of thought and not merely of good intention—moreover, of thought about his job from what for most workers was an entirely new angle. Stakhanov's innovation at the Irmino mine in the Ukraine involved a simple principle : a separation of the two processes of coal-cutting and the propping of the workings, which obviated the need for each hewer to change frequently from one operation to another and enabled the picks and mechanical drills to be continuously utilised throughout the

---

[1] Speech at the Plenum of the Central Committee of the Communist Party of the C.P.S.U. Dec. 21, 1935.

shift. Previously the hewer had done only two and a half to three hours of actual hewing, the rest of the time being spent on propping. This happened on two shifts, the third being a repair shift ; and the result was that the pneumatic drills were operated for only five or six hours and were idle for the rest of the twenty-four. The new method enabled a team of Stakhanov and two timberers working with a mechanical drill to attain the remarkable output of 102 tons in a shift of five and three quarter hours, and subsequently even higher figures. Later this improvement was combined with another : an altered method of working a vertical seam so as to ease the strain on the hewer and to enable the coal as it was hewn to drop directly on to the conveyor, thereby facilitating a more rapid removal of the coal from the coalface.

This achievement of the pioneer (which Stakhanov tells us at first met with scepticism even from other workers in his own mine) quickly found imitators in other industries almost before it had had time to be publicised. Evdokia Vinogradova and her fellow-worker of the same name introduced a new system of team-work in the minding of Northrop automatic looms, and with nine unskilled assistants managed as many as 220 looms ; thereby attaining a per head output 50 per cent. higher than the best Lancashire or New England figure. Smetanin at the Shorokhod boot and shoe factory at Leningrad claimed to beat the records of the Czech Bata factory for lasting shoes. Krivonoss raised the steam-output of his locomotive, and hence his train-speed, by the use of anti-scale emulsion, by insulating pipes and cylinders and by a number of other small improvements. Marie Demchenko in agriculture (in sugar-beet production), workers on Marten-ovens at Makeyevka, workers in a vegetable cannery, miners in Siberia followed with comparable achievements. In the Donetz metal industry Eremenko and Konenev increased the output of an electrical furnace to between 44 and 48 tons a day, whereas European practice had previously regarded 38 tons as a maximum. In the making of electrical equipment for tractors productivity per man was raised to a level 50 per cent. higher than that of leading American factories ; in the Gorki motor works the production-time for making a valve was reduced by 20 per cent., and of pistons by 40 per cent., on that which operated in the Ford works in America ; at Taganrog the output of a boiler-making plant was increased to such an extent (four or five times) as to obviate the construction of a new works that had been planned.[1] A few

---

[1] B. Marcus on " The Stakhanov Movement " in *International. Labour Review*, July 1936, 11–12 ; Reports of First Conference of Stakhanovites, No. 14, 1935.

months later (in November, 1935) an all-Union Conference of Stakhanovites was held in Moscow ; and Stalin, addressing them, announced that their spontaneous initiative had succeeded in " smashing antiquated standards of output and introducing amendments into the estimated capacity of industry and the economic plans prepared by the leaders of industry ". Before long there was hardly a factory that had not its group of Stakhanovites : i.e. workers who had substantial achievements to their credit, entitling them to be ranked as such and to be awarded special bonuses for their attainments. In the larger factories their number often ran into thousands ; for example, the Kaganovitch ball-bearing works in Moscow, which, by August, 1936, out of 19,000 workers had over 2,000 Stakhanovites.[1]

We have said that the major part of these achievements represented, not just " shock " methods and temporary " spurts ", but permanent improvements in working methods. Once pioneered these methods could easily be copied even by much less enterprising or well-trained workers, thereby raising the whole level of productivity. This is evident from a number of examples. In the building trade the Russian bricklayer had traditionally prepared his own mortar and carried as well as laid his own bricks. Now these separate tasks were divided among separate members of a team. Moreover, the lay-out of bricklaying was so altered (by having bricks placed on a raised plank beside the bricklayer, etc.) that on the average he had to lift each brick only one foot instead of more than one yard, and the energy expended in laying a given quantity of bricks was reduced to less than a third of its previous amount. " In the Kuntsovskaia worsted factory the woman weaver Chekunova changed over from working two looms to eight looms and increased her output from 40 to 172 metres [by] persuading the head of the workshop to alter the construction of the beam of the loom and to have the driving-belt cleaned periodically, which prevented slipping, and this increased the speed of the loom from 130 to 145 revolutions per minute ; at the same time she had the shuttles made larger." In a factory engaged on X-ray apparatus " the milling-machine-minder Kolobov has increased his productivity six times by taking the initiative in having the faces of the bolts shaped by means of a milling-machine, and not, as before, a planing-machine ; in this way they can be worked simultaneously on both sides by the use of two milling-machines. In the Uritsky factory the metal turner Likhoradov succeeded in turning 11 metal bands per shift instead of 2·5 by using two supports instead of one and

[1] Cf. Georges Friedmann, *De la Sainte Russie à l'U.R.S.S.*, 104.

arranging his cutting tools in a certain manner. In the agricultural machinery factory at Rostov the turner Prusachenko has increased his productivity $6\frac{1}{2}$ times simply by using a shaped chisel instead of an ordinary one."[1]   Nossikov, a forgeman at the Voroshilovgrad locomotive works, who doubled or trebled the standard output, explained his improvement as follows : " Before I used to take the billets from the furnace myself and place them under the hammer. But now I stand the whole time at the hammer and some-body else hands me the billets. While I was moving from place to place the hammer would be striking unproductively." Under the new arrangement the forgeman stood at the hammer while an assistant took the billets from the furnace and placed them under the hammer, so that the hammer could work productively all the time.[2] Stakhanov himself made the statement : " To extract 100 tons of coal and more per 6-hour shift does not call for an excep-tional effort. All that is needed is to *organise the work* properly." Smetanin made a similar comment : " Many people think that increased productivity of labour can be obtained only at the cost of physical strain. Nothing can be more mistaken. Labour productivity can be increased only by a perfect mastery of tech-nique." On another occasion Smetanin said : " In order to work well you must know your machine well : you must know its inner life. . . . I did my 1,400 pairs, not as a result of physical strain but solely by maintaining a rhythm and because I made a careful study of each operation."[3] Another Stakhanovite in an Ivanovo textile mill, Kirianova, added : " If the Stakhanov movement is to make progress, more intelligent methods must be applied. . . . I have arrived at excellent results by abolishing unnecessary move-ments and that is the whole secret of my work."[4]

The movement was not without weaknesses and exaggerations; and in certain directions it even became something of a mania. Sometimes it represented short-term accelerations of *tempo* at the expense of long-term achievement. In some weaving establish-ments an increase in the number of looms tended was at the expense of the efficiency of each loom.[5] Sometimes it was allowed to lead to changes in output with too little regard for the dislocation thereby caused (e.g. through increased demands upon raw material or equipment) to other parts of the Plan. Mechanical attempts to

---

[1] B. Marcus, *loc. cit.*, 27, 29–30.
[2] Quoted by Ordzhonikidze, speech to Plenum of C.C. of C.P.S.U., Dec. 21, 1935.   [3] First Conference of Stakhanovites, Nov. 14, 1935.
[4] B. Marcus, *loc. cit.*, 23–4.
[5] Cf. Liubimov, speech at Plenum of C.C. of C.P.S.U., Dec. 21, 1935.

imitate it in barbers' shops or among laboratory workers and translators were later held up to ridicule in the Soviet press. But these examples, though they often provided good copy for foreign journalists, did not outweigh the solid achievements of the movement. Even in spheres like scientific work, where some of its hasty applications may have been ridiculous, there was probably room for the principle that thought should be applied to the method of work as well as to the work itself. Very soon attention was being turned to securing "a reciprocal adjustment of the work, not only of the various departments or workshops of a single undertaking, but of all related undertakings that co-operate in the same branch of production";[1] and we hear of an interesting example of a woman worker in a Kalinin spinning-mill organising for the first time a vertical system of "liaison brigades" of Stakhanovite groups at all the various stages of production.

Some years before, a campaign had been set on foot to encourage a system of patronage or tutorship by fast workers over slow. The new achievements of the enterprising vanguard of workers gave added importance to these efforts; and public statements laid great stress on the fact that it was part of the duty of a Stakhanovite not to rest content with showing that he could excel, but to train more backward workers to follow his example and to lend them continually a helping hand. An instruction of the Central Committee of the Communist Party (28 December, 1937) was at pains to condemn the tendency to concentrate on record-outputs by individuals and stressed the need to increase the number of Stakhanovites and to turn the movement into a mass movement. Prior to this, on the occasion of the anniversary of the movement, the trade union press had complained that the ranks of Stakhanovites did not yet comprise the *majority* of workers (although in many industries they comprised between a third and a half) and urged trade unionists to assist all workers to become Stakhanovites and to see that attention was paid to improving quality as much as to increase of quantity.[2] Special enquiries were held into the causes of slow output, and workshop discussions were organised to consider the appropriate remedies. Of these an interesting example (occurring two years later), was a meeting that was called in the Ordzhonikidze Engineering Works of slow workers who did not attain the standard output. These amounted to 6 per cent. of all piece-workers. The meeting was described as an eye-

---

[1] B. Marcus, *op. cit.*, 15.   [2] E.g. *Trud*, Aug. 27, 1936.

opener to the management. Among the causes cited were too frequent changes of foremen, stoppages of machinery, too much of the workers' time being occupied in preparing the lay-out of the work, and inadequate training ; and the remedies adopted included improved training facilities and the allocation of each slow worker to a more experienced one for advice and guidance.[1] Instructors in the new methods were appointed in leading enterprises, and arrangements were made for an exchange of experience between advanced workers in different factories and for the institution of special Stakhanovite schools.[2] Stalin in a speech in 1935 declared: "We used to say that 'technique decided everything'. . . . This slogan helped us to put an end to the dearth in technique. . . . That is very good. But it is not enough, it is not enough by far. . . . Without people who have mastered technique, technique is dead. In the charge of people who have mastered technique, technique can and should perform miracles. . . . It is time to realise that of all the valuable capital the world possesses the most valuable and most decisive is people." From then on some shift of emphasis was noticeable from machines to the training of people and to the elaboration of incentive-payments that encouraged individual innovation.

The type of man and woman of which these innovators were is not without interest. The majority were fairly young, between 25 and 30 : men and women of the new Soviet generation whose factory experience and the later part of whose schooling had fallen within the period of the Soviet régime. But, as Molotov pointed out, the bulk of them were not members of the Communist Party. A few of them were between 30 and 45 and had had long years of industrial experience. But the most common characteristic among them was that they had benefited from some kind of technical training—had passed at least what is known as the " technical minimum examination ". Not all of them, however, had. Busygin, for example, had come from the village in comparatively recent years, from a poor peasant family, and had worked first as a woodworker on the construction of the Gorki motor plant and later as a greaser in the forge. When he started working on the steam hammer, he was at first shifted from job to job, until he complained

---

[1] *Industria*, Feb. 14, 1938.
[2] Cf. *Industrial and Labour Information*, vol. LXXII, No. 4, 126. *Izvestia* of Sept. 23, 1939, gave some examples of co-operation between Stakhanovite instructors and the technical staff in the Ural Engineering Construction Works at Sverdlovsk which led to an adaptation of technical drawings for new tools, etc., to instructors' suggestions, made on the basis of experiments that they had conducted in working methods.

that he was never left on a job long enough to become proficient at it, and was nearly fired as a " trouble-maker " for his pains. Previously he had been only " semi-literate ", as he described himself (having read his first book, a volume of Pushkin stories, only a few weeks back, and " liked them very much ") ; and in the factory " nobody ever taught me ; I taught myself ".[1] As Stalin pointed out, they were not ambitious careerists or personal advertisers : they were " simple and modest people without the slightest ambition to acquire the laurels of national figures ".[2] They were serious, conscientious workers, possessed in a unique degree of a sense of pride in their work and of responsibility to their fellows— " people with culture and technical knowledge, who are able to appreciate the time factor in work and who have learned to count not only the minutes, but also the seconds ".[3] On the contrary to being jealous of the secret of their prowess, they were among the first to emphasise that their methods must be popularised and to exert themselves to teach these methods to others. In the course of 1939 the impetus of the movement they had started set in motion a new phase. This new phase originated simultaneously in two places, in engineering factories in the Urals and at Kharkov, and had its special emphasis in the mastering by the worker of several processes of production and of multiple machine-minding.[4]

The decisive test of the success of these changes must, of course, be sought in their effect upon labour productivity. Here unfortunately we can get no precise statistical test, since figures of output per head do not enable one to distinguish the effects of changes in working methods and of new machinery and equipment that were coming into service as a result of the constructional work of the preceding years. What with some reason, however, can be attributed in the main to Stakhanovism is the amount by which the increase of labour productivity in the two years following these innovations was in excess of what had been expected—the extent to which it exceeded the increase provided for in the Plan. Here we find at least *prima facie* evidence that the achievements of the movement were very substantial. We have seen that an outstanding deficiency of the First Five Year Plan period had been the failure of labour productivity to rise in the degree that had been

[1] Speech at First Conference of Stakhanovites, Nov. 14, 1935.
[2] *Ibid.*, Nov. 17, 1935.   [3] *Ibid.*
[4] An interesting example of later Stakhanovite improvements was in June, 1940, when a Leningrad weaver invented a remarkably cheap electrical device for flashing a signal when one of the looms required attention and stopping the loom automatically in case of a breakage, thereby increasing the number of looms he could tend. (U.S. Dept. of Commerce, *Russian Economic Notes*, Sept. 30, 1940.)

planned. The Second Five Year Plan had envisaged a more moderate rate of increase than the First had intended but had failed to achieve, namely 62 per cent. In contrast with the earlier period, this figure was actually exceeded, and by 1937 an increase of 78 per cent. over 1932 had been attained.[1] Molotov, in his Report to the Eighteenth Party Congress in March, 1939, declared that " our plans for increased labour productivity during the Second Five Year Plan period were exceeded because no plan could have made provision for the rise of the Stakhanov movement ". The increase was specially marked in the last two years of the Second Plan and in heavy industry. In steel the yearly output per worker, which was 253 tons in 1932, reached 575 tons in 1936 and 740 tons in 1937 (or slightly more than the German although less than half the American).[2] The year 1935, when Stakhanovism originated, was remarkable as being the year when " industry for the first time in a number of years completely fulfilled its plan for lowering production costs " and labour-productivity in large-scale industry rose by 12·9 per cent. compared with 10·7 per cent. in 1934 and 8·7 per cent. in 1933.[3] In the first seven months of the following year production in heavy industry increased by as much as 36 per cent. over the same period of the previous year, against 26 per cent. provided for in the Plan, with a labour-supply that had increased by no more than 6 per cent. The Plan had budgeted for an increased per head output in heavy industry for 1936 of 23 per cent. ; but in the first seven months alone this had increased by

[1] This is the figure quoted for large-scale industry in 1937 from *Planovoe Khoziaistvo* by Bettelheim, *La Planification Soviétique*, 309. Molotov in his Report to the Eighteenth Party Congress in March, 1939, mentions the higher figure of 82 per cent. for the end of the Second Plan period. Mr. Colin Clark makes an estimate for the *three* years, 1934–7, and concludes that " average income per head of the working population taken as a whole had risen by as much as 42 per cent. between 1934 and 1937 ". (*Critique of Russian Statistics*, 68.)

[2] Cf. Bettelheim, *op. cit.*, 310–11. Some plants such as Magnitogorsk showed much higher figures (due to their superior equipment) that surpassed the average American figures ; but these were still exceptional. Average coal output per man-*day* in 1936 varied from 1,020 kilograms in Donbas to 1,988 in Kuzbas, against 1,194 in England in 1936 and 1,710 in the Ruhr. (*Ibid.*) An article in *Plan* in 1937 gave 1,735 tons and 675 tons as the yearly output of pig-iron per worker in U.S.A. and in U.S.S.R respectively ; and spoke of labour productivity in iron and steel as a whole as being lower " by 2 to 2½ times than in U.S.A." (G. Paushkina in *Plan*, 1937, No. 10, 11.)

[3] The *Second Five-Year Plan*, Ed. Gosplan, 1936, xxxi. Marcus gives 10·6 and 12·7 per cent. as the increase per man-*hour* in 1934 and 1935. Output per man-*year* would tend to grow a little faster than per man-*hour* at this period owing to attempts to decrease absenteeism and hence the number of hours worked per man per year. (*Int. Lab. Review*, July, 1936, 7.) But the difference is very small, Marcus gives 7·37 as the average daily hours (including overtime) in 1928 and 264·2 as the average number of days worked per worker in a year ; for 1934 these figures were respectively 7·09 and 267, and for 1935 7·06 and 268.

28 per cent. Similarly in the coal industry output per worker had grown by the unexpected figure of 22·9 per cent. in the same period.[1] Over industry as a whole 1936 registered an increase in labour productivity approaching 20 per cent. : a rise in the rate of increase of more than 50 per cent. on the high figure of the previous year.

III

Another consequence of the Stakhanov movement was less immediately auspicious for the smooth working of economic plans. Operating as it did in conjunction with a wage-payment system which caused earnings to increase in greater proportion than output, it had the paradoxical result of raising the prime costs of output. Accordingly, while beating the production targets, it tended to disturb the financial provisions of the plan, based as these were on a level of wage-earnings appropriate to lower rates of output. When higher speeds of work are the product of greater effort, there is clearly everything to be said for increasing the remuneration of the workers at least proportionately to output, and probably for an increase of pay in greater proportion than output in so far as each additional increase in the speed of work is more difficult than the previous increase and the human strain becomes progressively greater. But when higher output is the result either of improved technical equipment or improved methods of work, the position is different. Once the new methods have been adopted, the higher rate of output does not necessarily involve greater effort on the workers' part ; at least not an increase in effort proportional to the increase of product. Moreover, the higher speeds can become general. Even the slow worker can copy the pioneers and learn the new methods ; and speeds which were formerly regarded as excep-

[1] *Industrial and Labour Information*, vol. LX, No. 2, 41. Mr. E. Strauss, who dismisses Stakhanovism as " a creation of official propaganda and official pressure " and " of course no movement of the masses of the working-class ", uses the curious argument that such progress as was achieved in 1936 must have been purchased at the expense of " a severe setback during 1937 " because the increase in labour-productivity was smaller again in 1937. (*Soviet Russia*, 297–83.) Since we are dealing here with rates of *increase* in productivity, we are concerned with the results of *improvements* introduced each year. It would be surprising, indeed, if Stakhanovism continued to register the same rate of improvement in all subsequent years as it did in the first year of its existence. Were we faced with an actual *decline* in productivity in later years, one could reasonably speak of a " setback "— of a short-period gain purchased at the expense of a loss of productivity in the long run—but not for the reason simply that the rate of improvement slackened off. Actually, the rate of improvement showed a new burst upwards in 1939, following the new wave of Stakhanovism that is mentioned above : in 1938 labour productivity increased 11 per cent. and in 1939 16·7 per cent.

tional cease fairly soon to be the preserve of the strong or the energetic. It does not follow, in this case, that those special gains which were justified as incentives and as a reward to those who had had the initiative to pioneer improved methods, when these were novel and unfamiliar, should continue to be earned by them indefinitely ; still less that these gains should be reaped also by those who at a later stage and at a safe distance walk in the steps of the pioneers.

During the period of the First Five Year Plan the increase in labour productivity that had occurred was no doubt primarily due to an improvement in the technical equipment which the worker used, as product of the capital investments of recent years. Kuibyshev in a report to the Sixteenth Party Congress in 1930 had pointed out that the increase in output per worker which had occurred during the past three years had been closely correlated with the growth in capital equipment per worker in those years, adding that "the dependence of these two series of figures upon one another is perfectly obvious".[1]

The Five Year Plan had adopted the principle that the gain in productivity resulting from the enormous investment that was occurring should to a large extent accrue in lowered money (prime) costs of production (and hence either in greater possibilities of investment or in lower ultimate prices to consumers). This required that wage-rates measured per unit of output should rise in smaller proportion than the increase in productivity. Partly this was a question as to whether workers should share in increased output *qua* consumers *via* lower prices or by direct increases in money wages. As we have remarked above, the latter may operate more powerfully as a production-incentive than the former, partly because changes in money-earnings are more immediately noticed by the producer than changes in their spending power, and partly because increases in money earnings can be related in each individual case to improvements in productivity, whereas the former cannot, since they diffuse the results of productivity over the whole community of consumers. Actually the Plan chose a compromise between the two: a compromise that proved to be an unstable one, since the increase of employment (and hence of total earnings) was

---

[1] V. V. Kuibyshev, *O Vipolnenii Piatiletnovo Plana Promishlennosti*, 63. Kuibyshev pointed out that productivity of labour had risen by 41 per cent. between 1926–7 and 1930 and the amount of capital equipment per worker by 39 per cent. During the First Five Year Plan the power-supply per worker (measured in kilowatt-hours per man-hour) increased by 33 per cent. (*Summary of the Fulfilment of the First Five Year Plan*, 275.)

such as to have inflationary consequences (see above, page 240), so that retail prices, especially of food, actually *rose*, and more rapidly than money wages could be raised.[1]   In a society where all income consists of work-income in some form (except for relatively small amounts of interest on deposits in a saving bank or in savings bonds), and property-income has ceased to exist as an income-category, there can be no issue concerning the sharing of the gain between two classes of industrial income, wages and profit.   Moreover, since the rate of investment is a policy-decision, forming one of the corner-stones of the Plan, the relation between changes in money-wages and changes in productivity cannot influence the amount that is devoted to capital construction, compared with the amount that is immediately consumed.   Since agriculture, however, rests on a system of collective farming and not of wages, the income of the agricultural population in terms of industrial goods will be dependent upon the relative prices of industrial and agricultural products; and consequently the price policy with regard to industrial goods may be an important determinant of the way in which the available supplies of consumption-goods are shared between the farming population and the industrial workers.[2]

If an increase of productivity is to result at all in lowered money costs of production, the output standards that form the basis of piece-rate scales will manifestly need to be revised from time to time as labour productivity rises.   This, in fact, became the practice in Soviet industry at the beginning of the '30's.[3]   There was little difficulty in this so long as the rise in productivity was wholly or mainly due to new equipment.   But the Stakhanov movement, which brought about large increases of output on the initiative of the worker himself, created a new situation.   Not only

[1] Had they been raised more, the greater, of course, would have been the degree of inflation.   The discontinuance of an official cost of living index at this period precludes any definite statement of the resulting fall in real wage-rates.   For an estimate see above, page 315.

[2] Here again, of course, it is true that, since it is the *relative* prices of industrial and agricultural products that matter, and the relation of each of these to wages, exactly the same result would follow if both money-wages and the purchase-prices of agricultural products were raised, industrial prices remaining constant, as if industrial prices were lowered, wages and agricultural purchase-prices being kept constant.   What is said in the text—that the policy pursued with regard to industrial prices can make a difference to the relative purchasing-power of town and country—only applies *given* a certain policy with regard to agricultural purchase-prices.

[3] A semi-official description of rate-fixing states that "a revision of the norm should be undertaken whenever there is a change in the technical processes of production or whenever the norm is rendered obsolete by the introduction of new methods of work, and should take place, as a rule, at least once a year." (Cit. Hubbard, *Soviet Labour and Industry*, 104.)

were these improvements in excess of what the estimates had allowed for, but they resulted (under progressive piece-rate scales and special bonuses) in a sharp increase in the unit-cost of production, at any rate as soon as the new methods had been adopted at all widely and had begun appreciably to affect the output and the earnings of the average worker. Many Stakhanovites trebled or even quadrupled their earnings within the space of a few months. Stakhanov himself, who formerly had earned 500 to 600 roubles a month, by September, 1935, was earning " 1000 roubles in eighteen shifts of work ", and others among his mates between 1000 and 1600. Busygin raised his earnings from between 300 and 350 to over 1000 ; Krivonoss from 400 to 900 ; Vinogradova from 216 to nearly 1200.[1] For a time there was a considerable confusion as to the proper treatment of output-standards in the new situation. In certain cases apparently industrial managements, faced with an inflated wage-bill, insisted on raising them (i.e. raising the output required to qualify a piece-worker to receive the basic wage). We find, for example, the organ of heavy industry, *Za Industrialisatsiu*, considering it necessary to remind industrial managers that an order of the Commissariat of Heavy Industry had provided that the new output-standards adopted in the spring of 1935 should not be revised within less than twelve months from that date.[2] Clearly any precipitate revision of standards would have served to discourage the pioneers of the new methods : at least, it would have made it very much harder for them to persuade their less enterprising workmates to follow suit. The efforts of some of the first Stakhanovites met with a certain amount of obstruction, not only from managements who, from innate conservatism or fear of resulting dislocation, looked askance at the new methods, but often from their fellow-workmen, who disliked any disturbance of time-honoured methods of work or retained old-time prejudices against " speeding-up ". Even Stakhanov himself had to face " certain workers who jeered at and hounded him because of his new-fangled ideas ". Any precipitate scaling-down of piece-rates would have stiffened the backs of such opposition and afforded justification for the complaints of those who grumbled that Stakhanovites' extra earnings were merely at the expense of the

[1] Report of First All-Union Conference of Stakhanovites, Nov. 14, 1935; cf. also G. Friedmann, *op. cit.*, 113.
[2] Cit. *Industrial and Labour Information*, vol. LVI, No. 9, 320. The Central Council of Trade Unions also issued a statement on Oct. 17 drawing attention to the fact that some managers had tried to revise the output-standards, and stating that the standards should be stabilised over a period of a year.

slow or even of the average worker whose pay-packet was now reduced. But it is equally clear that, once the new methods of work had been popularised, and the speed of work of the *majority* of workers in a plant had thereby been substantially enhanced, it would have been impossible to maintain the old output-standards intact. At any rate, if these had been so maintained, the whole structure of industrial costs would have been drastically inflated[1] just at the time when, following de-rationing, strenuous efforts were being made to reduce retail prices.

It was accordingly decided that, as soon as the new methods had come to be widely adopted among the workers, and opportunity had been given to more backward workers to improve their output, an upward revision of output-standards must occur. This was done in most industries in the course of April, 1936. By the end of August it was announced that in heavy industry between 70 and 80 per cent. of the piece-workers were able to attain or to exceed the new output-standards : that is, to assimilate the more rational-ised methods of work sufficiently to suffer no loss of earnings from the change.[2] There seems to be little ground, therefore, for the statements sometimes made that an outstanding result of Stak-hanovism was to create a labour aristocracy, whose higher earnings were at the expense of the majority of the unskilled. The minority, constituting perhaps a quarter or a third of the labour-force at the outside, may have suffered some reduction in earnings as a result of the change ; and to some extent these may have been the same persons as, previous to de-rationing, had spent a relatively large proportion of their earnings on rationed foodstuffs, and hence were adversely affected by the abolition of the low ration-price. Many Stakhanovites also, no doubt, suffered a reduction of earnings on the high levels at which they had been earning for the first few months following their achievements, although they continued to

---

[1] Part of the effect of Stakhanovism, it is true, was capital-saving. This had two aspects : first, it increased the output from a given plant ; secondly, it enabled a given volume of current investment to " go further " and hence ultimately to be more productive. An example of the latter was the statement of Liubimov, Commissar for Light Industry, with reference to the boot and shoe industry in a speech on Dec. 21, 1935 : " The Stakhanov movement in the shoe industry will enable us to fulfil the Five-Year Plan with the old factories and the new factories now under construction and to abandon the idea of constructing the two new shoe factories provided for in the Second Five-Year Plan at a cost of 36 million roubles each, thus saving 72 million roubles." (*Soviet Union, 1936*, 468.) Again, production at a Taganrog boiler-plant was increased four or five times, thereby making unnecessary the construction of a new works. (Marcus, *loc. cit.*, 12.) In such cases the net effect on costs would be that amortisation-charges per unit of output would tend to be lower. But this effect would almost certainly be small compared with the increase in unit wage-cost under a progressive piece-rate system.

[2] *Pravda*, Aug. 30, 1936.

benefit substantially as compared with their original position.[1] At the same time, an energetic campaign, as we have seen, was launched to afford opportunities for these slower or less-trained workers to attain to the new standards. In fact the situation we find, so far from being one where attempts are made to perpetuate the differential privileges of a better-paid minority, is the precise opposite.

Concerted efforts to augment the number of skilled workers and technicians at a quite unprecedented rate had been a characteristic of labour-policy from the beginning of the First Five Year Plan. Ambitious training-schemes were undertaken, impressive in their dimensions, both in special technical schools, which in 1936 were attended by nearly 700,000 students or nearly three times the number attending them in 1928, and in engineering and technical colleges of university standing for the training of qualified engineers and specialists. At the same time these were supplemented by factory schools where shorter courses of instruction were given for skilled workers by foremen and mechanics and the engineering staff of the enterprise, with a qualifying examination at the end of the course. As a result, over the period of two quinquennia the number of skilled mechanics increased fourfold and of engineers and industrial scientists increased sevenfold.[2]

Differentials of money wages were used in the 1930's, not only to increase the supply of skill and to encourage the attainment of new standards in quantity and style of work, but also to influence the supply of labour to different industries. Apart from building, it was the various branches of heavy industry where the demand for labour was expanding with exceptional rapidity. Prior to 1930

---

[1] M. Georges Friedmann, who made a special study of the Kaganovitch ball-bearing works at Moscow in 1936, found that in the foundry some workers, who had enjoyed an average wage of 300 roubles a month before the advent of Stakhanovism, had raised this to 700 or 800 by the spring of 1936 ; a level which was then lowered to 500 after the new output-standards had been introduced. But he found that "since the Stakhanov movement the average salary had been appreciably raised and there has not only been a gain to Stakhanovites properly so called ". In the textile factory " Red Rosa " he found a lower general level of wages, the median being just above 200 and the upper and lower quartiles about 300 and 145. About 17 per cent. had more than 350 roubles. These figures included apprentices and learners. (*Op. cit.*, 112–17.) The upward revision of standards in the spring of 1936 was probably in the neighbourhood of 30 per cent. of the average.

As regards the lowest-paid grades, a grant of 600 million roubles per annum was voted in the following year to raise wages in the lowest wage-categories to a minimum of 115 roubles a month for time-workers and 110 roubles for piece-workers. (Cf. *Industrial Labour Information*, vol. LXIV, No. 3, 274.)

[2] It is important to note the extent to which this technical intelligentsia, trained and reared as it has mainly been in recent years, is an intelligentsia of a new type. Already by 1933 65 per cent. of them consisted of former peasants or workers or else of children of peasant and worker families. (V. V. Prokofiev, *op. cit.*, 53.) By the end of the decade that proportion must have reached 80 per cent. or more.

coal and iron and steel had been relatively poorly paid (although engineering had traditionally been one of the better-paid industries, owing to the scarcity of skilled and responsible labour). In 1931 by an agreement between the Central Council of Trade Unions and Vesenkha wages in mining, iron and steel and heavy chemicals, and later in railways, were raised compared with wages elsewhere. As a result of this, according to a Soviet commentator, there occurred " an influx of labour into the leading branches of industry, the metallurgical, chemical and coal industries, i.e. those branches on which other branches of the national economy are dependent and where the conditions of work are much harder than in light industry ".[1] By 1937 the coal industry, which had occupied thirteenth place among industries in the scale of relative wages in 1928, had risen to second place ; heavy engineering had moved from ninth to fifth, and oil which had previously been eighth was in 1937 at the head of the list. As wage-differentials between industries were used to attract labour into the industries that were expanding most rapidly, so also geographical differences of pay were used to attract labour to regions, such as the Urals and Siberia, where life was primitive and labour was scarce.[2]

Labour recruitment prior to 1940 was largely done, in the case of technicians and skilled workers, through the familiar channels of advertisement ; and a worker or engineer was always free to terminate his employment in one enterprise and make a new contract of employment with another.[3] The high rate of labour-

---

[1] A. Nelepin, *Zarabotnaia Plata v Kapitalicheskikh Straniki i S.S.S.R.* (1932). It is to be noticed that this writer does not state that the raising of the relative rates in these industries was due solely to the temporary demand-supply situation, but justifies it also on the grounds of arduousness of conditions of work, which it is implied had not previously been reflected at all adequately in the wage-rate.

As a matter of fact by the end of the decade it was the textile industry that was complaining of being handicapped, no longer by shortage of raw materials, but by difficulties of obtaining labour ; and plant was standing idle for this reason to the extent of some 10 per cent. (Cf. D. Erlich in *Plan. Khoz.*, 1940, No. 9, 91.)

[2] In 1935 average monthly earnings for workers in large-scale industry ranged from 127 roubles in the Kursk region to 194 in Sverdlovsk, 221 in Eastern Siberia and 284 in Buriat-Mongolia. For engineers the range was from 316 in Kursk to 509 in Sverdlovsk, 570 in Eastern Siberia, 644 in Tadjikistan and 743 in Buriat-Mongolia. In iron and steel engineers earned 495 in Leningrad and 714 in Stalingrad. (*Trud v S.S.S.R.*, 82, 147.) These figures are of earnings and are influenced by differences in the type of industry in each place and the relative weight of different grades of work. But it seems clear that to a substantial extent the differences reflect differences in wage-rates for similar jobs.

[3] There were, however, certain exceptions to this. Technicians who had graduated as students of the special higher technical schools maintained by the Commissariat of Heavy Industry were under a special obligation to accept employment in the enterprise to which they were posted by the Commissariat, and to remain in that post (apart from transfer with official permission) for a period of three years. (*Industrial and Labour Information*, vol. LIX, No. 8, 278.)

turnover that prevailed was witness to the extent to which this was done. To a considerable extent enterprises competed with one another for labour, if not by raising their wage-scales (which were controlled, as we have seen, within the " limits " defined by wage-policy), by offering improved living conditions and other facilities or by various forms of up-grading and opportunities for training and promotion. For its unskilled labour industry to a large extent came to rely in the 1930's on labour supply agreements with collective farms. Among the things to which Stalin had directed attention in his Six Point speech of 1931 was the altered situation in the labour market due to the replacement of unemployment by labour-scarcity and the need to " recruit labour in an organised way," instead of " relying as we did formerly on an automatic influx of labour ". Under these labour supply agreements collective farms agreed to find among their members a certain quota of workers for the industrial enterprise at a given rate of wages for a minimum period of six or twelve months. In this way the labour reserve of the village was tapped to supply the needs of an expanding industry. In 1938 about a million and a half workers were employed in industry in the Russian republic on this type of contract. In each republic special labour recruitment committees were established to supervise and co-ordinate the movement of labour under this type of contract, with subordinate committees in each region to register demands for labour and to survey the available supply. Of the increased number of wage- and salary-earners between 1929 and 1939, amounting to some 15 million, it seems probable that at least two thirds was the result of migration from the village.[1]

Labour turnover and absenteeism, however, continued to be serious problems even in the late '30's, despite the efforts made to combat them by monetary inducements and the fostering of a new attitude towards work. Nor is it at all surprising that this should have been so, in view of the rapid influx into industry in these years of new labour from the village that was unused to factory work or even to the constraints of an urban existence. Some of the new plants (the Stalingrad tractor plant was an example in the early '30's) found acute difficulty in starting normal production, because they had become virtual training establishments from which other enterpises drew away newly recruited labour as soon as it had acquired a modicum of competence. This labour turnover reached its peak in 1930 and thereafter declined, especially after 1933 ; but

[1] Cf. the estimate of Mr. Hubbard, *op. cit.*, 143–4.

even so it remained surprisingly high.[1] As late as 1938 we find a lively correspondence in the Press in which managers, Stakhanovites and members of factory committees combined to cite examples of how production was being disorganised through slackness on the part of a minority of workers and by high labour turnover. Reference was made to " a small knot of disorganisers of production, shirkers, drifters and idlers, who, notwithstanding their relative insignificance in numbers, contribute great damage to socialist economy " and " impede all conscientious workers and employees in their struggle to create productive labour worthy of socialist society ".[2] The preamble of an official order (of Sovnarcom, 28 December, 1938) mentioned the continued prevalence of bad timekeeping, and of workers presenting themselves at the factory on only four or five days a week and migrating from one factory to another at frequent intervals. This order drew the attention of managers to the regulation that absence without just cause was a ground for dismissal, and that for this purpose absence could be held to include lateness of more than twenty minutes. It proceeded to stipulate that managers who failed to enforce dismissal in cases of three unjustified absences in a month, or four in two months, would in future render themselves liable to a penalty. Moreover, in future eleven months (instead of five and a half months) of service in the same undertaking would be necessary to qualify a worker for the customary two weeks' holiday with pay ; since unscrupulous persons had previously abused the regulation by going from one factory to another and, by spending five and a half months in each, securing two holiday-periods in the year.[3] Two further measures in the same year had a similar object : the introduction of work-books (by an order of 20 December, 1938), to be kept by the management as a record of the reasons for a worker leaving his previous employment and to be presented by a worker to the management when entering upon new employment,[4] and a revision of the social insurance regulations so as to grade the benefit to which a worker was entitled according to the

---

[1] The " accession rate " for all industries, expressed as a percentage of the average number of workers employed, was officially given as follows : for 1928, 100·8 ; for 1930, 176·4 ; for 1932, 127·1 ; for 1934, 100·5, after which it fell below 100. The rate was highest in mining and lowest in cotton. (*Socialist Construction : statistical abstract*, 388.)
[2] E. Vassiliev on " Socialist Labour Discipline " in *Plan. Khoz.*, 1940, No. 9, 19. The damage thereby caused was said to be particularly great " in conditions of contemporary production, the advanced technique of which strengthens the interdependence between technical processes and between individual sections of production ".   [3] *Industrial and Labour Information*, vol. LXIX, No. 4, 99.
[4] *Ibid.*, vol. LXIX. No. 3.

length of time that he had been associated with the same enterprise.

In June, 1940, four days after the French capitulation at Compiègne, measures were adopted which virtually put labour discipline in Soviet industry on a war footing. In the first place, the cherished seven-hour day (the shortest working-day of any country—in heavy occupations and in clerical it had been as low as six hours) was abandoned and a normal working day of eight hours was introduced instead.[1] Moreover, time-rates, output-standards and piece-rates were adjusted so as to leave weekly earnings the same. The result, therefore, was that the additional hour per day represented a contribution by all workers to the Soviet defence programme. The seven-day week was substituted for the six-day week, with each seventh day a rest day. The statement of the Central Council of Trade Unions accepting this lengthening of hours referred to " the danger of attack on the U.S.S.R." in the rapidly worsening international situation, and " the necessity, in the interests of peace, of increasing still further the defensive and economic strength of the Soviet Union, by developing industry, by producing more metal, fuel, railway rolling stock, metal and wood-working machines, motor-cars, planes, tanks, guns and ammunition, etc." The statement went on to speak of " a small percentage [of workers], some 3 or 4 per cent., that are young and new to industry, who neglect their obligations and disorganise production by straying from one plant to another ".[2] Coupled with the lengthening of working hours went an official order, not unlike the war-time Essential Work Order in Britain, which made it an offence, punishable in a court of law, for a worker to leave his employment without the permission of the management or to be guilty of persistent absenteeism.

On 2 October there followed a further order establishing new

[1] Occupations where six hours had previously been worked were now to work seven hours, with the exception of office-workers whose hours were lengthened from six to eight.

[2] *Industria*, June 26, 1940. Five days previously an editorial in *Industria* had cited examples of absenteeism and poor labour discipline. In the Red Triangle Rubber Factory the absence of nine press-operators without notice on one day had caused production to drop by 6,000 pairs of galoshes per shift. Five of the nine had been celebrating the night before and were not in a condition to work the next morning, and four of them stayed away in the hope of getting discharged and getting a better job elsewhere. While complaining that many managers winked at the conduct of loafers and paid little notice to what was stated of their past record in their work-book when engaging them, the editorial pointed out that sometimes a high labour turnover was " due to the fact that the directors and Party-members do not give enough attention to the proper organisation of production or to the cultural and living conditions of the workers ". It concluded by saying : " It is time that liberal treatment of loafers ceased."

types of vocational schools for young workers, and introducing compulsory enrolment of young persons for these schools. The preamble to the decree explained that, since " the future expansion of industry in U.S.S.R. calls for a constant flow of fresh labour to mining and transport, industry, factories and workshops ", " the State is faced with the task of systematically training new workers from among young people in the towns or on the collective farms in order to create the labour reserves that industry needs ". Three types of school were to be established : Trade Schools for boys and girls of 14 to 15, with a two-year course for training as high-grade skilled workers in the metal, chemical, mining and oil industries, in shipping and the postal and telephone services ; and Railway and Vocational Schools for young persons of 16 to 17, with a six-months' course in each case, in the latter for training in ordinary skilled and semi-skilled operations in mining, building, metal-working, etc. Pupils were to be maintained by the State during their schooling ; and entrants were to be selected by town Soviets and by the presidents of collective farms in the countryside, to a total number of 800,000 to a million each year. After completing their studies, pupils were under obligation to take work in State undertakings to which they were assigned for a period of four years, and in return they were to be exempted from any military obligations.[1] This coincided with the introduction of fees for pupils in High Schools and Universities (other than those attaining a certain standard of excellence), presumably with the aim of discouraging those who were not of what in this country would be described as scholarship standard from entering upon a university career and diverting them into the Trade Schools instead. In the course of the pre-war decade the need for high-grade engineers (university trained) had been satisfied more adequately than the need for middle-grade technicians (products of technical secondary schools), so that in many branches of industry the ratio of the latter to the former was abnormally small, with an " irrational utilisation " in consequence of the more expensively trained cadres on work which could have been performed by a lower grade of technician.[2]

On 19 October powers were further given to the industrial Commissariats to transfer workers and technicians from one enterprise to

---

[1] *Izvestia*, Oct. 3, 1940 ; *Industrial and Labour Information*, vol. XLII, No. 6, 404–5.

[2] The target ratio between the two grades had been regarded as being about 2 : 3, whereas in many branches of industry the actual ratio both before and at the conclusion of the war was said to be exactly the reverse of this. (S. Kaftanov in *Plan. Khoz.*, 1945, No. 5, 36–7.)

another, " wherever situated ". Declaring that " hitherto the
People's Commissariats have not had the right to make such
transfers and this has had a hampering effect on national economic
development ", and stressing the need for " a rational distribution
of engineers, technicians, foremen and the like among the different
undertakings ", the order bluntly stated that now, " if need arises,
workers must be transferred from one undertaking to another ".
This transfer, however, " must not have any material ill-effects
for the person concerned " ; and it was provided that the transferee
was entitled to be reimbursed for travelling expenses for himself
and his family, for the cost of transferring his belongings, and for
installation expenses ; to receive wages during the journey together
with wages for a further six days thereafter and a travelling allowance ; and that managements must not stand in the way of the
wives of transferred persons leaving their existing employment.
Anyone refusing to carry out such a transfer-order rendered himself
liable to similar penalties to those attaching to " leaving one's
employment without authorisation " under the order of 26 June.[1]
Thus a virtual mobilisation of labour preceded Hitler's attack on the
Soviet Union by almost one year. We shall see that it was to
be continued into the years of post-war reconstruction and even
after.

IV

A final word remains to be said in summary of the social
insurance system as this has grown up in the U.S.S.R. Since this
is a system applicable to employed persons, it serves as an adjunct
to the wage-system, and is usually considered to add something of
the order of magnitude of one third to money earnings. Co-
operative workers are not catered for by compulsory insurance,
but by voluntary insurance through mutual aid societies, to which
the State gives subsidies and sometimes grants of land. In a collective farm, for example, the formation of such a society rests upon
a vote of the meeting of collective farm members, and membership
of it remains voluntary when it has been formed. Administered
by elected officers, these societies come under the supervision of
the village Soviet and of the local office of the Commissariat of
Social Welfare ; and they are financed from members' contributions and contributions voted by the farm as a whole, supplemented

[1] *Industrial and Labour Information*, vol. XLIII, No. 2, 207. This order did
not apply to workers below the sixth category, i.e. to other than skilled workers.

by grants from the government and from certain other sources. Assistance when in need to persons who fall outside the scope either of compulsory social insurance for employed persons or of some form of voluntary insurance is the responsibility of the Commissariats of Social Welfare in each of the republics and of the social assistance departments of town and village Soviets, which maintain a staff of local inspectors and have local advisory boards drawn from active citizens and families of disabled persons.[1]

The Labour Code of 1922 had included (in Article 175) the following stipulation regarding social insurance : " The social insurance system shall cover all employed persons irrespective of whether the undertakings, institutions or businesses in which they are employed are State, public, co-operative, established under a concession or lease, of mixed character or private, or whether they are employed by private individuals ; and irrespective also of the nature and duration of their employment and the method of remuneration." At that time, however, the number of employed persons only composed one seventh of the occupied population ; certain categories of persons remained excluded from benefit (e.g. those disfranchised under the pre-1936 Constitution owing to their social origin) ; and the rights of salary earners were more limited than those of wage-earners. In the circumstances of the time benefits could not be extensive and could not be other than meagre. It was not until 1927 that old-age pensions were instituted, and then only for workers in certain industries. Unemployment benefit, which at that time existed and amounted to about a quarter or a third of the worker's normal earnings, was restricted to those with a considerable period of prior employment (one year in the case of trade unionists and three years for non-unionists ; with three to five years respectively in the case of non-manual workers), and it covered only between a quarter and a third of all unemployed persons. Since then the number of employed persons has grown to two thirds of all occupied persons. Old-age pensions have been extended to all wage-earners and (after 1937) to all salary-earners; and the old category of disfranchised, and hence excluded, persons disappeared. To-day only a few temporary or seasonal workers are not embraced within the scheme. Mr. and Mrs. Sidney Webb once said of this system (to which they referred as "a system of unlimited and universal security to the entire wage-earning popula-

---

[1] These bodies also supervise, and partly finance, special co-operatives and mutual aid societies for disabled persons (e.g. deaf and dumb and blind) and run rehabilitation centres and workshops for disabled persons.

tion ") that "in our judgement this provision of economic security has been . . . an important factor in making each workman conscious, not only of his Soviet citizenship, but also of his joint ownership with his fellows of the whole of the means of production ".[1]

This system, as it exists to-day, falls into three parts. The first, the provision of actual medical facilities, is administered by the Commissariat of Health in each republic and its local organs, and is financed by contributions from the central and from local budgets. The service applies both to earners and their families, and includes the service of specialists and the provision of medicines and appliances and hospital treatment as well as the advice of a general practitioner. The second consists of old-age pensions to those who have retired from work and pensions to the totally disabled, which come under the control of the Commissariats for Social Welfare in each republic. The third consists of a combined insurance, administered by the trade unions and covering disablement and maternity benefit, funeral allowances, superannuation pensions to those who have passed a certain age but continue at work, children's aid, the provision of rest-homes and sanatoria and assistance to travel. In each factory or place of employment these benefits are administered by elected social insurance committees attached to the factory committee. Of the total trade union insurance budget before the war between a third and a half represented expenditure on temporary disablement (or sickness) benefit; with maternity benefit and the provision of rest homes and sanatoria coming next in importance, and together making up a further fifth of total expenditure. The funds for these benefits are drawn from a levy on each enterprise in proportion to the size of its wage-bill.[2] Old-age pensions vary between 50 and 100 per cent. of the normal earnings of the worker in question (in the case of mining and certain unhealthy trades they are higher) according to the level of earnings (being 100 per cent. of the lowest earnings and 50 per cent. of the highest) with a ceiling of 1200 roubles a month.[3]; they are payable at the age of 60 in the case of men and of 55 for women (miners and certain other unhealthy trades are entitled to draw pension 5 years, or in some cases even 10 years, earlier); and the qualifying period is 25 years of employment in the case of men and 20 years in the case of

---

[1] *Soviet Communism*, 863.
[2] On the average this levy amounted pre-war to about 6½ per cent. of the wage bill. But it was graded between different employments according to the degree of risk which the employment entailed; the range being from slightly under 4 per cent. to just over 10 per cent.
[3] These figures are in *old* roubles, prior to the revaluation of 1961.

women.   Sickness benefit, prior to 1938, amounting to full wages at
the normal time-rate, was payable to all trade unionists with a record
of three years' employment, on production of a medical certificate.
In December, 1938, however, the benefit was graded according to the
applicants' length of service in the same enterprise, as a means of discouraging a high labour turnover; and from thenceforth only a
worker with six years of unbroken employment in the same occupation (except in mining, etc., where the period was two years) could
claim his full normal wage: a worker with less than six years' employment could claim only four fifths; with less than three years, three
fifths; and with less than two years, a half of his normal wage as sickness benefit.   Disablement benefit, payable to those who in the
opinion of a medical board have lost ability for regular employment
as a result of accident or illness, amounts to between 65 and 100 per
cent. of the normal wage of the applicant, varying with the degree of
disablement and the amount of attention the applicant requires.[1]

We have already mentioned that after 1933 the trade unions
became the main agency for the administration of social insurance.   Among the distinctive features of the system one may
in summary list the following.   Firstly, it is (like the post-war
British scheme) an all-in scheme of insurance, covering all the main
risks of human life that result in loss of earning power or exceptional
expenditure; and the major part (though not the whole) of the benefits is administered by a single agency.   Secondly, it is a non-
contributory scheme; the whole charge being borne either by the
State budget or local budgets or by the enterprises themselves in proportion to the numbers they employ.   Thirdly, all employed persons,
salary-earners' and wage-earners, agricultural wage-earners and
domestic workers as well as industrial workers, are included in the
scheme irrespective of their incomes; but benefits are generally graded
according to the normal earnings of the grade within which the
person in question would fall in his normal employment, and also
in certain cases according to his period of service in the undertaking where he is at present employed.   Fourthly, benefits payable
to non-trade unionists are in most cases lower than those payable
to trade union members.   Fifthly, unemployment benefit which
bulks so prominently in the insurance schemes of other countries is
no longer included.   Since 1930, when the construction projects of

---

[1] Karavaiev and Trephilov, *Posobia po Sotsialnomu Strakovaniu* (1935);
Industrial and Labour Information, vol. LXIII, 346–8; vol. LXII, 165–7; *International Labour Review*, vol. XXVIII, 539–46.   These percentages applied, after
1956, only to earnings up to 450–600 roubles, beyond which lower percentages
(10–20) applied to any excess of earnings above these figures.

the First Five Year Plan substituted labour-scarcity for unemployment, the unemployment benefit scheme has been officially suspended, as has also the labour exchange system in its traditional form.

The pre-war system of old-age and disability pensions, however, was subject to an earnings-ceiling of 300 roubles a month (this corresponding to a fairly high wage in the middle-30's). The result was that, in face of war-time inflation, the real value of pensions subject to this low ceiling (and also of those fixed in relation to pre-inflation earnings) was drastically reduced. In 1947 higher pension rates were established for " basic categories " of workers and technicians in " leading branches of the national economy " ; and pensions for the war-disabled and servicemen's families that had lost a breadwinner were on a more generous scale. But large categories of pensioners remained unaffected by these provisions and suffered acutely. The new Law on State Pensions of July 1956 was designed to deal with these and some other anomalies. The old ceiling of 300 roubles monthly now became the minimum-level for any old-age pension, and a new pension-maximum of 1200 roubles monthly was set. The earnings to which a pension-rate was geared were to be the actual earnings (on the average of the preceding twelve months) and not merely the basic rate for the job, as previously ; pensions were to be related to the number of dependants in the family ; qualification by period of service was no longer required in the case of disability resulting from industrial accident or occupational disease ; and some other limitations were abolished. It was estimated that the changes would result in a doubling of old-age pensions in the standard case and in more than doubling disability pensions.[1]

Apart from the changes in working hours and the raising of the minimum wage in the lowest wage-categories, that were also announced in 1956 and have been mentioned above (page 323), there was at the time a final repeal of the war-time legislation restricting movement of labour. The eve-of-war Labour Decrees of 1940, which restricted a worker's right to leave his job and imposed penalties for lateness and absenteeism and infringements of factory discipline, had already been considerably modified by an amending Decree of July 14, 1951; subsequently to which the compulsory provisions seem not to have been enforced in practice. In 1956 the 1940 Decrees were finally repealed,[2] thus restoring the principle of

---

[1] Report of N. A. Bulganin to Supreme Supreme Soviet, July 11th, 1956.
[2] Decree of the Presidium of the Supreme Soviet dated 25 April 1956.

voluntary movement of labour.   All previous convictions for quitting employment without leave or for absenteeism were cancelled; and for the future any "factory, office or other worker" was declared free to leave his employment with a fortnight's notice.   At the same time a new law defining the Principles of Labour Legislation, and applying to "all factory and office workers", reasserted the status of the individual labour contract of employment and defined the rights of both management and worker under such a contract, including the conditions under which the management could terminate a contract, and the obligation on the management to obtain "the consent of the factory, plant or local trade union committee" to such a termination (with the exception only of those holding certain listed "leading posts").   The status and rights of trade unions and of factory committees were simultaneously defined.   In addition, provision was made for the institution of "permanently functioning production conferences", with a standing committee, in all enterprises, construction sites and shops employing 100 or more persons.

A GLOSSARY OF TERMS

Bedniak, Poor peasant.

Centres, Tsentralnie Upravlenya: SEE pages 86, 110.

Centrosoyus, Central Union of Consumers' Co-operative Societies.

Dessiatine = 2·7 acres = 1·09 hectares.

Glavki, Glavnie Upravlenya: sub-departments of the Supreme Economic Council, or boards, to administer an industry or a branch of industry. SEE pages 86, 110. Later used of the Chief Administrations for branches of industries, set up as sub-departments of a Ministry, and in 1957 transferred to the regional *Sovnarkhoze*.

GOELRO, State Commission for Electrification, instituted in 1920.

Gosbank, The State Bank. SEE especially pages 416–17.

Gosplan, State Economic Planning Commission: a permanent expert commission attached to STO, instituted in 1921.

Gubernia, An administrative unit, or province.

Gubsovnarhoz, The economic department of the gubernia Soviet; or provincial economic council.

Kolkhoz, Collective farm; whence *kolkhoznik*, a member of a collective farm.

Kulak (literally, "fist"), A rich peasant employing labour, making a living by trading and/or acting as village usurer.

Narcomfin, People's Commissariat of Finance.

Narcomlegprom, People's Commissariat of Light Industry.

Narcomprod, People's Commissariat of Supplies.

Narcomput, People's Commissariat of Ways and Communications.

Narcomtiazhprom, People's Commissariat of Heavy Industry.

Narcomtorg, People's Commissariat of Trade.

Narcomtrud, People's Commissariat of Labour.

Narcomvneshtorg, People's Commissariat of Foreign Trade (merged in Narcomtorg in 1925 but re-formed again in 1931).

Narcomzem, People's Commissariat of Agriculture.

Narodnik, A member of the *v Narod* movement. SEE page 61.

NEP, The New Economic Policy.

Nepman, Private trader or private entrepreneur.

Pood = 36·11 lb. (English) = 16·38 kilograms.

Prombank, The Bank for Industry: a long-term credit bank. SEE pages 416–17.

Rabkrin, Department of Workers' and Peasants' Inspection.

Selkhozbank, A bank instituted in 1929 to finance the collective farm movement, which absorbed the older Agricultural Bank.

Selskosoyus, Union of Agricultural Co-operatives.

Seredniak, "Middle peasant".

Smytchka, Union or alliance between working-class and peasantry. SEE page 65.

Sovkhoz, State farm.

Sovnarcom, Council of People's Commissaries (equivalent to Cabinet or Council of Ministers).

Sovnarkhoz, Economic Council, since 1957 used of the Regional Councils given power in that year. SEE pages 329, 377–8.

S.R., Member of Social Revolutionary Party. SEE page 78.

STO, Council of Labour and Defence: the supreme authority in the economic sphere. SEE page 113.

Thermidor, 9th Thermidor (July 27), 1794, when the Jacobins were overthrown.

Trust, An industrial administrative unit, grouping a number of factories. SEE pages 132–8.

Tsekombank, Central Municipal and Housing Bank.

TSIK, Central Executive Committee of the Congress of Soviets.

Uyezd, An administrative unit equivalent to a county.

Vendée, District in the west of France which was the seat of a royalist peasant rising in 1793 during the French Revolution, led by priests and nobles, and marked by considerable brutality.

Verst = 0·66 miles = 1·06 kilometres.

Vesenkha, Vishnii Soviet Narodnovo Khoziaistva, or Supreme Economic Council. SEE pages 86, 369–70.

INDEX OF AUTHORITIES